The Random House
Speller/Divider

The Random House

Speller/Divider

Edited by
Jess Stein

The Ballantine Reference Library
Ballantine Books · New York

Staff

Editor in Chief:	Jess Stein
Associate Editors:	Gloria Mihalyi Solomon Dorothy Gerner Stein
Editorial Assistants:	Barbara Hale Regina B. Wilson

Appreciative acknowledgment to Marilyn J. Abraham, Stuart Berg Flexner, Leonore C. Hauck, Keith Hollaman, John Hornor III, and P.Y. Su

http://www.randomhouse.com

Library of Congress Catalog Card Number: 81-65792

ISBN 0-345-29255-3

Manufactured in the United States of America

First Edition: August 1981

20   19   18

Contents

Preface

This book is an easy-to-use, reliable, up-to-date guide to spelling, word division, hyphenation, pronunciation stress, irregular inflected forms, and frequently confused words. It contains more than 50,000 words, making it larger and more comprehensive than any comparable book of its kind. Its reliability is assured by the fact that it is based on the scholarly resources of the permanent lexicographic staff of Random House, publishers of the widely acclaimed *Random House Dictionaries*.

Coverage extends far beyond the basic general, scientific, and technical vocabularies. This book includes hundreds of words that have come into frequent use only within the last few years. In addition, this book includes the names of the nations of the world, the states of the United States and the provinces of Canada, the major cities of the world, and the leading foreign currencies, as well as commonly encountered names of people of the past and present.

The user will find much help in the special sections at the back of this book. These sections include a dictionary of abbreviations, rules of spelling and word division, a basic manual of style, a table of weights and measures, and other material of daily value.

Every user of the English language, we confidently believe, will find this book to be an indispensable desk companion.

How to Use this Book

All the words and phrases covered in this book, including geographical and biographical names, are in a single alphabetical list to facilitate rapid reference. All the common one-syllable words in the English language are included without exception, a unique feature of this book among books of its kind. All common variant spellings are included, the first one being the spelling most frequently preferred in standard American English. Every form in this book, unless specifically restricted, is acceptable in good usage.

Word Division

Every entry, if more than one syllable, has been divided into syllables. These divisions are indicated by a centered dot or a stress mark. When a hyphen appears in the entry word, it is part of the word and should be shown when the word is used. While it is preferable to avoid dividing an already hyphenated word, it may be divided, if necessary, directly after the hyphen.

li · no'le · um   heav'y- heart'ed   broad'side'
mor · tal'i · ty   moth'er- in- law'   sleep'- in'

If the entry consists of two or more words, a large space is shown between the separate words.

New' York'er   bump'er stick'er

Important further information is given in the section entitled *Basic Rules of Word Division* at the back of this book.

Pronunciation Stress

The syllable that receives the main emphasis in the pronunciation of a word is followed by a boldface mark ('), called a primary stress.

Lat'in   com · ply'   pa · go'da

The syllable that receives a slightly lesser emphasis than the main one in a word is followed by a lighter mark ('), called a secondary stress.

home'com'ing   op'po · si'tion   tes'ti · mo'ni · al

vii

Inflected Forms

All irregular inflected forms—the past tense, past participle, and present participle of verbs; the plural of nouns; the comparative and superlative of adjectives and adverbs—are shown under the root word. All such irregular forms are shown fully spelled out to provide immediately clear information.

a · bridge'
  a · bridged', a · bridg'ing
fly
  flew, flown, fly'ing
er · ra'tum
  pl. er · ra'ta

shop
  shopped, shop'ping
eas'y
  eas'i · er, eas'i · est
cac'tus
  pl. cac'ti *or* cac'tus · es

If two inflected forms are shown for a verb, the first form is both the past tense and the past participle. If three inflected forms are shown for a verb, the first is the past tense, the second is the past participle, and the third is the present participle.

If an entry requires that irregular forms be shown for more than one of its parts of speech, each irregular part of speech group is preceded by a grammatical label.

emp'ty
  adj. emp'ti · er, emp'ti · est;
  v. emp'tied, emp'ty · ing; *pl.*
  emp'ties

Only irregular forms are shown. This does not mean, however, that a given entry does not have other parts of speech, which may have been omitted because they are perfectly regular in form.

Words Often Confused

Some words are confused with others because they sound alike but differ in spelling and meaning. In such cases, a brief identification of the meaning follows the entry word and a cautionary cross-reference to the similar word is placed underneath.

be (*exist*)
  (SEE bee)
bee (*insect*)
  (SEE be)

man'ner (*way; sort*)
  (SEE manor)
man'or (*estate*)
  (SEE manner)

In some cases, the spellings or pronunciations of two or more different words may be so close that they are often confused. In such cases, distinctions are made in the same manner as above.

ac · cept' (*receive*)
  (SEE except)
ex · cept' (*excluding*)
  (SEE accept)

des'ert (*barren region*)
  (SEE dessert)
des · sert' (*food*)
  (SEE desert)

A

a
aard'vark'
aard'wolf'
  pl. aard'wolves'
Aar'on
a'ba·ca'
a·back'
ab'a·cus
  pl. ab'a·cus·es or
  ab'a·ci'
a·baft'
ab'a·lo'ne
a·ban'don
a·ban'doned
a·ban'don·ment
a·base'
  a·based', a·bas'ing
a·base'ment
a·bash'
a·bat'a·ble
a·bate'
  a·bat'ed, a·bat'ing
a·bate'ment
ab'a·tis
  pl. ab'a·tis or
  ab'a·tis'es
ab'at·toir'
ab·ax'i·al
ab'ba·cy
  pl. ab'ba·cies
ab·ba'tial
ab'bé
ab'bess
ab'bey
ab'bot
ab·bre'vi·ate'
  ab·bre'vi·at'ed,
  ab·bre'vi·at'ing
ab·bre'vi·a'tion
ab·bre'vi·a'tor
ab·cou'lomb
ab'di·cate'
  ab'di·cat'ed,
  ab'di·cat'ing
ab'di·ca'tion
ab'di·ca'tor
ab'do·men
ab·dom'i·nal

ab·dom'i·nous
ab·duct'
ab·duc'tion
ab·duc'tor
a·beam'
a'be·ce·dar'i·an
a·bed'
A'bel
a·bele'
Ab'er·deen'
ab·er'rant
ab'er·ra'tion
a·bet'
  a·bet'ted, a·bet'ting
a·bet'ment
a·bet'tor or a·bet'ter
a·bey'ance
ab·far'ad
ab·hen'ry
ab·hor'
  ab·horred', ab·hor'ring
ab·hor'rence
ab·hor'rent
a·bid'ance
a·bide'
  a·bode' or a·bid'ed,
  a·bid'ing
Ab'i·djan'
ab'i·et'ic
a·bil'i·ty
  pl. a·bil'i·ties
a'bi·o·gen'e·sis
a'bi·o'sis
ab'ject
ab·jec'tion
ab'ju·ra'tion
ab·jure'
  ab·jured', ab·jur'ing
ab·la'tion
ab'la·tive
ab'laut
a·blaze'
a'ble
  a'bler, a'blest
a'ble-bod'ied
a·bloom'
ab·lu'tion

a'bly
ab'ne·gate'
  ab'ne·gat'ed,
  ab'ne·gat'ing
ab'ne·ga'tion
ab·nor'mal
ab·nor·mal'i·ty
  pl. ab·nor·mal'i·ties
ab·nor'mal·ly
ab·nor'mi·ty
  pl. ab·nor'mi·ties
a·board'
a·bode'
ab·ohm'
a·bol'ish
ab'o·li'tion
ab'o·li'tion·ism'
ab'o·li'tion·ist
ab'o·ma'sum
  pl. ab'o·ma'sa
A'-bomb'
a·bom'i·na·ble
a·bom'i·na·bly
a·bom'i·nate'
  a·bom'i·nat'ed,
  a·bom'i·nat'ing
a·bom'i·na'tion
a·bom'i·na'tor
ab'o·rig'i·nal
ab'o·rig'i·ne
a·born'ing
a·bort'
a·bor'ti·cide'
a·bor'ti·fa'cient
a·bor'tion
a·bor'tion·ist
a·bor'tive
a·bound'
a·bout'
a·bout'-face'
  a·bout'-faced',
  a·bout'-fac'ing
a·bove'
a·bove'board'
a·bove'ground'
ab'ra·ca·dab'ra
a·brade'
  a·brad'ed, a·brad'ing

A′bra•ham

a•bra′sion

a•bra′sive

a•bra′sive•ly

ab′re•act′

ab′re•ac′tion

a•breast′

a•bri′
  pl. a•bris′

a•bridge′
  a•bridged′, a•bridg′ing

a•bridg′er

a•bridg′ment
  or a•bridge′ment

a•broad′

ab′ro•gate′
  ab′ro•gat′ed,
  ab′ro•gat′ing

ab′ro•ga′tion

ab•rupt′

Ab′sa•lom

ab′scess

ab•scise′
  ab•scised′, ab•scis′ing

ab•scis′sa
  pl. ab•scis′sas *or*
  ab•scis′sae

ab•scis′sion

ab•scond′

ab′sence

ab′sent (*adj.*)

ab•sent′ (*v.*)

ab′sen•tee′

ab′sen•tee′ism

ab′sent–mind′ed

ab′sinthe

ab′so•lute′

ab′so•lute′ly

ab′so•lu′tion

ab′so•lut′ism

ab′so•lut′ist

ab′so•lu•tis′tic

ab•solve′
  ab•solved′, ab•solv′ing

ab•solv′a•ble

ab•solv′er

ab•sorb′

ab•sorbed′

ab•sor′be•fa′cient

ab•sorb′en•cy

ab•sorb′ent

ab•sorp′tion

ab•sorp′tive

ab•stain′

ab•ste′mi•ous

ab•sten′tion

ab′sti•nence

ab′sti•nent

ab′stract (*adj., n.*)

ab•stract′ (*v.*)

ab•stract′ed

ab•strac′tion

ab•strac′tion•ism

ab•strac′tion•ist

ab•struse′

ab•struse′ness

ab•stru′si•ty

ab•surd′

ab•surd′i•ty
  pl. ab•surd′i•ties

a•bu′li•a

a•bun′dance

a•bun′dant

a•buse′
  a•bused′, a•bus′ing

a•bus′er

a•bu′sive

a•but′
  a•but′ted, a•but′ting

a•but′ment

a•but′tal

a•but′ter

ab•volt′

ab•watt′

a•bysm′

a•bys′mal

a•bys′mal•ly

a•byss′

a•byss′al

Ab′ys•sin′i•a

a•ca′cia

ac′a•deme′

ac′a•de′mi•a

ac′a•dem′ic

ac′a•dem′i•cal•ly

a•cad′e•mi′cian

ac′a•dem′i•cism′

a•cad′e•my
  pl. a•cad′e•mies

A•ca′di•an

a•can′thus
  pl. a•can′thus•es *or*
  a•can′thi

a′cap•pel′la

A′ca•pul′co

a•car′pous

ac•cede′ (*agree*)
  ac•ced′ed, ac•ced′ing
  (SEE exceed)

ac•ced′ence

ac•ced′er

ac•cel′er•an′do

ac•cel′er•ant

ac•cel′er•ate′
  ac•cel′er•at′ed,
  ac•cel′er•at′ing

ac•cel′er•a′tion

ac•cel′er•a′tive

ac•cel′er•a′tor

ac•cel′er•om′e•ter

ac′cent

ac•cen′tu•al

ac•cen′tu•ate′
  ac•cen′tu•at′ed,
  ac•cen′tu•at′ing

ac•cen′tu•a′tion

ac•cept′ (*receive*)
  (SEE except)

ac•cept′a•ble

ac•cept′a•bly

ac•cept′a•bil′i•ty

ac•cept′ance

ac•cept′ant

ac′cep•ta′tion

ac•cept′ed

ac•cep′tor

ac′cess (*approach*)
  (SEE excess)

ac•ces′si•ble

ac•ces′si•bil′i•ty

ac•ces′si•bly

ac•ces′sion

ac•ces′so•ry
  pl. ac•ces′so•ries

ac•ciac′ca•tu′ra

ac′ci•dence

ac'ci · dent

ac'ci · den'tal

ac'ci · den'tal · ly

ac · claim'

ac'cla · ma'tion
(approval)
(SEE acclimation)

ac · cli'mate
ac · cli'mat · ed,
ac · cli'mat · ing

ac'cli · ma'tion
(adaptation)
(SEE acclamation)

ac · cli'ma · ti · za'tion

ac · cli'ma · tize'
ac · cli'ma · tized',
ac · cli'ma · tiz'ing

ac · cliv'i · ty
pl. ac · cliv'i · ties

ac'co · lade'

ac · com'mo · date'
ac · com'mo · dat'ed,
ac · com'mo · dat'ing

ac · com'mo · da'tion

ac · com'mo · da'tive

ac · com'pa · ni · ment

ac · com'pa · nist

ac · com'pa · ny
ac · com'pa · nied,
ac · com'pa · ny · ing

ac · com'plice

ac · com'plish

ac · com'plished

ac · com'plish · ment

ac · cord'

ac · cord'ance

ac · cord'ant

ac · cord'ing

ac · cord'ing · ly

ac · cor'di · on

ac · cor'di · on · ist

ac · cost'

ac · count'

ac · count'a · ble

ac · count'a · bil'i · ty

ac · count'a · bly

ac · count'an · cy

ac · count'ant

ac · count'ing

ac · cout'er

ac · cou'ter · ment

Ac'cra

ac · cred'it

ac · cred'i · ta'tion

ac · cre'tion

ac · cru'al

ac · crue'
ac · crued', ac · cru'ing

ac · crue'ment

ac · cul'tur · a'tion

ac · cu'mu · late'
ac · cu'mu · lat'ed,
ac · cu'mu · lat'ing

ac · cu'mu · la'tion

ac · cu'mu · la'tive

ac · cu'mu · la'tor

ac'cu · ra · cy
pl. ac'cu · ra · cies

ac'cu · rate

ac'cu · rate · ly

ac'cu · rate · ness

ac · curs'ed

ac · cus'ant

ac'cu · sa'tion

ac · cu'sa · tive

ac · cu'sa · to'ri · al

ac · cu'sa · to'ry

ac · cuse'
ac · cused', ac · cus'ing

ac · cus'er

ac · cus'tom

ac · cus'tomed

ace
aced, ac'ing

a · cen'tric

a · cerb'

ac'er · bate' (v.)
ac'er · bat'ed,
ac'er · bat'ing

ac · er'bate (adj.)

a · cer'bi · ty

ac'er · ose'

ac'e · tab'u · lum

ac'e · tal'

ac'e · tate'

a · ce'tic (vinegary)
(SEE ascetic)

a · cet'i · fy'
a · cet'i · fied',
a · cet'i · fy'ing

ac'e · tone'

a · ce'tyl

a · ce'tyl · cho'line

a · cet'y · lene'

a · ce'tyl · sal'i · cyl'ic

ace'y–deuc'y

A · chae'an

ache
ached, ach'ing

a · chene'

Ach'e · ron'

a · chieve'
a · chieved', a · chiev'ing

a · chieve'ment

a · chiev'er

A · chil'les

ach'ro · mat'ic

a · cic'u · lar

ac'id

ac'id head'

a · cid'ic

a · cid'i · fi · ca'tion

a · cid'i · fy'
a · cid'i · fied',
a · cid'i · fy'ing

ac'i · dim'e · ter

a · cid'i · ty

ac'i · doph'i · lus

ac'i · do'sis

a · cid'u · lous

ack'–ack'

ac · knowl'edge
ac · knowl'edged,
ac · knowl'edg · ing

ac · knowl'edge · a · ble

ac · knowl'edg · ment
or ac · knowl'-
edge · ment

a · clin'ic

ac'me

ac'ne

ac'o · lyte'

A'con · ca'gua

ac'o · nite'

a'corn

a'cot · y · le'don

a · cous'tic

a · cous'ti · cal

a·cous′ti·cal·ly

a·cous′tics

ac·quaint′

ac·quaint′ance

ac·quaint′ed

ac′qui·esce′
ac′qui·esced′,
ac′qui·esc′ing

ac′qui·es′cence

ac′qui·es′cent

ac·quire′
ac·quired′, ac·quir′ing

ac′qui·si′tion

ac·quis′i·tive

ac·quit′
ac·quit′ted,
ac·quit′ting

ac·quit′tal

ac·quit′tance

a′cre

A′cre

a′cre·age

a′cre-foot′

ac′rid

a·crid′i·ty

Ac′ri·lan′
(Trademark)

ac′ri·mo′ni·ous

ac′ri·mo′ny

ac′ro·bat′

ac′ro·bat′ic

ac′ro·bat′ics

ac′ro·meg′a·ly

ac′ro·nym

ac′ro·pho′bi·a

a·crop′o·lis

a·cross′

a·cross′-the-board′

a·cros′tic

a·cryl′ic

act

act′a·ble

ac′tin

act′ing

ac·tin′ic

ac′tin·ism′

ac·tin′i·um

ac′ti·nom′e·ter

ac′ti·non′

ac′tion

ac′tion·a·ble

Ac′ti·um

ac′ti·vate′
ac′ti·vat′ed,
ac′ti·vat′ing

ac′ti·va′tion

ac′ti·va′tor

ac′tive

ac′tive·ly

ac′tiv·ism′

ac′tiv·ist

ac·tiv′i·ty
pl. ac·tiv′i·ties

ac′to·my′o·sin

ac′tor

ac′tress

ac′tu·al

ac′tu·al′i·ty
pl. ac′tu·al′i·ties

ac′tu·al·ly

ac′tu·ar′i·al

ac′tu·ar′y
pl. ac′tu·ar′ies

ac′tu·ate′
ac′tu·at′ed, ac′tu·at′ing

ac′tu·a′tion

ac′tu·a′tor

a·cu′i·ty

a·cu′men

a·cu′mi·nous

ac′u·punc′ture (n.)

ac′u·punc′ture (v.)
ac′u·punc′tured,
ac′u·punc′tur·ing

a·cut′ance

a·cute′

a·cute′ly

a·cute′ness

ac′yl

ad (advertisement)
(SEE add)

ad ab·sur′dum

ad′age

a·da′gio

Ad′am

ad′a·mant

ad′a·man′tine

Ad′am·ic

Ad′am·ite′

Ad′ams

Ad′am's ap′ple

a·dapt′ (modify)
(SEE adept and adopt)

a·dapt′a·ble

a·dapt′a·bil′i·ty

ad′ap·ta′tion

a·dap′tive

a·dap′ter or
a·dap′tor

add (total)
(SEE ad)

Ad′dams

ad′dax

ad′dend

ad·den′dum
pl. ad·den′da or
ad·den′dums

add′er (one who
adds)
(SEE BELOW)

ad′der (snake)
(SEE ABOVE)

ad′der's-tongue′

ad·dict′

ad·dic′tion

ad·dic′tive

Ad′dis A′ba·ba

ad·di′tion (act of
adding)
(SEE edition)

ad·di′tion·al

ad·di′tion·al·ly

ad′di·tive

ad′dle
ad′dled, ad′dling

ad′dle·brained′

ad·dress′ (v.)

ad′dress (n.)

ad′dress·ee′

ad·dress′er or
ad·dres′sor

Ad·dres′so·graph′
(Trademark)

ad·duce′
ad·duced′, ad·duc′ing

ad·duct′

ad·duc′tion
ad·duc′tive
Ad′e·laide′
A′den
ad′e·nine
ad′e·noid′
ad′e·noi′dal
ad′e·noid·ec′to·my
  pl.
  ad′e·noid·ec′to·mies
a·den′o·sine′
ad·ept′ (adj.)
  (skilled)
  (SEE adapt and adopt)
ad′ept (n.)
ad′e·qua·cy
ad′e·quate
ad′e·quate·ly
ad·here′
  ad·hered′, ad·her′ing
ad·her′ence
ad·her′ent
ad·he′sion
ad·he′sive
ad hoc′
ad ho′mi·nem′
ad′i·a·bat′ic
ad′i·aph′o·rous
a·dieu′
ad in′fi·ni′tum
ad i·ni′ti·um
ad in′te·rim
ad′i·os′
ad′i·pose′
Ad′i·ron′dack
ad·ja′cen·cy
  pl. ad·ja′cen·cies
ad·ja′cent
ad′jec·ti′val
ad′jec·ti′val·ly
ad′jec·tive
ad·join′
ad·join′ing
ad·journ′
ad·journ′ment
ad·judge′
  ad·judged′, ad·judg′ing

ad·ju′di·cate′
  ad·ju′di·cat′ed,
  ad·ju′di·cat′ing
ad·ju′di·ca′tion
ad·ju′di·ca′tive
ad·ju′di·ca′tor
ad′junct
ad·junc′tive
ad′ju·ra′tion
ad·jure′
  ad·jured′, ad·jur′ing
ad·just′
ad·just′a·ble
ad·just′er or
  ad·just′or
ad·just′ment
ad′ju·tant
ad′ju·tant gen′e·ral
  pl. ad′ju·tants
  gen′e·ral
ad–lib′
  ad-libbed′, ad-lib′bing
ad lib′i·tum
ad′man′
  pl. ad′men′
ad·min′is·ter
ad·min′is·tra·ble
ad·min′is·tra′tion
ad·min′is·tra′tive
ad·min′is·tra′tor
ad·min′is·tra′trix
ad′mi·ra·ble
ad′mi·ra·bly
ad′mi·ral
ad′mi·ral·ty
  pl. ad′mi·ral·ties
ad′mi·ra′tion
ad·mire′
  ad·mired′, ad·mir′ing
ad·mir′er
ad·mis′si·bil′i·ty
ad·mis′si·ble
ad·mis′sion
ad·mis′sive
ad·mit′
  ad·mit′ted, ad·mit′ting
ad·mit′tance
ad·mit′ted·ly
ad·mix′
ad·mix′ture

ad·mon′ish
ad′mo·ni′tion
ad·mon′i·to′ry
ad′nate
ad nau′se·am
ad′noun
a·do′
a·do′be
ad′o·les′cence
ad′o·les′cent
A·do·nai′
A·do′nis
a·dopt′ (take)
  (SEE adapt and adept)
a·dop′tion
a·dop′tive
a·dor′a·ble
a·dor′a·bly
ad′o·ra′tion
a·dore′
  a·dored′, a·dor′ing
a·dor′er
a·dorn′
a·dorn′ment
ad·re′nal
A·dren′a·lin
  (Trademark)
a·dren′a·line
a·dre′no·cor′ti·
  co·trop′ic
A′dri·at′ic
a·drift′
a·droit′
ad·sorb′
ad·sorb′ent
ab·sorp′tion
ad′u·late′
  ad′u·lat′ed, ad′u·lat′ing
ad′u·la′tion
ad′u·la′tor
ad′u·la·to′ry
a·dult′
a·dul′ter·ant
a·dul′ter·ate′
  a·dul′ter·at′ed,
  a·dul′ter·at′ing
a·dul′ter·a′tion
a·dul′ter·er

a·dul′ter·ess
a·dul′ter·ine
a·dul′ter·ous
a·dul′ter·y
  pl. a·dul′ter·ies
a·dult′hood
ad·um′bral
ad·um′brate
  ad·um′brat·ed,
  ad·um′brat·ing
ad′um·bra′tion
ad va·lor′em
ad·vance′
  ad·vanced′,
  ad·vanc′ing
ad·vanc′er
ad·vanced′
ad·vance′ment
ad·van′tage
  ad·van′taged,
  ad·van′tag·ing
ad′van·ta′geous
ad·vec′tion
ad′vent
Ad′vent·ist
ad′ven·ti′tious
ad·ven′tive
ad·ven′ture
  ad·ven′tured,
  ad·ven′tur·ing
ad·ven′tur·er
ad·ven′ture·some
ad·ven′tur·ess
ad·ven′tur·ism′
ad·ven′tur·ous
ad′verb
ad·ver′bi·al
ad·ver′bi·al·ly
ad′ver·sar′y
  pl. ad′ver·sar′ies
ad·ver′sa·tive
ad·verse′ (*opposed*)
  (SEE averse)
ad·verse′ly
ad·ver′si·ty
  pl. ad·ver′si·ties
ad·vert′
ad·vert′ent
ad′ver·tise′
  ad′ver·tised′,
  ad′ver·tis′ing

ad′ver·tis′er
ad′ver·tise′ment
ad′ver·tis′ing
ad·vice′
  (*recommendation*)
  (SEE advise)
ad·vis′a·bil′i·ty
ad·vis′a·ble
ad·vise′ (*recommend*)
  ad·vised′, ad·vis′ing
  (SEE advice)
ad·vis′ed·ly
ad·vis·ee′
ad·vise′ment
ad·vis′er or ad·vi′sor
ad·vi′so·ry
ad′vo·ca·cy
  pl. ad′vo·ca·cies
ad′vo·cate′
  ad′vo·cat′ed,
  ad′vo·cat′ing
adz
ad·zu′ki
Ae·ge′an
ae′gis
Ae·ne′as
Ae·ne′id
ae·o′li·an
ae′on
aer′ate
  aer′at·ed, aer′at·ing
aer·a′tion
aer′a·tor
aer′i·al
aer′i·al·ist
aer′i·al·ly
aer′ie (*nest*)
  (SEE airy)
aer′o·bat′ics
aer′obe
aer·o′bic
aer′o·bi·o′sis
aer′o·dy·nam′ic
aer′o·dy·nam′i
  ·cal·ly
aer′o·dy·nam′ics
aer′o·em′bo·lism′
aer·om′e·ter
aer′o·naut′

aer′o·nau′tic
aer′o·nau′ti·cal
aer′o·nau′tics
aer′o·pause′
aer′o·sol′
aer′o·space′
aer′o·sphere′
aer′o·stat′
Aes′chy·lus
Aes′cu·la′pi·us
Ae′sop
aes′thete
aes·thet′ic
aes·thet′i·cal·ly
aes·thet′i·cism′
aes·thet′ics
a·far′
af′fa·bil′i·ty
af′fa·ble
af′fa·bly
af·fair′
af·faire′ d′hon·neur′
af·fect′ (*influence*)
  (SEE effect)
af′fec·ta′tion
af·fect′ed
af·fect′ing
af·fec′tion
af·fec′tion·ate
af·fec′tion·ate·ly
af·fec′tive
af′fen·pin′scher
af′fer·ent
af·fi′ance
  af·fi′anced,
  af·fi′anc·ing
af′fi·da′vit
af·fil′i·ate′ (*v.*)
  af·fil′i·at′ed,
  af·fil′i·at′ing
af·fil′i·ate (*n.*)
af·fil′i·a′tion
af·fin′i·ty
  af·fin′i·ties
af·firm′
af′fir·ma′tion
af·firm′a·tive
af·fix′ (*v.*)

af'fix (n.)
af·fla'tus
af·flict'
af·flic'tion
af'flu·ence
af'flu·ent
af·ford'
af·ford'a·ble
af·for'est
af·fray'
af'fri·cate
af·fright'
af·front'
Af'ghan
af·ghan'i
Af·ghan'i·stan
a·fi'cio·na'do
  pl. a·fi'cio·na'dos
a·field'
a·fire'
a·flame'
a·float'
a·flut'ter
a·foot'
a·fore'men'tioned
a·fore'said'
a·fore'thought'
a for'ti·o'ri
a·foul'
a·fraid'
A'–frame'
a·fresh'
Af'ri·ca
Af'ri·can
Af'ri·kaans'
Af'ri·kan'der
Af'ro
Af'ro-A·mer'i·can
aft
af'ter
af'ter·birth'
af'ter·burn'er
af'ter·care'
af'ter·damp'
af'ter·deck'
af'ter·ef·fect'
af'ter·glow'

af'ter·growth'
af'ter·im'age
af'ter·life'
af'ter·math'
af'ter·most'
af'ter·noon' (n.)
af'ter·noon' (adj.)
af'ter·taste'
af'ter·tax'
af'ter·thought'
af'ter·ward'
af'ter·wards'
af'ter·word'
af'ter·world'
a·gain'
a·gainst'
a·gam'ic
A·ga'ña
a·gape' (wide open)
  (SEE BELOW)
a·ga'pe (love)
  pl. a·ga'pae or
  a·ga'pai'
  (SEE ABOVE)
a'gar
ag'a·ric
ag'ate
a·ga've
age
  aged, ag'ing or age'ing
a'ged (elderly)
age'ism
age'ist
age'less
a'gen·cy
  pl. a'gen·cies
a·gen'da
a·gen'dum
  pl. a·gen'da or
  a·gen'dums
a'gent
a·gent'
  pro·vo·ca·teur'
age'–old'
ag'er·a'tum
ag·glom'er·ate' (v.)
  ag·glom'er·at'ed,
  ag·glom'er·at'ing

ag·glom'er·ate (n.,
  adj.)
ag·glom'er·a'tion
ag·glu'ti·nate'
  ag·glu'ti·nat'ed,
  ag·glu'ti·nat'ing
ag·glu'ti·na'tion
ag·glu'ti·na'tive
ag·glu'ti·nin
ag·gran'dize,
  ag·gran'dized,
  ag·gran'diz·ing
ag·gran'dize·ment
ag·gran'diz'er
ag'gra·vate'
  ag'gra·vat'ed,
  ag'gra·vat'ing
ag'gra·va'tion
ag'gra·va'tor
ag'gre·gate (adj., n.)
ag'gre·gate' (v.)
  ag'gre·gat'ed,
  ag'gre·gat'ing
ag'gre·ga'tion
ag·gress'
ag·gres'sion
ag·gres'sive
ag·gres'sive·ly
ag·gres'sive·ness
ag·gres'sor
ag·grieve'
  ag·grieved', ag·griev'ing
a·ghast'
ag'ile
ag'ile·ness
a·gil'i·ty
ag'i·o'
ag'i·tate'
  ag'i·tat'ed, ag'i·tat'ing
ag'i·ta'tion
ag'i·ta'tor
a·gleam'
ag'let
a·gley'
a·glim'mer
a·glit'ter
a·glow'
ag'nate
ag·no'men
  pl. ag·nom'i·na

ag·nos'tic

ag·nos'ti·cism'

Ag'nus De'i

a·go'

a·gog'

à go'go

a·gon'ic

ag'o·nize'
ag'o·nized',
ag'o·niz'ing

ag'o·ny
pl. ag'o·nies

ag'o·ra
pl. ag'o·rae'

ag'o·ra·pho'bi·a

a·gou'ti
pl. a·gou'tis or
a·gou'ties

a·grar'i·an

a·gree'
a·greed', a·gree'ing

a·gree'a·bil'i·ty

a·gree'a·ble

a·gree'a·bly

a·greed'

a·gree'ment

ag'ri·busi'ness

ag'ri·cul'tur·al

ag'ri·cul'ture

ag'ri·cul'tur·ist

ag'ro·nom'ic

a·gron'o·mist

a·gron'o·my

a·ground'

a'gue

a·ha'

a·head'

a·hem'

a·hoy'

aid (help)
(SEE aide)

aide (assistant)
(SEE aid)

aide'-de-camp'

aide-mé·moire'
pl. aides-mé·moire'

ai'grette

ai'ki·do

ail (be ill)
(SEE ale)

ai·lan'thus

ai'ler·on'

ail'ment

aim

aim'less

air (atmosphere)
(SEE heir)

air' bag'

air'borne'

air'brush'

air'burst'

air'bus

air'-con·di'tion

air' con·di'tion·er

air' con·di'tion·ing

air'-cool'

air'craft'

air' cur'tain

air'drome'

air'drop'
air'dropped',
air'drop'ping

air'-dry'
air'-dried', air'-dry'ing

Aire'dale'

air' ex·press'

air'field'

air'flow'

air'foil'

air' force'

air' freight'

air'glow'

air' gun'

air'i·ly

air'i·ness

air' lane'

air'less

air'lift'

air'line'

air'lin'er

air' lock'

air' mail'

air'man
pl. air'men

air'-mind'ed

air'plane'

air' pock'et

air'port'

air' pres'sure

air' raid'

air' ri'fle

air' right'

air'ship'

air'sick'

air' space'

air'speed'

air'strip'

air'tight'

air'waves'

air'way'

air'wor'thy

air'y
air'i·er, air'i·est
(SEE aerie)

aisle (passage)
(SEE isle)

a·jar'

a·kim'bo

a·kin'

Ak'ron

ak'va·vit'

Al'a·bam'a

Al'a·bam·an

Al'a·bam'i·an

al'a·bas'ter

à' la carte'

a·lack'

a·lac'ri·ty

à' la king'

al'a·me'da

Al'a·mo'

à' la mode'

a'lar

a·larm'

a·larm' clock'

a·larm'ism

a·larm'ist

a·las'

A·las'ka

A·las'kan

a'late

alb

al'ba·core'

Al·ba'ni·a

Al·ba'ni·an

Al'ba·ny
al'ba·tross'
al·be'do
al·be'it
Al·ber'ta
al'bi·nism'
al·bi'no
　pl. al·bi'nos
Al'bi·on
al'bum
al·bu'men (egg
　white)
　(SEE albumin)
al·bu'min (protein)
　(SEE albumen)
Al'bu·quer'que
al·cai'de
　pl. al·cai'des
al·cal'de
　pl. al·cal'des
Al'ca·traz'
al·chem'i·cal
al'che·mist
al'che·my
　pl. al'che·mies
al'co·hol'
al'co·hol'ic
al'co·hol·ism'
al'cove
al'de·hyde'
al' den'te
al'der
al'der·man
　pl. al'der·men
ale (beverage)
　(SEE ail)
a·lee'
a·lem'bic
A·len·çon'
a·lert'
Al·eut'
A·leu'tian
ale'wife'
　pl. ale'wives'
Al'ex·an'der
Al'ex·an'dri·a
a·lex'i·a
al·fal'fa
al·for'ja

al·fres'co
al'ga
　pl. al'gae
al'gal
al'ge·bra
al'ge·bra'ic
al'ge·bra'ist
Al·ge'ri·a
Al·ge'ri·an
al'gid
Al·giers'
AL'GOL
Al·gon'qui·an
　pl. Al·gon'qui·ans or
　Al·gon'qui·an
Al·gon'quin
　pl. Al·gon'quins or
　Al·gon'quin
al'go·rithm'
Al·ham'bra
a'li·as
　pl. a'li·as·es
al'i·bi'
　pl. al'i·bis'
al'i·dade'
al'ien
al'ien·a·ble
al'ien·ate'
　al'ien·at'ed,
　al'ien·at'ing
al'ien·a'tion
al'ien·ee'
al'ien·ist
al'lien·or
a·light'
a·lign'
a·lign'ment
a·like'
al'i·ment (n.)
al'i·ment' (v.)
al'i·men'ta·ry
al'i·mo'ny
a·line'
　a·lined', a·lin'ing
a·line'ment
al'i·phat'ic
al'i·quant
al'i·quot
a·live'

a·li'yah
　pl. a·li'yahs or a·li'yos
　or a'li·yoth'
a·liz'a·rin
al'ka·hest'
al'ka·li'
　pl. al'ka·lis' or
　al'ka·lies'
al'ka·lim'e·ter
al'ka·line'
al'ka·lin'i·ty
al'ka·lin'i·za'tion
al'ka·lin·ize'
　al'ka·lin·ized',
　al'ka·lin·iz'ing
al'ka·li·za'tion
al'ka·lize'
　al'ka·lized',
　al'ka·liz'ing
al'ka·loid'
al'ka·lo'sis
al'kane
al'kene
al'kyd
al'kyl
al'kyne
all (whole)
　(SEE awl)
al'la bre've
Al'lah
all'-A·mer'i·can
al·lan'to·is
all'-a·round'
all' clear'
al·lay'
　al·layed', al·lay'ing
all'-day'
al'le·ga'tion
al·lege'
　al·leged', al·leg'ing
al·leged'
al·leg'ed·ly
Al'le·ghe'ny
al·le'giance
al'le·gor'ic
al'le·gor'i·cal
al'le·go'rist
al'le·go'ry
　pl. al'le·go'ries
al'le·gret'to

al·le′gro
  pl. al·le′gros

al·lele′

al·lel′ic

al′le·lu′ia

al′le·mande′

al′ler·gen′

al′ler·gen′ic

al·ler′gic

al′ler·gist

al′ler·gy
  pl. al′ler·gies

al·le′vi·ate′
  al·le′vi·at′ed,
  al·le′vi·at′ing

al·le′vi·a′tor

al·le′vi·a′tion

al′ley (street)
  pl. al′leys
  (SEE ally)

al′ley·way′

al·li′ance

al·lied′

al′li·ga′tor

al·lit′er·ate′
  al·lit′er·at′ed,
  al·lit′er·at′ing

al·lit′er·a′tion

al·lit′er·a′tive

all′-night′

al′lo·cate′
  al′lo·cat′ed,
  al′lo·cat′ing

al′lo·ca′tion

al′lo·morph′

al′lo·mor′phic

al′lo·nym

al′lo·phone′

al′lo·phon′ic

al·lot′

al·lot′ted, al·lot′ting

al·lot′ment

al′lo·trope′

al′lo·trop′ic

al·lot′ro·py

all′-out′

all′ov′er (adj.)

all′o′ver (n.)

al·low′

al·low′a·ble

al·low′ance

al′loy (n.)

al·loy′ (v.)

all′ read′y (prepared)
  (SEE already)

all′ right′

all′-round′

all′spice′

all′-star′

all′-time′

al·lude′ (refer)
  al·lud′ed, al·lud′ing
  (SEE elude)

al·lure′
  al·lured′, al·lur′ing

al·lure′ment

al·lu′sion (reference)
  (SEE illusion)

al·lu′sive (suggestive)
  (SEE elusive and
  illusive)

al·lu′vi·al

al·lu′vi·um
  pl. al·lu′vi·ums or
  al·lu′vi·a

al·ly′
  al·lied′, al·ly′ing

al′ly (n.) (friend)
  pl. al′lies
  (SEE alley)

all′-year′

al′lyl

al′ma ma′ter

al′ma·nac′

al·might′y

al′mond

al′mond-eyed′

al′mon·er

al′most

alms

alms′house′

Al′ni·co′
  (Trademark)

al′oe
  pl. al′oes

a·loft′

a·lo′ha

a·lone′

a·long′

a·long′shore′

a·long′side′

a·loof′

al′o·pe′ci·a

a·loud′

al·pac′a

al′pen·glow′

al′pen·horn′

al′pen·stock′

al′pha

al′pha·bet′

al′pha·bet′ic

al′pha·bet′i·cal

al′pha·bet′i·cal·ly

al′pha·bet·ize′
  al′pha·bet·ized′,
  al′pha·bet·iz′ing

al′pha·mer′ic

al′pha·nu·mer′ic

al′pine

Alps

al·read′y (previously)
  (SEE all ready)

Al′sace-Lor·raine′

Al·sa′tian

al′so

al′so-ran′

al′tar (platform)
  (SEE alter)

al′tar boy′

al′tar·piece′

al′ter (change)
  (SEE altar)

al′ter·a′tion

al′ter·a′tive

al′ter·ca′tion

al′ter e′go

al′ter·nate′
  al′ter·nat′ed,
  al′ter·nat′ing

al′ter·nate (adj., n.)

al′ter·nate·ly

al′ter·na′tion

al·ter′na·tive

al′ter·na′tor

alt′horn′

al·though′ or al·tho′

al·tim′e·ter

al·tim'e·try
al'ti·tude'
al'ti·tu'di·nal
al'to
  pl. al'tos
al'to·cu'mu·lus
  pl. al'to·cu'mu·lus
al'to·geth'er
al'to·stra'tus
  pl. al'to·stra'tus
al'tru·ism'
al'tru·ist
al'tru·is'tic
al'tru·is'ti·cal·ly
al'um
a·lu'mi·na
al'u·min'i·um (*esp.*
  Brit.)
al·lu'mi·nize'
  a·lu'mi·nized',
  a·lu'mi·niz'ing
a·lu'mi·num
a·lum'na
  pl. a·lum'nae
a·lum'nus
  pl. a·lum'ni
al·ve'o·lar
al·ve'o·lus
  pl. al·ve'o·li'
al'ways
a·lys'sum
am
a'mah
a·main'
a·mal'gam
a·mal'ga·mate'
  a·mal'ga·mat·ed,
  a·mal'ga·mat'ing
a·mal'ga·ma'tor
a·mal'ga·ma'tion
a'man·dine'
am'a·ni'ta
a·man'u·en'sis
  pl. a·man'u·en'ses
am'a·ranth'
am'a·ran'thine
am'a·ryl'lis
a·mass'
am'a·teur'
am'a·teur'ish

am'a·teur·ism'
A·ma'ti
am'a·tive
am'a·to'ry
a·maze'
  a·mazed', a·maz'ing
a·maze'ment
a·maz'ing
Am'a·zon'
Am'a·zo'ni·an
am·bas'sa·dor
am·bas'sa·do'ri·al
am·bas'sa·dress
am'ber
am'ber·gris'
am'ber·oid'
am'bi·ance
am'bi·dex'ter·i·ty
am'bi·dex'trous
am'bi·ence
am'bi·ent
am'bi·gu'i·ty
  pl. am'bi·gu'i·ties
am·big'u·ous
am'bit
am·bi'tion
am·bi'tious
am·biv'a·lence
am·biv'a·lent
am'bi·vert'
am'ble
  am'bled, am'bling
am·bro'sia
am·bro'sial
am'bu·lance
am'bu·lant
am'bu·late
  am'bu·lat·ed,
  am'bu·lat·ing
am'bu·la·to'ry
  pl. am'bu·la·to'ries
am'bus·cade'
  am'bus·cad'ed,
  am'bus·cad'ing
am'bush
a·me'ba
  a·me'bas or a·me'bae
a·me'bic

a·mel'io·rate'
  a·mel'io·rat'ed,
  a·mel'io·rat'ing
a·mel'io·ra'tion
a'men'
a·me'na·bil'i·ty
a·me'na·ble
a·me'na·bly
a'men' cor'ner
a·mend' (*change*)
  (SEE emend)
a·mend'ment
a·mends'
a·men'i·ty
  pl. a·men'i·ties
A'mer·a'sian
a·merce'
  a·merced', a·merc'ing
A·mer'i·ca
A·mer'i·can
A·mer'i·ca'na
A·mer'i·can·ism'
A·mer'i·can·ist
A·mer'i·can·i·
  za'tion
A·mer'i·can·ize'
  A·mer'i·can·ized',
  A·mer'i·can·iz'ing
am'er·i'ci·um
Am'er·ind
Am'er·in'di·an
am'e·thyst
a'mi·a·bil'i·ty
a'mi·a·ble
a'mi·a·bly
am'i·ca·bil'i·ty
am'i·ca·ble
am'i·ca·bly
am'ice
a·mi'cus cu'ri·ae'
a·mid'
am'ide
a·mid'ships
a·midst'
a·mi'ga
  pl. a·mi'gas
a·mi'go
  pl. a·mi'gos
a·mine'

a·mi′no

A′mish

a·miss′

am′i·ty

Am·man′

am′me·ter

am′mo

am·mo′nia

am·mo·nite′

am·mo′ni·um

am′mu·ni′tion

am·ne′sia

am·ne′si·ac′

am′nes·ty
  pl. am′nes·ties; *v.*
  am′nes·tied,
  am′nes·ty·ing

am′ni·o·cen·te′sis

am′ni·on
  pl. am′ni·ons or
  am′ni·a

am′ni·ot′ic

a·moe′ba
  pl. a·moe′bae or
  a·moe′bas

a·moe′bic

a·mok′

a·mong′

a·mongst′

a·mon′til·la′do

a·mor′al

a′mo·ral′i·ty
  pl. a′mo·ral′i·ties

a·mor′al·ly

am′o·ret′to

am′o·rous

a·mor′phism

a·mor′phous

am′or·ti·za′tion

am′or·tize′
  am′or·tized′,
  am′or·tiz′ing

A′mos

a·mount′

a·mour′

a·mour-pro′pre

am′per·age

am·pere′

am′per·sand′

am·phet′a·mine′

am·phib′i·an

am·phib′i·ous

am·phi·bole

am′phi·the′a·ter *or*
  am′phi·the′a·tre

am′pho·ra
  pl. am′pho·rae or
  am′pho·ras

am′pi·cil′lin

am′ple
  am′pler, am′plest

am′pli·fi·ca′tion

am′pli·fi′er

am′pli·fy′
  am′pli·fied′,
  am′pli·fy′ing

am′pli·tude′

am′ply

am′pule, am′pul, or
  am′poule

am′pu·tate′
  am′pu·tat′ed,
  am′pu·tat′ing

am′pu·ta′tion

am′pu·tee′

Am′ster·dam′

Am′trak′

a·muck′

am′u·let

A′mund·sen

A·mur′

a·muse′
  a·mused′, a·mus′ing

a·muse′ment

am′yl

am′yl·ase′

am′y·lop′sin

an

An′a·bap′tist

a·nab′a·sis

a·nab′o·lism′

an′a·bol′ic

a·nach′ro·nism′

a·nach′ro·nis′tic

an′a·con′da

an′a·dem′

a·nae′mi·a

a·nae′mic

an·aer′obe

an′aer·o′bic

an′aes·the′sia

an′aes·the′si·ol′o·gist

an′aes·the′si·ol′o·gy

an′aes·thet′ic

an·aes′the·tist

an·aes′the·ti·za′tion

an·aes′the·tize′
  an·aes′the·tized′,
  an·aes′the·tiz′ing

an′a·gram′

a′nal

an′a·lects′

an′al·ge′si·a

an′al·ge′sic

an′a·log′i·cal

a·nal′o·gous

an′a·logue′ *or*
  an′a·log′

a·nal′o·gy
  pl. a·nal′o·gies

a·nal′y·sand′

a·nal′y·sis
  pl. a·nal′y·ses

an′a·lyst (*one who*
  analyzes)
  (SEE annalist)

an′a·lyt′ic

an′a·lyt′i·cal

an′a·lyze′
  an′a·lyzed′,
  an′a·lyz′ing

an′a·mor′phic

An′a·ni′as

an′a·pest′

an′a·pes′tic

an·ar′chic

an·ar′chi·cal

an′ar·chism′

an′ar·chist

an′ar·chis′tic

an′ar·chy
  pl. an′ar·chies

an·as′tig·mat′

an′as·tig·mat′ic

a·nath′e·ma
  pl. a·nath′e·mas

a · nath′e · ma · tize′
　a · nath′e · ma · tized′,
　a · nath′e · ma · tiz′ing
an′a · tom′ic
an′a · tom′i · cal
a · nat′o · mist
a · nat′o · mize′
　a · nat′o · mized′,
　a · nat′o · miz′ing
a · nat′o · my
　pl. a · nat′o · mies
an′ces · tor
an · ces′tral
an′ces · try
　pl. an′ces · tries
an′chor
an′chor · age
an′cho · rite′
an′cho · rit′ic
an′chor man′
　pl. an′chor men′
an′chor wom′an
　pl. an′chor wo′men
an′cho · vy
　pl. an′cho · vies
an · cien′ ré · gime′
an′cient
an′cil · lar′y
and
an · dan′te
　pl. an · dan′tes
an′dan · ti′no
　pl. an′dan · ti′nos
An · de′an
An′des
and′i′ron
and/or
An · dor′ra
An · dor′ran
an′dro · gen
an′dro · gen′ic
an · drog′y · nous
an · drog′y · ny
an′droid
An · drom′e · da
an′ec · do′tal
an′ec · dote′
an′e · cho′ic
a · ne′mi · a
a · ne′mic

an′e · mom′e · ter
a · nem′o · ne
a · nent′
an′er · oid′
an′es · the′sia
an′es · the′si · ol′o · gist
an′es · the′si · ol′o · gy
an′es · thet′ic
an · es′the · tist
an · es′the · ti · za′tion
an · es′the · tize′
　an · es′the · tized′,
　an · es′the · tiz′ing
an′eu · rysm′
a · new′
an′gel (heavenly
　spirit)
　(SEE angle)
an′gel dust′
an′gel · fish′
　pl. an′gel · fish′ or
　an′gel · fish′es
an · gel′ic
an · gel′i · ca
an · gel′i · cal
an · gel′i · cal · ly
An′ge · lus
an′ger
an · gi′na pec′to · ris
an′gi · o · sperm′
an′gle (convergence)
　an′gled, an′gling
　(SEE angel)
an′gler
an′gle · worm′
An′gli · can
An′gli · can · ism′
An′gli · cism′
An′gli · ci · za′tion
An′gli · cize′
　An′gli · cized′,
　An′gli · ciz′ing
an′gling
An′glo-A · mer′i · can
An′glo · phile′
An′glo · phil′i · a
An′glo · phobe′
An′glo · pho′bi · a
An′glo-Sax′on

An · go′la
An · go′lan
An · go′ra
an′gos · tu′ra
an′gri · ly
an′gri · ness
an′gry
　an′gri · er, an′gri · est
angst
ang′strom
an′guish
an′guished
an′gu · lar
an′gu · lar′i · ty
　pl. an′gu · lar′i · ties
an · hy′dride
an · hy′drous
an′il
an′i · line
an′i · mad · ver′sion
an′i · mad · vert′
an′i · mal
an′i · mal′cule
an′i · mate′ (v.)
　an′i · mat′ed,
　an′i · mat′ing
an′i · mate (adj.)
an′i · mat′ed
an′i · ma′tion
a′ni · ma′to
an′i · ma′tor or
　an′i · ma′ter
an′i · mism′
an′i · mist
an′i · mis′tic
an′i · mos′i · ty
　pl. an′i · mos′i · ties
an′i · mus
an′i′on
an′i · on′ic
an′ise
an′i · seed′
an′i · sette′
An′ka · ra
ankh
an′kle
an′kle · bone′
an′klet

an'ky•lose'
  an'ky•losed',
  an'ky•los'ing

an'ky•lo'sis

an'nal•ist (*historian*)
  (SEE analyst)

an'nals

An•nap'o•lis

an•neal'

an'ne•lid

an•nex' (*v.*)

an'nex (*n.*)

an'nex•a'tion

an•ni'hi•late'
  an•ni'hi•lat'ed,
  an•ni'hi•lat'ing

an•ni'hi•la'tion

an•ni'hi•la'tor

an'ni•ver'sa•ry
  pl. an'ni•ver'sa•ries

an'no Dom'i•ni'

an'no•tate'
  an'no•tat'ed,
  an'no•tat'ing

an'no•ta'tion

an'no•ta'tive

an'no•ta'tor

an•nounce'
  an•nounced',
  an•nounc'ing

an•nounce'ment

an•nounc'er

an•noy'

an•noy'ance

an•noy'ing

an'nu•al

an'nu•al•ly

an•nu'i•tant

an•nu'i•ty
  pl. an•nu'i•ties

an•nul'
  an•nulled', an•nul'ling

an'nu•lar

an•nul'ment

an'nu•lus
  pl. an'nu•li' or
  an'nu•lus•es

an•nun'ci•ate'
  an•nun'ci•at'ed,
  an•nun'ci•at'ing

an•nun'ci•a'tion

an•nun'ci•a'tor

an'ode

an•od'ic

an'o•dize'
  an'o•dized',
  an'o•diz'ing

an'o•dyne'

a•noint'

a•nom'a•lis'tic

a•nom'a•lous

a•nom'a•ly
  pl. a•nom'a•lies

an'o•mie'

a•non'

a•non'y•mous

an'o•nym'i•ty

a•noph'e•les
  pl. a•noph'e•les

a'no•rak'

an'o•rex'i•a

an•oth'er

an•ox'i•a

An'schluss

an'swer

an'swer•a•ble

ant (*insect*)
  (SEE aunt)

ant•ac'id

an•tag'o•nism'

an•tag'o•nist

an•tag'o•nis'tic

an•tag'o•nize'
  an•tag'o•nized',
  an•tag'o•niz'ing

ant•arc'tic

Ant•arc'ti•ca

ant' bear'

an'te
  an'ted or an'teed,
  an'te•ing

ant'eat'er

an'te•bel'lum

an'te•ced'ence

an'te•ced'ent

an'te•cham'ber

an'te•date'
  an'te•dat'ed,
  an'te•dat'ing

an'te•di•lu'vi•an

an'te•lope'
  pl. an'te•lopes' or
  an'te•lope'

an'te me•rid'i•em

an•ten'na
  pl. an•ten'nas or
  an•ten'nae

an'te•pe'nult

an'te•pe•nul'ti•mate

an•te'ri•or

an'te•room'

an'them

an'ther

ant'hill' or ant' hill'

an•thol'o•gize'
  an•thol'o•gized',
  an•thol'o•giz'ing

an•thol'o•gy
  pl. an•thol'o•gies

an•thol'o•gist

an'thra•cite'

an'thrax
  pl. an'thra•ces'

an'thro•po•cen'tric

an'thro•poid'

an'thro•pol'o•gist

an'thro•pol'o•gy

an'thro•po•log'ic

an'thro•po•log'i•cal

an'thro•pom'e•try

an'thro•po•mor'phic

an'thro•po•mor'
  phism

an'ti
  pl. an'tis

an'ti•air'craft'

an'ti-A•mer'i•can

an'ti•bac•te'ri•al

an'ti•bal•lis'tic

an'ti•bi•ot'ic

an'ti•bod'y
  pl. an'ti•bod'ies

an'tic
  an'ticked, an'tick•ing

An'ti•christ'

an•tic'i•pate'
  an•tic'i•pat'ed,
  an•tic'i•pat'ing

an•tic'i•pa'tion

an•tic'i•pa'tor

an•tic'i•pa•to'ry

an'ti•cler'i•cal

an'ti•cli•mac'tic

an·ti·cli′max

an′ti·clin′al

an′ti·cline′

an′ti·co·ag′u·lant

an′ti·cy′clone

an′ti·de·pres′sant

an′ti·do′tal

an′ti·dote′

an′ti·freeze′

an′ti·fric′tion

an′ti·gen

an′ti·gen′ic

an′ti·he′ro
   pl. an′ti·he′roes

an′ti·his′ta·mine′

an′ti·in′tel·lec′tu·al

an′ti·knock′

an′ti·la′bor

An·til′les

an′ti·log′a·rithm′

an′ti·ma·cas′sar

an′ti·mag·net′ic

an′ti·mat′ter

an′ti·mis′sile

an′ti·mo′ny

an′ti·neu·tri′no
   pl. an′ti·neu·tri′nos

an′ti·neu′tron

an′ti·ox′i·dant

an′ti·par′ti·cle

an′ti·pas′to
   pl. an′ti·pas′tos or
   an′ti·pas′ti

an′ti·pa·thet′ic

an·tip′a·thy
   pl. an·tip′a·thies

an′ti·per′son·nel′

an′ti·per′spi·rant

an′ti·phon′

an·tiph′o·nal

an·tiph′o·ny
   pl. an·tiph′o·nies

an·tip′o·dal

an·tip′o·des′

an′ti·pope′

an′ti·pov′er·ty

an′ti·pro′ton

an′ti·py·ret′ic

an′ti·py·re′sis

an′ti·quar′i·an

an′ti·quar′y
   pl. an′ti·quar′ies

an′ti·quate′
   an′ti·quat′ed,
   an′ti·quat′ing

an′ti·quat′ed

an·tique′
   an·tiqued′, an·ti′quing

an·tiq′ui·ty
   pl. an·tiq′ui·ties

an′ti–Sem′ite

an′ti–Se·mit′ic

an′ti–Sem′i·tism′

an′ti·sep′sis

an′ti·sep′tic

an′ti·sep′ti·cal·ly

an′ti·slav′er·y

an′ti·so′cial

an·tis′tro·phe

an′ti·sub′ma·rine′

an′ti·tank′

an·tith′e·sis
   pl. an·tith′e·ses′

an′ti·thet′ic

an′ti·thet′i·cal

an′ti·tox′in

an′ti·trade′

an′ti·trust′

an′ti·un′ion

an′ti·ven′in

an′ti·viv′i·sec′tion

ant′ler

ant′lered

an′to·nym

an·ton′y·mous

an′trum
   pl. an′tra

Ant′werp

an′u·ret′ic

an·u′ri·a

a′nus
   pl. a′nus·es

an′vil

anx·i′e·ty
   pl. anx·i′e·ties

anx′ious

an′y

an′y·bod′y
   pl. an′y·bod′ies

an′y·how′

an′y·one′

an′y·place′

an′y·thing′

an′y·time′

an′y·way′

an′y·where′

an′y·wise′

An′zac

A′-O.K.′ or A′-OK′
   or A′-O·kay′

A′ one′ or A′-one or
   A-1

a·or′ta
   pl. a·or′tas or a·or′tae

a·or′tic

a′ou·dad′

a·pace′

a·pache′ (*gangster*)
   (SEE Apache)

A·pach′e (*Indian*)
   pl. A·pach′es or
   A·pach′e
   (SEE apache)

a′pa·re′jo
   pl. a′pa·re′jos

a·part′

a·part′heid

a·part′ment

ap′a·thet′ic

ap′a·thet′i·cal·ly

ap′a·thy
   pl. ap′a·thies

ap′a·tite′ (*mineral*)
   (SEE appetite)

ape
   aped, ap′ing

a·peak′

ape′-man′

Ap′en·nines′

a·per′i·ent

a·pe′ri·tif′

ap′er·ture

a′pex
   pl. a′pex·es or
   a′pi·ces′

a·pha′sia

a·pha′si·ac′

a·pha′sic

a · phe'li · on

a'phid

aph'o · rism'

aph'o · rist'

aph'o · ris'tic

a · pho'tic

aph'ro · dis'i · ac

Aph'ro · di'te

a'pi · an

a'pi · a · rist

a'pi · ar'y
    pl. a'pi · ar'ies

ap'i · cal

a'pi · cul'ture

a · piece'

ap'ish

ap'la · nat'ic

a · plen'ty

a · plomb'

ap · ne'a

a · poc'a · lypse

a · poc'a · lyp'tic

a · poc'a · lyp'ti · cal

a · poc'o · pe

a · poc'ry · pha

a · poc'ry · phal

ap'o · ge'al

ap'o · ge'an

ap'o · gee'

a'po · lit'i · cal

A · pol'lo
    pl. A · pol'los

a · pol'o · get'ic

a · pol'o · get'i · cal · ly

ap'o · lo'gi · a

a · pol'o · gist

a · pol'o · gize'
    a · pol'o · gized',
    a · pol'o · giz'ing

a · pol'o · giz'er

a · pol'o · gy
    pl. a · pol'o · gies

ap'o · plec'tic

ap'o · plex'y

a · port'

ap'o · si'o · pe'sis

a · pos'ta · sy
    pl. a · pos'ta · sies

a · pos'tate

a' pos · te'ri · o'ri

a · pos'tle

a · pos'to · late

ap'os · tol'ic

a · pos'tro · phe

a · poth'e · car'y
    pl. a · poth'e · car'ies

ap'o · thegm' (saying)
    (SEE apothem)

ap'o · them' (geometric
    line)
    (SEE apothegm)

a · poth'e · o'sis
    pl. a · poth'e · o'ses

Ap'pa · la'chi · a

Ap'pa · la'chi · an

ap · pall'

Ap'pa · loo'sa

ap'pa · nage

ap'pa · rat'us
    pl. ap'pa · rat'us or
    ap'pa · rat'us · es

ap · par'el
    ap · par'eled,
    ap · par'el · ing

ap · par'ent

ap'pa · ri'tion

ap · peal'

ap · peal'ing

ap · pear'

ap · pear'ance

ap · pease'
    ap · peased', ap · peas'ing

ap · pease'ment

ap · peas'er

ap · pel'lant

ap · pel'late

ap'pel · la'tion

ap'pel · lee'

ap · pend'

ap · pend'age

ap'pen · dec'to · my
    pl. ap'pen · dec'to · mies

ap · pen'di · ci'tis

ap · pen'dix
    pl. ap · pen'dix · es or
    ap · pen'di · ces'

ap'per · cep'tion

ap'per · tain'

ap · pe · stat'

ap'pe · tite' (hunger)
    (SEE apatite)

ap'pe · tiz'er

ap'pe · tiz'ing

Ap'pi · an

ap · plaud'

ap · plause'

ap'ple

ap'ple · cart'

ap'ple · jack'

ap'ple–pol'ish

ap'ple · sauce'

ap · pli'ance

ap'pli · ca · bil'i · ty

ap'pli · ca · ble

ap'pli · cant

ap'pli · ca'tion

ap'pli · ca'tor

ap · plied'

ap'pli · qué'

ap · ply'
    ap · plied', ap · ply'ing

ap · pog'gia · tu'ra
    pl. ap · pog'gia · tu'ras or
    (It.) ap · pog'gia · tu're

ap · point'

ap · point · ee'

ap · poin'tive

ap · point'ment

Ap'po · mat'tox

ap · por'tion

ap · por'tion · ment

ap · pose'
    ap · posed', ap · pos'ing

ap'po · site (suitable)
    (SEE opposite)

ap'po · si'tion

ap · pos'i · tive

ap · prais'al

ap · praise' (evaluate)
    ap · praised',
    ap · prais'ing
    (SEE apprise)

ap · prais'er

ap · pre'ci · a · ble

ap · pre'ci · a · bly

ap · pre'ci · ate'
    ap · pre'ci · at'ed,
    ap · pre'ci · at'ing

ap‧pre‧ci‧a′tion

ap‧pre′ci‧a′tor

ap‧pre′cia‧tive

ap′pre‧hend′

ap′pre‧hen′sion

ap′pre‧hen′sive

ap‧pren′tice
  ap‧pren′ticed,
  ap‧pren′tic‧ing

ap‧pren′tice‧ship

ap‧prise′ (*inform*)
  ap‧prised′, ap‧pris′ing
  (SEE appraise)

ap‧proach′

ap‧proach′a‧ble

ap‧proach′a‧bil′ity

ap′pro‧ba′tion

ap‧pro′pri‧ate (*adj.*)

ap‧pro′pri‧ate′ (*v.*)
  ap‧pro′pri‧at′ed,
  ap‧pro′pri‧at′ing

ap‧pro′pri‧ate‧ly

ap‧pro′pri‧a′tion

ap‧pro′pri‧a′tor

ap‧prov′al

ap‧prove′
  ap‧proved′, ap‧prov′ing

ap‧prox′i‧mate (*adj.*)

ap‧prox′i‧mate′ (*v.*)
  ap‧prox′i‧mat′ed,
  ap‧prox′i‧mat′ing

ap‧prox′i‧mate‧ly

ap‧prox′i‧ma′tion

ap‧pur′te‧nance

a‧prax′i‧a

a′près‧ski′

ap′ri‧cot′

A′pril

a′ pri‧o′ri

a′pron

ap′ro‧pos′

apse

apt

ap′ter‧ous

ap′ti‧tude′

apt′ly

A′qa‧ba′

aq′ua
  pl. aq′uae or aq′uas

aq′ua‧cade′

Aq′ua‧Lung′
  (*Trademark*)

aq′ua‧ma‧rine′

aq′ua‧naut′

aq′ua‧plane′
  aq′ua‧planed′,
  aq′ua‧plan′ing

aq′ua re′gi‧a

a‧quar′i‧um
  pl. a‧quar′i‧ums or
  a‧quar′i‧a

A‧quar′i‧us

a‧quat′ic

aq′ua‧tint′

aq′ua vi′tae

aq′ue‧duct′

a′que‧ous

aq′ui‧fer

aq′ui‧line′

A‧qui′nas

a‧quiv′er

Ar′ab

ar′a‧besque′

A‧ra′bi‧a

A‧ra′bi‧an

Ar′a‧bic

Ar′ab‧ist

ar′a‧ble

a‧rach′nid

Ar′a‧ma′ic

A‧rap′a‧ho′
  pl. A‧rap′a‧hos′ or
  A‧rap′a‧ho′

ar′ba‧lest

ar′bi‧ter

ar′bi‧trage′

ar‧bit′ra‧ment

ar′bi‧trar′i‧ly

ar′bi‧trar′i‧ness

ar′bi‧trar′y
  pl. ar′bi‧trar′ies

ar′bi‧trate′
  ar′bi‧trat′ed,
  ar′bi‧trat′ing

ar′bi‧tra′tion

ar′bi‧tra′tor

ar′bor

ar‧bo′re‧al

ar‧bo‧re′tum
  pl. ar′bo‧re′tums or
  ar′bo‧re′ta

ar′bor‧i‧cul′ture

ar′bor vi′tae (*brain
  structure*)
  (SEE arborvitae)

ar′bor‧vi′tae (*tree*)
  (SEE arbor vitae)

ar‧bu′tus
  pl. ar‧bu′tus‧es

arc (*curve*)
  arced or arcked, arc′ing
  or arck′ing
  (SEE ark)

ar‧cade′
  ar‧cad′ed, ar‧cad′ing

Ar‧ca′di‧a

Ar‧ca′di‧an

ar‧cane′

arch
  pl. arch′es

ar′chae‧o‧log′i‧cal

ar′chae‧ol′o‧gist

ar′chae‧ol′o‧gy

ar′chae‧op′ter‧yx

ar‧cha′ic

ar′cha‧ism′

ar′cha‧is′tic

arch‧an′gel

arch′bish′op

arch′bish′op‧ric

arch′dea′con

arch′di′o‧cese′

arch′di‧oc′e‧san

arch′du′cal

arch′duch′ess

arch′duch′y

arch′duke′

arch‧en′e‧my
  pl. arch‧en′e‧mies

ar′che‧o‧log′i‧cal

ar′che‧ol′o‧gist

ar′che‧ol′o‧gy

Ar′che‧o‧zo′ic

arch′er

arch′er‧y

ar′che‧type′

arch′fiend′

ar′chi‧e‧pis′co‧pal

ar′chi·man′drite
Ar′chi·me′des
ar′chi·pel′a·go′
ar′chi·tect′
ar′chi·tec·ton′ic
ar′chi·tec·ton′ics
ar′chi·tec′tur·al
ar′chi·tec′ture
ar′chi·trave′
ar′chive
ar′chi·vist
ar′chon
arch′priest′
arch′way′
arc′ light′
arc′tic
Arc·tu′rus
ar′cu·ate
ar′den·cy
ar′dent
ar′dor
ar′du·ous
are
ar′e·a (space)
  (SEE aria)
ar′e·a code′
ar′e·a·way′
ar′e·ca
a·re′na
aren't
Ar′es (god of war)
  (SEE Aries)
ar′ga·li
  pl. ar′ga·lis
ar′gent
Ar′gen·ti′na
Ar′gen·tine′
Ar′gen·tin′e·an
ar′gol
ar′gon
Ar′go·naut′
ar′go·sy
  pl. ar′go·sies
ar′got
ar′gu·a·ble
ar′gue
  ar′gued, ar′gu·ing
ar′gu·ment

ar′gu·men·ta′tion
ar′gu·men′ta·tive
Ar′gus
ar′gyle
Ar′gy·rol′
  (Trademark)
a′ri·a (melody)
  (SEE area)
a′ri·a da ca′po
Ar′i·an·ism′
ar′id
a·rid′i·ty
Ar′ies (zodiac sign)
  (SEE Ares)
a·right′
ar′il
a·rise′
  a·rose′, a·ris′en,
  a·ris′ing
a·ris′ta
  pl. a·ris′tae
ar′is·toc′ra·cy
  pl. ar′is·toc′ra·cies
a·ris′to·crat′
a·ris′to·crat′ic
Ar′is·to·te′lian
Ar′is·tot′le
a·rith′me·tic
a·rith′met′i·cal
a′rith·met′i·cal·ly
a·rith′me·ti′cian
Ar′i·zo′na
Ar′i·zo′nan
ark (boat)
  (SEE arc)
Ar′kan·sas′
Ar·kan′san
arm
Ar·ma′da
ar′ma·dil′lo
  pl. ar′ma·dil′los
Ar′ma·ged′don
ar′ma·ment
ar′ma·ture
arm′band′
arm′chair′
Ar·me′ni·a
Ar·me′ni·an
arm′ful′
  pl. arm′fuls′

arm′hole′
ar′mi·stice
arm′let
arm′load′
ar·moire′
ar′mor
ar′mored
ar′mor·er
ar·mo′ri·al
ar′mor·y
  pl. ar′mor·ies
arm′pit′
arm′rest′
ar′my
  pl. ar′mies
ar′my ant′
ar′my worm′
ar′ni·ca
a·ro′ma
ar′o·mat′ic
ar′o·mat′i·cal·ly
a·rose′
a·round′
a·rous′al
a·rouse′
  a·roused′, a·rous′ing
ar·peg′gi·o
  pl. ar·peg′gi·os
ar·raign′
ar·raign′ment
ar·range′
  ar·ranged′, ar·rang′ing
ar·range′ment
ar·rang′er
ar′rant
ar′ras
ar·ray′
ar·rear′age
ar·rears′
ar·rest′
ar·rest′ing
ar·rhyth′mi·a
ar·ri′val
ar·rive′
  ar·rived′, ar·riv′ing
ar·riv′er
ar′ri·ve·der′ci
ar′ro·gance
ar′ro·gant

ar'ro·gate'
  ar'ro·gat'ed,
  ar'ro·gat'ing
ar'ro·ga'tion
ar·ron'disse·ment
ar'row
ar'row·head'
ar'row·root'
ar·roy'o
  pl. ar·roy'os
ar'se·nal
ar'se·nate'
ar'se·nic (*n.*)
ar·se'nic (*adj.*)
ar'son
ar'son·ist
art
Art' De'co
Ar'te·mis
ar'te·mis'i·a
ar·te'ri·al
ar·te'ri·o·scle·ro'sis
ar·te'ri·o·scle·rot'ic
ar'ter·y
  pl. ar'ter·ies
ar·te'sian
art'ful
art'ful·ly
ar·thri'tis
ar·thrit'ic
ar'thro·pod'
Ar'thur
Ar·thu'ri·an
ar'ti·choke'
ar'ti·cle
  ar'ti·cled, ar'ti·cling
ar·tic'u·lar
ar·tic'u·late (*adj.,*
  n.)
ar·tic'u·late' (*v.*)
  ar·tic'u·lat'ed,
  ar·tic'u·lat'ing
ar·tic'u·late·ly
ar·tic'u·la'tion
ar'ti·fact'
ar'ti·fice
ar·tif'i·cer
ar'ti·fi'cial
ar'ti·fi'cial·ly

ar'ti·fi'ci·al'i·ty
  pl. ar'ti·fi'ci·al'i·ties
ar·til'ler·y
ar·til'ler·y·man
  pl. ar·til'ler·y·men
art'i·ness
ar'ti·san
art'ist
ar·tiste'
ar·tis'tic
ar·tis'ti·cal·ly
art'ist·ry
art'less
Art' Nou·veau'
art'work'
art'y
  art'i·er, art'i·est
A·ru'ba
ar'um
Ar'y·an
ar'yl
as
as'a·fet'i·da
as·bes'tos
as·cend'
as·cend'ance or
  as·cend'ence
as·cend'an·cy or
  as·cend'en·cy
as·cend'ant or
  as·cend'ent
as·cen'sion
as·cent' (*climb*)
  (SEE assent)
as'cer·tain'
as·cet'ic (*austere*)
  (SEE ascetic)
as·cet'i·cism'
Asch'heim–Zon'dek
a·scor'bic
as'cot
as·crib'a·ble
as·cribe'
  as·cribed', as·crib'ing
as·crip'tion
a·sep'sis
a·sep'tic
a·sex'u·al
ash
  pl. ash'es

ash'can'
ash'en
Ash'ke·naz'im
  sing. Ash'ke·naz'i
ash'lar
a·shore'
ash'ram
ash'tray'
A'sia
A'sian
A'si·at'ic
a·side'
as'i·nine'
as'i·nin'i·ty
ask
a·skance'
a·skew'
a·slant'
a·sleep'
As·ma'ra
a·so'cial
asp
as·par'a·gus
as'pect
as'pen
as·per'i·ty
  pl. as·per'i·ties
as·perse'
  as·persed', as·pers'ing
as·per'sion
as'phalt
as'pho·del'
as·phyx'i·a
as·phyx'i·ate'
  as·phyx'i·at'ed,
  as·phyx'i·at'ing
as·phyx'i·a'tion
as'pic
as'pi·dis'tra
as'pir·ant
as'pi·rate' (*v.*)
  as'pi·rat'ed,
  as'pi·rat'ing
as'pi·rate (*n., adj.*)
as'pi·ra'tion
as'pi·ra'tor
as·pire'
  as·pired', as·pir'ing

as·pi·rin

ass

as·sail′

as·sail′a·ble

as·sail′ant

as·sas′sin

as·sas′si·nate′
 as·sas′si·nat·ed,
 as·sas′si·nat·ing

as·sas′si·na′tion

as·sault′

as·say′ (evaluate)
 (SEE essay)

as·se·gai′
 pl. as′se·gais′
 as′se·gaied′,
 as′se·gai′ing

as·sem′blage

as·sem′ble
 as·sem′bled,
 as·sem′bling

as·sem′bler

as·sem′bly
 pl. as·sem′blies

as·sem′bly line′

as·sem′bly·man
 pl. as·sem′bly·men

as·sent′ (agreement)
 (SEE ascent)

as·sert′

as·ser′tion

as·ser′tive

as·sess′

as·sess′a·ble

as·sess′ment

as·ses′sor

as′set

as·sev′e·rate′
 as·sev′e·rat·ed,
 as·sev′e·rat·ing

as·sev′e·ra′tion

as′si·du′i·ty
 pl. as′si·du′i·ties

as·sid′u·ous

as·sign′

as·sign′a·ble

as′sig·na′tion

as·sign·ee′

as·sign′er or
 as·sign′or

as·sign′ment

as·sim′i·la·ble

as·sim′i·late′
 as·sim′i·lat′ed,
 as·sim′i·lat′ing

as·sim′i·la′tion

As·si′si

as·sist′

as·sis′tance

as·sis′tant

as·siz′es

as·so′ci·ate′ (v.)
 as·so′ci·at′ed,
 as·so′ci·at′ing

as·so′ci·ate (n., adj.)

as·so′ci·a′tion

as·so′ci·a′tive

as′so·nance

as′so·nant

as·sort′

as·sort′ed

as·sort′ment

as·suage′
 as·suaged′, as·suag′ing

as·sume′
 as·sumed′, as·sum′ing

as·sumed′

as·sump′sit

as·sump′tion

as·sump′tive

as·sur′ance

as·sure′
 as·sured′, as·sur′ing

As·syr′i·a

As·syr′i·an

a·stat′ic

as′ta·tine′

as′ter

as′ter·isk

as′ter·ism′

a·stern′

as′ter·oid′

as·the′ni·a

as·then′ic

asth′ma

asth·mat′ic

as·tig·mat′ic

as·tig·mat′i·cal·ly

a·stig′ma·tism′

a·stir′

As′ti spu·man′te

as·ton′ish

as·tound′

a·strad′dle

as′tra·khan′

as′tral

a·stray′

a·stride′

as·trin′gent

as·trin′gen·cy

as′tro·dome′

as′tro·gate′
 as′tro·gat′ed,
 as′tro·gat′ing

as′tro·ga′tion

as′tro·ga′tor

as′tro·labe′

as·trol′o·ger

as′tro·log′i·cal

as·trol′o·gy

as′tro·naut′

as′tro·nau′ti·cal

as′tro·nau′tics

as·tron′o·mer

as′tro·nom′ic

as′tro·nom′i·cal

as·tron′o·my

as′tro·phys′i·cal

as′tro·phys′i·cist

as′tro·phys′ics

as·tute′

A·sun·ción′

a·sun′der

As′wan

a·sy′lum

a·sym·met′ric

a·sym·met′ri·cal

a·sym′me·try

as′ymp·tote′

as′ymp·tot′ic

at

at′a·rax′i·a

at′a·vism′

at′a·vis′tic

a·tax′i·a

a·tax′ic

ate

at'el·ier'
a tem'po
Ath'a·na'sian
a'the·ism'
a'the·ist
a'the·is'tic
a'the·is'ti·cal·ly
A·the'na
ath'e·nae'um or
   ath'e·ne'um
A·the'ni·an
Ath'ens
ath'er·o·scle·ro'sis
ath'er·o·scle·rot'ic
a·thirst'
ath'lete
ath·let'ic
ath·let'i·cal·ly
ath·let'ics
a·thwart'
a·tilt'
a·tin'gle
At·lan'ta
At·lan'tic
At·lan'tis
at'las
at'mos·phere'
at'mos·pher'ic
at'mos·pher'i·cal·ly
at'oll
at'om
a'tom bomb'
a·tom'ic
a·tom'ics
a·tom'ic bomb'
at'om·ism'
at'om·i·za'tion
at'om·ize'
   at'om·ized',
   at'om·iz'ing
at'om·iz'er
a'ton·al
a'to·nal'i·ty
a·ton'al·ly
a·tone'
   a·toned', a·ton'ing
a·ton'er

a·tone'ment
at'o·ny
a·top'
a·trip'
a'tri·um
   pl. a'tri·a
a·tro'cious
a·troc'i·ty
   pl. a·troc'i·ties
at'ro·phy
   at'ro·phied,
   at'ro·phy·ing
at'ro·pine'
at·tach'
at·tach'a·ble
at'ta·ché'
at·tach'ment
at·tack'
at·tain'
at·tain'a·ble
at·tain'der
at·tain'ment
at·taint'
at'tar
at·tempt'
at·tend'
at·tend'ance
at·tend'ant
at·ten'tion
at·ten'tive
at·ten'tive·ly
at·ten'u·ate' (v.)
   at·ten'u·at'ed,
   at·ten'u·at'ing
at·ten'u·ate (adj.)
at·ten'u·a'tion
at·test'
at·tes·ta'tion
at'tic (top floor)
   (SEE Attic)
At'tic (Greek)
   (SEE attic)
At'ti·la
at·tire'
   at·tired', at·tir'ing
at'ti·tude'
at'ti·tu'di·nal
at·tor'ney
   pl. at·tor'neys

at·tor'ney-at-law'
   pl. at·tor'neys-at-law'
at·tor'ney gen'er·al
   pl. at·tor'neys
   gen'er·al
at·tract'
at·trac'tion
at·trac'tive
at·trib'ut·a·ble
at·trib'ute (v.)
   at·trib'ut·ed,
   at·trib'ut·ing
at'trib·ute' (n.)
at'tri·bu'tion
at·trib'u·tive
at·trib'u·tive·ly
at·tri'tion
at·tune'
   at·tuned', at·tun'ing
a·twit'ter
a·typ'i·cal
au·bade'
au'burn
Au'bus·son
Auck'land
au con·traire'
au cou·rant'
auc'tion
auc'tion·eer'
auc·to'ri·al
au·da'cious
au·dac'i·ty
   pl. au·dac'i·ties
au'di·bil'i·ty
au'di·ble
au'di·bly
au'di·ence
au'di·o
au'di·o fre'quen·cy
au'di·ol'o·gy
au'di·ol'o·gist
au'di·om'e·ter
au'di·o·phile'
au'di·o·tape'
au'di·o·vis'u·al
au'dit
au·di'tion
au'di·tor

au'di·to'ri·um
  pl. au'di·to'ri·ums or au'di·to'ri·a

au'di·to'ry
  pl. au'di·to'ries

Au'du·bon'

Auf'klä'rung

auf Wie'der·seh'en

Au·ge'an

au'ger (*drill*)
  (SEE augur)

aught (*zero*)
  (SEE ought)

aug·ment' (*v.*)

aug'ment (*n.*)

aug'men·ta'tion

aug·ment'a·tive

au grat'in

Augs'burg

au'gur (*predict*)
  (SEE auger)

au'gu·ry
  pl. au'gu·ries

au·gust' (*majestic*)
  (SEE August)

Au'gust (*month*)
  (SEE august)

Au·gus'ta

Au·gus'tan

Au'gus·tine'

Au'gus·tin'i·an

Au·gus'tus

au jus'

auk

au lait'

auld' lang syne'

au na·tu·rel'

aunt (*relative*)
  (SEE ant)

au pair

au'ra
  pl. au'ras or au'rae

au'ral (*of hearing*)
  (SEE oral)

au'ral·ly

au're·ate

au're·ole'

Au're·o·my'cin
  (*Trademark*)

au re·voir'

au'ric

au'ri·cle (*outer ear*)
  (SEE oracle)

au·ric'u·lar

au·rif'er·ous

au'rochs

Au·ro'ra

au·ro'ra aus·tra'lis

au·ro'ra bo're·al'is

au·ro'ral

aur'ous

Ausch'witz

aus'cul·tate'
  aus'cul·tat'ed,
  aus'cul·tat'ing

aus'cul·ta'tion

aus'pice
  pl. aus'pic·es

aus·pi'cious

Aus'sie

aus·tere'

aus·tere'ly

aus·ter'i·ty
  pl. aus·ter'i·ties

Aus'tin

aus'tral

Aus'tral·a'sia

Aus·tral'ia

Aus·tral'ian

Aus'tra·loid'

Aus'tri·a

Aus'tri·an

Aus'tro–Hun·gar'i·an

Aus'tro·ne'sia

au'tar·chy
  pl. au'tar·chies

au·then'tic

au·then'ti·cal·ly

au·then'ti·cate'
  au·then'ti·cat'ed,
  au·then'ti·cat'ing

au·then'ti·ca'tion

au·then'ti·ca'tor

au'then·tic'i·ty

au'thor

auth'or·ess

au·thor'i·tar'i·an

au·thor'i·tar'i·an·ism'

au·thor'i·ta'tive

au·thor'i·ty
  pl. au·thor'i·ties

au'thor·i·za'tion

au'thor·ize'
  au'thor·ized',
  au'thor·iz'ing

au'thor·ship'

au'tism

au·tis'tic

au'to
  pl. au'tos

au'to·bahn'

au'to·bi·og'ra·pher

au'to·bi'o·graph'ic

au'to·bi'o·graph'i·cal

au'to·bi·og'ra·phy
  pl. au'to·bi·og'ra·phies

au·toch'tho·nous

au'to·clave'

au·toc'ra·cy
  pl. au·toc'ra·cies

au'to·crat'

au'to·crat'ic

au'to·crat'i·cal·ly

au'to–da–fé'
  pl. au'tos–da–fé'

au'to·er'o·tism'

au·tog'e·nous

au'to·gi'ro
  pl. au'to·gi'ros

au'to·graph'

au'to·harp'

au'to·hyp·no'sis

au'to·in·tox'i·ca'tion

au'to·mat'

au'to·mate'
  au'to·mat'ed,
  au'to·mat'ing

au'to·mat'ic

au'to·mat'i·cal·ly

au'to·ma'tion

au·tom'a·tism

au·tom'a·ton'
  pl. au·tom'a·tons' or au·tom'a·ta

au'to·mo·bile'

au'to·mo·bil'ist

au'to·mo'tive

au'to·nom'ic

au·ton'o·mous
au·ton'o·my
  pl. au·ton'o·mies
au'to·pi'lot
au'to·plas'ty
au'top·sy
  pl. au'top·sies
au'to·stra'da
au'to·sug·ges'tion
au'tumn
au·tum'nal
aux·il'ia·ry
  pl. aux·il'ia·ries
aux'in
a·vail'
a·vail'a·bil'i·ty
  pl. a·vail'a·bil'i·ties
a·vail'a·ble
av'a·lanche'
Av'a·lon'
a·vant'-garde'
av'a·rice
av'a·ri'cious
a·vast'
av'a·tar'
A've Ma·ri'a
a·venge'
  a·venged', a·veng'ing
a·veng'er
av'e·nue'
a·ver'
  a·verred', a·ver'ring
av'er·age
  av'er·aged,
  av'er·ag·ing
A·ver'nus
a·verse' (unwilling)
  (SEE adverse)
a·ver'sion
a·vert'
a'vi·an
a'vi·ar'y
  pl. a'vi·ar'ies
a'vi·a'tion

a'vi·a'tor
a'vi·a'trix
  pl. a'vi·a'tri·ces'
av'id
a·vid'i·ty
A·vi·gnon'
a'vi·on'ic
a'vi·on'ics
a·vi'ta·min·o'sis
av'o·ca'do
  pl. av'o·ca'dos
av'o·ca'tion
av'o·cet'
a·void'
a·void'a·ble
a·void'ance
av'oir·du·pois'
a·vouch'
a·vow'
a·vow'al
a·vowed'
a·vun'cu·lar
aw (exclamation)
  (SEE awe)
a·wait'
a·wake'
  a·woke' or a·waked',
  a·wak'ing
a·wak'en
a·wak'en·ing
a·ward'
a·ware'
a·ware'ness
a·wash'
a·way' (apart)
  (SEE aweigh)
awe (respect)
  awed, aw'ing
  (SEE aw)
a·wea'ry
a·weath'er
a·weigh' (raised)
  (SEE away)

awe'some
awe'-strick'en
awe'-struck'
aw'ful (causing fear)
  (SEE offal)
aw'ful·ly
a·while'
a·whirl'
awk'ward
awl (drill)
  (SEE all)
aw'less
awn
awn'ing
a·woke'
A.W.O.L.
a·wry'
ax or axe
  axed, ax'ing
ax'i·al
ax·il'la
  pl. ax·il'lae
ax'i·om
ax'i·o·mat'ic
ax'i·o·mat'i·cal·ly
ax'is
  pl. ax'es
ax'le
ax'le·tree'
Ax'min·ster
ax'o·lotl'
ax'on
a'ya·tol'lah
aye (yes)
  (SEE eye)
aye'-aye'
a·zal'ea
az'i·muth
az'o
A·zores'
Az'tec
az'ure
az'ur·ite'

B

baa
  baaed, baa'ing

Ba'al
  pl. Ba'al·im

Baath
ba'ba
ba'ba au rhum'
Bab'bitt

bab'ble
  bab'bled, bab'bling
babe
Ba'bel

ba'bies'–breath'

bab'i•ru'sa

bab'ka

ba•boon'

ba•bush'ka

ba'by
  pl. ba'bies; v. ba'bied,
  ba'by•ing

Bab'y•lon

Bab'y•lo'ni•a

Bab'y•lo'ni•an

ba'by's–breath'

ba'by–sit'
  ba'by-sat', ba'by-
    •sit'ting

ba'by sit'ter

ba'by talk'

bac'ca•lau're•ate

bac'ca•rat'

bac'cha•nal'

bac'cha•na'li•a

bac'cha•na'li•an

Bac'chic

Bac'chus

Bach

bach'e•lor

bach'e•lor's–but'ton

ba•cil'lus
  pl. ba•cil'li

bac'i•tra'cin

back

back'ache'

back'bend'

back'bite'
  back'bit', back'bit'ing

back'bit'er

back'board'

back'bone'

back'break'ing

back' burn'er

back'court'

back'drop'

back'er

back'field'

back'fire'
  back'fired', back'fir'ing

back' for•ma'tion

back'gam'mon

back'ground'

back'hand'

back'hand'ed

back'ing

back'lash'

back'light'

back'log'

back'pack'

back'rest'

back'side'

back'slap'per

back'slide'
  back'slid', back'slid' or
  back'slid'den,
  back'sli'ding

back'slid'er

back'space'
  back'spaced',
  back'spac'ing

back'spin'

back'stage'

back' stairs'

back'stay'

back'stitch

back'stop'
  back'stopped',
  back'stop'ping

back'stretch'

back'stroke'
  back'stroked',
  back'strok'ing

back'swept'

back'swing'

back' talk'

back'track'

back'up'

back'ward

back'wards

back'wash'

back'wa'ter

back'woods'

back'woods'man
  pl. back'woods'men

ba'con

Ba•co'ni•an

bac•te'ri•a
  sing. bac•te'ri•um

bac•te'ri•al

bac•te'ri•cid'al

bac•te'ri•cide'

bac•te'ri•o•log'ic

bac•te'ri•o•log'i•cal

bac•te'ri•ol'o•gist

bac•te'ri•ol'o•gy

Bac'tri•an cam'el

bad (not good)
  worse, worst
  (SEE bade)

bade (pt. of bid)
  (SEE bad)

badge
  badged, badg'ing

badg'er

bad'i•nage'
  bad'i•naged',
  bad'i•nag'ing

bad'lands'

bad'ly
  worse, worst

bad'man'
  pl. bad'men'

bad'min•ton

bad'mouth'

bad'–tem'pered

Bae'de•ker

Baf'fin

baf'fle
  baf'fled, baf'fling

bag
  bagged, bag'ging

ba•gasse'

bag'a•telle'

ba'gel

bag'ful'
  pl. bag'fuls'

bag'gage

bag'gage•mas'ter

bag'ger

bag'gy
  bag'gi•er, bag'gi•est

Bagh'dad

bag'man
  pl. bag'men

bagn'io

bag'pipe'
  bag'piped', bag'pip'ing

bag'pip'er

ba•guette'

bah

Ba•ha'i'

Ba•ha'ma

Ba·ha′mi·an

Bah·rain′

baht
　pl. bahts or baht

bail (*money; dip*)
　(SEE bale)

bail′ee′

bail′iff

bail′i·wick

bail′or

bail′out′

bails′man
　pl. bails′men

bairn

bait (*lure*)
　(SEE bate)

baize
　baized, baiz′ing

bake
　baked, bak′ing

Ba′ke·lite′
　(*Trademark*)

bak′er

bak′er's doz′en

bak′er·y
　pl. bak′er·ies

ba′kla·va′

bak′sheesh

bal′a·lai′ka

bal′ance
　bal′anced, bal′anc·ing

bal′a·ta

Bal·bo′a

bal·bo′a

bal·brig′gan

bal′co·ny
　pl. bal′co·nies

bald

bal′da·chin

bal′der·dash′

bald′head′ed

bald′pate′

bal′dric

bale (*bundle*)
　baled, bal′ing
　(SEE bail)

ba·leen′

bale′ful

Ba′li

Ba′li·nese′
　pl. Ba′li·nese′

balk

Bal′kan

balk′line′

balk′y
　balk′i·er, balk′i·est

ball (*round object*)
　(SEE bawl)

bal′lad

bal·lade′

bal′lad·eer′

bal′lad·ry

ball′-and-sock′et

bal′last

ball′ bear′ing

bal′le·ri′na
　pl. bal′le·ri′nas or (*It.*)
　bal′le·ri′ne

bal·let′

bal·let′o·mane′

bal·lis′tic

bal·lis′tics

bal·loon′

bal·loon′ist

bal′lot
　bal′lot·ed, bal′lot·ing

ball′ park′

ball′ peen′

ball′play′er

ball′point′

ball′room′

bal′ly·hoo′
　pl. bal′ly·hoos′; v.
　bal′ly·hooed′,
　bal′ly·hoo′ing

balm

bal′ma·caan′

balm′y
　balm′i·er, balm′i·est

ba·lo′ney

bal′sa

bal′sam

Bal′tic

Bal′ti·more′

bal′us·ter

bal′us·trade′

Bal′zac

bam·boo′
　pl. bam·boos′

bam·boo′zle
　bam·boo′zled,
　bam·boo′zling

ban
　banned, ban′ning

ba′nal

ba·nal′i·ty
　pl. ba·nal′i·ties

ba·nan′a

band (*musicians*)
　(SEE banned)

band′age
　band′aged, band′ag·ing

Band′-Aid′
　(*Trademark*)

ban·dan′na or
　ban·dan′a

band′box′

ban·deau′
　pl. ban·deaux′

ban′de·role′ or
　ban′de·rol′

ban′di·coot′

ban′dit
　pl. ban′dits or
　ban·dit′ti

ban′dit·ry

band′mas′ter

ban′do·leer′ or
　ban′do·lier′

band′ saw′

band′stand′

band′wag′on

ban′dy
　ban′died, ban′dy·ing

ban′dy·leg′ged

bane

bane′ful

Banff

bang

Bang′kok

Ban′gla·desh′

ban′gle

Ban·gui′

bang′-up′

ban′ish

ban′is·ter or
　ban′nis·ter

ban′jo
　pl. ban′jos or ban′joes

ban′jo·ist

bank

bank′a·ble

bank′book′

bank′ card′

bank′er

bank′ing

bank′ note′ or
  bank′note′

bank′roll′

bank′rupt

bank′rupt·cy
  pl. bank′rupt·cies

ban′ner

banns

ban′quet
  ban′quet·ed,
  ban′quet·ing

ban·quette′

ban′shee

ban′tam

ban′tam·weight′

ban′ter

Ban′tu
  pl. Ban′tus or Ban′tu

ban′yan

ban·zai′

ba′o·bab′

bap′tism

bap·tis′mal

Bap′tist

bap′tis·ter·y
  pl. bap′tis·ter·ies

bap·tize′
  bap·tized′, bap·tiz′ing

bap·tiz′er

bar
  barred, bar′ring

Bar·ab′bas

barb

Bar·ba′dos

bar·bar′i·an

bar·bar′ic

bar·ba′rism′

bar·bar′i·ty
  pl. bar·bar′i·ties

bar′ba·rous

Bar′ba·ry

bar′be·cue′
  bar′be·cued′,
  bar′be·cu′ing

bar′bel

bar′bell′

bar′bel·late′

bar′ber

bar′ber′ry
  pl. bar′ber′ries

bar′ber·shop′

bar·bette

bar′bi·can

bar′bi·tal′

bar·bi′tu·rate′

Bar′bi·zon

barb′wire′

bar′ car′

bar′ca·role′ or
  bar′ca·rolle′

Bar′ce·lon′a

bard (*poet*)
  (SEE *barred*)

bare (*naked*)
  adj. bar′er, bar′est;
  v. bared, bar′ing
  (SEE *bear*)

bare′back′

bare′faced′

bare′foot′

bare′foot′ed

bare′hand′ed

bare′head′ed

bare′knuck′le

bare′leg′ged

bare′ly

bar′fly′
  pl. bar′flies′

bar′gain

barge
  barged, barg′ing

bar′ graph′

bar′ic

bar′ite

bar′i·tone′

bar′i·um

bark (*sound*)
  (SEE *barque*)

bar′keep′er

bar′ken·tine′

bark′er

bar′ley

bar′ley·corn′

bar′maid′

bar′man
  pl. bar′men

bar mitz′vah

barn

bar′na·cle

barn′ dance′

barn′storm′

Bar′num

barn′yard′

bar′o·graph′

ba·rom′e·ter

bar′o·met′ric

bar′o·met′ri·cal

bar′on (*nobleman*)
  (SEE *barren*)

bar′on·ess

bar′on·et

ba·ro′ni·al

bar′o·ny
  pl. bar′o·nies

ba·roque′

ba·rouche′

barque (*ship*)
  (SEE *bark*)

bar′rack

bar′racks

bar′ra·cu′da
  pl. bar′ra·cu′da or
  bar′ra·cu′das

bar·rage′
  bar·raged′, bar·rag′ing

bar′ra·try

barred (*pt. of bar*)
  (SEE *bard*)

bar′rel
  bar′reled, bar′rel·ing

bar′rel–chest′ed

bar′rel·head′

bar′rel·house′

bar′ren (*empty*)
  (SEE *baron*)

bar′ren·ness

bar·rette′

bar′ri·cade′
  bar′ri·cad′ed,
  bar′ri·cad′ing

bar′ri·cad′er

bar′ri·er

bar′ring

bar′rio
  pl. bar′rios

bar'ris•ter

bar'room'

bar'row

bar'stool'

bar'ten'der

bar'ter

ba'sal

ba•salt'

ba•sal'tic

bas'cule

base (*foundation;
    bad*)
  v. based, bas'ing
  adj. bas'er, bas'est
  (SEE bass, *singer*)

base'ball'

base'board'

base'born'

base' hit'

base'less

base' line'

base'ly

base'man
  pl. base'men

base'ment

base'ness

Ba•sen'ji

bash

bash'ful

ba'sic

ba•sic'i•ty

ba'si•cal•ly

bas'il

bas'i•lar

ba•sil'i•ca

bas'i•lisk'

ba'sin

ba'sis
  pl. ba'ses

bask (*lie in warmth*)
  (SEE Basque)

bas'ket

bas'ket•ball'

bas'ket•ful'
  pl. bas'ket•fuls'

bas'ket•ry

bas'ket•work'

basque

Basque

bas'–re•lief'

bass (*singer*)
  (SEE base)

bass (*fish*)
  pl. bass or bass'es

bass' clef'

bass' drum'

bas'set

Basse–Terre'

bas'si•net'

bass'ist

bas'so
  pl. bas'sos or (*It.*) bas'si

bas•soon'

bas•soon'ist

bas'so pro•fun'do

bass'wood'

bast

bas'tard

bas'tard•ize'
  bas'tard•ized',
  bas'tard•iz'ing

bas'tar•dy

baste
  bast'ed, bast'ing

Bas•tille'

bas'ti•na'do
  pl. bas'ti•na'does

bas'tion

bat
  bat'ted, bat'ting

Ba•taan'

batch

bate (*decrease*)
  bat'ed, bat'ing
  (SEE bait)

ba•teau'
  pl. ba•teaux'

bath

bathe
  bathed, bath'ing

bath'er

ba•thet'ic

bath'house'

Bath'i•nette'
  (*Trademark*)

bath mitz'vah

bath'ing cap'

bath'ing suit'

bath'o•lith

ba'thos

bath'robe'

bath'room'

Bath•she'ba

bath'tub'

bath'y•scaphe'

bath'y•sphere'

ba•tik'

ba•tiste'

bat'man
  pl. bat'men

ba•ton'

Bat'on Rouge'

bats'man
  pl. bats'men

bat•tal'ion

bat'ten

bat'ter

bat'ter•ing ram'

bat'ter•y
  pl. bat'ter•ies

bat'ting

bat'tle
  bat'tled, bat'tling

bat'tle–ax' or
  bat'tle–axe'

bat'tle cry'

bat'tle•dore'
  bat'tle•dored',
  bat'tle•dor'ing

bat'tle•field'

bat'tle•front'

bat'tle jack'et

bat'tle line'

bat'tle•ment

bat'tle–scarred'

bat'tle•ship'

bat'tle star'

bat'ty
  bat'ti•er, bat'ti•est

bau'ble

baud

baux'ite

Ba•var'i•a

Ba•var'i•an

bawd'i•ness

bawd'y
  bawd'i•er, bawd'i•est

bawl (*shout*)
  (SEE ball)

bay (*inlet of sea*)
(SEE bey)

bay'ber'ry
pl. bay'ber'ries

bay' leaf'

bay'o·net
bay'o·net·ed or
bay'o·net·ted,
bay'o·net·ing or
bay'o·net·ting

bay'ou
pl. bay'ous

bay' rum'

bay' win'dow

ba·zaar'
(*marketplace*)
(SEE bizarre)

ba·zoo'ka

be (*exist*)
was or were, been,
being
(SEE bee)

beach (*shore*)
(SEE beech)

beach' ball'

beach'boy'

beach' bug'gy

beach'comb'er

beach'head'

bea'con

bead

bead'ing

bea'dle

bead'work'

bead'y
bead'i·er, bead'i·est

bea'gle

beak

beak'er

beam

bean

bean'bag'

bean' ball'

bean'er·y
pl. bean'e·ries

bean'ie

bean'pole'

bean'stalk'

bear (*carry*)
bore, borne or born,
bear'ing
(SEE bare)

bear (*animal*)
pl. bears or bear
(SEE bare)

bear'a·ble

bear'cat'

beard

beard'ed

bear'er

bear' hug'

bear'ing

bear'ish

bear'skin'

beast

beast'ly
beast'li·er, beast'li·est

beat (*strike*)
beat, beat'en or beat,
beat'ing
(SEE beet)

beat'en

beat'er

be·a·tif'ic

be·at'i·fi·ca'tion

be·at'i·fy'
be·at'i·fied',
be·at'i·fy'ing

beat'ing

be·at'i·tude'

beat'nik

beat'–up'

beau (*suitor*)
pl. beaus or beaux
(SEE bow, *weapon*)

Beau' Brum'mell

Beau'fort

beau geste'
pl. *beaux gestes'*

Beau'jo·lais'

beau' monde'

beaut

beau'te·ous

beau·ti'cian

beau'ti·fi·ca'tion

beau'ti·ful

beau'ti·ful·ly

beau'ti·fy'
beau'ti·fied',
beau'ti·fy'ing

beau'ty
pl. beau'ties

bea'ver
pl. bea'vers or bea'ver

be'bop'

be·calm'

be·came'

be·cause'

bé'cha·mel'

beck

Beck'et

beck'on

be·cloud'

be·come'
be·came', be·come',
be·com'ing

bed
bed'ded, bed'ding

be·daub'

be·daz'zle
be·daz'zled,
be·daz'zling

bed' board'

bed'bug'

bed'cham'ber

bed' check'

bed'clothes'

bed'ding

be·deck'

be·dev'il
be·dev'iled,
be·dev'il·ing

be·dew'

bed'fel'low

bed'frame'

be·di'zen

bed'lam

Bed'ling·ton

Bed'ou·in
pl. Bed'ou·ins or
Bed'ou·in

bed'pan'

bed'post'

be·drag'gle
be·drag'gled,
be·drag'gling

bed'rail'

bed'rid'den

bed'rock'

bed'roll'

bed'room'

bed'side'

bed'sore'

bed'stand'

bed′spread′
bed′stead′
bed′time′
bee (*insect*)
  (SEE be)
beech (*tree*)
  (SEE beach)
beech′nut′
beef
  pl. beeves or beefs
beef′burg′er
beef′eat′er
beef′steak′
beef′y
  beef′i·er, beef′i·est
bee′hive′
bee′keep′er
bee′line′
Be·el′ze·bub′
beep
beep′er
beer (*beverage*)
  (SEE bier)
beer′ gar′den
Beer·she′ba
bees′wax′
beet (*plant*)
  (SEE beat)
Bee′tho·ven
bee′tle (*insect*)
  bee′tled, bee′tling
  (SEE betel)
be·fall′
  be·fell′, be·fall′en,
  be·fall′ing
be·fit′
  be·fit′ted, be·fit′ting
be·fog′
  be·fogged′, be·fog′ging
be·fore′
be·fore′hand′
be·foul′
be·friend′
be·fud′dle
  be·fud′dled,
  be·fud′dling
beg
  begged, beg′ging
be·gan′
be·get′
  be·got′, be·got′ten or
  be·got′, be·get′ting

be·get′ter
beg′gar
be·gin′
  be·gan′, be·gun′,
  be·gin′ning
be·gin′ner
be·gin′ning
be·gone′
be·gon′ia
be·gor′ra
be·grime′
  be·grimed′, be·grim′ing
be·grudge′
  be·grudged′,
  be·grudg′ing
be·guile′
  be·guiled′, be·guil′ing
be·guil′er
be·guine′
be′gum
be·gun′
be·half′
be·have′
  be·haved′, be·hav′ing
be·hav′ior
be·hav′ior·al
be·hav′ior·ism′
be·hav′ior·ist
be·head′
be·he′moth
be·hest′
be·hind′
be·hind′hand′
be·hold′
  be·held′, be·hold′ing
be·hold′en
be·hoove′
  be·hooved′,
  be·hoov′ing
beige
be′ing
Bei·rut′
be·la′bor
be·lat′ed
be·lay′
  be·layed′, be·lay′ing
bel′ can′to
belch
be·lea′guer
Bel′fast

be·get′ter
beg′gar
bel′fry
  pl. bel′fries
Bel′gian
Bel′gium
Bel·grade′
be·lie′
  be·lied′, be·ly′ing
be·li′er
be·lief′
be·liev′a·ble
be·lieve′
  be·lieved′, be·liev′ing
be·liev′er
be·lit′tle
  be·lit′tled, be·lit′tling
Be·lize′
bell (*metal
  instrument*)
  (SEE belle)
bel′la·don′na
bell′–bot′tom
bell′boy′
bell′ cap′tain
belle (*woman*)
  (SEE bell)
belles–let′tres
bell′hop′
bel′li·cose′
bel′li·cos′i·ty
bel·lig′er·ence
bel·lig′er·en·cy
bel·lig′er·ent
Bel·li′ni
bell′ jar′
bell′man
  pl. bell′men
bel′low
bel′lows
bell′weth′er
bel′ly
  pl. bel′lies; *v.*
  bel′lied, bel′ly·ing
bel′ly·ache′
  bel′ly·ached′,
  bel′ly·ach′ing
bel′ly·but′ton
bel′ly dance′
bel′ly flop′
bel′ly laugh′
be·long′

be·long'ing

be·lov'ed

be·low'

belt

belt'ed

belt'ing

belt'way

be·lu'ga

bel've·dere'

be'ma
pl. be'ma·ta

be·mire'
be·mired', be·mir'ing

be·moan'

be·muse'
be·mused', be·mus'ing

be·mused'

Ben'a·dryl
(Trademark)

bench

bench' war'rant

bend
bent, bend'ing

bend'er

be·neath'

ben'e·dict

Ben'e·dic'tine

ben'e·dic'tion

ben'e·fac'tion

ben'e·fac'tor

ben'e·fac'tress

ben'e·fice
ben'e·ficed,
ben'e·fic·ing

be·nef'i·cence

be·nef'i·cent

ben'e·fi'cial

ben'e·fi'cial·ly

ben'e·fi'ci·ar'y
pl. ben'e·fi'ci·ar'ies

ben'e·fit
ben'e·fit·ed or
ben'e·fit·ted,
ben'e·fit·ing or
ben'e·fit·ting

be·nev'o·lence

be·nev'o·lent

Ben·gal'

Ben·ga'li

Ben-Gu·rion'

be·night'ed

be·nign'

be·nig'nant

be·nig'ni·ty
pl. be·nig'ni·ties

Be·nin'

ben'i·son

ben'ny
pl. ben'nies

bent

ben'thic

ben'thos

bent'wood'

be·numb'

Ben'ze·drine'
(Trademark)

ben'zene

ben'zine

ben'zo·caine'

ben·zo'ic

ben'zo·in

ben'zol

ben'zyl

be·queath'

be·quest'

be·rate'
be·rat'ed, be·rat'ing

Ber'ber

ber·ceuse'

Berch'tes·ga·den

be·reave'
be·reaved' or be·reft',
be·reav'ing

be·reave'ment

be·reft'

be·ret'

berg

ber'ga·mot'

ber'i·ber'i

Ber'ing

ber·ke'li·um

Berk'shire

Ber·lin'

Ber'li·oz'

berm

Ber·mu'da

Ber·mu'di·an

Bern

Ber·ni'ni

Ber·noul'li

ber'ry (fruit)
pl. ber'ries; v.
ber'ried, ber'ry·ing
(SEE bury)

ber·serk'

berth (bed)
(SEE birth)

Ber'til·lon'

ber'yl

be·ryl'li·um

be·seech'
be·sought',
be·seech'ing

be·seem'

be·set'
be·set', be·set'ting

be·side'

be·sides'

be·siege'
be·sieged', be·sieg'ing

be·sieg'er

be·smear'

be·smirch'

be'som

be·sot'
be·sot'ted, be·sot'ting

be·span'gle
be·span'gled,
be·span'gling

be·spat'ter

be·speak'
be·spoke', be·spok'en
or be·spoke',
be·speak'ing

be·spec'ta·cled

be·spread'
be·spread',
be·spread'ing

be·sprin'kle
be·sprin'kled,
be·sprin'kling

Bes'se·mer

best

bes'tial

bes·ti·al'i·ty
pl. bes·ti·al'i·ties

bes'ti·ar'y
pl. bes'ti·ar'ies

be·stir'
be·stirred', be·stir'ring

best' man'

be·stow'

be·strew'
  be·strewed',
  be·strewed' or
  be·strewn',
  be·strew'ing

be·stride'
  be·strode' or be·strid',
  be·strid'den or
  be·strid', be·strid'ing

best' sell'er

best'-sell'ing

bet
  bet or bet'ted, bet'ting

be'ta

be·take'
  be·took', be·tak'en,
  be·tak'ing

be'ta·tron

be'tel (*plant*)
  (SEE beetle)

Be'tel·geuse'

bête noir'

beth'el

be·think'
  be·thought',
  be·think'ing

Beth'le·hem

be·tide'
  be·tid'ed, be·tid'ing

be·times'

be·tok'en

bet'o·ny

be·tray'

be·tray'al

be·troth'

be·troth'al

be·trothed'

bet'ter (*superior*)
  (SEE bettor)

bet'ter·ment

bet'tor (*one who bets*)
  (SEE better)

be·tween'

be·twixt'

beurre' noir'

bev'a·tron'

bev'el
  bev'eled or bev'elled,
  bev'el·ing or
  bev'el·ling

bev'er·age

bev'y
  pl. bev'ies

be·wail'

be·ware'
  be·wared', be·war'ing

be·whisk'ered

be·wil'der

be·witch'

be·yond'

bez'el

B'-girl'

bhang

Bhu·tan'

Bhu'tan·ese'

bi·a'ly
  pl. bi·a'lys

bi·an'nu·al (*twice a year*)
  (SEE biennial)

bi·an'nu·al·ly

bi'as
  bi'ased or bi'assed,
  bi'as·ing or bi'as·sing

bi·ath'lon

bib
  bibbed, bib'bing

bib'cock'

bi'be·lot

Bi'ble

Bi'ble Belt'

Bib'li·cal

bib'li·og'ra·pher

bib'li·o·graph'ic

bib'li·o·graph'i·cal

bib'li·og'ra·phy
  pl. bib'li·og'ra·phies

bib'li·o·phile'

bib'u·lous

bi·cam'er·al

bi·car'bo·nate

bi·cen'te·nar'y
  pl. bi·cen'te·nar'ies

bi'cen·ten'ni·al

bi'ceps

bi·chlo'ride

bick'er

bi'col'or

bi·con'cave

bi·con'vex

bi·cor'po·ral

bi·cus'pid

bi'cy·cle
  bi'cy·cled, bi'cy·cling

bi'cy·clist

bid
  bade or bad or bid;
  bid'den or bid, bid'ding

bid'da·ble

bid'der

bid'ding

bid'dy
  pl. bid'dies

bide
  bid'ed or bode, bid'ed,
  bid'ing

bi·det'

Bie'der·mei'er

bi·en'ni·al

bi·en'ni·al·ly

bier (*coffin stand*)
  (SEE beer)

bi·fo'cal

bi'fur·cate'
  bi'fur·cat'ed,
  bi'fur·cat'ing

bi'fur·ca'tion

big
  big'ger, big'gest

big'a·mist

big'a·mous

big'a·my
  pl. big'a·mies

Big' Ap'ple

Big' Dip'per

big'gie

big'-heart'ed

big'horn'
  pl. big'horns' or
  big'horn'

bight (*loop*)
  (SEE bite)

big'ot

big'ot·ed

big'ot·ry
  pl. big'ot·ries

big' shot'

big'wig'

bike
  biked, bik'ing
bike'way'
bi·ki'ni
bi·la'bi·al
bi·lat'er·al
bi·lat'er·al·ly
bile
bilge
  bilged, bilg'ing
bilge' wa'ter
bi·lin'gual
bi·lin'gual·ism
bi·lin'gual·ly
bil'ious
bilk
bilk'er
bill
bill'board'
bil'let
  bil'let·ed, bil'let·ing
bil'let-doux'
bill'fold'
bill'head'
bil'liard
bil'liards
bill'ing
bil'lings·gate'
bil'lion
  pl. bil'lions or bil'lion
bil'lion·aire'
bil'lionth
bil'low
bil'low·y
bil'ly
  pl. bil'lies
bil'ly goat'
bi'mah
bi'met·al'lic
bi·met'al·lism'
bi·met'al·list
bi·month'ly
  pl. bi·month'lies
bin
  binned, bin'ning
bi'na·ry
  pl. bi'na·ries
bin·au'ral
bind
  bound, bind'ing

bind'er
bind'er·y
  pl. bind'er·ies
bind'ing
bind'weed'
binge
bin'go
bin'na·cle
bin·oc'u·lar
bi·no'mi·al
bi'o·as'tro·nau'tics
bi'o·chem'i·cal
bi'o·chem'ist
bi'o·chem'is·try
bi'o·de·grad'a·bil'
  i·ty
bi'o·de·grad'a·ble
bi'o·e·col'o·gy
bi'o·en'gi·neer'ing
bi'o·feed'back'
bi'o·gen'e·sis
bi'o·ge·og'ra·pher
bi'o·ge·og'ra·phy
bi·og'ra·pher
bi'o·graph'ic
bi'o·graph'i·cal
bi·og'ra·phy
  pl. bi·og'ra·phies
bi'o·log'ic
bi'o·log'i·cal
bi·ol'o·gist
bi·ol'o·gy
bi'o·lu'mi·nes'cence
bi'o·mass'
bi'o·met'rics
bi·on'ic
bi·on'ics
bi'o·phys'ics
bi'op·sy
  pl. bi'op·sies
bi'o·rhythm'
bi'o·sci'ence
bi'o·sphere'
bi·o'ta
bi'o·te·lem'e·try
bi·ot'ic

bi'o·tin
bi'o·tite'
bip'a·rous
bi·par'ti·san
bi·par'tite
bi'par·ti'tion
bi'ped
bi'plane'
bi·po'lar
bi·ra'cial
bi·ra'cial·ism'
birch
birch' beer'
birch'en
bird
bird'bath'
bird'brain'
bird'cage'
bird' call' or bird'call'
bird' dog'
bird'house'
bird'ie
  bird'ied, bird'ie·ing
bird'lime'
  bird'limed', bird'lim'ing
bird'man'
  pl. bird'men'
bird'seed'
bird's'-eye'
  pl. bird's-eyes'
bi·ret'ta
birl
birth (*being born*)
  (SEE berth)
birth'day'
birth'mark'
birth'place'
birth' rate'
birth'right'
birth'stone'
bis'cuit
bis'cuit tor·to'ni
bi·sect' (*v.*)
bi'sect (*n.*)
bi·sec'tion
bi·sec'tor
bi·sex'u·al

bish'op
  bish'oped, bish'op·ing

bish'op·ric

Bis'marck

bis'muth

bi'son
  pl. bi'son

bisque

Bis·sau'

bis'tre *or* bis'ter

bis'tro
  pl. bis'tros

bit
  bit'ted, bit'ting

bitch

bitch'y
  bitch'i·er, bitch'i·est

bite (*cut with teeth*)
  bit, bit'ten *or* bit,
  bit'ing
  (SEE bight)

bit'er

bit'ing

bit'ten

bit'ter

bit'tern

bit'ter·root'

bit'ters

bit'ter·sweet' (*n.*)

bit'ter·sweet' (*adj.*)

bi·tu'men

bi·tu'mi·nous

bi·va'lent

bi'valve'

biv'ou·ac'
  biv'ou·acked',
  biv'ou·ack'ing

bi·week'ly
  pl. bi·week'lies

bi·year'ly

bi·zarre' (*strange*)
  (SEE bazaar)

bi·zarre'ly

Bi·zet'

blab
  blabbed, blab'bing

blab'ber

blab'ber·mouth'

black

black'-and-blue'

black'ball'

black' bass'

black' bear'

black' belt'

black'ber'ry
  pl. black'ber'ries

black'bird'

black'board'

black' bod'y

black' book'

black'damp'

black'en

black' eye'

black'-eyed'

black'face

Black'foot'
  pl. Black'feet' *or*
  Black'foot'

black'guard

black'head'

black'-heart'ed

black' hole'

black'ing

black'jack'

black'leg'

black' let'ter

black'list'

black'mail'

black' mar'ket

black'out'

black' rot'

black'smith'

black'snake'

black'strap'

black'thorn'

black' tie'

black'top'

black' wid'ow

blad'der

blad'der·wort'

blade

blah

blain

blam'a·ble

blame
  blamed, blam'ing

blam'er

blame'less

blame'wor'thy

blanch

blanc·manage'

bland

blan'dish

blan'dish·ment

bland'ly

blank

blan'ket
  blan'ket·ed,
  blan'ket·ing

blank'e·ty-blank'

blank'ly

blare
  blared, blar'ing

blar'ney
  blar'neyed, blar'ney·ing

Blar'ney stone'

bla·sé'

blas·pheme'
  blas·phemed',
  blas·phem'ing

blas'phe·mous

blas'phe·my
  pl. blas'phe·mies

blast

blast'ed

blas·te'ma
  pl. blas·te'mas *or*
  blas·te'ma·ta

blast'-off'

blas'tu·la
  pl. blas'tu·las *or*
  blas'tu·lae'

bla'tan·cy
  pl. bla'tan·cies

bla'tant

blath'er

blath'er·skite'

blaze
  blazed, blaz'ing

blaz'er

bla'zon

bla'zon·ry

bleach

bleach'ers

bleak

bleak'ly

blear'i·ness

blear'y
  blear'i·er, blear'i·est

bleat
bleat'er
bled
bleed
 bled, bleed'ing
bleed'er
bleed'ing heart'
bleep
blem'ish
blench
blend
 blend'ed or blent,
 blend'ing
blend'er
bleph'a·ri'tis
bless
 blessed or blest,
 bless'ing
bless'ed
bless'ing
blew
blight
blimp
blind
blind' date'
blind'fold'
blind'man's' buff'
blind' spot'
blink
blink'er
blintze or blintz
blip
bliss
bliss'ful
bliss'ful·ly
blis'ter
blithe
blithe'ly
blithe'ness
blithe'some
blitz
blitz'krieg'
bliz'zard
bloat
bloat'er
blob
 blobbed, blob'bing
bloc (group)
 (SEE block)

block (solid piece)
 (SEE bloc)
block·ade'
 block·ad'ed,
 block·ad'ing
block·ad'er
block·ade'-run'ner
block'age
block'bust'er
block'head'
block'house'
bloke
blond or blonde
blood
blood' bank'
blood' bath'
blood' cell'
blood'cur'dling
blood'ed
blood'hound'
blood'less
blood'let'ting
blood'line'
blood'mo·bile'
blood' pres'sure
blood'root'
blood'shed'
blood'shot'
blood'stain'
blood'stone'
blood'stream'
blood'suck'er
blood'thirst'y
blood'worm'
blood'y
 blood'i·er, blood'i·est
 blood'ied, blood'y·ing
bloom
bloom'er
bloom'ers
bloom'ing
bloop'er
blos'som
blot
 blot'ted, blot'ting
blotch
blotch'y
 blotch'i·er, blotch'i·est
blot'ter

blouse
 bloused, blous'ing
blou'son
blow
 blew, blown, blow'ing
blow'-by'-blow'
blow'er
blow'gun'
blow'hole'
blown
blow'off'
blow'out'
blow'pipe'
blow'torch'
blow'up'
blow'y
blowz'y
 blowz'i·er, blowz'i·est
blub'ber
blub'ber·y
blu'cher
bludg'eon
blue (color)
 adj. blu'er, blu'est; v.
 blued, blu'ing or
 blue'ing
 (SEE blew, pt. of
 blow)
blue'bell'
blue'ber'ry
 pl. blue'ber'ries
blue'bird'
blue' blood'
blue'bon'net
blue'book
blue'bot'tle
blue' chip'
blue'-col'lar
blue'fin'
blue'fish'
 pl. blue'fish' or
 blue'fish'es
blue'grass'
blue'jack'et
blue' jay'
blue' jeans'
blue'nose'
blue'-pen'cil
 blue'-pen'ciled, blue'-
 pen'cil·ing

blue'point'
blue'print'
blues
blue'stock'ing
blue'stone'
blu'ets
bluff
bluff'er
blu'ing
blu'ish
blun'der
blun'der·buss'
blunt
blunt'ly
blur
  blurred, blur'ring
blurb
blur'ry
blurt
blush
blush'er
blus'ter
blus'ter·y
B'nai' B'rith'
bo'a
  pl. bo'as
boar (animal)
  (SEE bore)
board (wood)
  (SEE bored, pt. of
  bore)
board'er (lodger)
  (SEE border)
board'ing
board'ing·house'
board'walk'
boast
boast'ful
boast'ful·ly
boat
boat'el
boat'er
boat' hook'
boat'house'
boat'load'
boat'man
  pl. boat'men
boat'swain

boat'yard'
bob
  bobbed, bob'bing
bob'bin
bob'ble
  bob'bled, bob'bling
bob'by
  pl. bob'bies
bob'by pin'
bob'by·socks'
bob'by·sox'er
bob'cat'
  pl. bob'cats' or bob'cat'
bob'o·link'
bob'sled'
  bob'sled'ded,
  bob'sled'ding
bob'tail'
bob'white'
Boc·cac'ci·o'
Boc'che·ri'ni
boc'cie
bock' beer'
bode
  bod'ed, bod'ing
bo·de'ga
bod'ice
bod'i·less
bod'i·ly
bod'kin
bod'y
  pl. bod'ies; v.
  bod'ied, bod'y·ing
bod'y·guard'
bod'y shirt'
bod'y snatch'er
Boer
bof'fo
bog
  bogged, bog'ging
bo'gey (golf score)
  pl. bo'geys; v.
  bo'geyed, bo'gey·ing
  (SEE bogy)
bo'gey·man'
  pl. bo'gey·men'
bog'gle
  bog'gled, bog'gling
bog'gy
bo'gle
Bo·go·tá'

bo'gus
bo'gy (evil spirit)
  pl. bo'gies
  (SEE bogey)
Bo·he'mi·an
boil
boil'er
boil'er·mak'er
Boi'se
bois'ter·ous
bo'la
  pl. bo'las
bold
bold'face'
  bold'faced', bold'fac'ing
bold'–faced'
bold'ly
bole (tree trunk)
  (SEE boll and bowl)
bo·le'ro
  pl. bo·le'ros
Bol'i·var
bol'i·var
  pl. bol'i·vars or (Sp.)
  bo'li·va'res
Bo·liv'i·a
Bo·liv'i·an
boll (seed pod)
  (SEE bole and bowl)
bol'lix
bo'lo
bo·lo'gna
Bol'she·vik
  pl. Bol'she·viks or
  Bol'she·vik'i
Bol'she·vism'
Bol'she·vist
bol'ster
bolt
bolt'er
bo'lus
  pl. bo'lus·es
bomb
bom·bard' (v.)
bom'bard (n.)
bom'bar·dier'
bom'bast
bom·bas'tic
Bom·bay'
bom'ba·zine'

bom·bé′
bomb′er
bomb′load′
bomb′proof′
bomb′shell′
bomb′ shel′ter
bomb′sight′
bo′na fide′
bo·nan′za
Bo′na·parte′
bon′bon′
bond
bond′age
bond′hold′er
bold′ pa′per
bond′ serv′ant
bonds′man
  pl. bonds′men
bonds′wom′an
  pl. bonds′wom′en
bone
  boned, bon′ing
bone′ ash′
bone′black′
bone′ chi′na
bone′-dry′
bone′fish′
  pl. bone′fish′es or
  bone′fish′
bone′head′
bone′less
bone′ meal′
bon′er
bon′fire′
bon′go
  pl. bon′gos or bon′goes
bon′ho·mie′
bo·ni′to
  pl. bo·ni′to or
  bo·ni′tos
bon′ mot′
Bonn
bon′net
bon′ny or bon′nie
  bon′ni·er, bon′ni·est
bon′ny·clab′ber
bon′sai
  pl. bon′sai
bo′nus
  pl. bo′nus·es

bon vi·vant′
  pl. bons vi·vants′
bon′ vo·yage′
bon′y
  bon′i·er, bon′i·est
boo
  pl. boos; v. booed,
  boo′ing
boob
boo′-boo′
  pl. boo′-boos′
boo′by
  pl. boo′bies
boo′by·prize′
boo′by trap′
boo′dle
  boo′dled, boo′dling
boog′ie-woog′ie
boo′hoo′
  v. boo′hooed′,
  boo′hoo′ing
  pl. boo′hoos′
book
book′bind′er·y
  pl. book′bind′er·ies
book′bind′ing
book′case′
book′ club′
book′end′
book′ie
book′ing
book′ish
book′ jack′et
book′keep′er
book′keep′ing
book′let
book′mak′er
book′man
  pl. book′men
book′mark′
book′mo·bile′
book′plate′
book′rack′
book′sel′ler
book′shelf′
book′stall′
book′store′
book′worm′
Bool′e·an
boom

boom′er·ang′
boom′ town′
boon
boon′docks′
boon′dog′gle
  boon′dog′gled,
  boon′dog′gling
Boone
boor
boor′ish
boost
boost′er
boot
boot′black′
boot′ camp′
boot′ee or boot′ie
  (baby's shoe)
  (SEE booty)
boot′er·y
  pl. boot′er·ies
booth
boot′jack′
boot′leg′
  boot′legged′,
  boot′leg′ging
boot′leg′ger
boot′less
boot′lick′
boot′strap′
boo′ty (plunder)
  pl. boo′ties
  (SEE bootee and
  bootie)
booze
  boozed, booz′ing
booz′er
bop
  bopped, bop′ping
bor′age
bo′rate
  bo′rat·ed, bo′rat·ing
bo′rax
  pl. bo′rax·es or
  bo′ra·ces′
Bor·deaux′
Bor·de·laise′
bor·del′lo
  pl. bor·del′los
bor′der (edge)
  (SEE boarder)
bor′der·land′

bor'der·line'

bore (*drill; weary*)
 bored, bor'ing
 (SEE boar)

bore (*pt. of bear*)

bo're·al

bore'dom

bor'er

Bor'gia

bo'ric

bor'ing

born (*brought forth*)
 (SEE borne)

born'-a·gain'

borne (*pt. of bear*)
 (SEE born)

Bor'ne·o

Bor'o·din

bo'ron

bor'ough (*town*)
 (SEE burrow *and* burro)

bor'row

borscht or borsch or borsht

bor'stal

bort

bor'zoi
 pl. bor'zois

Bosc

bosh

bosk'y
 bosk'i·er, bosk'i·est

bos'om

bos'om·y

boss

bos'sa no'va

boss'i·ness

boss'ism

boss'y
 boss'i·er, boss'i·est

Bos'ton

Bos·to'ni·an

bo'sun

bo·tan'ic

bo·tan'i·cal

bot'a·nist

bot'a·ny
 pl. bot'a·nies

botch

botch'er

bot'fly'
 pl. bot'flies'

both

both'er

both'er·some

Bo·tswa'na

Bot'ti·cel'li

bot'tle
 bot'tled, bot'tling

bot'tle·neck'

bot'tom

bot'tom·less

bot'tom line'

bot'tom·most'

bot'u·lism'

bou·clé'

bou'doir

bouf·fant'

bou'gain·vil'lae·a

bough (*branch of tree*)
 (SEE bow, bend down)

bought

boule

bouil'la·baisse'

bouil'lon (*soup*)
 (SEE bullion)

boul'der

boul'e·vard'

bou'le·var·dier'

bounce
 bounced, bounc'ing

bounc'er

bound

bound'a·ry
 pl. bound'a·ries

bound'en

bound'er

bound'less

boun'te·ous

boun'ti·ful

boun'ti·ful·ly

boun'ty
 pl. boun'ties

bou·quet'

bour'bon

bour·geois'
 pl. bour·geois'

bour·geoi·sie'

bourn

Bourse

bout

bou·tique'

bou'ton·niere'

bou·zou'ki

bo'vid

bo'vine

bow (*bend down*)
 (SEE bough)

bow (*weapon*)
 (SEE beau)

bowd'ler·i·za'tion

bowd'ler·ize'
 bowd'ler·ized',
 bowd'ler·iz'ing

bow'el
 bow'eled, bow'el·ing

bow'er

Bow'er·y

bow'fin'

bow'head'

bow'ie knife'

bowl (*dish*)
 (SEE bole *and* boll)

bow'leg'

bow'leg'ged

bowl'er

bow'line

bowl'ing

bow'man
 pl. bow'men

bow'sprit

bow'string'
 bow'stringed' or
 bow'strung',
 bow'string·ing

bow' tie'

bow'wow'

box

box'car'

box' el'der

box'er

box'ful'
 pl. box'fuls'

box'ing

box' of'fice

box' score'

box'wood'

boy (*male child*)
(SEE buoy)

boy'cott

boy'friend'

boy'hood

boy'ish

boy'sen • ber'ry
  pl. boy'sen • ber'ries

bo'zo
  pl. bo'zos

brace
  braced, brac'ing

brace'let

brac'er

bra • ce'ro
  pl. bra • ce'ros

bra'chi • o • pod'

brack'en

brack'et

brack'ish

bract

brad

brad'awl'

brae

brag
  bragged, brag'ging

brag'ga • do'cio
  pl. brag'ga • do'ci • os

brag'gart

brag'ger

Brah'ma

Brah'man (*Hindu priest; cattle*)
(SEE Brahmin)

Brah'min (*cultured person*)
(SEE Brahman)

Brahms

braid

braid'ing

brail

Braille
  Brailled, Braill'ing

brain

brain'child

brain'less

brain'storm'

brain' trust'

brain'wash'

brain'y
  brain'i • er, brain'i • est

braise (*cook*)
  braised, brais'ing
(SEE braze)

brake (*slow; thicket*)
  braked, brak'ing
(SEE break)

brake'man
  pl. brake'men

brake' shoe'

bram'ble
  bram'bled, bram'bling

bram'bly
  bram'bli • er,
  bram'bli • est

Bramp'ton

bran
  branned, bran'ning

branch

branch' wa'ter

brand

bran'dish

brand'-new'

bran'dy
  pl. bran'dies
  bran'died, bran'dy • ing

brant
  pl. brants or brant

Braque

brash

brash'ly

Bra • sil'ia

brass

brass' hat'

brass'ie

bras • siere'

brass'y
  brass'i • er, brass'i • est

brat

brat'ty
  brat'ti • er, brat'ti • est

brat'wurst'

Braun'schwei'ger

bra • va'do
  pl. bra • va'does or
  bra • va'dos

brave
  adj. brav'er, brav'est;
  v. braved, brav'ing

brave'ly

brav'er • y
  pl. brav'er • ies

bra • vis'si • mo'

bra'vo
  pl. bra'vos or bra'voes;
  v.
  bra'voed, bra'vo • ing

bra • vu'ra
  pl. bra • vu'ras or (*It.*)
  bra • vu're

brawl

brawl'er

brawn

brawn'y
  brawn'i • er, brawn'i • est

bray

bray'er

braze (*solder*)
  brazed, braz'ing
(SEE braise)

bra'zen

bra'zen • ness

bra'zier

Bra • zil'

bra • zil'

Bra • zil'ian

Bra • zil' nut'

Braz'za • ville

breach (*gap; violation*)
(SEE breech)

bread (*food*)
(SEE bred)

bread'-and-but'ter

bread'bas'ket

bread'board'

bread'fruit'

bread'stuff'

breadth (*width*)
(SEE breath)

bread'win'ner

break (*fracture*)
  broke, bro'ken,
  break'ing
(SEE brake)

break'a • ble

break'age

break'down'

break'er

break'e'ven

break'fast

break'front'

break'-in'

break'neck'
break'out'
break'point'
break'through'
break'up'
break'wa'ter
bream
breast
breast'bone'
breast'plate
breast'stroke'
breast'work'
breath (*air*)
  (SEE breadth)
Breath'a · lyz'er
  (*Trademark*)
breathe
  breathed, breath'ing
breath'er
breath'less
breath'tak'ing
breath'y
  breath'i · er, breath'i · est
Brecht
breech (*rear part*)
  (SEE breach)
breech'block'
breech'cloth'
breech'es
breech'load'er
breed
  bred, breed'ing
breed'er
breed'ing
breeze
  breezed, breez'ing
breeze'way
breez'y
breth'ren
Bret'on
Breu'ghel
breve
bre · vet'
bre'vi · ar'y
  pl. bre'vi · ar'ies
brev'i · ty
brew
brew'er

brew'er · y
  pl. brew'er · ies
brew'house'
brew'ing
Brezh'nev
bri'ar
bribe
  bribed, brib'ing
brib'er
brib'er · y
  pl. brib'er · ies
bric'-a-brac'
brick
brick'lay'er
brid'al (*wedding*)
  (SEE bridle)
bride
bride'groom'
brides'maid'
bridge
  bridged, bridg'ing
bridge'a · ble
bridge'head'
bridge' lamp'
bridge' ta'ble
Bridge'town'
bridge'work'
bridg'ing
bri'dle
  bri'dled, bri'dling
bri'dle path'
Brie
brief
brief'case'
brief'ing
bri'er
brig
bri · gade'
  bri · gad'ed, bri · gad'ing
brig'a · dier'
brig'a · dier gen'er · al
  pl. brig'a · dier
  gen'er · als
brig'and
brig'an · tine'
bright
bright'en
bright'ness
bril'liance
bril'lian · cy

bril'liant
bril'lian · tine'
brim
  brimmed, brim'ming
brim'ful'
brim'stone'
brin'dle
brin'dled
brine
  brined, brin'ing
bring
  brought, bring'ing
brink
brink'man · ship'
brin'y
  brin'i · er, brin'i · est
bri'oche
bri · quette'
  bri · quett'ed,
  bri · quett'ing
Bris'bane
brisk
bris'ket
brisk'ly
bris'ling
bris'tle
  bris'tled, bris'tling
bris'tly
Brit'ain (*country*)
  (SEE Briton)
Bri · tan'nic
britch'es
Brit'i · cism'
Brit'ish
Brit'ish Co · lum'bi · a
Brit'ish · er
Brit'ish Isles'
Brit'on (*Englishman*)
  (SEE Britain)
Brit'ta · ny
brit'tle
broach (*mention*)
  (SEE brooch)
broad
broad'ax' or
  broad'axe'
broad'band'
broad'cast'
  broad'cast' or
  broad'cast'ed,
  broad'cast'ing

broad′cast′er
broad′cloth′
broad′en
broad′ jump′
broad′leaf′
  pl. broad′leaves′
broad′loom′
broad′mind′ed
broad′side′
  broad′sid′ed,
  broad′sid′ing
broad′sword′
broad′tail′
Broad′way′
bro·cade′
  bro·cad′ed, bro·cad′ing
broc′co·li
bro·chette′
bro·chure′
bro′gan
brogue
broil
broil′er
broke
bro′ken
bro′ken·down′
bro′ken·heart′ed
bro′ker
bro′ker·age
bro·me′li·ad′
bro′mic
bro′mide
bro·mid′ic
bro′mine
bron′chi·a
bron′chi·al
bron′chi·ole′
bron·chi′tis
bron′cho·scope′
bron′chus
  pl. bron′chi
bron′co
  pl. bron′cos
bron′co·bust′er
Bron′të
bron′to·saur′
bron′to·saur′us
Bronx

bronze
  bronzed, bronz′ing
brooch (*clasp*)
  (SEE broach)
brood
brood′er
brood′y
  brood′i·er, brood′i·est
brook
Brook′lyn
brook′ trout′
broom (*sweeper*)
  (SEE brougham)
broom′corn′
broom′stick′
broth
broth′el
broth′er
broth′er·hood′
broth′er-in-law′
  pl. broth′ers-in-law′
broth′er·li·ness
broth′er·ly
brough′am (*vehicle*)
  (SEE broom)
brought
brou·ha′ha
brow
brow′beat′
  brow′beat′,
  brow′beat′en,
  brow′beat′ing
brown
brown′ bear′
brown′ belt′
brown′ bet′ty
Brown′i·an
brown′ie
Brown′ing
brown′out′
brown′stone′
browse
  browsed, brows′ing
bru′cel·lo′sis
Bruck′ner
bru′in
bruise
  bruised, bruis′ing
bruis′er
bruit (*rumor*)
  (SEE brute *and* brut)

brum′ma·gem
brunch
Bru·nei′
bru·net′ or
  bru·nette′
brunt
brush
brush′ fire′
brush′-off′
brush′up′
brush′wood′
brush′work′
brusque
brusque′ly
Brus′sels
Brus′sels sprout′
brut (*dry*)
  (SEE brute *and* bruit)
bru′tal
bru·tal′i·ty
  pl. bru·tal′i·ties
bru′tal·ize′
  bru′tal·ized′,
  bru′tal·iz′ing
brute (*person*)
  (SEE bruit *and* brut)
brut′ish
Bru′tus
bry′o·phyte′
bub′ble
  bub′bled, bub′bling
bub′ble gum′
bub′bler
bub′bly
  bub′bli·er, bub′bli·est
bu′bo
  pl. bu′boes
bu·bon′ic
buc′ca·neer′
Bù·chan′an
Bu′cha·rest′
Buch′en·wald′
buck
buck′a·roo′
  pl. buck′a·roos′
buck′board′
buck′et
buck′et·ful′
  pl. buck′et·fuls
buck′et seat′

buck'et shop'

buck'eye'
  pl. buck'eyes'

buck'ish

buck'le
  buck'led, buck'ling

buck'ler

buck'ram

buck'saw'

buck'shot'

buck'skin'

buck' slip'

buck'thorn'

buck'tooth'
  pl. buck'teeth'

buck'toothed'

buck'wheat'

bu·col'ic

bud
  bud'ded, bud'ding

Bu'da·pest'

bud'der

Bud'dha

Bud'dhism

Bud'dhist

bud'dy
  pl. bud'dies

budge
  budged, budg'ing

budg'er·i·gar'

budg'et
  budg'et·ed, budg'et·ing

budg'et·ar'y

budg'ie

Bue'nos Ai'res

buff

buf'fa·lo'
  pl. buf'fa·loes' or
  buf'fa·los' or
  buf'fa·lo'; *v.*
  buf'fa·loed',
  buf'fa·lo'ing

Buf'fa·lo'

buff'er

buf'fet (*strike*)
  buf'fet·ed, buf'fet·ing

buf·fet' (*sideboard*)

buf'fo
  pl. buf'fi or buf'fos

buf·foon'

buf·foon'er·y

bug
  bugged, bug'ging

bug'a·boo'
  pl. bug'a·boos'

bug'bear'

bug'eyed'

bug'ger

bug'gy
  pl. bug'gies

bu'gle
  bu'gled, bu'gling

bu'gler

build
  built, build'ing

build'er

build'ing

build'-up'

built

built'-in'

bulb

bulb'ar

bulb'ous

bul'bul

Bul·gar'i·a

Bul·gar'i·an

bulge
  bulged, bulg'ing

bulg'y
  bulg'i·er, bulg'i·est

bul'gur

bulk

bulk'head'

bulk' mail'

bulk'y
  bulk'i·er, bulk'i·est

bull

bul'la
  pl. bul'lae

bull'dog'
  bull'dogged',
  bull'dog'ging

bull'doze'
  bull'dozed', bull'doz'ing

bull'doz'er

bul'let
  bul'let·ed, bul'let·ing

bul'le·tin
  bul'le·tined,
  bul'le·tin·ing

bul'let·proof'

bull'fight'

bull'finch'

bull'frog'

bull'head'

bull'head'ed

bull' horn' or
  bull'horn'

bul'lion (*metal*)
  (SEE bouillon)

bull'ish

bull'ock

bull' pen'

bull'ring'

bull'roar'er

bull's'-eye'
  pl. bull's'-eyes'

bull'ter'rier

bull'whip'

bul'ly
  pl. bul'lies; *v.*
  bul'lied, bul'ly·ing

bul'rush'

bul'wark

bum
  bummed, bum'ming

bum'ble
  bum'bled, bum'bling

bum'ble·bee'

bum'mer

bump

bump'er

bump'er guard'

bump'er stick'er

bump'kin

bump'tious

bump'y
  bump'i·er, bump'i·est

bum's' rush'

bun

bunch

Bunche

bunch'y
  bunch'i·er, bunch'i·est

bun'co
  pl. bun'cos; *v.*
  bun'coed, bun'co·ing

bun'dle
  bun'dled, bun'dling

bung

bun'ga·low'

bung'hole'

bun'gle
  bun'gled, bun'gling

bun'gler

bun'ion

bunk

bunk'er

Bunk'er Hill'

bunk'house'

bun'ko
  pl. bun'kos
  bun'koed, bun'ko·ing

bun'kum or
  bun'combe

bun'ny
  pl. bun'nies

Bun'sen

bunt

bun'ting

bu'oy (floating
  marker)
  (SEE boy)

buoy'an·cy

buoy'ant

bur (seedcase)
  (SEE burr)

bur'ble
  bur'bled, bur'bling

bur'den

bur'den·some

bur'dock

bu'reau
  pl. bu'reaus or bu'reaux

bu·reauc'ra·cy
  pl. bu·reauc'ra·cies

bu'reau·crat'

bu'reau·crat'ic

bu·rette'

burg' (town)
  (SEE burgh)

bur'gee

bur'geon

Burg'er

burg'er (hamburger)
  (SEE burgher)

bur'gess

burgh (Scottish town)
  (SEE burg)

burgh'er (citizen)
  (SEE burger)

bur'glar

bur'glar·ize'
  bur'glar·ized',
  bur'glar·iz'ing

bur'gla·ry
  pl. bur'gla·ries

bur·glar'i·ous

bur'go·mas'ter

bur'goo

Bur'gun·dy
  pl. Bur'gun·dies

bur'i·al

bu'rin

burke
  burked, burk'ing

burl

bur'lap

bur·lesque'
  bur·lesqued',
  bur·les'quing

bur'ley
  pl. bur'leys

Bur'ling·ton

bur'ly
  bur'li·er, bur'li·est

Bur'ma

Bur·mese'
  pl. Bur·mese'

burn
  burned or burnt,
  burn'ing

burn'er

bur'nish

bur·noose'

burn'out'

burn'sides'

burp

burp' gun'

burr (tool;
  pronunciation)
  (SEE bur)

bur'ro (donkey)
  pl. bur'ros
  (SEE borough and
  burrow)

bur'row (hole)
  (SEE burro and
  borough)

bur'sa
  pl. bur'sae or bur'sas

bur'sar

bur·si'tis

burst
  burst, burst'ing

Bu·run'di

Bu·run'di·an

bur'weed'

bur'y (inter)
  v. bur'ied, bur'y·ing;
  pl. bur'ies
  (SEE berry)

bus (vehicle)
  pl. bus'es or bus'ses; v.
  bussed or bused,
  bus'sing or bus'ing
  (SEE buss)

bus'boy'

bus'by
  pl. bus'bies

bush

bushed

bush'el

bush'el·ful'
  pl. bush'el·fuls'

Bu'shi·do'

bush'ing

bush'man
  pl. bush'men

bush'mas'ter

bush'whack'

bush'whack'er

bush'y
  bush'i·er, bush'i·est

bus'i·ly

busi'ness

busi'ness·like'

busi'ness·man'
  pl. busi'ness·men'

busi'ness·wom'an
  pl. busi'ness·wom'en

bus'kin

bus'man
  pl. bus'men

buss (kiss)
  (SEE bus)

bust

bus'tard

bust'er

bus'tle
  bus'tled, bus'tling

bus'y
  adj. bus'i·er, bus'i·est;
  v.
  bus'ied, bus'y·ing

bus'y · bod'y
  pl. bus'y · bod'ies

but (except)
  (SEE butt)

bu'ta · di'ene

bu'tane

butch

butch'er

butch'er · y
  pl. butch'er · ies

but'ler

butt (end; target;
  join)
  (SEE but)

butte

but'ter

but'ter–and–eggs'
  pl. but'ter–and–eggs'

but'ter · ball'

but'ter · cup'

but'ter · fat'

but'ter · fin'gered

but'ter · fin'gers
  pl. but'ter fin'gers

but'ter · fish'
  pl. but'ter · fish'es or
  but'ter · fish'

but'ter · fly'
  pl. but'ter · flies'

but'ter · milk'

but'ter · nut'

but'ter · scotch'

but'ter · y
  pl. but'ter · ies

butt' joint'

but'tock

but'ton

but'ton–down'

but'ton · hole'
  but'ton · holed',
  but'ton · hol'ing

but'ton · hook'

but'ton · wood'

but'tress

bu'tyl

Bu'tyl (Trademark)

bux'om

Bux'te · hu'de

buy (purchase)
  bought, buy'ing
  (SEE by and bye)

buy'er

buzz

buz'zard

buzz'er

buzz' saw'

buzz'word

bwa'na

by (near)
  pl. byes
  (SEE buy and bye)

by'–and–by'

bye (sports position)
  (SEE buy and by)

bye'–bye'

by'–e · lec'tion

by'gone'

by'law'

by'line'
  by'lined', by'lin'ing

by'lin'er

by'pass'
  by'passed', by'passed' or
  by'past', by'pass'ing

by'path'

by'play'

by'prod'uct

byre

by'–road'

By'ron

By · ron'ic

by'stand'er

by'street'

byte

by'way'

by'word'

by'–your–leave'

Byz'an · tine'

C

cab

ca · bal'
  ca · balled', ca · bal'ling

cab'a · la

ca'bal · le'ro
  pl. ca'bal · le'ros

ca · ban'a or ca · ba'ña

cab'a · ret'

cab'bage
  cab'baged, cab'bag · ing
  etc.

cab'by or cab'bie
  pl. cab'bies

cab'driv'er

cab'er

cab'in

cab'in boy'

cab'i · net

cab'i · net · mak'er

cab'i · net · work'

ca'ble
  ca'bled, ca'bling

ca'ble car'

ca'ble · gram'

ca'ble–stitch'

cab'man
  pl. cab'men

cab'o · chon'

ca · boo'dle

ca · boose'

Ca · bri'ni

cab'ri · ole'

cab'ri · o · let'

ca · ca'o
  pl. ca · ca'os

cac'cia · to're

cache (hide)
  cached, cach'ing
  (SEE cash)

cache'pot'

ca · chet'

cack'le
  cack'led, cack'ling

cac'o · mis'tle

ca · coph'o · nous

ca · coph'o · ny
  pl. ca · coph'o · nies

cac'tus
  pl. cac'tus · es or cac'ti

cad

ca·dav'er

ca·dav'er·ous

cad'die
  cad'died, cad'dy·ing

cad'dis·fly'
  pl. cad'dis·flies'

cad'dish

cad'dy
  pl. cad'dies; (*v.*)
  cad'died, cad'dy·ing

cade

ca'dence
  ca'denced, ca'denc·ing

ca·den'za

ca·det'

cadge
  cadged, cadg'ing

cad'mi·um

ca'dre

ca·du'ce·us
  pl. ca·du'ce·i'

Cae'sar

Cae·sar'e·an *or*
  Cae·sar'i·an

Cae'sar·ism'

cae·su'ra
  pl. cae·su'ras *or*
  cae·su'rae

cae·su'ral

ca·fé'

ca'fé au lait'

caf·e·te'ri·a

caf·feine'

caf'tan

cage
  caged, cag'ing

cage'y *or* cag'y
  cag'i·er, cag'i·est

cag'i·ly

cag'i·ness

ca·hoots'

cai'man
  pl. cai'mans

Cain

cairn

Cai'ro

cais'son

cai'tiff

ca·jole'
  ca·joled', ca·jol'ing

ca·jol'er

ca·jol'er·y
  pl. ca·jol'er·ies

Ca'jun

cake
  caked, cak'ing

cake'walk'

cal'a·bash

cal'a·boose'

ca·la'di·um

cal'a·mine'

ca·lam'i·tous

ca·lam'i·ty
  pl. ca·lam'i·ties

ca·lash'

cal·car'e·ous

cal·cif'er·ous

cal'ci·fi·ca'tion

cal'ci·fied',
  cal'ci·fy'ing

cal'ci·mine'
  cal'ci·mined',
  cal'ci·min'ing

cal'ci·na'tion

cal'cine
  cal'cined, cal'sin·ing

cal'cite

cal·cit'ic

cal'ci·um

cal'cu·la·ble

cal'cu·late'
  cal'cu·lat'ed,
  cal'cu·lat'ing

cal'cu·la'tion

cal'cu·la'tor

cal'cu·lus
  pl. cal'cu·li' *or*
  cal'cu·lus·es

Cal·cut'ta

cal·de'ra

cal'dron *or* caul'dron

Cal'e·do'ni·a

cal'en·dar (*time
  chart*)
  (SEE calender *and*
  colander)

cal'en·der (*press*)
  (SEE calendar *and*
  colander)

cal'ends

calf
  pl. calves

calf'skin'

Cal'ga·ry

cal'i·ber *or* cal'i·bre

cal'i·brate'
  cal'i·brat'ed,
  cal'i·brat'ing

cal'i·bra'tion

cal'i·bra'tor

cal'i·co'
  pl. cal'i·coes' *or*
  cal'i·cos'

Cal'i·for'nia

Cal'i·for'nian

cal'i·for'ni·um

cal'i·pash'

cal'i·pee'

cal'i·per *or* cal'li·per

ca'liph

ca'liph·ate'

cal'is·then'ics

call

cal'la

call'a·ble

call'back'

call' box'

call'er

call' girl'

cal·lig'ra·pher

cal·li·graph'ic

cal·lig'ra·phy

call'-in'

cal·li'o·pe

cal'li·pyg'i·an

cal·los'i·ty
  pl. cal·los'i·ties

cal'lous (*unfeeling*)
  (SEE callus)

cal'low

call'-up'

cal'lus (*hard tissue*)
  pl. cal'lus·es; (*v.*)
  cal'lused, cal'lus·ing
  (SEE callous)

calm

cal'ma·tive

calm'ly

cal'o·mel'

ca·lor'ic

cal'o·rie

cal'o·rif'ic

cal'o·rim'e·ter

cal'u·met'

ca·lum'ni·ate'
  ca·lum'ni·at'ed,
  ca·lum'ni·at'ing

ca·lum'ni·a'tion

ca·lum'ni·a'tor

ca·lum'ni·ous

cal'um·ny
  pl. cal'um·nies

Cal'va·dos'

Cal'va·ry (Biblical
  place)
  pl. Cal'va·ries
  (SEE cavalry)

calve
  calved, calv'ing

Cal'vin

Cal'vin·ism'

Cal'vin·ist

Cal'vin·is'tic

ca·lyp'so

ca'lyx
  pl. ca'lyx·es or
  cal'y·ces'

cam

ca'ma·ra'de·rie

cam'ber

cam'bi·um
  pl. cam'bi·ums or
  cam'bi·a

Cam·bo'di·a

Cam·bo'di·an

Cam'bri·an

cam'bric

cam'bridge

came

cam'el

ca·mel'lia

ca·mel'o·pard'

Cam'e·lot'

Cam'em·bert'

cam'e·o
  pl. cam'e·os

cam'er·a
  pl. cam'er·as or
  cam'er·ae'

cam'er·a·man'
  pl. cam'er·a·men'

cam'er·a ob·scu'ra

Cam'e·roon'

Cam'i·on

cam'i·sole'

cam'o·mile'

cam'ou·flage'
  cam'ou·flaged',
  cam'ou·flag'ing

cam'ou·flag'er

camp

cam·paign'

cam'pa·ni'le
  pl. cam'pa·ni'les or
  cam'pa·ni'li

camp'craft'

camp'er

camp'fire'

camp' fol'low·er

camp'ground'

cam'phor

cam'pho·rate'
  cam'pho·rat'ed,
  cam'pho·rat'ing

cam'phor ball'

cam·phor'ic

camp'o·ree'

camp'site'

camp'stool'

cam'pus
  pl. cam'pus·es

camp'y

camp'i·er, camp'i·est

cam'shaft'

Ca·mus'

can (be able to)
  could
  (SEE BELOW)

can (preserve)
  canned, can'ning
  (SEE ABOVE)

Ca'naan

Ca'naan·ite'

Can'a·da

Ca·na'di·an

Ca·na'di·an·ism'

ca·naille'

ca·nal'
  ca·nalled' or ca·naled',
  ca·nal'ling or
  ca·nal'ing

ca·nal'i·za'tion

ca·nal'ize
  ca·nal'ized,
  ca·nal'iz·ing

Ca·nal' Zone'

can'a·pé (appetizer)
  (SEE canopy)

ca·nard'

ca·nar'y
  pl. ca·nar'ies

ca·nas'ta

Can'ber·ra

can'can'

can'cel
  can'celed or can'celled,
  can'cel·ing or
  can'cel·ling

can'cel·la'tion

can'cer

Can'cer

can'cer·ous

can·de'la

can'de·la'brum
  pl. can'de·la'bra or
  can'de·la'brums

can'did

can'di·da·cy

can'di·date'

can'died

can'dle
  can'dled, can'dling

can'dle·light'

can'dle·pin'

can'dle·pow'er

can'dle·stick'

can'dle·wick'

can'dor

can'dy
  pl. can'dies
  can'died, can'dy·ing

can'dy·tuft'

cane
  caned, can'ing

cane'brake'

cane' sug'ar

ca'nine

Ca'nis Ma'jor

Ca'nis Mi'nor

can'is·ter

can'ker

can'ker·ous

can′ker sore′

can′ker • worm′

can′na

can′na • bis

can′nel

can′ner • y
  pl. can′ner • ies

can′ni • bal

can′ni • bal • ism′

can′ni • bal • is′tic

can′ni • bal • i • za′tion

can′ni • bal • ize′
  can′ni • bal • ized′,
  can′ni • bal • iz′ing

can′ni • ly

can′ni • nes

can′non (*gun*)
  pl. can′nons *or* can′non
  (SEE canon)

can′non • ade′
  can′non • ad′ed,
  can′non • ad′ing

can′non • ball′

can′non bone′

can′non • eer′

can′not

can′ny
  can′ni • er, can′ni • est

ca • noe′

ca • noe′ist

can′on (*rule*)
  (SEE cannon)

ca • non′ic

ca • non′i • cal

can′on • ic′i • ty

can′on • i • za′tion

can′on • ize′
  can′on • ized,
  can′on • iz′ing

can′o • py (*overhead cover*)
  pl. can′o • pies; (*v.*)
  can′o • pied,
  can′o • py • ing
  (SEE canapé)

canst

cant (*jargon*)
  (SEE can't)

can't (*cannot*)
  (SEE cant)

can • ta′bi • le′

can′ta • loupe′

can • tan′ker • ous

can • ta′ta

can • teen′

can′ter (*gallop*)
  (SEE cantor)

Can′ter • bur′y

cant′ hook

can′thus
  pl. can′thi

can′ti • cle

can′ti • lev′er

can • ti′na

can′tle

can′to
  pl. can′tos

can′ton

Can′ton

Can′ton • ese′
  pl. Can′ton • ese′

can • ton′ment

can′tor (*singer*)
  (SEE canter)

can′vas (*cloth*)
  (SEE canvass)

can′vas • back′
  pl. can′vas • backs′ *or*
  can′vas • back′

can′vass (*solicit*)
  (SEE canvas)

can′yon

caou′tchouc

cap
  capped, cap′ing

ca′pa • bil′i • ty
  pl. ca′pa • bil′i • ties

ca′pa • ble

ca′pa • bly

ca • pa′cious

ca • pac′i • tance

ca • pac′i • tate′
  ca • pac′i • tat′ed,
  ca • pac′i • tat′ing

ca • pac′i • ta′tion

ca • pac′i • tive

ca • pac′i • tor

ca • pac′i • ty
  pl. ca • pac′i • ties

ca • par′i • son

cape

Cape′ Horn′

ca′per

Ca • per • na′um

cape′skin′

Cape′ Town′

cap′ful
  pl. cap′fuls

cap′il • lar′i • ty

cap′il • lar′y
  pl. cap′il • lar′ies

cap′i • tal (*city; wealth*)
  (SEE capitol)

cap′i • tal • ism′

cap′i • tal • ist

cap′i • tal′is • tic

cap′i • tal • i • za′tion

cap′i • tal • ize′
  cap′i • tal • ized′,
  cap′i • tal • iz′ing

cap′i • ta′tion

Cap′i • tol (*U.S. Congress building*)

cap′i • tol (*building*)
  (SEE capital)

ca • pit′u • late′
  ca • pit′u • lat′ed,
  ca • pit′u • la′ting

ca • pit′u • la′tion

ca′po
  pl. ca′pos

ca′pon

ca • pote′

cap′puc • ci′no

Ca′pri

ca • pric′ci • o

ca • price′

ca • pri′cious

Cap′ri • corn′

cap′ri • ole′
  cap′ri • oled′,
  cap′ri • ol′ing

cap′si • cum

cap′size
  cap′sized, cap′siz • ing

cap′stan

cap′stone′

cap′su • late′

cap′sule
  cap′suled, cap′sul • ing

cap′su • lar

cap′tain

cap'tain · cy
  pl. cap'tain · cies

cap'tion

cap'tious

cap'ti · vate'
  cap'ti · vat'ed,
  cap'ti · vat'ing

cap'ti · va'tion

cap'tive

cap'tiv'i · ty
  pl. cap · tiv'i · ties

cap'tor

cap'ture
  cap'tured, cap'tur · ing

cap'u · chin

cap'y · ba'ra

car

car'a · cole'
  car'a · coled',
  car'a · col'ing

Ca · ra'cas

car'a · cul

ca · rafe'

car'a · mel

car'a · pace'

car'at (*weight*)
  (SEE caret *and* carrot)

car'a · van'
  car'a · vaned' or
  car'a · vanned',
  car'a · van'ing or
  car'a · van'ning

car'a · van'sa · ry
  pl. car'a · van'sa · ries

car'a · vel'

car'a · way'

car'bide

car'bine

car'bo · hy'drate

car'bo · lat'ed

car · bol'ic

car'bon

car'bo · na'ceous

car'bon · ate'
  car'bon · at'ed,
  car'bon · at'ing

car'bon · a'tion

car'bon · a'tor

car · bon'ic

car'bon · if'er · ous

car'bon · i · za'tion

car'bon · ize'
  car'bon · ized',
  car'bon · iz'ing

Car'bo · run'dum
  (*Trademark*)

car'boy

car'bun · cle

car · bun'cu · lar

car'bu · re'tion

car'bu · re'tor

car'cass

car · cin'o · gen

car'cin · o · gen'ic

car'ci · no'ma
  pl. car'ci · no'mas or
  car'ci · no'ma · ta

car' coat'

card

car'da · mom

card'board'

car'di · ac'

car'di · gan

car'di · nal

car'di · nal · ate'

car'di · o · gram'

car'di · o · graph'

car'di · oid'

car'di · ol'o · gist

car'di · ol'o · gy

car'di · o · pul'mo · nar'y

car'di · o · vas'cu · lar

card'sharp'

care
  cared, car'ing

ca · reen'

ca · reer'

ca · reer'ism

ca · reer'ist

care'free'

care'ful

care'ful · ly

care'less

ca · ress'
  pl. ca · ress'es

car'et (*insertion mark*)
  (SEE carat *and* carrot)

care'tak'er

care'worn'

car'fare'

car'go
  pl. car'goes or car'gos

car'hop'

Car'ib
  pl. Car'ibs or Car'ib

Car'ib · be'an

car'i · bou'
  pl. car'i · bous' or
  car'i · bou'

car'i · ca · ture
  car'i · ca · tured,
  car'i · ca · tur · ing

car'i · ca · tur · ist

car'ies (*decay*)
  pl. car'ies
  (SEE carry)

car'il · lon'
  car'il · lonned',
  car'il · lon'ning

car'il · lon · neur'

ca · ri'na
  pl. ca · ri'nas or
  ca · ri'nae

Ca · ri'na

car'load'

car · min'a · tive

car'mine

car'nage

car'nal

car'nal · ly

car · nal'i · ty

car · na'tion

car · nau'ba

Car · ne'gie

car · nel'ian

car'ni · val

car'ni · vore'

car · niv'o · rous

car'no · tite'

car'ob

car'ol (*song*)
  car'oled, car'ol · ing
  (SEE carrel)

Car'o · li'na

Car'o · lin'i · an

car'om

car'o · tene'

ca · rot'id

ca · rous'al (*revelry*)
  (SEE carrousel)

ca·rouse′
  ca·roused′, ca·rous′ing

ca·rous′er

carp
  pl. carp or carps

Car·pa′thi·an

car′pel

car′pen·ter

car′pen·try

car′pet
  car′pet·ed, car′pet·ing

car′pet·bag′
  car′pet·bagged′,
  car′pet·bag′ging

car′pet·bag′ger

car·pol′o·gy

car′pool′

car′port′

car′pus
  pl. car′pi

car·ra·geen′

car′rel (*study nook*)
  (SEE carol)

car′riage

car′ri·er

car′ri·on

car′rot (*vegetable*)
  (SEE carat *and* caret)

car′rou·sel′ (*merry-
  go-round*)
  (SEE carousel)

car′ry
  (*v.*) car′ried,
  car′ry·ing;
  pl. car′ries

car′ry·all′

car′ry·ing-on′
  pl. car′ry·ings-on′

car′ry-on′

car′ry-o′ver

car′sick′

Car′son Cit′y

cart

cart′age

carte′ blanche′

car·tel′

Car′ter

Car·te′sian

Car′thage

Car′tha·gin′i·an

Car·thu′sian

car′ti·lage

car′ti·lag′i·nous

car′to·gram′

car·tog′ra·pher

car′to·graph′ic

car·tog′ra·phy

car′ton

car·toon′

car·toon′ist

car·touche′

car′tridge

cart′wheel′

Ca·ru′so

carve
  carved, carv′ing

carv′er

Car′ver

car′y·at′id
  pl. car′y·at′ids or
  car′y·at′i·des′

ca·sa′ba

Ca′sa·blan′ca

Cas′a·no′va

cas·cade′
  cas·cad′ed, cas·cad′ing

cas·car′a

case
  cased, cas′ing

case′book′

case′bound′

case′hard′en

ca′sein

case′load′

case′mate′

case′ment

case′work′

cash (*money*)
  (SEE cache)

cash′-and-car′ry

cash′book′

cash′box′

cash′ew

cash′ flow′

cash·ier′

cash′-in′

cash′mere

cas′ing

ca·si′no (*amusement
  place*)
  pl. ca·si′nos
  (SEE cassino)

cask (*barrel*)
  (SEE casque)

cas′ket

Cas′pi·an

casque (*helmet*)
  (SEE cask)

cas·sa′va

cas′se·role′
  cas′se·roled′,
  cas′se·rol′ing

cas·sette′

cas′sia

cas·si′no (*card
  game*)
  pl. cas·si′nos
  (SEE casino)

Cas′si·o·pe′ia

cas′so·war′y
  pl. cas′so·war′ies

cas′sock

cast (*throw*)
  cast, cast′ing
  (SEE caste)

cas′ta·net′

cast′a·way′

caste (*social class*)
  (SEE cast)

cas′tel·lan

cas′tel·lat′ed

cast′er (*wheel*)
  (SEE castor)

cas′ti·gate′
  cas′ti·gat′ed,
  cas′ti·gat′ing

cas′ti·ga′tion

Cas·tile′

Cas·til′ian

cast′ i′ron

cas′tle
  cas′tled, cas′tling

cast′off′

cas′tor (*bean*)
  (SEE caster)

cas′tor oil′

cas′trate
  cas′trat·ed, cas′trat·ing

cas·tra′tion

cas′u·al

cas′u · al · ly

cas′u · al · ty
  pl. cas′u · al · ties

cas′u · ist

cas′u · is′tic

cas′u · ist · ry
  pl. cas′u · ist · ries

ca′sus bel′li
  pl. ca′sus bel′li

cat

cat′a · bol′ic

ca · tab′o · lism′

cat′a · clysm′

cat′a · clys′mic

cat′a · combs′

cat′a · falque′

Cat′a · lan′

cat′a · lep′sy

cat′a · lep′tic

cat′a · log′
  cat′a · loged′,
  cat′a · log′ing

cat′a · logue′
  cat′a · logued′,
  cat′a · logu′ing

cat′a · logu′er or
  cat′a · log′er

ca · tal′pa

ca · tal′y · sis
  pl. ca · tal′y · ses′

cat′a · lyst

cat′a · lyt′ic

cat′a · lyze′
  cat′a · lyzed′,
  cat′a · lyz′ing

cat′a · ma · ran′

cat′a · mount′

cat′a · moun′tain

cat′a · pult′

cat′a · ract′

ca · tarrh′

ca · tarrh′al

ca · tas′tro · phe

cat′a · stroph′ic

cat′a · to′ni · a

cat′a · ton′ic

Ca · taw′ba

cat′bird′

cat′boat′

cat′call′

catch
  caught, catch′ing

catch′all′

catch′-as-catch′-can′

catch′er

catch′ment

catch′word′

catch′y
  catch′i · er, catch′i · est

cat′e · chet′i · cal

cat′e · chism′

cat′e · chist

cat′e · chize′
  cat′e · chized′,
  cat′e · chiz′ing

cat′e · chu′men

cat′e · gor′i · cal

cat′e · gor′i · cal · ly

cat′e · go · ri · za′tion

cat′e · go · rize′
  cat′e · go · rized′,
  cat′e · go · riz′ing

cat′e · go′ry
  pl. cat′e · go′ries

cat′e · nar′y
  pl. cat′e · nar′ies

cat′e · nate′
  cat′e · nat′ed,
  cat′e · nat′ing

cat′e · na′tion

ca′ter

cat′er-cor′ner

cat′er-cor′nered

cat′er · er

cat′er · pil′lar

cat′er · waul′

cat′fish′
  pl. cat′fish′ or
  cat′fish′es

cat′gut′

ca · thar′sis

ca · thar′tic

Ca · thay′

ca · the′dral

Cath′er

Cath′er · ine

cath′e · ter

cath′ode

cath′ode ray′

cath′o · lic
  (*universal*)

Cath′o · lic (*religion*)

Ca · thol′i · cism′

cath′o · lic′i · ty

cat′i′on

cat′i · on′ic

cat′kin

cat′nap′
  cat′napped′, cat′nap′ping

cat′nip

cat′-o′-nine′-tails′
  pl. cat′-o′-nine′-tails′

CAT′ scan′ner

Cats′kill

cat′s′-paw′ or
  cats′paw′

cat′sup

cat′tail′

cat′ti · ly

cat′ti · ness

cat′tle

cat′tle · man
  pl. cat′tle · men

cat′ty
  cat′ti · er, cat′ti · est

cat′ty-cor′ner

cat′ty-cor′nered

cat′walk′

Cau · ca′sian

Cau′ca · soid′

Cau′ca · sus

cau′cus
  pl. cau′cus · es

cau′dal

cau · dil′lo

caught

caul

caul′dron

cau′li · flow′er

caulk

caulk′er

caus′al

cau · sal′i · ty
  pl. cau · sal′i · ties

cau · sa′tion

caus′a · tive

cause
  caused, caus′ing

cause′ cé · lè′bre

cau′se · rie′

cause'way'

caus'tic

caus'ti·cal·ly

cau'ter·i·za'tion

cau'ter·ize'
cau'ter·ized',
cau'ter·iz'ing

cau'ter·y
pl. cau'ter·ies

cau'tion

cau'tion·ar'y

cau'tious

cav'al·cade'

cav'a·lier'

cav'al·ry
pl. cav'al·ries

cav'a·ti'na

cave
caved, cav'ing

ca've·at' emp'tor

cave'–in'

cave' man'

cav'en·dish

cav'ern

cav'ern·ous

cav'i·ar'

cav'il
cav'iled or cav'illed,
cav'il·ing or cav'il·ling

cav'i·ta'tion

cav'i·ty
pl. cav'i·ties

ca·vort'

ca'vy
pl. ca'vies

caw

Cax'ton

cay (island)
(SEE key and quay)

cay·enne' (pepper)

Cay·enne' (city)

cay·use'

cease
ceased, ceas'ing

cease'–fire'

cease'less

ce'cum
pl. ce'ca

ce'dar

ce'dar chest'

cede (yield)
ced'ed, ced'ing
(SEE seed)

ce·dil'la

ceil'ing

cel'a·don'

cel'an·dine'

cel'e·brant

cel'e·brate'
cel'e·brat'ed,
cel'e·brat'ing

cel'e·bra'tion

cel'e·bra'tor

ce·leb'ri·ty
pl. ce·leb'ri·ties

ce·ler'i·ty

cel'er·y

ce·les'ta

ce·leste'

ce·les'tial

ce·li·ac'

cel'i·ba·cy

cel'i·bate

cell (room)
(SEE sell)

cel'lar (basement)
(SEE seller)

cel'lar·age

cel'lar·et'

cell'block'

Cel·li'ni

cel'list

cel'lo
pl. cel'los

cel'lo·phane'

cel'lu·lar

Cel'lu·loid'
(Trademark)

cel'lu·lose'

Cel'si·us

Celt

Celt'ic

cem'ba·lo'
pl. cem'ba·li' or
cem'ba·los'

ce·ment'

cem'e·ter'y
pl. cem'e·ter·ies

cen'a·cle

ce'no·bite'

ce'no·bit'ic

cen'o·taph'

cen'o·taph'ic

Ce'no·zo'ic

cen'ser (container)
(SEE censor and
censure)

cen'sor (judge)
(SEE censer and
censure)

cen·so'ri·al

cen·so'ri·ous

cen'sor·ship'

cen'sur·a·ble

cen'sure (rebuke)
cen'sured, cen'sur·ing
(SEE censer and
censor)

cen'sur·er

cen'sus
pl. cen'sus·es

cent (coin)
(SEE scent and sent)

cen'taur

Cen·tau'rus

cen·ta'vo
pl. cen·ta'vos

cen'te·nar'i·an

cen'te·nar'y
pl. cen'te·nar'ies

cen·ten'ni·al

cen'ter

cen'ter·board'

cen'ter field'

cen'ter·fold'

cen'ter·piece'

cen·tes'i·mo'
pl. (It.) cen·tes'i·mi or
(Sp.) cen·tes'i·mos

cen'ti·are'

cen'ti·grade'

cen'ti·gram' or
cen'ti·gramme'

cen'ti·li'ter or
cen'ti·li'tre

cen'time

cen'ti·me'ter or
cen'ti·me'tre

cen'ti·mo'

cen'ti·pede'

cen'tral

cen'tral·ism'

cen'tral · ist

cen'tral · is'tic

cen · tral'i · ty
   pl. cen · tral'i · ties

cen'tral · i · za'tion

cen'tral · ize'
   cen'tral · ized',
   cen'tral · iz'ing

cen · trif'u · gal

cen'tri · fuge'
   cen'tri · fuged',
   cen'tri · fug'ing

cen · trif'u · ga'tion

cen'tri · ole'

cen'trip'e · tal

cen'trist

cen'tro · some'

cen · tu'ri · on

cen'tu · ry
   pl. cen'tu · ries

ce · phal'ic

ceph'a · li · za'tion

ce'phe · id

ce · ram'ic

ce · ram'i · cist

cer'a · mist

ce're · al (*grain*)
   (SEE serial)

cer'e · bel'lum
   pl. cer'e · bel'lums or
   cer'e · bel'la

cer'e · bral

cer'e · bra'tion

cer'e · bro · spi'nal

cer'e · brum
   pl. cer'e · brums or
   cer'e · bra

cere'cloth'

cer'e · mo'ni · al

cer'e · mo'ni · al · ly

cer'e · mo'ni · us

cer'e · mo'ny
   pl. cer'e · mo'nies

Ce'res

ce · rise'

ce'ri · um

cer'met

cer'tain

cer'tain · ly

cer'tain · ty
   pl. cer'tain · ties

---

cer'ti · fi'a · ble

cer · tif'i · cate (*n.*)

cer · tif'i · cate' (*v.*)
   cer · tif'i · cat'ed,
   cer · tif'i · cat'ing

cer · ti · fi · ca'tion

cer'ti · fied'

cer'ti · fy'
   cer'ti · fied', cer'ti · fy'ing

cer'ti · o · ra'ri

cer'ti · tude'

ce · ru'le · an

ce · ru'men

Cer · van'tes

cer've · lat'

cer'vi · cal

cer'vix
   pl. cer'vix · es or
   cer · vi'ces

ce'si · um

cess

ces · sa'tion

ces'sion (*yielding*)
   (SEE session)

cess'pool'

ce · ta'cean

Cey · lon'

Cey'lo · nese'

Cé · zanne'

Chab · lis'

cha'-cha'
   pl. cha'-chas'; (*v.*)
   cha'-chaed',
   cha'-cha'ing

cha · conne'

Chad

chafe (*rub*)
   chafed, chaf'ing
   (SEE chaff)

chaff (*husks of
   grain*)
   (SEE chafe)

chaf'fer

chaf'finch

chaf'ing dish'

Cha · gall'

cha · grin'
   cha · grined' or
   cha · grinned',
   cha · grin'ing or
   cha · grin'ning

---

chain

chain' gang'

chain' saw'

chain' stitch'

chain' store'

chair

chair'man
   pl. chair'men; (*v.*)
   chair'maned or
   chair'manned,
   chair'man · ing or
   chair'man · ning

chair'per'son

chair'wom'an
   pl. chair'wom'en

chaise

chaise' longue'

chal · ced'o · ny
   pl. chal · ced'o · nies

cha · let'

chal'ice

chalk

chalk'board'

chalk'y
   chalk'i · er, chalk'i · est

chal'lah
   pl. chal'lahs or (*Heb.*)
   chal · loth'

chal'lenge
   chal'lenged,
   chal · leng · ing

chal · leng · er

chal'lis

chal'lis

cham'ber

cham'ber · lain

cham'ber · maid'

cham'bray

cha · me'le · on

cham'fer

cham'ois
   pl. cham'ois

cham'o · mile'

champ

cham · pagne' (*wine*)
   (SEE champaign)

cham'paign' (*flat
   land*)
   (SEE champagne)

cham · pi'gnon

cham'pi · on

cham'pi·on·ship'

Champs É·ly·sées'

chance
  chanced, chanc'ing

chan'cel

chan'cel·ler·y
  pl. chan'cel·ler·ies

chan'cel·lor

chan'cer·y
  chan'cer·ies

chan'cre

chanc'y
  chanc'i·er, chanc'i·est

chan'de·lier'

chan'dler

chan'dler·y
  pl. chan'dler·ies

change
  changed, chang'ing

change'a·ble

change'ful

change'less

change'ling

change'o'ver

chan'nel
  chan'neled or
  chan'nelled,
  chan'nel·ing or
  chan'nel·ling

chan'son

chant

chant'er

chan'te·relle'

chan·teuse'

chant'ey (song)
  pl. chant'eys
  (SEE shanty)

chan'ti·cleer'

Chan·til'ly

chan'try
  pl. chan'tries

chan'ty (song)
  pl. chan'ties
  (SEE shanty)

Cha'nu·kah'

cha'os

cha·ot'ic

cha·ot'i·cal·ly

chap
  chapped, chap'ping

chap'ar·ral'

chap'book'

cha·peau'
  pl. cha·peaux' or
  cha·peaus'

chap'el

chap'er·on' or
  chap'er·one'

chap'lain

chap'let

Chap'lin

chaps

chap'ter

char (burn)
  charred, char'ring
  (SEE chard)

char'ac·ter

char'ac·ter·is'tic

char'ac·ter·is'ti·
  cal·ly

char'ac·ter·i·za'tion

char'ac·ter·ize'
  char'ac·ter·ized',
  char'ac·ter·iz'ing

cha·rades'

char'broil

char'coal

chard (beet)
  (SEE pt. of char)

charge
  charged, charg'ing

charge'a·ble

char·gé' d'af·faires'

charg'er

char'i·ly

char'i·ness

char'i·ot

char'i·ot·eer'

cha·ris'ma
  pl. cha·ris'ma·ta

char'is·mat'ic

char'i·ta·ble

char'i·ty
  pl. char'i·ties

char'la·tan

Char'le·magne'

Charles'ton

char'ley horse'

Char'lotte

char'lotte

Char·lot'te
  A·ma'li·e

Char'lotte·town'

charm

charm'er

char'nel

char'nel house

Char'on

chart

char'ter

char'tist

Char'tres

char·treuse'

char'wom'an
  pl. char'wom'en

char'y (careful)
  char'i·er, char'i·est
  (SEE cherry)

Cha·ryb'dis

chase (pursue)
  chased, chas'ing
  (SEE chaste)

chas'er

chasm

chas'mal

chas·sé'
  chas·séd, chas·sé'ing

chas'sis
  pl. chas'sis

chaste (virtuous)
  chast'er, chast'est
  (SEE pt. of. chase)

chas'ten

chas·tise'
  chas·tised', chas·tis'ing

chas·tise'ment

chas'ti·ty

chas'u·ble

chat
  chat'ted, chat'ting

châ·teau' or
  cha·teau'
  pl. châ·teaus' or
  châ·teaux'

Châ·teau·bri·and'

chat'e·laine'

chat'tel

chat'ter

chat'ter·box'
  pl. chat'ter·box'es

chat'ty
  chat'ti·er, chat'ti·est

Chau'cer

chauf'feur
Chau · tau'qua
chau'vin · ism'
chau'vin · ist
chau'vin · ist'ic
chau'vin · is'ti · cal · ly
cheap (*inexpensive*)
  (SEE cheap)
cheap'en
cheap'skate'
cheat
cheat'er
check (*verify*)
  (SEE Czech)
check'a · ble
check'book'
check'er
check'er · board'
check'ered
check'–in'
check' list'
check' mark'
check'mate'
  check'mat'ed,
  check'mat'ing
check'off'
check'out'
check'point'
check'rein'
check'room'
check'up'
Ched'dar
cheek
cheek'bone'
cheek'y
  cheek'i · er, cheek'i · est
cheep (*chirp*)
  (SEE cheap)
cheer
cheer'ful
cheer'ful · ly
cheer'ful · ness
cheer'i · ly
cheer'i · ness
cheer'i · o'
  pl. cheer'i · os'
cheer'lead'er
cheer'less

cheer'y
  cheer'i · er, cheer'i · est
cheese
cheese'burg'er
cheese'cake'
cheese'cloth'
cheese'par'ing
chees'y
  chees'i · er, chees'i · est
chee'tah
chef
chef-d'oeu'vre
  pl. chefs-d'oeu'vre
Che'khov
chem'ic
chem'i · cal
chem'i · cal · ly
chem'i · lum'i · nes'
  cence
che · min' de fer'
che · mise'
chem'ist
chem'is · try
  pl. chem'is · tries
chem'o · sphere'
chem'o · sur'ger · y
chem'o · syn'the · sis
chem'o · syn · thet'ic
chem'o · ther'a · py
chem'ur · gy
che · nille'
cher'ish
Cher'o · kee'
  pl. Cher'o · kees' or
  Cher'o · kee'
che · root'
cher'ry (*fruit*)
  pl. cher'ries
  (SEE chary)
cher'ry · stone'
cher'ub
  pl. cher'ubs or
  cher'u · bim
che · ru'bic
cher'vil
Ches'a · peake'
chess'board'
chess'man'
  pl. chess'men'
chest

ches'ter · field'
chest'nut'
chev'a · lier'
chev'i · ot
chev'ron
chew
chew'ing gum'
che · wink'
chew'y
  chew'i · er, chew'i · est
Chey · enne'
  pl. Chey · ennes' or
  Chey · enne'
chi
  pl. chis
Chiang' Kai'-shek'
Chi · an'ti
chi · a'ro · scu'ro
  pl. chi · a'ro · scu'ros
chic (*stylish*)
  (SEE sheik *and* chick)
Chi · ca'go
chi · can'er · y
  pl. chi · can'er · ies
Chi · ca'no
  pl. Chi · ca'nos
chi'chi'
chick (*bird*)
  (SEE chic *and* sheik)
chick'a · dee'
Chick'a · saw'
  pl. Chick'a · saws' or
  Chick'a · saw'
chick'en
chick'en feed'
chick'en-heart'ed
chick'en pox'
chick'pea'
chick'weed'
chic'le
chic'o · ry
  pl. chic'o · ries
chide
  chid'ed or chid,
  chid'ed or chid or
  chid'den, chid'ing
chief
chief'ly
chief'tain
chif · fon'
chif'fo · nier'

chif'fo•robe'

chig'ger

chi'gnon

chig'oe

Chi•hua'hua

chil'blain'

child
  pl. chil'dren

child'bear'ing

child'birth'

child'hood

child'ish

child'like'

child'proof

Chil'e (*nation*)
  (SEE chili *and* chilly)

Chil'e•an

chil'i (*food*)
  pl. chil'ies
  (SEE Chile *and* chilly)

chil'i con car'ne

chill

chill'er

chill'i•ness

chill'y (*cold*)
  chill'i•er, chill'i•est
  (SEE Chile *and* chili)

chime
  chimed, chim'ing

chim'er

chi•me'ra
  pl. chi•me'ras

chi•mer'i•cal

chim'ney
  pl. chim'neys

chim'ney sweep'

chimp

chim'pan•zee'

chin
  chinned, chin'ning

chi'na

Chi'na

chi'na•ber'ry
  pl. chi'na•ber'ries

Chi'na•town'

chi'na•ware'

chin•chil'la

chinch'y
  chinch'i•er,
  chinch'i•est

chin'cough'

Chi•nese'
  pl. Chi•nese'

chink

chi'no
  pl. chi'nos

Chi•nook'
  pl. Chi•nooks' or
  Chi•nook'

chin'qua•pin

chintz

chintz'y
  chintz'i•er, chintz'i•est

chin'–up'

chip
  chipped, chip'ping

chip'board'

chip'munk

Chip'pen•dale'

chip'per

chip'py
  pl. chip'pies

chi•rop'o•dist

chi•rop'o•dy

chi'ro•prac'tic

chi'ro•prac'tor

chirp

chirp'er

chirr

chir'rup
  chir'ruped, chir'rup•ing

chis'el
  chis'eled or chis'elled,
  chis'el•ing or
  chis'el•ling

chis'el•er

Chis'holm Trail'

chit

chit'chat'
  chit'chat'ted,
  chit'chat'ting

chit'lings or chit'lins

chi'ton

chit'ter

chit'ter•lings

chiv'al•ric

chiv'al•rous

chiv'al•ry
  pl. chiv'al•ries

chive

chiv'vy
  (*v.*)chiv'vied,
  chiv'vy•ing;
  pl. chiv'vies

chlo'ral

chlo'rate

chlor'dane

chlo'ric

chlo'ride

chlo'rin•ate'
  chlo'rin•at'ed,
  chlo'rin•at'ing

chlo'rin•a'tion

chlo'rine

chlo'ro•form'

chlo'ro•phyll

chlo'ro•plast'

chlo•ro'sis

chock

chock'–a–block'

chock'–full'

choc'o•late

Choc'taw
  pl. Choc'taws or
  Choc'taw

choice
  choic'er, choic'est

choir (*singers*)
  (SEE quire)

choir'boy'

choir'girl'

choir'mas'ter

choke
  choked, chok'ing

choke'cher'ry
  pl. choke'cher'ries

choke'damp'

chok'er

chol'er (*anger*)
  (SEE collar)

chol'er•a

chol'er•ic

cho•les'ter•ol'

cho'line

chol'la
  pl. chol'las

choose
  chose, cho'sen,
  choos'ing

choos'er

choos'y or choos'ey
  choos'i•er, choos'i•est

chop
  chopped, chop'ping

chop'house'

Cho'pin

chop'per

chop'pi・ly

chop'pi・ness

chop'py
  chop'pi・er, chop'pi・est

chop'stick'

chop' su'ey

cho'ral (adj.)
  (SEE coral)

cho・rale' or cho・ral'
  (n.)
  (SEE corral)

cho'ral・ly

chord (tones)
  (SEE cord)

chor'date

chore
  chored, chor'ing

cho・re'a

cho're・o・graph'

cho're・og'ra・pher

cho're・o・graph'ic

cho're・og'ra・phy

cho'ric

cho'rine

cho'ri・on

chor'is・ter

cho'roid

chor'tle
  chor'tled, chor'tling

cho'rus
  pl. cho'rus・es; (v.)
  cho'rused, cho'rus・ing

cho'sen

Chou' En'-lai'

chow' chow' (dog)

chow'-chow' (food)

chow'der

chow' mein'

Christ

chris'ten

chris'ten・ing

Chris'ten・dom

Chris'tian

Chris'ti・an'i・ty
  pl. Chris'ti・an'i・ties

Christ'mas
  pl. Christ'mas・es

chro'ma

chro'mate

chro・mat'ic

chro・mat'i・cism'

chro'ma・tin

chro'ma・tog'ra・phy

chrome
  chromed, chrom'ing

chro'mic

chro'mite

chro'mi・um

chro'mo・lith'o・graph'

chro'mo・li・thog'
  ra・phy

chro'mo・so'mal

chro'mo・some'

chro'mo・sphere'

chro'mous

chron'ic

chron'i・cal・ly

chron'i・cle
  chron'i・cled,
  chron'i・cling

chron'i・cler

chron'o・graph'

chron'o・log'ic

chron'o・log'i・cal

chro・nol'o・gist

chro・nol'o・gy
  pl. chro・nol'o・gies

chro・nom'e・ter

chrys'a・lid

chrys'a・lis
  pl. chrys'a・lis・es or
  chry・sal'i・ses'

chry・san'the・mum

chub
  pl. chub or chubs

chub'bi・ness

chub'by
  chub'bi・er, chub'bi・est

chuck

chuck'hole'

chuck'le
  chuck'led, chuck'ling

chuck' wag'on

chug
  chugged, chug'ging

chuk'ka (boot)
  (SEE chukker)

chuk'ker (polo
  period)
  (SEE chukka)

chum
  chummed, chum'ming

chum'mi・ly

chum'mi・ness

chum'my
  chum'mi・er,
  chum'mi・est

chump

chunk

Chung'king'

chunk'y
  chunk'i・er, chunk'i・est

church
  pl. church'es

church'go'er

Church'ill

church'man
  pl. church'men

church'ward'en

church'wom'an
  pl. church'wom'en

church'yard'

churl

churl'ish

churn

churr

chute (channel)
  chut'ed, chut'ing
  (SEE shoot)

chut'ney
  pl. chut'neys

chutz'pa or chutz'pah

chyle

chyme

cia'o

ci・ca'da
  pl. ci・ca'das or
  ci・ca'dae

cic'a・trix
  pl. cic'a・tri'ces

Cic'e・ro'

cic'e・ro'ne

ci'der

ci・gar'

cig'a・rette'

cig'a・ril'lo
  pl. cig'a・ril'los

cil′i•a
  sing. cil′i•um

cil′i•ar′y

cil′i•ate

cinch

cin•cho′na

Cin′cin•nat′i

cinc′ture
  cinc′tured, cinc′tur•ing

cin′der

cin′der block′

Cin′der•el′la

cin′e•ma

cin′e•mat′ic

cin′e•ma•tog′ra•pher

cin′e•mat′o•graph′ic

cin′e•ma•tog′ra•phy

cin•é•ma′ vé•ri•té′

cin′e•rar′i•a

cin′na•bar

cin′na•mon

cinque′foil′

ci′pher

cir′ca

cir′cle
  cir′cled, cir′cling

cir′clet

cir′cuit

cir•cu′i•tous

cir′cuit•ry

cir′cu•lar

cir′cu•lar′i•ty

cir′cu•lar•i•za′tion

cir′cu•lar•ize′
  cir′cu•lar•ized′,
  cir′cu•lar•iz′ing

cir′cu•late′
  cir′cu•lat′ed,
  cir′cu•lat′ing

cir′cu•la′tion

cir′cu•la′tor

cir′cu•la•to′ry

cir′cum•cise′
  cir′cum•cised′,
  cir′cum•cis′ing

cir′cum•ci′sion

cir•cum•fer•ence

cir′cum•flex′

cir′cum•lo•cu′tion

cir′cum•loc•u•to′ry

cir′cum•lu′nar

cir′cum•nav′i•gate′
  cir′cum•nav′i•gat′ed,
  cir′cum•nav′i•gat′ing

cir′cum•nav′i•ga′tion

cir′cum•nav′i•ga′tor

cir′cum•po′lar

cir′cum•scribe′
  cir′cum•scribed′,
  cir′cum•scrib′ing

cir′cum•scrip′tion

cir′cum•so′lar

cir′cum•spect′

cir′cum•spec′tion

cir′cum•stance′
  cir′cum•stanced′,
  cir′cum•stanc′ing

cir′cum•stan′tial

cir′cum•stan′tial•ly

cir′cum•stan′ti•ate′
  cir′cum•stan′ti•at′ed,
  cir′cum•stan′ti•at′ing

cir′cum•stan′ti•a′tion

cir′cum•vent′

cir′cum•ven′tion

cir′cus
  pl. cir′cus•es

cirque

cir•rho′sis

cir•rhot′ic

cir′ro•cu′mu•lus
  pl. cir′ro•cu′mu•lus

cir′ro•stra′tus
  pl. cir′ro•stra′tus

cir′rus
  pl. cir′ri or cir′rus

cis•lu′nar

Cis•ter′cian

cis′tern

cit′a•del

ci•ta′tion

cite (*mention*)
  cit′ed, cit′ing
  (SEE sight *and* site)

cit′i•fi•ca′tion

cit′i•fy′
  cit′i•fied′, cit′i•fy′ing

cit′i•zen

cit′i•zen•ry
  pl. cit′i•zen•ries

cit′i•zens band′

cit′i•zen•ship′

cit′rate

cit′ric

cit′ri•cul′ture

cit′ron

cit′ron•el′la

cit′rus
  pl. cit′rus•es

cit′y
  pl. cit′ies

cit′y•scape′

cit′y–state′

civ′et

civ′ic

civ′ies

civ′il

ci•vil′ian

ci•vil′i•ty
  pl. ci•vil′i•ties

civ•i•liz′a•ble

civ′i•li•za′tion

civ′i•lize′
  civ′i•lized′, civ′i•liz′ing

civ′i•liz′er

civ′il•ly

civ′vies

clab′ber

clack (*chatter*)
  (SEE claque)

clad
  clad, clad′ding

claim

claim′ant

clair•voy′ance

clair•voy′ant

clam
  clammed, clam′ming

clam′bake′

clam′ber

clam′mi•ness

clam′my
  clam′mi•er,
  clam′mi•est

clam′or

clam′or•ous

clamp

clam′shell′

clan

clan·des'tine

clang

clang'or

clank

clan'nish

clans'man
  pl. clans'men

clans'wom·an
  pl. clans'wom·en

clap
  clapped, clap'ping

clap'board

clap'per

clap'trap'

claque (*applauders*)
  (SEE clack)

clar'et

clar'i·fi·ca'tion

clar'i·fy'
  clar'i·fied, clar'i·fy'ing

clar'i·net'

clar'i·net'ist

clar'i·on

clar'i·ty

clash

clasp

clasp' knife'

class

clas'sic

clas'si·cal

clas'si·cal·ly

clas'si·cism'

clas'si·cist

clas'si·fi'a·ble

clas'si·fi·ca'tion

clas'si·fy'
  clas'si·fied',
  clas'si·fy'ing

class'mate'

class'room'

class'work'

class'y
  class'i·er, class'i·est

clat'ter

clau'di·ca'tion

clause

claus'tro·pho'bi·a

claus'tro·pho'bic

clav'i·chord'

clav'i·cle

cla·vic'u·lar

cla·vier'

claw

claw' ham'mer

clay

clay'ey

clay'more'

clean

clean'-cut'

clean'er

clean'li·ness

clean'ly
  clean'li·er, clean'li·est

clean'ness

cleanse
  cleansed, cleans'ing

clean'ser

clean'-shav'en

clean'up'

clear

clear'a·ble

clear'ance

clear'-cut'

clear'-eyed'

clear'head'ed

clear'ing

clear'ing house'

clear'ly

clear'ness

clear'sight'ed

cleat

cleav'age

cleave (*adhere*)
  cleaved, cleav'ing
  (SEE BELOW)

cleave (*split*)
  cleft or cleaved or
  clove, cleft or cleaved
  or clo'ven, cleav'ing
  (SEE ABOVE)

cleav'er

clef

cleft

clem'a·tis

clem'en·cy
  pl. clem'en·cies

Clem'ens

clem'ent

clench

Cle'o·pa'tra

clere'sto'ry
  pl. clere'sto'ries

cler'gy
  pl. cler'gies

cler'gy·man
  pl. cler'gy·men

cler'ic

cler'i·cal

cler'i·cal·ism'

clerk

Cleve'land

clev'er

clev'is

clew

cli·ché'

click

click'er

cli'ent

cli'en·tele'

cliff

cliff'-hang'er

cli·mac'ter·ic

cli·mac'tic (*of*
  climax)
  (SEE climatic)

cli'mate

cli·mat'ic (*of*
  weather)
  (SEE climactic)

cli·mat'i·cal·ly

cli'ma·to·log'ic

cli'ma·to·log'i·cal·ly

cli'ma·tol'o·gist

cli'ma·tol'o·gy

cli'max
  pl. cli'max·es

climb (*ascend*)
  (SEE clime)

climb'a·ble

climb'er

clime (*region*)
  (SEE climb)

clinch

clinch'er

cling
  clung, cling'ing

cling'stone'

clin'ic

clin'i · cal

clin'i · cal · ly

cli · ni'cian

clink

clink'er

cli · nom'e · ter

clip (*cut*)
clipped, clipped or clipt,
clip'ping
(SEE BELOW)

clip (*grip*)
clipped, clip'ping
(SEE ABOVE)

clip'board'

clip'-fed'

clip'-on'

clip'per

clip'ping

clique

cli'quish

clit'o · ral

clit'o · ris

clo · a'ca
pl. clo · a'cae

cloak

cloak'-and-dag'ger

cloak'room'

clob'ber

cloche

clock

clock'wise'

clock'work'

clod

clod'dish

clod'hop'per

clog
clogged, clog'ging

cloi'son · né'

clois'ter

clone
cloned, clon'ing

clop
clopped, clop'ping

close (*shut*)
closed, clos'ing, (*adj.*)
clos'er, clos'est
(SEE clothes)

close'-by'

closed'-end'

close'fist'ed

close'-fit'ting

close'ly

close'-mouthed'

close'ness

close'out'

clos'et

close'-up'

clo'sure
clo'sured, clo'sur · ing

clot
clot'ted, clot'ting

cloth
pl. cloths

clothe
clothed or clad,
clothing

clothes (*garments*)
(SEE close)

clothes'horse'

clothes'line'

clothes'pin'^

clothes'press'

cloth'ier

cloth'ing

clo'ture
clo'tured, clo'tur · ing

cloud

cloud'burst'

cloud'i · ness

cloud'y
cloud'i · er, cloud'i · est

clout

clove

clo'ven-hoofed'

clo'ver

clo'ver · leaf'
pl. clo'ver · leaves'

clown

clown'ish · ly

cloy

cloy'ing · ly

club
clubbed, club'bing

club'by
club'bi · er, club'bi · est

club' car'

club'foot'

club'foot'ed

club'house'

cluck

clue
clued, clu'ing

clum'ber

clump

clump'y
clump'i · er, clump'i · est

clum'si · ly

clum'si · ness

clum'sy
clum'si · er, clum'si · est

clung

clus'ter

clutch
pl. clutch'es

clut'ter

Clydes'dale'

clys'ter

coach
pl. coach'es

coach'man
pl. coach'men

coach'work'

co · ac'tion

co · ad'ju · tor

co · ag'u · lant

co · ag'u · late' (*v.*)
co · ag'u · lat'ed,
co · ag'u · lat'ing

co · ag'u · late (*adj.*)

co · ag'u · la'tion

coal

coal'er

co'a · lesce'
co'a · lesced',
co'a · lesc'ing

co'a · les'cence

co'a · les'cent

coal' field'

coal' gas'

co'a · li'tion

coal' tar'

coarse (*rough*)
coars'er, coars'est
(SEE course)

coarse'ly

coars'en

coarse'ness

coast

coast'al

coast'er

Coast' Guard'

coast'line'

coast'ward

coast'wise'

coat (*garment*)
(SEE cote)

co·a'ti
　pl. co·a'tis

coat'ing

coat' of arms'

coat' of mail'

coat'room'

coat'tail'

co·au'thor

coax

coax'er

co·ax'i·al

cob

co'balt

cob'ble
　cob'bled, cob'bling

cob'bler

cob'ble·stone'

CO'BOL

co'bra

cob'web'
　cob'webbed',
　cob'web'bing

co'ca

co·caine'

coc'cus
　pl. coc'ci

coc'cyx
　pl. coc·cy'ges

co·chair'man
　pl. co·chair'men

co'chin

coch'i·neal'

coch'le·a

cock

cock·ade'

cock'a·doo'dle-·doo'

cock'a·ma'mie

cock'a·too'
　pl. cock'a·toos'

cock'a·trice

cock'boat'

cock'chaf'er

cock'crow'

cock'er

cock'er·el

cock'eye'
　pl. cock'eyes'

cock'eyed'

cock'fight'

cock'horse'

cock'i·ly

cock'i·ness

cock'le
　cock'led, cock'ling

cock'le·bur

cock'le·shell'

cock'ney
　pl. cock'neys

cock'pit'

cock'roach'
　pl. cock'roach'es

cocks'comb'

cock'sure'

cock'tail'

cock'y
　cock'i·er, cock'i·est

co'co (*coconut*)
　pl. co'cos
　(SEE cocoa)

co'coa (*beverage*)
　(SEE coco)

co'co·nut'

co·coon'

co·cotte'

Coc·teau'

cod
　pl. cod or cods

co'da

cod'dle
　cod'dled, cod'dling

code
　cod'ed, cod'ing

co'deine

co'dex
　pl. co'di·ces'

cod'fish'
　pl. cod'fish' or
　cod'fish'es

codg'er

cod'i·cil

cod'i·fi·ca'tion

cod'i·fy'
　cod'i·fied', cod'i·fy'ing

cod'ling

cod'-liv'er oil'

co'ed'

co·ed'i·tor

co'ed·u·ca'tion

co'ef·fi'cient

coe'la·canth'

coe·len'ter·ate'

co·en'zyme

co·e'qual

co'e·qual'i·ty
　pl. co'e·qual'i·ties

co·erce'
　co·erced', co·erc'ing

co·erc'er

co·er'cion

co·er'cive

co'e·ta'ne·ous

co·e'val

co'ex·ist'

co'ex·ist'ence

co'ex·ist'ent

co'ex·tend'

co'ex·ten'sive

cof'fee

cof'fee·cake'

cof'fee·house'

cof'fee klatsch'

cof'fee·pot'

cof'fee shop'

cof'fer

cof'fer dam'

cof'fin

cog
　cogged, cog'ging

co'gen·cy

co'gent

cog'i·tate'
　cog'i·tat'ed,
　cog'i·tat'ing

cog'i·ta'tion

co'gnac

cog'nate

cog·ni'tion

cog'ni·tive

cog'ni·zance

cog'ni·zant

cog·no'men
　pl. cog·no'mens or
　cog·nom'i·na

co'gno·scen'ti
  sing. co'gno·scen'te

cog'wheel'

co·hab'it

co·hab'i·ta'tion

co·heir'

co·here'
  co·hered', co·her'ing

co·her'ence

co·her'ent

co·he'sion

co·he'sive

co'hort

co'hosh

coif

coif feur' (hairdresser)

coif fure' (hair style)
  coif fured', coif·fur'ing

coil

coin (money)
  (SEE quoin)

coin'age

coin' box'

co'in·cide'
  co'in·cid'ed,
  co'in·cid'ing

co·in'ci·dence

co·in'ci·dent

co·in'ci·den'tal

co'in·sur'ance

co'in·sure'
  co'in·sured',
  co'in·sur'ing

co·i'tion

co'i·tus

coke
  coked, cok'ing

co'la

col'an·der (strainer)
  (SEE calendar and calender)

col'chi·cine'

cold

cold'-blood'ed

cold' cream'

cold' frame'

cold'-heart'ed

cold' pack'

cold' sore'

Cole'ridge

cole'slaw'

co'le·us
  pl. co'le·us·es

col'ic

col'ick·y

col'i·se'um (public building)
  (SEE Colosseum)

co·li'tis

col·lab'o·rate'
  col·lab'o·rat'ed,
  col·lab'o·rat'ing

co·lab'o·ra'tion

col·lab'o·ra'tor

col·lage'

col'la·gen

col·lapse'
  col·lapsed', col·laps'ing

col·laps'i·ble

col'lar (part around neck)
  (SEE choler)

col'lar·bone'

col'lard

col·late'
  col·lat'ed, col·lat'ing

col·lat'er·al

col·la'tion

col·la'tor

col'league'

col·lect' (v., adj., adv.)

col'lect (n.)

col·lect'ed

col·lect'i·ble or
  col·lect'a·ble

col·lec'tion

col·lec'tive

col·lec'tive·ly

col·lec'tiv·ism'

col·lec'ti·vist

col·lec'ti·vize'
  col·lec'ti·vized',
  col·lec'ti·viz'ing

col·lec'tor

col'leen

col'lege

col·le'gi·al

col·le'gian

col·le'giate

col·lide'
  col·lid'ed, col·lid'ing

col'lie

col'lier

col'lier·y
  pl. col'lier·ies

col·lin'e·ar

col'lins

col·li'sion

col'lo·cate'
  col'lo·cat'ed,
  col'lo·cat'ing

col'lo·ca'tion

col·lo'di·on

col'loid

col·loi'dal

col·lo'qui·al

col·lo'qui·al·ism'

col·lo'qui·um
  pl. col·lo'qui·ums or
  col·lo'qui·a

col'lo·quy
  pl. col'lo·quies

col·lude'
  col·lud'ed, col·lud'ing

col·lu'sion

col·lu'sive

co·logne'

Co·lom'bi·a

Co·lom'bi·an

Co·lom'bo

co'lon (punctuation; intestine)
  pl. co'lons or co'la

co·lon' (money)
  pl. co·lons' or (Sp.)
  co·lo'nes

colo'nel (officer)
  (SEE kernel)

colo'nel·cy

co·lo'ni·al

co·lo'ni·al·ism'

co·lo'ni·al·ist

col'o·nist

col'o·ni·za'tion

col'o·nize'
  col'o·nized',
  col'o·niz'ing

col'o·niz'er

col'on·nade'

col'o‧ny
  pl. col'o‧nies

col'o‧phon'

col'or

Col'o‧rad'o

Col'o‧rad'an

col'or‧a'tion

col'o‧ra‧tu'ra

col'or-blind'

col'or‧cast'
  col'or‧cast',
  col'or‧cast'ing

col'ored

col'or‧fast'

col'or‧ful

col'or‧im'e‧ter

col'or‧ing

col'or‧ist

col'or‧less

co‧los'sal

Col'os‧se'um
  (*Roman
  amphitheater*)
  (SEE coliseum)

co‧los'sus
  pl. co‧los'si or
  co‧los'sus‧es

co‧los'to‧my
  pl. co‧los'to‧mies

colt

colt'ish

col'um‧bar'i‧um

Co‧lum'bi‧a

Co‧lum'bi‧an

col'um‧bine'

co‧lum'bi‧um

Co‧lum'bus

col'umn

co‧lum'nar

col'umn‧ist

co'ma (*unconscious
  state*)
  pl. co'mas
  (SEE comma)

co‧mak'er

Co‧man'che
  pl. Co‧man'ches or
  Co‧man'che

com'a‧tose'

comb

com‧bat' (*v.*)
  com‧bat'ed,
  com‧bat'ing

com'bat (*n.*)

com‧bat'ant

com‧bat'ive

comb'er

com'bi‧na'tion

com'bi‧na'tive

com‧bine' (*v.*)
  com‧bined',
  com‧bin'ing

com'bine (*n.*)

com‧bin'er

comb'ings

com'bo
  pl. com'bos

com‧bus'ti‧ble

com‧bus'tion

com‧bus'tive

come
  came, come, com'ing

come'back'

co‧me'di‧an

co‧me'di‧enne'

com'e‧do'
  pl. com'e‧dos' or
  com'e‧do'nes

come'down'

com'e‧dy
  pl. com'e‧dies

come'-hith'er

come'li‧ness

come'ly

come'-on'

com'er

co‧mes'ti‧ble

com'et

come'up'pance

com'fort

com'fort‧a‧ble

com'fort‧a‧bly

com'fort‧er

com'fy
  com'fi‧er, com'fi‧est

com'ic

com'i‧cal

Com'in‧form'

Com'in‧tern'

com'i‧ty
  pl. com'i‧ties

com'ma
  (*punctuation
  mark*)
  (SEE coma)

com‧mand'

com‧man'dant

com'man‧deer'

com‧mand'er

com‧man'der in
  chief'

com‧mand'er‧y
  pl. com‧mand'er‧ies

com‧mand'ing

com‧mand'ment

com‧man'do
  pl. com‧man'dos or
  com‧man'does

com‧me'dia dell'ar'te

com‧mem'o‧rate'
  com‧mem'o‧rat'ed,
  com‧mem'o‧rat'ing

com‧mem'o‧ra'tion

com‧mem'o‧ra'tive

com‧mence'
  com‧menced',
  com‧menc'ing

com‧mence'ment

com‧mend'

com‧mend'a‧ble

com'men‧da'tion

com‧men'sal

com‧men'sal‧ism'

com‧men'su‧ra‧ble

com‧men'su‧rate

com'ment

com'men‧tar'y
  pl. com'men‧tar'ies

com'men‧ta'tor

com'merce

com‧mer'cial

com‧mer'cial‧ism'

com‧mer'cial‧i‧
  za'tion

com‧mer'cial‧ize'
  com‧mer'cial‧ized',
  com‧mer'cial‧iz'ing

com‧mer'cial‧ly

com'mie

com·min'gle
　com·min'gled,
　com·min'gling

com·mis'er·ate'
　com·mis'er·at'ed,
　com·mis'er·at'ing

com·mis'er·a'tion

com'mis·sar'

com'mis·sar'i·at

com'mis·sar'y
　pl. com'mis·sar'ies

com·mis'sion

com·mis'sion·er

com·mit'
　com·mit'ted,
　com·mit'ting

com·mit'ment

com·mit'tal

com·mit'tee

com·mit'tee·man
　pl. com·mit'tee·men

com·mit'tee·per'son

com·mit'tee·wom'an
　pl.
　com·mit'tee·wom'en

com·mix'

com·mix'ture

com·mode'

com·mo'di·ous

com·mod'i·ty
　pl. com·mod'i·ties

com'mo·dore'

com'mon

com'mon·al·ty
　pl. com'mon·al·ties

com'mon·er

com'mon·ly

com'mon·ness

com'mon·place'

com'mon sense'

com'mon·weal'

com'mon·wealth'

com·mo'tion

com·mu'nal

com·mu·nal'i·ty

com·mune' (v.)
　com·muned',
　com·mun'ing

com'mune (n.)

com·mu·ni·ca·
　bil'i·ty

com·mu'ni·ca·ble

com·mu'ni·cant

com·mu'ni·cate'
　com·mu'ni·cat'ed,
　com·mu'ni·cat'ing

com·mu'ni·ca'tion

com·mu'ni·ca'tor

com·mu'ni·ca'tive

com·mun'ion

com·mu'ni·qué'

com'mun·ism'

com'mun·ist

com'mu·nis'tic

com·mu'ni·ty
　pl. com·mu'ni·ties

com'mu·ta'tion

com'mu·ta·tive

com'mu·ta·tor

com·mute'
　com·mut'ed,
　com·mut'ing

com·mut'er

com·pact' (adj., v.)

com'pact (n.)

com·pac'tor

com·pan'ion

com·pan'ion·a·ble

com·pan'ion·ship'

com·pan'ion·way'

com'pa·ny
　pl. com'pa·nies

com'pa·ra·ble

com·par'a·tive

com·par'a·tive·ly

com·pare'
　com·pared',
　com·par'ing

com·par'er

com·par'i·son

com·part'ment

com·part·men'tal

com·part·men'
　tal·ize'
　com·part·men'
　tal·ized',
　com·part·men'
　tal·iz'ing

com'pass

com·pas'sion

com·pas'sion·ate
　(adj.)

com·pas'sion·ate'
　(v.)
　com·pas'sion·at'ed,
　com·pas'sion·at'ing

com·pat'i·bil'i·ty

com·pat'i·ble

com·pa'tri·ot

com·peer'

com·pel'
　com·pelled',
　com·pel'ling

com·pen'di·ous

com·pen'di·um
　pl. com·pen'di·ums or
　com·pen'di·a

com'pen·sate'
　com'pen·sat'ed,
　com'pen·sat'ing

com'pen·sa'tion

com'pen·sa'tor

com·pen'sa·to·ry

com·pete'
　com·pet'ed,
　com·pet'ing

com'pe·tence

com'pe·ten·cy

com'pe·tent

com'pe·ti'tion

com·pet'i·tive

com·pet'i·tor

com'pi·la'tion

com·pile'
　com·piled', com·pil'ing

com·pil'er

com·pla'cence (self-
　satisfaction)
　(SEE complaisance)

com·pla'cen·cy
　pl. com·pla'cen·cies

com·pla'cent (self-
　satisfied)
　(SEE complaisant)

com·plain'

com·plain'ant

com·plaint'

com·plai'sance
　(agreeableness)
　(SEE complacence)

com·plai'sant
　(agreeable)
　(SEE complacent)

com'ple·ment (n.)
(full amount)
(SEE compliment)

com'ple·ment' (v.)

com'ple·men'ta·ry
(completing)
pl. com'ple·men'ta·ries
(SEE complimentary)

com·plete'
com·plet'ed,
com·plet'ing

com·plete'ly

com·plete'ness

com·ple'tion

com·plex' (adj.)

com'plex (n.)

com·plex'ion

com·plex'i·ty
pl. com·plex'i·ties

com·pli'ance

com·pli'an·cy

com·pli'ant

com'pli·cate' (v.)
com'pli·cat'ed,
com'pli·cat'ing

com'pli·cate (adj.)

com'pli·cat'ed

com'pli·ca'tion

com·plic'i·ty
pl. com·plic'i·ties

com·pli'er

com'pli·ment (n.)
(praise)
(SEE complement)

com'pli·ment' (v.)

com'pli·men'ta·ry
(praising)
(SEE complimentary)

com·ply'
com·plied',
com·ply'ing

com·po'nent

com·port' (v.)

com'port (n.)

com·pose'
com·posed',
com·pos'ing

com·posed'

com·pos'er

com·pos'ite

com'po·si'tion

com·pos'i·tor

com'post

com·po'sure

com'pote

com'pound (adj. n.)

com·pound' (v.)

com'pre·hend'

com'pre·hen'si·
bil'i·ty

com'pre·hen'si·ble

com'pre·hen'sion

com'pre·hen'sive

com·press' (v.)

com'press (n.)

com·press'i·bil'i·ty
pl.
com·press'i·bil'i·ties

com·press'i·ble

com·pres'sion

com·pres'sive

com·pres'sor

com·prise'
com·prised',
com·pris'ing

com'pro·mise'
com'pro·mised',
com'pro·mis'ing

com'pro·mis'er

comp·trol'ler

com·pul'sion

com·pul'sive

com·pul'so·ry

com·punc'tion

com'pu·ta'tion

com·put'a·ble

com·pute'
com·put'ed,
com·put'ing

com·put'er

com·pu'ter·i·za'tion

com·pu'ter·ize'
com·pu'ter·ized',
com·pu'ter·iz'ing

com'rade

com'rade·ship'

con
conned, con'ning

Co·na·kry'

con a·mo're

co·na'tion

com·pos'i·tor

con bri'o

con·cat'e·nate'
con·cat'e·nat'ed,
con·cat'e·nat'ing

con·cat'e·na'tion

con·cave' (adj., v.)
con·caved',
con·cav'ing

con'cave (n.)

con·cav'i·ty
pl. con·cav'i·ties

con·ceal'

con·ceal'ment

con·cede'
con·ced'ed,
con·ced'ing

con·ceit'

con·ceit'ed

con·ceiv'a·bil'i·ty

con·ceiv'a·ble

con·ceiv'a·bly

con·ceive'
con·ceived',
con·ceiv'ing

con'cen·trate'
con'cen·trat'ed,
con'cen·trat'ing

con'cen·tra'tion

con'cen·tra'tive

con'cen·tra'tor

con·cen'tric

con'cen·tric'i·ty

con'cept

con·cep'tion

con·cep'tu·al

con·cep'tu·al·ize'
con·cep'tu·al·ized',
con·cep'tu·al·iz'ing

con·cep'tu·al·ly

con·cern'

con·cerned'

con·cern'ing

con'cert (n., adj.)

con·cert' (v.)

con·cert'ed

con'cer·ti'na

con'cer·ti'no
pl. con'cer·ti'ni

con'cer·tize'
con'cer·tized',
con'cer·tiz'ing

con·cert·mas'ter

con·cer'to
  pl. con·cer'tos or (*It.*)
  con·cer'ti

con·ces'sion

con·ces'sion·aire'

con·ces'sive

conch   (*sea animal*)
  pl. conchs or con'ches
  (SEE conk)

con·chol'o·gy

con·cierge'

con·cil'i·ate'
  con·cil'i·at'ed,
  con·cil'i·at'ing

con·cil'i·a'tion

con·cil'i·a'tor

con·cil'i·a·to'ry

con·cise'

con·cise'ly

con·cise'ness

con'clave

con·clude'
  con·clud'ed,
  con·clud'ing

con·clu'sion

con·clu'sive

con·coct'

con·coc'tion

con·com'i·tance

con·com'i·tant

con'cord

Con'cord

con·cord'ance

con·cord'ant

con·cor'dat

Con·corde'
  (*Trademark*)

con'course

con·cres'cence

con'crete
  con'cret·ed,
  con'cret·ing

con·cre'tion

con·cu·bine'

con·cu'pis·cence

con·cu'pis·cent

con·cur'
  con·curred',
  con·cur'ring

con·cur'rence

con·cur'rent

con·cus'sion

con·demn'

con'dem·na'tion

con·den'sate

con'den·sa'tion

con·den'sa·ble

con·dense'
  con·densed',
  con·dens'ing

con·dens'er

con'de·scend'

con'de·scen'sion

con·dign'

con'di·ment

con·di'tion

con·di'tion·al

con·di'tioned

con·di'tion·er

con'do

con·dole'
  con·doled', con·dol'ing

con·do'lence

con·dol'er

con' do·lo're

con'dom

con'do·min'i·um
  pl. con'do·min'i·ums

con'do·na'tion

con·done'
  con·doned',
  con·don'ing

con'dor

con'dot·tie're
  pl. con'do·tie'ri

con·duce'
  con·duced',
  con·duc'ing

con·du'cive

con'duct   (*n.*)

con·duct'   (*v.*)

con·duct'ance

con·duc'tion

con·duc'tive

con'duc·tiv'i·ty
  pl. con'duc·tiv'i·ties

con·duc'tor

con'duit

cone
  coned, con'ing

Con'el·rad'

Con'es·to'ga

con·fab'u·late'
  con·fab'u·lat'ed,
  con·fab'u·lat'ing

con·fab'u·la'tion

con·fect'

con·fec'tion

con·fec'tion·er'y
  pl. con·fec'tion·er'ies

con·fed'er·a·cy
  pl. con·fed'er·a·cies

con·fed'er·ate   (*adj.,
  n.*)

con·fed'er·ate'   (*v.*)
  con·fed'er·at'ed,
  con·fed'er·at'ing

con·fed'er·a'tion

con·fed'er·a'tive

con·fer'
  con·ferred',
  con·fer'ring

con'fer·ee'

con'fer·ence

con·fess'

con·fess'ed·ly

con·fes'sion

con·fes'sion·al

con·fes'sor

con·fet'ti
  sing. con·fet'to

con'fi·dant'   (*friend*)
  (SEE confident)

con·fide'
  con·fid'ed, con·fid'ing

con'fi·dence

con'fi·dence man'

con'fi·dent   (*sure*)
  (SEE confidant)

con'fi·den'tial

con'fi·den'tial·ly

con·fid'er

con·fig'u·ra'tion

con·fig'u·ra·tive

con·fine'
  con·fined', con·fin'ing

con·fine'ment

con·fin'er

con·firm'

con'fir • ma'tion
con • firmed'
con • fis'ca • ble
con'fis • cate'
  con'fis • cat'ed,
  con'fis • cat'ing
con'fis • ca'tion
con'fis • ca'tor
con • fis'ca • to'ry
con'fla • gra'tion
con • flict' (v.)
con'flict (n.)
con • flic'tive
con'flu • ence
con'flu • ent
con'flux
con'form'
con • form'a • ble
con • form'ance
con'for • ma'tion
con • form'ist
con • form'i • ty
  pl. con • form'i • ties
con • found'
con'fra • ter'ni • ty
  pl. con'fra • ter'ni • ties
con'frere
con • front'
con'fron • ta'tion
Con • fu'cian • ism'
Con • fu'cius
con • fuse'
  con • fused', con • fus'ing
con • fus'ed • ly
con • fu'sion
con'fu • ta'tion
con • fute'
  con • fut'ed, con • fut'ing
con'ga
  pl. con'gas; (v.)
  con'gaed, con'ga • ing
con'gé
con • geal'
con'ge • ner
con • gen'ial
con • ge'ni • al'i • ty
con • gen'i • tal
con'ger
con • ge'ries

con • gest'
con • ges'tion
con • ges'tive
con • glo'bate
  con • glo'bat • ed,
  con • glo'bat • ing
con'glo • ba'tion
con • glom'er • ate (n., adj.)
con • glom'er • ate' (v.)
  con • glom'er • at'ed,
  con • glom'er • at'ing
con • glom'er • a'tion
Con'go
Con'go • lese'
  pl. Con'go • lese'
con'gou
con • grat'u • late'
  con • grat'u • lat'ed,
  con • grat'u • lat'ing
con • grat'u • la'tion
con • grat'u • la'tor
con • grat'u • la • to'ry
con'gre • gate' (v.)
  con'gre • gat'ed,
  con'gre • gat'ing
con'gre • gate (adj.)
con'gre • ga'tion
con'gre • ga'tion • al
con'gre • ga'
  tion • al • ism'
con'gre • ga'tion • al • ist
con'gress (n.)
con'gress' (v)
con • gres'sion • al
con'gress • man
  pl. con'gress • men
con'gress • wom'an
  pl. con'gress • wom'en
con'gru • ence
con'gru • en • cy
con'gru • ent
con • gru'i • ty
  pl. con • gru'i • ties
con'gru • ous
con'ic
con'i • cal
con'i • cal • ly
co'ni • fer
co • nif'er • ous

con • jec'tur • a • ble
con • jec'tur • al
con • jec'ture
  con • jec'tured,
  con • jec'tur • ing
con • join'
con • joint'
con'ju • gal
con'ju • gate' (v.)
  con'ju • gat'ed,
  con'ju • gat'ing
con'ju • gate (adj., n.)
con'ju • ga'tion
con'ju • ga'tor
con • junct'
con • junc'tion
con'junc • ti'va
  pl. con'junc • ti'vas or
  con'junc • ti'vae
con'junc • ti'val
con • junc'tive
con • junc'ti • vi'tis
con • junc'ture
con'jur • a'tion
con'jure
  con'jured, con'jur • ing
con'jur • er or
  con'jur • or
conk (strike)
  (SEE conch)
con' man'
con • nect'
Con • nect'i • cut
con • nec'tion
con • nec'tive
con • nec'tor
conn'ing tow'er
con • nip'tion
con • niv'ance
con • nive'
  con • nived', con • niv'ing
con • niv'er
con'nois • seur'
con'no • ta'tion
con'no • ta'tive
con • note'
  con • not'ed,
  con • not'ing
con • nu'bi • al
co'noid

co · noi′dal
con′quer
con′quer · a · ble
con′quer · or
con′quest
con · quis′ta · dor′
  pl. con · quis′ta · dors′ or
  (*Sp.*) con · quis′ta · do′res
Con′rad
con · san · guin′e · ous
con · san · guin′i · ty
con′science
con · sci · en′tious
con′scion · a · ble
con′scious
con · script′ (*v.*)
con′script (*n., adj.*)
con · scrip′tion
con′se · crate′
  con′se · crat′ed,
  con′se · crat′ing
con · se · cra′tion
con · se · cu′tion
con · sec′u · tive
con · sen′su · al
con · sen′sus
  pl. con · sen′sus · es
con · sent′
con′se · quence
con′se · quent′
con · se · quen′tial
con · serv′a · ble
con′ser · va′tion
con′ser · va′tion · ist
con · serv′a · tism′
con · serv′a · tive
con · serv′a · to′ry
  pl. con · serv′a · to′ries
con · serve′ (*v.*)
  con · served′,
  con · serv′ing
con′serve (*n.*)
con · sid′er
con · sid′er · a · ble
con · sid′er · ate
con · sid′er · a′tion
con · sid′ered
con · sid′er · ing

con · sign′
con · sign · ee′
con · sign′ment
con · sign′or or
  con · sign′er
con · sist′ (*v.*)
con′sist (*n.*)
con · sist′ence
con · sist′en · cy
  pl. con · sist′en · cies
con · sist′ent
con · sis′to · ry
  pl. con′sis · to′ries
con · sis · to′ri · al
con · sol′a · ble
con′so · la′tion
con · sol′a · to′ry
con · sole′ (*v.*)
  con · soled′, con · sol′ing
con′sole (*n.*)
con · sol′er
con · sol′i · date′
  con · sol′i · dat′ed,
  con · sol′i · dat′ing
con · sol′i · da′tion
con′som · mé′
con′so · nance
con′so · nant
con′so · nan′tal
con′sort (*n.*)
con · sort′ (*v.*)
con · sor′ti · um
  pl. con · sor′ti · a
con · spec′tus
  pl. con · spec′tus · es
con · spic′u · ous
con · spir′a · cy
  pl. con · spir′a · cies
con · spir′a · tor
con · spir′a · to′ri · al
con · spire′
  con · spired′,
  con · spir′ing
con · spir′er
con′sta · ble
con · stab′u · lar′y
  pl. con · stab′u · lar′ies
con′stan · cy
con′stant
con′stel · la′tion

con′ster · na′tion
con′sti · pate′
  con′sti · pat′ed,
  con′sti · pat′ing
con′sti · pa′tion
con · stit′u · en · cy
  pl. con · stit′u · en · cies
con · stit′u · ent
con′sti · tute′
  con′sti · tut′ed,
  con′sti · tut′ing
con′sti · tu′tion
con′sti · tu′tion · al
con′sti · tu′
  tion · al · ism′
con′sti · tu′tion · al′i · ty
con′sti · tu′tion · al · ly
con · strain′
con · strain′a · ble
con · strained′
con · straint′
con · strict′
con · stric′tion
con · stric′tive
con · stric′tor
con · struct′ (*v.*)
con′struct (*n.*)
con · struc′tion
con · struc′tion · ist
con · struc′tive
con · struc′tor or
  con · struc′ter
con · strue′ (*v.*)
  con · strued′,
  con · stru′ing
con′strue (*n.*)
con · sub · stan′ti · a′tion
con′sue · tude′
con′sul (*official*)
  (SEE counsel *and*
  concil)
con′su · lar
con′su · late
con′sul gen′er · al
  pl. con′suls gen′er · al
con · sult′ (*v.*)
con′sult (*n.*)
con · sult′ant
con′sul · ta′tion
con · sult′a · tive

con·sum'a·ble

con·sume'
  con·sumed',
  con·sum'ing

con·sum'er

con·sum'er·ism'

con·sum'er·ist

con'sum·mate' (v.)
  con'sum·mat'ed,
  con'sum·mat'ing

con·sum'mate (adj.)

con'sum·ma'tion

con·sump'tion

con·sump'tive

con'tact

con·ta'gion

con·ta'gious

con·ta'gium
  pl. con·ta'gia

con·tain'

con·tain'er

con·tain'ment

con·tam'i·nant

con·tam'i·nate' (v.)
  con·tam'i·nat'ed,
  con·tam'i·nat'ing

con·tam'i·nate
  (adj.)

con·tam'i·na'tion

con'tam·i·na'tor

con·temn'

con'tem·plate'
  con'tem·plat'ed,
  con'tem·plat'ing

con'tem·pla'tion

con·tem'pla·tive

con'tem·pla'tor

con·tem'po·ra'ne·ous

con·tem'po·rar'y
  pl. con·tem'po·rar'ies

con·tempt'

con·tempt'i·ble

con·temp'tu·ous

con·tend'

con·tend'er

con'tent (n.)

con·tent' (adj.)

con·tent'ed

con·ten'tion

con·ten'tious

con·tent'ment

con·ter'mi·nous

con'test (n.)

con·test' (v.)

con·test'a·ble

con·test'ant

con'text

con·tex'tu·al

con·tex'ture

con'ti·gu'i·ty
  pl. con'ti·gu'i·ties

con·tig'u·ous

con'ti·nence

con'ti·nent

con'ti·nen'tal

con·tin'gen·cy
  pl. con·tin'gen·cies

con·tin'gent

con·tin'u·al

con·tin'u·al·ly

con·tin'u·ance

con·tin'u·ant

con·tin'u·a'tion

con·tin'ue
  con·tin'ued,
  con·tin'u·ing

con·tin'u·er

con'ti·nu'i·ty
  pl. con'ti·nu'i·ties

con·tin'u·ous

con·tin'u·um
  pl. con·tin'u·a

con'to

con·tort'

con·tor'tion

con·tor'tion·ist

con·tor'tive

con'tour

con'tra

con'tra·band'

con'tra·bass'
  pl. con'tra·bass'es

con'tra·bas·soon'

con'tra·cep'tion

con'tra·cep'tive

con'tract (n.)

con·tract' (v.)

con·tract'i·ble

con·trac'tile

con·trac'tion

con·trac'tive

con'trac·tor

con·trac'tu·al

con·trac'tu·al·ly

con·trac'ture

con'tra·dict'

con'tra·dict'er

con'tra·dic'tion

con'tra·dic'tive

con'tra·dic'to·ry
  pl. con'tra·dic'to·ries

con'tra·dis·tinc'tion

con'trail

con'tra·in'di·cate'
  con'tra·in'di·cat'ed,
  con'tra·in'di·cat'ing

con'tra·in'di·ca'tion

con·tral'to
  pl. con·tral'tos

con'tra·po·si'tion

con'tra·pun'tal

con'tra·ri'e·ty
  pl. con'tra·ri'e·ties

con'tra·ri·ly

con'tra·ri·ness

con'tra·ri·wise'

con'tra·ry
  pl. con'tra·ries

con·trast' (v.)

con'trast (n.)

con·tras'tive

con·trast'y

con'tra·vene'
  con'tra·vened',
  con'tra·ven'ing

con'tra·ven'tion

con'tre·temps'
  pl. con'tre·temps'

con·trib'ute
  con·trib'ut·ed,
  con·trib'ut·ing

con'tri·bu'tion

con·trib'u·tor

con·trib'u·to'ry
  pl. con·trib'u·to'ries

con·trite'

con·tri'tion

con·triv'ance

con·trive'
  con·trived',
  con·triv'ing

con·trol'
  con·trolled,
  con·trol'ling

con·trol'la·ble

con·trol'ler

con·trol' tow'er

con'tro·ver'sial

con'tro·ver'sy
  pl. con'tro·ver·sies

con'tro·vert'

con'tro·vert'i·ble

con·tu·ma'cious

con·tu·mac'i·ty

con'tu·ma·cy
  pl. con'tu·ma·cies

con'tu·me'li·ous

con'tu·me·ly
  pl. con'tu·me·lies

con·tuse'
  con·tused', con·tus'ing

con·tu'sion

co·nun'drum

con'ur·ba'tion

con'va·lesce'
  con'va·lesced',
  con'va·lesc'ing

con'va·les'cence

con'va·les'cent

con·vect'

con·vec'tion

con·vec'tive

con·vene'
  con·vened',
  con·ven'ing

con·ven'ience

con·ven'ient

con'vent

con·ven'ti·cle

con·ven'tion

con·ven'tion·al

con·ven'tion·al'i·ty
  pl.
  con·ven'tion·al'i·ties

con·ven'tio·neer'

con·ven'tu·al

con·verge'
  con·verged',
  con·verg'ing

con·ver'gence

con·ver'gen·cy

con·ver'gent

con·vers'a·ble

con·ver'sant

con'ver·sa'tion

con'ver·sa'tion·al

con'ver·sa'tion·al·ist

con·verse' (v.)
  con·versed',
  con·vers'ing

con'verse (n.)

con·verse' (adj.)

con·verse'ly

con·ver'sion

con·vert' (v.)

con'vert (n.)

con·vert'er or
  con·vert'or

con·vert'i·ble

con·vert'i·plane'

con·vex' (adj.)

con'vex (n.)

con·vex'i·ty
  pl. con·vex'i·ties

con·vey'

con·vey'ance

con·vey'er or
  con·vey'or

con·vict' (v., adj.)

con'vict (n.)

con·vic'tion

con·vince'
  con·vinced',
  con·vinc'ing

con·vinc'er

con·vinc'ing

con·viv'i·al

con·viv'i·al'i·ty

con·viv'i·al·ly

con'vo·ca'tion

con·voke'
  con·voked',
  con·vok'ing

con'vo·lute'
  con'vo·lut'ed,
  con'vo·lut'ing

con'vo·lu'tion

con'voy

con·vulse'
  con·vulsed',
  con·vuls'ing

con·vul'sion

con·vul'sion·ar'y

con·vul'sive

co'ny
  pl. co'nies

coo (v.)
  cooed, coo'ing

coo (interj.)

cook

cook'book'

cook'er

cook'e·ry
  pl. cook'e·ries

cook'house'

cook'ie

cook'out'

Cook's' tour'

cook'stove'

cook'top'

cook'y
  pl. cook'ies

cool

cool'ant

cool'er

cool'head'ed

Cool'idge

coo'lie (laborer)
  (SEE coolly and
  coulee)

cool'ly (calmly)
  (SEE coolie and
  coulee)

coon

coon' dog'

coon'skin'

co'-op'

coop (cage)
  (SEE coupe and coup)

Coo'per

coop'er·age

co·op'er·ate'
  co·op'er·at'ed,
  co·op'er·at'ing

co·op'er·a'tion

co·op'er·a'tive

co·op'er·a'tor

co·opt'

co·or'di·nate (*adj.*, *n.*)

co·or'di·nate' (*v.*)
co·or'di·nat'ed,
co·or'di·nat'ing

co·or'di·na'tion

co·or'di·na'tor

coot

coot'ie

co'–own'

cop
copped, cop'ping

co'pa·cet'ic

co'pal

co·part'ner

cope
coped, cop'ing

Co'pen·ha'gen

Co·per'ni·can

Co·per'ni·cus

cope'stone'

cop'i·er

co'pi·lot

cop'ing

cop'ing saw'

co'pi·ous

co·pla'nar

co·pol'y·mer

cop'out'

cop'per

cop'per·as

cop'per·head'

cop'per·plate'

cop'per·smith'

cop'per·tone'

cop'per·y

cop'pice

cop'ra

cop'ro·phil'i·a

co'–pros·per'i·ty

copse

Copt

cop'ter

Cop'tic

cop'u·la
pl. cop'u·las or
cop'u·lae'

cop'u·lar

cop'u·late' (*v.*)
cop'u·lat'ed,
cop'u·lat'ing

cop'u·late (*adj.*)

cop'u·la'tion

cop'u·la'tive

cop'y
pl. cop'ies; (*v.*)
cop'ied, cop'y·ing

cop'y·book'

cop'y·cat'
cop'y·cat'ted,
cop'y·cat'ting

cop'y–ed'it

cop'y·hold'er

cop'y·ist

cop'y·read'er

cop'y·right'

cop'y·writ'er

coq au vin'

co·quet'
co·quet'ted,
co·quet'ting

co'quet·ry
pl. co'quet·ries

co·quette'

co·quet'tish

co·quille'

co·qui'na

cor'a·cle

cor'al (*marine skeleton*)
(SEE choral)

cor'al·line

cor' an·glais'

cor'bel
cor'beled, cor'bel·ing

cord (*rope*)
(SEE chord)

cord'age

cor'date

cor·del'is

cor'dial

cor·dial'i·ty
pl. cor·dial'i·ties

cor'dial·ly

cor'dil·le'ra

cor'dil·le'ran

Cor'dil·le'ras

cord'ite

cord'less

cor·do'ba

cor'don

cor·don bleu'
pl. cor·dons bleus'

cor·don sa·ni·taire'

Cor'do·van

cor'du·roy'

cord'wood'

core (*center*)
cored, cor'ing
(SEE corps)

co're·li'gion·ist

cor'er

co're·spond'ent
(*defendant*)
(SEE correspondent)

cor'gi

co'ri·a'ceous

co'ri·an'der

Cor'inth

Co·rin'thi·an

co'ri·um
pl. co'ri·a

cork

cork'age

cork'board'

cor'ker

cork'ing

cork'screw'

cork'y
cork'i·er, cork'i·est

corm

cor'mo·rant

corn

corn'ball'

Corn' Belt'

corn' bread'

corn' cake'

corn'cob'

corn'crib'

cor'ne·a

corned

cor'ne·ous

cor'ner

cor'ner·stone'

cor·net'

cor·net'ist

corn'fed'

corn'flakes' or corn'
   flakes'

corn'flow'er

corn' grits'

corn'husk'

corn'husk'er

cor'nice
  cor'niced, cor'nic · ing

Cor'nish

corn' meal'

corn' oil'

corn' pone'

corn' silk'

corn'stalk'

corn'starch'

cor·nu·co'pi·a

cor·nu·co'pi·an

corn'y
  corn'i·er, corn'i·est

co·rol'la

cor'ol·lar'y
  pl. cor'ol·lar'ies

co·ro'na
  pl. co·ro'nas or
  co·ro'nae

cor'o·nach

co·ro'na·graph'

cor'o·nal

cor'o·nar'y
  pl. cor'o·nar'ies

cor'o·na'tion

cor'o·ner

cor'o·net

Co·rot'

cor'por·al

cor'po·rate

cor'po·ra'tion

cor'po·ra'tive

cor'po·ra'tor

cor·po're·al

corps (group)
  pl. corps
  (SEE core and corps)

corps' de bal·let'

corpse (dead body)
  (SEE corps)

corps'man
  pl. corps'men

cor'pu·lence

cor'pu·lent

cor'pus
  pl. cor'po·ra

Cor'pus Chris'ti

cor'pus·cle

cor·pus'cu·lar

cor'pus de·lic'ti

cor'pus ju'ris

cor·ral' (enclosure)
  cor·ralled', cor·ral'ling
  (SEE chorale)

cor·ra'sion

cor·rect'

cor·rect'a·ble

cor·rect'i·ble

cor·rec'tion

cor·rec'tive

cor're·late'
  cor're·lat'ed,
  cor're·lat'ing

cor're·la'tion

cor·rel'a·tive

cor're·spond'

cor're·spond'ence

cor're·spond'ent
  (writer)
  (SEE correspondent)

cor're·spond'ing

cor·ri'da

cor'ri·dor

cor·ri·gen'dum
  pl. cor·ri·gen'da

cor·rob'o·rate' (v.)
  cor·rob'o·rat'ed,
  cor·rob'o·rat'ing

cor·rob'o·rate (adj.)

cor·rob'o·ra'tion

cor·rob'o·ra'tive

co·rob'o·ra'tor

cor·rode'
  cor·rod'ed, cor·rod'ing

cor·ro'sion

cor·ro'sive

cor'ru·gate' (v.)
  cor'ru·gat'ed,
  cor'ru·gat'ing

cor'ru·gate (adj.)

cor'ru·ga'tion

cor·rupt'

cor·rupt'i·ble

cor·rup'tion

cor·rup'tive

cor·sage'

cor'sair

cor'set
  cor'set·ed, cor'set·ing

Cor'si·ca

cor·tege' or cor·tège'

cor'tex
  pl. cor'ti·ces'

cor'ti·cal

cor'ti·cate

cor'ti·sone'

co·run'dum

co·rus'cant

cor'us·cate'
  cor'us·cat'ed,
  cor'us·cat'ing

cor'us·ca'tion

cor·vée'

cor·vette'

cor'y·phée'

co·ry'za

cos

Co'sa Nos'tra

co·se'cant

co·sig'na·to'ry
  pl. co·sig'na·to'ries

co'sign'er

co'sine

cos·met'ic

cos'me·ti'cian

cos'me·tol'o·gy

cos'mic

cos'mi·cal·ly

cos'mic ray'

cos·mog'o·ny
  pl. cos·mog'o·nies

cos·mog'ra·phy
  pl. cos·mog'ra·phies

cos'mo·line'

cos'mo·log'i·cal

cos·mol'o·gist

cos·mol'o·gy

cos'mo·naut'

cos'mo·pol'i·tan

cos·mop'o·lite'

cos'mos
  pl. cos'mos or
  cos'mos·es

Cos'mo·tron'

Cos'sack

cos'set

cost
  cost, cost'ing

cos'ta
  pl. cos'tae

cos'tal

co'·star' (n.)

co'-star' (v.)
  co'-starred', co'-
  star'ring

Cos'ta Ri'ca

Cos'ta Ri'can

cost-'effec'tive

cos'tive

cost'li·ness

cost'ly
  cost'li·er, cost'li·est

cost'-plus'

cost'-push'

cos'trel

cos'tume (n.)

cos·tume' (v.)
  cos·tumed',
  cos·tum'ing

cos·tum'er

cot

co·tan'gent

cote (shelter)
  cot'ed, cot'ing
  (SEE coat)

co'te·rie

co·thur'nus

co·til'lion

cot'tage

cot'tag·er

cot'ter

cot'ter pin'

cot'ton

cot'ton belt'

cot'ton can'dy

cot'ton·mouth'

cot'ton·pick'in'

cot'ton·seed'

cot'ton·tail'

cot'ton·wood'

cot'ton·y

cot'y·le'don

cot'y·le'don·al

couch

couch'ant

cou'gar
  pl. cou'gars or cou'gar

cough

cough' drop'

could

could'n't

cou'lee (ravine)
  (SEE coolly and coolie)

cou'lomb

cou'ma·rin

coun'cil (assembly)
  (SEE counsel and
  consul)

coun'ci·lor or
  coun'cil·lor
  (council member)
  (SEE counselor)

coun'sel (advice)
  coun'seled or
  coun'selled,
  coun'sel·ing or
  coun'sel·ling
  (SEE council and
  consul)

coun'se·lor or
  coun'sel·lor
  (adviser)
  (SEE councilor)

count

count'a·ble

count'down'

coun'te·nance
  coun'te·nanced,
  coun'te·nanc·ing

count'er

coun'ter·act'

coun'ter·ac'tion

coun'ter·at·tack'
  (n.)

coun'ter·at·tack'
  (v.)

coun'ter·bal'ance
  (n.)

coun'ter·bal'ance
  (v.)
  coun'ter·bal'anced,
  coun'ter·bal'anc·ing

coun'ter·blow'

coun'ter·charge' (n.)

coun'ter·charge' (v.)
  coun'ter·charged',
  coun'ter·charg'ing

coun'ter·claim' (n.)

coun'ter·claim' (v.)

coun'ter·clock'wise'

coun'ter·cul'ture

coun'ter·es·
  pi·o·nage'

coun'ter·feit'

coun'ter·feit·er

coun'ter·in·sur'gent

coun'ter·in·tel'li·
  gence

coun'ter·ir'ri·tant

coun'ter·man'
  pl. coun'ter·men'

coun'ter·mand' (v.)

coun'ter·mand' (n.)

coun'ter·meas'ure

coun'ter·of·fen'sive

coun'ter·pane'

coun'ter·part'

coun'ter·point'

coun'ter·poise'
  coun'ter·poised',
  coun'ter·pois'ing

coun'ter·pro·pos'al

coun'ter·punch'

Coun'ter Ref'or·
  ma'tion

coun'ter·rev'o·lu'tion

coun'ter·rev'o·lu'
  tion·ar'y
  pl. coun'ter·rev'o·lu'
  tion·ar'ies

coun'ter·shaft'

coun'ter·sign'

coun'ter·sig'na·ture

coun'ter·sink'
  coun'ter·sank',
  coun'ter·sunk',
  coun'ter·sink'ing

coun'ter·spy'
  pl. coun'ter·spies'

coun'ter·state'ment

coun'ter·ten'or

coun'ter·thrust'

coun'ter • vail'
coun'ter • weigh'
coun'ter • weight'
coun'tess
count'less
coun'tri • fied'
coun'try
  pl. coun'tries
coun'try club'
coun'try • folk'
coun'try • man
  pl. coun'try • men
coun'try • side'
coun'try • wom'an
  pl. coun'try • wom'en
coun'ty
  pl. coun'ties
coup (*daring act*)
  (SEE coop *and* coupe)
coup de grace'
  pl. coups de grace'
coup' d'é • tat'
  pl. coups' de'é • tat'
coup *or* cou • pé'
  (*automobile*)
  (SEE coup *and* coop)
cou'ple
  cou'pled, cou'pling
cou'pler
cou'plet
cou'pling
cou'pon
cour'age
cou • ra'geous
cou'ri • er
course (*route*)
  coursed, cours'ing
  (SEE coarse)
cours'er
cours'ing
court
cour'te • ous
cour'te • san
cour'te • sy
  (*politeness*)
  pl. cour'te • sies
  (SEE curtsy *and*
  curtsey)
court'house'
cour'ti • er
court'li • ness

court'ly
  court'li • er, court'li • est
court'mar'tial
  pl. courts'mar'tial;
  v. court'mar'tialed,
  court'mar'tial • ing
court'room'
court'ship'
court'yard'
cous'in (*relative*)
  (SEE cozen)
cou • ture'
cou • tu'ri • er
cou • vade'
co • va'lence
co • va'lent
cove
  coved, cov'ing
cov'en
cov'e • nant
cov'e • nan • tor
cov'er
cov'er • age
cov'er • all
Cov'er • dale'
cov'er • let
cov'ert
cov'er • ture
cov'er-up'
cov'et
  cov'et • ed, cov'et • ing
cov'et • ous
cov'ey
  pl. cov'eys
cow
cow'ard
cow'ard • ice
cow'ard • ly
cow'bell'
cow'bird'
cow'boy'
cow'catch'er
cow'er
cow'girl'
cow'hand'
cow'herd'
cow'hide'
  cow'hid'ed, cow'hid'ing
cowl

cow'lick'
cowl'ing
cow'man
  pl. cow'men
co • work'er
cow'poke'
cow'pox'
cow'punch'er
cow'rie *or* cow'ry
  pl. cow'ries
cow'slip'
cox'comb'
cox'swain
coy
coy'ly
coy'ness
coy • o'te
  pl. coy • o'tes
coz'en (*dupe*)
  (SEE cousin)
co'zi • ly
co'zi • ness
co'zy
  (*v.*) co'zi • er, co'zi • est;
  pl. co'zi • es
crab
  crabbed, crab'bing
crab' ap'ple
crab'bed
crab'by
  crab'bi • er, crab'bi • est
crab' grass'
crack
crack'brain'
crack'down'
cracked
crack'er
crack'er • bar'rel
crack'er • jack'
Crack'er Jack'
  (*Trademark*)
crack'ing
crack'le
  crack'led, crack'ling
crack'le • ware'
crack'ling
crack'nel
crack'pot'
crack'-up'

Crac'ow

cra'dle
cra'dled, cra'dling

cra'dle · song'

craft

craft'i · ness

crafts'man
pl. crafts'men

craft'y
craft'i · er, craft'i · est

crag

crag'gy
crag'gi · er, crag'gi · est

cram
crammed, cram'ming

cramp

cram'pon

cran'ber'ry
pl. cran'ber'ries

crane
craned, cran'ing

cra'ni · al

cra'ni · om'e · try

cra'ni · um
pl. cra'ni · ums or
cra'ni · a

crank

crank'case'

crank'i · ly

crank'i · ness

crank'shaft'

crank'y
crank'i · er, crank'i · est

cran'ny
pl. cran'nies

crap

crape'hang · er

crap'pie

craps

crap'shoot'er

crash

crash'land'

crass

crass'ly

crate
crat'ed, crat'ing

cra'ter

cra · vat'

crave
craved, crav'ing

cra'ven

crav'er

crav'ing

craw

craw'fish'
pl. craw'fish' or
craw'fish'es

crawl

crawl'y
crawl'i · er, crawl'i · est

cray'fish'
pl. cray'fish' or
cray'fish'es

cray'on

craze
crazed, craz'ing

cra'zi · ly

cra'zi · ness

cra'zy
pl. cra'zies (adj.)
cra'zi · er, cra'zi · est

creak (squeak)
(SEE creek)

creak'y
creak'i · er, creak'i · est

cream

cream' cheese'

cream'er

cream'er · y
pl. cream'er · ies

cream'y
cream'i · er, cream'i · est

crease
creased, creas'ing

cre · ate'
cre · at'ed, cre · at'ing

cre · a'tion

cre · a'tive

cre'a · tiv'i · ty

cre · a'tor

crea'ture

crèche
pl. crèch'es

cre'dence

cre · den'tial

cre · den'za

cred'i · bil'i · ty

cred'i · ble

cred'it

cred'it · a · bil'i · ty

cred'it · a · ble

cred'it · a · bly

cred'it card'

cred'i · tor

cred'it un'ion

cre'do
pl. cre'dos

cre · du'li · ty

cred'u · lous

Cree
pl. Crees or Cree

creed

creek (brook)
(SEE creak)

Creek
pl. Creeks or Creek

creel

creep
crept, creep'ing

creep'er

creep'y
creep'i · er, creep'i · est

cre'mate
cre'mat · ed, cre'mat · ing

cre · ma'tion

cre'ma · tor

cre'ma · to'ri · um
pl. cre'ma · to'ri · ums or
cre'ma · to'ri · a

cre'ma · to'ry
pl. cre'ma · to'ries

crème' de ca · ca'o

crème' de menthe'

cren'el · at'ed

cren'el · a'tion

Cre'ole

cre'o · sol'

cre'o · sote'

crepe
creped, crep'ing

crêpe' su · zette'
pl. crêpe' su · zettes'

crept

cre · pus'cu · lar

cre · scen'do
pl. cre · scen'dos or (It.)
cre · scen'di

cres'cent

cre'sol

cress

cres'set

crest

crest'fall'en

cre·ta'ceous

Cre'tan (of Crete)
(SEE cretin)

Crete

cre'tin (invalid)
(SEE Cretan)

cre'tin·ism'

cre·tonne'

cre·vasse'
cre·vassed',
cre·vas'sing

crev'ice

crew

crew' cut'

crew'el

crew' neck'

crib
cribbed, crib'bing

crib'bage

crick

crick'et

cri'er

crime

Cri·me'a

Cri·me'an

crim'i·nal

crim'i·nal'i·ty
pl. crim'i·nal'i·ties

crim'i·nal·ly

crim'i·no·log'i·cal

crim'i·nol'o·gist

crim'i·nol'o·gy

crimp

crim'son

cringe
cringed, cring'ing

crin'gle

crin'kle
crin'kled, crin'kling

crin'kly
crin'kli·er, crin'kli·est

cri'noid

crin'o·line

cri·ol'lo

crip'ple
crip'pled, crip'pling

cri'sis
pl. cri'ses

crisp

crisp'en

crisp'er

crisp'ly

crisp'y
crisp'i·er, cris'pi·est

criss'cross'

cri·te'ri·on
pl. cri·te'ri·a or
cri·te'ri·ons

crit'ic

crit'i·cal

crit'i·cal·ly

crit'i·cism'

crit'i·cize'
crit'i·cized',
crit'i·ciz'ing

cri·tique'

crit'ter

croak

croak'er

Cro·a'tia

cro·chet'
cro·cheted',
cro·chet'ing

crock

crock'er·y

croc'o·dile'

croc'o·dil'i·an

cro'cus
pl. cro'cus·es

Croe'sus

crois·sant'

Croix de Guerre'

Cro–Mag'non

crom'lech

Crom'well

crone

cro'ny
pl. cro'nies

crook

crook'ed

croon

croon'er

crop
cropped, crop'ping

crop'–dust'

crop'–dust'er

crop'per

cro·quet' (game)
cro·queted',
cro·quet'ing
(SEE croquette)

cro·quette' (food)
(SEE croquet)

cro'sier

cross

cross'arm'

cross'bar'

cross'beam'

cross'bones'

cross'bow'

cross'breed'
cross'bred',
cross'breed'ing

cross'–coun'try (adj.)

cross'–coun'try (n.)

cross'cur'rent

cross'cut'
cross'cut', cross'cut'ting

cross'–ex·am'i·
na'tion

cross'–ex·am'ine
cross'–ex·am'ined,
cross'–ex·am'in·ing

cross'–eye'

cross'–eyed'

cross'–fer'ti·li·za'tion

cross'–fer'ti·lize'
cross'–fer'ti·lized',
cross'–fer'ti·liz'ing

cross' fire' or
cross'fire'

cross'–grained'

cross'hatch'

cross'ing

cross'–leg'ged

cross'o'ver

cross'patch'

cross'piece'

cross'–pol'li·nate'
cross'–pol'li·nat'ed,
cross'–pol'li·nat'ing

cross'–pol'li·na'tion

cross'–pur'pose

cross'–ques'tion

cross're·fer'
cross're·ferred',
cross're·fer'ring

cross' ref'er·ence

cross'road'

cross' sec'tion

cross'-stitch'

cross' street'

cross' talk'

cross'tie'

cross'town'

cross'walk'

cross' wind'

cross'wise'

cross'word' puz'zle

crotch

crotch'et

crotch'et·i·ness

crotch'et·y

Cro'ton bug'

crouch

croup

crou'pi·er

crou'ton

crow

Crow

crow'bar'

crowd

crow'foot'
  pl. crow'foots' or
  crow'feet'

crown

crown' glass'

crown'piece'

crown' saw'

crow's'-foot'
  pl. crow's'-feet'

crow's'-nest'

cru'cial

cru'ci·ble

cru'ci·fer

cru'ci·fix
  pl. cru'ci·fix·es

cru'ci·fix'ion

cru'ci·form'

cru'ci·fy'
  cru'ci·fied',
  cru'ci·fy'ing

crud

crud'dy
  crud'di·er, crud'di·est

crude

crude'ly

crude'ness

crude' oil'

cru'di·ty
  pl. cru'di·ties

cru'el

cru'el·ly

cru'el·ty
  pl. cru'el·ties

cru'et

cruise (*sail*)
  cruised, cruis'ing
  (SEE cruse)

cruise' mis'sile

cruis'er

crul'ler

crumb

crum'ble
  crum'bled, crum'bling

crum'bly
  crum'bli·er,
  crum'bli·est

crumb'y
  crumb'i·er, crumb'i·est

crum'my
  crum'mi·er,
  crum'mi·est

crump

crum'pet

crum·ple
  crum'pled, crum'pling

crunch

crunch'y
  crunch'i·er,
  crunch'i·est

crup'per

cru·sade'
  cru·sad'ed, cru·sad'ing

cru·sad'er

cruse (*container*)
  (SEE cruise)

crush

crush'a·ble

crust

crus·ta'cean

crus'tal

crust'y
  crust'i·er, crust'i·est

crutch
  pl. crutch'es

crux
  pl. crux'es or cru'ces

cru·zei'ro
  pl. cru·zei'ros

cry
  (v.) cried, cry'ing,
  pl. cries

cry'ba'by
  pl. cry'ba'bies

cry'ing

cry'o·gen'ic

cry'o·gen'ics

cry·om'e·ter

cry·on'ics

cry'o·sur'ger·y

crypt

crypt'a·nal'y·sis

crypt·an'a·lyst

cryp'tic

cryp'to·gram'

cryp'to·graph'

cryp·tog'ra·pher

cryp'to·graph'ic

cryp·tog'ra·phy

crys'tal
  crys'taled, crys'tal·ing

crys'tal gaz'ing

crys'tal·line

crys'tal·li·za'tion

crys'tal·lize'
  crys'tal·lized',
  crys'tal·liz'ing

crys'tal·log'ra·phy

crys'tal·loid'

cub

Cu'ba

Cu'ban

cu'ba·ture

cub'by·hole'

cube
  cubed, cub'ing

cu'beb

cube' root'

cu'bic

cu'bi·cal (*cube-
  shaped*)
  (SEE cubicle)

cu'bi·cle (*room*)
  (SEE cubical)

Cub'ism or cub'ism

Cub'ist or cub'ist

cu'bit

cu'boid

cuck′old

cuck′oo
  pl. cuck′oos
  cuck′ooed, cuck′oo·ing

cu′cum·ber

cud

cud′dle
  cud′dled, cud′dling

cudg′el
  cudg′eled, cudg′el·ing

cue (*hint*)
  cued, cu′ing
  (SEE queue)

cue′ ball′

cuff

cuff′ link′

cui·rass′

cui·sine′

cul′-de-sac′

cu′li·nar′y

cull

cul′mi·nate′
  cul′mi·nat′ed,
  cul′mi·nat′ing

cul′mi·na′tion

cu·lottes′

cul′pa·bil′i·ty

cul′pa·ble

cul′pa·bly

cul′prit

cul′tic

cult′ist

cul′ti·va·ble

cul′ti·vate′
  cul′ti·vat′ed,
  cul′ti·vat′ing

cul′ti·va′tion

cul′ti·va′tor

cul′tur·al

cul′tur·al·ly

cul′ture
  cul′tured, cul′tur·ing

cul′tured

cul′ture shock′

cul′ver·in

cul′vert

cum′ber

cum′ber·some

cum′brance

cum′in

cum lau′de

cum′mer·bund′

cu′mu·la′tive

cu′mu·lo·nim′bus
  pl. cu′mu·lo·nim′bus

cu′mu·lus
  pl. cu′mu·lus

cunc·ta′tion

cunc·ta′tor

cu·ne′i·form′

cun′ning

cup
  cupped, cup′ping

cub′bear′er

cup′board

cup′cake′

cup′ful′
  pl. cup′fuls′

cup′hold′er

Cu′pid

cu·pid′i·ty

cu′po·la

cupped

cup′ping

cu′pre·ous

cu′pric

cu′prous

cur

cur′a·ble

Cu′ra·çao′

cu·ra′re

cu′rate

cur′a·tive

cu·ra′tor

curb

curb′ing

curb′stone′

curd

cur′dle
  cur′dled, cur′dling

curd′y
  curd′i·er, curd′i·est

cure
  cured, cur′ing

cu·ré′

cure′-all′

cur′er

cu·ret′tage

cu·rette′
  cu·ret′ted, cu·ret′ting

cur′few

cu′ri·a
  pl. cu′ri·ae′

cu′rie

Cu′rie

cu′ri·o
  pl. cu′ri·os

cu′ri·o′sa

cu′ri·os′i·ty
  pl. cu′ri·os′i·ties

cu′ri·ous

cu′ri·um

curl

curl′er

cur′lew

curl′i·cue′

curl′ing

curl′y
  curl′i·er, curl′i·est

cur·mudg′eon

cur′rant (*berry*)
  (SEE current)

cur′ren·cy
  pl. cur′ren·cies

cur′rent (*present*)
  (SEE currant)

cur·ric′u·lar

cur·ric′u·lum
  pl. cur·ric′u·lums or
  cur·ric′u·la

cur′rish

cur′ry
  pl. cur′ries; (*v.*)
  cur′ried, cur′ry·ing

cur′ry·comb′

curse
  cursed, curs′ing

curs′ed

cur′sive

cur′so·ri·ly

cur·so′ri·al

cur′so·ry

curt

curt′ly

cur′tail′ (*v.*)

cur′tail (*n.*)

cur′tain

curt′sey (*bow*)
  pl. curt′seys; (v.)
  curt′seyed, curt′sey·ing
  (SEE courtesy *and*
  curtsy)

curt′sy (*bow*)
  pl. curt′sies
  curt′sied, curt′sy·ing
  (SEE courtesy *and*
  curtsey)

cur·va′ceous

cur′va·ture

curve
  curved, curv′ing

curv′ed·ly

cur′vet (*n.*)

cur·vet′ (*v.*)
  cur·vet′ted or
  cur·vet′ed, cur·vet′ting
  or cur·vet′ing

cur′vi·lin′e·ar

curv′y
  curv′ier, curv′i·est

cush′ion

cush′y
  cush′i·er, cush′i·est

cusp

cus′pid

cus′pi·date′

cus′pi·dor′

cuss

cuss′ed

cus′tard

cus·to′di·al

cus·to′di·an

cus′to·dy
  pl. cus′to·dies

cus′tom

cus′tom·ar′i·ly

cus′tom·ar′y
  pl. cus′tom·ar′ies

cus′tom–built′

cus′tom·er

cus′tom house′

cus′tom–made′

cus′toms un′ion

cut
  cut, cut′ting

cu·ta′ne·ous

cut′a·way′

cut′back′

cut′down′

cute
  cut′er, cut′est

cute′ly

cut′ glass′

cu′ti·cle

cut′ie

cut′lass
  pl. cut′lass·es

cut′ler

cut′ler·y

cut′let

cut′off′

cut′out′

cut′ rate′

cut′ter

cut′throat′

cut′ting

cut′tle·bone′

cut′tle·fish′
  pl. cut′tle·fish′ or
  cut′tle·fish′es

cut′up′

cut′wa′ter

cut′worm′

cu·vette′

cy′a·nide′
  cy′a·nid′ed,
  cy′a·nid′ing

cy·an′o·gen

cy′a·no′sis

cy′an

cy·an′ic

cy′a·nide′

cy′a·not′ic

cy′ber·net′ic

cy′ber·net′ics

cy′cla·mate′

cyc′la·men

cy′cle
  cy′cled, cy′cling

cy′cler

cy′clic

cy′cli·cal

cy′cli·cal·ly

cy′clist

cy′clo·hex′ane

cy′cloid

cy·clom′e·ter

cy′clone

cy·clon′ic

cy′clo·pe′di·a

Cy′clops

cy′clo·ram′a

cy′clo·tron′

cyg′net (*swan*)
  (SEE signet)

Cyg′nus

cyl′in·der

cy·lin′dri·cal

cyl′in·droid′

cym′bal (*musical
  instrument*)
  (SEE symbol)

cyme

Cym′ry

cyn′ic

cyn′i·cal

cyn′i·cism′

cy′no·sure′

cy′press (*tree*)
  pl. cy′press·es
  (SEE Cyprus)

Cyp′ri·ot or
  Cyp′ri·ote

Cy′prus (*nation*)
  (SEE cypress)

Cy·ril′lic

cyst

cys·tec′to·my
  pl. cys·tec′to·mies

cyst′ic

cys·ti′tis

cyst′oid

cys′to·scope′

cys·tos′co·py
  pl. cys·tos′co·pies

cy·tol′o·gist

cy·tol′o·gy

cy′to·plasm′

cy′to·plas′mic

czar

czar′das

czar′e·vitch

cza·rev′na

cza · ri'na
czar'ism
czar'ist

Czech (*native of
Czechoslovakia*)
(SEE check)

Czech'o · slo'vak
Czech'o · slo · va'ki · a
Czech'o · slo · va'ki · an

D

dab
dabbed, dab'bing
dab'ber
dab'ble
dab'bled, dab'bling
dab'bler
da ca'po
Dac'ca
dace
pl. dace or dac'es
da'cha
Da'chau
dachs'hund'
Da'cron (*Trademark*)
dac'tyl
dac · tyl'ic
dad
dad'dy
pl. dad'dies
dad'dy–long'legs'
da'do
pl. da'does or da'dos
daf'fo · dil
daff'y
daff'i · er, daff'i · est
daft
dag'ger
da · guerre'o · type'
da · guerre'o · typed',
da · guerre'o · typ' · ing
dahl'ia
Da · ho'man
Da · ho'mey
dai'ly
pl. dai'lies
dain'ti · ly
dain'ti · ness
dain'ty
adj. dain'ti · er,
dain'ti · est;
pl. dain'ties
dai'qui · ri
pl. dai'qui · ris
dair'y
pl. dair'ies

dair'y farm
dair'y · ing
dair'y · maid'
dair'y · man
pl. dair'y · men
da'is
dai'sy
pl. dai'sies
Da · kar'
Da · ko'ta
Da · ko'tan
Da'lai La'ma
dale
Da'li
Dal'las
dal'li · ance
dal'ly
dal'lied, dal'ly · ing
Dal · ma'tian
dal se'gno
dam (*barrier*)
dammed, dam'ming
(SEE damn)
dam'age
dam'aged, dam'ag · ing
dam'a · scene'
dam'a · scened',
dam'a · scen'ing
Da · mas'cus
dam'ask
dame
dam'mar
damn (*condemn*) (SEE
dam)
dam'na · ble
dam'na · bly
dam · na'tion
damned
superl. damned'est or
damnd'est
Dam'o · cles'
damp
damp'en

damp'en · er
damp'er
damp'ness
dam'sel
dam'sel fly'
pl. dam'sel flies
dam'son
dance
danced, danc'ing
danc'er
dan'de · li'on
dan'der
Dan'die Din'mont
dan'di · fi · ca'tion
dan'di · fy'
dan'di · fied',
dan'di · fy'ing
dan'dle
dan'dled, dan'dling
dan'druff
dan'dy
pl. dan'dies; *adj.*
dan'di · er, dan'di · est
Dane
dan'ger
dan'ger · ous
dan'gle
dan'gled, dan'gling
Dan'iel
Dan'ish
dank
dank'ness
danse maca'bre
dan · seur'
dan · seuse'
Dan'te
Dan'ube
Dan · u'bi · an
Dan'zig
dap'per
dap'ple
dap'pled, dap'pling
Dar'da · nelles'

dare
  dared, dar'ing
dare'dev'il
dar'er
dare'say'
Dar' es Sa·laam'
dar'ing
Dar·jee'ling
dark
Dark Ag'es
dark'en
dark' horse'
dark'room'
dar'ling
darn
  darned
dar'nel
darn'er
darn'ing
darn'ing nee'dle
dart
dart'board'
dart'er
dar'tle
  dar'tled, dar'tling
Dar'von (*Trademark*)
Dar'win
Dar·win'i·an
Dar'win·ism'
Dar'win·ist
dash
  pl. dash'es
dash'board'
dash'er
da·shi'ki
dash'ing
das'tard
da'ta
dat'a bank'
da'ta·ma'tion
da'ta proc·ess·ing
  da'ta proc'ess·or
date
  dat'ed, dat'ing
date'less
date' line'
date'line'
  date'lined', date'lin'ing
date' palm'

da'tive
da'tum
  pl. da'ta *or* da'tums
daub
daub'er
daugh'ter
daugh'ter-in-law'
  pl. daugh'ters-in-law'
daunt
daunt'less
dau'phin
dau'phine
dav'en·port'
Da'vid
da Vin'ci
Da'vis
dav'it
Da'vy Jones'
daw
daw'dle
  daw'dled, daw'dling
daw'dler
dawn
day
day'bed'
day'book'
day'break'
day' camp'
day' care'
day' coach'
day'dream'
day'light'
day'light'–sav'ing
  time'
day' lil'y
  pl. day' lil'ies
day' school'
day'star'
day'time'
daze
  dazed, daz'ing
daz'zle
  daz'zled, daz'zling
D'–day'
dea'con
dea'con·ess
dea'con·ry
de·ac'ti·vate'
  de·ac'ti·vat'ed,
  de·ac'ti·vat'ing

de·ac'ti·va'tion
dead
dead'beat' (*adj.*)
dead'beat' (*n.*)
dead'en
dead' end'
dead'eye'
dead'head'
dead' heat'
dead' let'ter
dead'line'
dead'li·ness
dead'lock'
dead'ly
  dead'li·er, dead'li·est
dead'pan'
  dead'panned',
  dead'pan'ning
Dead' Sea'
dead' weight'
dead'wood'
deaf
deaf'en
deaf'–mute'
deal
  dealt, deal'ing
deal'er
deal'er·ship'
dean
dean'er·y
  pl. dean'er·ies
dean's' list'
dear (*beloved*)
  (SEE deer)
dearth
death
death'bed'
death'blow'
death' knell'
death'less
death'ly
death' row'
death's'–head'
death'trap'
death'watch'
de·ba'cle
de·bar'
  de·barred', de·bar'ring
de·bark'

de'bar·ka'tion
de·bar'ment
de·base'
  de·based', de·bas'ing
de·bat'a·ble
de·bate'
  de·bated', de·bat'ing
de·bat'er
de·bauch'
deb'au·chee'
de·bauch'er·y
  pl. de·bauch'er·ies
de·ben'ture
de·bil'i·tate'
  de·bil'i·tat'ed,
  de·bil'i·tat'ing
de·bil'i·ta'tion
de·bil'i·ta'tive
de·bil'i·ty
  pl. de·bil'i·ties
deb'it
  deb'it·ed, deb'it·ing
deb'o·nair'
de·bouch'
de·bride'ment
de·brief'
de·bris'
debt
debt'or
de·bug'
  de·bugged', de·bug'ging
de·bunk
De·bus·sy'
de·but'
deb'u·tante'
dec'ade
dec'a·dence
dec'a·dent
de·caf'fein·ate'
  de·caf'fein·at'ed,
  de·caf'fein·at'ing
dec'a·gon'
dec'a·gram' or
  dec'a·gramme'
dec'a·he'dron
  pl. dec'a·he'drons or
  dec'a·he'dra
de'cal
de·cal'ci·fi·ca'tion
de·cal'ci·fy
  de·cal'ci·fied',
  de·cal'ci·fy'ing

de·cal'co·ma'ni·a
dec'a·li'ter or
  dec'a·li'tre
Dec'a·logue' or
  Dec'a·log'
dec'a·me'ter or
  dec'a·me'tre
de·camp'
dec'a·nal
de·cant'
de'can·ta'tion
de·cant'er
de·cap'i·tate'
  de·cap'i·tat'ed,
  de·cap'i·tat'ing
de·cap'i·ta'tion
de·cap'i·ta'tor
dec'are
de·cath'lon
de·cay'
de·cease'
  de·ceased', de·ceas'ing
de·ce'dent
de·ceit'
de·ceit'ful
de·ceit'ful·ly
de·ceit'ful·ness
de·ceive
  de·ceived', de·ceiving
de·ceiv'er
de·cel'er·ate'
  de·cel'er·at'ed,
  de·cel'er·at'ing
de·cel'er·a'tion
de·cel'er·a'tor
De·cem'ber
de'cen·cy
  pl. de'cen·cies
de·cen'ni·al
de·cent· (proper)
  (SEE descent and
  dissent)
de·cen'tral·i·za'tion
de·cen'tral·ize'
de·cen'tral·ized',
  de·cen'tral·iz'ing
de·cep'tion
de·cep'tive
de·cep'tive·ly
dec'i·are'

dec'i·bel'
de·cide'
  de·cid'ed, de·cid'ing
de·cid'ed
de·cid'u·ate
de·cid'u·ous
dec'i·gram' or
  dec'i·gramme'
dec'i·li'ter or
  dec'i·li'tre
de·cil'lion
dec'i·mal
de'ci·mal·ly
dec'i·mate'
  dec'i·mat'ed,
  dec'i·mat'ing
dec'i·ma'tion
dec'i·me'ter or
  dec'i·me'tre
de·ci'pher
de·ci'pher·a·ble
de·ci'sion
de·ci'sive
de·ci'sive·ly
deck
deck' chair'
deck' hand'
deck'house'
deck'le
de·claim'
dec'la·ma'tion
de·clam'a·tor'y
dec'la·ra'tion
de·clar'a·tive
de·clar'a·to'ry
de·clare'
  de·clared', de·clar'ing
dé'clas·sé'
de·clas'si·fi·ca'tion
de·clas'si·fy'
  de·clas'si·fied',
  de·clas'si·fy'ing
de·clen'sion
de·clin'a·ble
dec'li·na'tion
de·cline'
  de·clined', de·clin'ing
de·cliv'i·ty
  pl. de·cliv'i·ties
de·coct'

de·coc'tion
de·code'
 de·cod'ed, de·cod'ing
de·cod'er
dé'colle'tage'
dé'colle·té'
de·col'o·nize'
 de·col'o·nized',
 de·col'o·niz'ing
de'com·mis'sion
de'com·pose'
 de'com·posed',
 de'com·pos'ing
de'com·po·si'tion
de'com·press'
de'com·pres'sion
de'con·tam'i·nate'
 de'con·tam'i·nat'ed',
 de'con·tam'i·nat'ing
de'con·gest'
de'con·gest'ant
de'con·tam'i·na'tion
de'con·trol'
 de'con·trolled',
 de'control'ling
dé·cor' or de·cor'
dec'o·rate'
 dec'o·rat'ed,
 dec'o·rat'ing
dec'o·ra'tion
dec'o·ra·tive
dec'o·ra'tor
dec'o·rous
de·co'rum
de'cou·page'
de·coy'
de·crease'
 de·creased',
 de·creas'ing
de·cree'
 de·creed', de·cree'ing
dec're·ment
de·crep'it
de·crep'i·tude'
de'cre·scen'do
 pl. de'cre·scen'dos or
 IT. de'cre·scen'di
de·cre'tal
de·crim'i·nal·ize'
 de·crim'i·nal·ized',
 de·crim'i·nal·iz'ing
de·cry'
 de·cried', de·cry'ing

ded'i·cate'
 ded'i·cate'ed,
 ded'i·cat'ing
ded'i·ca'tion
ded'i·ca'tor
ded'i·ca·to'ry
de·duce'
 de·duced', de·duc'ing
de·duc'i·ble
de·duct'
de·duct'i·ble
de·duc'tion
de·duc'tive
deed
dee'jay'
deem
de–em'pha·size'
 de-em'pha·sized',
 de-em'pha·siz'ing
deep
deep'-dish'
deep'en
Deep'freeze
 (*Trademark*)
deep'-fry'
 deep'-fried', deep'-
 fry'ing
deep'-root'ed
deep'-sea'
deep'-seat'ed
deep'-six'
deer (*animal*)
 pl. deer or deers
 (SEE dear)
deer'hound'
deer'skin'
deer'stalk'er'
de·es'ca·late'
 de·es'ca·lat'ed,
 de·es'ca·lat'ing
de·es'ca·la'tion
de·face'
 de·faced', de·fac'ing
de·face'ment
de fac'to
de·fal'cate
 de·fal'cat·ed,
 de·fal'cat·ing
de'fal·ca'tion
def'a·ma'tion
de·fam'a·to'ry

de·fame'
 de·famed', de·fam'ing
de·fault'
de·fault'er
de·feat'
de·feat'ism
de·feat'ist
def'e·cate'
 def'e·cat'ed,
 def'e·cat'ing
def'e·ca'tion
de'fect (*n.*)
de·fect' (*v.*)
de·fec'tion
de·fec'tive
de·fec'tor
de·fend'
de·fend'ant
de·fend'er
de·fen'es·tra'tion
de·fense'
de·fense'less
de·fen'si·ble
de·fen'sive
de·fer'
 de·ferred', de·fer'ring
def'er·ment
de·fer'ra·ble
de·fer'ral
de·fer'rer
de·fi'ance
de·fi'ant
de·fi'cien·cy
 pl. de·fi'cien·cies
de·fi'cient
def'i·cit
de'fi·lade'
de·file'
 de·filed', de·fil'ing
de·file'ment
de·fil'er
de·fin'a·ble
de·fine'
 de·fined', de·fin'ing
de·fin'er
def'i·nite

def'er·ence (*respect*)
 (SEE difference)
def'er·en'tial

def'i · ni'tion
de · fin'i · tive
de · flate'
  de · flat'ed, de · flat'ing
de · fla'tion
de · fla'tion · ar'y
de · fla'tor
de · flect'
de · flec'tion
de · flec'tive
de · flec'tor
def'lo · ra'tion
de · flow'er
De · foe'
de · fog'
  de · fogged', de · fog'ging
de · fog'ger
de · fo'li · ant
de · fo'li · ate (v.)
  de · fo'li · at'ed,
  de · fo'li · at'ing
de · fo'li · ate (adj.)
de · fol'i · a'tion
de · for'est
de · for'est · a'tion
de · form'
de'for · ma'tion
de · formed'
de · form'ity
  pl. de · form'i · ties
de · fraud'
de'frau · da'tion
de · fray'
de · fray'a · ble
de · fray'al
de · frock'
de · frost'
de · frost'er
deft
deft'ly
de · funct'
de · fuse'
  de · fused', de · fus'ing
de · fy'
  de · fied', de · fy'ing
De · gas'
de Gaulle'
de · gauss
de · gen'er · a · cy

de · gen'er · ate (v.)
  de · gen'er · at'ed,
  de · gen'er · at'ing
de · gen'er · ate
  (adj.,n.)
de · gen'er · a'tion
de · gen'er · a'tive
de · glu'ti · nate'
  de · glu'ti · nat'ed,
  de · glu'ti · nat'ing
de · glu'ti · na'tion
de'glu · ti'tion
de · grad'a · ble
deg'ra · da'tion
de · grade'
  de · grad'ed, de · grad'ing
de · gree'
de · gree'-day'
de · his'cence
de · horn'
de · hu'man · i · za'tion
de · hu'man · ize'
  de · hu'man · ized',
  de · hu'man · iz'ing
de'hu · mid'i · fi ·
  ca'tion
de'hu · mid'i · fi'er
de'hu · mid'i · fy'
  de'hu · mid'i · fied',
  de'hu · mid'ify'ing
de · hy'drate
  de · hy'drat · ed,
  de · hy'drat · ing
de'hy · dra'tion
de · hy'dro · gen · ate'
  de · hy'dro · gen · at'ed,
  de · hy'dro · gen · at'ing
de · hy'dro · gen · a'tion
de · ice'
  de · iced', de · ic'ing
de · ic'er
de'i · fi · ca'tion
de'i · fy'
  de'i · fied', de'i · fy'ing
deign
De'i gra'ti · a'
de'ism
de'ist
de · is'tic
de'i · ty
  pl. de'i · ties
dé · jà vu'

de · ject'ed
de · jec'tion
de ju're
Del'a · ware'
Del'a · war'e · an
de · lay'
de'le
  de'led, de'le · ing
de · lec'ta · bil'i · ty
de · lec'ta · ble
de'lec · ta'tion
del'e · gate'
  del'e · gat'ed,
  del'e · gat'ing
del'e · ga'tion
de · lete'
  de · let'ed, de · let'ing
del'e · te · ri · ous
de · le'tion
delft
Del'hi
del'i
  pl. del'is
de · lib'er · ate (adj.)
de · lib'er · ate' (v.)
  de · lib'er · at'ed,
  de · lib'er · at'ing
de · lib'er · ate · ness
de · lib'er · a'tion
de · lib'er · a'tive
De · libes'
del'i · ca · cy
  pl. del'i · ca · cies
del'i · cate
del'i · cate · ly
del'i · ca · tes'sen
de · li'cious
de · light'
de · light'ful
de · light'ful · ly
de · lim'it
de · lin'e · ate'
  de · lin'e · at'ed,
  de · lin'e · at'ing
de · lin'e · a'tion
de · lin'e · a'tive
de · lin'e · a'tor
de · lin'quen · cy
  pl. de · lin'quen · cies
de · lin'quent

del'i·quesce'
  del'i·quesced',
  del'i·quesc'ing
del'i·ques'cence
del'i·ques'cent
de·lir'i·ous
de·lir'i·um
  pl. de·lir'i·ums or
  de·lir'i·a
de·lir'i·um tre'mens
De'li·us
de·liv'er
de·liv'er·er
de·liv'er·ance
de·liv'er·y
  pl. de·liv'er·ies
dell
de·louse'
  de·loused', de·lous'ing
Del'phi
Del'phic
del·phin'i·um
  pl. del·phin'i·ums or
  del·phin'i·a
del'ta
del·ta'ic
del'ta ray'
del'ta wave'
del'ta wing'
del'toid
de·lude'
  de·lud'ed, de·lud'ing
del'uge
  del'uged, del'ug·ing
de·lu'sion
de·lu'sive
de·lu'so·ry
de·luxe'
delve
  delved, delv'ing
delv'er
de·mag'net·ize'
  de·mag'net·ized',
  de·mag'net·iz'ing
de·mag'net·i·za'tion
dem'a·gog'ic
dem'a·gogue' or
  dem'a·gog'
dem'a·gogu'er·y
dem'a·go'gy
de·mand'

de·mand'ing
de·mand'–pull'
de·mar'cate
  de·mar'cat·ed,
  de·mar'cat·ing
de'mar·ca'tion
de'march'e'
de·mean'
de·mean'or
de·ment'ed
de·men'tia
de·men'tia prae'cox
de·mer'it
Dem'e·rol'
  (*Trademark*)
de·mesne'
De·me'ter
dem'i·god'
dem'i·john'
de·mil'i·ta·ri·za'tion
de·mil'i·ta·rize'
  de·mil'i·ta·rized',
  de·mil'i·ta·riz'ing
dem'i·monde'
dem'i·qua'ver
de·mise'
  de·mised', de·mis'ing
dem'i·tasse'
dem'i·urge'
dem'i·ur'gic
dem'o
de·mo'bi·li·za'tion
de·mo'bi·lize'
  de·mo'bi·lized',
  de·mo'bi·liz'ing
de·moc'ra·cy
  pl. de·moc'ra·cies
dem'o·crat'
dem'o·crat'ic
dem'o·crat'i·cal·ly
de·moc'ra·tize'
  de·moc'ra·tized',
  de·moc'ra·tiz'ing
de·mod'u·late'
  de·mod'u·lat'ed,
  de·mod'u·lat'ing
de·mod'u·la'tion
de·mog'ra·pher
de'mo·graph'ic
de'mo·graph'i·cal·ly

de·mog'ra·phy
de·mol'ish
dem'o·li'tion
de'mon or dae'mon
de·mon'e·ti·za'tion
de·mon'e·tize'
  de·mon'e·tized',
  de·mon'e·tiz'ing
de·mo'ni·ac'
de'mon·i'a·cal·ly
de·mon'ic
de·mon'i·cal·ly
de'mon·ol'o·gy
de·mon'stra·ble
de·mon'strant
dem'on·strate'
  dem'on·strat'ed,
  dem'on·strat'ing
dem'on·stra'tion
de·mon'stra·tive
dem'on·stra'tor
de·mor'al·i·za'tion
de·mor'al·ize'
  de·mor'al·ized',
  de·mor'al·iz'ing
de·mor'al·iz'er
de·mote'
  de·mot'ed, de·mot'ing
de·mot'ic
de·mo'tion
de·mount'
de·mul'cent
de·mur' (*object*)
  de·murred',
  de·mur'ring(SEE
  demure)
de·mure' (*modest*)
  de·mur'er,
  de·mur'est(SEE
  demur)
de·mur'rage
de·mur'rer
de·my'
  pl. de·mies'
den
  denned, den'ning
de·nar'i·us
  pl. de·nar'i·i'
de·na'tion·al·i·
  za'tion
de·na'tion·al·ize'
  de·na'tion·al·ized',
  de·na'tion·al·iz'ing

de·nat'u·ral·ize'
  de·nat'u·ral·ized',
  de·nat'u·ral·iz'ing

de·na'ture
  de·na'tured,
  de·na'tur·ing

den'dri·form'

den'drite

den'dro·chro·
  nol'o·gy

den·drol'o·gist

den·drol'o·gy

den'gue

de·ni'a·ble

de·ni'al

de·ni'er

de·nier'

den'i·grate'
  den'i·grat·ed,
  den'i·grat'ing

den'i·gra'tion

den'im

de·ni'tri·fi·ca'tion

de·ni'tri·fy'
  de·ni'tri·fied',
  de·ni'tri·fy'ing

den'i·zen

Den'mark

de·nom'i·nate'
  de·nom'i·nat·ed,
  de·nom'i·nat'ing

de·nom'i·na'tion

de·nom'i·na'tion·al

de·nom'i·na'tive

de·nom'i·na'tor

de'no·ta'tion

de'no·ta'tive

de·note'
  de·not'ed, de·not'ing

dé'noue·ment' or
  dénoue·ment

de·nounce'
  de·nounced',
  de·nounc'ing

de no'vo

dense
  dens'er, dens'est

dense'ly

dense'ness

den·sim'e·ter

den·si·tom'e·ter

den'si·ty
  pl. den'si·ties

dent

den'tal

den'tal·ly

den'tate

den'ti·frice

den'tin or den'tine

den'tin·al

den'tist

den'tist·ry

den·ti'tion

den'ture

de·nu'cle·ar·i·
  za'tion

de·nu'cle·ar·ize'
  de·nu'cle·ar·ized',
  de·nu'cle·ar·iz'ing

den'u·da'tion

de·nude'
  de·nud'ed, de·nud'ing

de·nu'mer·a·ble

de·nun'ci·a'tion

de·nun'ci·a·to'ry

Den'ver

de·ny'
  de·nied', de·ny'ing

de·o'dor·ant

de·o'dor·ize'
  de·o'dor·ized',
  de·o'dor·iz'ing

de·o'dor·iz'er

De'o vo·len'te

de·ox'i·di·za'tion

de·ox'i·dize'
  de·ox'i·dized',
  de·oz'i·diz'ing

de·ox'i·diz'er

de·ox'y·gen·ate'
  de·ox'y·gen·at'ed,
  de·ox'y·gen·at'ing

de·ox'y·ri'
  bo·nu·cle'ic

de·part'

de·part'ed

de·part'ment

de·part·men'tal

de·part·men'tal·ize
  de·part·men'tal·ized',
  de·part·men'tal·iz'ing

de·par'ture

de·pend'

de·pend'a·bil'i·ty

de·pend'a·ble

de·pend'ence

de·pend'en·cy
  pl. de·pend'en·cies

de·pend'ent

de·per'son·al·ize'
  de·per'son·al·ized',
  de·per'son·al·iz'ing

de·pict'

de·pic'tion

de·pil'ato'ry
  pl. de·pil'a·to'ries

de·plane'
  de·planed', de·plan'ing

de·plet'a·ble

de·plete'
  de·plet'ed, de·plet'ing

de·ple'tion

de·plor'a·ble

de·plor'a·bly

de·plore'
  de·plored', de·plor'ing

de·ploy'

de·ploy'ment

de·plume'
  de·plumed',
  de·plum'ing

de·po'lar·i·za'tion

de·po'lar·ize'
  de·po'lar·ized',
  de·po'lar·iz'ing

de·po'nent

de·pop'u·late' (v.)
  de·pop'u·lat'ed,
  de·pop'u·lat'ing

de·pop'u·late (adj.)

de·pop'u·la'tion

de·pop'u·la'tor

de·port'

de'por·ta'tion

de·por'tee

de·port'ment

de·pos'a·ble

de·pose'
  de·posed', de·pos'ing

de·pos'it

dep'o·si'tion

de·pos'i·tor

de·pos'i·to'ry
  pl. de·pos'i·to'ries

de'pot

dep'ra · va'tion
(*corruption*)
(SEE deprivation)

de · prave'
de · praved', de · prav'ing

de · prav'i · ty
pl. de · prav'i · ties

dep're · cate'
dep're · cat'ed,
dep're · cat'ing

dep're · ca'tion

dep're · ca'tive

dep're · ca'tor

dep're · ca · to'ry

de · pre'ci · ate'
de · pre'ci · at'ed,
de · pre'ci · at'ing

de · pre'ci · a'tion

de · pre'ci · a'tor

de · pre'ci · a · to'ry

dep're · date'
dep're · dat'ed,
dep're · dat'ing

dep're · da'tion

de · press'

de · pres'sant

de · pressed'

de · pres'sion

de · pres'sive

de · pres'sor

dep'ri · va'tion
(*withholding*)
(SEE depravation)

de · prive'
de · prived', de · priv'ing

de · pro'gram
de · pro'grammed,
de · pro'gram · ming

de · pro'gram · mer

depth

dep'u · ta'tion

de · pute'
de · put'ed, de · put'ing

dep'u · tize'
dep'u · tized',
dep'u · tiz'ing

dep'u · ty
pl. dep'u · ties

de · rac'in · ate'
de · rac'i · nat'ed,
de · rac'i · nat'ing

de · rail'

de · rail'leur

de · range'
de · ranged', de · rang'ing

de · range'ment

Der'by (*race*)
pl. Der'bies

der'by (*hat*)
pl. der'bies

der'e · lict

der'e · lic'tion

de · ride'
de · rid'ed, de · rid'ing

de ri · gueur'

de · ri'sion

de · ri'sive

der'i · va'tion

de · riv'a · tive

de · rive'
de · rived', de · riv'ing

der'ma

derm'a · bra'sion

der'mal

der'ma · ti'tis

der'ma · tol'o · gist

der'ma · tol'o · gy

der'mis

der · nier cri'

der'o · gate' (*v.*)
der'o · gat'ed,
der'o · gat'ing

der'o · gate (*adj.*)

der'o · ga · tion

de · rog'a · to'ri · ly

de · rog'a · to'ry

der'rick

der'ri · ère' or
der'ri · ere'

der'ring–do'

der'rin · ger

der'vish

de · sal'i · nate'
de · sal'i · nat'ed,
de · sal'i · nat'ing

de · sal'i · na'tion

de · sa'lin · i · za'tion

de · sa'lin · ize'
de · sa'lin · ized',
de · sa'lin · iz'ing

de · salt'

des'cant (*n.,adj.*)

des · cant' (*v.*)

Des · cartes'

de · scend'

de · scend'ant (*n.*)

de · scend'ent (*adj.*)

de · scend'er

de · scent' (*downward
movement*)
(SEE decent *and*
dissent)

de · scribe'
de · scribed',
de · scrib'ing

de · scrib'a · ble

de · scrip'tion

de · scrip'tive

de · scrip'tor

de · scry'
de · scried', de · scry'ing

des'e · crate'
des'e · crat'ed,
des'e · crat'ing

des'e · cra'tion

de · seg're · gate'
de · seg're · gat'ed,
de · seg're · gat'ing

de · seg're · ga'tion

de · sen'si · ti · za'tion

de · sen'si · tize'
de · sen'si · tized',
de · sen'si · tiz'ing

des'ert (*n.*) (*barren
region*)
(SEE dessert)

de · sert' (*v.*)
(*abandon*)
(SEE dessert)

de · sert' (*n.*)
(*reward*)
(SEE dessert)

de · ser'tion

de · serve'
de · served', de · serv'ing

de · serv'ed · ly

de · serv'ing

de · sex'

des'ic · cant

des'ic · cate'
des'ic · cat'ed,
des'ic · cat'ing

des'ic · ca'tion

des'ic·ca'tive

des'ic·ca'tor

de·sid'er·a'tum
  pl. de·sid'er·a'ta

de·sign'

des'ig·nate'
  des'ig·nat'ed,
  des'ig·nat'ing

des'ig·na'tion

de·sign'ed·ly

des'ig·nee'

de·sign'er

de·sign'ing

de·sir'a·bil'i·ty

de·sir'a·ble

de·sire'
  de·sired', de·sir'ing

de·sir'er

de·sir'ous

de·sist'

desk

Des Moines'

des'o·late (adj.)

des'o·late' (v.)
  des'o·lat'ed,
  des'o·lat'ing

des'o·late·ly

des'o·la'tion

De So'to

des·ox'y·ri'bo·
  nu·cle'ic

de·spair'

des·patch

des'per·a'do
  pl. des'per·a'does or
  des'per·a'dos

des'per·ate
  (reckless)
  (SEE disparate)

des'per·ate·ly

des'per·a'tion

des'pi·ca·ble

des'pi·ca·bly

de·spise'
  de·spised', de·spis'ing

de·spis'er

de·spite'
  de·spit'ed, de·spit'ing

de·spoil'

de·spo'li·a'tion

de·spond'

de·spond'en·cy

de·spond'ent

des'pot

des·pot'ic

des·pot'i·cal·ly

des'pot·ism'

des·sert' (food)(SEE
  desert)

des·sert'spoon'

des'ti·na'tion

des'tine
  des'tined, des'tin·ing

des'ti·ny
  pl. des'ti·nies

des'ti·tute'
  des'ti·tut'ed,
  des'ti·tut'ing

des'ti·tu'tion

de·stroy'

de·stroy'er

de·struct'

de·struct'i·bil'i·ty

de·struct'i·ble

de·struc'tion

de·struc'tive

de·struc'tor

des'ue·tude'

des'ul·to'ry

de·tach'

de·tach'a·ble

de·tach'ment

de·tail'

de·tain'

de·tect'

de·tect'a·ble

de·tec'tion

de·tec'tive

de·tec'tor

de·tent'

dé·tente'

de·ten'tion

de·ter'
  de·terred', de·ter'ring

de·ter'gent

de·te'ri·o·rate'
  de·te'ri·o·rat'ed,
  de·te'ri·o·rat'ing

de·te'ri·o·ra'tion

de·ter'mi·na·ble

de·ter'mi·nant

de·ter'mi·nate
  (adj.)

de·ter'mi·nate' (v.)
  de·ter'mi·nat'ed,
  de·ter'mi·nat'ing

de·ter'mi·na'tion

de·ter'mi·na'tive

de·ter'mine
  de·ter'mined,
  de·ter'min·ing

de·ter'mined

de·ter'mined·ly

de·ter'min·er

de·ter'min·ism'

de·ter'rence

de·ter'rent

de·test'

de·test'a·ble

de·test'a·bly

de'tes·ta'tion

de·throne'
  de·throned',
  de·thron'ing

de·throne'ment

det'o·nate'
  det'o·nat'ed,
  det'o·nat'ing

det'o·na'tion

det'o·na'tor

de'tour

de·tract'

de·trac'tion

de·trac'tor

de·train'

det'ri·ment

det'ri·men'tal

det'ri·men'tal·ly

de·tri'tus

De·troit'

de trop'

deuce

De'us

deu·te'ri·um

deu'ter·on'

Deu'ter·on'o·my

Deut'sche mark'

deut'zi·a

De' Va·le'ra

de·val'u·ate'
  de·val'u·at'ed,
  de·val'u·at'ing

de·val'u·a'tion

de·val'ue
  de·val'ued,
  de·val'u·a'ting

dev'as·tate'
  dev'as·tat'ed,
  dev'as·tat'ing

dev'as·ta'tion

de·vein'

de·vel'op
  de·vel'oped,
  de·vel'op·ing

de·vel'op·er

de·vel'op·ment

de·vel'op·men'tal

de·vel'op·men'tal·ly

de'vi·ance

de'vi·ant

de'vi·ate' (v.)
  de'vi·at'ed, de'vi·at'ing

de·vi·ate (adj.,n.)

de'vi·a'tion

de'vi·a'tor

de·vice'
  (contrivance)
  (SEE devise)

dev'il
  dev'iled or dev'illed,
  dev'il·ing or dev'il·ling

dev'il·fish'
  pl. dev'il·fish or
  dev'il·fish'es

dev'il·ish

dev'il–may–care'

dev'il·ment

dev'il·ry
  pl. dev'il·ries

dev'il's ad'vo·cate

Dev'il's Is'land

dev'il·try
  pl. dev'il·tries

de'vi·ous

de·vis'a·ble

de·vise' (contrive)
  de·vised', de·vis'ing
  (SEE device)

de·vi·see'

de·vis'er or (Law)
  de·vis'or

de·vi'tal·ize'
  de·vi'tal·ized',
  de·vi'tal·iz'ing

de·void'

de·voir'

dev'o·lu'tion

de·volve'
  de·volved', de·volv'ing

De·vo'ni·an

de·vote'
  de·vot'ed, de·vot'ing

dev'o·tee'

de·vo'tion

de·vo'tion·al

de·vour'

de·vour'er

de·vout'

dew (moisture)
  (SEE do and due)

dew'ber'ry
  pl. dew'ber'ries

dew'claw'

dew'drop'

Dew'ey

dew'lap'

DEW line'

dew' point'

dew'y

dew'y–eyed'

Dex'a·myl
  (Trademark)

Dex'e·drine
  (Trademark)

dex'ter

dex·ter'i·ty

dex'ter·ous or
  dex'trous

dex'tral

dex'trin

dex'trose

dhar'ma

dhole

dho'ti

dhow

di'a·be'tes

di'a·be'tes mel·li'tus

di'a·bet'ic

di'a·bol'ic

di'a·bol'i·cal·ly

di'a–chron'ic

di·ac'o·nal

di·ac'o·nate

di'a·crit'ic

di'a·crit'i·cal

di'a·dem'

di'ag·nose'
  di'ag·nosed',
  di'ag·nos'ing

di'ag·no'sis
  pl. di'ag·no'ses

di'ag·nos'tic

di'ag·nos'ti·cal·ly

di'ag·nos·ti'cian

di·ag'o·nal

di·ag'o·nal·ly

di'a·gram'
  di'a·gramed' or
  di'a·grammed',
  di'a·gram'ing or
  di'a·gram'ming

di'a·gram·mat'i·cal·ly

di'al
  di'aled or di'alled,
  di'al·ing or di'al·ling

di'al·er

di'a·lect'

di'a·lec'tal

di'a·lec'tic

di'a·lec'ti·cal

di'a·lec·tol'o·gy

di'a·logue' or
  di'a·log'

di'al tone'

di·al'y·sis
  pl. di·al'y·ses

di·am'e·ter

di'a·met'ri·cal

di'a·met'ri·cal·ly

dia'mond

dia'mond·back'

Di·an'a

di·an'thus
  pl. di·an'thus·es

di'a·pa'son

dia'per

di·aph'a·nous

di'a·phone'

di·a·pho·ret'ic

di·a·phragm'

di·ar·rhe'a or
  di·ar'rhoe'a

di'a·rist

di'a·ry
  pl. di'a·ries

Di·as'po·ra

di·as'to·le'

di'as·tol'ic

di'a·stroph'ic

di·as'tro·phism'

di'a·ther'my

di'a·tom

di'a·to·ma'ceous

di'a·tom'ic

di'a·ton'ic

di'a·ton'i·cal·ly

di'a·tribe'

di·az'e·pam'

di·az'o

dib'ble
  dib'bled, dib'bling

dice
  (*sing.*) die (v.).
  diced, dic'ing

di·cen'tra

dic'er

dice'y
  dic'i·er, dic'i·est

di·chot'o·mous

di·chot'o·my
  pl. di·chot'o·mies

dick·cis'sel

dick'ens

Dick'ens

dick'er

dick'ey
  pl. dick'eys

di·cot'y·le'don

di·cot'y·le'don·ous

di·cou'ma·rin

Dic'ta·phone'
  (*Trademark*)

dic'tate
  dic'tat·ed, dic'tat·ing

dic·ta'tion

dic'ta·tor

dic·ta·to'ri·al

dic·ta'tor·ship'

dic'tion

dic'tion·ar·y
  pl. dic'tion·ar·ries

dic'tum
  pl. dic'ta or dic'tums

did

di·dac'tic

di·dac'ti·cal·ly

di·dac'ti·cism'

did'dle
  did'dled, did'dling

Di'de·rot'

did·n't

di'do
  pl. di'dos or di'does

di·dym'i·um

die (*cease being*)
  died, dy'ing
  (SEE dye)

die (*stamp*)
  pl. dies or dice; (v.)
  died, die'ing
  (SEE dye)

die'back'

die'–hard'

di'e·lec'tric

di'en·ceph'a·lon

di·er'e·sis
  pl. di·er'e·ses'

die'sel

di'et
  di'et·ed, di'et·ing

di'e·tar'y
  pl. di'e·tar'ies

di'e·tet'ic

di·eth'yl·stil·bes'trol

di'e·ti'tian or
  di'e·ti'cian

dif'fer

dif'fer·ence
  (*unlikeness*)
  dif'fer·enced,
  dif'fer·enc·ing
  (SEE deference)

dif'fer·ent

dif'fer·en'ti·a

dif'fer·en'tial

dif'fer·en'ti·ate'
  dif'fer·en'ti·at'ed,
  dif'fer·en'ti·at'ing

dif'fer·en'ti·a'tion

dif'fi·cult'

dif'fi·cul'ty
  pl. dif'fi·cul'ties

dif'fi·dence

dif'fi·dent

dif·fract'

dif·frac'tion

dif·frac'tive

dif·fuse'
  dif·fused', dif·fus·ing

dif·fus'er

dif·fus'i·ble

dif·fu'sion

dif·fu'sive

dig
  dug, dig'ging

di·gam'ma

dig'a·my

di·gest' (v.)

di'gest (n.)

di·gest'i·ble

di·gest'i·bil'i·ty

di·ges'tion

di·ges'tive

dig'ger

dig'gings

dig'it

dig'it·al

dig'i·tal'is

dig'i·tal·ly

dig'i·tox'in

dig'ni·fied'

dig'ni·fy'
  dig'ni·fied',
  dig'ni·fy'ing

dig'ni·tar'y
  pl. dig'ni·tar'ies

dig'ni·ty
  pl. dig'ni·ties

di'graph

di·gress'

di·gres'sion

di·gres'sive

di·he'dral

dike
  diked, dik'ing

dik'er

Di·lan'tin
  (*Trademark*)

di·lap′i·dat′ed
di·lap′i·da′tion
dil′a·ta′tion
di·late′
  di·lat′ed, di·lat′ing
di·la′tive
di·la′tor
dil′a·to′ry
di·lem′ma
dil′et·tante′
  pl. dil′et·tantes or
  dil′et·tan′ti
dil′et·tant′ism
del′i·gence
dil′i·gent
dill
dil′ly
dil′ly
  pl. dil′lies
dil′ly·dal′ly
  dil′ly·dal′lied,
  dil′ly·dal′ly·ing
dil′u·ent
di·lute′
  di·lut′ed, di·lut′ing
di·lu′tion
di·lu′vi·al
dim
  adj. dim′mer, dim′mest;
  (v.) dimmed,
  dim′ming
dime
di·men′sion
di·men′sion·al
dime′ store′
di·min′ish
di·min′u·en′do
  pl. di·min′u·en′dos
dim′i·nu′tion
di·min′u·tive
dim′i·ty
  pl. dim′i·ties
dim′mer
di′morph
di·mor′phic
di·mor′phism
dim′-out′
dim′ple
  dim′pled, dim′pling
dim′wit′

din
  dinned, din′ning
di·nar′
dine (eat)
  dined, din′ing
  (SEE dyne)
din′er (eater)
  (SEE dinner)
di·ner′o
di·nette′
ding
ding′bat′
ding′-dong′
din′ghy (boat)
  pl. din′ghies (SEE dingy)
din′gi·ness
din′gle
din′go
  pl. din′goes
din′gus
  pl. din′gus·es
din′gy (dark)
  din′gi·er, din′gi·est
  (SEE dinghy)
din′ing room′
dink
dink′y
  adj. dink′i·er,
  dink′i·est;
  pl. dink′ies
din′ner (meal)
  (SEE diner)
din′ner jack′et
din′ner·ware′
di′no·saur′
di′no·sau′ri·an
dint
di·oc′e·san
di′o·cese′
di′ode
Di′o·ny′sian
Di′o·ny′sus
di·op′ter
di′op·tom′e·ter
di·op′tric
di′o·ram′a
di·ox′ide
dip
  dipped, dip′ping
di′phase′
diph·the′ri·a

diph′the·rit′ic
diph′thong
diph·thong′al
di·plod′o·cus
  pl. di·plod′o·cus·es
dip′loid
di·plo′ma
  pl. di·plo′mas or (Lat.)
  di·plo′ma·ta;
  (v.) di·plo′maed,
  di·plo′ma·ing
di·plo′ma·cy
dip′lo·mat′ (official)
  (SEE diplomate)
dip′lo·mate′
  (specialist)
  (SEE diplomat)
dip′lo·mat′ic
dip′lo·mat′i·cal·ly
di·plo′ma·tist
di′pole′
dip′per
dip′py
  dip′pi·er, dip′pi·est
dip′so·ma′ni·a
dip′so·ma′ni·ac′
dip′so·ma·ni′a·cal
dip′stick′
dip′ter·ous
dip′tych
dire (dreadful)
  dir′er, dir′est
  (SEE dyer)
di·rect′
di·rec′tion
di·rec′tion·al
di·rec′tive
di·rect′ly
di·rect′ mail′
di·rec′tor
di·rec′to·rate
di·rec′to·ry
  pl. di·rec′to·ries
di·rec′tress
dire′ful
dirge
dir·ham′
dir′i·gi·ble
dirk
dirn′dl

dirt
dirt'–cheap'
dirt' farm'er
dirt'i·ness
dirt'y
  dirt'i·er, dirt'i·est
dis·a·bil'i·ty
  pl. dis·a·bil'i·ties
dis·a'ble
  dis·a'bled, dis·a'bling
dis·a·buse'
  dis·a·bused',
  dis·a·bus'ing
dis'ac·cus'tom
dis·ad·van'tage
  dis·ad·van'taged,
  dis·ad·van'tag·ing
dis·ad·van'taged
dis·ad'van·ta'geous
dis·af·fect'
dis·af·fec'tion
dis·af·firm'
dis·af·fir·ma'tion
dis·a·gree'
  dis·a·greed',
  dis·a·gree'ing
dis·a·gree'a·ble
dis·a·gree'a·bly
dis·a·gree'ment
dis·al·low'
dis·ap·pear'
dis·ap·pear'ance
dis·ap·point'
dis·ap·point'ed
dis·ap·point'ment
dis·ap·pro·ba'tion
dis·ap·prov'al
dis·ap·prove'
  dis·ap·proved',
  dis·ap·prov'ing
dis·arm'
dis·ar'ma·ment
dis·ar·range'
  dis·ar·ranged',
  dis·ar·rang'ing
dis·ar·ray'
dis·as·sem'ble
  dis·as·sem'bled,
  dis·as·sem'bling
dis·as·so'ci·ate'
  dis·as·so'ci·at'ed,
  dis·as·so'ci·at'ing

dis·as·so'ci·a'tion
dis·as'ter
dis·as'trous
dis·a·vow'
dis·a·vow'al
dis·band'
dis·bar'
  dis·barred', dis·bar'ring
dis·bar'ment
dis·be·lief'
dis·be·lieve'
  dis·be·lieved',
  dis·be·liev'ing
dis·be·liev'er
dis·bur'den
dis·burse' (pay out)
  dis·bursed',
  dis·burs'ing
  (SEE disperse)
dis·burse'ment
disc or disk
dis·card' (v.)
dis'card (n.)
dis·cern'
dis·cern'i·ble
dis·cern'ing
dis·cern'ment
dis·charge' (v.)
  dis·charged',
  dis·charg'ing
dis'charge (n.)
dis·charge'a·ble
dis·ci'ple
  dis·ci'pled, dis·ci'pling
dis'ci·pli·nar'i·an
dis'ci·pli·nar'y
dis'ci·pline
  dis'ci·plined,
  dis'ci·plin·ing
dis'ci·plin'er
dis·claim'
dis·claim'er
dis·close'
  dis·closed', dis·clos'ing
dis·clos'er
dis·clo'sure
dis'co
  pl. dis'cos
dis·cog'ra·pher
dis·cog'ra·phy
dis'coid

dis·col'or
dis·col'or·a'tion
dis·com·bob'u·late'
  dis·com·bob'u·lat'ed,
  dis·com·bob'u·lat'ing
dis·com'fit
  dis·com'fit·ed,
  dis·com'fit·ing
dis·com'fi·ture
dis·com'fort
dis·com·mode'
  dis·com·mod'ed,
  dis·com·mod'ing
dis·com·pose'
  dis·com·posed',
  dis·com·pos'ing
dis·com·po'sure
dis·con·cert'
dis·con·nect'
dis·con·nec'tion
dis·con'so·late
dis·con·tent'
dis·con·tin'u·ance
dis·con·tin'u·a'tion
dis·con·tin'ue
  dis·con·tin'ued,
  dis·con·tin'u·ing
dis·con·ti·nu'i·ty
  pl. dis·con·ti·nu'i·ties
dis·con·tin'u·ous
dis'co·phile'
dis'cord (n.)
dis·cord' (v.)
dis·cord'ance
dis·cord'ant
dis'co·theque' or
  dis'co·théque
dis'count
dis'count·a·ble
dis·count'e·nance
  dis·count'e·nanced,
  dis·count'e·nanc·ing
dis'count house'
dis·cour'age
  dis·cour'aged,
  dis·cour'ag·ing
dis·cour'age·ment
dis'course (n.)
dis·course' (v.)
  dis·coursed',
  dis·cours'ing

dis·cours'er
dis·cour'te·ous
dis·cour'te·sy
  pl. dis·cour'te·sies
dis·cov'er
dis·cov'er·er
dis·cov'er·a·ble
dis·cov'er·y
  pl. dis·cov'er·ies
dis·cred'it
  dis·cred'it·ed,
  dis·cred'it·ing
dis·cred'it·a·ble
dis·creet' (*prudent*)
  (SEE discrete)
dis·crep'an·cy
  pl. dis·crep'an·cies
dis·crep'ant
dis·crete' (*separate*)
  (SEE discreet)
dis·cre'tion
dis·cre'tion·ar'y
dis·crim'i·nate' (*v.*)
  dis·crim'i·nat'ed,
  dis·crim'i·nat'ing
dis·crim'i·nate
  (*adj.*)
dis·crim'i·nat'ing
dis·crim'i·na'tion
dis·crim'i·na'tive
dis·crim'i·na'tor
dis·crim'i·na·to'ry
dis·cur'sive
dis'cus (*disk*)
  pl. dis'cus·es or dis'ci
  (SEE discuss)
dis·cuss' (*talk*
  about)
  (SEE discus)
dis·cus'sant
dis·cus'sion
dis·dain'
dis·dain'ful
dis·dain'ful·ly
dis·ease'
  dis·eased', dis·eas'ing
dis·em·bark'
dis·em'bar·ka'tion
dis·em·bod'i·ment
dis·em·bod'y
  dis·em·bod'ied,
  dis·em·bod'y·ing

dis·em·bow'el
  dis·em'bow'eled,
  dis·em·bow'el·ing
dis·en·chant'
dis·en·chant'ment
dis·en·cum'ber
dis·en·gage'
  dis·en·gaged',
  dis·en·gag'ing
dis·en·tan'gle
  dis·en·tan'gled,
  dis·en·tan'gling
dis·es·tab'lish
dis·es·teem'
dis·fa'vor
dis·fig'ure
  dis·fig'ured,
  dis·fig'ur·ing
dis·fran'chise
  dis·fran'chised,
  dis·fran'chis·ing
dis·gorge'
  dis·gorged', dis·gorg'ing
dis·grace'
  dis·graced', dis·grac'ing
dis·grace'ful
dis·grace'ful·ly
dis·grace'er
dis·grun'tle
  dis·grun'tled,
  dis·grun'tling
dis·guise'
  dis·guised', dis·guis'ing
dis·gust'
dis·gust'ed
dis·gust'ing
dish
  pl. dish'es
dis'ha·bille'
dis·har·mo'ni·ous
dis·har'mo·ny
  pl. dis·har'mo·nies
dish'cloth'
dis·heart'en
di·shev'el
  di·shev'eled or
  di·shev'elled,
  di·shev'el·ing or
  di·shev'el·ling
dish'ful
  pl. dish'fuls
dis·hon'est
dis·hon'es·ty
  pl. dis·hon'es·ties

dis·hon'or
dis·hon'or·a·ble
dis·hon'or·a·bly
dish'pan'
dish'rag'
dish'tow'el
dish'wash'er
dish'wa'ter
dis·il·lu'sion
dis'in·cen'tive
dis·in'clin·a'tion
dis'in·cline'
  dis'in·clined',
  dis'in·clin'ing
dis'in·fect'
dis'in·fec'tion
dis'in·fect'ant
dis'in·gen'u·ous
dis'in·her'it
dis·in'te·grate'
  dis·in'te·grat'ed,
  dis·in'te·grat'ing
dis·in'te·gra'tion
dis'in·ter'
  dis'in·terred',
  dis'in·ter'ring
dis·in'ter·est'ed
dis·join'
dis·joint'
dis·joint'ed
dis·junc'tive
disk
disk' jock'ey
dis·like'
  dis·liked', dis·lik'ing
dis'lo·cate'
  dis'lo·cat'ed,
  dis'lo·cat'ing
dis'lo·ca'tion
dis·lodge'
  dis·lodged',
  dis·lodg'ing
dis·loy'al
dis·loy'al·ty
  pl. dis·loy'al·ties
dis'mal
dis'mal·ly
dis·man'tle
  dis·man'tled,
  dis·man'tling
dis·mast'

dis·may′·

dis·mem′ber

dis·miss′

dis·miss′al

dis·miss′i·ble

dis·mount′

dis′o·be′di·ence

dis′o·be′di·ent

dis′o·bey′

dis·or′der

dis·or′dered

dis·or′der·ly

dis·or′gan·i·za′tion

dis·or′gan·ize′
  dis·or′gan·ized′,
  dis·or′gan·iz′ing

dis·or′gan·iz′er

dis·o′ri·ent

dis·o′ri·en·ta′tion

dis·own′

dis·par′age
  dis·par′aged,
  dis·par′ag·ing

dis·par′age·ment

dis′pa·rate (*different*)
  (SEE desperate)

dis·par′i·ty
  pl. dis·par′i·ties

di·pas′sion·ate

dis·pas′sion·ate·ly

dis·patch′

dis·patch′er

dis·pel′
  dis·pelled′, dis·pel′ling

dis·pen′sa·bil′i·ty

dis·pen′sa·ble

dis·pen′sa·ry
  pl. dis·pen′sa·ries

dis′pen·sa′tion

dis·pense′
  dis·pensed′,
  dis·pens′ing

dis·pens′er

dis·per′sal

dis·perse′ (*scatter*)
  dis·persed′, dis·pers′ing
  (SEE disburse)

dis·per′sion

dis·per′sive

dis·pir′it

dis·pir′it·ed

dis·place′
  dis·placed′, dis·plac′ing

dis·place′ment

dis·play′

dis·please′
  dis·pleased′,
  dis·pleas′ing

dis·pleas′ure

dis·port′

dis·pos′a·bil′i·ty

dis·pos′a·ble

dis·pos′al

dis·pose′
  dis·posed′, dis·pos′ing

dis·pos′er

dis′po·si′tion

dis·pos·sess′

dis·pos·es′sion

dis·proof′

dis′pro·por′tion

dis′pro·por′tion·ate

dis·prove′
  dis·proved′,
  dis·prov′ing

dis·put′a·ble

dis·pu′tant

dis′pu·ta′tion

dis′pu·ta′tious

dis·pute′
  dis·put′ed, dis·put′ing

dis·qual′i·fi·ca′tion

dis·qual′i·fy′
  dis·qual′i·fied′,
  dis·qual′i·fy′ing

dis·qui′et

dis·qui′e·tude′

dis·qui·si′tion

Dis·rae′li

dis′re·gard′

dis′re·gard′ful

dis′re·pair′

dis·rep′u·ta·ble

dis·rep′u·ta·bly

dis′re·pute′

dis′re·spect′

dis′re·spect′ful

dis′re·spect′ful·ly

dis·robe′
  dis·robed′, dis·rob′ing

dis·rob′er

dis·rupt′

dis·rup′tion

dis·rup′tive

dis′sat·is·fac′tion

dis·sat′is·fied′

dis·sat′is·fy′
  dis·sat′is·fied′,
  dis·sat′is·fy′ing

dis·sect′

dis·sec′tion

dis·sem′ble
  dis·sem′bled,
  dis·sem′bling

dis·sem′bler

dis·sem′i·nate′
  dis·sem′i·nat′ed,
  dis·sem′i·nat′ing

dis·sem′i·na′tion

dis·sen′sion

dis·sent′ (*disagree*)
  (SEE decent and
  descent)

dis·sent′er

dis′ser·ta′tion

dis·serv′ice

dis·sev′er

dis·sev′er·ment

dis′si·dence

dis′si·dent

dis·sim′i·lar

dis·sim′i·lar′i·ty
  pl. dis·sim′i·lar′i·ties

dis′si·mil′i·tude′

dis·sim′u·late′
  dis·sim′u·lat′ed,
  dis·sim′u·lat′ing

dis·sim′u·la′tion

dis′si·pate′
  dis′si·pat′ed,
  dis′si·pat′ing

dis′si·pat′ed

dis′si·pa′tion

dis·so′ci·ate′
  dis·so′ci·at′ed,
  dis·so′ci·at′ing

dis·so′ci·a′tion

dis·so′ci·a′tive

dis·sol′u·ble

dis′so·lute′

dis′so·lu′tion

dis·solve'
  dis·solved', dis·solv'ing

dis'so·nance

dis'so·nant

dis·suade'
  dis·suad'ed,
  dis·suad'ing

dis·sua'sion

dis·sua'sive

dis·sym'me·try

dis'taff

dis'tal

dis'tance
  dis'tanced, dis'tanc·ing

dis'tant

dis·taste'

dis·taste'ful

dis·tem'per

dis·tend'

dis·ten'si·ble

dis·ten'tion or
  dis·ten'sion

dis'tich

dis·till'
  pl. ditch'es

dis'til·late

dis'til·la'tion

dis·till'er

dis·till'er·y
  pl. dis·till'er·ies

dis·tinct'

dis·tinc'tion

dis·tinc'tive

dis·tin·gué'

dis·tin'guish

dis·tin'guish·a·ble

dis·tin'guish·a·bly

dis·tin'guished

dis·tort'

dis·tort'ed

dis·tor'tion

dis·tract'

dis·tract'ed

dis·trac'tion

dis·trait'

dis·traught'

dis·tress'

dis·tress'ful

dis·trib'·ute
  dis·trib'ut·ed,
  dis·trib'ut·ing

dis·trib'u·tee'

dis'tri·bu'tion

dis·trib'u·tive

dis·trib'u·tor or
  dis·trib'u·ter

dis·trib'u·tor·ship'

dis'trict

dis·trust'

dis·trust'ful

dis·turb'

dis·turb'ance

di·sul'fide

dis·un'ion

dis'u·nite'
  dis'u·nit'ed,
  dis'u·nit'ing

dis·u·ni·ty
  pl. dis·u'ni·ties

dis·use'
  dis·used', dis·us'ing

ditch
  pl. ditch'es

ditch'wa·ter

di'the·ism'

dith'er

dith'y·ramb'

dit'to
  pl. dit'tos; (v.)
  dit'toed, dit'to·ing

dit'ty
  pl. dit'ties (v.)
  dit'tied, dit'ty·ing

dit'ty bag'

di'u·re'sis

di'u·ret'ic

di·ur'nal

di'va
  pl. di'vas or di've

di'va·ga'tion

di·va'lent

di·van'

dive
  dived or dove, dived,
  div'ing

div'er

di·verge'
  di·verged', di·verg'ing

di·ver'gence

di·ver'gent

di'vers (various)
  (SEE diverse)

di·verse' (different)
  (SEE divers)

di·ver'si·fi·ca'tion

di·ver'si·fy'
  di·ver'si·fied',
  di·ver'si·fy·ing

di·ver'sion

di·ver'sion·ar'y

di·ver'si·ty
  pl. di·ver'si·ties

di·vert'

di·ver'ti·men'to
  pl. di·ver'ti·men'ti

di·ver'tisse·ment

di·vest'

di·vid'a·ble

di·vide'
  di·vid'ed, di·vid'ing

div'i·dend'

di·vid'er

div'i·na'tion

di·vine'
  di·vined', di·vin'ing

di·vin'er

di·vin'ing rod'

di·vin'i·ty
  pl. di·vin'i·ties

di·vis'i·bil'i·ty

di·vis'i·ble

di·vi'sion

di·vi'sion·al

di·vi'sive

di·vi'sor

di·vorce'
  di·vorced', di·vorc'ing

di·vor·cé'

di·vor·cee' or
  di·vor·cée'

di·vorce'ment

div'ot

di·vulge'
  di·vulged', di·vulg'ing

di·vulg'er

div'vy
  (v.)div'vied,
  div'vy·ing;
  pl. div'vies

Dix'ie

Dix'ie·land'

diz'·zi·ly

diz'zi·ness

diz'zy
  adj. diz'zi·er,
  diz'zi·est; (*v.*)
  diz'zied, diz'zy·ing

Dja·kar'ta

Dji·bou'ti

do (*perform*)
  did, done, doing
  pl. dos, do's
    (SEE dew *and* due)

do (*musical tone*)
  pl. dos
    (SEE dough *and* doe)

dob'bin

Do'ber·man pin'scher

do'cent

doc'ile

do·cil'i·ty

dock

dock'age

dock'er

dock'et
  dock'et·ed, dock'et·ing

dock'hand'

dock'yard'

doc'tor

doc'tor·al

doc'tor·ate

doc'tri·naire'

doc'tri·nal

doc'trine

doc'u·ment

doc'u·men·ta·ry
  pl. doc'u·men'ta·ries

doc'u·men·ta'tion

dod'der

do·dec'a·gon'

do·dec'a·he'dron
  pl. do·dec'a·he'drons
  or do·dec'a·he'dra

dodge
  dodged, dodg'ing

dodg'er

do'do
  pl. do'dos or do'does

doe (*animal*)
  pl. does or doe
    (SEE dough *and* do)

do'er

does

doe'skin'

does'n't

doff

dog
  dogged, dog'ging

dog'bane'

dog'cart'

dog'catch'er

dog' col'lar

doge

dog'-ear'

dog'-eared'

dog'face'

dog'fight'

dog'fish'
  pl. dog'fish' or
  dog'·fish'es

dog'ged

dog'ger·el

dog'gie bag'

dog'gone'

dog'gy or doggie
  pl. dog'gies; (*adj.*)
  dog'gie·er, dog'gi·est

dog'house

do'gie

dog'leg'

dog'ma
  pl. dog'mas or
  dog'ma·ta

dog·mat'ic

dog·mat'i·cal·ly

dog'ma·tism'

dog'ma·tist

do'-good'er

dog' sled'

dog' tag'

dog'-tired'

dog'tooth'

dog'trot'

dog'watch'
  pl. dog'watch'es

dog'wood'

do'gy or do'gie

Do'ha

doi'ly
  pl. doi'lies

do'ing

do'-it-your·self'

Dol'by (*Trademark*)

dol'ce vi'ta

dol'drums

dole
  doled, dol'ing

dole'ful

doll

dol'lar

doll'house'

dol'lop

doll'y
  pl. doll'ies; (*v.*)
  doll'ied, doll'y·ing

dol'man (*robe*)
  pl. dol'mans
    (SEE below)

dol'men (*structure*)
    (SEE above)

do'lo·mite'

do'lor

dol'or·ous

dol'phin

dolt

dolt'ish

do·main'

dome
  domed, dom'ing

do·mes'tic

do·mes'ti·cal·ly

do·mes'ti·cate'
  do·mes'ti·cat'ed,
  do·mes'ti·cat'ing

do·mes'ti·ca'tion

do'mes·tic'i·ty
  pl. do'mes·tic'i·ties

dom'i·cile'
  dom'i·ciled,
  dom'i·cil'ing

dom'i·cil'i·ar·y

dom'i·nance

dom'i·nant

dom'i·nate'
  dom'i·nat'ed,
  dom'i·nat'ing

dom'i·na'tion

dom'i·na'tor

dom'i·neer'

Do·min'i·ca

Do·min'i·can

dom'i · nie

do · min'ion

dom'i · no'
　pl. dom'i · noes' or
　dom'i · nos'

don
　donned, don'ning

do'ña

do'nate
　do'nat · ed, do'nat · ing

Don'a · tel'lo

do · na'tion

done (completed)
　(SEE dun)

do · nee'

Don'i · zet'ti

don'jon

Don Juan'

don'key
　pl. don'keys

don'na

Donne

don'ny · brook'

do'nor

do'-noth'ing

Don' Quix · o'te

don't

do'nut or dough'nut

doo'dad

doo'dle
　doo'dled, doo'dling

doo'dle · bug'

doo'dler

doo'hick'ey
　pl. doo'hick'eys

doom

dooms'day'

door

door'bell'

door'jamb'

door'keep'er

door'knob'

door'man'
　pl. door'men'

door'mat'

door'nail'

door'plate'

door' prize'

door'step'

door'stop'

door'way'

door'yard'

dop'ant

dope
　doped, dop'ing

dope'ster

dope'y
　dop'i · er, dop'i · est

Dop'pler

Do'ri · an

Dor'ic

dor'man · cy

dor'mant

dor'mer

dor'mie

dor'mi · to'ry
　pl. dor'mi · to'ries

dor'mouse'
　pl. dor'mice'

dor'sal

dor'sum
　pl. dor'sa

do'ry
　pl. do'ries

dos-à-dos

dos'age

dose
　dosed, dos'ing

do · sim'e · ter

dos'si · er'

Dos'to · ev'sky

dot
　dot'ted, dot'ting

dot'age

do'tard

dote
　dot'ed, dot'ing

dot'er

dot'tle

dot'ty
　dot'ti · er, dot'ti · est

Dou'ay

dou'ble
　dou'bled, dou'bling

dou'ble-bar'reled

dou'ble bass'

dou'ble bas · soon'

dou'ble bed'

dou'ble-breasted

dou'ble-check'

dou'ble cross' (n.)

dou'ble-cross' (v.)

dou'ble-deal'er

dou'ble-deal'ing

dou'ble-deck'er

dou'ble-dig'it

dou'ble-dip'per

dou'ble-edged'

dou'ble en · ten'dre

dou'ble · head'er

dou'ble he'lix

dou'ble-hung'

dou'ble-joint'ed

dou'ble-knit'

dou'ble-park'

dou'ble play'

dou'ble-quick'

dou'ble-reed'

dou'ble-space'
　dou'ble-spaced',
　dou'ble-spac'ing

dou'ble star'

dou'blet

dou'ble take'

dou'ble-talk'

dou'ble · think'
　dou'ble · thought',
　dou'ble · think'ing

dou'ble time'

dou'ble-time'
　dou'ble-timed', dou'ble-
　tim'ing

dou'ble-tongue'
　dou'ble-tongued',
　dou'ble-tongu'ing

dou'ble-tree'

dou · bloon'

dou'bly

doubt

doubt'er

doubt'ful

doubt'ful · ly

doubt'less

dou · ceur'

douche
　douched, douch'ing

dough (bread)
　(SEE do and doe)

dough'boy'

dougn'nut or do'nut

dough'ty
  dough'ti·er,
  dough'ti·est

dough'y
  dough'ier, dough'i·est

dour

douse or dowse
  doused, dous'ing

dove

dove'cote' or dove'cot'

Do'ver

dove'tail'

dow'a·ger

dowd'i·ly

dowd'i·ness

dow'dy
  adj. dow'di·er,
  dow'di·est;
  pl. dow'dies

dow'el
  dow'eled, dow'el·ing

dow'er

down

down'beat'

down'cast'

down'court

down'er

down'fall'

down'grade'
  down'grad'ed,
  down'grad'ing

down'heart'ed

down'hill'

down'play'

down'pour'

down'range'   (adj.)

down'range'   (adv.)

down'right'

down'shift'

down'size'
  down'sized',
  down'siz'ing

down'stage'   (adv.,n.)

down'stage'   (adj.)

down'stairs'   (adv., n.)

down'stairs'   (adj.)

down'state'   (n., adv.)

down'state'   (adj.)

down'stream'

down'stroke'

down'swing'

down'time'

down'-to-earth'

down'town'

down'trod'den

down'turn'

down' un'der

down'ward

down'wards

down'wind'

down'y
  down'i·er, down'i·est

dow'ry
  pl. dow'ries

dowse or douse
  dowsed, dows'ing

dows'er

dox·ol'o·gy
  pl. dox·ol'o·gies

doy·en'

doy·enne'

doze
  dozed, doz'ing

doz'en
  pl. doz'ens or doz'en

doz'enth

doz'er

drab
  drab'ber, drab'best

drab'ly

dra·cae'na

drach'ma
  pl. drach'mas or
  drach'ma·ta

Dra·co'ni·an

draft   (version)
  (SEE draught)

draft·ee'

draft'er

drafts'man
  pl. drafts'men

draft'y
  draft'i·er, draft'i·est

drag
  dragged, drag'ging

drag'ger

drag'gle
  drag'gled, drag'gling

drag'gle·tailed'

drag'line'

drag'net'

drag'o·man

drag'on

drag'on·fly'
  pl. drag'on·flies'

dra·goon'

drag' race'

drag' strip'

drain

drain'age

drain'pipe'

drake

dram
  drammed, dram'ming

dra'ma

Dram'a·mine'
  (Trademark)

dra·mat'ic

dra·mat'i·cal·ly

dra·mat'ics

dram'a·tis per·so'nae

dram'a·tist

dram'a·ti·za'tion

dram'a·tize'
  dram'a·tized',
  dram'a·tiz'ing

dram'a·tur'gy

drank

drape
  draped, drap'ing

drap'er

dra'per·y
  pl. dra'per·ies

dras'tic

dras'ti·cal·ly

drat

draught   (drink)
  (SEE draft)

draw
  drew, drawn, draw'ing

draw'back'

draw'bridge'

draw'ee'

draw'er

draw'ing

draw'ing board'

draw'ing room'

draw'knife'
  pl. draw'knives'

drawl

drawn

draw'string'

dray

dray'age

dread

dread'ful

dread'ful • ly

dread'nought'

dream
  dreamed or dreamt,
  dream'ing

dream'er

dream'i • ly

dream'land'

dream' world'

drear'i • ly

drear'i • ness

dream'y
  dream'i • er, dream'i • est

drear'y
  drear'i • er, drear'i • est

dredge
  dredged, dredg'ing

dredg' er

dregs

Drei'ser

drench

Dres'den

dress

dres • sage'

dress'er

dress'ing

dress'ing–down'

dress'ing gown'

dress'mak'er

dress'mak'ing

dress'–up'

dress'y
  dress'i • er, dress'i • est

drew

drib

drib'ble
  drib'bled, drib'bling

drib'let

dri'er or dry'er

drift

drift'age

drift'er

drift'wood'

drill

drill'mas'ter

drill' press'

drily

drink
  drank, drunk or drank,
  drink'ing

drink'a • ble

drink'er

drip
  dripped or dript,
  drip'ping

drip'–dry'   (adj.)

drip'–dry'   (v.)
  drip'–dried', drip'–
  dry'ing

drip' pan'

drip'pings

drive
  drove, driv'en, driv'ing

drive'–in'

driv'el
  driv'eled, driv'el • ing

driv'en

driv'er

drive' shaft'

drive'way'

driv'ing

driz'zle
  driz'zled, driz'zling

drogue

droll

droll'er • y
  pl. droll'er • ies

drolly

drom'e • dar'y
  pl. drom'e • dar'ies

drone
  droned, dron'ing

drool

droop   (sag)
  (SEE drupe)

droop'y
  droop'i • er, droop'i • est

drop
  dropped or dropt,
  drop'ping

drop' cloth'

drop' forge'

drop' kick'   (n.)

drop'–kick'   (pl.)

drop'let

drop'out'

drop'per

drop'pings

drop' shot'

drop'sy

drosh'ky
  pl. drosh'kies

dross

drought

drouth

drove

dro'ver

drown

drowse
  drowsed, drows'ing

drows'i • ly

drows'i • ness

drow'sy
  drow'si • er, drow'si • est

drub
  drubbed, drub'bing

drub'bing

drudge
  drudged, drudg'ing

drudg'er • y

drug
  drugged, drug'ging

drug'get

drug'gist

drug'store'

Dru'id

drum
  drummed, drum'ming

drum'beat'

drum' corps'

drum'head'

drum'lin

drum'mer

drum'stick'

drunk

drunk'ard

drunk'en

drunk'en • ness

drunk • om'e • ter

drupe   (fruit)
  (SEE droop)

Druse

dry
adj. dri'er, dri'est;
(*v.*) dried, dry'ing;
pl. drys

dry'ad
pl. dry'ads or
dry'a·des'

dry' cell'

dry'-clean'

dry'-clean'ing

dry'-dock' (*v.*)

dry' dock' (*n.*)

dry'er or dri'er

dry'ly

dry'ness

dry' nurse'

dry'point'

dry' rot'

dry' run'

dry'wall'

du'al (*double*)
(SEE duel)

du'al·ism'

du·al'i·ty

du'al·ly

du'al-pur'pose

dub
dubbed, dub'bing

dub'ber

du·bi'e·ty
pl. du·bi'e·ties

du'bi·ous

Dub'lin

Du'bon·net'
(*Trademark*)

Du·buque'

du'cal

duc'at

du'ce

duch'ess
pl. duch'ess·es

duch'y
pl. duch'ies

duck

duck'bill'

duck'board'

duck'ling

duck'pin'

duck'weed'

duct

duc'tile

duc·til'i·ty

duct'less

dud

dude

dudg'eon

due (*payable*)
(SEE do and dew)

du'el (*combat*)
du'eled, du'el·ing
(SEE dual)

du'el·er

du'el·ist

du·en'na

dues

du·et'

duf'fel

duf'fel bag'

duff'er

duf'fle coat'

dug

du'gong

dug'out'

duke

duke'dom

dul'cet

dul'ci·mer

dull

dull'ard

dull'ness or dul'ness

dul'ly

Du·luth'

du'ly

Du·mas'

dumb

dumb'bell'

dumb'ly

dumb'ness

dum·found' or
dumb·found'

dumb'struck'

dumb'wait'er

dum'dum'

dum'my
pl. dum'mies; (*v.*)
dum'mied, dum'my·ing

dump

dump'cart

dump'ling

dump' truck'

dump'y
dump'i·er, dump'i·est

dun
dunned, dun'ning

dun (*demand
payment*)
(SEE done)

dunce

dune

dune' bug'gy

dung

dun'ga·ree'

dun'geon

dung'hill'

dunk

dunk'er

du'o
pl. du'os

du'o·dec'i·mal

du'o·dec'i·mo'
pl. du'o·dec'i·mos'

du'o·de'nal

du'o·de'num
pl. du'o·de'na or
du'o·de'nas

du'o·tone'

dupe
duped, dup'ing

dup'er·y
pl. dup'er·ies

du'ple

du'plex

du'pli·cate (*adj.,n.*)

du'pli·cate' (*v.*)
du'pli·cat'ed,
du'pli·cat'ing

du'pli·ca'tion

du'pli·ca'tor

du·plic'i·ty
pl. du·plic'i·ties

du'ra·bil'i·ty

du'ra·ble

du'ra ma'ter

dur'ance

du·ra'tion

du·ress'

Dü'rer

dur'ing
Du'roc
du'rum
dusk
dusk'i · ness
dusk'y
  dusk'i · er, dusk'i · est
dust
dust' bowl'
dust' cov'er
dust'er
dust'i · ness
dust'pan'
dust' storm'
dust'y
  dust'i · er, dust'i · est
Dutch
Dutch' door'
Dutch'man
  pl. Dutch'men
Dutch'man's–breech'es
  pl. Dutch'man's–
  breech'es
Dutch' o'ven
Dutch' treat'
du'te · ous
du'ti · a · ble
du'ti · ful
du'ti · ful · ly

du'ty
  pl. du'ties
Dvo'řák
dwarf
dwarf'ish
dwarf'ism
dwell
  dwelt or dwelled,
  dwell'ing
dwell'ing
dwin'dled
  dwin'dled, dwin'dling
dy'ad
dy · ad'ic
dyb'buk
  pl. dyb'buks or
  dyb · bu'kim
dye (color)
  pl. dyes; (v.)
  dyed, dye'ing
  (SEE die)
dyed'–in–the–wool'
dy'er (one who
  colors)
  (SEE dire)
dye'stuff'
dy'ing (ceasing to
  live)
  (SEE dyeing)
dy · nam'ic

dy · nam'i · cal · ly
dy · nam'ics
dy'na · mism'
dy'na · mist
dy'na · mite'
  dy'na · mit'ed,
  dy'na · mit'ing
dy'na · mo'
  pl. dy'na · mos'
dy'na · mo · e · lec'tric
dy'na · mom'e · ter
dy'nast
dy'nas · ty
  pl. dy'nas · ties
dyne (unit of force)
  (SEE dine)
dys'en · ter'ic
dys'en · ter'y
dys · func'tion
dys · gen'ic
dys · lex'i · a
dys · lex'ic
dys'men · or · rhe'a
dys · pep'sia
dys · pep'tic
dys · pro'si · um
dys · troph'ic
dys'tro · phy

E

each
ea'ger
ea'gle
  ea'gled, ea'gling
ea'gle–eyed'
ea'gle scout'
ea'glet
ear
ear'ache'
ear'drum'
ear'ful
  pl. ear'fuls
earl
earl'dom
ear'li · ness
ear'ly
  ear'li · er, ear'li · est

ear'ly bird'
ear'mark'
ear'muff'
earn (gain)
  (SEE urn)
ear'nest
earn'ing
ear'phone'
ear'piece'
ear'plug'
ear'ring'
ear'shot'
ear'split'ting
earth
earth'bound'
earth'en

earth'en · ware'
earth'i · ness
earth'ling
earth'ly
  earth'li · er, earth'li · est
earth'nut'
earth'quake'
earth'shak'ing
earth'ward
earth'wards
earth'work'
earth'worm'
earth'y
  earth'i · er, earth'i · est
ear'wax'
ear'wig'
  ear'wigged', ear'wig'ging

ease
  eased, eas'ing

ea'sel

ease'ment

eas'i·ly

eas'i·ness

east

east'bound'

East'er

east'er·ly

east'ern

east'ern·er

east'ward

east'wards

eas'y
  eas'i·er, eas'i·est

eas'y chair'

eas'y·go'ing

eas'y street'

eat
  ate, eat'en, eat'ing

eat'a·ble

eat'er·y
  pl. eat'er·ies

eau' de Co·logne'
  pl. eaux' de Co·logne'

eaves

eaves'drop'
  eaves'dropped',
  eaves'drop'ping

eaves'drop'per

ebb

eb'on·ite'

eb'on·y
  pl. eb'o·nies

e·bul'lience

e·bul'lient

eb'ul·li'tion

ec'ce ho'mo

ec·cen'tric

ec·cen'tri·cal·ly

ec'cen·tric'i·ty
  pl. ec'cen·tric'i·ties

ec·cle'si·as'tic

ec·cle'si·as'ti·cal

ec·dys'i·ast'

ech'e·lon'

e·chid'na

e·chi'no·derm'

ech'o
  pl. ech'oes; (v.)
  ech'oed, ech'o·ing

ech'o·la'li·a

ech'o·lo·ca'tion

é·clair'

é·clat'

ec·lec'tic

ec·lec'ti·cism'

e·clipse'
  e·clipsed', e·clips'ing

e·clip'tic

ec'logue

ec'o·log'ic

ec'o·log'i·cal

ec'o·log'i·cal·ly

e·col'o·gist

e·col'o·gy

e·con'o·met'rics

e'co·nom'ic

e'co·nom'i·cal

e'co·nom'i·cal·ly

e'co·nom'ics

e·con'o·mist

e·con'o·mize'
  e·con'o·mized',
  e·con'o·miz'ing

e·con'o·miz'er

e·con'o·my
  pl. e·con'o·mies

ec'o·sys'tem

ec'o·tone'

ec'o·type'

ec'ru

ec'sta·sy
  pl. ec'sta·sies

ec·stat'ic

ec·stat'i·cal·ly

ec'to·derm'

ec'to·morph'

ec'to·plasm'

Ec'ua·dor'

Eu'ua·do'ran

Ec'ua·do'ri·an

ec'u·men'i·cal

ec'u·men'i·cal·ly

ec'ze·ma

ec·zem'a·tous

E'dam

Ed'da

ed'dy
  pl. ed'dies; (v.)
  ed'died, ed'dy·ing

Ed'dy

e'del·weiss'

e·de'ma
  pl. e·de'ma·ta

e·dem'a·tous

E'den

edge
  edged, edg'ing

edge'ways'

edge'wise'

edg'i·ness

edg'ing

edg'y
  edg'i·er, edg'i·est

ed'i·bil'i·ty

ed'i·ble

e'dict

ed'i·fi·ca'tion

ed'i·fice

ed'i·fy'
  ed'i·fied', ed'i·fy'ing

Ed'in·burgh'

Ed'i·son

ed'it
  ed'it·ed, ed'it·ing

e·di'tion (printing)
  (SEE addition)

ed'i·tor

ed'i·to'ri·al

ed'i·to'ri·al·i·za'tion

ed'i·to'ri·al·ize'
  ed'i·to'ri·al·ized',
  ed'i·to'ri·al·iz'ing

ed'i·to'ri·al·ly

ed'i·tor in chief'
  pl. ed'i·tors in chief'

ed'i·tor·ship'

Ed'mon·ton

ed'u·ca·bil'i·ty

ed'u·ca·ble

ed'u·cate'
  ed'u·cat'ed,
  ed'u·cat'ing

ed'u·ca'tion

ed'u·ca'tion·al

ed'u·ca'tion·al·ly

ed'u·ca'tion·ist

ed'u·ca'tor

e·duce'
  e·duced', e·duc'ing

e·duc'i·ble

eel
  pl. eel or eels

e'er (*ever*)
  (SEE air *and* ere *and* heir)

ee'rie *or* ee'ry
  ee'ri·er, ee'ri·est

ee'ri·ly

ee'ri·ness

ef·face'
  ef·faced', ef·fac'ing

ef·face'a·ble

ef·face'ment

ef·fect' (*result*)
  (SEE affect)

ef·fec'tive

ef·fec'tive·ly

ef·fec'tive·ness

ef·fec'tu·al

ef·fec'tu·al·ly

ef·fec'tu·ate'
  ef·fec'tu·at'ed,
  ef·fec'tu·at'ing

ef·fem'i·na·cy

ef·fem'i·nate

ef·fen'di

ef'fer·ent

ef'fer·vesce'
  ef'fer·vesced',
  ef'fer·vesc'ing

ef'fer·ves'cence

ef'fer·ves'cent

ef·fete'

ef'fi·ca'cious

ef'fi·ca·cy
  pl. ef'fi·ca·cies

ef·fi'cien·cy
  pl. ef·fi'cien·cies

ef·fi'cient

ef'fi·gy
  pl. ef'fi·gies

ef'flo·resce'
  ef'flo·resced',
  ef'flo·resc'ing

ef'flo·res'cence

ef'flo·res'cent

ef'flu·ence

ef'flu·ent

ef·flu'vi·um
  pl. ef·flu'vi·a *or*
  ef·flu'vi·ums

ef'flux

ef'fort

ef'fort·less

ef·fron'ter·y
  pl. ef·fron'ter·ies

ef·ful'gence

ef·ful'gent

ef·fu'sion

ef·fu'sive

eft

e·gad'

e·gal'i·tar'i·an

e·gal'i·tar'i·an·ism'

egg

egg'beat'er

egg'drop

egg'head'

egg'nog'

egg'plant'

egg' roll'

egg'shell'

e'gis *or* ae'gis

eg'lan·tine'

e'go
  pl. e'gos

e'go·cen'tric

e'go·cen·tric'i·ty

e'go·ism'

e'go·ist

e'go·is'tic

e'go·is'ti·cal

e'go·is'ti·cal·ly

e'go·tism'

e'go·tist

e'go·tis'tic

e'go·tis'ti·cal

e'go·tis'ti·cal·ly

e'go trip'

e·gre'gious

e'gress (*n.*)

e·gress' (*v.*)

e'gret

E'gypt

E·gyp'tian

E'gyp·tol'o·gist

E'gyp·tol'o·gy

ei'der

ei'der·down'

ei'der duck'

Eif'fel

eight

eight'ball'

eight'een'

eight'eenth'

eighth

eight'i·eth

eight'-track'

eight'y
  pl. eight'ies

Ein'stein

ein·stein'i·um

Eir'e

Ei'sen·how'er

ei'ther

e·jac'u·late' (*v.*)
  e·jac'u·lat'ed,
  e·jac'u·lat'ing

e·jac'u·late (*n.*)

e·jac'u·la'tion

e·jac'u·la'tor

e·ject'

e·jec'tion

e·jec'tor

eke
  eked, ek'ing

e·lab'o·rate (*adj.*)

e·lab'o·rate' (*v.*)
  e·lab'o·rat'ed,
  e·lab'o·rat'ing

e·lab'o·rate·ly

e·lab'o·rate·ness

e·lab'o·ra'tion

é·lan'

é·lan vi·tal'

e'land
  pl. e'lands or e'land

e·lapse'
  e·lapsed', e·laps'ing

e·las'tic

e·las·tic'i·ty

e·late'
  e·lat'ed, e·lat'ing

e·la'tion

El'ba

El·ber'ta

el'bow

el'bow grease'

el'bow·room'

eld'er (older)
(SEE BELOW)

el'der (tree)
(SEE ABOVE)

el'der·ber'ry
pl. el'der·ber'ries

eld'er·ly

El'Do·ra'do

e·lect'

e·lec'tion

e·lec'tion·eer'

e·lec'tive

e·lec'tor

e·lec'tor·al

e·lec'tor·ate

E·lec'tra

e·lec'tric

e·lec'tri·cal

e·lec'tri·cal·ly

e·lec'tric eel'

e·lec·tri'cian

e·lec·tric'i·ty

e·lec'tri·fi·ca'tion

e·lec'tri·fy'
e·lec'tri·fied',
e·lec'tri·fy'ing

e·lec'tro·car·
di·o·gram'

e·lec'tro·car·
di·o·graph'

e·lec'tro·chem'i·cal

e·lec'tro·chem'is·try

e·lec'tro·cute'
e·lec'tro·cut'ed,
e·lec'tro·cut'ing

e·lec'tro·cu'tion

e·lec'trode

e·lec'tro·dy·nam'ics

e·lec'tro·en·
ceph'a·lo·gram'

e·lec'tro·en·
ceph'a·lo·graph'

e·lec·trol'o·gist

e·lec·trol'y·sis

e·lec'tro·lyte'

e·lec'tro·lyt'ic

e·lec'tro·lyze'
e·lec'tro·lyzed',
e·lec'tro·lyz'ing

e·lec'tro·mag'net

e·lec'tro·mag·net'ic

e·lec'tro·mag'
net·ism'

e·lec·trom'e·ter

e·lec'tro·mo'tive

e·lec'tron

e·lec'tro·neg'a·tive

e·lec·tron'ic

e·lec·tron'i·cal·ly

e·lec·tron'ics

e·lec'tro·plate'
e·lec'tro·plat'ed,
e·lec'tro·plat'ing

e·lec'tro·pos'i·tive

e·lec'tro·scope'

e·lec'tro·shock'

e·lec'tro·stat'ic

e·lec'tro·stat'ics

e·lec'tro·ther'a·py

e·lec'tro·type'
e·lec'tro·typed',
e·lec'tro·typ'ing

e·lec'tro·va'lence

e·lec'tro·va'lent

el'ee·mos'y·nar·y

el'e·gance

el'e·gant

el'e·gi'ac

el'e·gist

el'e·gize'
el'e·gized', el'e·giz'ing

el'e·gy
pl. el'e·gies

el'e·ment

el'e·men'tal

el'e·men'ta·try

el'e·phant

el'e·phan·ti'a·sis

el'e·phan'tine

el'e·vate'
el'e·vat'ed, el'e·vat'ing

el'e·va'tion

el'e·va'tor

e·lev'en

e·lev'enth

elf
pl. elves

elf'in

elf'ish

El'gar

El Gre'co

e·lic'it (draw out)
e·lic'it·ed, e·lic'it·ing
(SEE illicit)

e·lic'i·ta'tion

e·lic'i·tor

e·lide'
e·lid'ed, e·lid'ing

el'i·gi·bil'i·ty

el'i·gi·ble

E·li'jah

e·lim'i·nate'
e·lim'i·nat'ed,
e·lim'i·nat'ing

e·lim'i·na'tion

e·lim'i·na'tor

e·li'sion

e·lite'

e·lit'ism

e·lit'ist

e·lix'ir

E·liz'a·beth

E·liz'a·be'than

elk
pl. elks or elk

ell

el·lipse'

el·lip'sis
pl. el·lip'ses

el·lip'soid

el·lip·soi'dal

el·lip'tic

el·lip'ti·cal

elm

el'o·cu'tion

el'o·cu'tion·ist

E'lo·him'

e·lon'gate
e·lon'gat·ed,
e·lon'gat·ing

e·lon·ga'tion

e • lope'
　e • loped', e • lop'ing

e • lope'ment

el'o • quence

el'o • quent

El Pas'o

El Sal'va • dor

else

else'where'

e • lu'ci • date'
　e • lu'ci • dat'ed,
　e • lu'ci • dat'ing

e • lu'ci • da'tion

e • lu'ci • da'tor

e • lude'　(*avoid*)
　e • lud'ed, e • lud'ing
　(SEE allude)

e • lu'sive　(*evasive*)
　(SEE allusive *and*
　illusive)

e • lu'sive • ly

e • lu'sive • ness

el'ver

É • ly • sée'

E • ly'sian

E • ly'si • um

em

e • ma'ci • at'ed

e • ma'ci • a'tion

em'a • nate'
　em'a • nat'ed,
　em'a • nat'ing

em'a • na'tion

em'a • na'tive

e • man'ci • pate'
　e • man'ci • pat'ed,
　e • man'ci • pat'ing

e • man'ci • pa'tion

e • man'ci • pa'tor

e • mas'cu • late'　(v.)
　e • mas'cu • lat'ed,
　e • mas'cu • lat'ing

e • mas'cu • late　(adj.)

e • mas'cu • la'tion

e • mas'cu • la'tor

em • balm'

em • bank'

em • bank'ment

em • bar'go
　pl. em • bar'goes;　(v.)
　em • bar'goed,
　em • bar'go • ing

em • bark'

em'bar • ka'tion

em • bar'rass

em • bar'rass • ment

em'bas • sy
　pl. em'bas • sies

em • bat'tle
　em • bat'tled,
　em • bat'tling

em • bed'
　em • bed'ded,
　em • bed'ding

em • bel'ish

em • bel'ish • ment

em'ber

em • bez'zle
　em • bez'zled,
　em • bez'zling

em • bez'zle • ment

em • bez'zler

em • bit'ter

em • blaze'
　em • blazed',
　em • blaz'ing

em • bla'zon

em'blem

em'blem • at'ic

em'blem • at'i • cal • ly

em • bod'i • ment

em • bod'y
　em • bod'ied,
　em • bod'y • ing

em • bold'en

em'bo • lec'to • my

em • bol'ic

em'bo • lism'

em'bo • lus
　pl. em'bo • li'

em • boss'

em'bou • chure'

em • brace'
　em • braced',
　em • brac'ing

em • brace'a • ble

em • bra'sure

em'bro • ca'tion

em • broi'der

em • broi'der • y
　pl. em • broi'der • ies

em • broil'

em • broil'ment

em'bry • o'
　pl. em'bry • os'

em'bry • o • log'ic

em'bry • ol'o • gist

em'bry • ol'o • gy

em'bry • on'ic

em'cee'
　em'ceed', em'cee'ing

e • mend'　(*correct*)
　(SEE amend)

e'men • da'tion

em'er • ald

e • merge'
　e • merged', e • merg'ing

e • mer'gence

e • mer'gen • cy
　pl. e • mer'gen • cies

e • mer'gent

e • mer'i • tus
　pl. e • mer'i • ti'

Em'er • son

em'er • y

em'er • y board'

em'e • sis

e • met'ic

em'i • grant

em'i • grate'
　em'i • grat'ed,
　em'i • grat'ing

em'i • gra'tion

é'mi • gré'

em'i • nence

em'i • nent
　(*important*)
　(SEE imminent)

e • mir'　or e • meer'

e • mir'ate

em'is • sar'y
　pl. em'is • sar'ies

e • mis'sion

e • mis'sive

e • mit'
　e • mit'ted, e • mit'ting

e • mit'ter

e • mol'lient

e • mol'u • ment

e • mote'
　e • mot'ed, e • mot'ing

e • mo'tion

e • mo'tion • al

e·mo′tion·al·ism′
e·mo′tion·al·ist′
e·mo′tion·al·ly
e·mo′tive
em·path′ic
em′pa·thize′
  em′pa·thized′,
  em′pa·thiz′ing
em′pa·thy
em·pen·nage′
em′per·or
em′pha·sis
  pl. em′pha·ses′
em′pha·size′
  em′pha·sized′,
  em′pha·siz′ing
em·phat′ic
em·phat′i·cal·ly
em′phy·se′ma
em′pire
em·pir′ic
em·pir′i·cal
em·pir′i·cal·ly
em·pir′i·cism′
em·pir′i·cist
em·place′ment
em·ploy′
em·ploy′a·bil′i·ty
em·ploy′a·ble
em·ploy′ee
em·ploy′er
em·ploy′ment
em·po′ri·um
  pl. em·po′ri·ums or
  em·po′ri·a
em·pow′er
em′press
emp′ti·ness
emp′ty
  (adj.) emp′ti·er,
  emp′ti·est; (v.)
  emp′tied, emp′ty·ing;
  pl. .emp′ties
emp′ty–hand′ed
em·py′re·al
em′py·re′an
e′mu
em′u·late′
  em′u·lat′ed,
  em′u·lat′ing

em′u·la′tion
em′u·lous
e·mul′si·fi′er
e·mul′si·fi·ca′tion
e·mul′si·fy′
  e·mul′si·fied′,
  e·mul′si·fy′ing
e·mul′sion
en·a′ble
  en·a′bled, en·a′bling
en·act′
en·act′ment
en·ac′tor
e·nam′el
  e·nam′eled or
  e·nam′elled,
  e·nam′el·ing or
  e·nam′el·ling
e·nam′el·ware′
en·am′or
en bloc′
en·camp′
en·camp′ment
en·cap′su·late′
  en·cap′su·lat′ed,
  en·cap′su·lat′ing
en·cap′su·la′tion
en·case′
  en·cased′, en·cas′ing
en·caus′tic
en·ceinte′
en′ce·phal′ic
en·ceph′a·lit′ic
en·ceph′a·li′tis
en·ceph′a·lo·gram′
en·ceph′a·lo·
  my′e·li′tis
en·ceph′a·lon′
  pl. en·ceph′a·la
en·chain′
en·chant′
en·chant′ment
en·chant′ress
en′chi·la′da
en·ci′pher
en·cir′cle
  en·cir′cled, en·cir′cling
en·cir′cle·ment
en′clave
en·clit′ic

en·close′
  en·closed′, en·clos′ing
en·clo′sure
en·code′
  en·cod′ed, en·cod′ing
en·co′mi·ast′
en·co′mi·um
  pl. en·co′mi·ums or
  en·co′mi·a
en·com′pass
en′core
  en′cored, en′cor·ing
en·coun′ter
en·cour′age
  en·cour′aged,
  en·cour′ag·ing
en·cour′age·ment
en·cour′ag·er
en·croach′
en·croach′ment
en·crust′
en′crus·ta′tion
en·cum′ber
en·cum′brance
en·cyc′li·cal
en·cy′clo·pe′di·a or
  en·cy′clo·pae′di·a
en·cy′clo·pe′dic
en·cy′clo·pe′dist
end
end′–all′
en·dan′ger
en·dear′
en·dear′ment
en·deav′or
en·dem′ic
end′ing
en′dive
end′less
end′most′
en′do·crine
en′do·cri·nol′o·gy
en′do·derm′
en·dog′a·mons
en·dog′a·my
en′do·morph′
en′do·plasm′
en·dorse′
  en·dorsed′, en·dors′ing

en·dor·see'
en·dorse'ment
en·dors'er
en'do·scope'
en·dos'co·py
en'do·skel'e·ton
en'do·the'li·al
en'do·the'li·um
  pl. en'do·the'li·a
en'do·ther'mic
en·dow'
en·dow'er
en·dow'ment
end' pa'per
end' run'
end' ta'ble
en·due'
  en·dued', en·du'ing
en·dur'a·ble
en·dur'ance
en·dure'
  en·dured', en·dur'ing
end'ways'
end'wise'
end' zone'
en'e·ma
en'e·my
  pl. en'e·mies
en'er·get'ic
en'er·get'i·cal·ly
en'er·gize'
  en'er·gized',
  en'er·giz'ing
en'er·giz'er
en'er·gy
  pl. en'er·gies
en'er·vate' (v.)
  en'er·vat'ed,
  en'er·vat'ing
en·er'vate (adj.)
en'er·va'tion
en'er·va'tor
E·nes'co
en·fant ter·ri'ble
en·fee'ble
  en·fee'bled,
  en·fee'bling
en·fee'ble·ment
en'fi·lade'
  en'fi·lad'ed,
  en'fi·lad'ing

en·fold'
en·force'
  en·forced', en·forc'ing
en·force'a·bil'i·ty
en·force'a·ble
en·force'ment
en·forc'er
en·fran'chise
  en·fran'chised,
  en·fran'chis·ing
en·fran'chise·ment
en·gage'
  en·gaged', en·gag'ing
en·gage'ment
en·gag'er
en garde'
En'gels
en·gen'der
en'gine
en'gi·neer'
en'gi·neer'ing
Eng'land
Eng'lish
Eng'lish·man
  pl. Eng'lish·men
Eng'lish wom'an
  pl. Eng'lish wom'en
en·graft'
en'gram
en·grave'
  en·graved', en·grav'ing
en·grav'er
en·grav'ing
en·gross'
en·gross'ment
en·gulf'
en·hance'
  en·hanced',
  en·hanc'ing
en·hance'ment
en'har·mon'ic
en·heart'en
e·nig'ma
  pl. e·nig'mas or
  e·nig'ma·ta
en'ig·mat'ic
en'ig·mat'i·cal·ly
en·join'
en·joy'
en·joy'a·ble

en·joy'a·bly
en·joy'ment
en·large'
  en·larged', en·larg'ing
en·large'ment
en·larg'er
en·light'en
en·light'en·ment
en·list'
en·list·ee'
en·list'ment
en·liv'en
en masse'
en·mesh'
en'mi·ty
  pl. en'mi·ties
en·no'ble
  en·no'bled, en·no'bling
en·no'ble·ment
en·nui'
e·nor'mi·ty
  pl. e·nor'mi·ties
e·nor'mous
e·nough'
en' pas·sant'
en·plane'
  en·planed', en·plan'ing
en·quire'
  en·quired', en·quir'ing
en·quir'y
  pl. en·quir'ies
en·rage'
  en·raged', en·rag'ing
en·rich'
en·rich'ment
en·roll' or en·rol'
  en·rolled', en·rol'ling
en·roll'ee
en·roll'ment
en route'
en·sconce'
  en·sconced',
  en·sconc'ing
en·sem'ble
en·shrine'
  en·shrined',
  en·shrin'ing
en·shroud'
en'sign

en'si·lage
  en'si·laged,
  en'si·lag·ing
en·slave'
  en·slaved', en·slav'ing
en·slave'ment
en·snare'
  en·snared', en·snar'ing
en·snare'ment
en·sue'
  en·sued', en·su'ing
en·sure'
  en·sured', en·sur'ing
en·tab'la·ture
en·tail'
en·tail'ment
en·tan'gle
  en·tan'gled,
  en·tan'gling
en·tan'gle·ment
en·tente'
en·tente' cor·diale'
en'ter
en·ter'ic
en'ter·i'tis
en'ter·prise'
en'ter·pris'ing
en'ter·tain'
en'ter·tain'er
en'ter·tain'ing
en'ter·tain'ment
en·thrall'
en·throne'
  en·throned',
  en·thron'ing
en·thuse'
  en·thused', en·thus'ing
en·thu'si·asm'
en·thu'si·ast'
en·thu'si·as'tic
en·thu'si·as'ti·cal·ly
en·tice'
  en·ticed', en·tic'ing
en·tice'ment
en·tire'
en·tire'ly
en·tire'ty
  pl. en·tire'ties
en·ti'tle
  en·ti'tled, en·ti'tling

en'ti·ty
  pl. en'ti·ties
en·tomb'
en·tomb'ment
en'to·mo·log'i·cal
en'to·mol'o·gist
en'to·mol'o·gy
  pl. en'to·mol'o·gies
en'tou·rage'
en·tr'acte'
en'trails
en·train'
en'trance (n.)
en·trance' (v.)
  en·tranced',
  en·tranc'ing
en'trance·way'
en'trant
en·trap'
  en·trapped',
  en·trap'ping
en·trap'ment
en·treat'
en·treat'y
  pl. en·treat'ies
en·tre·chat'
en'trée or en'tree
en·trench'
en·trench'ment
en'tre·pre·neur'
en'tre·pre·neur'i·al
en'tro·py
en·trust'
en'try
  pl. en'tries
en'try·way'
en·twine'
  en·twined',
  en·twin'ing
en·twist'
e·nu'mer·ate'
  e·nu'mer·at'ed,
  e·nu'mer·at'ing
e·nu'mer·a'tion
e·nu'mer·a'tive
e·nu'mer·a'tor
e·nun'ci·ate'
  e·nun'ci·at'ed,
  e·nun'ci·at'ing
e·nun'ci·a'tion

e·nun'ci·a'tor
en·u·re'sis
en·u·ret'ic
en·vel'op
  en·vel'oped,
  en·vel'op·ing
en've·lope'
en·vel'op·ment
en·ven'om
en'vi·able
en'vi·a·bly
en'vi·ous
en·vi'ron·ment
en·vi'ron·men'tal
en·vi'ron·men'tal·ist
en·vi'rons
en·vis'age
  en·vis'aged,
  en·vis'ag·ing
en·vi'sion
en'voy
en'vy
  (v.) en'vied,
  en'vy·ing; pl. en'vies
en·wrap'
  en·wrapped',
  en·wrap'ping
en'zy·mat'ic
en'zyme
E'o·cene'
e'o·hip'pus
e'o·lith
e'o·lith'ic
e'on
ep'au·let' or
  ep'au·lette'
é·pée'
é·pée'ist
e·pergne'
e·phed'rine
e·phem'er·a
  pl. e·phem'er·as or
  e·phem'er·ae
e·phem'er·al
e·phem'er·is
  pl. e'phe·mer'i·des'
E·phe'sian
E'phra·im
ep'ic (poem)
  (SEE epoch)

ep'i·can'thic
ep'i·can'thus
ep'i·cene'
ep'i·cen'ter
ep'i·cure'
e'pi·cu·re'an
ep'i·dem'ic
ep'i·de'mi·ol'o·gy
ep'i·der'mal
ep'i·der'mis
ep'i·glot'tis
   pl. ep'i·glot'tis·es or
   ep'i·glot'ti·des'
ep'i·gone'
ep'i·gram'
ep'i·gram·mat'ic
ep'i·graph'
e·pig'ra·phy
ep'i·lep'sy
ep'i·lep'tic
ep'i·lep'toid
ep'i·logue'
ep'i·neph'rine
E·piph'a·ny
   pl. E·piph'a·nies
ep'i·phyte'
ep'i·phyt'ic
e·pis'co·pa·cy
   pl. e·pis'co·pa·cies
e·pis'co·pal
E·pis'co·pa'lian
e·pis'co·pate
ep'i·sode'
ep'i·sod'ic
ep'i·sod'i·cal·ly
e·pis'te·mol'o·gy
e·pis'tle
e·pis'to·lar'y
ep'i·taph'
ep·i·the'li·al
ep'i·the'li·um
   pl. ep'i·the'li·ums or
   ep'i·the'li·a
ep'i·thet'
e·pit'o·me
e·pit'o·mize'
   e·pit'o·mized',
   e·pit'o·miz'ing

e plu'ri·bus' u'num
ep'och (*era*)
   (SEE epic)
ep'och·al
ep'och–·mak'ing
ep'o·nym
ep·on'y·mous
ep'os
ep·ox'y
   pl. ep·ox'ies
ep'si·lon'
Ep'som
eq·ua·bil'i·ty
eq'ua·ble
eq'ua·bly
e'qual
   e'qualed, e'qual·ing
e·qual'i·tar'i·an
e·qual'i·ty
   pl. e·qual'i·ties
e'qual·i·za'tion
e'qual·ize'
   pl. e'qual·ized',
   e'qual·iz'ing
e'qual·iz'er
e'qual·ly
e'qua·nim'i·ty
e·quate'
   e·quat'ed, e·quat'ing
e·qua'tion
e·qua'tor
e'qua·to'ri·al
eq'uer·ry
   pl. eq'uer·ries
e·ques'tri·an
e·ques'tri·enne'
e'qui·an'gu·lar
e'qui·dis'tant
e'qui·lat'er·al
e·quil'i·brist
e'qui·lib'ri·um
   pl. e'qui·lib'ri·ums or
   e'qui·lib'ri·a
e'quine
e'qui·noc'tial
e'qui·nox'
   pl. e'qui·nox'es
e·quip'
   e·quipped', e·quip'ping
eq'ui·page

e·quip'ment
e'qui·poise'
e'qui·pol'lent
eq'ui·ta·ble
eq'ui·ta·bly
eq'ui·ta'tion
eq'ui·ty
   pl. eq'ui·ties
e·quiv'a·lence
e·quiv'a·len·cy
e·quiv'a·lent
e·quiv'o·cal
e·quiv'o·cal·ly
e·quiv'o·cate'
   e·quiv'o·cat'ed,
   e·quiv'o·cat'ing
e·quiv'o·ca'tion
e·quiv'o·ca·tor
e'ra
e·rad'i·ca·ble
e·rad'i·cate'
   e·rad'i·cat'ed,
   e·rad'i·cat'ing
e·rad'i·ca'tion
e·rad'i·ca'tor
e·ras'a·ble
e·rase'
   e·rased', e·ras'ing
e·ras'er
e·ras'ure
er'bi·um
ere (*before*)
   (SEE air *and* e'er *and*
   heir)
e·rect'
e·rec'tile
e·rec'tion
e·rec'tor
ere·long'
er'e·mite'
erg
er'go
er'go·nom'ic
er'go·nom'ics
er·gos'ter·ol'
er'got
E'rie
er'mine
   pl. er'mines or er'mine

e·rode'
  e·rod'ed, e·rod'ing

e·rod'ent

e·rog'e·nous

E'ros

e·ro'sion

e·ro'sive

e·rot'ic

e·rot'i·ca

e·rot'i·cal·ly

e·rot'i·cism'

err

er'rand

er'rant

er·rat'ic

er·rat'i·cal·ly

er·ra'tum
  pl. er·ra'ta

er·ro'ne·ous

er'ror

er'satz

erst'while'

er'u·bes'cent

e·ruct'

e·ruc·ta'tion

er'u·dite'

er'u·di'tion

e·rupt'

e·rup'tion

e·rup'tive

er'y·sip'e·las

er'y·the'ma

e·ryth'ro·blast'

e·ryth'ro·cyte'

e·ryth'ro·my'cin

E'sau

es·ca·drille'

es·ca·late'
  es·ca·lat'ed,
  es·ca·lat'ing

es·ca·la'tion

es·ca·la'tor

es·cal'lop

es·cap'a·ble

es·ca·pade'

es·cape'
  es·caped', es·cap'ing

es·cap·ee'

es·cape'ment

es·cap'ism

es·cap'ist

es·car·got'

es'ca·role'

es·carp'

es·carp'ment

es·cha·tol'o·gy

es·cheat'

es·chew'

es'cri·toire'

es'cort (n.)

es·cort' (v.)

es'crow

es·cu'do
  pl. es·cu'dos

es'cu·lent

es·cutch'eon

es'ker

Es'ki·mo'
  pl. Es'ki·mos' or
  Es'ki·mo'

e·soph'a·ge'al

e·soph'a·gus
  pl. e·soph'a·gi'

es'o·ter'ic

es'o·ter'i·cal·ly

es·pa·drille'

es·pal'ier

es·par'to

es·pe'cial

es·pe'cial·ly

Es'per·an'to

es·pi'al

es'pi·o·nage'

es'pla·nade'

es·pous'al

es·pouse'
  es·poused', es·pous'ing

es·pres'so

es·prit'

es·prit' de corps'

es·py'
  es·pied', es·py'ing

es·quire'
  es·quired', es·quir'ing

es'say (n.)

es·say' (v.) (try)
  (SEE assay)

es'say·ist

es'sence

Es'sene

es·sen'tial

es·sen'tial·ly

es·sen'ti·al'i·ty
  pl. es·sen'ti·al'i·ties

es·tab'lish

es·tab'lish·ment

es·tan'cia

es·tate'
  es·tat'ed, es·tat'ing

es·teem'

es'ter

Es'ther

es·thete'

es·thet'ic

es'ti·ma·ble

es'ti·mate' (v.)
  es'ti·mat'ed,
  es'ti·mat'ing

es'ti·mate (n.)

es'ti·ma'tion

es'ti·ma'tor

es'ti·val

es'ti·vate'
  es'ti·vat'ed,
  es'ti·vat'ing

es'ti·va'tion

Es·to'ni·a

Es·to'ni·an

es·top'pel

es·trange'
  es·tranged',
  es·trang'ing

es·trange'ment

es'tro·gen

es'trus

es'tu·ar'y
  pl. es'tu·ar'ies

e'ta

é·ta·gère'

et cet'er·a

etch

etch'er

etch'ing

e·ter'nal

e·ter'nal·ly

e·ter'ni·ty
  pl. e·ter'ni·ties

eth'ane
eth'a · nol'
e'ther
e · the're · al
e · the're · al · ly
e'ther · ize'
  e'ther · ized',
  e'ther · iz'ing
eth'ic
eth'i · cal
eth'i · cal · ly
eth'ics
E'thi · o'pi · a
E'thi · o'pi · an
eth'moid
eth'nic
eth'ni · cal · ly
eth · nic'i · ty
eth'no · cen'tric
eth'no · cen'trism
eth'no · log'ic
eth · nol'o · gist
eth · nol'o · gy
e'thos
eth'yl
eth'yl · ene'
e'ti · ol'o · gy
  pl. e'ti · ol'o · gies
et'i · quette
Et'na
E'ton
E · trus'can
é'tude
et'y · mo · log'i · cal
et'y · mol'o · gist
et'y · mol'o · gy
  pl. et'y · mol'o · gies
et'y · mon'
eu'ca · lyp'tus
  pl. eu'ca · lyp'ti or
  eu'ca · lyp'tus · es
Eu'cha · rist
eu'chre
  eu'chred, eu'chring
Eu'clid
Eu · clid'e · an
eu · gen'ic
eu · gen'i · cal · ly
eu · gen'ics

eu'lo · gis'tic
eu'lo · gize'
  eu'lo · gized',
  eu'lo · giz'ing
eu'lo · gy
  pl. eu'lo · gies
eu'nuch
eu'phe · mism'
eu'phe · mis'tic
eu'phe · mis'ti · cal · ly
eu · phon'ic
eu · pho'ni · ous
eu · pho'ni · um
eu'pho · ny
  pl. eu'pho · nies
eu · pho'ri · a
eu · phor'ic
Eu · phra'tes
eu'phu · ism'
Eur · a'sian
eu · re'ka
Eu · rip'i · des'
Eu'ro · dol'lar
Eu'rope
Eu'ro · pe'an
eu · ro'pi · um
Eu · sta'chian
eu'tha · na'sia
eu · then'ics
e · vac'u · ate'
  e · vac'u · at'ed,
  e · vac'u · at'ing
e · vac'u · a'tion
e · vac'u · a'tor
e · vac'u · ee'
e · vade'
  e · vad'ed, e · vad'ing
e · val'u · ate'
  e · val'u · at'ed,
  e · val'u · at'ing
e · val'u · a'tion
ev'a · nes'cence
ev'a · nes'cent
e'van · gel'ic
e'van · gel'i · cal
e'van · gel'i · cal · ly
e · van'ge · lism'
e · van'ge · list
e · van'ge · lis'tic

e · van'ge · lis'ti · cal · ly
e · van'ge · lize'
  e · van'ge · lized',
  e · van'ge · lis'ing
e · vap'o · rate'
  e · vap'o · rat'ed,
  e · vap'o · rat'ing
e · vap'o · ra'tion
e · vap'o · ra'tor
e · va'sion
e · va'sive
eve
e'ven
e'ven–hand'ed
eve'ning
e'ven · ness
e'ven · song'
e · vent'
e · vent'ful
e'ven · tide'
e · ven'tu · al
e · ven'tu · al'i · ty
  pl. e · ven'tu · al'i · ties
e · ven'tu · al · ly
e · ven'tu · ate'
  e · ven'tu · at'ed,
  e · ven'tu · at'ing
ev'er
ev'er · bloom'ing
Ev'er · est
Ev'er · glades'
ev'er · green'
ev'er · last'ing
ev'er · more'
e · ver'si · ble
e · vert'
eve'ry
eve'ry · bod'y
eve'ry · day'
eve'ry · one'
eve'ry · place'
eve'ry · thing'
eve'ry · where'
e · vict'
e · vict'ee
e · vic'tion
e · vic'tor
ev'i · dence
  ev'i · denced,
  ev'i · denc'ing

ev'i·dent

ev'i·den'tial

e'vil

e'vil·do'er

e'vil·ly

e'vil-mind'ed

e·vince'
e·vinced', e·vinc'ing

e·vin'ci·ble

e·vis'cer·ate'
e·vis'cer·at'ed,
e·vis'cer·at'ing

e·vis'cer·a'tion

ev'i·ta·ble

ev'o·ca'tion

e·voc'a·tive

e·voke'
e·voked', e·vok'ing

ev'o·lu'tion

ev'o·lu'tion·ar'y

ev'o·lu'tion·ism'

ev'o·lu'tion·ist

e·volve'
e·volved', e·volv'ing

ev'zone

ewe (*sheep*)
(SEE you *and* yew)

ew'er

ex·ac'er·bate'
ex·ac'er·bat'ed,
ex·ac'er·bat'ing

ex·ac'er·ba'tion

ex·act'

ex·ac'tion

ex·act'i·tude'

ex·ag'ger·ate'
ex·ag'ger·at'ed,
ex·ag'ger·at'ing

ex·ag'ger·a'tion

ex·ag'ger·a'tor

ex·alt'

ex'al·ta'tion

ex·alt'ed

ex·am'

ex·am'i·na'tion

ex·am'ine
ex·am'ined,
ex·am'in·ing

ex·am'i·nee'

ex·am'in·er

ex·am'ple
ex·am'pled,
ex·am'pling

ex·as'per·ate'
ex·as'per·at'ed,
ex·as'per·at'ing

ex·as'per·a'tion

Ex·cal'i·bur

ex ca·the'dra

ex'ca·vate'
ex'ca·vat'ed,
ex'ca·vat'ing

ex'ca·va'tion

ex'ca·va'tor

ex·ceed' (*surpass*)
(SEE accede)

ex·ceed'ing·ly

ex·cel'
ex·celled', ex·cel'ling

ex'cel·lence

ex'cel·len·cy
pl. ex'cel·len·cies

ex'cel·lent

ex·cel'si·or

ex·cept' (*excluding*)
(SEE accept)

ex·cept'ing

ex·cep'tion

ex·cep'tion·a·ble

ex·cep'tion·al

ex·cep'tion·al·ly

ex'cerpt (*n.*)

ex·cerpt' (*v.*)

ex·cess' (*n.*)
(*surplus*)
(SEE access)

ex'cess (*adj.*)

ex·ces'sive

ex·ces'sive·ly

ex·change'
ex·changed',
ex·chang'ing

ex·change'a·ble

ex·cheq'uer

ex'cise (*n.*)

ex·cise' (*v.*)
ex·cised', ex·cis'ing

ex·ci'sion

ex·cit'a·bil'i·ty

ex·cit'a·ble

ex·ci'tant

ex'ci·ta'tion

ex·cit'a·tive

ex·cite'
ex·cit'ed, ex·cit'ing

ex·cite'ment

ex·cit'er

ex·claim'

ex'cla·ma'tion

ex·clam'a·to'ry

ex'clave

ex·clude'
ex·clud'ed, ex·clud'ing

ex·clud'er

ex·clu'sion

ex·clu'sive

ex·clu'sive·ness

ex'clu·siv'i·ty

ex'com·mu'ni·cate'
(*v.*)
ex'com·mu'ni·cat'ed,
ex'com·mu'ni·cat'ing

ex'com·mu'ni·cate
(*n., adj.*)

ex'com·mu'ni·ca'tion

ex'com·mu'ni·ca'tor

ex·co'ri·ate'
ex·co'ri·at'ed,
ex·co'ri·at'ing

ex·co'ri·a'tion

ex'cre·ment

ex·cres'cence

ex·cres'cent

ex·cre'ta

ex·cre'tal

ex·crete'
ex·cret'ed, ex·cret'ing

ex·cre'tion

ex'cre·to'ry

ex·cru'ci·at'ing

ex'cul·pate'
ex'cul·pat'ed,
ex'cul·pat'ing

ex'cul·pa'tion

ex·cul'pa·to'ry

ex·cur'sion

ex·cur'sion·ist

ex·cus'a·ble

ex·cus'a·bly

ex·cuse'
ex·cused', ex·cus'ing

ex·e·cra·ble

ex·e·crate'
  ex'e·crat'ed,
  ex'e·crat'ing

ex·e·cra·tion

ex·e·cra·tor

ex·e·cute'
  ex'e·cut'ed,
  ex'e·cut'ing

ex·e·cu'tion

ex·e·cu'tion·er

ex·ec'u·tive

ex·ec'u·tor

ex·ec'u·trix
  pl. ex·ec'u·tri'ces or
  ex·ec'u·trix·es

ex·e·ge'sis
  pl. ex'e·ge'ses

ex·e·get'ic

ex·em'plar

ex·em'pla·ry

ex·em'pli·fi·ca'tion

ex·em'pli·fy'
  ex·em'pli·fied',
  ex·em'pli·fy'ing

ex·empt'

ex·empt'i·ble

ex·emp'tion

ex·er·cise' (exert)
  ex'er·cised',
  ex'er·cis'ing
  (SEE exorcise)

ex'er·cis·er

ex·ert'

ex·er'tion

ex·e·unt

ex·ha·la'tion

ex·hale'
  ex·haled', ex·hal'ing

ex·haust'

ex·haust'i·ble

ex·haus'tion

ex·haus'tive

ex·hib'it

ex·hi·bi'tion

ex·hi·bi'tion·ism'

ex·hi·bi'tion·ist

ex·hi·bi'tion·is'tic

ex·hib'i·tor

ex·hil'a·rant

ex·hil'a·rate'
  ex·hil'a·rat'ed,
  ex·hil'a·rat'ing

ex·hil'a·ra'tion

ex·hort'

ex'hor·ta'tion

ex·hu·ma'tion

ex·hume'
  ex·humed',
  ex·hum'ing

ex'i·gen·cy
  pl. ex'i·gen·cies

ex'i·gent

ex·ig'u·ous

ex'ile
  ex'iled, ex'il·ing

ex·il'ic

ex·ist'

ex·ist'ence

ex·ist'ent

ex'is·ten'tial

ex'is·ten'tial·ism'

ex'is·ten'tial·ist

ex'it

ex li'bris

ex'o·bi·ol'o·gy

ex'o·crine

ex'o·dus

ex of·fi·ci·o

ex·og'a·mous

ex·og'a·my

ex·og'e·nous

ex·on'er·ate'
  ex·on'er·at'ed,
  ex·on'er·at'ing

ex·on'er·a'tion

ex·or'bi·tance

ex·or'bi·tant

ex·or·cise' (expel)
  ex'or·cised',
  ex'or·cis'ing
  (SEE exercise)

ex'or·cis·er

ex'or·cism'

ex'or·cist'

ex·or'di·um

ex'o·skel'e·ton

ex'o·sphere'

ex'o·ther'mic

ex·ot'ic

ex·ot'i·cal·ly

ex·ot'i·cism'

ex·pand'

ex·panse'

ex·pan'si·ble

ex·pan'sion

ex·pan'sion·ism'

ex·pan'sion·ist

ex·pan'sive

ex par'te

ex·pa'ti·ate'
  ex·pa'ti·at'ed,
  ex·pa'ti·at'ing

ex·pa'ti·a'tion

ex·pa'tri·ate' (v.)
  ex·pa'tri·at'ed,
  ex·pa'tri·at'ing

ex·pa'tri·ate (adj., n.)

ex·pa'tri·a'tion

ex·pect'

ex·pect'a·ble

ex·pect'a·bly

ex·pect'an·cy
  pl. ex·pec'tan·cies

ex·pect'ant

ex'pec·ta'tion

ex·pec'to·rant

ex·pec'to·rate'
  ex·pec'to·rat'ed,
  ex·pec'to·rat'ing

ex·pec'to·ra'tion

ex·pe'di·ence

ex·pe'di·en·cy
  pl. ex·pe'di·en·cies

ex·pe'di·ent

ex·pe'di·en'tial

ex'pe·dite'
  ex'pe·dit'ed,
  ex'pe·dit'ing

ex'pe·dit'er

ex'pe·di'tion

ex'pe·di'tion·ar'y

ex'pe·di'tious

ex·pel'
  ex·pelled', ex·pel'ling

ex'pel·lee'

ex·pel'ler

ex·pend'

ex·pend'a·ble

ex·pend'i·ture
ex·pense'
ex·pen'sive
ex·pen'sive·ly
ex·pe'ri·ence
  ex·pe'ri·enced,
  ex·pe'ri·enc·ing
ex·per'i·en'tial
ex·per'i·ment (n.)
ex·per'i·ment' (v.)
ex·per'i·men'tal
ex·per'i·men'tal·ly
ex·per'i·men·ta'tion
ex'pert (n., v.)
ex·pert' (adj.)
ex'per·tise'
ex'pi·a·ble
ex'pi·ate'
  ex'pi·at'ed, ex'pi·at'ing
ex'pi·a'tion
ex'pi·a·to'ry
ex'pi·ra'tion
ex·pire'
  ex·pired', ex·pir'ing
ex·plain'
ex'pla·na'tion
ex·plan'a·to'ry
ex'ple·tive
ex'pli·ca·ble
ex'pli·cate'
  ex'pli·cat'ed,
  ex'pli·cat'ing
ex'pli·ca'tion
ex'pli·ca'tor
ex·plic'it
ex·plode'
  ex·plod'ed, ex·plod'ing
ex'ploit (n.)
ex·ploit' (v.)
ex·ploit'a·ble
ex'ploi·ta'tion
ex·ploit'a·tive
ex'plo·ra'tion
ex·plor'a·to'ry
ex·plore'
  ex·plored', ex·plor'ing
ex·plor'er
ex·plo'sion
ex·plo'sive

ex·po'nent
ex'po·nen'tial
ex·port' (v.)
ex'port (n., adj.)
ex'por·ta'tion
ex·port'er
ex·pose'
  ex·posed', ex·pos'ing
ex'po·sé'
ex'po·si'tion
ex·pos'i·tor
ex·pos'i·to'ry
ex' post' fac'to
ex·pos'tu·late'
  ex·pos'tu·lat'ed,
  ex·pos'tu·lat'ing
ex·pos'tu·la'tion
ex·po'sure
ex·pound'
ex·press'
ex·press'age
ex·press'i·ble
ex·pres'sion
Ex·pres'sion·ism'
Ex·pres'sion·ist
Ex·pres'sion·is'tic
ex·pres'sive
ex·press'way'
ex·pro'pri·ate'
  ex·pro'pri·at'ed,
  ex·pro'pri·at'ing
ex·pro'pri·a'tion
ex·pro'pri·a'tor
ex·pul'sion
ex·punge'
  ex·punged',
  ex·pung'ing
ex·pung'er
ex'pur·gate'
  ex'pur·gat'ed,
  ex'pur·gat'ing
ex'pur·ga'tion
ex'pur·ga'tor
ex·qui·site
ex'tant (existing)
  (SEE extent)
ex·tem'po·ra'ne·ous
ex·tem'po·rar'y
ex·tem'po·re

ex·tem'po·rize'
  ex·tem'po·rized',
  ex·tem'po·riz'ing
ex·tend'
ex·tend'i·bil'i·ty
ex·tend'i·ble
ex·ten'si·ble
ex·ten'sion
ex·ten'sive
ex·ten'sor
ex·tent' (amount)
  (SEE extant)
ex·ten'u·ate'
  ex·ten'u·at'ed,
  ex·ten'u·at'ing
ex·ten'u·a'tion
ex·te'ri·or
ex·ter'mi·nate'
  ex·ter'mi·nat'ed,
  ex·ter'mi·nat'ing
ex·ter'mi·na'tion
ex·ter'mi·na'tor
ex'tern
ex·ter'nal
ex·ter'nal·ly
ex·tinct'
ex·tinc'tion
ex·tin'guish
ex·tin'guish·able
ex·tin'guish·er
ex'tir·pate'
  ex'tir·pat'ed,
  ex'tir·pat'ing
ex'tir·pa'tion
ex·tol' or ex·toll'
  ex·tolled', ex·tol'ling
ex·tol'ler
ex·tort'
ex·tor'tion
ex·tor'tion·ate
ex·tor'tion·er
ex·tor'tion·ist
ex'tra
ex·tract' (v.)
ex'tract (n.)
ex·trac'tion
ex·trac'tive
ex·trac'tor
ex'tra·cur·ric'u·lar
ex'tra·dit'a·ble

ex'tra·dite'
  ex'tra·dit'ed,
  ex'tra·dit'ing

ex'tra·di'tion

ex'tra·ga·lac'tic

ex'tra·ju·di'cial

ex'tra·le'gal

ex'tra·mar'i·tal

ex'tra·mu'ral

ex·tra'ne·ous

ex·traor'di·nar'i·ly

ex·traor'di·nar'y

ex'trap'o·late'
  ex·trap'o·lat'ed,
  ex·trap'o·lat'ing

ex·trap'o·la'tion

ex'tra·sen'so·ry

ex'tra·ter'ri·to'ri·al

ex'tra·u'ter·ine

ex·trav'a·gance

ex·trav'a·gant

ex·trav'a·gan'za

ex'tra·ve·hic'u·lar

ex·treme'
  ex·trem'er, ex·trem'est

ex·treme'ly

ex·trem'ism

ex·trem'ist

ex·trem'i·ty
  pl. ex·trem'i·ties

ex'tri·ca·ble

ex'tri·cate'
  ex'tri·cat'ed,
  ex'tri·cat'ing

ex'tri·ca'tion

ex·trin'sic

ex'tro·ver'sion

ex'tro·vert'

ex·trude'
  ex·trud'ed, ex·trud'ing

ex·tru'sion

ex·u'ber·ance

ex·u'ber·ant

ex'u·date'

ex'u·da'tion

ex·ude'
  ex·ud'ed, ex·ud'ing

ex·ult'

ex·ult'ant

ex'ul·ta'tion

ex'urb

ex·ur'ban·ite'

ex·ur'bi·a

eye (sight organ)
  pl. eyes; (v.)
  eyed, eye'ing
  (SEE aye and I)

eye'ball'

eye' bank'

eye'brow'

eye'cup'

eye'drop'per

eye' drops'

eye'ful'
  pl. eye'fuls'

eye'glass'
  pl. eye'glass·es

eye'lash'
  pl. eye'lash·es

eye'let (hole)
  (SEE islet)

eye'lid'

eye·o'pen·er

eye'piece'

eye'sight'

eye'sore'

eye'spot'

eye'stalk'

eye'strain'

eye'tooth'
  pl. eye'teeth'

eye'wash'
  pl. eye'wash·es

eye'wit'ness

E·ze'kiel

ey'rie

Ez'ra

F

fa·ba'ceous

Fa'bi·an

fa'ble
  fa'bled, fa'bling

fa'bled

fab'ric

fab'ri·cate'
  fab'ri·cat'ed,
  fab'ri·cat'ing

fab'ri·ca'tion

fab'ri·ca'tor

fab'u·list

fab'u·lous

fa·çade' or fa·cade'

face
  faced, fac'ing

face' card'

face'less

face'-lift'

fac'er

face'-sav'ing

fac'et
  fac'et·ed, fac'et·ing

fa·ce'tious

face' val'ue

fa'cial

fac'ile

fa·cil'i·tate'
  fa·cil'i·tat'ed,
  fa·cil'i·tat'ing

fa·cil'i·ta'tion

fa·cil'i·ty
  pl. fa·cil'i·ties

fac'ing

fac·sim'i·le
  fac·sim'i·led,
  fac·sim'i·le·ing

fact

fact'-find'ing

fac'tion

fac'tion·al

fac'tion·al·ly

fac'tion·al·ism'

fac'tious

fac·ti'tious (artificial)
  (SEE fictitious)

fac'tor

fac'tor·a·ble

fac·to'ri·al

fac'to·ry
  pl. fac'to·ries

fac • to′tum

fac′tu • al

fac′tu • al • ly

fac′ul • ty
  pl. fac′ul • ties

fad

fad′dish

fad′dist

fade
  fad′ed, fad′ing

fade′-in′

fade′-out′

fa′do

fa′er • ie or fa′er • y

Faer′oe

fag
  fagged, fag′ging

fag′ end′

fag′ot or fag′got

fag′ot • ing or
  fag′got • ing

Fahr′en • heit′

fa • ïence′ or fa • ience′

fail (be
  unsuccessful)
  (SEE faille)

fail′ing

faille (fabric)
  (SEE fail and file)

fail′-safe′

fail′ure

faint (weak)
  (SEE feint)

faint′heart′ed

fair (just; market)
  (SEE fare)

fair′ground′

fair′-haired′

fair′ish

fair′ly

fair′mind′ed

fair′-spo′ken

fair′-trade′
  fair′-trad′ed,
  fair′-trad′ing

fair′way′

fair′-weath′er

fair′y (being)
  pl. fair′ies
  (SEE ferry)

fair′y • land′

fair′y tale′

fait ac • com • pli′
  pl. faits ac • com • plis′

faith

faith′ful

faith′ful • ly

faith′ful • ness

faith′ heal′er

faith′less

fake
  faked, fak′ing

fak′er (pretender)
  (SEE fakir)

fak′er • y
  pl. fak′er • ies

fa • kir′ (ascetic)
  (SEE faker)

fal′con

fal′con • er

fal′con • ry

Falk′land

fall
  fell, fall′en, fall′ing

fal • la′cious

fal′la • cy
  pl. fal′la • cies

fal′li • bil′i • ty

fal′li • ble

fal′li • bly

fall′ing-out′
  pl. fall′ings-out′ or
  fall′ing-outs′

fall′-off′

Fal • lo′pi • an

fall′out′

fal′low

false
  fals′er, fals′est

false′ a • larm′

false′-heart′ed

false′hood

false′ly

false′ness

fal • set′to
  pl. fal • set′tos

fals′ie

fal′si • fi • ca′tion

fal′si • fi′er

fal′si • fy′
  fal′si • fied′, fal′si • fy′ing

fal′si • ty
  pl. fal′si • ties

fal′ter

fame
  famed, fam′ing

fa • mil′ial

fa • mil′iar

fa • mil′i • ar′i • ty
  pl. fa • mil′i • ar′i • ties

fa • mil′iar • i • za′tion

fa • mil′iar • ize′
  fa • mil′iar • ized′,
  fa • mil′iar • iz′ing

fam′i • ly
  pl. fam′i • lies

fam′ine

fam′ished

fa′mous

fan
  fanned, fan′ning

fa • nat′ic

fa • nat′i • cal

fa • nat′i • cal • ly

fa • nat′i • cism′

fan′ci • er

fan′ci • ful

fan′ci • ful • ly

fan′ci • ly

fan′cy
  pl. fan′cies; (adj.)
  fan′ci • er, fan′ci • est;
  (v.)
  fan′ci • ed, fan′cy • ing

fan′cy–free′

fan′cy • work′

fan • dan′go
  pl. fan • dan′gos

fan′fare

fang

fan′jet′

fan′light′

fan′ mail′

fan′ny
  pl. fan′nies

fan′tail′

fan • ta′sia

fan′ta • size′
  fan′ta • sized′,
  fan′ta • siz′ing

fan′tast

fan · tas'tic

fan · tas'ti · cal · ly

fan'ta · sy
  pl. fan'ta · sies; (*v.*)
  fan'ta · sied,
  fan'ta · sy · ing

far
  far'ther *or* fur'ther,
  far'thest *or* fur'thest

far'ad

Far'a · day

fa · rad'ic

far'an · dole'

far'a · way'

farce
  farced, farc'ing

far · ceur

far'ci · cal

fare (*charge; food*)
  fared, far'ing
  (SEE fair)

Far' East'

far'er

fare'-thee-well'

fare'well'

far'-fetched'

far'-flung'

fa · ri'na

far'i · na'ceous

far'i · nose'

farm'er

farm' hand'

farm'house'

farm'land'

farm'stead'

farm'yard'

far'o

far'-off'

far'-out'

far · ra'go
  pl. far · ra'goes

far'-reach'ing

far'row

far'see'ing

far'sight'ed

far'ther

far'thest

far'thing

fas'ci · a
  pl. fas'ci · ae'

fas'ci · cle

fas'ci · nate'
  fas'ci · nat'ed,
  fas'ci · nat'ing

fas'ci · na'tion

fas'ci · na'tor

fas'cism

fas'cist

fa · scis'tic

fash'ion

fash'ion · a · ble

fash'ion · a · bly

fast

fast'back'

fas'ten

fas'ten · er

fas'ten · ing

fast'-food'

fas · tid'i · ous

fast'ness

fat
  (*adj.*) fat'ter, fat'test;
  (*v.*) fat'ted, fat'ting

fa'tal

fa'tal · ism'

fa'tal · ist

fa'tal · is'tic

fa'tal · is'ti · cal · ly

fa · tal'i · ty
  pl. fa · tal'i · ties

fa'tal · ly

fat'back'

fate (*destiny*)
  fat'ed, fat'ing
  (SEE fete)

fat'ed

fate'ful

fate'ful · ly

fat' farm'

fat'head'

fa'ther

fa'ther · hood'

fa'ther-in-law'
  pl. fa'thers-in-law'

fa'ther · land'

fa'ther · less

fa'ther · li · ness

fa'ther · ly

Fa'ther's Day'

fath'om
  pl. fath'oms *or* fath'om

fath'om · a · ble

fath'om · less

fa · tigue'
  fa · tigued', fa · ti'guing

fat'-sol'u · ble

fat'ten

fat'ty
  fat'ti · er, fat'ti · est

fa · tu'i · ty
  pl. fa · tu'i · ties

fat'u · ous

fau'ces

fau'cet

Faulk'ner

fault'find'er

fault'i · ly

fault'less

fault'y
  fault'i · er, fault'i · est

faun (*deity*)
  (SEE fawn)

fau'na
  pl. fau'nas *or* fau'nae

Faust

faux pas'
  pl. faux pas'

fa'vor

fa'vor · a · ble

fa'vor · a · bly

fa'vor · ite

fa'vor · it · ism'

fawn (*deer; grovel*)
  (SEE faun)

fay (*fairy*)
  (SEE fey)

faze (*daunt*)
  fazed, faz'ing
  (SEE phase)

fe'al · ty
  pl. fe'al · ties

fear'ful

fear'ful · ly

fear'less

fear'some

fea'si · bil'i · ty

fea'si · ble

fea'si · bly

feast'er

feat (*deed*)
  (SEE feet)

feath'er

feath'er bed'

feath'er • bed'ding

feath'er • brain'

feath'er • edge'

feath'er • weight'

feath'er • y

fea'ture
  fea'tured, fea'tur • ing

feb'ri • fuge'

fe'brile

Feb'ru • ar'y
  pl. Feb'ru • ar'ies

fe'cal

fe'ces

feck'less

fe'cund

fe'cun • date'
  fe'cun • dat'ed,
  fe'cun • dat'ing

fe • cun'di • ty

fed

fe • da • yeen'

fed'er • al

fed'er • al • ism'

fed'er • al • ist

fed'er • al • i • za'tion

fed'er • al • ize'
  fed'er • al • ized',
  fed'er • al • iz'ing

fed'er • ate' (*v.*)
  fed'er • at'ed,
  fed'er • at'ing

fed'er • ate (*adj.*)

fed'er • a'tion

fed'er • a'tive

fe • do'ra

fee
  feed, fee'ing

fee'ble
  fee'bler, fee'blest

fee'ble–mind'ed

fee'ble • ness

fee'bly

feed
  fed, feed'ing

feed'back'

feed' bag'

feed'er

feed'lot'

feel
  felt, feel'ing

feel'er

feel'ing

feet (*pl. of foot*)
  (SEE feat)

feign

feint (*deception*)
  (SEE faint)

feist'y
  feist'i • er, feist'i • est

feld'spar'

fe • lic'i • tate'
  fe • lic'i • tat'ed,
  fe • lic'i • tat'ing

fe • lic'i • ta'tion

fe • lic'i • ta'tor

fe • lic'i • tous

fe • lic'i • ty
  pl. fe • lic'i • ties

fe'line

fell

fel'lah
  pl. fel'lahs or (*Ar.*)
  fel'la • hin'

fel'loe (*rim*)
  (SEE fellow)

fel'low (*person*)
  (SEE felloe)

fel'low • man'
  pl. fel'low • men'

fel'low • ship'
  fel'low • shiped',
  fel'low • ship'ing

fel'ly
  pl. fel'lies

fel'on

fe • lo'ni • ous

fel'o • ny
  pl. fel'o • nies

felt

fe'male

fem'i • nine

fem'i • nin'i • ty

fem'i • nism'

fem'i • nist

femme fa • tale'
  pl. *femmes fa • tales'*

fem'o • ral

fe'mur
  pl. fe'murs or fem'o • ra

fen
  pl. fen

fence
  fenced, fenc'ing

fenc'er

fenc'ing

fend

fend'er

fen • nel

fen'u • greek'

fe'ral

fer'bam

fer'-de-lance'

fer'ment (*n.*)

fer • ment' (*v.*)

fer'men • ta'tion

fer'mi • um

fern

fe • ro'cious

fe • roc'i • ty

fer're • ous

fer'ret
  fer'ret • ed, fer'ret • ing

fer'ric

Fer'ris wheel'

fer'rite

fer'ro • mag • net'ic

fer'ro • mag'ne • tism'

fer'ro • type'
  fer'ro • typed',
  fer'ro • typ'ing

fer'rous

fer'rule (*metal ring*)
  fer'ruled, fer'rul • ing
  (SEE ferule)

fer'ry (*boat*)
  pl. fer'ries; (*v.*)
  fer'ried, fer'ry • ing
  (SEE fairy)

fer'ry • boat'

fer'tile

fer • til'i • ty

fer'ti • li • za'tion

fer'ti • lize'
  fer'ti • lized',
  fer'ti • liz'ing

fer'ti • liz'er

fer'ule (*rod*)
  fer'uled, fer'ul·ing
  (SEE ferrule)

fer'ven·cy

fer'vent

fer'vid

fer'vor

fes'cue

fes'tal

fes'ter

fes'ti·val

fes'tive

fes·tiv'i·ty
  pl. fes·tiv'i·ties

fes·toon'

Fest'schrift'
  pl. Fest'schrift'en or
  Fest'schrifts'

fe'tal

fetch

fetch'ing

fete or fête (*festival;
  honor*)
  fet'ed or fêt'ed, fet'ing
  or fêt'ing
  (SEE fate)

fet'i·cide'

fet'id

fet'ish or fet'ich

fet'ish·ism' or
  fet'ich·ism'

fet'ish·ist or
  fet'ich·ist

fet'lock'

fet'ter

fet'tle
  fet'tled, fet'tling

fet'tu·ci'ni

fe'tus
  pl. fe'tus·es

feud

feu'dal

feu'dal·ism'

feu'dal·ist

feu'dal·is'tic

feu'da·to'ry
  pl. feu'da·to'ries

feuil'le·ton

fe'ver

fe'ver·ish

few

fey (*strange*)
  (SEE fay)

fez
  pl. fez'zes

fi'an·cé' (*masc.*)

fi'an·cée' (*fem.*)

fi·as'co
  pl. fi·as'cos or
  fi·as'coes

fi'at

fi'at mon'ey

fib
  fibbed, fib'bing

fib'ber

fi'ber or fi'bre

fi'ber·board' or
  fi'bre·board'

Fi'ber·glas'
  (*Trademark*)

fi'ber·glass'

fi'ber op'tics

fi'bril

fib'ril·late
  fib'ril·lat·ed,
  fib'ril·lat·ing

fi'bril·la'tion

fi'brin

fi'broid

fi·bro'sis

fi'brous

fib'u·la
  pl. fib'u·lae or
  fib'u·las

fib'u·lar

fiche

fich'u
  pl. fich'us

fick'le

fick'le·ness

fic'tion

fic'tion·al

fic·ti'tious
  (*imaginary*)
  (SEE factitious)

fid'dle
  fid'dled, fid'dling

fid'dler

fid'dler crab'

fid'dle·sticks'

fi·del'i·ty
  pl. fi·del'i·ties

fidg'et
  fidg'et·ed, fidg'et·ing

fidg'et·y

fi·du'ci·ar'y
  pl. fi·du'ci·ar'ies

fie

fief

field

field' day'

field'er

field' glass'es

field' goal'

field' gun'

field' hock'ey

field' house'

field' mouse'

field'piece'

field'stone'

field' trip'

fiend

fiend'ish

fierce
  fierc'er, fierc'est

fierce'ly

fierce'ness

fier'y
  fier'i·er, fier'i·est

fi·es'ta

fife
  fifed, fif'ing

fif'teen'

fif'teenth'

fifth

fif'ti·eth

fif'ty
  pl. fif'ties

fif'ty–fif'ty

fig

fight
  fought, fight'ing

fight'er

fig' leaf'

fig'ment

fig'ur·a·tive

fig'ure

fig'ure·head'

fig'ur·ine'

Fi'ji
fil'a·ment
fil'bert
filch
file (*cabinet; tool*)
  filed, fil'ing
  (SEE faille)
fil'er
fil·et' mi·gnon'
fil'i·al
fil'i·bus'ter
fil'i·bus'ter·er
fil'i·cide'
fil'i·gree'
  fil'i·greed',
  fil'i·gree'ing
fil'ing
Fil'i·pi'no
  pl. Fil'i·pi'nos
fill
fill'er
fil'let
fill'-in'
fill'ing
fill'ing sta'tion
fil'lip
fil'ly
  pl. fil'lies
film
film'dom
film'strip
film'y
  film'i·er, film'i·est
fils
  pl. *fils*
fil'ter (*strainer*)
  (SEE philter)
fil'ter·a·ble
fil'ter tip'
filth
filth'i·ness
filth'y
  filth'i·er, filth'i·est
fil'tra·ble
fil'trate
  fil'trat·ed, fil'trat·ing
fil'tra'tion
fin
  finned, fin'ning
fi·na'gle
  fi·na'gled, fi·na'gling

fi·na'gler
fi'nal
fi·na'le
fi'nal·ist
fi·nal'i·ty
  pl. fi·nal'i·ties
fi'na·lize'
  fi'na·lized', fi'na·liz'ing
fi'nal·ly
fi·nance'
  fi·nanced', fi·nanc'ing
fi·nan'cial
fi·nan'cial·ly
fin'an·cier'
finch
find
  found, find'ing
find'er
fin de siè'cle
find'ing
fine
  (*adj.*) fin'er, fin'est;
  (*v.*) fined, fin'ing
fine'–drawn'
fine'ly
fine'ness
fin'er·y
  pl. fin'er·ies
fine'spun'
fi·nesse'
  fi·nessed', fi·ness'ing
fin'ger
fin'ger·board'
fin'ger bowl'
fin'ger·ing
fin'ger·nail'
fin'ger paint'
fin'ger–paint'
fin'ger·print'
fin'ger·tip'
fin'i·al
fin'ick·i·ness
fin'ick·y
fin'is
fin'ish
fin'ished
fi'nite
fink
Fin'land

Fin'land·er
Finn
fin'nan had'die
Finn'ish
fin'ny
  fin'ni·er, fin'ni·est
fiord
fir (*tree*)
  (SEE fur)
fire
  fired, fir'ing
fire' a·larm'
fire'arm'
fire'ball'
fire'boat
fire'box
fire'brand'
fire'break
fire'brick
fire'bug'
fire'crack'er
fire'damp'
fire'dog'
fire' drill'
fire'–eat'er
fire' en'gine
fire' es·cape'
fire' fight'
fire' fight'er
fire'fly'
  pl. fire'flies'
fire'guard'
fire'house'
fire'less
fire'light'
fire'man
  pl. fire'men
fire'place'
fire'plug'
fire' pow'er
fire'proof'
fire'–re·sist'ant
fire'side'
fire'trap'
fire' wall'
fire'wa'ter
fire'wood'
fire'works'

fir'ing line'

fir'ma·ment

firm'ly

first' aid'

first'born'

first' class'

first'hand'

first'ly

first'-night'er

first'-rate'

first'-string'

firth

fis'cal

fish
 pl. fish or fish'es

fish'bowl'

fish' cake'

fish'er (angler)
 (SEE fissure)

fish'er·man
 pl. fish'er·men

fish'er·y
 pl. fish'er·ies

fish'hook'

fish'ing rod'

fish' meal'

fish'mong'er

fish'net'

fish'tail'

fish'wife'
 pl. fish'wives'

fish'y
 fish'i·er, fish'i·est

fis'sile

fis'sion

fis'sion·a·ble

fis'sure
 fis'sured, fis'sur·ing

fist'ful'
 pl. fist'fuls'

fist'i·cuff'

fis'tu·la
 pl. fis'tu·las or
 fis'tu·lae

fit
 (adj.) fit'ter, fit'test,
 (v.) fit or fit'ted,
 fit'ting

fitch

fit'ful

fit'ful·ly

fit'ted

fit'ter

fit'ting

five

five'-and-ten'

five'-star'

fix
 fixed or fixt, fix'ing

fix'a·ble

fix·a'tion

fix'a·tive

fixed

fix'ings

fix'i·ty

fix'ture

fizz

fiz'zle
 fiz'zled, fiz'zling

fjord

flab

flab'ber·gast'

flab'bi·ness

flab'by
 flab'bi·er, flab'bi·est

flac'cid

flac'on

flag
 flagged, flag'ging

flag'el·lant

flag'el·late'
 flag'el·lat'ed,
 flag'el·lat'ing

flag'el·la'tion

fla·gel'lum
 pl. fla·gel'la or
 fla·gel'lums

flag'eo·let'

flag'ging

flag'man
 pl. flag'men

flag'on

flag'pole'

fla'grance

fla'gran·cy

fla'grant

fla·gran'te de·lic'to

flag'ship'

flag'staff'
 pl. flag'staves' or
 flag'staffs'

flag'stone'

flag'-wav'ing

flail

flair (aptitude)
 (SEE flare)

flak

flake
 flaked, flak'ing

flak'i·ness

flak'y
 flak'i·er, flak'i·est

flam·bé'

flam'beau
 pl. flam'beaux or
 flam'beaus

flam·boy'ance

flam·boy'an·cy

flam·boy'ant

flame
 flamed, flam'ing

fla·men'co
 pl. fla·men'cos

flame'-out'

flame'proof'

flame'throw'er

flam'ing

fla·min'go
 pl. fla·min'gos or
 fla·min'goes

flam'ma·bil'i·ty

flam'ma·ble

flan

flange
 flanged, flang'ing

flank

flank'er

flan'nel
 flan'neled, flan'nel·ing

flan'nel·et'

flap
 flapped, flap'ping

flap'jack'

flap'per

flare (flame)
 flared, flar'ing
 (SEE flair)

flare'-up'

flash

flash'back'

flash'bulb'

flash' card'

flash'cube'

flash'gun'

flash'i • ly

flash'i • ness

flash'light'

flash'y
flash'i • er, flash'i • est

flask

flat
(adj.) flat'ter, flat'test;
(v.) flat'ted, flat'ting

flat'bed

flat'boat'

flat'car'

flat'fish'
pl. flat'fish' or
flat'fish'es

flat'foot'
pl. flat'feet' or
flat'foots'

flat'foot'ed

flat'head'
pl. flat'head' or
flat'heads'

flat'i'ron

flat'ten

flat'ter

flat'ter • y
pl. flat'ter • ies

flat'top'

flat'u • lence

flat'u • lent

flat'ware'

flat'work'

flat'worm'

Flau • bert'

flaunt

flau'tist

fla'vor

fla'vor • ful

fla'vor • ing

fla'vor • some

flaw

flaw'less

flax

flax'en

flax'seed'

flay

flea (insect)
(SEE flee)

flea'bag'

flea'bite'

flea'bit'ten

flea' mar'ket

fleck

fled

fledg'ling

flee (run from)
fled, flee'ing
(SEE flea)

fleece
fleeced, fleec'ing

fleec'y
fleec'i • er, fleec'i • est

fleet

fleet'ing

Flem'ing

Flem'ish

flesh

flesh'i • ness

flesh'ly
flesh'li • er, flesh'li • est

flesh'pot'

flesh'y
flesh'i • er, flesh'i • est

fleur'–de–lis'
pl. fleurs'–de–lis'

flew (move in air)
(SEE flu and flue)

flex

flex'i • bil'i • ty

flex'i • ble

flex'i • bly

flex'i • time'

flex'or

flex'time'

flex'ure

flib'ber • ti • gib'bet

flick

flick'er

fli'er

flight

flight' deck'

flight'i • ness

flight'–test'

flight'wor'thy

flight'y
flight'i • er, flight'i • est

flim'flam'
flim'flammed',
flim'flam'ming

flim'si • ly

flim'si • ness

flim'sy
flim'si • er, flim'si • est

flinch

fling
flung, fling'ing

flint

flint' glass'

flint'lock'

flint'y

flip
flipped, flip'ping

flip' chart'

flip'–flop'
flip'–flopped',
flip'–flop'ping

flip'pan • cy
pl. flip'pan • cies

flip'pant

flip'per

flirt

flir • ta'tion

flir • ta'tious

flit
flit'ted, flit • ting

flitch

flit'ter

fliv'ver

float

float'er

flock

flock'ing

floe (ice)
(SEE flow)

flog
flogged, flog'ging

flog'ger

flood

flood'gate'

flood'light'
flood'light'ed or
flood'lit', flood'light'ing

flood' plain'

floor

floor'board'

floor'ing

floor'shift'

floor' show'

floor'walk'er

floo'zy
  pl. floo'zies

flop
  flopped, flop'ping

flop'house'

flop'py
  flop'pi·er, flop'pi·est

flo'ra
  pl. flo'ras or flo'rae

flo'ral

Flor'ence

Flor'en·tine'

flo·res'cence

flo·res'cent

flo'ret

flo'ri·cul'ture

flor'id

Flor'i·da

Flo·rid'i·an

flor'in

flo'rist

floss

floss'y
  floss'i·er, floss'i·est

flo·ta'tion

flo·til'la

flot'sam

flounce
  flounced, flounc'ing

floun'der

floun'der (v.)
  pl. floun'der or
  floun'ders

flour (grain)
  (SEE flower)

flour'ish

flour'y

flout

flow (stream)
  (SEE floe)

flow'chart'

flow'er (blossom)
  (SEE flour)

flow'ered

flow'er·i·ness

flow'er·pot'

flow'er·y

flow'ing

flown

flu (illness)
  (SEE flue and flew)

flub
  flubbed, flub'bing

fluc'tu·ate'
  fluc'tu·at'ed,
  fluc'tu·at'ing

fluc'tu·a'tion

flue (duct)
  (SEE flu and flew)

flu'en·cy

flu'ent

fluff

fluff'i·ness

fluff'y
  fluff'i·er, fluff'i·est

flu'id

flu·id'ics

flu·id'i·ty

flu'id ounce'

fluke
  fluked, fluk'ing

fluk'y
  fluk'i·er, fluk'i·est

flume
  flumed, flum'ing

flung

flunk

flun'ky
  pl. flun'kies

flu'o·resce'
  flu'o·resced',
  flu'o·resc'ing

flu'o·res'cence

flu'o·res'cent

fluor'i·date'
  fluor'i·dat'ed,
  fluor'i·dat'ing

fluor'i·da'tion

flu'o·ride'

fluor'i·nate'
  fluor'i·nat'ed,
  fluor'i·nat'ing

fluor'i·na'tion

flu'o·rine'

flu'o·rite'

fluor'o·scope'

fluor·os'co·py

flur'ry
  pl. flur'ries
  flur'ried, flur'ry·ing

flush

flush'es

flus'ter

flute
  flut'ed, flut'ing

flut'ist

flut'ter

flut'ter·y

flu'vi·al

flux

fly
  (v.) flew, flown,
  fly'ing; (pl.) flies

fly' ball'

fly'blown'

fly'by'
  pl. fly'bys'

fly'–by–night'

fly'cast'er

fly'catch'er

fly'ing

fly'ing fish'

fly'ing sau'cer

fly'leaf'
  pl. fly'leaves'

fly'pa'per

fly' rod'

fly'speck'

fly' swat'ter

fly'trap'

fly'weight'

fly'wheel'

foal

foam

foam'i·ness

foam'y
  foam'i·er, foam'i·est

fob
  fobbed, fob'bing

fo'cal

fo'cal·ly

fo'cus
  pl. fo'cus·es or fo'ci;
  (v.) fo'cused or
  fo'cussed, fo'cus·ing or
  fo'cus·sing

fod'der

foe

foehn or fohn

foe'tal

foe′tus

fog
  fogged, fog′ging

fog′bound′

fog′gi · ness

fog′gy
  fog′gi · er, fog′gi · est

fog′horn′

fog′ light′

fo′gy
  pl. fo′gies

foi′ble

foie gras′

foil

foist

fold

fold′a · way′

fold′er

fol′de · rol′

fo′li · age

fo′li · ar

fo′li · a′tion

fo′lic

fo′li · o′
  pl. fo′li · os′; (v.)
  fo′li · oed′, fo′li · o′ing

folk

folk′ dance′

folk′lore′

folk′-rock′

folk′ sing′er

folk′ song′

folk′sy
  folk′si · er, folk′si · est

folk′ tale′

folk′way′

fol′li · cle

fol′low

fol′low · er

fol′low · ing

fol′low-through′

fol′low-up′

fol′ly
  pl. fol′lies

fo · ment′

fo′men · ta′tion

fon′dant

fon′dle
  fon′dled, fon′dling

fond′ness

fon · due′

font

fon · ti′na

food

food′ stamp′

food′stuff′

fool

fool′er · y
  pl. fool′er · ies

fool′har′di · ly

fool′har′di · ness

fool′har′dy
  fool′har′di · er,
  fool′har′di · est

fool′ish

fool′proof′

fools′cap′ (paper)
  (SEE BELOW)

fool′s′ cap′ (jester's
  hat)
  (SEE ABOVE)

fool′s′ gold′

foot
  pl. feet or foots

foot′age

foot′ball′

foot′bridge′

foot′-can′dle

foot′fall′

foot′hill′

foot′hold′

foot′ing

foot′less

foot′lights′

foot′lock′er

foot′-loose′

foot′man
  pl. foot′men

foot′mark′

foot′note′
  foot′not′ed, foot′not′ing

foot′path′

foot′-pound′

foot′print′

foot′race′

foot′rest′

foot′sie

foot′sore′

foot′step′

foot′stool′

foot′-ton′

foot′wear′

foot′work′

fop

fop · per · y
  pl. fop′per · ies

fop′pish

for (with purpose of;
  since)
  (SEE four and fore)

for′age
  for′aged, for′ag · ing

for′ag · er

fo · ra′men
  pl. fo · ram′i · na

for′as · much′

for′ay

for · bear′ (v.)
  (refrain)
  for · bore′, for · borne′,
  for · bear′ing
  (SEE forebear)

for′bear′ (n.)

for · bear′ance

for · bid′
  for · bade′ or for · bad′,
  for · bid′den or for · bid′,
  for · bid′ding

force
  forced, forc′ing

force′-feed′
  force′-fed′, force′-
  feed′ing

force′ful

force′ful · ly

force′ful · ness

force′meat′

for′ceps
  pl. for′ceps or
  for′ci · pes′

for′ci · ble

for′ci · bly

ford

Ford

fore (front)
  (SEE for or four)

fore′-and-aft′

fore′arm′ (n.)

fore · arm′ (v.)

fore'bear' *(ancestor)*
(SEE forebear)

fore • bode'
fore • bod'ed,
fore • bod'ing

fore'brain'

fore'cast'
fore'cast' or fore'cast'ed,
fore'cast'ing

fore'cast'er

fore'cas'tle

fore • close'
fore • closed',
fore • clos'ing

fore • clos'ure

fore'court'

fore • doom'

fore'fa'ther

fore'fin'ger

fore'foot'
pl. fore'feet'

fore'front'

fore • go'
fore • went', fore • gone',
fore • go'ing

fore • gone'

fore'ground'

fore'hand'

fore'hand'ed

fore'head'

for'eign

for'eign–born'

for'eign • er

fore'knowl'edge

fore'la'dy
pl. fore'la'dies

fore'leg'

fore'limb'

fore'lock'

fore'man
pl. fore'men

fore'mast'

fore'most'

fore'name'

fore'noon' *(n.)*

fore'noon' *(adj.)*

fo • ren'sic

fo • ren'si • cal • ly

fore'or • dain'

fore'part'

fore'play'

fore'quar'ter

fore'run'ner

fore'said'

fore'sail'

fore • see'
fore • saw', fore • seen',
fore • see'ing

fore • see'a • ble

fore • shad'ow

fore'sheet'

fore • short'en

fore'sight'

fore'sight'ed

fore • skin'

fore • speak'
fore • spoke',
fore • spo'ken,
fore • speak'ing

for'est

for • stall'

for'es • ta'tion

for'est • er

for'est • ry

fore'taste' *(n.)*

fore • taste' *(v.)*
fore • tast'ed,
fore • tast'ing

fore • tell'
fore • told', fore • tell'ing

fore'thought'

fore'to'ken *(n.)*

fore • to'ken *(v.)*

fore'top'

for • ev'er

for • ev'er • more'

fore • warn'

fore'wing'

fore'wom'an
pl. fore'wom'en

fore'word' *(preface)*
(SEE forward)

for'feit

for'fei • ture

for • gath'er

forge
forged, forg'ing

forg'er

for'ger • y
pl. for'ger • ies

for • get'
for • got', for • got'ten or
for • got', for • get'ting

for • get'–me–not'

for • get'ta • ble

for • get'ter

for • get'ful

for • giv'a • ble

for • give'
for • gave', for • giv'en,
for • giv'ing

for • give'ness

for • go'
for • went', for • gone',
for • go'ing

for • go'er

for • got'

for • got'ten

fork

forked

fork'lift'

for • lorn'

form

for'mal

form • al'de • hyde'

for'mal • ism'

for'mal • ist

for • mal'i • ty
pl. for • mal'i • ties

for'mal • i • za'tion

for'mal • ize'
for'mal • ized',
for'mal • iz'ing

for'mal • ly

for'mat
for'mat • ed or
for'mat • ted,
for'mat • ing or
for'mat • ting

for • ma'tion

form'a • tive

for'mer

form'er

form'er • ly

form'fit'ting

for'mic

For • mi'ca
(Trademark)

for'mi • da • ble

for'mi • da • bly

form' let'ter

For · mo'sa
For · mo'san
for'mu · la
  pl. for'mu · las or
  for'mu · lae
for'mu · la'ic
for'mu · late'
  for'mu · lat'ed,
  for'mu · lat'ing
for'mu · la'tion
for'mu · la'tor
for'ni · cate' (*v.*)
  for'ni · cat'ed,
  for'ni · cat'ing
for'ni · cate (*adj.*)
for'ni · ca'tion
for'ni · ca'tor
for · sake'
  for · sook', for · sak'en,
  for · sak'ing
for · sooth'
for · swear'
  for · swore', for · sworn',
  for · swear'ing
for · syth'i · a
fort (*fortified place*)
  (SEE forte)
forte (*skill*)
  (SEE fort)
for'te (*music*)
forth (*onward*)
  (SEE fourth)
forth'com · ing
forth'right' (*adj., n.*)
forth'right' (*adv.*)
forth'with'
for'ti · eth
for'ti · fi · ca'tion
for'ti · fy'
  for'ti · fied', for'ti · fy'ing
for'tis
  pl. for'tes
for · tis'si · mo'
for'ti · tude'
for'ti · tu'din · ous
fort'night'
fort'night'ly
FOR'TRAN
for'tress
  pl. for'tress · es
Fort' Sum'ter
for · tu'i · tous

for · tu'i · ty
  pl. for · tu'i · ties
for'tu · nate
for'tune
for'tune · tell'er
Fort' Worth'
for'ty
  pl. for'ties
for'ty-nin'er
fo'rum
  pl. fo'rums or fo'ra
for'ward (*onward*)
  (SEE foreword)
for'ward · er
fos'sil
fos'sil fu'el
fos'sil · ize'
  fos'sil · ized',
  fos'sil · iz'ing
fos'ter
fos'ter child'
fos'ter home'
fos'ter par'ent
fought
foul (*filthy*)
  (SEE fowl)
fou · lard'
foul'ly
foul' ball'
foul'mouthed'
foul' play'
foul'-up'
found
foun · da'tion
found'er
found'ling
found'ry
  pl. found'ries
fount
foun'tain
foun'tain · head'
foun'tain pen'
four (*number*)
  (SEE for *and* fore)
four'flush'er
four'fold'
four'-foot'ed
four'-hand'ed
four'-in-hand'

four'post · er
four'ra · gère'
four'score'
four'some
four'square'
four'teen'
four'teenth'
fourth (*number*)
  (SEE forth)
fo've · a
  pl. fo've · ae'
fowl (*bird*)
  pl. fowls or fowl
  (SEE foul)
fowl'er
fox
foxed
fox'-fire'
fox'glove'
fox'hole'
fox'hound'
fox'i · ly
fox'i · ness
fox' trot'
fox'y
  fox'i · er, fox'i · est
foy'er
fra'cas
frac'tion
frac'tion · al
frac'tion · al · ly
frac'tious
frac'ture
  frac'tured, frac'tur · ing
frag
  fragged, frag'ging
frag'ile
fra · gil'i · ty
frag'ment
frag'men · tar'y
frag'men · ta'tion
fra'grance
fra'grant
frail
frail'ty
  pl. frail'ties
frame
  framed, fram'ing
fram'er

frame′ house′

frame′-up′

frame′work′

franc (*coin*)
(SEE frank)

France

fran′chise
fran′chised,
fran′chis・ing

fran′chi・see′

fran′chi・ser

fran′ci・um

fran′gi・ble

fran′gi・pan′i
pl. fran′gi・pan′is or
fran′gi・pan′i

frank (*candid*)
(SEE franc)

Frank′en・stein′

Frank′fort

frank′furt・er

frank′in・cense′

Frank′lin

fran′tic

fran′ti・cal・ly

frap・pé′

fra・ter′nal

fra・ter′nal・ism′

fra・ter′nal・ly

fra・ter′ni・ty
pl. fra・ter′ni・ties

frat′er・ni・za′tion

frat′er・nize′
frat′er・nized′,
frat′er・niz′ing

frat′ri・ci′dal

frat′ri・cide′

Frau
pl. *Frau′en* or (*Eng.*)
Fraus

fraud

fraud′u・lence

fraud′u・lent

fraught

Fräu′lein
pl. *Fräu′lein* or (*Eng.*)
Fräu′leins

fray

fraz′zle
fraz′zled, fraz′zling

freak

freak′ish

freck′le
freck′led, freck′ling

Fred′er・ic・ton

free
(*adj.*) fre′er, fre′est;
(*v.*) freed, free′ing

free′bie

free′boot′er

free′born′

freed′man
pl. freed′men

free′dom

freed′wom′an
pl. freed′wom′en

free′ fall′

free′-for-all′

free′ hand′

free′-hand′ed

free′hold′

free′hold′er

free′ lance′

free′load′

free′ly

free′man
pl. free′men

Free′ma′son

free′ma′son・ry

free′ port′

free′si・a

free′-spo′ken

free′stand′ing

free′stone′

free′style′

free′think′er

free′think′ing

Free′town′

free′way′

free′wheel′

free′wheel′ing

free′ will′

freeze (*chill*)
froze, fro′zen, freez′ing
(SEE frieze)

freeze′-dry′
freeze′-dried′

freez′er

freight

freight′age

freight′ car′

freight′er

French

French′ Ca・na′di・an

French′man
pl. French′men

French′wom′an
pl. French′wom′en

fre・net′ic

fre・net′i・cal・ly

fre′num
pl. fre′na

fren′zied

fren′zy

Fre′on (*Trademark*)

fre′quen・cy
pl. fre′quen・cies

fre′quent

fre・quen′ta・tive

fres′co
pl. fres′coes or fres′cos;
(*v.*) fres′coed,
fres′co・ing

fres′co・er

fres′co・ist

fresh

fresh′en

fresh′et

fresh′man
pl. fresh′men

fresh′-wa′ter

fret
fret′ted, fret′ting

fret′ful

fret′ful・ly

fret′ful・ness

fret′ saw′

fret′work′

Freud

Freud′i・an

fri′a・ble

fri′ar (*priest*)
(SEE fryer)

fric′as・see′
fric′as・seed′,
fric′as・see′ing

fric′a・tive

fric′tion

Fri′day

fried′-cake′

friend

friend'less

friend'li · ness

friend'ly
friend'li · er,
friend'li · est

friend'ship

frieze (decoration)
(SEE freeze)

frig'ate

fright

fright'en

fright'ful

fright'ful · ly

frig'id

fri · gid'i · ty

fri'jol
pl. fri · jo'les

frill

frill'y
frill'i · er, frill'i · est

fringe
fringed, fring'ing

frip'per · y
pl. frip'per · ies

Fris'bee (Trademark)

frisk

frisk'i · ly

frisk'i · ness

frisk'y
frisk'i · er, frisk'i · est

frit'il · lar'y
pl. frit'il · lar'ies

frit'ter

fri · vol'i · ty
pl. fri · vol'i · ties

friv'o · lous

friz
frizzed, friz'zing

friz'zi · ness

friz'zle
friz'zled, friz'zling

friz'zy
friz'zi · er, friz'zi · est

fro

frock

frock' coat'

frog'man'
pl. frog'men'

frol'ic
fol'icked, frol'ick · ing

frol'ick · er

frol'ic · some

from

frond

front

front'age

fron'tal

fron · tier'

fron · tiers'man
pl. fron · tiers'men

fron'tis · piece'

fron'ton

frost

frost'bite'
frost'bit', frost'bit'ten,
frost'bit'ing

frost'ed

frost'i · ly

frost'i · ness

frost'ing

frost'y
frost'i · er, frost'i · est

froth

froth'i · ness

froth'y
froth'i · er, froth'i · est

frown

frowz'y
frowz'i · er, frowz'i · est

froze

fro'zen

fruc'tose

frug

fru'gal

fru · gal'i · ty

fru'gal · ly

fruit
pl. fruits or fruit

fruit'cake'

fruit' fly'

fruit'ful

fruit'ful · ly

fru · i'tion

fruit'less

fruit'y
fruit'i · er, fruit'i · est

frump

frump'ish

frump'y

frus'trate
frus'trat · ed,
frus'trat · ing

frus · tra'tion

frus'tum
pl. frus'tums or frus'ta

fry
(v.) fried, fry'ing; pl.
fries

fry'er (one who
fries)
(SEE friar)

fry'ing pan'

fry'pan'

fuch'sia

fud'dy · dud'dy
pl. fud'dy · dud'dies

fudge
fudged, fudg'ing

fu'el
fu'eled or fu'elled,
fu'el · ing or fu'el · ling

fu'el cell'

fu'gal

fu'gi · tive

fugue

Füh'rer or fueh'rer

ful'crum
pl. ful'crums or ful'cra

ful · fill' or ful · fil'
ful · filled', ful · fil'ling

ful · fill'ment

full

full'back'

full'-blood'ed

full'-blown'

full'-bod'ied

full' dress'

full'er

ful'ler's earth'

full'-fash'ioned

full'-fledged'

full'-length'

full' moon'

full'-ness

full'-scale'

full'-time'

ful'ly

ful'mi · nate'
ful'mi · nat'ed,
ful'mi · nat'ing

ful'mi·na'tion
ful'mi·na'tor
ful'some
fum'ble
  fum'bled, fum'bling
fume
  fumed, fum'ing
fu'mi·gant
fu'mi·gate'
  fu'mi·gat'ed,
  fu'mi·gat'ing
fu'mi·ga'tion
fu'mi·ga'tor
fun
  funned, fun'ning
func'tion
func'tion·al
func'tion·al·ly
func'tion·ar'y
  pl. func'tion·ar'ies
func'tion·less
fund
fun'da·ment
fun'da·men'tal
fun'da·men'tal·ism'
fun'da·men'tal·ist
fun'da·men'tal·ly
fu'ner·al
fu'ner·ar'y
fu·ne're·al
fun'gal
fun'gi·ble
fun'gi·cid'al
fun'gi·cide'
fun'gous
fun'gus
  pl. fun'gi or fun'gus·es
fu·nic'u·lar
funk

funk'y
  funk'i·er, funk'i·est
fun'nel
  fun'neled or fun'nelled,
  fun'nel·ing or
  fun'nel·ling
fun'ni·ly
fun'ni·ness
fun'ny
  (adj.) fun'ni·er,
  fun'ni·est; pl. fun'nies
fur (animal hair)
  furred, fur'ring
  (SEE fir)
fur'be·low'
fur'bish
fur'cu·la
  pl. fur'cu·lae'
fu'ri·ous
furl
fur'long
fur'lough
fur'nace
  fur'naced, fur'nac·ing
fur'nish
fur'nish·ings
fur'ni·ture
fu'ror
furred
fur'ri·er
fur'ring
fur'row
fur'ry
  fur'ri·er, fur'ri·est
fur'ther
fur'ther·ance
fur'ther·more'
fur'ther·most'
fur'thest
fur'tive
fur'tive·ness

fu'ry
  pl. fu'ries
furze
fuse
  fused, fus'ing
fu·see'
fu'se·lage
fu'sel
fu'si·bil'i·ty
fu'si·ble
fu'sil·lade'
  fu'sil·lad'ed,
  fu'sil·lad'ing
fu'sion
fuss
fuss'budg'et
fuss'i·ly
fuss'i·ness
fuss'y
  fuss'i·er, fuss'i·est
fus'tian
fus'ti·ness
fus'ty
  fus'ti·er, fus'ti·est
fu'tile
fu·til'i·ty
  pl. fu·til'i·ties
fu'ture
fu'tur·ism'
fu'tur·ist
fu'tur·is'tic
fu·tu'ri·ty
  pl. fu·tu'ri·ties
fu'tu·rol'o·gy
fuze
  fuzed, fuz'ing
fuzz
fuzz'i·ly
fuzz'i·ness
fuzz'y
  fuzz'i·er, fuzz'i·est
fyl'fot

G

gab
  gab, gab'bing
gab'ar·dine'
gab'ber
gab'ble
  gab'bled, gab'bling

gab'by
  gab'bi·er, gab'bi·est
gab'fest'
ga'ble
Ga·bon'

Ga'bon·ese'
Ga'bo·rone'
Ga'bri·el
gad
  gad'ded, gad'ding

gad'a·bout'

gad'fly'
  pl. gad'flies'

gadg'et

gadg'e·teer'

gadg'et·ry

gad'o·lin'i·um

Gael'ic

gaff (hook)
  (SEE gaffe)

gaffe (blunder)
  (SEE gaff)

gaf'fer

gag
  gagged, gag'ging

gage (challenge)
  (SEE gauge)

gag'gle
  gag'gled, gag'gling

gag'ster

gai'e·ty
  pl. gai'e·ties

gail·lar'di·a

gai'ly

gain

gain'er

gain'ful

gain'ful·ly

gain'say'
  gain'said', gain'say'ing

gait (walk)
  (SEE gate)

gait'er

ga'la

ga·lac'tic

Gal'a·had'

Ga·lá'pa·gos'

gal'ax·y
  pl. gal'ax·ies

gale

ga·le'na

Gal'i·lee'

Gal'i·le'o

gall

gal'lant

gal'lant·ry
  pl. gal'lant·ries

gall'blad'der

gal'le·on

gal'ler·y
  pl. gal'ler·ies

gal'ley
  pl. gal'leys

Gal'lic

gal'li·mau'fry
  pl. gal'li·mau'fries

gal'li·um

gal'li·vant'

gal'lon

gal'lop
  gal'loped, gal'lop·ing

gal'lows

gall'stone'

ga·lore'

ga·losh'es

gal·van'ic

gal'va·nism'

gal'va·ni·za'tion

gal'va·nize'
  gal'va·nized',
  gal'va·niz'ing

gal'va·nom'e·ter

Gam'bi·a

Gam'bi·an

gam'bit

gam'ble (bet)
  gam'bled, gam'bling
  (SEE gambol)

gam'bler

gam'bol (frolic)
  gam'boled or
  gam'bolled, gam'bol·ing
  or gam'bol·ling
  (SEE gamble)

game
  (adj.) gam'er, gam'est;
  (v.) gamed, gam'ing

game'cock'

game'keep'er

gam'e·lan'

game'ly

game'ness

game' room'

games'man·ship'

gam'ete

gam'in

gam'i·ness

gam'ma

gam'mon

gam'ut

gam'y
  gam'i·er, gam'i·est

gan'der

Gan'dhi

gang

gang'bus'ter

Gan'ges'

gang'land'

gan'gling

gan'gli·on
  pl. gan'gli·a or
  gan'gli·ons

gang'ly

gang'plank'

gan'grene
  gan'grened,
  gan'gren·ing

gan'gre·nous

gang'ster

gang'way'

gan'net

gant'let

gan'try
  pl. gan'tries

gaol

gap
  gapped, gap'ping

gape
  gaped, gap'ing

gap'er

gar
  pl. gar or gars

ga·rage'
  ga·raged', ga·rag'ing

garb

gar'bage

gar·ban'zo

gar'ble
  gar'bled, gar'bling

gar·çon'

gar'den

gar'den·er

gar·de'nia

Gar'field

gar'fish'
  pl. gar'fish' or
  gar'fish·es

gar·gan'tu·an

gar'gle
  gar'gled, gar'gling

gar'goyle

Gar'i · bal'di
gar'ish
gar'land
gar'lic
gar'lic · y
gar'ment
gar'ner
gar'net
gar'nish
gar'nish · ee'
  gar'nish · eed',
  gar'nish · ee'ing
gar'nish · ment
gar'ni · ture
gar'ret
gar'ri · son
gar · rote'
  gar · rot'ed, gar · rot'ing
gar · ru'li · ty
gar'ru · lous
gar'ter
gar'ter snake'
gas
  pl. gas'es; (v.) gassed,
  gas'sing
gas'e · ous
gash
gas'i · fy'
  gas'i · fied', gas'i · fy'ing
gas' jet'
gas'ket
gas'light'
gas' mask'
gas'o · hol'
gas'o · line'
gasp
Gas · pé'
gas'ser
gas'sy
  gas'si · er, gas'si · est
gas' tank'
gas'tric
gas · tri'tis
gas'tro · en'ter · i'tis
gas'tro · en'ter · ol'
  o · gist
gas'tro · en'ter · ol'o · gy
gas'tro · in · tes'ti · nal
gas'tro · nom'ic

gas · tron'o · my
gas'tro · pod'
gas'works'
gate (*opening*)
  gat'ed, gat'ing
  (SEE gait)
gate'–crash'er
gate'fold'
gate'house'
gate'keep'er
gate' leg'
gate'post'
gate'way'
gath'er
gath'er · er
gath'er · ing
Gat'ling
gauche (*graceless*)
  (SEE gouache)
gau'che · rie'
gau'cho
  pl. gau'chos
gaud'i · ly
gaud'i · ness
gaud'y
  gaud'i · er, gaud'i · est
gauge (*measure*)
  gauged, gaug'ing
  (SEE gage)
Gau · guin'
Gaul
gaunt
gaunt'let
gauss
gauze
gauz'y
  gauz'i · er, gauz'i · est
gave
gav'el
ga'vi · al
ga · votte'
gawk
gawk'y
  gawk'i · er, gawk'i · est
gay
gay'e · ty
gay'ly
gay'ness
Ga'za

gaze
  gazed, gaz'ing
ga · ze'bo
  pl. ga · ze'bos or
  ga · ze'boes
ga · zelle'
  pl. ga · zelles' or
  ga · zelle'
gaz'er
ga · zette'
  ga · zet'ted, ga · zet'ting
gaz'et · teer'
gear
gear'box'
  pl. gear'box'es
gear'shift'
gear'wheel'
geck'o
  pl. geck'os or geck'oes
gee
gee'zer
ge · fil'te fish'
Ge · hen'na
Gei'ger
gei'sha
  pl. gei'sha or gei'shas
gel (*jelly*)
  gelled, gel'ling
  (SEE jell)
gel'a · tin or gel'a · tine
ge · lat'i · nous
geld
geld'ing
gel'id
ge · lid'i · ty
gem
Gem'i · ni'
gems'bok'
  pl. gems'boks' or
  gems'bok'
gem'stone'
ge · müt'lich
gen'darme
gen · dar'me · rie
gen'der
gene
ge'ne · a · log'i · cal
ge'ne · a · log'i · cal · ly
ge'ne · al'o · gist
ge'ne · al'o · gy
  pl. ge'ne · al'o · gies

gen'er · al

gen'er · al · is'si · mo'
  pl. gen'er · al · is'si · mos'

gen'er · al · ist

gen'er · al'i · ty
  pl. gen'er · al'i · ties

gen'er · al · i · za'tion

gen'er · al · ize'
  gen'er · al · ized',
  gen'er · al · iz'ing

gen'er · al · ly

gen'er · al · ship'

gen'er · ate'
  gen'er · at'ed,
  gen'er · at'ing

gen'er · a'tion

gen'er · a'tive

gen'er · a'tor

ge · ner'ic

ge · ner'i · cal · ly

gen'er · os'i · ty
  pl. gen'er · os'i · ties

gen'er · ous

gen'e · sis
  pl. gen'e · ses'

gen'et

ge · net'ic

ge · net'i · cal · ly

ge · net'i · cist

ge · net'ics

Ge · ne'va

Gen'ghis Khan'

gen'ial

gen'ial · ly

ge'ni · al'i · ty

gen'ie

gen'i · tal

gen'i · ta'lia

gen'i · tals

gen'i · tive

gen'i · to · u'ri · nar'y

gen'ius
  pl. gen'ius · es or
  gen'i · i'

Gen'o · a

gen'o · cid'al

gen'o · cide'

gen'o · type'

gen'o · typ'ic

gen're

gen · teel'

gen'tian

gen'tile

gen · til'i · ty

gen'tle
  (*adj.*) gen'tler,
  gen'tlest; (*v.*) gen'tled,
  gen'tling

gen'tle · folk'

gen'tle · man
  pl. gen'tle · men

gen'tle · man · ly

gen'tle · wom'an
  pl. gen'tle · wom'en

gen'tly

gen'try

gen'u · flect'

gen'u · flec'tion or
  gen'u · flex'ion

gen'u · ine

gen'u · ine · ly

gen'u · ine · ness

ge'nus
  pl. gen'e · ra or
  ge'nus · es

ge'o · cen'tric

ge'o · chem'i · cal

ge'o · chem'is · try

ge'ode

ge'o · des'ic

ge · od'e · sy

ge'o · det'ic

ge'o · duck

ge · og'ra · pher

ge'o · graph'ic

ge'o · graph'i · cal

ge'o · graph'i · cal · ly

ge · og'ra · phy
  pl. ge · og'ra · phies

ge'o · log'ic

ge'o · log'i · cal

ge'o · log'i · cal · ly

ge · ol'o · gist

ge · ol'o · gy
  pl. ge · ol'o · gies

ge'o · mag'net · ism

ge'o · met'ric

ge'o · met'ri · cal

ge'o · met'ri · cal · ly

ge · om'e · tri'cian

ge · om'e · try

ge'o · mor'phic

ge'o · mor · phol'o · gy

ge'o · phys'i · cal

ge'o · phys'i · cist

ge'o · phys'ics

ge'o · pol'i · tics

George'town'

Geor'gia

Geor'gian

ge'o · ther'mal

ge · ot'ro · pism'

ge · ra'ni · um

ger'bil

ger'i · at'ric

ger'i · at'rics

germ

Ger'man

ger · mane'

Ger · man'ic

ger · ma'ni · um

Ger'ma · ny

germ' cell'

ger'mi · cid'al

ger'mi · cide'

ger'mi · nal

ger'mi · nate'
  ger'mi · nat'ed,
  ger'mi · nat'ing

ger'mi · na'tion

Ge · ron'i · mo'

ger · on · tol'o · gist

ger · on · tol'o · gy

ger'ry · man'der

ger'und

ger · un'dive

ges'so

ge · stalt'
  pl. ge · stalts' or
  ge · stal'ten

Ge · sta'po

ges'tate
  ges'tat · ed, ges'tat · ing

ges · ta'tion

ges · tic'u · late'
  ges · tic'u · lat'ed,
  ges · tic'u · lat'ing

ges · tic'u · la'tion

ges'ture
  ges'tured, ges'tur·ing

ge·sund'heit

get
  got, got or got'ten,
  get'ting

get'a·way'

Geth·sem'a·ne

get'-to·geth'er

Get'tys·burg'

get'up'

gew'gaw

gey'ser

Gha'na

Gha'na·ian

Gha'ni·an

ghast'li·ness

ghast'ly

ghat

gher'kin

ghet'to
  pl. ghet'tos or ghet'toes

Ghi·ber'ti

ghost

ghost'li·ness

ghost'ly

ghost' town'

ghost'write'
  ghost'wrote',
  ghost'writ'ten,
  ghost'writ'ing

ghost' writ'er

ghoul

ghoul'ish

gi'ant

gi'ant·ess

gi'ant·ism'

gib'ber

gib'be·rel'lic

gib'ber·ish

gib'bet
  gib'bet·ed, gib'bet·ing

gib'bon

gib'bous

gibe (taunt)
  gibed, gib'ing
  (SEE jibe)

gib'er

gib'let

Gi·bral'tar

gid'di·ly

gid'di·ness

gid'dy
  (adj.) gid'di·er,
  gid'di·est; (v.)
  gid'died, gid'dy·ing

gift

gift'ed

gift'-wrap'
  gift'-wrapped' or gift'-
  wrapt', gift'-wrap'ping

gig
  gigged, gig'ging

gi·gan'tic

gi·gan'ti·cal·ly

gi·gan'tism

gig'gle
  gig'gled, gig'gling

gig'gly

gig'o·lo'
  pl. gig'o·los'

Gi'la

gild (coat with gold)
  gild'ed or gilt, gild'ing
  (SEE guild)

Gil'e·ad

gill

gill'-like'

gil'ly·flow'er

gilt (gold)
  (SEE guilt)

gilt'-edged'

gim'bals

gim'crack'

gim'let

gim'mick

gim'mick·ry

gim'mick·y

gimp

gin
  ginned, gin'ning

gin'ger

gin'ger ale'

gin'ger·bread'

gin'ger·ly

gin'ger·snap'

ging'ham

gin·gi'val

gin'gi·vi'tis

gink'go
  pl. gink'goes

gin' mill'

gin'seng

Gin'za

Giot'to

gi·raffe'

gird
  gird'ed or girt, gird'ing

gird'er

gir'dle
  gir'dled, gir'dling

girl

girl'hood

girl'ie

girl'ish

girl' scout'

girth

gis'mo
  pl. gis'mos

gist

give
  gave, giv'en, giv'ing

give'-and-take'

give'a·way'

giv'en

giz'zard

gla'brous

gla·cé'
  gla·céed', gla·cé'ing

gla'cial

gla'cier (ice mass)
  (SEE glazier)

glad
  glad'der, glad'dest

glad'den

glade

glad'i·a'tor

glad'i·o'lus
  pl. glad'i·o'lus or
  glad'i·o'li or
  glad'i·o'lus·es

glad'some

Glad'stone'

glam'or·i·za'tion or
  glam'our·i·za'tion

glam'or·ize' or
  glam'our·ize'
  glam'or·ized' or
  glam'our·ized',
  glam'or·iz'ing or
  glam'our·iz'ing

glam'or·ous or
  glam'our·ous

glam'our or glam'or

glance
  glanced, glanc'ing

gland

glan'ders

glan'du·lar

glare
  glared, glar'ing

Glas'gow

glass

glass'ful'
  pl. glass'fuls'

glass'ine

glass'i·ness

glass'mak'ing

glass'ware'

glass' wool'

glass'y
  glass'i·er, glass'i·est

glau·co'ma

glau·co'ma·tous

glaze
  glazed, glaz'ing

glaz'er

gla'zier (glass dealer)
  (SEE glacier)

gleam

glean

glean'er

glee

glee' club'

glee'ful

glee'ful·ly

glen

glen·gar'ry
  pl. glen·gar'ries

glib
  glib'ber, glib'best

glide
  glid'ed, glid'ing

glid'er

glim'mer

glimpse
  glimpsed, glimps'ing

glint

glis·san'do
  pl. glis·san'di

glis'ten

glis'ter

glitch

glit'ter

gloam'ing

gloat

glob

glob'al

glob'al·ly

globe

globe'–trot'ter

glob'u·lar

glob'ule

glob'u·lin

glock'en·spiel'

gloom

glom'i·ly

gloom'i·ness

gloom'y
  gloom'i·er, gloom'i·est

glo'ri·fi·ca'tion

glo'ri·fy'
  glo'ri·fied', glo'ri·fy'ing

glo'ri·ous

glo'ry
  pl. glo'ries; (v.)
  glo'ried, glo'ry·ing

gloss

glos'sa·ry
  pl. glos'sa·ries

gloss'i·ness

gloss'o·la'li·a

gloss'y
  (adj.) gloss'i·er,
  gloss'i·est; pl. gloss'ies

glot'tal

glot'tis
  pl. glot'tis·es or
  glot'ti·des'

Glouces'ter

glove
  gloved, glov'ing

glov'er

glow

glow'er

glow'ing

glow'worm'

glox·in'i·a

glu'cose

glue
  glued, glu'ing

glue'y
  glu'i·er, glu'i·est

glum
  glum'mer, glum'mest

glu'on

glut
  glut'ted, glut'ting

glu'ta·mate'

glu'ten

glu'te·nous (of
  gluten)
  (SEE glutinous)

glu'te·us
  pl. glu'te·i'

glu'ti·nous (sticky)
  (SEE glutenous)

glut'ton

glut'ton·ous

glut'ton·y

glyc'er·in or
  glyc'er·ine

glyc'er·ol'

gly'co·gen

gly'co·gen'ic

G'–man'
  pl. G'–men'

gnarl

gnarled

gnash

gnat

gnaw
  gnawed, gnawed or
  gnawn, gnaw'ing

gneiss

gnome

gnom'ish

gnos'tic

gnu
  pl. gnus or gnu

go
  (v.) went, gone,
  go'ing; pl. goes

goad

go'–a·head'

goal

goal'ie

goal'keep'er

goal' line'

goal' post'

goat

goat·ee'

goat'herd'

goat'skin'

gob
  gobbed, gob'bing

gob'bet

gob'ble
  gob'bled, gob'bling

gob'ble·dy·gook' or
  gob'ble·de·gook'

gob'bler

go'-be·tween'

gob'let

gob'lin

go'-cart'

God

god'child'
  pl. god'chil'dren

god'daugh'ter

god'dess

god'fa'ther

god'for·sak'en

God'head'

Go·di'va

god'less

god'like'

god'li·ness

god'ly
  god'li·er, god'li·est

god'moth'er

god'par'ent

god'send'

god'son'

God'speed'

Goe'the

go'fer

go'-get'ter

gog'gle
  gog'gled, gog'gling

go'-go'

go'ing

go'ings-on'

goi'ter

gold

gold'brik'

gold' dig'ger

gold'en

gold'en age'

gold'en·rod'

gold'field'

gold'-filled'

gold'finch'

gold'fish'
  pl. gold'fish' or
  gold'fish'es

gold' mine'

gold'min'er

gold' rush'

gold'smith'

go'lem

golf

golf' ball'

golf' club'

golf'er

Gol'go·tha

Go·li'ath

gol'ly

go'nad

gon'do·la

gon'do·lier'

gone

gon'er

gon'fa·lon

gong

gon'o·coc'cus
  pl. gon'o·coc'ci

gon'or·rhe'a

goo

goo'ber

good
  bet'ter, best

good'by'
  pl. good'by'

good'bye'

good' day'

good'-heart'ed

good'-hu'mored

good'-look'ing

good'ly
  good'li·er, good'li·est

good'-na'tured

good'ness

good'-sized'

good' will'

good'y·good'y
  pl. good'y·good'ies

goo'ey
  goo'i·er, goo'i·est

goof

goof'i·ness

goof'y
  goof'i·er, goof'i·est

goo'gol

gook

goon

goo'ney bird'

goose
  pl. geese or goos'es;
  (v.) goosed, goos'ing

goose'ber'ry
  pl. goose'ber'ries

goose' egg'

goose' flesh'

goose'neck'

goose'-step'
  goose'-stepped', goose'-
  step'ping

go'pher

Gor'di·an

gore
  gored, gor'ing

gorge
  gorged, gorg'ing

gor'geous

Gor'gon·zo'la

go·ril'la (animal)
  (SEE guerilla)

gorse

gor'y
  gor'i·er, gor'i·est

gosh

gos'hawk'

Go'shen

gos'ling

gos'pel

gos'sa·mer

gos'sip
  gos'siped, gos'sip·ing

gos'sip·y

got

Goth

Goth'ic

got'ten

Göt'ter·däm'mer·ung'

gouache (painting)
  (SEE gauche)

Gou'da

gouge
  gouged, goug'ing

goug'er

gou'lash

gou'ra·mi
 pl. gou'ra·mi or
 gou'ra·mis

gourd (*fruit*)
 (SEE gourde)

gourde (*coin*)
 (SEE gourd)

gour'mand

gour'met

gout

gout'y
 gout'i·er, gout'i·est

gov'ern

gov'ern·a·ble

gov'ern·ance

gov'ern·ess

gov'ern·ment

gov'ern·men'tal

gov'er·nor

gov'er·nor gen'er·al
 pl. gov'er·nors
 gen'er·al or gov'er·nor
 gen'er·als

gown

Go'ya

grab
 grabbed, grab'bing

grab'ber

grace
 graced, grac'ing

grace'ful

grace'ful·ly

grace'less

grace' note'

gra'cious

grack'le

grad

gra·da'tion

grade
 grad'ed, grad'ing

gra'di·ent

grad'u·al

grad'u·al·ly

grad'u·al·ism'

grad'u·ate (*n., adj.*)

grad'u·ate' (*v.*)
 grad'u·at'ed,
 grad'u·at'ing

grad'u·a'tion

graf·fi'ti
 sing. graf·fi'to

graft

graft'er

gra'ham

Grail

grain

grain'field'

grain'y
 grain'i·er, grain'i·est

gram or gramme

gram' at'om

gram'mar

gram·mar'i·an

gram·mat'i·cal

gram·mat'i·cal·ly

Gram'-neg'a·tive

gram'pus
 pl. gram'pus·es

Gra·na'da

gra'na·ry
 pl. gra'na·ries

Gran Cha'co

grand

gran'dam

grand'aunt'

grand'child'
 pl. grand'chil'dren

grand'dad'

grand'daugh'ter

gran·dee'

gran'deur

grand'fa'ther

gran·dil'o·quence

gran·dil'o·quent

gran'di·ose'

gran'di·os'i·ty

grand'ma'

grand'moth'er

grand'neph'ew

grand'niece'

grand'pa'

grand'par'ent

Grand Prix'

grand'son'

grand'stand'
 grand'stand'ed,
 grand'stand'ing

grand'un'cle

grange

gran'ite

gran'ny
 pl. gran'nies

gra·no'la

grant

Grant

gran·tee'

grant'-in-aid'
 pl. grants'-in-aid'

gran'tor

gran'u·lar

gran'u·lar'i·ty

gran'u·late'
 gran'u·lat'ed,
 gran'u·lat'ing

gran'u·la'tion

gran'ule

grape

grape'fruit'

grape'shot'

grape'vine'

graph

graph'eme

graph'ic

graph'i·cal·ly

graph'ics

graph'ite

gra·phit'ic

graph·ol'o·gy

grap·nel

grap'ple
 grap'pled, grap'pling

grasp

grasp'ing

grass

grass'hop'per

grass'land'

grass' roots'

grass'y
 grass'i·er, grass'i·est

grate (*metal frame*)
 grat'ed, grat'ing
 (SEE great)

grat'er

grate'ful

grate'ful·ly

grat'i·fi·ca'tion

grat'i·fy'
 grat'i·fied', grat'i·fy'ing

grat'ing

grat'is

grat'i · tude'

gra · tu'i · tous

gra · tu'i · ty
  pl. gra · tu'i · ties

gra · va'men
  pl. gra · va'mi · na

grave
  grav'er, grav'est

grave'dig'ger

grav'el
  grav'eled or grav'elled,
  grav'el · ing or
  grav'el · ling

grave'ly

grav'el · ly

grave'rob'ber

grave'stone'

grave'yard'

grav'id

gra · vim'e · ter

grav'i · met'ric

grav'i · tate'
  grav'i · tat'ed,
  grav'i · tat'ing

grav'i · ta'tion

grav'i · ty
  pl. grav'i · ties

gra · vure'

gra'vy
  pl. gra'vies

gra'vy boat'

gray

gray'beard'

gray'ish

gray'ling

gray' mat'ter

graze
  grazed, graz'ing

grease
  greased, greas'ing

grease' paint'

greas'i · ness

greas'y
  greas'i · er, greas'i · est

great (*large*)
  (SEE grate)

great'-aunt'

great'coat'

great'-grand'child'
  pl. great'-grand'chil'dren

great'-grand'daugh'ter

great'-grand'fa'ther

great'-grand'moth'er

great'-grand'par'ent

great'-grand'son'

great'-heart'ed

great'ly

great'-neph'ew

great'ness

great'-niece'

great'-un'cle

grebe

Gre'cian

Gre'co-Ro'man

Greece

greed

greed'i · ly

greed'i · ness

greed'y
  greed'i · er, greed'i · est

Greek

green

green'back'

green' belt'

Green' Be · ret'

green'er · y
  pl. green'er · ies

green'-eyed'

green'gage'

green'gro'cer

green'horn'

green'house'

green'ing

Green'land

green'ness

green'room'

greens'keep'er

green'sward'

Green'wich

greet

greet'er

greet'ing

gre · gar'i · ous

Gre · go'ri · an

grem'lin

gre · nade'

Gre · na'da

gren'a · dier'

gren'a · dine'

grew

grey

grey'hound'

grid

grid'dle
  grid'dled, grid'dling

grid'dle · cake'

grid'i'ron

grief

grief'-strick'en

Grieg

griev'ance

grieve
  grieved, griev'ing

griev'ous

grif'fin

grill (*utensil*)
  (SEE grille)

grille or grill
  (*grating*)
  (SEE grill)

grill'work'

grim
  grim'mer, grim'mest

grim'ace
  grim'aced, grim'ac · ing

grime
  grimed, grim'ing

grim'i · ness

grim'y
  grim'i · er, grim'i · est

grin
  grinned, grin'ning

grind
  ground, grind'ing

grind'er

grind'stone'

grin'go
  pl. grin'gos

gri'ot

grip (*hold*)
  gripped or gript,
  grip'ping
  (SEE gripe *and* grippe)

gripe (*complain*)
  griped, grip'ing
  (SEE grip *and* grippe)

grippe (*influenza*)
   (SEE grip and gripe)

gris'gris'
   pl. gris'gris

gris'li · ness

gris'ly (*gruesome*)
   gris'li · er, gris'li · est
   (SEE gristly and
   grizzly)

grist

gris'tle

gris'tli · ness

gris'tly (*of cartilage*)
   gris'tli · er, gris'tli · est
   (SEE grisly and grizzly)

grist'mill'

grit
   grit'ted, grit'ting

grits

grit'ti · ness

grit'ty
   grit'ti · er, grit'ti · est

griz'zle
   griz'zled, griz'zling

griz'zly (*gray*)
   (*adj.*) griz'zli · er,
   griz'zli · est; pl. griz'zlies
   (SEE grisly and gristly)

groan (*moan*)
   (SEE grown)

groats

gro'cer

gro'cer · y
   pl. gro'cer · ies

grog

grog'gi · ly

grog'gi · ness

grog'gy
   grog'gi · er, grog'gi · est

groin

grom'met

groom

groove
   grooved, groov'ing

groov'y
   groov'i · er, groov'i · est

grope
   groped, grop'ing

gros'beak'

gros'grain'

gross

gro · tesque'

gro · tesque'ly

grot'to
   pl. grot'toes or grot'tos

grouch

grouch'i · ly

grouch'i · ness

grouch'y
   grouch'i · er,
   grouch'i · est

ground

ground'er

ground' floor'

ground' glass'

ground' hog'

ground'keep'er

ground'less

ground'nut'

ground' rule'

ground'swell'

ground'work'

group

group'er

grou'pie

grouse
   pl. grouse or grous'es

grouse
   groused, grous'ing

grout

grove

grov'el
   grov'eled or grov'elled,
   grov'el · ing or
   grov'el · ling

grow
   grew, grown, grow'ing

grow'er

growl

growl'er

grown (*mature*)
   (SEE groan)

grown'-up' (*adj.*)

grown'up' (*n.*)

growth

grub
   grubbed, grub'bing

grub'i · ly

grub'bi · ness

grub'by
   grub'bi · er, grub'bi · est

grub'stake'
   grub'staked',
   grub'stak'ing

grudge
   grudged, grudg'ing

grudg'ing · ly

gru'el

gru'el · ing or
   gru'el · ling

grue'some

gruff

gruff'ly

grum'ble
   grum'bled, grum'bling

grum'bler

grump

grump'i · ly

grump'i · ness

grump'y
   grump'i · er, grump'i · est

grun'ion

grunt

Gru · yère'

G'-string'

gua'ca · mo'le

Gua'dal · ca · nal'

Gua'de · loupe'

Guam

gua · na'co

gua'no

gua'ra · ní'
   pl. gua'ra · ní' or
   gua'ra · nís'

guar'an · tee'
   guar'an · teed',
   guar'an · tee'ing

guar'an · tor'

guar'an · ty'
   pl. guar'an · ties'
   (*v.*) guar'an · tied',
   guar'an · ty'ing

guard

guard'ed

guard'house'

guard'i · an

guard'rail'

guard'room'

guards'man
   pl. guards'men

Guar · ne'ri · us
   pl. Guar · ne'ri · us · es

Gua'te · ma'la

Gua'te · ma'lan

gua'va

gu'ber · na · to'ri · al

gudg'eon

guer'don

Guern'sey
  pl. Guern'seys

guer · ril'la (*soldier*)
  (SEE gorilla)

guess
  pl. guess'es

guess'ti · mate

guess'work'

guest

guest'house'

guest' room'

guf · faw'

Gui · an'a

Gui'a · nese'

guid'a · ble

guid'ance

guide
  guid'ed, guid'ing

guide'book'

guide'line'

guide'post'

gui'don

guild (*organization*)
  (SEE gild)

guil'der

guild'hall'

guile

guile'ful

guile'ful · ly

guile'less

guil'lo · tine' (*n.*)

guil'lo · tine' (*v.*)
  guil'lo · tined',
  guil'lo · tin'ing

guilt (*blame*)
  (SEE gilt)

guilt'i · ly

guilt'i · ness

guilt'less

guilt'y
  guilt'i · er, guilt'i · est

guimpe

Guin'ea

Guin'e · an

guin'ea pig'

guise
  guised, guis'ing

gui · tar'

gui · tar'ist

gulch

gulf

gulf'weed'

gull

gul'let

gul'li · bil'i · ty

gul'li · ble

gul'li · bly

gul'ly
  pl. gul'lies; (*v.*)
  gul'lied, gul'ly · ing

gulp

gum
  gummed, gum'ming

gum'bo
  pl. gum'bos

gum'boil'

gum'drop'

gum'mi · ness

gum'my
  gum'mi · er, gum'mi · est

gump'tion

gum'shoe'
  gum'shoed',
  gum'shoe'ing

gum'wood'

gun
  gunned, gun'ning

gun'boat'

gun'cot'ton

gun'fight'
  gun'fought',
  gun'fight'ing

gun'fire'

gung' ho'

gunk

gun'lock'

gun'man
  pl. gun'men

gun'-met'al

gun' moll'

gun'ner

gun'ner · y

gun'ny
  pl. gun'nies

gun'ny · sack'

gun'point'

gun'pow'der

gun'run'ner

gun'run'ning

gun'ship'

gun'shot'

gun'shy'

gun'sling'er

gun'smith'

gun'wale

gup'py
  pl. gup'pies

gur'gle
  gur'gled, gur'gling

Gur'kha
  pl. Gur'khas or
  Gur'kha

gu'ru

gush

gush'er

gush'y
  gush'i · er, gush'i · est

gus'set

gust

gus'ta · to'ry

gust'i · ly

gust'i · ness

gus'to

gust'y
  gust'i · er, gust'i · est

gut
  gut'ted, gut'ting

Gu'ten · berg'

gut'less

guts'y
  guts'i · er, guts'i · est

gut'ta-per'cha

gut'ter

gut'ter · snipe'

gut'tur · al

gut'tur · al · ly

guy
  guyed, guy'ing

Guy · a'na

Guy'a · nese'

guz'zle
  guz'zled, guz'zling

gym
gym·na'si·um
  pl. gym·na'si·ums or gym·na'si·a
gym'nast
gym·nas'tic
gym·nas'tics
gym'no·sperm'
gyn'e·co·log'i·cal
gy'ne·col'o·gist
gy'ne·col'o·gy

gyp
  gypped, gyp'ping
gyp'per
gyp'sum
Gyp'sy
  pl. Gyp'sies
gy'rate·
  gy'rat·ed, gy'rat·ing
gy·ra'tion
gy'ra·tor
gyr'fal'con

gy'ro
  pl. gy'ros
gy'ro·com'pass
gy'ro·mag·net'ic
gy'ro·scope'
gy'ro·scop'ic
gy'ro·sta'bi·liz'er
gy'ro·stat'
gyve (*shackle*)
  gyved, gyv'ing
  (SEE jive)

H

ha'ba·ne'ra
ha'be·as cor'pus
hab'er·dash'er
hab'er·dash'er·y
  pl. hab'er·dash'er·ies
hab'it
hab'it·a·bil'i·ty
hab'it·a·ble
hab'it·a·bly
ha'bi·tant
hab'i·tat'
hab'i·ta'tion
hab'it-form'ing
ha·bit'u·al
ha·bit'u·al·ly
ha·bit'u·ate'
  ha·bit'u·at'ed,
  ha·bit'u·at'ing
ha·bit'u·a'tion
ha·bit'u·é'
ha·chure'
ha'ci·en'da
  pl. ha'ci·en'das
hack
hack'a·more'
hack'le
  hack'led, hack'ling
hack'man
  pl. hack'men
hack'ney
  pl. hack'neys
hack'neyed
hack'saw'
hack'work'
had

Ha·das'sah
had'dock
  pl. had'dock or
  had'docks
Ha'des
had'n't
haf'ni·um
haft
hag
Hag·ga'dah
  pl. Hag·ga'doth or
  Hag·ga'dahs
hag'gard
hag'gis
hag'gle
  hag'gled, hag'gling
hag'gler
Hag'i·og'ra·pha
hag'i·og'ra·pher
hag'i·og'ra·phy
hag'rid'den
Hague
hai'ku
hail (*ice; shout*)
  (SEE hale)
hail'stone'
hail'storm'
hair (*furlike growth*)
  (SEE hare)
hair'breadth'
hair'brush'
  pl. hair'brush'es
hair'cloth'
hair'cut'
hair'do'
  pl. hair'dos'

hair'dress'er
hair'dress'ing
hair'less
hair'line'
hair' net'
hair'piece'
hair'pin'
hair'-rais'ing
hair's-breadth'
hair'spray'
hair'spring'
hair' trig'ger
hair·i·ness
hair'y (*having hair*)
  hair'i·er, hair'i·est
  (SEE harry)
Hai'ti
Hai'tian
hajj
  pl. hajj'es
haj'ji
  pl. haj'jis
hake
  pl. hake or hakes
ha'kim
Ha·la'kah
ha·la'tion
hal'berd
hal'cy·on
hale (*haul; healthy*)
  (*adj.*) hal'er, hal'est;
  (*v.*) haled, hal'ing
hal'er
half
  pl. halves

half'-and-half'

half'back'

half'-baked'

half'-breed'

half' broth'er

half'-caste'

half'-cocked'

half' dol'lar

half'heart'ed

half'-hour'

half'-life'
　pl. half'-lives'

half'-mast'

half'-moon'

half' note'

half' rest'

half' sis'ter

half'-slip'

half'-staff'

half' step'

half' time'

half'tone'

half'-track'

half'-truth'

half'way'

half'-wit'

half'-wit'ted

hal'i • but
　pl. hal'i • but or
　hal'i • buts

hal'ide

Hal'i • fax'

hal'ite

hal'i • to'sis

hall (corridor)
　(SEE haul)

hal'le • lu'jah

hall'mark'

hal • lo'
　pl. hal • los'; (v.)
　hal • loed', hal • lo'ing

hal'low

Hal'low • een'

hal • lu'ci • nate'
　hal • lu'ci • nat'ed,
　hal • lu'ci • nat'ing

hal • lu'ci • na'tion

hal • lu'ci • na • to'ry

hal • lu'cin • o • gen'

hal • lu'ci • no • gen'ic

hall'way'

ha'lo
　pl. ha'los or ha'loes;
　(v.) ha'loed, ha'lo • ing

hal'o • gen

hal'oid

halt

hal'ter

hal • vah'

halve
　halved, halv'ing

hal'yard

ham
　hammed, ham'ming

Ham'burg

ham'burg'er

Ham'il • ton

ham'let

Ham'mar • skjöld'

ham'mer

ham'mer • head'

ham'mer lock'

ham'mer • toe'

ham'mock

Ham'mu • ra'bi

ham'per

ham'ster

ham'string'
　ham'strung',
　ham'string'ing

hand

hand'bag'

hand'ball'

hand'bar'row

hand'bill'

hand'book'

hand'car'

hand'cart'

hand'clasp'

hand'cuff'

Han'del

hand'ful'
　pl. hand'fuls'

hand'gun'

hand'i • cap'
　han'di • capped',
　han'di • cap'ping

hand'i • cap'per

hand'i • craft'

hand'i • crafts'man

hand'i • ly

hand'i • ness

hand'i • work'

hand'ker • chief

han'dle
　han'dled, han'dling

han'dle • bar'

han'dler

hand'made' (made
　by hand)
　(SEE handmaid)

hand'maid'
　(attendant)
　(SEE handmade)

hand'maid'en

hand'-me-down'

hand'off

hand'out'

hand'pick'

hand'rail'

hand'saw'

hands'-down'

hand'set'
　hand'set', hand'set'ting

hand'shake'

hand'some
　(attractive)
　(SEE hansom)

hand'spike'

hand'spring'

hand'stand'

hand'-to-hand'

hand'-to-mouth'

hand'work'

hand'wo'ven

hand'writ'ing

hand'y
　hand'i • er, han'di • est

han'dy • man'
　pl. han'dy • men'

hang
　hung or hanged,
　hang'ing

hang'ar (airplane
　shed)
　(SEE hanger)

hang' dog'

hang'er (*that which hangs*)
(SEE hangar)
hang'er-on'
hang' glid'er
hang' glid'ing
hang'ing
hang'man
pl. hang'men
hang'nail'
hang'out'
hang'o'ver
hang'-up'
hank
han'ker
han'ky or han'kie
pl. han'kies
han'ky-pan'ky
Ha·noi'
han'som (*carriage*)
(SEE handsome)
Ha'nuk·kah
hap·haz'ard (*adj.,
adv.*)
hap'haz'ard (*n.*)
hap'less
hap'loid
hap'pen
hap'pen·ing
hap'pen·stance'
hap'pi·ly
hap'pi·ness
hap'py
hap'pi·er, hap'pi·est
hap'py-go-luck'y
ha'ra-ki'ri
ha·rangue'
ha·rangued',
ha·rangu'ing
ha·rangu'er
har'ass
har'ass·ment
Har'bin
har'bin·ger
har'bor
har'bor·age
har'bor mas'ter
hard
hard'-and-fast'

hard'back'
hard'ball'
hard'-bit'ten
hard'-boiled'
hard·bound'
hard'-core' (*adj.*)
hard'cov'er
hard'en
har'dened
hard' hat'
hard'-head'ed
hard'-heart'ed
har'di·hood'
har'di·ly
har'di·ness
Har'ding
hard'-line'
hard'-lin'er
hard'ly
hard'-of-hear'ing
hard'pan'
hard'-pressed'
hard' rock'
hard'scrab'ble
hard'-shell'
hard'ship
hard'tack'
hard'top'
hard'ware'
hard'wood'
hard'work'ing
har'dy
har'di·er, har'di·est
Har'dy
hare (*animal*)
pl. hares or hare
(SEE hair)
hare'brained'
Ha're Krish'na
hare'lip'
hare'lipped'
har'em
har'i·cot'
hark
hark'en
Har'lem
har'le·quin

har'lot
harm
harm'ful
harm'ful·ly
harm'less
har·mon'ic
har·mon'i·ca
har·mon'i·cal·ly
har·mon'ics
har·mo'ni·ous
har·mo'ni·um
har'mo·ni·za'tion
har'mo·nize'
har'mo·nized',
har'mo·niz'ing
har'mo·ny
pl. har'mo·nies
har'ness
harp
harp'ist
har·poon'
harp'si·chord'
Har'py
pl. Har'pies
har'ri·dan
har'ri·er
Har'ris·burg'
Har'ri·son
har'row
har'ry (*torment*)
har'ried, har'ry·ing
(SEE hairy)
harsh
harsh'ly
hart (*deer*)
pl. harts or hart
(SEE heart)
har'te·beest'
pl. har'te·beests' or
har'te·beest'
Hart'ford
har'um-scar'um
har'vest
har'ves·ter
has'-been'
ha'sen·pfef'fer
hash
hash'ish or hash'eesh
has'n't

hasp
has'sle
 has'sled, has'sling
has'sock
haste
 hast'ed, hast'ing
has'ten
hast'i·ly
hast'i·ness
hast'y
 hast'i·er, hast'i·est
hat
hat'box'
 pl. hat'box'es
hatch
hatch'back'
hat'check'
hatch'er·y
 pl. hatch'er·ies
hatch'et
hatch'et man'
 pl. hatch'et men'
hatch'ing
hatch'way'
hate
 hat'ed, hat'ing
hate'ful
hate'ful·ly
ha'tred
hat'ter
hau'berk
haugh'ty
 haugh'ti·er,
 haugh'ti·est
haugh'ti·ly
haugh'ti·ness
haul (drag)
 (SEE hall)
haul'age
haunch
 pl. haunch'es
haunt
haunt'ed
haunt'ing
haute cou·ture'
haute cui·sine'
hau·teur'
Ha·van'a
have
 had, hav'ing

ha'ven
have'-not'
have'n't
hav'er·sack'
hav'er·sack'
hav'oc
 hav'ocked, hav'ock·ing
haw
Ha·wai'i
Ha·wai'ian
hawk
hawk'er
hawk'ish
haw'ser
haw'thorn'
Haw'thorne'
hay (grass)
 (SEE hey)
hay'cock'
Haydn
Hayes
hay' fe'ver
hay'fork'
hay'loft'
hay'mow'
hay'rack'
hay'seed'
hay'stack'
hay'wire'
haz'ard
haz'ard·ous
haze
 hazed, haz'ing
ha'zel
ha'zel·nut'
ha'zi·ly
ha'zi·ness
ha'zy
 ha'zi·er, ha'zi·est
H'-bomb'
he
head
head'ache'
head'band'
head'board'
head'cheese'
head'dress'
 pl. head'dress'es

head'er
head'first'
head'gear'
head'hunt'er
head'hunt'ing
head'i·ly
head'i·ness
head'ing
head'land
head'less
head'light'
head'line'
 head'lined', head'lin'ing
head'lin'er
head'long'
head'mas'ter
head'mis'tress
 pl. head'mis'tress·es
head'note'
head'-on'
head'phone'
head'piece'
head'quar'ters
 pl. head'quar'ters
head'rest'
head'set'
head' shop'
heads'man
 pl. heads'man
head'stall'
head' start'
head'stone'
head'strong'
head'wait'er
head'wa'ters
head'way'
head'wind'
head'work'
head'y
 head'i·er, head'i·est
heal (cure)
 (SEE heel)
heal'er
health'ful
health'ful·ly
health'i·ly
health'i·ness
health'y
 health'i·er, health'i·est

heap

hear (*listen*)
heard, hear'ing
(SEE here)

heard (*pt. of* hear)
(SEE herd)

hear'er

hear'ing

heark'en

hear'say'

hearse

heart (*body organ*)
(SEE hart)

heart'ache'

heart' at·tack'

heart'beat'

heart'break'

heart'bro'ken

heart'burn'

heart'en

heart'felt'

hearth

hearth'stone'

heart'i·ly

heart'i·ness

heart'land'

heart'less

heart'rend'ing

heart'sick'

heart'strings'

heart'-to-heart'

heart'warm'ing

heart'wood'

heart'y
heart'i·er, heart'i·est

heat

heat'ed

heat'ed·ly

heat'er

heath

hea'then
pl. hea'thens or
hea'then

heath'er

heat'stroke'

heat' wave'

heave
heaved or (*esp. naut.*)
hove, heav'ing

heave'-ho'

heav'en

heav'en·ly

heav'en·ward

heav'i·er-than-air'

heav'i·ly

heav'i·ness

heav'y
heav'i·er, heav'i·est
pl. heav'ies

heav'y-du'ty

heav'y-hand'ed

heav'y-heart'ed

heav'y·set'

heav'y·weight'

He·bra'ic

He'brew

heck

heck'le
heck'led, heck'ling

heck'ler

hec'tare

hec'tic

hec'ti·cal·ly

hec'to·gram'

hec'to·graph'

hec'to·li'ter or
hec'to·li'tre

hec'to·me'terswor
hec'to·me'tre

Hec'tor

hedge
hedged, hedg'ing

hedge'hog'

hedge'hop'
hedge'hopped',
hedge'hop'ping

hedge'row'

he'don·ism'

he'don·ist

he'do·nis'tic

hee'bie-jee'bies

heed

heed'ful

heed'ful·ly

heed'less

hee'haw'

heel (*foot; tilt*)
(SEE heal)

heel'-and-toe'

heft

heft'y
heft'i·er, heft'i·est

He'gel

He·ge'li·an

he·gem'o·ny
pl. he·gem'o·nies

He·gi'ra

heif'er

height

height'en

Heim'lich

Hei'ne

hei'nous

heir (*inheritor*)
(SEE air *and* ere)

heir'ess

heir'loom'

heist

held

Hel'e·na

Hel'ens

hel'i·cal

hel'i·coid'

Hel'i·con'

hel'i·cop'ter

he'li·o·cen'tric

he'li·o·graph'

he'li·o·trope'

hel'i·pad'

hel'i·port'

he'li·um

he'lix
pl. hel'i·ces' or
he'lix·es

hell

hell'bent'

hell'cat'

hel'le·bore'

Hel·len'ic

Hel'len·ism'

Hel'len·ist

Hel'len·is'tic

hell'fire'

hell'gram·mite'

hell'hole'

hel'lion

hell'ish
hel'lo
helm
hel'met
helms'man
  pl. helms'men
hel'ot
help
help'er
help'ful
help'ful·ly
help'ing
help'less
help'mate'
Hel'sin·ki
hel'ter-skel'ter
helve
  helved, helv'ing
hem
  hemmed, hem'ming
he'-man'
  pl. he'-men'
hem'a·tite'
hem'a·to·log'i·cal
hem'a·tol'o·gist
hem'a·tol'o·gy
Hem'ing·way'
he·mip'ter·ous
hem'i·sphere'
hem'i·spher'ic
hem'line'
hem'lock'
he'mo·glo'bin
he'mo·phil'i·a
he'mo·phil'i·ac'
hem'or·rhage
  hem'or·rhaged,
  hem'or·rhag·ing
hem'or·rhag'ic
hem'or·rhoid'
he'mo·stat'
hemp
hem'stitch'
  pl. hem'stitch'es
hen
hence
hence'forth'
hench'man
  pl. hench'men

hen'na
hen'peck'
hen'ry
  pl. hen'ries or hen'rys
hep'a·rin
he·pat'ic
he·pat'i·ca
hep'a·ti'tis
Hep'ple·white'
hep'ta·gon'
hep·tag'o·nal
hep·tam'e·ter
her
her'ald
he·ral'dic
her'ald·ry
  pl. her'ald·ries
herb
her·ba'ceous
herb'age
herb'al
herb'al·ist
her·bar'i·um
  pl. her·bar'i·ums or
  her·bar'i·a
her'bi·cid'al
herb'i·cide'
her'biv·ore'
her·biv'o·rous
her·cu·le'an
Her'cu·les'
herd (flock)
  (SEE heard)
herd'er
here (present)
  (SEE hear)
here'a·bout'
here'a·bouts'
here·af'ter
here·by'
he·red'i·tar'y
he·red'i·ty
  pl. he·red'i·ties
Her'e·ford
here·in'
here'in·af'ter
here·of'
here·on'

her'e·sy
  pl. her'e·sies
her'e·tic
he·ret'i·cal
here·to'
here'to·fore'
here·un'der
here·un·to'
here'up·on'
here·with'
her'it·a·ble
her'it·age
her·maph'ro·dite'
her·maph'ro·dit'ic
Her'mes
her·met'ic
her·met'i·cal·ly
her'mit
her'mit·age
her'ni·a
  pl. her'ni·as or
  her'ni·ae'
her'ro
  pl. he'roes
Her'od
He·rod'o·tus
he·ro'ic
her'o·in (drug)
  (SEE heroine)
her'o·ine (heroic
  woman)
  (SEE heroin)
her'o·ism'
her'on
her'pes
her·pe·tol'o·gist
her·pe·tol'o·gy
her'ring
her'ring·bone'
hers
her·self'
hertz
  pl. hertz or hertz'es
hes'i·tance
hes'i·tan·cy
  pl. hes'i·tan·cies
hes'i·tant
hes'i·tate'
  hes'i·tat'ed,
  hes'i·tat'ing

hes'i·tat'er

hes'i·ta'tion

Hes'sian

het'er·o·dox'

het'er·o·dox'y
  pl. het'er·o·dox'ies

het'er·o·dyne'
  het'er·o·dyned',
  het'er·o·dyn'ing

het'er·o·ge·ne'i·ty

het'er·o·ge'ne·ous

het'er·o·sex'u·al

het'er·o·sex'u·al'i·ty

heu·ris'tic

hew (*cut*)
  hewed, hewed or hewn,
  hew'ing
  (SEE hue)

hex
  pl. hex'es

hex'a·chlo'ro·phene'

hex'a·gon'

hex·ag'o·nal

hex'a·gram'

hex'a·he'dral

hex'a·he'dron
  pl. hex'a·he'drons or
  hex'a·he'dra

hex·am'e·ter

hey (*shout*)
  (SEE hay)

hey'day'

hi (*hello*)
  (SEE high *and* hie)

hi·a'tus
  pl. hi·a'tus·es or
  hi·a'tus

hi·ba'chi

hi'ber·nate'
  hi'ber·nat'ed,
  hi'ber·nat'ing

hi'ber·na'tion

hi'ber·na'tor

Hi·ber'ni·a

hi·bis'cus
  pl. hi·bis'cus·es

hic'cough

hic'cup
  hic'cuped or
  hic'cupped, hic'cup·ing
  or hic'cup·ping

hick

hick'ey

hick'o·ry
  pl. hick'o·ries

hid

hi·dal'go
  pl. hi·dal'gos

hide
  hid, hid'den or hid,
  hid'ing

hid'er

hide'-and-seek'

hide'a·way'

hide'bound'

hid'e·ous

hide'out'

hie (*hurry*)
  hied, hie'ing or hy'ing
  (SEE high *and* hi)

hi'er·ar'chic

hi'er·ar'chi·cal

hi'er·ar'chi·cal·ly

hi'er·ar'chy
  pl. hi'er·ar'chies

hi'er·o·glyph'

hi'er·o·glyph'ic

hi'-fi'

hig'gle·dy-pig'gle·dy

high (*tall*)
  (SEE hie *and* hi)

high'ball'

high'born'

high'boy'

high'bred'

high'brow'

high'chair'

high'-class'

high'er-up'

high'fa·lu'tin or
  hi'fa·lu'tin

high' fi·del'i·ty

high'-flown'

high'-fly'ing

high'-grade'

high'-hand'ed

high' jump'

high'-keyed'

high'land

High'land·er

high'-lev'el

high'light'
  high'light'ed,
  high'light'ing

high'ly

High' Mass'

high'mind'ed

high'ness

high'-oc'tane

high'-pitched'

high'-pres'sure
  high'-pres'sured,
  high'-pres'sur·ing

high' priest'

high'-rise'

high'road'

high' school'

high'-sound'ing

high'-speed'

high'-spir'it·ed

high'-strung'

high'tail'

high'-ten'sion

high'-test'

high'-toned'

high'-wa'ter mark'

high'way'

high'way'man
  pl. high'way'men

hi'jack'

hi'jack'er

hike
  hiked, hik'ing

hik'er

hi·lar'i·ous

hi·lar'i·ty

hill

hill'bil'ly
  pl. hill'bil'lies

hill'ock

hill'side'

hill'top'
  hill'topped', hill'top'ping

hill'y
  hill'i·er, hill'i·est

hilt

him (*that man*)
  (SEE hymn)

Him'a·la'yas

him·self'

hind

hin'der
Hin'di
hind'most'
hind'quar'ter
hin'drance
hind'sight'
Hin'du
Hin'du·ism'
Hin'du·sta'ni
hinge
  hinged, hing'ing
hin'ny
  pl. hin'nies; (*v.*)
  hin'nied, hin'ny·ing
hint
hin'ter·land'
hip
  hipped, hip'ping
hip'bone'
hip'pie
hip'po
  pl. hip'pos
Hip·poc'ra·tes'
Hip'po·crat'ic
hip'po·drome'
hip'po·pot'a·mus
  pl. hip'po·pot'a·
  mus·es or
  hip'po·pot'a·mi'
hip'py
  (*adj.*) hip'pi·er,
  hip'pi·est;
  pl. hip'pies
hip'ster
hir'cine
hire
  hired, hir'ing
hire'ling
Hi'ro·shi'ge
Hi'ro·shi'ma
hir'sute
his
His·pan'ic
His'pan·io'la
hiss
his'ta·mine'
his'ta·min'ic
his'to·log'i·cal
his·tol'o·gist
his·tol'o·gy

his·tol'y·sis
his'to·lyt'ic
his·to'ri·an
his·tor'ic
his·tor'i·cal
his·tor'i·cal·ly
his'to·ric'i·ty
his·to'ri·og'ra·pher
his·to'ri·og'ra·phy
  pl. his·to'ri·og'ra·phies
his'to·ry
  pl. his'to·ries
his'tri·on'ic
his'tri·on'ics
hit
  hit, hit'ting
hit'-and-run'
hitch
hitch'hike'
  hitch'hiked',
  hitch'hik'ing
hitch'-hik'er
hith'er
hith'er·to'
Hit'ler
hit'-or-miss'
hit'ter
Hit'tite
hive
  hived, hiv'ing
hives
ho (*shout*)
  (SEE hoe)
hoa'gy or hoa'gie
  pl. hoa'gies
hoar (*white*)
  (SEE whore)
hoard (*accumulate*)
  (SEE horde)
hoar'frost'
hoarse (*gruff*)
  hoars'er, hoars'est
  (SEE horse)
hoarse'ly
hoars'en
hoarse'ness
hoar'i·ness
hoar'y
  hoar'i·er, hoar'i·est
hoax
  pl. hoax'es

hoax'er
hob
Hobbes
hob'ble
  hob'bled, hob'bling
hob'by
  pl. hob'bies
hob'by–horse'
hob'by·ist
hob'gob'lin
hob'nail'
hob'nob'
  hob'nobbed',
  hob'nob'bing
ho'bo
  pl. ho'bos or ho'boes
hock
hock'ey
ho'cus-po'cus
  ho'cus-po'cused,
  ho'cus-po'cus·ing
hod
hodge'podge'
hoe (*implement*)
  hoed, hoe'ing
  (SEE ho)
hoe'cake'
hoe'down'
hog
  hogged, hog'ging
ho'gan
Ho'garth
hog'back'
hog'gish
hogs'head'
hog'tie'
  hog'tied', hog'ty'ing
hog'wash'
hog'-wild'
hoi' pol·loi'
hoist
hoi'ty-toi'ty
ho'key
ho'kum
Ho'ku·sai'
hold
  held, hold'ing
hold'er
hold'ing
hold'out'

hold'o'ver

hold'up'

hole (cavity)
  holed, hol'ing
  (SEE whole)

hol'i·day

ho'li·er-than-thou'

ho'li·ness

ho'lism

ho·lis'tic

Hol'land

Hol'land·er

hol'an·daise'

Hol'land·er

hol'ler

hol'low

hol'ly
  pl. hol'lies

hol'ly·hock'

Hol'ly·wood'

Holmes

hol'mi·um

hol'o·caust'

ho'lo·gram'

hol'o·graph'

ho·log'ra·phy

Hol'stein

hol'ster

ho'ly (sacred)
  (adj.) ho'li·er,
  ho'li·est;
  pl. ho'lies
  (SEE wholly)

Ho'ly Ci'ty

Ho'ly Fa'ther

Ho'ly Ghost'

Ho'ly Spir'it

ho'ly·stone'

hom'age

hom'bre

hom'burg

home
  homed, hom'ing

home'bod'y
  pl. home'bod'ies

home'bred'

home'-brew'

home'com'ing

home'-grown'

home'land'

home'less

home'li·ness

home'ly
  home'li·er, home'li·est

home'made'

home'mak'er

ho·me·o·path'ic

ho·me·op'a·thist

ho·me·op'a·thy

ho·me·o·sta'sis

home'own'er

home' plate'

hom'er

Ho'mer

Ho·mer'ic

home'room'

home' run'

home'sick'

home'spun'

home'stead'

home'stead'er

home'stretch'

home'town'

home'ward

home'work'

hom'ey
  hom'i·er, hom'i·est

home'y·ness

hom'i·ci'dal

hom'i·cide'

hom'i·let'ic

hom'i·let'ics

hom'i·ly
  pl. hom'i·lies

hom'ing

hom'i·nid

hom'i·noid'

hom'i·ny

ho'mo·ge·ne'i·ty

ho'mo·ge'ne·ous

ho·mog'e·ni·za'tion

ho·mog'e·nize'
  ho·mog'e·nized',
  ho·mog'e·niz'ing

ho·mog'e·nous

hom'o·graph'

ho·mol'o·gous

hom'o·nym

ho·mon'y·mous

hom'o·phone'

ho·mop'ter·ous

Ho'mo sa'pi·ens

ho'mo·sex'u·al

ho'mo·sex'u·al'i·ty

ho·mun'cu·lus
  pl. ho·mun'cu·li'

hom'y
  hom'i·er, hom'i·est

hon'cho'
  pl. hon'chos'

Hon·du'ran

Hon·du'ras

hone
  honed, hon'ing

hon'est

hon'es·ty
  pl. hon'es·ties

hon'ey
  pl. hon'eys; (v.)
  hon'eyed or hon'ied,
  hon'ey·ing

hon'ey·bee'

hon'ey·bunch'

hon'ey·comb'

hon'ey·dew'

hon'eyed

hon'ey·moon'

hon'ey·suck'le

Hong' Kong' or
  Hong'Kong'

honk

honk'y-tonk'

Hon'o·lu'lu

hon'or

hon'or·a·ble

hon'or·a·bly

hon'o·rar'i·um
  pl. hon'o·rar'i·ums or
  hon'o·rar'i·a

hon'or·ar'y

hon'or·if'ic

hon'or roll'

hooch

hood

hood'ed

hood'lum

hoo′doo
pl. hoo′doos
(v.) hoo′dooed,
hoo′doo·ing

hood′wink′

hoo′ey

hoof
pl. hoofs or hooves

hook

hook′ah

hook′er

hook′up′

hook′worm′

hook′y

hoo′li·gan

hoop

hoop′la

hoo′poe

hoose′gow

Hoo′sier

hoot

hoot′en·an′ny
pl. hoot′en·an′nies

Hoo′ver

hop
hopped, hop′ping

hope
hoped, hop′ing

hope′ chest′

hope′ful

hope′ful·ly

hope′less

Ho′pi
pl. Ho′pis or Ho′pi

hop′per

hop′sack′ing

hop′scotch′

ho′ra

Hor′ace

Ho·ra′tian

horde (throng)
hord′ed, hord′ing
(SEE hoard)

hore′hound′

ho·ri′zon

hor′i·zon′tal

hor′i·zon′tal·ly

hor·mo′nal

hor′mone

Hor′muz

horn

horn′bill′

horn′book′

horned

hor′net

horn′pipe′

horn′-rimmed′

horn′swog′gle
horn′swog′gled,
horn′swog′gling

horn′y
horn′i·er, horn′i·est

hor′o·log′ic

ho·rol′o·gy

hor′o·scope′

hor·ren′dous

hor′ri·ble

hor′ri·bly

hor′rid

hor′ri·fy′
hor′ri·fied′,
hor′ri·fy′ing

hor′ror

hors de com·bat′

hors d'oeu′vre
pl. hors d'oeu′vre or
hors d'oeu′vres

horse (animal)
pl. hors′es or horse;
(v.) horsed, hors′ing
(SEE hoarse)

horse′back′

horse′flesh′

horse′fly′
pl. horse′flies′

horse′hair′

horse′hide′

horse′laugh′

horse′man
pl. horse′men

horse′play′

horse′pow′er

horse′rad′ish

horse′ sense′

horse′shoe′
horse′shoed′,
horse′shoe′ing

horse′whip′
horse′whipped′,
horse′whip′ping

horse′wom′an
pl. horse′wom′en

hors′y or hors′ey
hors′i·er, hors′i·est

hor′ta·tive

hor′ta·to′ry

hor′ti·cul′tur·al

hor′ti·cul′ture

hor′ti·cul′tur·ist

ho·san′na
pl. ho·san′nas; (v.)
ho·san′naed,
ho·san′na·ing

hose
pl. hose or hos′es;
(v.) hosed, hos′ing

Ho·se′a

ho′sier·y

hos′pice

hos′pi·ta·ble

hos′pi·ta·bly

hos′pi·tal

hos′pi·tal′i·ty
pl. hos′pi·tal′i·ties

hos′pi·tal·i·za′tion

hos′pi·tal·ize′
hos′pi·tal·ized′,
hos′pi·tal·iz′ing

host

hos′tage
hos′taged, hos′tag·ing

hos′tel (inn)
(SEE hostile)

hos′tel·er

hos′tel·ry

host′ess
pl. host′ess·es

hos′tile
(antagonistic)
(SEE hostel)

hos′tile·ly

hos·til′i·ty
pl. hos·til′i·ties

hos′tler

hot
hot′ter, hot′test

hot′bed′

hot′-blood′ed

hot′box′
pl. hot′box′es

hot′ cake′

hot′ cross′ buns′

hot' dog'
ho · tel'
hot'foot'
   pl. hot'foots'
hot'head'ed
hot'house'
hot'line'
hot' plate'
hot' rod'
hot' rod'der
hot'shot'
Hot'ten · tot'
hound
hour (time)
   (SEE our)
hour'glass'
   pl. hour'glass'es
hour'ly
house
   housed, hous'ing
house'boat'
house'boy'
house'break'er
house'bro'ken
house'clean'
house'clean'ing
house'coat'
house'fly'
   pl. house'flies'
house'ful'
   pl. house'fuls'
house'hold'
house'keep'er
house'lights'
house'maid'
house'man'
   pl. house'men'
house'moth'er
house' slip'per
house'top'
house'warm'ing
house'wife'
   pl. house'wives'
house'work'
hous'ing
Hous'ton
hov'el
   hov'eled, hov'el · ing
hov'er

Hov'er · craft'
   (Trademark)
how
how · be'it
how'dah
how'–do-you-do'
how'dy
   pl. how'dies
how · ev'er
how'itz · er
howl
howl'er
howl'ing
how'so · ev'er
hoy'den
Hoyle
hua · ra'che
hub'bub
hub'cap'
hu'bris
huck'le · ber'ry
   pl. huck'le · ber'ries
huck'ster
hud'dle
   hud'dled, hid'dling
Hud'son
hue (color)
   (SEE hew)
huff
huff'ish
huff'y
   huff'i · er, huff'i · est
huff'i · ly
huff'i · ness
hug
   hugged, hug'ging
huge
   hug'er, hug'est
huge'ly
huge'ness
hug'ger
hug'ger-mug'ger
Hu'go
Hu'gue · not'
huh
hu'la
hu'la hoop'
hu'la skirt'
hu'la-hu'la

hulk
hulk'ing
hull
hul'la · ba · loo'
   pl. hul'la · ba · loos'
hum
   hummed, hum'ming
hu'man
hu · mane'
hu · mane'ly
hu · mane'ness
hu'man · ism'
hu'man · ist
hu'man · is'tic
hu · man'i · tar'i · an
hu · man'i · tar'
   i · an · ism'
hu · man'i · ty
   pl. hu · man'i · ties
hu'man · i · za'tion
hu'man · ize'
   hu'man · ized',
   hu'man · iz'ing
hu'man · kind'
hu'man · ly
hu'man · ness
hu'man · oid'
hum'ble
   (adj.) hum'bler,
   hum'blest; (v.)
   hum'bled, hum'bling
hum'bug'
   hum'bugged',
   hum'bug'ging
hum'ding'er
hum'drum'
hu · mec'tant
hu'mer · al
hu'mer · us (bone)
   pl. hu'mer · i'
   (SEE humorous)
hu'mid
hu · mid'i · fi · ca'tion
hu · mid'i · fi'er
hu · mid'i · fy'
   hu · mid'i · fied',
   hu · mid'i · fy'ing
hu · mid'i · ty
hu'mi · dor'
hu · mil'i · ate'
   hu · mil'i · at'ed,
   hu · mil'i · at'ing

hu·mil′i·a′tion
hu·mil′i·ty
hum′ming·bird′
hum′mock
hu·mon′gous
hu′mor
hu′mor·esque′
hu′mor·ist
hu′mor·ous   (*funny*)
  (SEE humerus)
hump
hump′back′
humph
hu′mus
Hun
hunch
hunch′back′
hunch′backed′
hun′dred
  pl. hun′dreds or
  hun′dred
hun′dredth
hun′dred·weight′
  pl. hun′dred·weights′
  or hun′dred·weight′
hung
Hun·gar′i·an
Hun′ga·ry
hun′ger
hun′gri·ly
hun′gri·ness
hun′gry
  hun′gri·er, hun′gri·est
hunk
hun′ker
hunk′y-do′ry
Hun′nish
hunt
hunt′er
hunt′ing
hunt′ress
  pl. hunt′ress·es
hunts′man
  pl. hunts′men
hur′dle   (*barrier*)
  hur′dled, hur′dling
  (SEE hurtle)
hur′dy-gur′dy
  pl. hur′dy-gur′dies
hurl

hurl′er
hurl′y-burl′y
  pl. hurl′y-bur′lies
Hu′ron
hur·rah′
hur′ri·cane′
hur′ried
hur′ried·ly
hur′ry
  (*v.*) hur′ried,
  hur′ry·ing;
  pl. hur′ries
hurt
  hurt, hurt′ing
hurt′ful
hurt′ful·ly
hurt′ful·ness
hur′tle   (*fling*)
  hur′tled, hur′tling
  (SEE hurdle)
hus′band
hus′band·man
  pl. hus′band·men
hus′band·ry
hush
hush′-hush′
hush′ pup′py
husk
husk′er
husk′i·ly
husk′i·ness
husk′y   (*hoarse; big*)
  husk′i·er, husk′i·est
hus′ky   (*dog*)
  pl. hus′kies
Huss
hus·sar′
hus′sy
  pl. hus′sies
hus′tings
hus′tle
  hus′tled, hus′tling
hus′tler
hut
  hut′ted, hut′ting
hutch
  pl. hutch′es
Hux′ley
huz·zah′ or huz·za′
hy′a·cinth

hy′brid
hy′brid·i·za′tion
hy′brid·ize′
  hy′brid·ized′,
  hy′brid·iz′ing
hy·dran′gea
hy′drant
hy′drate
  hy′drat·ed, hy′drat·ing
hy·dra′tion
hy′dra·tor
hy·drau′lic
hy·drau′lics
hy′dride
hy′dro·car′bon
hy′dro·ce·phal′ic
hy′dro·ceph′a·lus
hy′dro·chlo′ric
hy′dro·cor′ti·sone′
hy′dro·dy·nam′ic
hy′dro·dy·nam′ics
hy′dro·e·lec′tric
hy′dro·e·lec·tric′i·ty
hy′dro·foil′
hy′dro·gen
hy′dro·gen·ate′
  hy′dro·gen·at′ed,
  hy′dro·gen·at′ing
hy′dro·gen·a′tion
hy·drog′e·nous
hy′dro·log′ic
hy·drol′o·gist
hy·drol′o·gy
hy·drol′y·sis
  pl. hy·drol′y·ses′
hy′dro·lyt′ic
hy·drom′e·ter
hy′dro·pho′bi·a
hy′dro·phone′
hy′dro·plane′
  hy′dro·planed′,
  hy′dro·plan′ing
hy′dro·pon′ics
hy′dro·sphere′
hy′dro·stat′ic
hy′dro·stat′ics
hy′dro·ther′a·py
hy′drous
hy·drox′ide

hy·e′na

hy′giene

hy′gi·en′ic

hy′gi·en′i·cal·ly

hy·gien′ist

hy·grom′e·ter

hy·grom′e·try

hy′gro·scope′

hy′gro·scop′ic

hy′men

hy′me·ne′al

hymn (*song*)
(SEE him)

hym′nal

hym′nist

hym′no·dy

hym·nol′o·gy

hype
hyped, hyp′ing

hy′per·a·cid′i·ty

hy′per·ac′tive

hy′per·bar′ic

hy·per′bo·la (*curve*)
(SEE hyperbole)

hy·per′bo·le
(*exaggeration*)
(SEE hyperbola)

hy′per·bol′ic

hy′per·crit′i·cal
(*very critical*)
(SEE hypocritical)

hy′per·crit′i·cal·ly
(*very critically*)
(SEE hypocritically)

hy′per·gly·ce′mi·a
(*high glucose*)
(SEE hypoglycemia)

hy′per·son′ic

hy′per·ten′sion

hy′per·ten′sive

hy′per·thy′roid

hy′per·thy′roid·ism′

hy′per·troph′ic

hy·per′tro·phy
pl. hy·per′tro·phies

hy′per·ven′ti·la′tion

hy′phen

hy′phen·ate′ (*v.*)
hy′phen·at′ed,
hy′phen·at′ing

hy′phen·ate (*adj.,
n.*)

hy′phen·a′tion

hyp·no′sis
pl. hyp·no′ses

hyp·not′ic

hyp·not′i·cal·ly

hyp′no·tism′

hyp′no·tist

hyp′no·tize′
hyp′no·tized′,
hyp′no·tiz′ing

hy′po
pl. hy′pos

hy′po·chon′dri·a

hy′po·chon′dri·ac′

hy·poc′ri·sy
pl. hy·poc′ri·sies

hyp′o·crite

hyp′o·crit′i·cal
(*insincere*)
(SEE hypercritical)

hyp′o·crit′i·cal·ly
(*insincerely*)
(SEE hypercritically)

hy′po·der′mic

hy′po·gly·ce′mi·a
(*low glucose*)
(SEE hyperglycemia)

hy·pot′e·nuse

hy′po·thal′a·mus
pl. hy′po·thal′a·mi′

hy·poth′e·cate′
hy·poth′e·cat′ed,
hy·poth′e·cat′ing

hy·poth′e·sis
pl. hy·poth′e·ses′

hy·poth′e·size′
hy·poth′e·sized′,
hy·poth′e·siz′ing

hy′po·thet′i·cal

hy′po·thet′i·cal·ly

hy′po·thy′roid·ism′

hy′rax
pl. hy′rax·es or
hy′ra·ces′

hy′son

hys′sop

hys′ter·ec′to·my
pl. hys′ter·ec′to·mies

hys·ter·e′sis

hys·te′ri·a

hys·ter′ic

hys·ter′i·cal

hys·ter′i·cal·ly

hys·ter′ics

I

i′amb

i·am′bic

i·at′ro·gen′ic

I·be′ri·a

i·be′ri·an

i′bex
pl. i′bex·es or ib′i·ces′
or i′bex

i·bi′dem

i′bis
pl. i′bis·es or i′bis

Ib′sen

Ic′a·rus

ice
iced, ic′ing

ice′berg

ice′boat′

ice′bound′

ice′box′
pl. ice′box·es

ice′break′er

ice′cap′

ice′-cold′

ice′ cream′

ice′ cube′

ice′house′

Ice′land

Ice·lan′dic

ice′man′
pl. ice′men′

ice′ pack′

ice′-skate′
  ice′-skat′ed, ice′-skat′ing
ich·neu′mon
ich′thy·o·log′ic
ich′thy·o·log′i·cal
ich′thy·ol′o·gist
ich′thy·ol′o·gy
i′ci·cle
i′ci·ly
i′ci·ness
ic′ing
i′con
i·con′o·clasm′
i·con′o·clast′
i·con′o·clas′tic
i′co·nog′ra·phy
  pl. i′co·nog′ra·phies
i′cy
  i′ci·er, i′ci·est
id
I′d
I′da·ho′
i·de′a
i·de′al
i·de′al·ism′
i·de′al·ist
i·de′al·is′tic
i·de′al·is′ti·cal·ly
i·de′al·i·za′tion
i·de′al·ize′
  i·de′al·ized′,
  i·de′al·iz′ing
i·de′al·ly
i′de·ate′
  i′de·at′ed, i′de·at′ing
i′de·a′tion
i·*dée fixe′*
  pl. i·*dées fixes′*
i′dem
i·den′ti·cal
i·den′ti·cal·ly
i·den′ti·fi′a·ble
i·den′ti·fi·ca′tion
i·den′ti·fi′er
i·den′ti·fy′
  i·den′ti·fied′,
  i·den′ti·fy′ing
i·den′ti·ty
  pl. i·den′ti·ties

id′e·o·gram′
id′e·o·graph′
i′de·o·log′ic
i′de·o·log′i·cal
i′de·ol′o·gist
i′de·ol′o·gy
  pl. i′de·ol′o·gies
ides
id′i·o·cy
  pl. id′i·o·cies
id′i·om
id′i·o·mat′ic
id′i·o·mat′i·cal·ly
id′i·o·syn′cra·sy
  pl. id′i·o·syn′cra·sies
id′i·o·syn·crat′ic
id′i·o·syn·crat′i·cal·ly
id′i·ot
id′i·ot′ic
id′i·ot′i·cal·ly
id′i·ot·ism′
i′dle (*doing nothing*)
  (*adj.*) i′dler, i′dlest;
  (*v.*) i′dled, i′dling
  (SEE idol *and* idyll)
i′dle·ness
i′dler
i′dly
i′dol (*worshipped
  image*)
  (SEE idle *and* idyll)
i·dol′a·ter
i·dol′a·trous
i·dol′a·try
  pl. i·dol′a·tries
i′dol·i·za′tion
i′dol·ize′
  i′dol·ized′, i′dol·iz′ing
i′dyll or i′dyl (*poem*)
  (SEE idle *and* idol)
i·dyl′lic
if
if′fy
ig′loo
  pl. ig′loos
ig′ne·ous
ig·nit′a·ble or
  ig·nit′i·ble
ig·nite′
  ig·nit′ed, ig·nit′ing

ig·ni′tion
ig·no′ble
ig·no′bly
ig′no·min′i·ous
ig′no·min′y
  pl. ig′no·min′ies
ig′no·ra′mus
  pl. ig′no·ra′mus·es
ig′no·rance
ig′no·rant
ig·nore′
  ig·nored′, ig·nor′ing
i·gua′na
i′ke·ba·na
i′kon
il′e·i′tis
il′e·um (*intestine*)
  pl. il′e·a
  (SEE ilium)
Il′i·ad
il′i·um (*bone*)
  pl. il′i·a
  (SEE ileum)
ilk
ill
  worse, worst
I′ll
ill′-ad·vised′
ill′-be′ing
ill′-bred′
il·le′gal
il′le·gal′i·ty
  pl. il′le·gal′i·ties
il·le′gal·ly
il·leg′i·bil′i·ty
il·leg′i·ble
il·leg′i·bly
il′le·git′i·ma·cy
  pl. il′le·git′i·ma·cies
il′le·git′i·mate (*adj.,
  n.*)
il′le·git′i·mate′ (*v.*)
  il′le·git′i·mat′ed,
  il′le·git′i·mat′ing
il′le·git′i·mate·ly
ill′-fat′ed
ill′-fa′vored
ill′-got′ten
ill′-hu′mored
il·lib′er·al

il·lic'it (*unlawful*)
(SEE elicit)

il·lim'it·able

il·lim'it·a·bly

Il'li·nois'

Il'li·nois'an

il·liq'uid

il·lit'er·a·cy
pl. il·lit'er·a·cies

il·lit'er·ate

il·lit'er·ate·ly

ill'-man'nered

ill'-na'tured

ill'ness

il·log'ic

il·log'i·cal

il·log'i·cal'i·ty
pl. il·log'i·cal'i·ties

il·log'i·cal·ly

ill'-starred'

ill'-tem'pered

ill'-timed'

ill'-treat'

il·lu'mi·nate (*v.*)
il·lu'mi·nat·ed,
il·lu'mi·nat·ing

il·lu'mi·nate (*adj., n.*)

il·lu'mi·na'tion

il·lu'mi·na'tor

il·lu'mine
il·lu'mined,
il·lu'min·ing

ill'-us'age

ill'-use'
ill'-used', ill'-us'ing

il·lu'sion (*false idea*)
(SEE allusion)

il·lu'sion·ist

il·lu'sive (*deceptive*)
(SEE allusive *and* elusive)

il·lu'so·ry

il'lus·trate'
il'lus·trat·ed,
il'lus·trat·ing

il'lus·tra'tion

il·lus'tra·tive

il·lus'tra·tor

il·lus'tri·ous

il'ly

I'm

im'age
im'aged, im'ag·ing

im'age·ry
pl. im'age·ries

im·ag'i·na·ble

im·ag'i·na·bly

im·ag'i·nar'y
pl. im·ag'i·nar'ies

im·ag'i·na'tion

im·ag'i·na·tive

im·ag'ine
im·ag'ined,
im·ag'in·ing

im'ag·ism'

im'ag·ist

i·mam'

i·mam'ate

im·bal'ance

im'be·cile

im'be·cil'i·ty
pl. im'be·cil'i·ties

im·bibe'
im·bibed', im·bib'ing

im·bro'glio
pl. im·bro'glios

im·brue'
im·brued', im·bru'ing

im·bue'
im·bued', im·bu'ing

im'i·ta·ble

im'i·tate'
im'i·tat·ed, im'i·tat'ing

im'i·ta'tion

im'i·ta'tive

im'i·ta'tor

im·mac'u·late

im·mac'u·late·ly

im'ma·nent (*being within*)
(SEE imminent *and* eminent)

im'ma·te'ri·al

im'ma·ture'

im'ma·tu'ri·ty

im·meas'ur·a·ble

im·meas'ur·a·bly

im·me'di·a·cy

im·me'di·ate

im·me'di·ate·ly

im'me·mo'ri·al

im·mense'

im·mense'ly

im·men'si·ty
pl. im·men'si·ties

im·merse'
im·mersed',
im·mers'ing

im·mer'sion

im'mi·grant

im'mi·grate'
im'mi·grat·ed,
im'mi·grat'ing

im'mi·gra'tion

im'mi·nence

im'mi·nent (*impending*)
(SEE immanent *and* eminent)

im·mis'ci·ble

im·mo'bile

im'mo·bil'i·ty

im·mo'bi·li·za'tion

im·mo'bi·lize'
im·mo'bi·lized',
im·mo'bi·liz'ing

im·mod'er·ate

im·mod'er·a'tion

im·mod'est

im·mod'es·ty

im'mo·late'
im'mo·lat·ed,
im'mo·lat'ing

im'mo·la'tion

im·mor'al

im'mo·ral'i·ty
pl. im'mo·ral'i·ties

im·mor'al·ly

im·mor'tal

im·mor'tal·ly

im'mor·tal'i·ty

im·mor'tal·ize'
im·mor'tal·ized',
im·mor'tal·iz'ing

im·mov'a·bil'i·ty

im·mov'a·ble

im·mov'a·bly

im·mune'

im·mu'ni·ty
pl. im·mu'ni·ties

im'mu·nize'
  im'mu·nized',
  im'mu·niz'ing
im'mu·nol'o·gist
im'mu·nol'o·gy
im·mure'
  im·mured',
  im·mur'ing
im·mu'ta·bil'i·ty
im·mu'ta·ble
im·mu'ta·bly
imp
im'pact (n.)
im·pact' (v.)
im·pact'ed
im·pac'tion
im·pair'
im·pair'ment
im·pal'a
  pl. im·pal'as or
  im·pal'a
im·pale'
  im·paled', im·pal'ing
im·pale'ment
im·pal'pa·bil'i·ty
im·pal'pa·ble
im·pal'pa·bly
im·pan'el
  im·pan'eled,
  im·pan'el·ing
im·part'
im·part'a·ble
im·par'tial
im·par'ti·al'i·ty
im·par'tial·ly
im·pass'a·ble (*not*
  passable)
  (SEE impossible)
im·pass'a·bly
im'passe
im·pass'i·ble
  (*unfeeling*)
  (SEE impassable)
im·pass'i·bly
im·pas'sioned
im·pas'sive
im·pas'sive·ly
im'pas·siv'i·ty
im·pa'tience
im·pa'ti·ens'
  pl. im·pa'ti·ens'

im·pa'tient
im·peach'
im·peach'a·ble
im·peach'ment
im·pec'ca·bil'i·ty
im·pec'ca·ble
im·pec'ca·bly
im'pe·cu'ni·ous
im·ped'ance
im·pede'
  im·ped'ed, im·ped'ing
im·ped'er
im·ped'i·ment
im·ped'i·men'ta
im·pel'
  im·pelled', im·pel'ling
im·pend'
im·pend'ing
im·pen'e·tra·
  bil'i·ty
im·pen'e·tra·ble
im·pen'e·tra·bly
im·pen'i·tence
im·pen'i·tent
im·per'a·tive
im'per·ceiv'a·ble
im'per·cep'ti·bil'i·ty
im'per·cep'ti·ble
im'per·cep'ti·bly
im'per·cep'tive
im·per'fect
im'per·fec'tion
im·per'fo·rate
im·pe'ri·al
im·pe'ri·al·ism'
im·pe'ri·al·ist
im·pe'ri·al·is'tic
im·pe'ri·al·ly
im·per'il
  im·per'iled or
  im·per'illed,
  im·per'il·ing or
  im·per'il·ling
im·pe'ri·ous
im·per'ish·a·bil'i·ty
im·per'ish·a·ble
im·per'ish·a·bly
im·per'ma·nence

im·per'ma·nen·cy
im·per'ma·nent
im·per'me·a·bil'i·ty
im·per'me·a·ble
im·per'me·a·bly
im·per'son·al
im·per'son·al·ly
im·per'son·al'i·ty
  pl. im·per'son·al'i·ties
im·per'son·ate' (v.)
  im·per'son·at'ed,
  im·per'son·at'ing
im·per'son·ate
  (*adj.*)
im·per'son·a'tion
im·per'son·a'tor
im·per'ti·nence
im·per'ti·nent
im'per·turb'a·bil'i·ty
im'per·turb'a·ble
im'per·turb'a·bly
im·per'vi·ous
im'pe·ti'go
im·pet'u·os'i·ty
  pl. im·pet'u·os'i·ties
im·pet'u·ous
im'pe·tus
  pl. im'pe·tus·es
im·pi'e·ty
  pl. im·pi'e·ties
im·pinge'
  im·pinged',
  im·ping'ing
im·pinge'ment
im'pi·ous
imp'ish
im·plac'a·bil'i·ty
im·plac'a·ble
im·plac'a·bly
im·plant' (v.)
im'plant (n.)
im'plan·ta'tion
im·plau'si·bil'i·ty
  pl. im·plau'si·bil'i·ties
im·plau'si·ble
im·plau'si·bly
im'ple·ment (n.)
im'ple·ment' (v.)
im'ple·men·ta'tion

im'pli·cate'
  im'pli·cat'ed,
  im'pli·cat'ing

im'pli·ca'tion

im·plic'it

im·plied'

im·plode'
  im·plod'ed,
  im·plod'ing

im·plore'
  im·plored', im·plor'ing

im·plo'sion

im·plo'sive

im·ply'
  im·plied', im·ply'ing

im'po·lite'

im·pol'i·tic

im·pon'der·a·bil'i·ty

im·pon'der·a·ble

im·pon'der·a·bly

im·port' (v.)

im'port (n.)

im·port'a·bil'i·ty

im·port'a·ble

im·por'tance

im·por'tant

im'por·ta'tion

im·port'er

im·por'tu·nate

im'por·tune'
  im'por·tuned',
  im'por·tun'ing

im'por·tu'ni·ty
  pl. im'por·tu'ni·ties

im·pose'
  im·posed, im·pos'ing

im·pos'er

im·pos'ing

im'po·si'tion

im·pos'si·bil'i·ty
  pl. im·pos'si·bil'i·ties

im·pos'si·ble

im·pos'si·bly

im'post

im·pos'tor or
  im·pos'ter

im·pos'ture

im'po·tence

im'po·ten·cy

im'po·tent

im·pound'

im·pov'er·ish

im·pov'er·ish·ment

im·prac'ti·ca·bil'i·ty

im·prac'ti·ca·ble

im·prac'ti·ca·bly

im·prac'ti·cal

im·prac'ti·cal'i·ty

im'pre·cate'
  im'pre·cat'ed,
  im'pre·cat'ing

im'pre·ca'tion

im'pre·ca'tor

im'pre·ca·to'ry

im·pre·cise'

im·pre·ci'sion

im·preg'na·ble

im·preg'na·bly

im·preg'nate
  im·preg'nat·ed,
  im·preg'nat·ing

im'preg·na'tion

im·preg'na·tor

im'pre·sa'ri·o
  pl. im'pre·sa'ri·os or
  (It.) im'pre·sa'ri

im·press' (v.)

im'press (n.)

im·press'i·ble

im·pres'sion

im·pres'sion·
  a·bil'i·ty

im·pres'sion·a·ble

im·pres'sion·a·bly

Im·pres'sion·ism'

Im·pres'sion·ist

Im·pres'sion·is'tic

im·pres'sive

im·pres'sive·ly

im·press'ment

im'pri·ma'tur

im'print (n.)

im·print' (v.)

im·pris'on

im·pris'on·ment

im·prob'a·bil'i·ty
  pl. im·prob'a·bil'i·ties

im·prob'a·ble

im·prob'a·bly

im·promp'tu

im·prop'er

im'pro·pri'e·ty
  pl. im'pro·pri'e·ties

im·prov'a·ble

im·prov'a·bil'i·ty

im·prove'
  im·proved',
  im·prov'ing

im·prove'ment

im·prov'i·dence

im·prov'i·dent

im·prov'i·sa'tion

im'pro·vise'
  im'pro·vised',
  im'pro·vis'ing

im'pro·vis'er

im·pru'dence

im·pru'dent

im'pu·dence

im'pu·dent

im·pugn'

im'pulse

im·pul'sion

im·pul'sive

im·pul'sive·ly

im·pu'ni·ty

im·pure'

im·pu'ri·ty
  pl. im·pu'ri·ties

im'pu·ta'tion

im·pute'
  im·put'ed, im·put'ing

in (within)
  (SEE inn)

in'a·bil'i·ty

in ab·sen'tia

in'ac·ces'si·bil'i·ty

in'ac·ces'si·ble

in'ac·ces'si·bly

in·ac'cu·ra·cy
  pl. in·ac'cu·ra·cies

in·ac'cu·rate

in·ac'tion

in·ac'ti·vate'
  in·ac'ti·vat'ed,
  in·ac'ti·vat'ing

in·ac'ti·va'tion

in·ac'tive

in'ac・tiv'i・ty

in・ad'e・qua・cy

in・ad'e・quate

in・ad'e・quate・ly

in'ad・mis'si・bil'i・ty

in'ad・mis'si・ble

in'ad・vert'ence

in'ad・vert'en・cy

in'ad・vert'ent

in'ad・vis'a・bil'i・ty

in'ad・vis'a・ble

in'ad・vis'a・bly

in・al'ien・a・ble

in・al'ter・a・bil'i・ty

in・al'ter・a・ble

in・al'ter・a・bly

in・am'o・ra'ta

in・ane'

in・an'i・mate

in・an'i・ty
　pl. in・an'i・ties

in・ap'pli・ca・bil'i・ty

in・ap'pli・ca・ble

in・ap'pli・ca・bly

in'ap・pre'ci・a・ble

in'ap・pre'ci・a・bly

in'ap・pre'ci・a・tive

in'ap・pro'pri・ate

in'ap・pro'pri・ate・ly

in・apt'　(unsuited)
　(SEE inept)

in・ap'ti・tude'

in・arch'

in'ar・tic'u・late

in'as・much' as'

in'at・ten'tion

in'at・ten'tive

in・au'di・bil'i・ty

in・au'di・ble

in・au'di・bly

in・au'gu・ral

in・au'gu・rate'
　in・au'gu・rat'ed,
　in・au'gu・rat'ing

in・au'gu・ra'tion

in'aus・pi'cious

in'-be・tween'

in'board'

in'born'

in'bound'

in'bred'

in'breed'
　in'bred', in'breed'ing

In'ca

in・cal'cu・la・bil'i・ty

in・cal'cu・la・ble

in・cal'cu・la・bly

in'can・des'cence

in'can・des'cent

in'can・ta'tion

in・ca'pa・bil'i・ty

in・ca'pa・ble

in・ca'pa・bly

in'ca・pac'i・tate'
　in'ca・pac'i・tat'ed,
　in'ca・pac'i・tat'ing

in'ca・pac'i・ty

in・car'cer・ate'　(v.)
　in・car'cer・at'ed,
　in・car'cer・at'ing

in・car'cer・ate　(adj.)

in・car'cer・a'tion

in・car'nate
　in・car'nat・ed,
　in・car'nat・ing

in'car・na'tion

in・cau'tious

in'cen・di・a・rism'

in・cen'di・ar'y
　pl. in・cen'di・ar'ies

in'cense
　in'censed, in'cens・ing

in・cense'
　in・censed', in・cens'ing

in・cen'tive

in・cep'tion

in・cep'tive

in・cer'ti・tude'

in・ces'sant

in'cest

in・ces'tu・ous

inch
　pl. inch'es

in・cho'ate

inch'worm'

in'ci・dence

in'ci・dent

in'ci・den'tal

in'ci・den'tal・ly

in・cin'er・ate'
　in・cin'er・at'ed,
　in・cin'er・at'ing

in・cin'er・a'tion

in・cin'er・a'tor

in・cip'i・ence

in・cip'i・en・cy

in・cip'i・ent

in・cise'
　in・cised', in・cis'ing

in・cised'

in・ci'sion

in・ci'sive

in・ci'sive・ly

in・ci'sive・ness

in・ci'sor

in'ci・ta'tion

in・cite'　(provoke)
　in・cit'ed, in・cit'ing
　(SEE insight)

in・cite'ment

in'ci・vil'i・ty
　pl. in'ci・vil'i・ties

in・clem'en・cy

in・clem'ent

in・clin'a・ble

in'cli・na'tion

in・cline'　(v.)
　in・clined', in・clin'ing

in'cline　(n.)

in・clined'

in'cli・nom'e・ter

in・clud'a・ble

in・clude'
　in・clud'ed, in・clud'ing

in・clud'ed

in・clu'sion

in・clu'sive

in・cog'ni・to'
　pl. in・cog'ni・tos'

in・cog'ni・zant

in'co・her'ence

in'co・her'ent

in'com・bus'ti・ble

in'come

in'com'ing

in'com・men'su・rate

in'com・mode'
　in'com・mod'ed,
　in'com・mod'ing

in·com·mo'di·ous
in·com·mu'ni·ca·
  bil'i·ty
in·com·mu'ni·ca·ble
in·com·mu'ni·ca·bly
in·com·mu'ni·ca'do
in·com·mu'ni·ca'tive
in·com·mut'a·bly
in·com·pa'ra·bil'i·ty
in·com·pa'ra·ble
in·com·pa'ra·bly
in·com·pat'i·bil'i·ty
in·com·pat'i·ble
in·com'pe·tence
in·com'pe·ten·cy
in·com'pe·tent
in'com·plete'
in'com·pre·hen'si·
  bil'i·ty
in'com·pre·
  hen'si·ble
in'com·pre·
  hen'si·bly
in'com·press'i·ble
in'con·ceiv'a·bil'i·ty
in'con·ceiv'a·ble
in'con·ceiv'a·bly
in'con·clu'sive
in·con'gru·ent
in·con'gru'i·ty
  pl. in'con·gru'i·ties
in·con'gru·ous
in'con·se·quent'
in'con·se·quen'tial
in'con·se·quen'tial·ly
in'con·sid'er·a·ble
in'con·sid'er·ate
in'con·sid'er·ate·ly
in'con·sist'ence
in'con·sist'en·cy
  pl. in'con·sist'en·cies
in'con·sist'ent
in'con·sol'a·bil'i·ty
in'con·sol'a·ble
in'con·sol'a·bly
in·con'so·nant
in'con·spic'u·ous

in·con'stan·cy
in·con'stant
in'con·test'a·bil'i·ty
in'con·test'a·ble
in'con·test'a·bly
in·con'ti·nence
in·con'ti·nent
in'con·tro·vert'i·
  bil'i·ty
in'con·tro·vert'i·ble
in'con·tro·vert'i·bly
in'con·ven'ience
  in'con·ven'ienced,
  in'con·ven'ienc·ing
in'con·ven'ient
in·cor'po·rate' *(v.)*
  in·cor'po·rat'ed,
  in·cor'po·rat'ing
in·cor'po·rate *(adj.)*
in·cor'po·rat'ed
in·cor'po·ra'tion
in·cor'po·ra'tor
in'cor·po're·al
in'cor·po're·al·ly
in'cor·po·re'i·ty
in'cor·rect'
in·cor'ri·gi·bil'i·ty
in·cor'ri·gi·ble
in·cor'ri·gi·bly
in'cor·rupt'
in'cor·rupt'i·bil'i·ty
in'cor·rupt'i·ble
in'cor·rupt'i·bly
in·crease' *(v.)*
  in·creased',
  in·creas'ing
in'crease *(n.)*
in·cred'i·bil'i·ty
in·cred'i·ble
in·cred'i·bly
in'cre·du'li·ty
in·cred'u·lous
in'cre·ment
in'cre·men'tal
in·crim'i·nate'
  in·crim'i·nat'ed,
  in·crim'i·nat'ing
in·crim'i·na'tion
in·crim'i·na·to'ry

in·crust'
in'crus·ta'tion
in'cu·bate'
  in'cu·bat'ed,
  in'cu·bat'ing
in'cu·ba'tion
in'cu·ba'tive
in'cu·ba'tor
in'cu·bus
in·cul'cate
  in·cul'cat·ed,
  in·cul'cat·ing
in'cul·ca'tion
in·cul'ca·tor
in·cul'pa·ble
in·cul'pate
  in·cul'pat·ed,
  in·cul'pat·ing
in'cul·pa'tion
in·cum'ben·cy
  pl. in·cum'ben·cies
in·cum'bent
in'cu·nab'u·la
  sing. in'cu·nab'u·lum
in·cur'
  in·curred', in·cur'ring
in·cur'a·bil'i·ty
in·cur'a·ble
in·cur'a·bly
in·cu'ri·ous
in·cur'sion
in·cur'sive
in'cus
  pl. in·cu'des or in'cus
in·debt'ed
in·de'cen·cy
  pl. in·de'cen·cies
in·de'cent
in'de·ci'pher·a·ble
in'de·ci'sion
in'de·ci'sive
in·dec'o·rous
in·deed'
in'de·fat'i·ga·bil'i·ty
in'de·fat'i·ga·ble
in'de·fat'i·ga·bly
in'de·fen'si·bil'i·ty
in'de·fen'si·ble
in'de·fen'si·bly
in'de·fin'a·ble

in·de·fin'a·bly
in·def'i·nite
in·def'i·nite·ly
in·def'i·nite·ness
in·del'i·bil'i·ty
in·del'i·ble
in·del'i·bly
in·del'i·ca·cy
  pl. in·del'i·ca·cies
in·del'i·cate
in·del'i·cate·ly
in·dem'ni·fi·ca'tion
in·dem'ni·fy'
  in·dem'ni·fied',
  in·dem'ni·fy'ing
in·dem'ni·ty
  pl. in·dem'ni·ties
in·dent' (*v.*)
in'dent (*n.*)
in'den·ta'tion
in·den'tion
in·den'ture
in·de·pend'ence
in·de·pend'en·cy
  pl. in·de·pend'en·cies
in·de·pend'ent
in'-depth'
in·de·scrib'a·bil'i·ty
in·de·scrib'a·ble
in·de·scrib'a·bly
in·de·struct'i·bil'i·ty
in·de·struct'i·ble
in·de·struct'i·bly
in·de·ter'min·a·ble
in·de·ter'mi·na·bly
in·de·ter'mi·na·cy
in·de·ter'mi·nate
in·de·ter'mi·nate·ly
in·de·ter'mi·na'tion
in'dex
  pl. in'dex·es or
  in'di·ces'
in'dex·er
In'di·a
In'di·an
In'di·an'a
In'di·an'i·an
In'di·an·ap'o·lis
In'di·an club'

In'dia pa'per
in'di·cate'
  in'di·cat'ed,
  in'di·cat'ing
in'di·ca'tion
in·dic'a·tive
in'di·ca'tor
in·di'ci·a
  pl. in·di'ci·a or
  in·di'ci·as
in·dict' (*accuse*)
  (SEE indite)
in·dict'a·ble
in·dict'er
in·dict'ment
In'dies
in·dif'fer·ence
in·dif'fer·ent
in'di·gence
in·dig'e·nous
in'di·gent
in·di·gest'i·bil'i·ty
in·di·gest'i·ble
in'di·ges'tion
in·dig'nant
in'dig·na'tion
in·dig'ni·ty
  pl. in·dig'ni·ties
in'di·go'
  pl. in'di·gos' or
  in'di·goes'
in'di·rect'
in'di·rec'tion
in·dis·cern'i·ble
in·dis·creet'
  (*imprudent*)
  (SEE indiscrete)
in·dis·crete' (*not
  separate*)
  (SEE indiscreet)
in·dis·cre'tion
in·dis·crim'i·nate
in·dis·pen'sa·bil'i·ty
in·dis·pen'sa·ble
in·dis·pen'sa·bly
in·dis·posed'
in·dis·po·si'tion
in·dis·put'a·ble
in·dis·put'a·bly
in·dis·sol'u·ble

in'dis·sol'u·bly
in'dis·tinct'
in'dis·tin'guish·a·ble
in'dis·tin'guish·a·bly
in·dite' (*write*)
  in·dit'ed, in·dit'ing
  (SEE indict)
in'di·um
in'di·vid'u·al
in'di·vid'u·al·ism'
in'di·vid'u·al·ist
in'di·vid'u·a·lis'tic
in'di·vid'u·al'i·ty
  pl. in'di·vid'u·al'i·ties
in'di·vid'u·al·
  i·za'tion
in'di·vid'u·al·ize'
  in'di·vid'u·al·ized',
  in'di·vid'u·al·iz'ing
in'di·vid'u·al·ly
in'di·vis'i·bil'i·ty
in'di·vis'i·ble
in'di·vis'i·bly
In'do·chi'na
In'do·chi·nese'
in·doc'tri·nate'
  in·doc'tri·nat'ed,
  in·doc'tri·nat'ing
in·doc'tri·na'tion
In'do-Eu'ro·pe'an
in'do·lence
in'do·lent
in·dom'i·ta·bil'i·ty
in·dom'i·ta·ble
in·dom'i·ta·bly
In'do·ne'sia
In'do·ne'sian
in'door'
in·doors'
in·dorse'
  in·dorsed', in·dors'ing
in·dorse'ment
in·du'bi·ta·bil'i·ty
in·du'bi·ta·ble
in·du'bi·ta·bly
in·duce'
  in·duced', in·duc'ing
in·duce'ment
in·duct'

in·duct'ance

in'duc·tee'

in·duc'tile

in·duc'tion

in·duc'tive

in·duc'tor

in·dulge'
  in·dulged', in·dulg'ing

in·dul'gence

in·dulg'er

in·dul'gent

in'du·rate' (v.)
  in'du·rat'ed,
  in'du·rat'ing

in'du·rate (adj.)

in'du·ra'tion

in·dus'tri·al

in·dus'tri·al·ly

in·dus'tri·al·ism'

in·dus'tri·al·ist

in·dus'tri·al·
  i·za'tion

in·dus'tri·al·ize'
  in·dus'tri·al·ized',
  in·dus'tri·al·iz'ing

in·dus'tri·ous

in'dus·try
  pl. in'dus·tries

in·e'bri·ate' (v.)
  in·e'bri·at'ed,
  in·e'bri·at'ing

in·e'bri·ate (n., adj.)

in'e·bri'e·ty

in·ed'i·ble

in·ed'u·ca·ble

in·ef'fa·bil'i·ty

in·ef'fa·ble

in·ef'fa·bly

in'ef·face'a·ble

in'ef·fec'tive

in'ef·fec'tu·al

in'ef·fec'tu·al·ly

in'ef·fi·ca'cious

in'ef·fi·cac'i·ty

in'ef·fi'cien·cy
  pl. in'ef·fi'cien·cies

in'ef·fi'cient

in'e·las'tic

in'e·las·tic'i·ty

in·el'e·gance

in·el'e·gant

in·el'i·gi·ble

in'e·luc'ta·ble

in'e·luc'ta·bly

in·ept'
  (incompetent)
  (SEE inapt)

in·ept'i·tude'

in'e·qual'i·ty
  pl. in'e·qual'i·ties

in·eq'ui·ta·ble

in·eq'ui·ta·bly

in·eq'ui·ty
  (injustice)
  pl. in·eq'ui·ties
  (SEE iniquity)

in'e·rad'i·ca·ble

in'e·rad'i·ca·bly

in·ert'

in·er'tia

in·er'tial

in'es·cap'a·ble

in'es·cap'a·bly

in'es·sen'tial

in·es'ti·ma·ble

in·es'ti·ma·bly

in·ev'i·ta·bil'i·ty

in·ev'i·ta·ble

in·ev'i·ta·bly

in'ex·act'

in'ex·cus'a·ble

in'ex·haust'i·bil'i·ty

in'ex·haust'i·ble

in'ex·haust'i·bly

in·ex'o·ra·ble

in·ex'o·ra·bly

in'ex·pe'di·ence

in'ex·pe'di·ent

in'ex·pen'sive

in'ex·pe'ri·ence

in'ex·pe'ri·enced

in·ex'pert

in·ex'pi·a·ble

in'ex·pli·ca·bil'i·ty

in·ex'pli·ca·ble

in·ex'pli·ca·bly

in'ex·press'i·bil'i·ty

in'ex·press'i·ble

in'ex·press'i·bly

in'ex·ten'si·ble

in ex·ten'so

in'ex·tin'guish·a·ble

in'ex·tin'guish·a·bly

in ex·tre'mis

in·ex'tri·ca·ble

in·ex'tri·ca·bly

in·fal'li·bil'i·ty

in·fal'li·ble

in·fal'li·bly

in'fa·mous

in'fa·my
  pl. in'fa·mies

in'fan·cy
  pl. in'fan·cies

in'fant

in·fan'ti·cide'

in'fan·tile'

in'fan·ti·lism'

in'fan·try
  pl. in'fan·tries

in'fan·try·man
  pl. in'fan·try·men

in·farct'

in·farc'tion

in·fat'u·ate' (v.)
  in·fat'u·at'ed,
  in·fat'u·at'ing

in·fat'u·ate (adj., n.)

in·fat'u·a'tion

in·fect'

in·fec'tion

in·fec'tious

in·fec'tive

in'fe·lic'i·tous

in'fe·lic'i·ty
  pl. in'fe·lic'i·ties

in·fer'
  in·ferred', in·fer'ring

in'fer·ence

in'fer·en'tial

in'fer·en'tial·ly

in·fe'ri·or

in·fe'ri·or'i·ty

in·fer'nal

in·fer'nal·ly

in · fer'no
　pl. in · fer'nos
in · fer'tile
in'fer · til'i · ty
in · fest'
in'fes · ta'tion
in'fi · del
in'fi · del'i · ty
　pl. in'fi · del'i · ties
in'field'
in'field'er
in'fight'ing
in · fil'trate
　in · fil'trat · ed,
　in · fil'trat · ing
in'fil · tra'tion
in'fil · tra'tor
in'fi · nite
in'fi · nite · ly
in'fin · i · tes'i · mal
in'fin · i · tes'i · mal · ly
in · fin'i · tive
in · fin'i · tude'
in · fin'i · ty
　pl. in · fin'i · ties
in · firm'
in · fir'ma · ry
　pl. in · fir'ma · ries
in · fir'mi · ty
　pl. in · fir'mi · ties
in · fix' (v.)
in'fix (n.)
in fla · gran'te
　de · lic'to
in · flame'
　in · flamed', in · flam'ing
in · flam'ma · ble
in'flam · ma'tion
in · flam'ma · to'ry
in · flat'a · ble
in · flate'
　in · flat'ed, in · flat'ing
in · fla'tion
in · fla'tion · ar'y
in · flect'
in · flec'tion
in · flec'tor
in · flexed'
in · flex'i · bil'i · ty

in · flex'i · ble
in · flex'i · bly
in · flict'
in · flic'tion
in'-flight'
in'flo · res'cence
in'flow'
in'flu · ence
　in'flu · enced,
　in'flu · enc · ing
in'flu · enc · er
in'flu · en'tial
in'flu · en'za
in'flux'
in · fold'
in · form'
in · for'mal
in'for · mal'i · ty
　pl. in'for · mal'i · ties
in · for'mal · ly
in · form'ant
in'for · ma'tion
in · form'a · tive
in · form'er
in · frac'tion
in · fran'gi · bil'i · ty
in · fran'gi · ble
in · fran'gi · bly
in'fra · red'
in'fra · son'ic
in'fra · struc'ture
in · fre'quence
in · fre'quen · cy
in · fre'quent
in · fringe'
　in · fringed', in · fring'ing
in · fringe'ment
in · fur'i · ate' (v.)
　in · fur'i · at · ed,
　in · fur'i · at'ing
in · fur'i · ate (adj.)
in · fu'ri · a'tion
in · fuse'
　in · fused', in · fus'ing
in · fus'er
in · fu'si · ble
in · fu'sion
in'gath · er

in · gen'ious (clever)
　(SEE ingenuous)
in'gé · nue' or
　in'ge · nue'
in'ge · nu'i · ty
　pl. in'ge · nu'i · ties
in · gen'u · ous
　(artless)
　(SEE ingenious)
in · gest'
in · gest'i · ble
in · ges'tion
in · glo'ri · ous
in'got
in · grain' (v.)
in'grain' (adj. n.)
in · grained'
in'grate
in · gra'ti · ate
　in · gra'ti · at'ed,
　in · gra'ti · at'ing
in · gra'ti · a'tion
in · grat'i · tude'
in · gre'di · ent
in'gress
in'group'
in'grown'
in'gui · nal
in · hab'it
in · hab'it · a · bil'i · ty
in · hab'it · a · ble
in · hab'it · an · cy
　pl. in · hab'it · an · cies
in · hab'i · tant
in · ha · la'tion
in'ha · la'tor
in · hale'
　in · haled', in · hal'ing
in · hal'er
in'har · mon'ic
in'har · mo'ni · ous
in · here'
　in · hered', in · her'ing
in · her'ence
in · her'ent
in · her'it
in · her'it · a · ble
in · her'i · tance

in·her'i·tor

in·hib'it

in'hi·bi'tion

in·hib'i·to'ry

in·hib'i·tor or
in·hib'i·ter

in·hos'pi·ta·ble

in·hos'pi·ta·bly

in'-house'

in·hu'man

in'hu·mane'

in'hu·man'i·ty
  pl. in'hu·man'i·ties

in·im'i·cal

in·im'i·cal·ly

in·im'i·ta·ble

in·im'i·ta·bly

in·iq'ui·tous

in·iq'ui·ty
  (*wickedness*)
  pl. in·iq'ui·ties
  (SEE inequity)

in·i'tial
  in·i'tialed or
  in·i'tialled,
  in·i'tial·ing or
  in·i'tial·ling

in·i'tial·ly

in·i'ti·ate' (*v.*)
  in·i'ti·at'ed,
  in·i'ti·at'ing

in·i'ti·ate (*adj., n.*)

in·i'ti·a'tion

in·i'ti·a·tive

in·i'ti·a'tor

in·i'ti·a·to'ry

in·ject'

in·jec'tion

in'ju·di'cious

in·junc'tion

in'jure
  in'jured, in'jur·ing

in'jured

in·ju'ri·ous

in'ju·ry
  pl. in'ju·ries

in·jus'tice

ink

ink'blot'

ink'ling

ink'stand'

ink'well'

ink'y
  (*adj.*) ink'i·er,
  ink'i·est; *pl.* ink'ies

in'laid'

in'land (*adj.*)

in'land' (*adv., n.*)

in'-law'

in'lay'
  in'laid', in'lay'ing

in'let
  in'let, in'let·ting

in lo'co pa·ren'tis

in'mate'

in me'di·as' res'

in me·mo'ri·am

in'most'

inn (*hotel*)
  (SEE in)

in'nards

in·nate'

in·nate'ly

in'ner

in'ner cit'y

in'ner-di·rect'ed

in'ner·most'

in·ner'vate
  in·ner'vat·ed,
  in·ner'vat·ing

in'ner·va'tion

in'ning

inn'keep'er

in'no·cence

in'no·cent

in·noc'u·ous

in·nom'i·nate

in'no·vate'
  in'no·vat'ed,
  in'no·vat'ing

in'no·va'tion

in'no·va'tive

in'no·va'tor

in·nu·en'do
  pl. in'nu·en'dos or
  in'nu·en'does

in·nu'mer·a·ble

in·nu'mer·a·bly

in·oc'u·late'
  in·oc'u·lat'ed,
  in·oc'u·lat'ing

in·oc'u·la'tion

in'of·fen'sive

in·op'er·a·ble

in·op'er·a·tive

in·op'por·tune'

in·or'di·nate

in·or'di·nate·ly

in'or·gan'ic

in'pa'tient

in'put'
  in'put'ted, in'put'ting

in'quest

in·qui'e·tude'

in·quire'
  in·quired', in·quir'ing

in·quir'er

in·quir'y
  pl. in·quir'ies

in'qui·si'tion

in·quis'i·tive

in·quis'i·tor

in re'

in'road'

in'rush'

in'sa·lu'bri·ous

in·sane'

in·san'i·tar'y

in·san'i·ty
  pl. in·san'i·ties

in·sa'tia·bil'i·ty

in·sa'tia·ble

in·sa'tia·bly

in·sa'ti·ate

in·scribe'
  in·scribed', in·scrib'ing

in·scrib'er

in·scrip'tion

in·scru'ta·bil'i·ty

in·scru'ta·ble

in·scru'ta·bly

in'seam'

in'sect

in·sec'ti·cide

in·sec'ti·vore'

in'sec·tiv'o·rous

in'se·cure'

in'se·cu'ri·ty
  pl. in'se·cu'ri·ties

in·sem'i·nate'
  in·sem'i·nat·ed,
  in·sem'i·nat'ing
in·sem'i·na'tion
in·sen'sate
in·sen'si·bil'i·ty
  pl. in·sen'si·bil'i·ties
in·sen'si·ble
in·sen'si·bly
in·sen'si·tive
in·sen'si·tiv'i·ty
in·sen'ti·ence
in·sen'ti·ent
in·sep'a·ra·bil'i·ty
in·sep'a·ra·ble
in·sep'a·ra·bly
in·sert' (v.)
in'sert (n.)
in·sert'a·ble
in·ser'tion
in'set' (n.)
in·set' (v.)
  in·set', in·set'ting
in'shore'
in'side' (prep., adv., adj.)
in'side' (n.)
in'sid'er
in·sid'i·ous
in'sight' (discernment) (SEE incite)
in·sig'ni·a
  pl. in·sig'ni·a or in·sig'ni·as
in'sig·nif'i·cance
in'sig·nif'i·cant
in'sin·cere'
in'sin·cere'ly
in'sin·cer'i·ty
  pl. in'sin·cer'i·ties
in·sin'u·ate'
  in·sin'u·at·ed,
  in·sin'u·at'ing
in·sin'u·a'tion
in·sip'id
in·sist'
in·sist'ence
in·sist'en·cy
in·sist'ent

in'so·far'
in'sole'
in'so·lence
in'so·lent
in·sol'u·bil'i·ty
in·sol'u·ble
in·sol'u·bly
in·solv'a·ble
in·sol'ven·cy
in·sol'vent
in·som'ni·a
in·som'ni·ac'
in'so·much'
in·sou'ci·ance
in·sou'ci·ant
in·spect'
in·spec'tion
in·spec'tor
in'spi·ra'tion
in'spi·ra'tion·al
in·spire'
  in·spired', in·spir'ing
in·spir'it
in'sta·bil'i·ty
in·stall' or in·stal'
in·stal·la'tion
in·stall'ment or in·stal'ment
in'stance
  in'stanced, in'stanc·ing
in'stant
in'stan·ta'ne·ous
in·stan'ter
in·state'
  in·stat'ed, in·stat'ing
in·stead'
in'step'
in'sti·gate'
  in'sti·gat'ed,
  in'sti·gat'ing
in'sti·ga'tion
in'sti·ga'tor
in·still' or in·stil'
  in·stilled', in·stil'ling
in'stil·la'tion
in'stinct (n.)
in·stinct' (adj.)
in·stinc'tive

in'sti·tute'
  in'sti·tut'ed,
  in'sti·tut'ing
in'sti·tu'tion
in'sti·tu'tion·al
in'sti·tu'tion·al·ize'
  in'sti·tu'tion·al·ized',
  in'sti·tu'tion·al·iz'ing
in'sti·tu'tor
in·struct'
in·struc'tion
in·struc'tion·al
in·struc'tive
in·struc'tor
in'stru·ment
in'stru·men'tal
in'stru·men'tal·ist
in'stru·men·tal'i·ty
  pl. in'stru·men·tal'i·ties
in'stru·men'tal·ly
in'stru·men·ta'tion
in'sub·or'di·nate
in'sub·or'di·na'tion
in'sub·stan'tial
in'sub·stan'ti·al'i·ty
in'sub·stan'tial·ly
in·suf'fer·a·ble
in·suf'fer·a·bly
in·suf·fi'cien·cy
  pl. in·suf·fi'cien·cies
in·suf·fi'cient
in'su·lar
in'su·lar'i·ty
in'su·late'
  in'su·lat'ed,
  in'su·lat'ing
in'su·la'tion
in'su·la'tor
in'su·lin
in·sult' (v.)
in'sult (n.)
in·su'per·a·bil'i·ty
in·su'per·a·ble
in·su'per·a·bly
in·sup·port'a·ble
in·sup·port'a·bly
in·sup·press'i·ble
in·sup·press'i·bly

in·sur'a·bil'i·ty

in·sur'a·ble

in·sur'ance

in·sure'
in·sured', in·sur'ing

in·sur'er

in·sur'gence

in·sur'gen·cy

in·sur'gent

in'sur·mount'a·ble

in'sur·mount'a·bly

in'sur·rec'tion

in'sur·rec'tion·ar'y
pl. in·sur·rec'tion·ar'ies

in'sur·rec'tion·ist

in'sus·cep'ti·bil'i·ty

in'sus·cep'ti·ble

in'sus·cep'ti·bly

in·tact'

in·tagl'io
pl. in·tagl'ios or (It.)
in·ta'gli

in'take'

in·tan'gi·bil'i·ty

in·tan'gi·ble

in·tan'gi·bly

in'te·ger

in'te·gral

in'te·grate'
in'te·grat'ed,
in'te·grat'ing

in'te·grat'ed

in'te·gra'tion

in'te·gra'tion·ist

in'te·gra'tive

in'te·gra'tor

in·teg'ri·ty

in·teg'u·ment

in'tel·lect'

in'tel·lec'tu·al

in'tel·lec'tu·al·ism'

in'tel·lec'tu·al·ize'
in'tel·lec'tu·al·ized',
in'tel·lec'tu·al·iz'ing

in'tel·lec'tu·al·ly

in·tel'li·gence

in·tel'li·gent

in·tel'li·gent'si·a

in·tel'li·gi·bil'i·ty
pl. in·tel'li·gi·bil'i·ties

in·tel'li·gi·ble

in·tel'li·gi·bly

in·tem'per·ance

in·tem'per·ate

in·tem'per·ate·ly

in·tend'

in·tend'ed

in·tense'

in·tense'ly

in·ten'si·fi·ca'tion

in·ten'si·fi'er

in·ten'si·fy'
in·ten'si·fied',
in·ten'si·fy'ing

in·ten'si·ty
pl. in·ten'si·ties

in·ten'sive

in·tent'

in·ten'tion

in·ten'tion·al

in·ten'tion·al·ly

in·ter'
in·terred', in·ter'ring

in'ter·act'

in'ter·ac'tion

in'ter·ac'tive

in'ter a'li·a'

in'ter–A·mer'i·can

in'ter·bor'ough

in'ter·breed'
in'ter·bred',
in'ter·breed'ing

in·ter'ca·lar'y

in·ter'ca·late'
in·ter'ca·lat'ed,
in·ter'ca·lat'ing

in·ter'ca·la'tion

in'ter·cede'
in'ter·ced'ed,
in'ter·ced'ing

in'ter·cept'   (v.)

in'ter·cept'   (n.)

in'ter·cep'tion

in'ter·cep'tor

in'ter·ces'sion
(*interceding*)
(SEE intersession)

in'ter·ces'sor

in'ter·ces'so·ry

in'ter·change'   (v.)
in'ter·changed',
in'ter·chang'ing

in'ter·change'   (n.)

in'ter·change'a·ble

in'ter·change'a·bly

in'ter·col·le'giate

in'ter·com'

in'ter·com·mu'ni·
cate'
in'ter·com·mu'ni·
cat'ed,
in'ter·com·mu'ni·
cat'ing

in'ter·com·mu'ni·ca'
tion

in'ter·con'ti·nen'tal

in'ter·cos'tal

in'ter·course'

in'ter·cul'tur·al

in'ter·de·nom'i·na'
tion·al

in'ter·de'part·men'tal

in'ter·de·pend'en·cy

in'ter·de·pend'ent

in'ter·dict'   (n.)

in'ter·dict'   (v.)

in'ter·dic'tion

in'ter·dis'ci·pli·nar'y

in'ter·est

in'ter·est·ed

in'ter·est·ing

in'ter·face'
in'ter·faced',
in'ter·fac'ing

in'ter·faith'

in'ter·fere'
in'ter·fered',
in'ter·fer'ing

in'ter·fer'ence

in'ter·fer'er

in'ter·fer'on

in'ter·fuse'
in'ter·fused',
in'ter·fus'ing

in'ter·fu'sion

in'ter·ga·lac'tic

in'ter·group'

in'ter·im

in·te'ri·or

in'ter·ject'
in'ter·jec'tion
in'ter·jec'tor
in'ter·lace'
  in'ter·laced',
  in'ter·lac'ing
in'ter·lard'
in'ter·leaf'
  pl. in'ter·leaves'
in'ter·leave'
  in'ter·leaved',
  in'ter·leav'ing
in'ter·li'brar·y
in'ter·lin'e·ar
in'ter·lin'ing
in'ter·link' (v.)
in'ter·link' (n.)
in'ter·lock' (v.)
in'ter·lock' (n.)
in'ter·lo·cu'tion
in'ter·loc'u·tor
in'ter·loc'u·to'ry
in'ter·lope'
  in'ter·loped',
  in'ter·lop'ing
in'ter·lop'er
in'ter·lude'
in'ter·lu'nar
in'ter·mar'riage
in'ter·mar'ry
  in'ter·mar'ried,
  in'ter·mar'ry·ing
in'ter·me'di·ar'y
  pl. in'ter·me'di·ar'ies
in'ter·me'di·ate
  (adj., n.)
in'ter·me'di·ate'
  (v.)
  in'ter·me'di·at'ed,
  in'ter·me'di·at'ing
in·ter'ment
in'ter·mez'zo
  pl. in'ter·mez'zos or
  in'ter·mez'zi
in·ter'mi·na·ble
in·ter'mi·na·bly
in'ter·min'gle
  in'ter·min'gled,
  in'ter·min'gling
in'ter·mis'sion
in'ter·mit'
  in'ter·mit'ted,
  in'ter·mit'ting

in'ter·mit'tent
in'ter·mix'
in'ter·mix'ture
in'ter·mu'ral
in·tern' (v.)
in'tern (n.) or
  in'terne
in·ter'nal
in·ter'nal·i·za'tion
in·ter'nal·ize'
  in·ter'nal·ized',
  in·ter'nal·iz'ing
in'ter·na'tion·al
in'ter·na'tion·al·ly
In·ter·na·tio·nale'
in'ter·na'tion·al·ism'
in'ter·na'tion·al·ist
in'ter·na'tion·al·
  i·za'tion
in'ter·na'tion·al·ize'
  in'ter·na'tion·al·ized',
  in'ter·na'tion·al·iz'ing
in·terne' or in·tern'
  (n.)
in'ter·ne'cine
in'tern·ee'
in'tern·ist
in·tern'ment
in'ter·nun'ci·o'
  pl. in'ter·nun'ci·os'
in'ter·of'fice
in'ter·pen'e·trate'
  in'ter·pen'e·trat'ed,
  in'ter·pen'e·trat'ing
in'ter·pen'e·tra'tion
in'ter·per'son·al
in'ter·per'son·al·ly
in'ter·phone'
in'ter·plan'e·tar'y
in'ter·play' (n.)
in'ter·play' (v.)
In'ter·pol'
in·ter'po·late'
  in·ter'po·lat'ed,
  in·ter'po·lat'ing
in·ter'po·la'tion
in·ter'po·la'tor
in'ter·pose'
  in'ter·posed',
  in'ter·pos'ing
in'ter·po·si'tion

in·ter'pret
in·ter'pre·ta'tion
in·ter'pre·ta'tive
in·ter'pret·er
in·ter'pre·tive
in'ter·ra'cial
in'ter·reg'num
  pl. in'ter·reg'nums or
  in'ter·reg'na
in'ter·re·late'
  in'ter·re·lat'ed,
  in'ter·re·lat'ing
in·ter'ro·gate'
  in·ter'ro·gat'ed,
  in·ter'ro·gat'ing
in·ter'ro·ga'tion
in'ter·rog'a·tive
in'ter·rog'a·tor
in'ter·rog'a·to'ry
  pl. in'ter·rog'a·to'ries
in'ter·rupt'
in'ter·rup'tion
in'ter·scho·las'tic
in'ter·sect'
in'ter·sec'tion
in'ter·ses'sion (*recess
  between sessions*)
  (SEE intercession)
in'ter·sperse'
  in'ter·spersed',
  in'ter·spers'ing
in'ter·sper'sion
in'ter·state'
  (*between states*)
  (SEE intrastate)
in'ter·stel'lar
in·ter'stice
in'ter·sti'tial
in'ter·twine'
  in'ter·twined',
  in'ter·twin'ing
in'ter·twist'
in'ter·ur'ban
in'ter·val
in'ter·vene'
  in'ter·vened',
  in'ter·ven'ing
in'ter·ven'tion
in'ter·ven'tion·ism'
in'ter·ven'tion·ist
in'ter·view'

in·ter·view'er

in'ter vi'vos

in·ter·vo·cal'ic

in·ter·weave' (v.)
   in'ter·wove' or
   in'ter·weaved',
   in'ter·wo'ven or
   in'ter·wove' or
   in'ter·weaved',
   in'ter·weav'ing

in·ter·weave' (n.)

in·tes'ta·cy

in·tes'tate

in·tes'ti·nal

in·tes'tine

in'ti·ma·cy
   pl. in'ti·ma·cies

in'ti·mate (adj., n.)

in'ti·mate' (v.)
   in'ti·mat'ed,
   in'ti·mat'ing

in'ti·ma'tion

in·tim'i·date'
   in·tim'i·dat'ed,
   in·tim'i·dat'ing

in·tim'i·da'tion

in'to

in·tol'er·a·ble

in·tol'er·a·bil'i·ty

in·tol'er·a·bly

in·tol'er·ance

in·tol'er·ant

in'to·na'tion

in·tone'
   in·ton'ed, in·ton'ing

in·to'ner

in to'to

in·tox'i·cant

in·tox'i·cate' (v.)
   in·tox'i·cat'ed,
   in·tox'i·cat'ing

in·tox'i·cate (adj.)

in·tox'i·ca'tion

in·trac'ta·bil'i·ty

in·trac'ta·ble

in·trac'ta·bly

in'tra·cu·ta'ne·ous

in'tra·mu'ral

in'tra·mus'cu·lar

in·tran'si·gence

in·tran'si·gent

in·tran'si·tive

in'tra·state' (*within a state*)
   (SEE interstate)

in'tra·u'ter·ine

in'tra·ve'nous

in·trep'id

in'tre·pid'i·ty

in'tri·ca·cy
   pl. in'tri·ca·cies

in'tri·cate

in·trigue'
   in·trigued', in·tri'guing

in·tri'guer

in·trin'sic

in·trin'si·cal·ly

in'tro·duce'
   in'tro·duced',
   in'tro·duc'ing

in'tro·duc'er

in'tro·duc'tion

in'tro·duc'to·ry

in'tro·spec'tion

in'tro·spec'tive

in'tro·ver'sion

in'tro·vert' (n., adj.)

in'tro·vert' (v.)

in·trude'
   in·trud'ed, in·trud'ing

in·trud'er

in·tru'sion

in·tru'sive

in'tu·i'tion

in·tu'i·tive

in'tu·mesce'
   in'tu·mesced',
   in'tu·mesc'ing

in'tu·mes'cence

in'un·date'
   in'un·dat'ed,
   in'un·dat'ing

in'un·da'tion

in·ure'
   in·ured', in·ur'ing

in va'cu·o'

in·vade'
   in·vad'ed, in·vad'ing

in·vad'er

in'va·lid (n.)

in·val'id (adj.)

in·val'i·date'
   in·val'i·dat'ed,
   in·val'i·dat'ing

in·val'i·da'tion

in·val'u·a·ble

in·val'u·a·bly

in·var'i·a·bil'i·ty

in·var'i·a·ble

in·var'i·a·bly

in·var'i·ance

in·var'i·ant

in·va'sion

in·va'sive

in·vect'ed

in·vec'tive

in·veigh'

in·vei'gle
   in·vei'gled, in·vei'gling

in·vent'

in·ven'tion

in·ven'tive

in·ven'tor

in'ven·to'ry
   pl. in'ven·to'ries; (v.)
   in'ven·to'ried,
   in'ven·to'ry·ing

in'ver·ness'

in·verse'
   in·versed', in·vers'ing

in·verse'ly

in·ver'sion

in·vert' (v.)

in'vert (adj., n.)

in·ver'te·brate

in·vest'

in·ves'ti·gate'
   in·ves'ti·gat'ed,
   in·ves'ti·gat'ing

in·ves'ti·ga'tion

in·ves'ti·ga'tor

in·ves'ti·ture

in·vest'ment

in·ves'tor

in·vet'er·a·cy

in·vet'er·ate

in·vid'i·ous

in·vig'or·ate'
   in·vig'or·at'ed,
   in·vig'or·at'ing

in·vig'or·a'tion

in‧vin'ci‧bil'i‧ty
in‧vin'ci‧ble
in‧vin'ci‧bly
in‧vi'o‧la‧bil'i‧ty
in‧vi'o‧la‧ble
in‧vi'o‧la‧bly
in‧vi'o‧late
in‧vis'i‧bil'i‧ty
in‧vis'i‧ble
in‧vis'i‧bly
in'vi‧ta'tion
in‧vite' (v.)
  in‧vit'ed, in‧vit'ing
in'vite (n.)
in vi'tro
in vi'vo
in'vo‧ca'tion
in'voice
  in'voiced, in'voic‧ing
in‧voke'
  in‧voked', in‧vok'ing
in‧vol'un‧tar'i‧ly
in‧vol'un‧tar'y
in'vo‧lute' (adj., n.)
in'vo‧lute' (v.)
  in'vo‧lut'ed,
  in'vo‧lut'ing
in'vo‧lu'tion
in‧volve'
  in‧volved', in‧volv'ing
in‧volved'
in‧volve'ment
in‧vul'ner‧a‧bil'i‧ty
in‧vul'ner‧a‧ble
in‧vul'ner‧a‧bly
in'ward
in'ward‧ly
in'wards
i'o‧dide'
i'o‧dine'
i'o‧dize'
  i'o‧dized', i'o‧diz'ing
i'on
I‧o'ni‧an
i‧on'ic
I‧on'ic
i'on‧i‧za'tion
i'on‧ize'
  i'on‧ized', i'on‧iz'ing

i‧on'o‧sphere'
i‧o'ta
I'OU'
I'o‧wa
I'o‧wan
ip'e‧cac'
ip'se dix'it
ip'so fac'to
I‧ran'
I‧ra'ni‧an
I‧raq'
I‧ra'qi
i‧ras'ci‧bil'i‧ty
i‧ras'ci‧ble
i‧ras'ci‧bly
i'rate
ire
ire'ful
Ire'land
i‧ren'ic
Ir‧gun'
ir'i‧des'cence
ir'i‧des'cent
i‧rid'i‧um
i'ris
  pl. i'ris‧es or ir'i‧des
I'rish
I'rish‧man
  pl. I'rish‧men
I'rish moss'
irk
irk'some
i'ron
i'ron‧bound'
i'ron‧clad' (adj.)
i'ron‧clad' (n.)
i'ron‧hand'ed
i‧ron'ic
i‧ron'i‧cal
i‧ron'i‧cal‧ly
i'ron lung'
i'ron‧stone'
i'ron‧ware'
i'ron‧wood'
i'ron‧work'
i'ro‧ny
  pl. i'ro‧nies

Ir'o‧quois'
  pl. Ir'o‧quois'
ir‧ra'di‧ate' (v.)
  ir‧ra'di‧at'ed,
  ir‧ra'di‧at'ing
ir‧ra'di‧ate (adj.)
ir‧ra'di‧a'tion
ir‧ra'tion‧al
ir‧ra'tion‧al'i‧ty
ir‧ra'tion‧al‧ly
ir're‧claim'a‧ble
ir'rec'on‧cil'
  a‧bil'i‧ty
ir'rec'on‧cil'a‧ble
ir'rec'on‧cil'a‧bly
ir're‧cov'er‧a‧ble
ir're‧cov'er‧a‧bly
ir're‧deem'a‧ble
ir're‧deem'a‧bly
ir're‧den'tist
ir're‧den'tism
ir're‧duc'i‧ble
ir‧ref'u‧ta‧bil'i‧ty
ir‧ref'u‧ta‧ble
ir‧ref'u‧ta‧bly
ir‧reg'u‧lar
ir‧reg'u‧lar'i‧ty
  pl. ir‧reg'u‧lar'i‧ties
ir‧rel'e‧vance
ir‧rel'e‧vant
ir're‧li'gious
ir're‧me'di‧a‧ble
ir're‧me'di‧a‧bly
ir're‧mov'a‧ble
ir're‧mov'a‧bly
ir‧rep'a‧ra‧bil'i‧ty
ir‧rep'a‧ra‧ble
ir‧rep'a‧ra‧bly
ir're‧place'a‧ble
ir're‧place'a‧bly
ir're‧press'i‧bil'i‧ty
ir're‧press'i‧ble
ir're‧press'i‧bly
ir're‧proach'a‧ble
ir're‧proach'a‧bly
ir're‧sist'i‧bil'i‧ty
ir're‧sist'i‧ble

ir·re·sist'i·bly
ir·res'o·lute'
ir·res'o·lu'tion
ir're·solv'a·ble
ir're·spec'tive
ir're·spon'si·bil'i·ty
ir're·spon'si·ble
ir're·spon'si·bly
ir're·triev'a·ble
ir're·triev'a·bly
ir·rev'er·ence
ir·rev'er·ent
ir're·vers'i·bil'i·ty
ir're·vers'i·ble
ir're·vers'i·bly
ir·rev'o·ca·bil'i·ty
ir·rev'o·ca·ble
ir·rev'o·ca·bly
ir'ri·gate'
 ir'ri·gat'ed, ir'ri·gat'ing
ir'ri·ga'tion
ir'ri·ga'tor
ir'ri·ta·bil'i·ty
 pl. ir'ri·ta·bil'i·ties
ir'ri·ta·ble
ir'ri·ta·bly
ir'ri·tant
ir'ri·tate'
 ir'ri·tat'ed, ir'ri·tat'ing
ir'ri·ta'tion
ir·rupt'
ir·rup'tion
Ir'ving
is
I'saac
I·sa'iah
is'chi·um
 pl. is'chi·a
Ish'ma·el
i'sin·glass'
I'sis

Is'lam
Is·lam'a·bad'
Is·lam'ic
is'land
isle (island)
 isled, isl'ing
 (SEE aisle)
is'let (small island)
 (SEE eyelet)
is'n't
i'so·bar'
i'so·bar'ic
i'so·late' (v.)
 i'so·lat'ed, i'so·lat'ing
i'so·late (adj.)
i'so·la'tion
i'so·la'tion·ism'
i'so·la'tion·ist
i'so·mer'
i'so·mer'ic
i·som'er·ism'
i'so·met'ric
i'so·met'ri·cal
i'so·met'ri·cal·ly
i'so·pro'pyl
i·sos'ce·les
i'so·therm'
i'so·ther'mal
i'so·tope'
i'so·top'ic
Is'ra·el
Is·rae'li
 pl. Is·rae'lis or Is·rae'li
Is'ra·el·ite'
Is'sei
 pl. Is'sei'
is'su·a·ble
is'su·ance
is'sue
 is'sued, is'su·ing
is'su·er
Is'tan·bul'
Isth'mi·an

isth'mus
 pl. isth'mus·es or
 isth'mi
it
I·tal'ian
i·tal'ic
i·tal'i·ci·za'tion
i·tal'i·cize'
 i·tal'i·cized',
 i·tal'i·ciz'ing
It'a·ly
itch
 pl. itch'es
itch'i·ness
itch'y
 itch'i·er, itch'i·est
i'tem
i'tem·i·za'tion
i'tem·ize'
 i'tem·ized', i'tem·iz'ing
it'er·ate'
 it'er·at'ed, it'er·at'ing
it'er·a'tion
it'er·a'tive
i·tin'er·ant
i·tin'er·ar'y
 pl. i·tin'er·ar'ies
it'll
its (possessive of it)
 (SEE it's BELOW)
it's (it is)
 (SEE its ABOVE)
it·self'
I'UD'
I've
i'vied
I·vo'rien
i'vo·ry
 pl. i'vo·ries
I'vo·ry Coast'
i'vo·ry tow'er
i'vy
 pl. i'vies

J

jab
 jabbed, jab'bing
jab'ber
ja·bot'

jac'a·ran'da
jack
jack'al
jack'a·napes'

jack'ass'
 pl. jack'ass'es
jack'boot'
jack'daw'

jack'et

jack'ham'mer

jack'-in-the-box'
    pl. jack'-in-the-box'es

jack'-in-the-pul'pit
    pl. jack'-in-the-pul'pits

jack'knife'
    pl. jack'knives'

jack'-of-all'-trades'
    pl. jacks'-of-all'-trades'

jack'-o'-lan'tern

jack'pot'

jack' rab'bit

jack'screw

Jack'son

Jack'son · ville'

jack'straw'

Ja'cob

Jac'o · be'an

Jac'o · bin

jac'quard

jade
    jad'ed, jad'ing

jad'ed

jade'ite

jae'ger

jag
    jagged, jag'ging

jag'ged

jag'uar

jai' a · lai'

jail

jail'bird'

jail'break'

jail'er or jail'or

jail'house'

Ja · kar'ta

ja · lop'y
    pl. ja · lop'ies

jal'ou · sie' (shutter)
    (SEE jealousy)

jam (push; jelly)
    jammed, jam'ming
    (SEE jamb)

Ja · mai'ca

Ja · mai'can

jamb (side of door)
    (SEE jam)

jam'ba · lay'a

jam'bo · ree'

James

jam'-packed'

jam' ses'sion

jam'-up'

jan'gle
    jan'gled, jan'gling

jan'i · tor

jan'i · to'ri · al

Jan'u · ar'y
    pl. Jan'u · ar'ies

Ja'nus

ja · pan'
    ja · panned', ja · pan'ning

Ja · pan'

Jap'a · nese'

jape
    japed, jap'ing

jap'er · y

jar
    jarred, jar'ring

jar'di · niere' or
    jar'di · nière'

jar'gon

jas'mine

Ja'son

jas'per

ja'to
    pl. ja'tos

jaun'dice
    jaun'diced, jaun'dic · ing

jaunt

jaun'ti · ly

jaun'ti · ness

jaun'ty
    jaun'ti · er, jaun'ti · est

Ja'va

Jav'a · nese'

jave'lin

jaw

jaw'bone'
    jaw'boned', jaw'bon'ing

jaw'break'er

jay

Jay'hawk'er

jay'vee'

jay'walk'

jay'walk'er

jazz

jazz'i · ly

jazz'i · ness

jazz'y
    jazz'i · er, jazz'i · est

jeal'ous

jeal'ous · y (envy)
    pl. jeal'ous · ies
    (SEE jalousie)

jeans

jeep

jeer

jeer'ing

Jef'fer · son

Jef'fer · so'ni · an

Je · ho'vah

Je'hu

je · june'

je · ju'num

jell (become
    jellylike)
    (SEE gel)

Jell'-O (Trademark)

jel'ly
    pl. jel'lies
    (v.) jel'lied, jel'ly · ing

jel'ly · bean'

jel'ly · fish'
    pl. jel'ly · fish' or
    jel'ly · fish'es

jel'ly roll'

jen'net

jen'ny
    pl. jen'nies

jeop'ard · ize'
    jeop'ard · ized',
    jeop'ard · iz'ing

jeop'ard · y
    pl. jeop'ard · ies

jer · bo'a

jer'e · mi'ad

Jer'e · mi'ah

Jer'i · cho'

jerk

jer'kin

jerk'wa'ter

jerk'i · ly

jerk'i · ness

jerk'y
    jerk'i · er, jerk'i · est

Jer'o · bo'am

jer'ry-build'
    jer'ry-built', jer'ry-
    build'ing

jer'sey
   pl. jer'seys
Je·ru'sa·lem
jess
jes'sa·mine
jest
jest'er
Jes'u·it
Jes'u·it'i·cal·ly
Je'sus
jet
   jet'ted, jet'ting
jet'-black'
je·té'
jet' en'gine
jet' lag'
jet'lin'er
jet' plane'
jet'port'
jet'-pro·pelled'
jet'sam
jet' set'
jet' stream'
jet'ti·son
jet'ty
   pl. jet'ties; (*v.*)
   jet'tied, jet'ty·ing
jeu d'es·prit'
   pl. *jeux d'es·prit'*
Jew
jew'el
   jew'eled, jew'el·ing
jew'el·er
jew'el·ry
jew'el·weed'
Jew'ish
Jew'ry
jew's'-harp'
Jez'e·bel
jib
jib
   jibbed, jib'bing
jibe
   jibed, jib'ing
jif'fy
   pl. jif'fies
jig
   jigged, jig'ging

jig'ger
jig'gle
   jig'gled, jig'gling
jig' saw'
jig'saw puz'zle
ji·had'
jilt
Jim' Crow'
jim'my
   pl. jim'mies; (*v.*)
   jim'mied, jim'my·ing
jim'son weed'
jin'gle
   jin'gled, jin'gling
jin'go
   pl. jin'goes
jin'go·ism'
jin'go·ist
jin'go·is'tic
jinn
   pl. jinns or jinn
jin·rik'i·sha
jinx
   pl. jinx'es
jit'ney
   pl. jit'neys; (*v.*)
   jit'neyed, jit'ney·ing
jit'ters
jit'ter·bug
   jit'ter·bugged',
   jit'ter·bug'ging
jit'ter·y
jiu·ji'tsu or
   jiu·ju'tsu
jive (*music*)
   jived, jiv'ing
   (SEE gyve)
job
   jobbed, job'bing
Job
job'ber
job'hold'er
job'less
job' lot'
jock
jock'ey
   pl. jock'eys; (*v.*)
   jock'eyed, jock'ey·ing
jock'strap'
jo·cose'

jo·cos'i·ty
   pl. jo·cos'i·ties
joc'u·lar
joc'u·lar'i·ty
   pl. joc'u·lar'i·ties
joc'und
jo·cun'di·ty
   pl. jo·cun'di·ties
jodh'purs
jog
   jogged, jog'ging
jog'ger
jog'gle
   jog'gled, jog'gling
Jo·han'nes·burg'
John' Doe'
john'ny·cake'
John'ny-jump'-up'
John'son
joie de vi'vre
join
join'er
joint
joint'ed
joist
joke
   joked, jok'ing
jok'er
jol'li·ty
   pl. jol'li·ties
jol'ly
   (*adj.*) jol'li·er,
   jol'li·est; (*v.*)
   jol'lied, jol'ly·ing;
   pl. jol'lies
Jol'ly Rog'er
jolt
Jo'nah
jon'quil
Jor'dan
Jor·da'ni·an
Jo'seph
josh
Josh'u·a
joss
jos'tle
   jos'tled, jos'tling
jot
   jot'ted, jot'ting

joule

jounce
jounced, jounc'ing

jour'nal

jour'nal·ese'

jour'nal·ism'

jour'nal·ist

jour'nal·is'tic

jour'ney
pl. jour'neys; (*v.*)
jour'neyed,
jour'ney·ing

jour'ney·man
pl. jour'ney·men

joust

Jove

jo'vi·al

jo'vi·al'i·ty

jo'vi·al·ly

jowl

joy

Joyce

joy'ful

joy'ful·ly

joy'ous

joy' ride'

joy'-ride'
joy'-rode', joy'-rid'den,
joy'-rid'ing

joy' stick'

ju'bi·lance

ju'bi·lant

ju'bi·la'tion

ju'bi·lee'

Ju'dah

Ju·da'ic

Ju·da'i·ca

Ju'da·ism'

Ju'das

Ju·de'a

judge
judged, judg'ing

judge' ad'vo·cate
pl. judge' ad'vo·cates

judg'ment or
judge'ment

ju'di·ca'ture

ju·di'cial

ju·di'ci·ar'y
pl. ju·di'ci·ar'ies

ju·di'cious

ju'do

jug
jugged, jug'ging

Jug'ger·naut

jug'gle
jug'gled, jug'gling

jug'gler

jug'u·lar

juice
juiced, juic'ing

juic'er

juic'i·ness

juic'y
juic'i·er, juic'i·est

ju·jit'su

ju'jube

juke'box'
pl. juke'box'es

ju'lep

ju'li·enne'

Ju·ly'
pl. Ju·lies'

jum'ble
jum'bled, jum'bling

jum'bo
jum'bos

jump

jump'er

jump'i·ness

jump'ing bean'

jump'ing jack'

jump'y
jump'i·er, jum'pi·est

jun'co
pl. jun'cos

junc'tion

junc'ture

June

Ju'neau

Jung

jun'gle

jun'ior

ju'ni·per

junk

Jun'ker

jun'ket

junk' food'

junk'ie or junk'y
pl. junk'ies

junk' mail'

junk'man
pl. junk'men

junk'yard'

Ju'no

jun'ta

Ju'pi·ter

Ju·ras'sic

ju·rid'i·cal

ju·rid'i·cal·ly

ju'ris·dic'tion

ju'ris·pru'dence

ju'rist

ju·ris'tic

ju'ror

ju'ry
pl. ju'ries

ju'ry·man
pl. ju'ry·men

ju'ry·rig'
ju'ry·rigged',
ju'ry·rig'ging

ju'ry·wom'an
pl. ju'ry·wom'en

just

jus'tice

jus·ti'ci·a·ble

jus'ti·fi'able

jus'ti·fi'a·bly

jus'ti·fi·ca'tion

jus'ti·fy'
jus'ti·fied', jus'ti·fy'ing

just'ly

jut
jut'ted, jut'ting

jute

Jut'land

ju've·nile

ju've·nil'i·a

jux'ta·pose'
jux'ta·posed',
jux'ta·pos'ing

jux'ta·po·si'tion

K

Kaa'ba
ka·bob'
ka·bu'ki
Ka'bul
ka·chi'na
Kad'dish
  pl. Kad·di'shim
kaf'fee klatsch
Kaf'ka
kai'ser
Ka'la·ha'ri
kale
ka·lei'do·scope'
ka·lei'do·scop'ic
ka'ma·ai'na
kame
ka'mi·ka'ze
Kam·pa'la
Kam'pu·che'a
Ka·nak'a
kan'ga·roo'
  pl. kan'ga·roos' or
  kan'ga·roo'
kan'ji
Kan'san
Kan'sas
Kant
Kant'i·an
ka'o·lin
ka'pok
kap'pa
ka·put'
Ka·ra'chi
kar'a·kul
kar'at (*measure*)
  (SEE caret *and* carrot)
ka·ra'te
kar'ma
ka'sha
Kash'mir
kash·ruth'
Kat'man·du'
ka'ty·did
kat'zen·jam'mer
kay'ak

kay'o'
  pl. kay'os'; (*v.*)
  kay'oed, kay'o·ing
ka·zoo'
  pl. ka·zoos'
ke·bab' or ke·bob'
keel
keel'boat'
keel'haul'
keel'less
keel'son
keen'ly
keep
  kept, keep'ing
keep'er
keep'sake'
keg
keg'ler
kelp
kel'vin
ken
  kenned or kent,
  ken'ning
Ken'ne·dy
ken'nel
  ken'neled, ken'nel·ing
ke'no
Ken·tuck'i·an
Ken·tuck'y
Ken'ya
Ken'yan
kep'i
  pl. kep'is
Ke'pone (*Trademark*)
kept
ker'a·tin
ke·rat'i·nous
ker'a·to'sis
  pl. ker'a·to'ses
ker'chief
ker'nel (*grain*)
  ker'neled, ker'nel·ing
  (SEE colonel)
ker'o·sene' or
  ker'o·sine'
ker·plunk'
kes'trel

ketch
  pl. ketch'es
ketch'up
ke'tene
ke'tone
ket'tle
ket'tle·drum'
key (*lock device*)
  pl. keys; (*v.*) keyed,
  key'ing
  (SEE cay *and* quay)
key·board
key' club'
key'hole'
Keynes
key'note'
  key'not'ed, key'not'ing
key'not'er
key'punch'
key'stone'
key'stroke'
khak'i
  pl. khak'is
khan
Khar·toum'
Khmer
Khy'ber Pass'
kib'ble
  kib'bled, kib'bling
kib·butz'
  pl. kib·but·zim'
Ki'bei'
  pl. Ki'bei'
kib'itz·er
ki'bosh
kick
kick'back'
kick'off'
kick'stand'
kid
  kid'ded, kid'ding
Kid'dush
kid'dy or kiddie
  pl. kid'dies
kid'nap
  kid'napped or
  kid'naped, kid'nap·ping
  or kid'nap·ing

kid'nap•per or
  kid'nap•er
kid'ney
  pl. kid'neys
kid'ney bean'
kid'ney stone'
kid'skin'
kiel•ba'sa
Kier'ke•gaard'
Ki'ev
Ki'ev•an
Ki•ga'li
kill
kill'deer'
kill'er
kil'li•fish'
  pl. kil'li•fish' or
  kil'li•fish'es
kill'ing
kill'–joy'
kiln
kiln'–dry'
  kiln'–dried',
  kiln'–dry'ing
kil'o
  pl. kil'os
kil'o•cy'cle
kil'o•gram'
kil'o•hertz'
kil'o•li'ter or
  kil'o•li'tre
ki•lom'e•ter or
  kil'o•me'tre
kil'o•volt'
kil'o•watt'
kil'o•watt'–hour'
kilt
kil'ter
ki•mo'no
  pl. ki•mo'nos
kin
kind
kin'der•gar'ten
kind'heart'ed
kin'dle
  kin'dled, kin'dling
kind'li•ness
kin'dling
kind'ly

kind'ness
kin'dred
kin•e•mat'ics
kin'e•scope'
  kin'e•scoped',
  kin'e•scop'ing
kin•es•the'sia
kin•es•thet'ic
ki•net'ic
ki•net'ics
kin'folk'
king
king'dom
king'fish'
  pl. king'fish' or
  king'fish'es
king'fish'er
king'let
king'ly
king'mak'er
king'pin'
king's Eng'lish
king'–size'
Kings'ton
kink
kin'ka•jou'
kink'y
  kink'i•er, kink'i•est
kins'folk'
kin'ship
Kin•sha•sa
kins'man
  pl. kins'men
kins'wom'an
  pl. kins'wom'en
ki•osk'
Ki'o•wa
  pl. Ki'o•was or
  Ki'o•wa
kip
kip'per
kirk
kirsch
kis'met
kiss
kiss'a•ble
kiss'er
kit
kitch'en

Kitch'en•er
kitch'en•ette'
kitch'en•ware'
kite
  kit'ed, kit'ing
kith
kith' and kin'
kitsch
kit'ten
kit'ten•ish
kit'ti•wake'
kit'ty
  pl. kit'ties
kit'ty–cor'nered
Ki•wa'nis
ki'wi
  pl. ki'wis
klan
Klans'man
  pl. Klans'men
klax'on
Kleen'ex
  (*Trademark*)
klep'to•ma'ni•a
klep'to•ma'ni•ac'
klieg' light'
Klon'dike
klutze
knack
knack'wurst
knap'sack'
knave (*rogue*)
  (SEE nave)
knav'er•y
  pl. knav'er•ies
knav'ish
knead (*mix*)
  (SEE need)
knee
  kneed, knee'ing
knee'cap'
knee'–deep'
knee'–high'
knee'hole'
knee' jerk'
kneel
  knelt or kneeled,
  kneel'ing
knee'pad'
knell

Knes'set

knew

knick'ers

knick'er · bock'ers

knick'knack'

knife
pl. knives; (v.) knifed, knif'ing

knight (soldier)
(SEE night)

knight'-er'rant
pl. knights'-er'rant

knight'hood

knight'ly

knish
pl. knish'es

knit
knit'ted or knit,
knit'ting

knit'ter

knob
knobbed, knob'bing

knob'by
knob'bi · er, knob'bi · est

knock

knock'a · bout'

knock'down'

knock'er

knock'-knee'

knock'-kneed'

knock'out'

knock'wurst

knoll

Knos'sos

knot (tie)
knot'ted, knot'ting
(SEE not)

knot'hole'

knot'ty
knot'ti · er, knot'ti · est

knout

know (understand)
knew, known, know'ing
(SEE no)

know'a · ble

know'-how'

know'ing

know'-it-all'

knowl'edge

knowl'edge · a · ble

knowl'edge · a · bly

known

know'-noth'ing

knuck'le
knuck'led, knuck'ling

knuck'le · head'

knurl

ko · a'la

kohl · ra'bi
pl. kohl · ra'bies

ko'la

ko · lin'sky
pl. ko · lin'skies

Kol' Ni'dre

kook

kook'a · bur'ra

kook'y
kook'i · er, kook'i · est

ko'peck

Ko · ran'

Ko · re'a

Ko · re'an

ko'ru · na'
pl. ko'ru · ny or ko'run
or ko'ru · nas'

Kos'ci · us'ko

ko · sher

ko'to
pl. ko'tos or (Japn.)
ko'to

kow'tow'

kraal

kraut

Krem'lin

krill
pl. krill

Krish'na

kro'na (Icelandic
money)
pl. kro'nor

kró'na (Swedish
money)
pl. kró'nur

kro'ne (Danish and
Norwegian money)
pl. kro'ner

kryp'ton

Kua'la Lum · pur'

Ku'blai Khan'

ku'chen

ku'dos

ku'du

kud'zu

Ku' Klux' Klan'

ku · lak'

küm'mel

kum'quat

kung' fu'

Kuo'min'tang'

Kurd

Ku · wait'

Ku · wai'ti

kvetch

kwa'cha

kwash'i · or'kor

kyat

ky'mo · graph'

Kyo'to

Kyr'i · e' e · le'i · son'

L

laa'ger

lab

la'bel
la'beled or la'belled,
la'bel · ing or la'bel · ling

la'bel · er

la'bi · al

la'bi · ate'

la'bile

la'bi · um
pl. la'bi · a

la'bor

lab'o · ra · to'ry
pl. lab'o · ra · to'ries

la'bored

la'bor · er

la · bo'ri · ous

la'bor-sav'ing

Lab'ra · dor'

la · bur'num

lab′y•rinth

lab′y•rin′thine

lac (*resin*)
(SEE lack)

lace
 laced, lac′ing

lac′er•ate′
 lac′er•at′ed,
 lac′er•at′ing

lac′er•a′tion

lace′wing′

lach′es

lach′ry•mal

lach′ry•mose′

lac′ing

lack (*deficiency*)
(SEE lac)

lack′a•dai′si•cal

lack′a•dai′si•cal•ly

lack′ey
 pl. lack′eys; (v.)
 lack′eyed, lack′ey•ing

lack′lus′ter

la•con′ic

la•con′i•cal•ly

lac′quer

lac′ri•mal

la•crosse′

lac′tase

lac′tate
 lac′tat•ed, lac′tat•ing

lac•ta′tion

lac′te•al

lac′tic

lac′to•ba•cil′lus
 pl. lac′to•ba•cil′li

lac′to•pro′tein

lac′tose

la•cu′na
 pl. la•cu′nae or
 la•cu′nas

la•cus′trine

lac′y
 lac′i•er, lac′i•est

lad

lad′der

lad′der back′

lad′dle

lade
 lad′ed, lad′en or lad′ed,
 lad′ing

lad′en

la′dies′ room′

la′dle
 la′dled, la′dling

la•drone′

la′dy
 pl. la′dies

la′dy•bug

la′dy•fin′ger

la′dy-in-wait′ing
 pl. la′dies-in-wait′ing

la′dy-kill′er

la′dy•like′

la′dy•love′

la′dy•ship′

la′dy′s maid′

la′dy′s-slip′per

la′e•trile′

La•fa•yette′

lag
 lagged, lag′ging

la′ger

lag′gard

la•gniappe′

la•goon′

La′gos

La Guar′di•a

La•hore′

la′ic

laid

laid′-back′

lain

lair (*den*)
(SEE layer)

laird

lais′sez faire′

la′i•ty

lake

lake′front′

lak′er

lam (*beat; flee*)
 lammed, lam′ming
(SEE lamb)

la′ma (*monk*)
(SEE llama)

La•maze′

lamb (*sheep*)
(SEE lam)

lam•baste′ or
 lam•bast′
 lam•bast′ed,
 lam•bast′ing

lamb′da

lam′ben•cy
 pl. lam′ben•cies

lam′bent

lamb′kin

lamb′skin′

lame
 (*adj.*) lam′er,
 lam′est; (*v.*)
 lamed, lam′ing

la•mé′

lame′brain′

lame′ duck′

la•mel′la
 pl. la•mel′lae or
 la•mel′las

la•ment′

lam′en•ta•ble

lam′en•ta•bly

lam′en•ta′tion

lam′i•na
 pl. lam′i•nae′ or
 lam′i•nas

lam′i•nal

lam′i•nar

lam′i•nate′
 lam′i•nat′ed,
 lam′i•nat′ing

lam′i•na′tion

lam′i•na′tor

lamp

lamp′black′

lamp′light′

lamp′light′er

lam•poon′

lam•poon′er

lam•poon′ist

lamp′post′

lam′prey
 pl. lam′preys

lamp′shade′

la•na′i

lance
 lanced, lanc′ing

lance′let

Lan′ce•lot

lanc'er

lan'cet

land

lan'dau

land'ed

land'fall'

land' grant'

land'hold'er

land'ing

land'ing craft'

land'ing strip'

land'la'dy
  pl. land'la'dies

land'locked'

land'lord'

land'lub'ber

land'mark'

land'mass'

land' mine'

land'own'er

land'scape'
  land'scaped',
  land'scap'ing

land'scap'ist

land'slide'
  land'slid', land'slid' or
  land'slid'den,
  land'slid'ing

lands'man
  pl. lands'men

land'ward

land'wards

lane

lang'syne' or lang'
  syne'

lan'guage

lan'guid

lan'guish

lan'guor

lan'guor • ous

lank

lank'i • ness

lank'y
  lank'i • er, lank'i • est

lan'o • lin

Lan'sing

lan • ta'na

lan'tern

lan'tha • num

lan'yard

La'os

La • o'tian

Lao'-tzu'

lap
  lapped, lap'ping

La Paz'

lap' dog'

la • pel'

lap'i • dar'y
  pl. lap'i • dar'ies

lap'in

lap'is laz'u • li

Lap'land'

Lap'land • er

Lapp

lap'pet

Lap'pish

lap' robe'

lapse
  lapsed, laps'ing

lar'ce • nist

lar'ce • nous

lar'ce • ny
  pl. lar'ce • nies

larch
  pl. larch'es

lard

lar'der

lar'es
  sing. lar

large
  larg'er, larg'est

large'ly

large'ness

large'-scale'

lar • gess' or lar • gesse'

lar • ghet'to
  pl. lar • ghet'tos

larg'ish

lar'go
  pl. lar'gos

lar'i • at

lark

lark'spur'

lar'ri • gan

lar'va
  pl. lar'vae

lar'val

la • ryn'ge • al

lar'yn • gi'tis

la • ryn'go • scope'

lar'ynx
  pl. la • ryn'ges or
  lar'ynx • es

la • sa'gna or la • sa'gne

las • civ'i • ous

la'ser (light beam)
  (SEE lazar)

lash

lash'ing

lass
  pl. lass'es

las'sie

las'si • tude'

las'so
  pl. las'sos or las'soes;
  (v.) las'soed, las'so • ing

last

Las'tex (Trademark)

last'ing

Las Ve'gas

lat'a • ki'a

latch
  pl. latch'es

latch'key'
  pl. latch'keys'

latch'string'

late
  (adj.) lat'er or lat'ter,
  lat'est or last; (adv.)
  lat'er, lat'est

late'com'er

la • teen'

late'ly

la'ten • cy

la'tent

lat'er • al

Lat'er • an

la • tex
  pl. lat'i • ces' or
  la'tex • es

lath (strip)

lathe (machine)
  lathed, lath'ing
  (SEE lath)

lath'er

lath'er • y

La'tin

La · ti′no
lat′i · tude′
lat′i · tu′di · nal
la · trine′
lat′ter
lat′ter–day′
lat′tice
  lat′ticed, lat′tic · ing
lat′tice · work′
Lat′vi · a
Lat′vi · an
lau · an′
laud
laud′a · bil′i · ty
laud′a · ble
laud′a · bly
lau′da · num
lau′da · to′ry
laugh
laugh′a · ble
laugh′ing · stock′
laugh′ter
launch
launch′er
launch′ pad′
lauch′ing pad′
laun′der
laun′der · ette′
laun′dress
  pl. laun′dress · es
Laun′dro · mat′
  (Trademark)
laun′dry
  pl. laun′dries
laun′dry · man′
  pl. laun′dry · men′
lau′re · ate
lau′rel
  lau′rel · ing
Lau · ren′tian
la′va
la · va′bo
  pl. la · va′boes
La · val′
la′va · liere′
la · va′tion
lav′a · to′ry
  pl. lav′a · to′ries

lave
  laved, lav′ing
lav′en · der
lav′ish
law
law′–a · bid′ing
law′break′er
law′ful
law′ful · ly
law′giv′er
law′less
law′mak′er
law′man′
  pl. law′men′
lawn
law · ren′ci · um
law′suit′
law′yer
lax
lax′a · tive
lax′i · ty
lay (put down;
  poem; secular)
  laid or layed, lay′ing
  (SEE lei)
lay′a · way
layed
lay′er (thickness)
  (SEE lair)
lay · ette′
lay′man
  pl. lay′men
lay′off′
lay′out′
lay′o′ver
laz′ar
laz′a · ret′to
  pl. laz′a · ret′tos
laze
  lazed, laz′ing
la′zi · ly
la′zi · ness
la′zy
  la′zi · er, la′zi · est
la′zy · bones′
la′zy Su′san
L′–do′pa
lea (meadow)
  (SEE lee)

leach (percolate)
  (SEE leech)
lead (guide; metal)
  led, lead′ing
  (SEE lied)
lead′en
lead′er
lead′er · ship′
lead′–in′
lead′ing
lead′off′
leaf (foliage)
  pl. leaves
  (SEE lief)
leaf · age
leaf′hop · per
leaf′let
leaf′stalk′
leaf′y
  leaf′i · er, leaf′i · est
league
  leagued, lea′guing
lea′guer
leak (opening)
  (SEE leek)
leak′age
leak′y
  leak′i · er, leak′i · est
lean (incline; thin)
  (SEE lien)
lean′ing
lean′ness
lean′–to′
  pl. lean′–tos′
leap
  leaped or leapt, leap′ing
leap′frog′
  leap′frogged′,
  leap′frog′ging
leap′ year′
learn
  learned or learnt,
  learn′ing
learn′ed
learn′er
learn′ing
lease
  leased, leas′ing
lease′hold′
leash
  pl. leash′es
least

least'wise'
leath'er
Leath·er·ette' (Trademark)
leath'ern
leath'er·neck'
Leath'er·oid' (Trademark)
leath'er·y
leave
    left, leav'ing
leaved
leav'en
leave'-tak'ing
leav'ings
Leb'a·nese'
    pl. Leb'a·nese'
Leb'a·non
Le'bens·raum'
lech'er
lech'er·ous
lech'er·y
    pl. lech'er·ies
lec'i·thin
Le Cor·bu·sier'
lec'tern
lec'tion
lec'tor
lec'ture
    lec'tured, lec'tur·ing
lec'tur·er
le'der·ho'sen
ledge
    ledged, ledg'ing
ledg'er
lee (shelter)
    (SEE lea)
Lee
leech (worm)
    pl. leech'es
    (SEE leach)
leek (plant)
    (SEE leak)
leer
leer'y
    leer'i·er, leer'i·est
lees
lee'ward
lee'way'
left

Left' Bank'
left' field'
left'-hand'
left'-hand'ed
left'-hand'er
left'ist
left'o'ver
left' wing'
left'-wing'er
left'y
    pl. left'ies
leg
    legged, leg'ging
leg'a·cy
    pl. leg'a·cies
le'gal
le'gal·ism'
le'gal·ist
le'gal·is'tic
le·gal'i·ty
    pl. le·gal'i·ties
le'gal·i·za'tion
le'gal·ize'
    le'gal·ized', le'gal·iz'ing
le'gal·ly
leg'ate
leg·a·tee'
le·ga'tion
le·ga'to
leg'end
leg'en·dar'y
    pl. leg'en·dar'ies
leg'er·de·main'
leg'ged
leg'ging or leg'gin
leg'gy
    leg'gi·er, leg'gi·est
Leg'horn'
leg'i·bil'i·ty
leg'i·ble
leg'i·bly
le'gion
le'gion·ar'y
    pl. le'gion·ar'ies
le'gion·naire'
leg'is·late'
    leg'is·lat'ed, leg'is·lat'ing
leg'is·la'tion

leg'is·la'tive
leg'is·la'tor
leg'is·la'ture
le·git'i·ma·cy
le·git'i·mate (adj.)
le·git'i·mate' (v.)
    le·git'i·mat'ed, le·git'i·mat'ing
le·git'i·mate·ly
le·git'i·mize'
    le·git'i·mized', le·git'i·miz'ing
leg'man'
    pl. leg'men'
leg'-of-mut'ton
leg'room'
leg'ume
le·gu'mi·nous
leg'work'
le'i (wreath)
    pl. le'is
    (SEE lay)
lei'sure
lei'sured
lei'sure·li·ness
lei'sure·ly
leit'mo·tif'
lek
lem'ming
lem'on
lem'on·ade'
lem·pi'ra
le'mur
lend
    lent, lend'ing
lend'er
lend'-lease'
    lend'-leased', lend'-leas'ing
length
length'en
length'ways'
length'wise'
length'y
    length'i·er, length'i·est
le'ni·ence
le'ni·en·cy
    pl. le'ni·en·cies
le'ni·ent
Len'in

Len'in·grad'
len'i·tive
len'i·ty
  pl. len'i·ties
lens
  pl. lens'es
lent
Lent
len·ta·men'te
Lent'en
len'til
len·tis'si·mo'
len'to
Le'o
Le·o·nar'do da Vin'ci
Le·on'ca·val'lo
le·one'
le'o·nine'
leop'ard
le'o·tard'
lep'er
lep'i·dop'ter·ous
lep're·chaun'
lep'ro·sy
lep'rous
lep'ton
  pl. lep'ta
les'bi·an
les'bi·an·ism'
lese' maj'es·ty
le'sion
Le·so'tho
less
les·see'
less'en (*reduce*)
  (SEE lesson)
less'er (*smaller*)
  (SEE lessor)
les'son (*instruction*)
  (SEE lessen)
les'sor (*lease giver*)
  (SEE lesser)
lest
let
  let, let'ting
let'down'
le'thal
le·thal'i·ty
le'thal·ly

le·thar'gic
leth'ar·gy
  pl. leth'ar·gies
Lett
let'ter
let'ter box'
let'tered
let'ter·head'
let'ter·ing
let'ter·man'
  pl. let'ter·men'
let'ter–per'fect
let'ter·press'
Let'tish
let'tuce
let'up'
le'u
  pl. lei
leu·ke'mi·a
leu'ko·cyte' or
  leu'co·cyte'
lev
  pl. lev'a
Le·vant'
Le'van·tine'
lev'ee (*embankment*)
  lev'eed, lev'ee·ing
  (SEE levy)
lev'el
  lev'eled or lev'elled,
  lev'el·ing or lev'el·ling
lev'el·er
lev'el·head'ed
lev'er
lev'er·age
Le'vi
le·vi'a·than
Le·vi's (*Trademark*)
lev'i·tate'
  lev'i·tat'ed, lev'i·tat'ing
lev'i·ta'tion
Le'vite
Le·vit'i·cus
lev'i·ty
  pl. lev'i·ties
lev'y (*tax*)
  pl. lev'ies; (*v.*) lev'ied,
  lev'y·ing
  (SEE levee)
lewd

lewd'ness
lex'i·cal
lex'i·cog'ra·pher
lex'i·co·graph'ic
lex'i·co·graph'i·cal
lex'i·cog'ra·phy
lex'i·con
Lex'ing·ton
Ley'den jar'
Lha'sa
li'a·bil'i·ty
  pl. li'a·bil'i·ties
li'a·ble (*likely*)
  (SEE libel)
li'ai·son'
li·a'na
li'ar (*one who lies*)
  (SEE lyre)
lib
li·ba'tion
li'bel (*defame*)
  li'beled or li'belled,
  li'bel·ing or li'bel·ling
  (SEE liable)
li'bel·er or li'bel·ler
li'bel·ous or
  li'bel·lous
lib'er·al
lib'er·al·ism'
lib'er·al'i·ty
  pl. lib'er·al'i·ties
lib'er·al·i·za'tion
lib'er·al·ize'
  lib'er·al·ized',
  lib'er·al·iz'ing
lib'er·al·ly
lib'er·ate'
  lib'er·at'ed,
  lib'er·at'ing
lib'er·a'tion
lib'er·a'tor
Li·be'ri·a
Li·be'ri·an
lib'er·tar'i·an
lib'er·tine'
lib'er·ty
  pl. lib'er·ties
li·bid'i·nal
li·bid'i·nous
li·bi'do

Li'bra

li·brar'i·an

li'brar·y
pl. li'brar·ies

li·bret'tist

li·bret'to
pl. li·bret'tos or
li·bret'ti

Li·bre·ville'

Lib'y·a

Lib'y·an

li'cense
li'censed, li'cens·ing

li'cen·see'

li·cen'ti·ate

li·cen'tious

li'chen (plant)
(SEE liken)

lic'it

lick

lick'e·ty–split'

lic'o·rice

lid

lid'ded

lie (tell untruth)
lied, ly'ing
(SEE lye)

lie (recline)
lay, lain, ly'ing
(SEE lye)

lieb'frau·milch'

Leich'ten·stein'

lied (song)
pl. lied'er
(SEE lead)

Lie'der·kranz'
(Trademark)

lie' de·tec'tor

lief (gladly)
(SEE leaf)

liege

lien (claim)
(SEE lean)

lieu

lieu·ten'an·cy
pl. lieu·ten'an·cies

lieu·ten'ant

life
pl. lives

life' belt'

life'blood'

life'boat'

life' buoy'

life'guard'

life' jack'et

life'less

life'like'

life' line'

life'long'

life' pre·serv'er

lif'er

life' raft'

life'sav'er

life'–size'

life'–sized'

life' span'

life'style' or life'
style'

life'time'

life'work'

lift

lift'–off'

lig'a·ment

lig'a·ture
lig'a·tured,
lig'a·tur·ing

light
light'ed or lit, light'ing

light'en

light'er

light'face'

light'–fin'gered

light'–foot'ed

light'–head'ed

light'–heart'ed

light'house'

light'ing

light'ly

light'ness

light'ning

light'proof'

light'ship'

light'weight'

light'–year'

lig'ne·ous

lig'nin

lig'nite

lig'num vi'tae

lik'a·ble or like'a·ble

like
(adj.) lik'er, lik'est;
(v.) liked, lik'ing

like'li·hood'

like'ly
like'li·er, like'li·est

like'–mind'ed

lik'en (compare)
(SEE lichen)

like'ness

like'wise'

lik'ing

li'lac

Lil'li·pu'tian

lilt

lil'y
pl. lil'ies

lil'y of the val'ley
pl. lil'ies of the val'ley

lil'y–white' (adj.)

Li'ma

li'ma bean'

limb (body part)
(SEE limn)

lim'ber

lim'bo
pl. lim'bos

Lim'burg·er

lime
limed, lim'ing

lime'ade'

lime'light'

lim'er·ick

lime'stone'

lim'it

lim'it·a·ble

lim'i·ta'tion

lim'it·ed

lim'it·less

limn

lim'ner

lim·nol'o·gy

Li·moges'

lim'ou·sine'

limp

lim'pet

lim'pid

lim·pid'i·ty

limp'ly
lim'y
  lim'i·er, lim'i·est
lin'age (*lines*)
  (SEE lineage)
linch'pin'
Lin'coln
Lin'coln·esque'
Lind'bergh
lin'den
line
  lined, lin'ing
lin'e·age (*ancestry*)
  (SEE linage)
lin'e·al
lin'e·a·ment
  (*feature*)
  (SEE liniment)
lin'e·ar
line'back'er
line' drive'
line'man
  pl. line'men
lin'en
lin'er
lines'man
  pl. lines'men
lines'-up'
lin'ger
lin'ge·rie'
lin'go
  pl. lin'goes
lin'gua fran'ca
  pl. lin'gua fran'cas or
  lin'guae fran'cae
lin'gual
lin·gui'ni
lin'guist
lin·guis'tic
lin·guis'tics
lin'i·ment
  (*medication*)
  (SEE lineament)
lin'ing
link
link'age
links (*golf course*)
  (SEE lynx)
link'up'
Lin·ne'an

lin'net
li·no'le·um
Lin'o·type'
  (*Trademark*)
lin'seed'
lin'sey-wool'sey
  pl. lin'sey-wool'seys
lint
lin'tel
li'on
li'on·ess
  pl. li'on·ess·es
li'on·heart'ed
li'on·i·za'tion
li'on·ize'
  li'on·ized', li'on·iz'ing
lip
li'pase
li'pid or li'pide
Lip'pi
lip'-read'
  lip'-read', lip'-read'ing
lip' ser'vice
lip'stick'
liq'ue·fac'tion
liq'ue·fi'a·ble
liq'ue·fi'er
liq'ue·fy'
  liq'ue·fied',
  liq'ue·fy'ing
li·ques'cence
li·ques'cent
li·queur'
liq'uid
liq'ui·date'
  liq'ui·dat'ed,
  liq'ui·dat'ing
liq'ui·da'tion
liq'ui·da'tor
li·quid'i·ty
liq'uor
li'ra
  pl. li're or li'ras
Lis'bon
lisle
lisp
lisp'er
lis'some or lis'som
list

lis'ten
lis'ten·er
list'ing
list'less
list' price'
Liszt
lit
lit'a·ny
  pl. lit'a·nies
li'tchi
  pl. li'tchis
li'ter
lit'er·a·cy
lit'er·al (*exact*)
  (SEE littoral)
lit'er·al·ly
lit'er·ar'y
lit'er·ate
lit'e·ra'ti
lit'er·a·ture
lithe
  lith'er, lith'est
lithe'some
lith'ic
lith'i·um
lith'o·graph'
li·thog'ra·pher
lith'o·graph'ic
lith'o·graph'i·cal
li·thog'ra·phy
lith'o·sphere'
Lith'u·a'ni·a
Lith'u·a'ni·an
lit'i·ga·ble
lit'i·gant
lit'i·gate'
  lit'i·gat'ed, lit'i·gat'ing
lit'i·ga'tion
lit'i·ga'tor
li·ti'gious
lit'mus
lit'ter
lit'ter·bag'
lit'ter·bug'
lit'tle
  (*adj.*) less or less'er,
  least or lit'tler (*adv.*)
  less, least

lit'tle·neck'
Lit'tle·Rock'
lit'to·ral (*shore*)
  (SEE literal)
li·tur'gi·cal
li·tur'gi·cal·ly
lit'ur·gist
lit'ur·gy
  pl. lit'ur·gies
liv'a·ble or live'a·ble
live (*v.*)
  lived, liv'ing
live (*adj.*)
  liv'er, liv'est
live'-in'
live'li·hood'
live'long'
live'li·ness
live'ly
liv'en
liv'er
liv'er·ied
liv'er·wort'
liv'er·wurst'
liv'er·y
  pl. liv'er·ies
liv'er·y·man
  pl. liv'er·y·men
live'stock'
liv'id
liv'ing
liv'ing room'
liz'ard
lla'ma (*animal*)
  (SEE lama)
lla'no
  pl. lla'nos
lo (*behold*)
  (SEE low)
load (*cargo*)
  (SEE lode)
load'ed
load'ing
load'stone
loaf
  pl. loaves
loaf'er
loam
loam'y

loan (*lend*)
  (SEE lone)
loan' word'
loath (*reluctant*)
  (SEE loathe)
loathe (*detest*)
  loathed, loath'ing
  (SEE loath)
loath'ing
loath'some
lob
  lobbed, lob'bing
lo'bar
lob'by
  pl. lob'bies; (*v.*)
  lob'bied, lob'by·ing
lob'by·ist
lobe
lo·bel'ia
lob'lol'ly
  pl. lob'lol'lies
lo'bo
  pl. lo'bos
lo·bot'o·my
  pl. lo·bot'o·mies
lob'ster
lo'cal
lo·cale'
lo·cal'i·ty
  pl. lo·cal'i·ties
lo'cal·i·za'tion
lo'cal·ize'
  lo'cal·ized',
  lo'cal·iz'ing
lo'cal·ly
lo'cate
  lo'cat·ed, lo'cat·ing
lo·ca'tion
loc'a·tive
loch
lock
Locke
lock'er
lock'er room'
lock'et
lock'jaw'
lock'out'
lock'smith'
lock' step'
lock'up'

lo'co
  pl. lo'cos; (*v.*) lo'coed,
  lo'co·ing
lo'co·mo'tion
lo'co·mo'tive
lo'co·weed'
lo'cus
  pl. lo'ci or lo'ca
lo'cust
lo·cu'tion
lode (*mineral
  deposit*)
  (SEE load)
lo'den
lode'star'
lode'stone'
lodge (*house*)
  lodged, lodg'ing
  (SEE loge)
lodg'er
lodg'ing
lodg'ment or
  lodge'ment
lo'ess
loft
loft'i·ly
loft'i·ness
loft'y
  loft'i·er, loft'i·est
log
  logged, log'ging
lo'gan·ber'ry
  pl. lo'gan·ber'ries
log'a·rithm'
log'a·rith'mic
loge (*theater seat*)
  (SEE lodge)
log'ger·head'
log'gia
  pl. log'gias or (*It.*)
  log'gie
log'ging
log'ic
log'i·cal
log'i·cal·ly
lo·gi'cian
lo·gis'tic
lo·gis'ti·cal
lo·gis'tics
log'jam'

lo′go
lo′gos
log′o·type′
log′roll′ing
lo′gy
  lo′gi·er, lo′gi·est
loin
loin′cloth′
loi′ter
loll
lol′a·pa·loo′za
lol′li·pop′ or
  lol′ly·pop′
Lo·mé′
Lon′don
lone (*solitary*)
  (SEE loan)
lone′li·ness
lone′ly
  lone′li·er, lone′li·est
lon′er
lone′some
long
Long′Beach′
long′boat′
long′bow′
long′-dis′tance
long′-drawn′
lon·gev′i·ty
lon·ge′vous
long′hair′
long′-haired′
long′hand′
long′ horn′
long′ing
lon′gi·tude′
lon′gi·tu′di·nal
lon′gi·tu′di·nal·ly
long′-lived′
long′play′ing
long′-range′
long′shore′man
  pl. long′shore′men
long′-sight′ed
long′stand′ing
long′-suf′fer·ing
long′-term′
long′time′

Lon·gueuil′
long′-wind′ed
look
look′er-on′
  pl. look′ers-on′
look′ing glass′
look′out′
look′see′
loom
loon
loon′y or loon′ey
  loon′i·er, loon′i·est
loop (*circular fold*)
  (SEE loupe)
loop′hole′
  loop′holed′, loop′hol′ing
loop′-the-loop′
loose (*not tight*)
  (*adj.*) loos′er, loos′est;
  (*v.*) loosed, loos′ing
  (SEE lose)
loose′-joint′ed
loose′-leaf′
loose′ly
loos·en
loose′ness
loot (*plunder*)
  (SEE lute)
loot′er
lop
  lopped, lop′ping
lope
  loped, lop′ing
lop′-eared′
lop′er
lop′sid′ed
lo·qua′cious
lo·quac′i·ty
lo′ran
lord
lord′ly
lor·do′sis
lord′ship
lore
Lor′e·lei′
lor·gnette′
lor′ry
  pl. lor′ries

Los An′ge·les
lose (*mislay*)
  lost, los′ing
  (SEE loose)
los′er
loss
  pl. loss′es
lost
lot
  lot′ted, lot′ting
Lo·thar′i·o
  pl. Lo·thar′i·os
lo′tion
lo′tos
  pl. lo′tos·es
lot′ter·y
  pl. lot′ter·ies
lot′to
lo′tus
  pl. lo′tus·es
loud
loud′-mouth′
loud′mouth′
loud′-mouthed′
loud′speak′er
Lou·i′si·an′a
Lou·i′si·an′an or
  Lou·i′si·an′i·an
Lou′is·ville′
lounge
  lounged, loung′ing
loupe (*magnifier*)
  (SEE loop)
lour
Lourdes
louse
  pl. lice or lous′es; (*v.*)
  loused, lous′ing
lous′y
  lous′i·er, lous′i·est
lout
lout′ish
lou′ver
Lou′vre
lov′a·ble
lov′a·bly
love
  loved, lov′ing
love′bird′
love′less
love′lorn′

love'li‧ness

love'ly
 love'li‧er, love'li‧est

love'-mak'ing

lov'er

love' seat'

love'sick'

lov'ing

low (not high)
 (SEE lo)

low'born'

low'boy'

low'bred'

low'brow' (n.)

low'brow' (adj.)

low'-cal'

Low' Church'

low'-down' (n.)

low'-down' (adj.)

low'er

low'er-case'
 low'er-cased', low'er-
 cas'ing

low'er‧most'

low'-key'

low'-keyed'

low'land

low'-lev'el

low'li‧ness

low'ly
 low'li‧er, low'li‧est

Low' Mass'

low'-mind'ed

low'-pitched'

low'-pres'sure

low' pro'file

low'-spir'it‧ed

low'-test'

low' tide'

lox

loy'al

loy'al‧ist

loy'al‧ly

loy'al‧ty
 pl. loy'al‧ties

Loy‧o'la

loz'enge

Lu‧an'da

lu‧au'

lub'ber

lu'bri‧cant

lu'bri‧cate'
 lu'bri‧cat'ed,
 lu'bri‧cat'ing

lu'bri‧ca'tion

lu'bri‧ca'tor

lu‧bri'cious

lu'bri‧cous

lu'cent

lu'cid

lu‧cid'i‧ty

Lu'ci‧fer

Lu'cite (Trademark)

luck

luck'i‧ly

luck'i‧ness

luck'y
 luck'i‧er, luck'i‧est

lu'cra‧tive

lu'cre

lu'cu‧bra'tion

lu'di‧crous

luff

Luft'waf'fe

lug
 lugged, lug'ging

Lu'ger (Trademark)

lug'gage

lu‧gu'bri‧ous

Luke

luke'warm'

lull

lull'a‧by'
 pl. lull'a‧bies'; (v.)
 lull'a‧bied',
 lull'a‧by'ing

lum‧ba'go

lum'bar (of loins)
 (SEE lumber)

lum'ber (wood)
 (SEE lumbar)

lum'ber‧jack'

lum'ber‧man
 pl. lum'ber‧men

lum'ber‧mill'

lum'ber‧yard'

lu'men
 pl. lu'mi‧na

lu'mi‧nance

lu'mi‧nar'y
 pl. lu'mi‧nar'ies

lu'mi‧nesce'
 lu'mi‧nesced',
 lu'mi‧nesc'ing

lu'mi‧nes'cence

lu'mi‧nes'cent

lu'mi‧nos'i‧ty
 pl. lu'mi‧nos'i‧ties

lu'mi‧nous

lum'mox

lump

lump'ish

lump'y
 lump'i‧er, lump'i‧est

lu'na‧cy
 pl. lu'na‧cies

lu'nar

lu'na‧tic

lunch

lunch'eon

lunch'eon‧ette'

lunch'room'

lunch'time'

lu‧nette'

lung

lunge
 lunged, lung'ing

lung'fish'
 pl. lung'fish' or
 lung'fish'es

lu'pine

lu'pus

lurch

lure
 lured, lur'ing

lu'rid

lurk

Lu‧sa'ka

lus'cious

lush
 pl. lush'es

lust

lus'ter or lus'tre

lust'ful

lus'trous

lust'i‧ly

lust'i‧ness

lust'y
 lust'i‧er, lust'i‧est

lute (*musical
　　instrument*)
　lut′ed, lut′ing
lu·te′ti·um or
　lu·te′ci·um
Lu′ther
Lu′ther·an
Lu′ther·an·ism′
lut′ist
Lux′em·bourg′ or
　Lux′em·burg
lux·u′ri·ance
lux·u′ri·ant
lux·u′ri·ate′
　lux·u′ri·at′ed,
　lux·u′ri·at′ing

lu·u′ri·ous
lux′u·ry
　pl. lux′u·ries
ly·cée′
ly·ce′um
lye (*chemical*)
　(SEE lie)
ly′ing
ly′ing-in′
　pl. ly′ings-in′ or ly′ing-
　ins′
lymph
lym·phat′ic
lym′pho·cyte′
lym′phoid
lym·pho′ma

lym·pho′ma
lynch
lynx (*animal*)
　pl. lynx′es or lynx
　(SEE links)
ly′on·naise′
lyre (*harp*)
　(SEE liar)
lyre′bird′
lyr′ic
lyr′i·cal
lyr′i·cal·ly
lyr′i·cism′
lyr′i·cist
ly·ser′gic

M

ma
ma′am
ma·ca′bre
mac·ad′am
mac′a·da′mi·a
mac·ad′am·ize′
　mac·ad′am·ized′,
　mac·ad′am·iz′ing
Ma·cao′
ma·caque′
mac′a·ro′ni
　pl. mac′a·ro′nis or
　mac′a·ro′nies
mac′a·roon′
ma·caw′
Mac′ca·bees′
mace
Mac′e·do′ni·an
mac′er·ate′
　mac′er·at′ed,
　mac′er·at′ing
mac′er·a′tion
mac′er·a′tor or
　mac′er·a′ter
Mach
ma·chet′e
Mach′i·a·vel′li·an
mach′i·nate′
　mach′i·nat′ed,
　mach′i·nat′ing
mach′i·na′tion

ma·chine′
　ma·chined′,
　ma·chin′ing
ma·chine′ gun′ (*n.*)
ma·chine′- gun′
　(*v.*)
　ma·chine′-gunned′,
　ma·chine′-gun′ning
ma·chin′er·y
　pl. ma·chin′er·ies
ma·chin′ist
ma·chis′mo
mach′ num′ber
ma′cho
　pl. ma′chos
mack′er·el
　pl. mack′er·el or
　mack′er·els
mack′i·naw′
mack′in·tosh′
　(*raincoat*)
　(SEE McIntosh)
mac′ra·mé′
mac′ro
mac′ro·bi·ot′ic
mac′ro·bi·ot′ics
mac′ro·cosm′
mac′ro·cos′mic
mac′ro·e′co·nom′ics
mac′ro·mol′e·cule′
ma′cron

mac′ro·scop′ic
mac′ro·scop′i·cal
mac′u·late′ (*v.*)
　mac′u·lat′ed,
　mac′u·lat′ing
mac′u·late (*adj.*)
mac′u·la′tion
mad
　mad′der, mad′dest
Mad′a·gas′can
Mad′a·gas′car
mad′am
mad′ame
　pl. mes·dames′
mad′cap′
mad′den
mad′der
made
Ma·dei′ra
mad′e·moi·selle′
　pl. mad′e·moi·selles′
　or mes·de·moi·selles′
made′-to- or′der
made′-up′
mad′house′
Mad′i·son
mad′ly
mad′man′
　pl. mad′men′
mad′ness

Ma·don'na

Mad'ras

mad'ras

Ma·drid'

mad'ri·gal

mad'ri·lène'

mad'wo·man
  pl. mad'wo·men

mael'strom

maes'tro
  pl. maes'tros or
  (*It.*) ma·es'tri

Ma'fi·a

Ma'fi·o'so
  pl. Ma'fi·o'si

mag'a·zine'

Ma·gel'lan

ma·gen'ta

mag'got

mag'got·y

Ma'gi
  sing. Ma'gus

mag'ic

mag'i·cal

mag'i·cal·ly

ma·gi'cian

mag·is·te'ri·al

mag'is·tra·cy
  pl. mag'is·tra·cies

mag'is·tral

mag'is·trate'

mag'ma
  pl. mag'mas or
  mag'ma·ta

Mag'na Char'ta or
  Mag'na Car'ta

mag'na cum lau'de

mag'na·nim'i·ty
  pl. mag'na·nim'i·ties

mag·nan'i·mous

mag'nate (*business
  leader*)
  (SEE magnet)

mag·ne'sia

mag·ne'si·um

mag'net (*attracter*)
  (SEE magnate)

mag·net'ic

mag'net·ism'

mag'net·ite'

mag'net·iz'a·ble

mag'net·i·za'tion

mag'net·ize'
  mag'net·ized',
  mag'net·iz'ing

mag'net·iz'er

mag·ne'to
  pl. mag·ne'tos

mag'ne·tom'e·ter

mag'ni·fi·ca'tion

mag·nif'i·cence

mag·nif'i·cent

mag'ni·fi'er

mag'ni·fy'
  mag'ni·fied',
  mag'ni·fy'ing

mag·nil'o·quence

mag·nil'o·quent

mag'ni·tude'

mag·no'lia

mag'num

mag'pie

mag'uey

Mag'yar

ma·ha·ra'jah or
  ma'ha·ra'ja

ma·ha·ra'nee or
  ma'ha·ra'ni

ma·hat'ma

Mah'di
  pl. Mah'dis

mah'-jong' or mah'-
  jongg'

Mah'ler

ma·hog'a·ny
  pl. ma·hog'a·nies

ma·hout'

maid (*servant*)
  (SEE made)

maid'en

maid'en·hair'

maid'en·hood'

maid'en·ly

maid'-in-wait'ing
  pl. maids'-in-wait'ing

maid' of hon'or

maid'ser'vant

mail (*letters; armor*)
  (SEE male)

mail'bag'

mail'box'
  pl. mail'box'es

mail·lot'

mail'man'
  pl. mail'men'

mail' or'der

maim

main (*chief*)
  (SEE mane and
  Maine)

Maine (*State*)
  (SEE main and mane)

main'frame'

main'land'

main' line'

main'ly

main'mast'

main'sail'

main'sheet'

main'spring'

main'stay'

main'stream'

main·tain'

main·tain'a·ble

main'te·nance

mai' tai'

maî'tre d'hô·tel'

maize (*grain*)
  (SEE maze)

ma·jes'tic

ma·jes'ti·cal·ly

maj'es·ty
  pl. maj'es·ties

ma·jol'i·ca

ma'jor

Ma·jor'ca

Ma·jor'can

ma'jor–do'mo
  pl. ma'jor–do'mos

ma'jor·ette'

ma·jor'i·ty
  pl. ma·jor'i·ties

ma·jus'cule

make
  made, mak'ing

mak'a·ble

make'-be·lieve'

mak'er

make'–read'y

make'shift'
make'up'
make'-work'
mal'a·chite'
mal'ad·just'ed
mal'ad·just'ment
mal'ad·min'is·ter
mal'ad·min'is·tra'tion
mal'a·droit'
mal'a·dy
  pl. mal'a·dies
Mal'a·ga
Mal'a·gas'y
  pl. Mal'a·gas'y or
  Mal'a·gas'ies
ma·laise'
mal'a·prop·ism'
mal'ap·ro·pos'
ma·lar'i·a
ma·lar'i·al
ma·lar'key or
  ma·lar'ky
Ma·la'wi
Ma·la'wi·an
Ma'lay
Ma·lay'a
Ma·lay'an
Ma·lay'sia
Ma·lay'sian
mal'con·tent'
mal de mer'
Mal'dive
Mal·div'i·an
male (*masculine*)
  (SEE mail)
Ma'lé
mal'e·dic'tion
mal'e·fac'tor
ma·lef'ic
ma·lef'i·cence
ma·lef'i·cent
male'ness
ma·lev'o·lence
ma·lev'o·lent
mal·fea'sance
mal·fea'sant
mal'for·ma'tion
mal·formed'

mal·func'tion
Ma'li
Ma'li·an
mal'ic
mal'ice
ma·li'cious
ma·lign'
ma·lig'nan·cy
  pl. ma·lig'nan·cies
ma·lig'nant
ma·lig'ni·ty
  pl. ma·lig'ni·ties
ma'li·hi'ni
ma·lin'ger
ma·lin'ger·er
mall (*promenade*)
  (SEE maul)
mal'lard
mal'le·a·bil'i·ty
mal'le·a·ble
mal'let
mal'le·us
  pl. mal'le·i'
mal'low
malm'sey
mal'nour'ished
mal'nu·tri'tion
mal'oc·clud'ed
mal'oc·clu'sion
mal·o'dor·ous
mal·prac'tice
Mal·raux'
malt
Mal'ta
malt'ase
malt'ed milk'
Mal·tese'
  pl. Mal·tese'
Mal'thus
Mal·thu'si·an
malt'ose
mal·treat'
ma'ma
mam'ba
mam'bo
  pl. mam'bos
mam'ma
mam'mal

mam·ma'li·an
mam'ma·ry
mam'mo·gram'
mam·mog'ra·phy
mam'mon
mam'moth
mam'my
  pl. mam'mies
man
  pl. men; (*v.*) manned,
  man'ning
man'a·cle
  man'a·cled,
  man'a·cling
man'age
  man'aged, man'ag·ing
man'age·a·bil'i·ty
man'age·a·ble
man'age·a·bly
man'age·ment
man'a·ger
man'a·ge'ri·al
Ma·na'gua
Ma·na'ma
ma·ña'na
man'-at-arms'
  pl. men'-at-arms'
man'a·tee'
Man·chu'
  pl. Man·chus' or
  Man·chu'
Man·chu'ri·a
Man·chu'ri·an
man'da·la
man·da'mus
  pl. man·da'mus·es
Man·da·lay'
man'da·rin
man'da·tar'y
  pl. man'da·tar'ies
man'date
  man'dat·ed,
  man'dat·ing
man'da·to'ry
  pl. man'da·to'ries
man'di·ble
Man·din'go
  pl. Man·din'gos or
  Man·din'goes
man'do·lin
man·drag'o·ra

man'drake

man'drel (*shaft*)
(SEE mandrill)

man'drill (*baboon*)
(SEE mandrel)

mane (*hair*)
(SEE main *and* Maine)

ma·nège' or
ma·nege'
(*horsemanship*)
(SEE ménage)

ma'nes

Ma·net'

ma·neu'ver
ma·neu'vered,
ma·neu'ver·ing

ma·neu'ver·a·
bil'i·ty

ma·neu'ver·a·ble

man'ful

man'ful·ly

man'ga·nese'

mange

man'ger

man'gle
man'gled, man'gling

man'gler

man'go
pl. man'goes or
man'gos

man'grove

man'gy
man'gi·er, man'gi·est

man'han'dle
man'han'dled,
man'han'dling

Man·hat'tan

man'hole'

man'hood

man'-hour'

man'hunt'

ma'ni·a

ma'ni·ac'

ma·ni'a·cal

ma·ni'a·cal·ly

man'ic

man'ic–de·pres'sive

ma'ni·cot'ti

man'i·cure'
man'i·cured',
man'i·cur'ing

man'i·cur'ist

man'i·fest'

man'i·fes·ta'tion

man'i·fes'to
pl. man'i·fes'toes

man'i·fold'

man'i·kin or
man'ni·kin

Ma·nil'a

ma·nip'u·la·ble

ma·nip'u·late'
ma·nip'u·lat'ed,
ma·nip'u·lat'ing

ma·nip'u·la'tion

ma·nip'u·la'tive

ma·nip'u·la'tor

Man'i·to'ba

man'i·tou'
pl. man'i·tous' or
man'i·tou'

man'kind'

man'like'

man'li·ness

man'ly
man'li·er, man'li·est

man'-made'

man'na

man'ne·quin

man'ner (*way; sort*)
(SEE manor)

man'nered

man'ner·ism'

man'ner·ly

man'nish

man'-of-war'
pl. men'-of-war'

ma·nom'e·ter

man'or (*estate*)
(SEE manner)

ma·no'ri·al

man'pow'er

man·qué'

man'sard

manse

man'serv'ant
pl. men'serv'ants

man'sion

man'-size'

man'-sized'

man'slaugh'ter

man'ta

man'ta ray'

man'tel (*shelf*)
(SEE mantle)

man'tel·piece'

man·til'la

man'tis
pl. man'tis·es or
man'tes

man·tis'sa

man'tle (*cloak*)
man'tled, man'tling
(SEE mantel)

man'u·al

man'u·al·ly

man'u·fac'ture
man'u·fac'tured,
man'u·fac'tur·ing

man'u·fac'tur·er

man'u·mis'sion

man'u·mit'
man'u·mit'ted,
man'u·mit'ting

ma·nure'
ma·nured', ma·nur'ing

man'u·script'

Manx

man'y
more, most

man'y·sid'ed

Mao'ism

Mao'ist

Ma'o·ri
pl. Ma'o·ris or
Ma'o·ri

mao'tai'

Mao' Tse-tung'

map
mapped, map'ping

ma'ple

ma'ple su'gar

ma'ple syr'up

mar
marred, mar'ring

mar'a·bou'

ma·rac'a

mar'a·schi'no

mar'a·thon'

ma·raud'

ma·raud'er

mar'ble
mar'bled, mar'bling

mar'ble cake'

mar'bling

mar·cel'
  mar·celled',
  mar·cel'ling

march
  pl. march'es

March

mar'chion·ess

Mar·co'ni

Mar'di gras'

mare (*horse*)

ma're (*lunar plains*)
  pl. ma'ri·a

mare's'-nest'

mar'ga·rine

mar'gay

mar'gin

mar'gin·al

mar'gi·na'li·a

mar'gin·al·ly

mar'grave

mar'que·rite'

mar'i·a'chi

mar'i·gold'

ma'ri·jua'na or
  ma'ri·hua'na

ma·rim'ba

ma·ri'na

mar'i·nade' (*n.*)

mar'i·nade' (*v.*)
  mar'i·nad'ed,
  mar'i·nad'ing

ma'ri·na'ra

mar'i·nate'
  mar'i·nat'ed,
  mar'i·nat'ing

ma·rine'

mar'i·ner

mar'i·on·ette'

Mar'ist

mar'i·tal

mar'i·time'

mar'jo·ram

mark

Mark

mark'down'

marked

mark'er

mar'ket

mar'ket·a·bil'i·ty

mar'ket·a·ble

mar'ket·ing

mar'ket·place'

mark'ing

mark'ka
  pl. mark'kaa

marks'man
  pl. marks'men

marks'man·ship'

mark'up'

marl

mar'lin (*fish*)
  (SEE marline)

mar'line (*rope*)
  (SEE marlin)

mar'line·spike'

mar'ma·lade'

mar·mo're·al

mar'mo·set'

mar'mot

ma·roon'

marque

mar·quee'

mar'que·try
  pl. mar'que·tries

mar'quis
  pl. mar'quis·es or
  mar·quis'

mar·quise'

mar'qui·sette'

mar'riage

mar'riage·a·ble

mar'ried

mar'ron

mar'row

mar'row·bone'

mar'ry (*wed*)
  mar'ried, mar'ry·ing
  (SEE merry)

Mars

Mar'seil·laise'

Mar·seilles

marsh

mar'shal (*arrange*)
  mar'shaled,
  mar'shal·ing
  (SEE martial)

marsh' gas'

marsh'mal'low

marsh'y
  marsh'i·er, marsh'i·est

mar·su'pi·al

mart

mar'ten (*animal*)
  (SEE martin)

mar'tial (*military*)
  (SEE marshal)

Mar'tian

mar'tin (*bird*)
  (SEE marten)

mar'ti·net'

mar'tin·gale'

mar·ti'ni
  pl. mar·ti'nis

Mar'ti·nique'

mar'tyr

mar'tyr·dom

mar'vel
  mar'veled or mar'velled,
  mar'vel·ing or
  mar'vel·ling

mar'vel·ous or
  mar'vel·lous

Marx

Marx'ism

Marx'ist

Mar'y

Mar'y·land

Mar'y·land·er

mar'zi·pan'

Ma·sac'cio

Ma·sa'da

Ma·sai'
  pl. Ma·sais or Ma·sai'

mas·car'a

mas'cot

mas'cu·line

mas'cu·lin'i·ty

ma'ser

Mas'e·ru'

mash

mash'er

mash'ie

mask (*disguise*)
  (SEE masque)

mas'och·ism'

mas′och · ist

mas′och · is′tic

ma′son

Ma′son-Dix′on line′

ma · son′ic

Ma′son jar′

ma′son · ry
  pl. ma′son · ries

masque (play)
  (SEE mask)

mas′quer · ade′
  mas′quer · ad′ed,
  mas′quer · ad′ing

mas′quer · ad′er

mass
  pl. mass′es

Mas′sa · chu′setts

mas′sa · cre
  mas′sa · cred,
  mas′sa · cring

mas · sage′
  mas · saged′, mas · sag′ing

mas · sé

Mas′se · net′

mas · seur′

mas · seuse′

mas′sif (mountain)
  (SEE massive)

mass′-pro · duce′
  mass′-pro · duced′,
  mass′-pro · duc′ing

mass′ pro · duc′tion

mast

mas · tec′to · my
  pl. mas · tec′to · mies

mas′ter

mas′ter-at-arms′
  pl. mas′ters-at-arms′

mas′ter · ful

mas′ter · ful · ly

mas′ter · ly

mas′ter · mind′

mas′ter · piece′

mas′ter stroke′

mas′ter · work′

mas′ter · y
  pl. mas′ter · ies

mast′head′

mas′tic

mas′ti · cate′
  mas′ti · cat′ed,
  mas′ti · cat′ing

mas′ti · ca′tion

mas′ti · ca · to′ry
  pl. mas′ti · ca · to′ries

mas′tiff

mas′to · don′

mas′toid

mas′toid · ec′to · my
  pl. mas′toid · ec′to · mies

mas′toid · i′tis

mas′tur · bate′
  mas′tur · bat′ed,
  mas′tur · bat′ing

mas′tur · ba′tion

mat
  mat′ted, mat′ting

mat′a · dor′

match

match′board′

match′book′

match′box′
  pl. match′box′es

match′less

match′lock′

match′mak′er

match′mak′ing

match′wood′

mate
  mat′ed, mat′ing

ma · té′

ma · te′ri · al (matter)
  (SEE matériel)

ma · te′ri · al · ism′

ma · te′ri · al · ist

ma · te′ri · al · is′tic

ma · te′ri · al · is′
  ti · cal · ly

ma · te′ri · al · i · za′tion

ma · te′ri · al · ize′
  ma · te′ri · al · ized′,
  ma · te′ri · al · iz′ing

ma · te′ri · al · ly

ma · te′ri · a med′i · ca

ma · té′ri · el′ or
  ma · te′ri · el′
  (equipment)
  (SEE material)

ma · ter′nal

ma · ter′nal · ly

ma · ter′ni · ty

math

math′e · mat′ic

math′e · mat′i · cal

math′e · mat′i · cal · ly

math′e · ma · ti′cian

math′e · mat′ics

Math′er

mat′i · nee′ or
  mat′i · née′

Ma · tisse′

ma′tri · arch′

ma′tri · ar′chal

ma′tri · ar′chy
  pl. ma′tri · ar′chies

mat′ri · cid′al

mat′ri · cide′

ma · tric′u · late′ (v.)
  ma · tric′u · lat′ed,
  ma · tric′u · lat′ing

ma · tric′u · late (n.)

ma · tric′u · la′tion

mat′ri · lin′e · al · ly

mat′ri · mo′ni · al

mat′ri · mo′ni · al · ly

mat′ri · mo′ny
  pl. mat′ri · mon′ies

ma′trix
  pl. ma′tri · ces or
  ma′trix · es

ma′tron

ma′tron · ly

matte (dull)
  (SEE mat)

mat′ter

mat′ter-of-fact′
  (adj.)

Mat′thew

mat′ting

mat′tock

mat′tress
  pl. mat′tress · es

mat′u · rate′
  mat′u · rat′ed,
  mat′u · rat′ing

mat′u · ra′tion

ma · ture′
  ma · tured′, ma · tur′ing

ma · tu′ri · ty

mat′zo
  pl. mat′zoth or mat′zos

maud′lin

maul (*handle roughly*)
(SEE mall)

maun'der

Maun'dy Thurs'day

Mau·ri·ta'ni·a or Mau're·ta'ni·a

Mau'ri·ta'ni·an or Mau're·ta'ni·an

Mau·ri'tian

Mau·ri'tius

mau'so·le'um
pl. mau'so·le'ums or mau'so·le'a

mauve

mav'er·ick

ma'vin or ma'ven

ma·vour'neen

maw

mawk'ish

max'i

max·il'la
pl. max·il'lae

max'il·lar'y
pl. max'il·lar'ies

max'im

max'i·mal

max'i·mal·ly

max'i·mize'
max'i·mized',
max'i·miz'ing

max'i·mum
pl. max'i·mums or max'i·ma

may

May

Ma'ya
pl. Ma'yas or Ma'ya

Ma'yan

May' ap'ple

may'be

May' Day'

May'flow'er

may'fly'
pl. may'flies'

may'hem

may'n't

may'on·naise'

may'or

may'or·al

may'or·al·ty
pl. may'or·al·ties

may'or·ess
pl. may'or·ess·es

May'pole' or may'pole'

maze (*network*)
mazed, maz'ing
(SEE maize)

ma'zel tov'

ma·zur'ka

Mc·Coy'

Mc'In·tosh' (*apple*)
(SEE mackintosh)

me

me'a cul'pa

mead (*beverage*)
(SEE meed)

mead'ow

mead'ow·lark'

mea'ger or mea'gre

meal

meal'time'

meal'y
meal'i·er, meal'i·est

meal'y-mouthed'

mean (*v.*) (*intend*)
meant, mean'ing
(SEE mien)

mean (*adj., ignoble;
n., midway point*)
(SEE mien)

me·an'der

mean'ing

mean'ing·ful

mean'ing·less

mean'ly

mean'ness

meant

mean'time'

mean'while'

mea'sles

mea'sly
mea'sli·er, mea'sli·est

meas·ur·a·bil'i·ty

meas'ur·a·ble

meas'ur·a·bly

meas'ure
meas'ured, meas'ur·ing

meas'ured

meas'ure·less

meas'ure·ment

meas'ur·er

meat (*flesh*)
(SEE meet *and* mete)

meat' ax'

meat'ball'

me·a'tus
pl. me·a'tus·es or me·a'tus

meat'i·ness

meat'y
meat'i·er, meat'i·est

Mec'ca

me·chan'ic

me·chan'i·cal

me·chan'i·cal·ly

me·chan'ics

mech'an·ism'

mech'a·nis'tic

mech'a·nis'ti·cal·ly

mech'a·ni·za'tion

mech'a·nize'
mech'a·nized',
mech'a·niz'ing

med'al (*award*)
med'aled, med'al·ing
(SEE meddle)

med'al·ist

me·dal'lion

med'dle (*interfere*)
med'dled, med'dling
(SEE medal)

med'dler

med'dle·some

med'e·vac'

me'di·a

me'di·al

me'di·an

me'di·ate' (*v.*)
me'di·at'ed,
me'di·at'ing

me'di·ate (*adj.*)

me'di·a'tion

me'di·a'tor

med'ic

med'i·ca·ble

med'i·ca·bly

Med'i·caid'

med'i·cal

med′i·cal·ly

me·dic′a·ment

Med′i·care′

med′i·cate′
 med′i·cat′ed,
 med′i·cat′ing

med′i·ca′tion

Med′i·ci

me·dic′i·nal

me·dic′i·nal·ly

med′i·cine
 med′i·cined,
 med′i·cin·ing

med′i·cine man′

med′i·co′
 pl. med′i·cos′

me′di·e′val

me′di·e′val·ist

Me·di′na

me′di·o′cre

me′di·oc′ri·ty
 pl. me′di·oc′ri·ties

med′i·tate′
 med′i·tat′ed,
 med′i·tat′ing

med′i·ta′tion

med′i·ta′tive

med′i·ta′tor

Med′i·ter·ra′ne·an

me′di·um
 pl. me′di·a or
 me′di·ums

med′ley
 pl. med′leys

Mé·doc′

me·dul′la
 pl. me·dul′las or
 me·dul′lae

meek

meek′ly

meer′schaum

meet (come upon;
 fitting)
 met, meet′ing
 (SEE meat and mete)

meet′ing

meet′ing house′

meg′a·cy′cle

meg′a·hertz′
 pl. meg′a·hertz′ or
 meg′a·hertz′es

meg′a·lith

meg′a·lith′ic

meg′a·lo·ma′ni·a

meg′a·lo·ma′ni·ac′

meg′a·lo·ma·ni′a·cal

meg′a·lop′o·lis

meg′a·phone′

meg′a·ton′

meg′a·volt′

meg′a·watt′

me·gil′lah
 pl. me·gil′lahs or (Heb)
 me·gil′loth

me′grim

mei·o′sis

Meis′sen

mel′a·mine′

mel′an·cho′li·a

mel′an·chol′ic

mel′an·chol′y
 pl. mel′an·chol′ies

Mel′a·ne′sia

Mel′a·ne′sian

mé·lange′ or
 me·lange′

mel′a·nin

mel′a·no′ma
 pl. mel′a·no′mas or
 mel′a·no′ma·ta

Mel′ba

Mel′bourne

meld

me′lee or mé·lée′

mel′io·rate′
 mel′io·rat′ed,
 mel′io·rat′ing

mel′io·ra′tion

mel′io·ra′tive

mel·lif′lu·ous

mel′low

me·lo′de·on

me·lod′ic

me·lod′i·cal·ly

me·lo′di·ous

mel′o·dra′ma

mel′o·dra·mat′ic

me′o·dra·
 mat′i·cal·ly

mel′o·dy
 pl. mel′o·dies

mel′on

melt
 melt′ed, melt′ed or
 mol′ten, melt′ing

melt′down′

melt′ing point′

mel′ton

Mel′ville

mem′ber

mem′ber·ship′

mem′brane

mem′bra·nous

me·men′to
 pl. me·men′tos or
 me·men′toes

mem′o
 pl. mem′os

mem′oir

mem′o·ra·bil′i·a
 sing. mem′o·rab′i·le

mem′o·ra·ble

mem′o·ra·bly

mem′o·ran′dum
 pl. mem′o·ran′dums or
 mem′o·ran′da

me·mo′ri·al

me·mo′ri·al·
 i·za′tion

me·mo′ri·al·ize′
 me·mo′ri·al·ized′,
 me·mo′ri·al·iz′ing

mem′o·ri·za′tion

mem′o·rize′
 mem′o·rized′,
 mem′o·riz′ing

mem′o·ry
 pl. mem′o·ries

Mem′phis

men′ace
 men′aced, men′ac·ing

men′ac·ing·ly

mé·nage′ or
 me·nage′
 (household)
 (SEE manège)

me·nag′er·ie

Menck′en

mend

Men′del

men·da′cious

men·dac'i·ty
  pl. men·dac'i·ties
men'de·le'vi·um
Men·de'li·an
Men'dels·sohn
men'di·cant
men'folk'
men'folks'
men·ha'den
  pl. men·ha'den
me'ni·al
me'ni·al·ly
men'in·gi'tis
me'ninx
  pl. me·nin'ges
me·nis'coid
me·nis'cus
  pl. me·nis'ci *or*
  me·nis'cus·es
Men'non·ite'
men'o·pau'sal
men'o·pause'
me·nor'ah
men'sal
mensch
men'ses
men's' room'
men'stru·al
men'stru·ate'
  men'stru·at'ed,
  men'stru·at'ing
men'stru·a'tion
men'sur·a·bil'i·ty
men'sur·a·ble
men'su·ral
men'su·ra'tion
men'tal
men·tal'i·ty
  pl. men·tal'i·ties
men'tal·ly
men'thol
men'tho·lat'ed
men'tion
men'tion·a·ble
men'tor
men'u
  pl. men'us
me·ow'
Meph'i·stoph'e·les'

me·phit'ic
me·phi'tis
me·pro'ba·mate'
mer'can·tile'
mer'can·til·ism'
mer'can·til·ist
Mer·ca'tor
mer'ce·nar'y
  pl. mer'ce·nar'ies
mer'cer·ize'
  mer'cer·ized',
  mer'cer·iz'ing
mer'chan·dise'
  mer'chan·dised',
  mer'chan·dis'ing
mer'chan·dis'er
mer'chan·dis'ing
mer'chant
mer'ci·ful
mer'ci·ful·ly
mer'ci·less
mer·cu'ri·al
mer·cu'ric
Mer·cu'ro·chrome'
  (*Trademark*)
mer·cu'rous
mer'cu·ry
  pl. mer'cu·ries
mer'cy
  pl. mer'cies
mere
  superl. mer'est
mere'ly
me·ren'gue
mer'e·tri'cious
mer·gan'ser
  pl. mer·gan'sers *or*
  mer·gan'ser
merge
  merged, merg'ing
merg'er
me·rid'i·an
me·ringue'
me·ri'no
  pl. me·ri'nos
mer'it
mer'i·toc'ra·cy
mer'i·to·crat'
mer'i·to'ri·ous
Mer'lin

mer'maid'
Mer'ri·mac'
mer'ri·ment
mer'ry (*joyous*)
  mer'ri·er, mer'ri·est
  (SEE marry)
mer'ri·ly
mer'ry-go-round'
mer'ry·mak'er
mer'ry·mak'ing
Mer·thi'o·late'
  (*Trademark*)
me'sa
mé'sal·li'ance
mes·cal'
mes'ca·line'
mes·dames'
mes'de·moi·selles'
mes'en·ter'ic
mes'en·ter'y
  pl. mes'en·ter'ies
mesh
mesh'work'
mes'mer·ism'
mes'mer·ize'
  mes'mer·ized',
  mes'mer·iz'ing
mes'mer·iz'er
mes'o·derm'
Mes'o·lith'ic
mes'o·morph'
mes'o·mor'phic
me'son
Mes'o·po·ta'mi·a
Mes'o·po·ta'mi·an
Mes'o·zo'ic
mes·quite'
mess
mes'sage
mes'sen·ger
mess' hall'
Mes·si'ah
Mes'si·an'ic
mes'sieurs
mess' kit'
mess'mate'
mess'i·ly
mess'i·ness

messy
  mess'i·er, mess'i·est

mes·ti'zo
  pl. mes·ti'zos or
  mes·ti'zoes

met

met'a·bol'ic

me·tab'o·lism'

me·tab'o·lize'
  me·tab'o·lized'
  me·tab'o·liz'ing

met'a·car'pal

met'a·car'pus
  pl. met'a·car'pi

met'al (chemical
  substance)
  met'aled, met'al·ing
  (SEE mettle)

me·tal'lic

met'al·loid'

met'al·lur'gic

met'al·lur'gi·cal

met'al·lur'gist

met'al·lur'gy

met'al·ware'

met'al·work'

met'a·mor'phic

met'a·mor'phism

met'a·mor'phose
  met'a·mor'phosed,
  met'a·mor'phos·ing

met'a·mor'pho·sis
  pl. met'a·mor'pho·ses'

met'a·mor'phous

met'a·phase'

met'a·phor'

met'a·phor'ic

met'a·phor'i·cal

met'a·phor'i·cal·ly

met'a·phys'i·cal

met'a·phy·si'cian

met'a·phys'ics

me·tas'ta·sis
  pl. me·tas'ta·ses'

me·tas'ta·size'
  pl. me·tas'ta·sized'
  me·tas'ta·siz'ing

met'a·tar'sal

met'a·tar'sus
  pl. met'a·tar'si

mete
  met'ed, met'ing

me·tem'psy·cho'sis

me'te·or

me'te·or'ic

me'te·or'i·cal·ly

me'te·or·ite'

me'te·or·oid'

me'te·or·o·log'i·cal

me'te·or·o·log'i·cal·ly

me'te·or·ol'o·gist

me'te·or·ol'o·gy

me'ter

me'ter maid'

meth'a·done' or
  meth'a·don'

meth'ane

meth'a·nol'

meth'a·qua'lone

me·thinks'
  me·thought'
  me·think'ing

meth'od

me·thod'ic

me·thod'i·cal

me·thod'i·cal·ly

Meth'od·ism'

Meth'od·ist

meth'od·o·log'i·cal

meth'od·ol'o·gy
  pl. meth'od·ol'o·gies

Me·thu'se·lah

meth'yl

me·tic'u·los'i·ty

me·tic'u·lous

me'tier

me·tis'
  pl. me·tis'

me·ton'y·my

me'·too'

me'·too'ism

met'ric

met'ri·cal

met'ri·cal·ly

met'ri·ca'tion

met'rics

met'ri·fi·ca'tion

met'ri·fy'
  met'ri·fied',
  met'ri·fy·ing

met'ro
  pl. met'ros

Met'ro·li'ner

me·trol'o·gy
  pl. me·trol'o·gies

met'ro·nome'

met'ro·nom'ic

me·trop'lis
  pl. me·trop'o·lis·es

met'ro·pol'i·tan

met'tle

met'tle·some

meu·niere'

Meur·sault'

mew

mewl (cry)
  (SEE mule)

mews (street)
  (SEE muse)

Mex'i·can

Mex'i·co'

me·zu'zah
  pl. me·zu'zahs or
  (Heb.) me·zu·zoth'

mez'za·nine'

mez'zo

mez'zo-so·pran'o
  pl. mez'zo-so·pran'os
  or mez'zo-so·pran'i

mez'zo·tint'

mho
  pl. mhos

mi

Mi·am'i

mi·as'ma
  pl. mi·as'ma·ta or
  mi·as'mas

mi·as'mal

mi·as'mic

mi'ca

Mi'cah

Mich'ael·mas

Mi'chel·an'ge·lo'

Mich'i·gan

Mich'i·gan'der

Mic'mac
  pl. Mic'macs or
  Mic'mac

mic'ro
mi'cro・am'pere
mi'crobe
mi・cro'bi・al
mi'cro・bi'o・log'i・cal
mi'cro・bi・ol'o・gist
mi'cro・bi・ol'o・gy
mi'cro・cir'cuit
mi'cro・com・put'er
mi'cro・cop'y
   pl. mi'cro・cop'ies
mi'cro・cosm'
mi'cro・cos'mic
mi'cro・cos'mi・cal
mi'cro・dot'
mi'cro・e'co・nom'ics
mi'cro・far'ad
mi'cro・fiche'
mi'cro・film'
mi'cro・form'
mi'cro・gram'
mi'cro・groove'
mi・crom'e・ter
mi'crohm'
mi'cro・li'ter or
   mi'cro・li'tre
mi'cro・me'ter or
   mi'cro・me'tre
mi'cron
   pl. mi'crons or mi'cra
Mi'cro・ne'sia
Mi'cro・ne'sian
mi'cro・or'gan・ism'
mi'cro・phone'
mi'cro・pho'to・graph'
mi'cro・print'
mi'cro・proc'es・sor
mi'cro・scope'
mi'cro・scop'ic
mi'cro・scop'i・cal
mi'cro・scop'i・cal・ly
mi・cros'co・pist
mi・cros'co・py
mi'cro・volt'
mi'cro・watt'
mi'cro・wave'
mic'tu・rate'
   mic'ur・rat'ed,
   mic'tu・rat'ing

mid・air'
mid'day'
mid'dle
   mid'dled, mid'dling
mid'dle age'
mid'dle-aged'
Mid'dle・Ag'es
mid'dle・brow'
mid'dle class'
Mid'dle East'
mid'dle・man'
   pl. mid'dle・men'
mid'dle-of-the-road'
mid'dle・weight'
Mid'dle West'
Mid'dle West'ern
mid'dling
mid'dy (*blouse*)
   pl. mid'dies
   (SEE midi)
Mid'east'
midge
midg'et
mid'i (*skirt*)
   (SEE middy)
mid'i'ron
mid'land
mid'most'
mid'night'
mid'point'
mid'rib'
mid'riff'
mid'sec'tion
mid'ship'man
   pl. mid'ship'men
mid'ships'
midst
mid'stream'
mid'sum'mer
mid'term'
mid'town'
mid'-Vic・to'ri・an
mid'way' (*adv., adj.*)
mid'way' (*n.*)
mid'week'
Mid'west'
Mid・west'ern
mid'wife'
   pl. mid'wives'

mid'wife'ry
mid'win'ter
mid'year'
mien (*bearing*)
   (SEE mean)
miff
Mig or MIG
might (*strength*)
   (SEE mite)
might'i・ly
might'i・ness
might'y
   might'i・er, might'i・est
mi'gnon・ette'
mi'graine
mi'grant
mi'grate
   mi'grat・ed, mi'grat・ing
mi・gra'tion
mi'gra・to'ry
mi・ka'do
   pl. mi・ka'dos
mike
mil (*unit of length*)
   (SEE mill)
mi・la'dy
   pl. mi・la'dies
Mil'an・ese'
   pl. Mil'an・ese'
milch
mild
mild'ly
mil'dew'
mile
mile'age
mile'post'
mil'er
mile'stone'
mi・lieu'
   pl. mi・lieus' or (*Fr.*)
   mi・lieux'
mil'i・tan・cy
mil'i・tant
mil'i・tar'i・ly
mil'i・ta・rism'
mil'i・ta・rist
mil'i・ta・ris'tic
mil'i・ta・ri・za'tion

mil′i·ta·rize′
  mil′i·ta·rized′,
  mil′i·ta·riz′ing
mil′i·tar′y
  pl. mil′i·tar′ies or
  mil′i·tar′y
mil′i·tate′
  mil′i·tat′ed,
  mil′i·tat′ing
mi·li′tia
mi·li′tia·man
  pl. mi·li′tia·men
milk
milk′i·ness
milk′maid′
milk′man′
  pl. milk′men′
milk′ shake′
milk′sop′
milk′ toast′
milk′weed′
milk′wort′
milk′y
  milk′i·er, milk′i·est
Milk′y Way′
mill (factory; money
  unit)
  (SEE mil)
mill′dam′
mil·len′ni·al
mil·len′ni·um
  pl. mil·len′ni·ums or
  mil·len′ni·a
mill′er
mil′let
mil′li·am′pere
mil′liard
mil′li·bar′
mil·lieme′
mil′li·gram′
mil′li·li′ter or
  mil′li·li′tre
mil′li·me′ter or
  mil′li·me′tre
mil′li·ner
mil′li·ner′y
mill′ing
mil′lion
mil′lion·aire′
mil′lionth
mil′li·pede′

mil′li·sec′ond
mil′li·volt′
mil′li·watt′
mill′pond′
mill′race′
mill′stone′
mill′stream′
mill′work′
mill′wright′
mi·lord′
milque′toast′
milt
Mil′ton
Mil′town′
  (Trademark)
Mil·wau′kee
mime
  mimed, mim′ing
mim′e·o·graph′
mim′er
mi·me′sis
mi·met′ic
mim′ic
  mim′icked,
  mim′ick·ing
mim′ick·er
mim′ic·ry
  pl. mim′ic·ries
mi·mo′sa
min′a·ret′
min′a·to′ry
mince
  minced, minc′ing
mince′meat′
mind
mind′ed
mind′ful
mind′ful·ly
mind′less
mine
mine
  mined, min′ing
mine′field′
mine′lay′er
min′er (one who
  mines)
  (SEE minor)
min′er·al
min′er·al·i·za′tion

min′er·al·ize′
  min′er·al·ized′,
  min′er·al·iz′ing
min′er·al·og′i·cal
min′er·al′o·gist
min′er·al′o·gy
Mi·ner′va
min′e·stro′ne
mine′sweep′er
Ming
min′gle
  min′gled, min′gling
min′i
min′i·a·ture
min′i·a·tur·i·za′tion
min′i·a·tur·ize′
  min′i·a·tur·ized′,
  min′i·a·tur·iz′ing
min′i·bus′
min′i·cab′
min′im
min′i·mal
min′i·mal·ly
min′i·mi·za′tion
min′i·mize′
  min′i·mized′,
  min′i·miz′ing
min′i·miz′er
min′i·mum
  pl. min′i·mums or
  min′i·ma
min′ing
min′ion
min′i·park′
min′i·se′ries
min′i·skirt′
min′i·skirt′ed
min′is·ter
min′is·te′ri·al
min′is·trant
min′is·tra′tion
min′is·try
  pl. min′is·tries
min′i·track′
mink
  pl. minks or mink
Min′ne·ap′o·lis
min′ne·sing′er
Min′ne·so′ta
Min′ne·so′tan

min′now
Mi · no′an
mi′nor (*lesser*)
  (SEE miner)
Mi · nor′ca
Mi · nor′can
mi · nor′i · ty
  pl. mi · nor′i · ties
Min′o · taur′
min′strel
min′strel · sy
mint
mint′age
mint′y
min′u · end′
min′u · et′
mi′nus
mi · nus′cu · lar
mi′nus · cule′
min′ute (*n.*)
mi · nute′ (*adj.*)
  mi · nut′er, mi · nut′est
min′ute · ly (*adj.*)
mi · nute′ly (*adv.*)
mi · nu′ti · ae′
  sing. mi · nu′ti · a
minx
Mi′o · cene′
mir′a · cle
mi · rac′u · lous
mi · rage′
mire
  mired, mir′ing
mir′ror
mirth
mirth′ful
mirth′ful · ly
MIRV
mir′y
  mir′i · er, mir′i · est
mis′ad · ven′ture
mis′al · li′ance
mis′an · thrope′
mis′an · throp′ic
mis′an · throp′i · cal · ly
mis · an′thro · py
mis′ap · pli · ca′tion

mis′ap · ply′
  mis′ap · plied′,
  mis′ap · ply′ing
mis′ap · pre · hend′
mis′ap · pre · hen′sion
mis′ap · pro′pri · ate′
  mis′ap · pro′pri · at′ed,
  mis′ap · pro′pri · at′ing
mis′ap · pro′pri · a′tion
mis′be · got′ten
mis′be · have′
  mis′be · haved′,
  mis′be · hav′ing
mis′be · ha′vior
mis′be · lief′
mis · brand′
mis · cal′cu · late′
  mis · cal′cu · lat′ed,
  mis · cal′cu · lat′ing
mis′cal · cu · la′tion
mis · call′
mis · car′riage
mis · car′ry
  mis · car′ried,
  mis · car′ry · ing
mis · cast′
  mis · cast′, mis · cast′ing
mis′ce · ge · na′tion
mis′cel · la′ne · a
mis′cel · la′ne · ous
mis′cel · la′ny
  pl. mis′cel · la′nies
mis · chance′
mis′chief
mis′chie · vous
mis′ci · bil′i · ty
mis′ci · ble
mis′con · ceive′
  mis′con · ceived′,
  mis′con · ceiv′ing
mis′con · cep′tion
mis · con′duct (*n.*)
mis′con · duct′ (*v.*)
mis′con · struc′tion
mis′con · strue′
  mis′con · strued′,
  mis′con · stru′ing
mis · count′
mis′cre · ant
mis · cue′
  mis · cued′, mis · cu′ing

mis · deal′
  mis · dealt′, mis · deal′ing
mis · deed′
mis′de · mean′or
mis · do′
  mis · did′, mis · done′,
  mis · do′ing
mis · do′er
mis · do′ing
mis′di · rect′
mis′di · rec′tion
mise en scène′
mi′ser
mis′er · able
mis′er · a · bly
mi′ser · ly
mis′er · y
  pl. mis′er · ies
mis · fea′sance
mis · fea′sor
mis · file′
  mis · filed′, mis · fil′ing
mis · fire′
  mis · fired′, mis · fir′ing
mis · fit′ (*v.*)
  mis · fit′ted,
  mis · fit · ting
mis′fit (*n.*)
mis · for′tune
mis · giv′ing
mis · gov′ern
mis · gov′ern · ment
mis · guid′ance
mis · guide′
  mis · guid′ed,
  mis · guid′ing
mis · han′dle
  mis · han′dled,
  mis · han′dling
mis′hap
mis · hear′
  mis · heard′,
  mis · hear′ing
mish′mash′
Mish′nah
  pl. Mish′na · yoth′
mis′in · form′
mis′in · for · ma′tion
mis′in · ter′pret
mis′in · ter′pre · ta′tion

mis·judge'
  mis·judged',
  mis·judg'ing

mis·judg'ment

mis·lay'
  mis·laid', mis·lay'ing

mis·lead'
  mis·led', mis·lead'ing

mis·man'age
  mis·man'aged,
  mis·man'ag·ing

mis·man'age·ment

mis·match'

mis·name'
  mis·named',
  mis·nam'ing

mis·no'mer

mi·sog'y·nist

mi·sog'y·nous

mi·sog'y·ny

mis·place'
  mis·placed',
  mis·plac'ing

mis·play'

mis'print (n.)

mis·print' (v.)

mis·pri'sion

mis'pro·nounce'
  mis'pro·nounced',
  mis'pro·nounc'ing

mis'pro·nun'ci·a'tion

mis'quo·ta'tion

mis·quote'
  mis·quot'ed,
  mis·quot'ing

mis·read'
  mis·read', mis·read'ing

mis'rep·re·sent'

mis'rep·re·sen·
  ta'tion

mis·rule'
  mis·ruled', mis·rul'ing

miss
  pl. misses

mis'sal (book)
  (SEE missile)

mis·shape'
  mis·shaped',
  mis·shaped' or
  mis·shap'en,
  mis·shap'ing

mis·shap'en

mis'sile (weapon)
  (SEE missal)

mis'sile·ry or
  mis'sil·ry

miss'ing

mis'sion

mis'sion·ar'y
  pl. mis'sion·ar'ies

mis'sion·er

Mis'sis·sau'ga

Mis'sis·sip'pi

Mis'sis·sip'pi·an

mis'sive

Mis·sour'i

Mis·sour'i·an

mis·spell'
  mis·spelled' or
  mis·spelt', mis·spell'ing

mis·spend'
  mis·spent',
  mis·spend'ing

mis·state'
  mis·stat'ed,
  mis·stat'ing

mis·state'ment

mis·step'
  mis·stepped',
  mis·step'ping

mist

mis·tak'a·ble

mis·take'
  mis·took', mis·tak'en,
  mis·tak'ing

mis·tak'en

mis'ter

mis'tle·toe'

mis'tral

mis·treat'

mis·treat'ment

mis'tress
  pl. mis'tress·es

mis·tri'al

mis·trust'

mist'i·ness

mist'y
  mist'i·er, mist'i·est

mis'un·der·stand'
  mis'un·der·stood',
  mis'un·der·stand'ing

mis·us'age

mis·use'
  mis·used', mis·us'ing

mite (small bit)
  (SEE might)

mi'ter or mi'tre

mit'i·ga·ble

mit'i·gate'
  mit'i·gat'ed,
  mit'i·gat'ing

mit'i·ga'tion

mit'i·ga'tive

mit'i·ga'tor

mi'to·chon'dri·on
  pl. mi'to·chon'dri·a

mi·to'sis

mi·tot'ic

mitt

mit'ten

mix
  mixed or mixt, mix'ing
  pl. mix'es

mix'a·ble

mixed

mixed'-up'

mix'er

mix'ture

mix'-up'

miz'zen or miz'en

miz'zen·mast' or
  miz'en·mast'

mne·mon'ic

mo'a

moan

moat (ditch)
  (SEE mote)

mob
  mobbed, mob'bing

mo'bile

Mo·bile'

mo'bile home'

mo·bil'i·ty

mo'bi·li·za'tion

mo'bi·lize'
  mo'bi·lized',
  mo'bi·liz'ing

Mö'bi·us strip'

mob·oc'ra·cy
  pl. mob·oc'ra·cies

mob'ster

moc'ca·sin

mo'cha

mock

mock'er·y
  pl. mock'er·ies

mock′-he·ro′ic

mock′ing·bird′

mock′up′

mod

mod′al (*of a mode*)
(SEE model)

mo·dal′i·ty
  pl. mo·dal′i·ties

mode

mod′el (*example*)
  mod′eled, mod′el·ing
  (SEE modal)

mod′er·ate (*adj., n.*)

mod′er·ate′ (*v.*)
  mod′er·at′ed,
  mod′er·at′ing

mod′er·a′tion

mod′e·ra′to

mod′er·a′tor

mod′ern

mod′ern·ism′

mod′ern·ist

mod′ern·is′tic

mo·der′ni·ty
  pl. mo·der′ni·ties

mod′ern·i·za′tion

mod′ern·ize′
  mod′ern·ized′,
  mod′ern·iz′ing

mod′ern·iz′er

mod′est

mod′es·ty
  pl. mod′es·ties

mod′i·cum

mod′i·fi·ca′tion

mod′i·fi′er

mod′i·fy′
  mod′i·fied′,
  mod′i·fy′ing

Mo·di′glia′ni

mod′ish

mo·diste′

mod′u·lar

mod′u·late
  mod′u·lat′ed,
  mod′u·lat′ing

mod′u·la′tion

mod′u·la′tive

mod′u·la′tor

mod′u·la·to′ry

mod′ule

mo′dus o′pe·ran′di
  pl. mo′di o′pe·ran′di

mo′dus vi·ven′di
  pl. mo′di vi·ven′di

Mo′ga·di′shu

Mo′gen Da′vid

mo′gul

mo′hair′

Mo·ham′med·an

Mo·ha′ve
  pl. Mo·ha′ves or
  Mo·ha′ve

Mo′hawk
  pl. Mo′hawks or
  Mo′hawk

Mo·he′gan
  pl. Mo·he′gans or
  Mo·he′gan

Mo·hi′can
  pl. Mo·hi′cans or
  Mo·hi′can

Mo′hole

moi′e·ty
  pl. moi′e·ties

moil

moi·ré′ or moi·re′

moist

mois′ten

mois′ture

mois′tur·ize′
  mois′tur·ized′,
  mois′tur·iz′ing

mois′tur·iz′er

mo′lar

mo·las′ses

mold

mold′a·ble

Mol·da′vi·an

mold′er

mold′i·ness

mold′ing

mold′y
  mold′i·er, mold′i·est

mole

mo·lec′u·lar

mol′e·cule′

mole′hill′

mole′skin′

mo·lest′

mo′les·ta′tion

mo·lest′er

Mo·lière′

moll

mol′li·fi·ca′tion

mol′li·fy′
  mol′li·fied′,
  mol′li·fy′ing

mol′lusk or mol′lusc

mol′ly
  pl. mol′lies

mol′ly·col′dle
  mol′ly·col′dled,
  mol′ly·cod′dling

Mo′loch

molt

mol′ten

mol′to

mo·lyb′de·num

mom

mo′ment

mo′men·tar′i·ly

mo′men·tar′y

mo·men′tous

mo·men′tum
  pl. mo·men′ta or
  mo·men′tums

mom′my

Mo·na′can

Mon′a·co′

mon′ad

mon′arch

mo·nar′chic

mo·nar′chi·cal

mon′ar·chism′

mon′ar·chist

mon′ar·chy
  pl. mon′ar·chies

mon′as·te′ri·al

mon′as·ter′y
  pl. mon′as·ter′ies

mo·nas′tic

mo·nas′ti·cal·ly

mo·nas′ti·cism′

mon′a·tom′ic

mon·au′ral

mon′a·zite′

Mon′day

Mon′e·gasque′

mon′e·tar′i·ly

mon′e·tar′ism

mon'e · tar'y
mon'e · ti · za'tion
mon'e · tize'
  mon'e · tized',
  mon'e · tiz'ing
mon'ey
  pl. mon'eys or mon'ies
mon'ey · bag'
mon'ey · chang'er
mon'eyed or mon'ied
mon'ey · lend'er
mon'ey · mak'er
mon'ey · mak'ing
mon'ger
Mon'gol
Mon · go'li · a
Mon · go'li · an
Mon · gol'ic
Mon'gol · ism'
Mon'gol · oid'
mon'goose
  pl. mon'goos'es
mon'grel
mon'i · ker
mon'ism
mon'ist
mo · nis'tic
mo · ni'tion
mon'i · tor
mon'i · to'ry
  pl. mon'i · to'ries
monk
mon'key
  pl. mon'keys
  mon'keyed,
  mon'key · ing
mon'key · shine'
mon'key wrench'
monk'ish
monks'hood
mon'o · chro · mat'ic
mon'o · chro · mat'i · cal
mon'o · chrome'
mon'o · cle
mon'o · cot'y · le'don
mo · noc'u · lar
mo · nod'ic
mon'o · dy
  pl. mon'o · dies

mo · nog'a · mist
mo · nog'a · mous
mo · nog'a · my
mon'o · gram'
mon'o · graph'
mo · nog'y · ny
mon'o · lith
mon'o · lith'ic
mon'o · logue' or
  mon'o · log'
mon'o · log'ist or
  mon'o · logu'ist
mon'o · ma'ni · a
mon'o · ma'ni · ac'
mon'o · mer
mo · no'mi · al
mon'o · nu'cle · o'sis
mon'o · phon'ic
mon'o · plane
mo · nop'o · dy
  pl. mo · nop'o · dies
mo · nop'o · list
mo · nop'o · lis'tic
mo · nop'o · lize'
  mo · nop'o · lized',
  mo · nop'o · liz'ing
mo · nop'o · li · za'tion
mo · nop'o · ly
  pl. mo · nop'o · lies
mon'o · rail'
mon'o · so'di · um
  glu'ta · mate'
mon'o · syl · lab'ic
mon'o · syl ·
  lab'i · cal · ly
mon'o · syl'la · ble
mon'o · the · ism'
mon'o · the'ist
mon'o · the · is'tic
mon'o · tone'
mo · not'o · nous
mo · not'o · ny
Mon'o · type
  (Trademark)
mon'o · va'lent
mon · ox'ide
Mon · roe'
Mon · ro'vi · a

Mon · sei · gneur'
  pl. Mes · sei · gneurs'
mon · sieur'
  pl. mes'sieurs or (Fr.)
  mes · sieurs'
Mon · si'gnor
  pl. Mon · si'gnors or
  (It.) Mon'si · gno'ri
mon · soon'
mon'ster
mon'strance
mon · stros'i · ty
  pl. mon · stros'i · ties
mon'strous
mon · tage'
Mon · taigne'
Mon · tan'a
Mon · tan'an
mon'tane
Mon'te Car'lo
Mon'tes · so'ri
Mon'te · vi · de'o
Mon'te · zu'ma
Mont · gom'er · y
month
month'ly
  pl. month'lies
Mon'ti · cel'lo
Mont · mar'tre
Mont · par · nasse'
Mont · pel'ier
Mon'tra · chet'
Mont're · al'
Mont'ser · rat'
mon'u · ment
mon'u · men'tal
mon'u · men'tal · ly
moo
  (v.) mooed, moo'ing
  pl. moos
mooch
mooch'er
mood
mood'i · ly
mood'i · ness
mood'y
  mood'i · er, mood'i · est
Moog
moon
moon'beam'

moon'calf'
  pl. moon'calves'

moon'light'
  moon'light'ed,
  moon'light'ing

moon'light'er

moon'light'ing

moon'lit'

moon'scape'

moon'shine'

moon'shin'er

moon'stone'

moon'strick'en

moon'struck'

moon'y
  moon'i·er, moon'i·est

moor (*open field;*
  attach)

Moor (*Muslim*)

moor'age

moor'ing

Moor'ish

moose (*deer*)
  pl. moose
  (SEE mousse and
  mouse)

moot (*debatable*)
  (SEE mute)

mop
  mopped, mop'ping

mope
  moped, mop'ing

mo'ped

mop'pet

mop'-up'

mo·raine'

mor'al

mor·ale'

mor'al·ist

mor'al·is'tic

mor'al·is'ti·cal·ly

mo·ral'i·ty
  pl. mo·ral'i·ties

mor'al·i·za'tion

mor'al·ize'
  mor'al·ized',
  mor'al·iz'ing

mor'al·iz'er

mor'al·ly

mo·rass'

mor'a·to'ri·um
  pl. mor'a·to'ri·a or
  mor'a·to'ri·ums

mo'ray
  pl. mo'rays

mor'bid

mor·bid'i·ty

mor'dan·cy

mor'dant (*caustic*)
  (SEE mordent)

mor'dent (*musical
  passage*)
  (SEE mordant)

more
  superl. most

mo·rel'

more·o'ver

mo'res

mor'ga·nat'ic

mor'ga·nat'i·cal·ly

morgue

mor'i·bund'

Mor'mon

Mor'mon·ism'

morn (*morning*)
  (SEE mourn)

morn'ing (*dawn*)
  (SEE mourning)

morn'ing-glo'ry
  pl. mor'ning-glo'ries

morn'ing star'

Mo'ro

Mo·roc'can

Mo·roc'co

mo'ron

mo·ron'ic

mo·ron'i·cal·ly

mo·rose'

mor'pheme

mor·phem'ic

Mor'phe·us

mor'phine

mor'phin·ism'

mor'pho·log'i·cal

mor'pho·log'i·cal·ly

mor·phol'o·gist

mor·phol'o·gy

mor'ris dance'

mor'row

Morse' code'

mor'sel

mor'tal

mor·tal'i·ty
  pl. mor·tal'i·ties

mor'tal·ly

mor'tar

mor'tar·board'

mort'gage
  mort'gaged,
  mort'gag·ing

mort'ga·gee'

mort'ga·gor

mor'tice
  mor'ticed, mor'ti·cing

mor·ti'cian

mor'ti·fi·ca'tion

mor'ti·fy'
  mor'ti·fied',
  mor'ti·fy'ing

mor'tise
  mor'tised, mor'tis·ing

mort'main'

mor'tu·ar'y
  pl. mor'tu·ar'ies

mo·sa'ic (*design*)

Mo·sa'ic (*of Moses*)

Mos'cow

Mo·selle'

Mo'ses

mo'sey
  mo'seyed, mo'sey·ing

Mos'lem

mosque

mos·qui'to
  pl. mos·qui'toes

moss

moss'back'

moss'y
  moss'i·er, moss'i·est

most

most'ly

mot

mote (*particle*)
  (SEE moat)

mo·tel'

mo·tet'

moth

moth'ball'

moth'-eat'en

moth'er

moth'er·hood'

moth'er–in–law'
  pl. moth'ers–in–law'

moth'er·land'

moth'er·li·ness

moth'er·ly

moth'er–of–pearl'

moth'proof'

mo·tif'

mo'tile

mo·til'i·ty

mo'tion

mo'tion·less

mo'tion pic'ture

mo'ti·vate'
  mo'ti·vat'ed,
  mo'ti·vat'ing

mo'ti·va'tion

mo'tive

mo·tiv'i·ty

mot'ley
  pl. mot'leys

mo'tor

mo'tor·bike'

mo'tor·boat'

mo'tor·cade'

mo'tor·car'

mo'tor·cy'cle
  mo'tor·cy'cled,
  mo'tor·cy'cling

mo'tor·cy'clist

mo'tor home'

mo'tor·ist

mo'tor·i·za'tion

mo'tor·ize'
  mo'tor·ized',
  mo'tor·iz'ing

mo'tor lodge'

mo'tor·man
  pl. mo'tor·men

mo'tor ship'

mo'tor truck'

mot'tle
  mot'tled, mot'tling

mot'to
  pl. mot'toes or mot'tos

mound

mount

mount'a·ble

moun'tain

moun'tain·eer'

moun'tain·ous

moun'tain·side'

moun'tain range'

moun'tain·top'

moun'te·bank'

mount'ed

Moun'tie

mount'ing

mourn (grieve)
  (SEE morn)

mourn'er

mourn'ful

mourn'ful·ly

mourn'ing (grief)
  (SEE morning)

mouse (rodent)
  pl. mice
  moused, mous'ing
  (SEE moose and mousse)

mous'er

mouse'trap'
  pl. mouse'trapped,
  mouse'trap'ping

mousse (dessert)
  (SEE moose and mouse)

mous·se·line'

Mous·sorg'sky

mous'tache

mous'y
  mous'i·er, mous'i·est

mouth

mouth'ful'
  pl. mouth'fuls'

mouth' or'gan

mouth'piece'

mouth'wash'

mouth'–wa'ter·ing

mou'ton (sheepskin)
  (SEE mutton)

mov'a·bil'i·ty or
  move'a·bil'i·ty

mov'a·ble or
  move'a·ble

mov'a·bly or
  move'a·bly

move
  moved, mov'ing

move'ment

mov'er

mov'ie

mov'ie·go'er

mov'ing

mov'ing pic'ture

mow
  mowed, mowed or
  mown, mow'ing

mow'er

mox'ie

Mo'zam·bi'can

Mo'zam·bique'

moz'za·rel'la

mu

much
  more, most

mu'ci·lage

mu'ci·lag'i·nous

muck

muck'rake'
  muck'raked',
  muck'rak'ing

muck'rak'er

muck'y
  muck'i·er, muck'i·est

mu'cous (adj.)

mu'cus (n.)

mud

mud'der

mud'di·ness

mud'dle
  mud'dled, mud'dling

mud'dle·head'ed

mud'dler

mud'dy
  mud'di·er, mud'di·est
  mud'died, mud'dy·ing

mud'guard'

mud'sling'er

mud'sling'ing

muen'ster

mu·ez'zin

muff

muf'fin

muf'fle
  muf'fled, muf'fling

muf'fler

muf'ti
  pl. muf'tis

mug
  mugged, mug'ging

mug'ger

mug'gi · ness

mug'ging

mug'gy
  mug'gi · er, mug'gi · est

mug'wump'

Mu · ham'mad

Muk'den

muk'luk

mu · la'to
  pl. mu · la'toes

mul'ber · ry
  pl. mul'ber · ries

mulch

mulct

mule (*animal*)
  (SEE mewl)

mule' skin'ner

mu'le · teer'

mul'ish

mull

mul'lah

mul'lein

mul'let
  pl. mul'let or mul'lets

mul'li · gan

mul'li · ga · taw'ny

mul'lion

mul'ti · col'ored

mul'ti · far'i · ous

mul'ti · form'

Mul'ti · graph'
  (*Trademark*)

mul'ti · lat'er · al

mul'ti · lat'er · al · ly

mul'ti · lin'gual

mul'ti · me'di · a

mul'ti · mil'lion · aire'

mul'ti · na'tion · al

mul'ti · par'tite

mul'ti · ple

mul'ti · ple–choice'

mul'ti · plex'

mul'ti · pli · cand'

mul'ti · pli · ca'tion

mul'ti · pli · ca'tive

mul'ti · plic'i · ty
  pl. mul'ti · plic'i · ties

mul'ti · pli'er

mul'ti · ply' (*v.*)
  mul'ti · plied',
  mul'ti · ply'ing

mul'ti · ply (*adv.*)

mul'ti · pur'pose

mul'ti · ra'cial

mul'ti · stage'

mul'ti · tude'

mul'ti · tu'di · nous

mul'ti · vi'ta · min

mum

mum'ble
  mum'bled, mum'bling

mum'bler

mum'ble · ty · peg

mum'bo jum'bo
  pl. mum'bo jum'bos

mum'mer

mum'mer · y
  pl. mum'mer · ies

mum'mi · fi · ca'tion

mum'mi · fy'
  mum'mi · fied',
  mum'mi · fy'ing

mum'my
  pl. mum'mies;
  (*v.*) mum'mied,
  mum'my · ing

mumps

munch

mun · dane'

Mu'nich

mu · nic'i · pal

mu · nic'i · pal · ly

mu · nic'i · pal'i · ty
  pl. mu · nic'i · pal'i · ties

mu · nif'i · cence

mu · nif'i · cent

mu · ni'tions

mu'ral

mu'ral · ist

mur'der

mur'der · er

mur'der · ess

mur'der · ous

mu'rex
  pl. mu'ri · ces' or
  mu'rex · es

murk

murk'i · ly

murk'i · ness

murk'y
  pl. murk'i · er,
  murk'i · est

mur'mur

mur'mur · er

mur'rain

mus'ca · dine

Mus'cat

mus'cat

mus'ca · tel'

mus'cle (*body part*)
  mus'cled, mus'cling
  (SEE mussel)

mus'cle · bound'

Mus'co · vite'

mus'cu · lar

mus'cu · lar'i · ty

mus'cu · la · ture

muse (*think*)
  mused, mus'ing
  (SEE mews)

Muse (*goddess*)
  (SEE mews)

mu · sette'

mu · se'um

mush

mush'room

mush'i · ness

mush'y
  mush'i · er, mush'i · est

mu'sic

mu'si · cal (*of music*)
  (SEE musicale)

mu'si · cale' (*concert*)
  (SEE musical)

mu'si · cal · ly

mu'sic box'

mu'sic hall'

mu · si'cian

mu'si · col'o · gist

mu'si · col'o · gy

musk

mus'keg

mus'kel · lunge'
  pl. mus'kel · lunge'

mus'ket

mus'ket · eer'

mus'ket•ry

musk'mel'on

musk'rat'

musk'y
  musk'i•er, musk'i•est

Mus'lim
  pl. Mus'lims *or*
  Mus'lim

mus'lin

mus'quash

muss

mus'sel (*shellfish*)
  (SEE muscle)

Mus'so•li'ni

muss'i•ly

muss'i•ness

muss'y
  muss'i•er, muss'i•est

must

mus'tache *or*
  mous'tache

mus'tang

mus'tard

mus'ter

mus'ti•ness

mus'ty
  mus'ti•er, mus'ti•est

mu'ta•bil'i•ty

mu'ta•ble

mu'tant

mu'tate
  mu'tat•ed, mu'tat•ing

mu'ta•tive

mu•ta'tion

mute (*silent*)
  mut'ed, mut'ing
  (SEE moot)

mute'ly

mute'ness

mu'ti•late'
  mu'ti•lat'ed,
  mu'ti•lat'ing

mu'ti•la'tion

mu'ti•la'tor

mu'ti•neer'

mu'ti•nous

mu'ti•ny
  pl. mu'ti•nies; (v.)
  mu'ti•nied,
  mu'ti•ny•ing

mutt

mut'ter

mut'ton (*meat*)
  (SEE mouton)

mut'ton•chops'

mu'tu•al

mu'tu•al'i•ty

mu'tu•al•ly

muu'muu'

mu•zhik'

muz'zle
  muz'zled, muz'zling

muz'zle•load'er

muz'zle•load'ing

my

my'as•the'ni•a

my•ce'li•um
  pl. my•ce'li•a

my'co•log'i•cal

my•col'o•gist

my•col'o•gy

my•co'sis

my'e•lin *or*
  my'e•line

my'e•li'tis

My'lar (*Trademark*)

my'na *or* my'nah

my'o•car'di•al

my'o•gen'ic

my•o'pi•a

my•op'ic

my•op'i•cal•ly

my'o•sin

myr'i•ad

myr'mi•don'

myrrh

myr'tle

my•self'
  pl. our•selves'

mys•te'ri•ous

mys'ter•y
  pl. mys'ter•ies

mys'tic

mys'ti•cal

mys'ti•cal•ly

mys'ti•cism'

mys'ti•fi•ca'tion

mys'ti•fy'
  mys'ti•fied',
  mys'ti•fy'ing

mys'ti•fi'er

mys•tique'

myth

myth'i•cal

myth'i•cal•ly

myth'o•log'ic

myth'o•log'i•cal

myth'o•log'i•cal•ly

my•thol'o•gist

my•thol'o•gize'
  my•thol'o•gized',
  my•thol'o•giz'ing

my•thol'o•gy
  pl. my•thol'o•gies

N

nab
  nabbed, nab'bing

na'bob

na•celle'

ma'cre

na'cre•ous

na'dir

nag
  nagged, nag'ging

Na'go•ya'

Na'hua•tl
  pl. Na'hua•tls *or*
  Na'hua•tl

nai'ad
  pl. nai'ads *or* nai'a•des'

nail

nail' file'

nail'head'

nail' pol'ish

nain'sook

Nai•ro'bi

na•ive' *or* na•ïve'

na•ive•té' *or*
  na•ïve•té'

na'ked

nam′by–pam′by
  pl. nam′by-pam′bies

name
  named, nam′ing

name′a · ble *or*
  nam′a · ble

name′–drop′ping

name′less

name′ly

name′sake′

name′tag′

Na · mib′i · a

Na · mib′i · an

nan · keen′ *or*
  nan · kin′

nan′ny
  pl. nan′nies

nan′ny goat′

na′no · sec′ond

Nan · tuck′et

Na · o′mi

nap
  napped, nap′ping

na′palm

nape

na′per · y

naph′tha

naph′tha · lene′

nap′kin

nap′kin ring′

Na′ples

Na · po′le · on

Na · po′le · on′ic

narc

nar′cis · sism′

nar′cis · sist

nar′cis · sis′tic

nar · cis′sus
  pl. nar · cis′sus *or*
  nar · cis′sus · es *or*
  nar · cis′si

nar′co
  pl. nar′cos

nar′co · lep′sy

nar · co′sis

nar · cot′ic

nar′co · tism′

nar′co · tize′
  nar′co · tized′,
  nar′co · tiz′ing

nar′is
  pl. nar′es

Nar′ra · gan′sett
  pl. Nar′ra · gan′setts *or*
  Nar′ra · gan′sett

nar′rate
  nar′rat · ed, nar′rat · ing

nar · ra′tion

nar′ra · tive

nar′ra · tor *or*
  nar′ra · ter

nar′row

nar′row gauge′

nar′row-mind′ed

nar′whal

nar′y

na′sal

na · sal′i · ty

na′sal · i · za′tion

na′sal · ize′
  na′sal · ized′,
  na′sal · iz′ing

na′sal · ly

nas′cence

nas′cent

Nash′ville

na′so · phar′ynx
  pl. na′so · pha · ryn′ges
  or na′so · phar′ynx · es

Nas′sau

na · stur′tium

nas′ti · ly

nas′ti · ness

nas′ty
  nas′ti · er, nas′ti · est

na′tal

na′tant

na · ta · to′ri · al

na · ta · to′ri · um
  pl. na · ta · to′ri · ums *or*
  na · ta · to′ri · a

na · ta · to′ry

Natch′ez

na′tion

na′tion · al

na′tion · al · ism′

na′tion · al · ist

na′tion · al · is′tic

na′tion · al · is′ti · cal · ly

na′tion · al′i · ty
  pl. na′tion · al′i · ties

na′tion · al · i · za′tion

na′tion · al · ize′
  na′tion · al · ized′,
  na′tion · al · iz′ing

na′tion · hood′

na′tion–state′

na′tion · wide′

na′tive

na′tive–born′

na · tiv′i · ty
  pl. na · tiv′i · ties

nat′ti · ly

nat′ti · ness

nat′ty
  nat′ti · er, nat′ti · est

nat′u · ral

nat′u · ral · ism′

nat′u · ral · ist

nat′u · ral · is′tic

nat′u · ral · is′ti · cal · ly

nat′u · ral · i · za′tion

nat′u · ral · ize′
  nat′u · ral · ized′,
  nat′u · ral · iz′ing

nat′u · ral · ly

na′ture

Nau′ga · hyde′
  (*Trademark*)

naught

naugh′ti · ly

naugh′ti · ness

naugh′ty
  naugh′ti · er,
  naugh′ti · est

Na · u′ru

nau′se · a

nau′se · ate′
  nau′se · at′ed,
  nau′se · at′ing

nau′seous

nau′ti · cal

nau′ti · cal · ly

nau′ti · lus
  pl. nau′ti · lus · es *or*
  nau′ti · li′

Nav′a · ho′
  pl. Nav′a · hos′ *or*
  Nav′a · hoes′ *or*
  Nav′a · ho′

na′val (*of a navy*)
  (SEE navel)

nave (*area in church*)
(SEE knave)

na'vel (*umbilicus*)
(SEE naval)

nav'i·ga·bil'i·ty

nav·i·ga·ble

nav'i·gate'
nav'i·gat'ed,
nav'i·gat'ing

nav'i·ga'tion

nav'i·ga'tor

na'vy
pl. na'vies

na'vy bean'

na'vy yard'

nay (*no*)
(SEE neigh *and* nee)

na·ya' pai·sa'
pl. na·ye' pai·se'

Naz'a·rene'

Naz'a·reth

Na'zi
pl. Na'zis

Na'zism

Ne·an'der·thal'

Ne'a·pol'i·tan

neap' tide'

near

near'by'

Near' East'

Near' East'ern

near'ly

near'ness

near'–sight'ed

near'–term'

neat

neath *or* 'neath

neat'ly

neat'ness

neat's'–foot' oil'

neb'bish

Ne·bras'ka

Ne·bras'kan

neb'u·la
pl. neb'u·lae' *or* neb'u·las

neb'u·lar

neb'u·lize'
neb'u·lized',
neb'u·liz'ing

neb'u·los'i·ty
pl. neb'u·los'i·ties

neb'u·lous

nec'es·sar'i·ly

nec'es·sar'y
pl. nec'es·sar'ies

ne·ces'si·tate'
ne·ces'si·tat'ed,
ne·ces'si·tat'ing

ne·ces'si·ta'tion

ne·ces'si·tous

ne·ces'si·ty
pl. ne·ces'si·ties

neck

neck'band'

neck'er·chief

neck'lace

neck'line'

neck'piece'

neck'tie'

neck'wear'

ne·crol'o·gist

ne·crol'o·gy
pl. ne·crol'o·gies

nec'ro·man'cer

nec'ro·man'cy

nec'ro·phil'i·a

ne·crop'o·lis
pl. ne·crop'o·lis·es

nec'rop·sy
pl. nec'rop·sies

ne·cro'sis

nec'tar

nec'tar·ine'

nee *or* née (*born*)
(SEE neigh *and* nay)

need (*require*)
(SEE knead)

need'ful

need'ful·ly

need'i·ness

nee'dle
nee'dled, nee'dling

nee'dle·point'

need'less

nee'dle·work'

need'n't

needs

need'y
need'i·er, need'i·est

ne'er

ne·er'–do–well'

ne·far'i·ous

ne·gate'
ne·gat'ed, ne·gat'ing

ne·ga'tion

neg'a·tive
neg'a·tived,
neg'a·tiv·ing

neg'a·tive·ly

neg'a·tiv·ism'

nag'a·tiv·ist

neg'a·tiv·is'tic

ne·glect'

ne·glect'ful

neg'li·gee' *or* neg'li·gée'

neg'li·gence

neg'li·gent

neg'li·gi·bil'i·ty

neg'li·gi·ble

neg'li·gi·bly

ne·go'ti·a·bil'i·ty

ne·go'ti·a·ble

ne·go'ti·ate'
ne·go'ti·at'ed,
ne·go'ti·at'ing

ne·go'ti·a'tion

ne·go'ti·a'tor

Ne·gril'lo
pl. Ne·gril'los *or* Ne·gril'lo

Ne·gri'to
pl. Ne·gri'tos *or* Ne·gri'toes

Neg'ri·tude'

Ne'gro
pl. Ne'groes

Ne'groid

neigh (*whinny*)
(SEE nay *and* nee)

neigh'bor

neigh'bor·hood'

neigh'bor·ing

neigh'bor·li·ness

neigh'bor·ly

nei'ther

nel'son

nem'a·to·cyst

nem'a·tode'

Nem'bu·tal'
  (Trademark)
nem'e·sis
  pl. nem'e·ses'
ne'o·clas'sic
ne'o·clas'si·cal
ne'o·clas'si·cism'
ne'o·co·lo'ni·al·ism'
ne'o·dym'i·um
Ne'o–
  Im·pres'sion·ism'
Ne'o–Lat'in
Ne'o·lith'ic
ne·ol'o·gism'
ne'o·my'cin
ne'on
Ne'o–Na'zi
ne'o·phyte'
ne'o·plasm'
Ne'o·pla'to·nism'
ne'o·prene'
Ne·pal'
Nep'a·lese'
  pl. Nep'a·lese'
ne·pen'the
neph'ew
neph'rite
ne·phri'tis
ne·phro'sis
ne·phrot'o·my
ne plus ul'tra
nep'o·tism'
nep'o·tis'tic
Nep'tune
Nep·tu'ni·an
nep·tu'ni·um
nerd
nerts
nerve
nerve' cen'ter
nerve' gas'
nerve'less
nerve'–rack'ing or
  nerve'–wrack'ing
nerv'ine
nerv'ous
nerv'y
  nerv'i·er, nerv'i·est

nes'cience
Nes'sel·rode'
nest
nest' egg'
nes'tle
  nes'tled, nes'tling
nest'ling
net
  net'ted, net'ting
neth'er
Neth'er·land'er
Neth'er·lands
neth'er·most'
neth'er world'
ne'tsu·ke
net'ting
net'tle
  net'tled, net'tling
net'tle·some
net'work'
Neuf'châ·tel'
neu'ral
neu·ral'gia
neu·ral'gic
neu'ras·the'ni·a
neu'ras·then'ic
neu·ri'tic
neu·ri'tis
neu'ro·log'i·cal
neu·rol'o·gist
neu·rol'o·gy
neu'ro·mus'cu·lar
neu'ron or neu'rone
neu'ro·psy·chi'a·try
neu'ro·psy·cho'sis
neu·ro'sis
  pl. neu·ro'ses
neu'ro·sur'ger·y
neu·rot'ic
neu·rot'i·cal·ly
neu'ter
neu'tral
neu'tral·ism'
neu'tral·ist
neu·tral'i·ty
neu·tral·i·za'tion
neu'tral·ize'
  neu'tral·ized',
  neu'tral·iz'ing

neu'tral·iz'er
neu·tri'no
  pl. neu·tri'nos
neu'tron
Ne·va'da
Ne·va'dan
nev'er
nev'er·more'
nev'er·the·less'
ne'void
ne'vus
  pl. ne'vi
new (recent)
  (SEE gnu and knew)
New'ark
new'born'
  pl. new'born' or
  new'borns'
New' Bruns'wick
New'burg
new'com'er
New' Deal'
New' Deal'er
New' Del'hi
new'el
New' Eng'land
New' Eng'land·er
new'fan'gled
new'fash'ioned
New'found·land'
New' Hamp'shire
new'ish
New' Jer'sey
New' Jer'sey·ite'
new'ly
new'ly·wed'
New' Mex'i·can
New' Mex'ico
new'ness
New' Or'le·ans
news
news'boy'
news'break'
news'cast'
news'cast'er
news'deal'er
news'let'ter
news'mak'er

news'man
  pl. news'men'

news'pa'per

news'pa'per•man'
  pl. news'pa'per•men

new'speak'

news'print'

news'reel'

news' room'

news'stand'

news'wor'thy

news'y
  news'i•er, news'i•est

newt

New'ton

New' Year's' Eve'

New' York'

New' York'er

New' Zea'land

New' Zea'land•er

next

next'–door' (adv.)

next'–door' (adj.)

nex'us
  pl. nex'us

Nez' Per'cé
  pl. Nez' Per'cés or Nez'
  Per'cé

ni'a•cin

Ni•ag'a•ra

Nia•mey'

nib
  nibbed, nib'bing

nib'ble
  nib'bled, nib'bling

Ni'be•lung'en•lied'

nib'lick

ni'–cad' or ni'cad'

Nic'a•ra'gua

Nic'a•ra'guan

nice (agreeable)
  nic'er, nic'est
  (SEE gneiss)

nice'ly

Ni'cene

Ni'cene Creed'

nice'ness

ni'ce•ty
  pl. ni'ce•ties

niche
  niched, nich'ing

nick

nick'el
  nick'eled, nick'el•ing

nick'el•o'de•on

nick'el plate'

nick'el-plate'
  nick'el-plat'ed, nick'el-
  plat•ing

nick'name'
  nick'named',
  nick'nam'ing

Nic'o•si'a

ni•co'ti•a'na

nic'o•tine'

nic'o•tin'ic

niece

Nie'tzsche

nif'ty
  nif'ti•er, nif'ti•est

Ni'ger

Ni'ger–Con'go

Ni•ge'ri•a

Ni•ge'ri•an

nig'gard

nig'gard•li•ness

nig'gard•ly

nig'gling

nigh

night (darkness)
  (SEE knight)

night'–blind'

night'cap'

night' clothes'

night' club'

night'dress'

night'fall'

night'gown'

night'hawk'

night'in•gale'

night' let'ter

night' light'

night'long'

night'ly

night'mare'

night' owl'

night'rid'er

night' school'

night' shift'

night'shade'

night'shirt'

night'spot'

night' stick'

night' ta'ble

night'time'

night'walk'er

night' watch'man

ni'hil•ism'

ni'hil•ist

ni'hil•is'tic

Ni•jin'sky

Ni'ke

nil

Nile

nim'ble
  nim'bler, nim'blest

nim'bly

nim'bo•stra'tus
  pl. nim'bo•stra'tus

nim'bus
  pl. nim'bi or
  nim'bus•es

Nim'rod

nin'com•poop'

nine

nine'pins'

nine'teen'

nine'teenth'

nine'ti•eth

nine'ty
  pl. nine'ties

nin'ny
  pl. nin'nies

ni•non'

ninth

ni•o'bi•um

nip
  nipped, nip'ping

nip'per

nip'ple

Nip•pon

Nip'pon•ese'
  pl. Nip'pon•ese'

nip'py
  nip'pi•er, nip'pi•est

nip'–up'

nir•va'na

Ni′sei′
  pl. Ni′sei′
ni′si
nit
ni′ter
nit′pick′
ni′trate
  ni′trat·ed, ni′trat·ing
ni·tra′tion
ni′tric
ni′tride
ni′tri·fi·ca′tion
ni′tri·fy′
  ni′tri·fied′, ni′tri·fy′ing
ni′trite
ni′tro·bac·te′ri·a
ni′tro·cel′lu·lose′
ni′tro·gen
ni·trog′e·nous
ni′tro·glyc′er·in or
  ni′tro·glyc′er·ine
ni′trous
nit′ty–grit′ty
nit′wit′
nix
nix′ie
  pl. nix′ies
Nix′on
no (*negative*)
  pl. noes or nos
Nō or No (*Japanese drama*)
No′ah
No·bel′
No·bel′ist
no·be′li·um
no·bil′i·ty
  pl. no·bil′i·ties
no′ble
  no′bler, no′blest
no′ble·man
  pl. no′ble·men
no·blesse′ o·blige′
no′ble·wom′an
  pl. no′ble·wom′en
no′bly
no′bod′y
  pl. no′bod′ies
noc·tur′nal

noc·tur′nal·ly
noc′turne
nod
  nod′ded, nod′ding
nod′al
node
nod′u·lar
nod′ule
nod′u·lous
No·el′
no′-fault′
no′-frills′
nog′gin
no′-good′
noise
  noised, nois′ing
noise′less
noise′mak′er
noi′some
nois′i·ly
nois′i·ness
nois′y
  nois′i·er, nois′i·est
no′-load′
no′lo con·ten′de·re
no′mad
no·mad′ic
no′ man s′ land′
nom′ de plume′
no′men·cla′ture
nom′i·nal
nom′i·nal·ly
nom′i·nate′ (*v.*)
  nom′i·nat′ed,
  nom′i·nat′ing
nom′i·nate (*adj.*)
nom′i·na′tion
nom′i·na′tive
nom′i·na′tor
nom′i·nee′
non′age
non·a·ge·nar′i·an
non′ag·gres′sion
non·a′gon′
non·al·co·hol′ic
non·a·ligned′
non·al·ler·gen′ic
non·a·lign′ment

non′be·liev′er
non′bel·lig′er·ent
nonce
non′cha·lance′
non′cha·lant′
non·cit′i·zen
non′com
non·com′bat·ant
non·com·bus′ti·ble
non·com·mer′cial
non·com·mis′sioned
non·com·mit′tal
non·com·pet′i·tive
non·com·pli′ance
non com′pos men′tis
non′con·duc′tor
non′con·form′ist
non′con·form′i·ty
non·con·ta′gious
non·con·tro·ver′sial
non′co·op′er·a′tion
non′de·script′
non′dis·crim′i·na′tion
non·dis·tinc′tive
non·dra·mat′ic
none (*not one*)
  (SEE nun)
non·en′ti·ty
  pl. non·en′ti·ties
non·es·sen′tial
none′such′
none′the·less′
non′-Eu·clid′e·an
non·ex·ist′ence
non′fer′rous
non·fic′tion
non·flam′ma·ble
non·hu′man
no·nil′lion
  pl. no·nil′lions or
  no·nil′lion
no·nil′lionth
non·in·ter·fer′ence
non·in·ter·ven′tion
non·in·ter·
  ven′tion·ist
non·in·tox′i·cat′ing

non·ko'sher
non'lead'ed
non'le'gal
non·mem'ber
non·met'al
non·me·tal'lic
no'-no'
   pl. no'-nos' or no'-no's'
non'ob·jec'tive
non'pa·reil'
non·par·tic'i·pat'ing
non·par'ti·san
non·pay'ment
non·per·form'ance
non'per'son
non·plus'
   pl. non·plused' or
   non·plussed',
   non·plus'ing or
   non·plus'sing
non·po'rous
non'pro·duc'tive
non·prof'it
non'pro·lif'er·a'tion
non'rep·re·sen·
   ta'tion·al
non·res'i·dent
non're·sis'tant
non're·stric'tive
non·rig'id
non·sched'uled
non'sec·tar'i·an
non'sense
non·sen'si·cal
non·sen'si·cal·ly
non se'qui·tur
non·sex'u·al
non·sked'
non·skid'
non·smok'er
non·stop'
non·strik'er
non·sup·port'
non·sur'gi·cal
non·tech'ni·cal
non·un'ion
non·us'er
non·ver'bal

non·vi'o·lence
non·vi'o·lent
non·white'
noo'dle
nook
noon
noon'day'
no' one'
noon'tide'
noon'time'
noose
   noosed, noos'ing
no'-par'
nope
nor
Nor'dic
Nor'folk
norm
nor'mal
nor'mal·cy
nor·mal'i·ty
nor'mal·i·za'tion
nor'mal·ize'
   nor'mal·ized',
   nor'mal·iz'ing
nor'mal·ly
Nor'man
nor'ma·tive
Norse
Norse'man
   pl. Norse'men
north
North' A·mer'i·ca
North' A·mer'i·can
north'bound'
North' Car'o·li'na
North' Car'o·lin'i·an
North' Da·ko'ta
North' Da·ko'tan
north'east'
north'east'er
north'east'er·ly
north'east'ward
north'east'wards
north'er
north'er·ly
north'ern

North'ern·er
North'ern Ire'land
north'ern·most'
north'land
North'man
   pl. North'men
north'-north'east'
north'-north'west'
North' Pole'
north'ward
north'wards
north'west'
north'west'er
north'west'er·ly
North'west
   Ter'ri·tor'ies
north'west'ward
Nor'way
Nor·we'gian
nose
   nosed, nos'ing
nose'bleed'
nose' cone'
nose' dive'
nose'-dive'
   nose'-dived' or nose'-
   dove', nose'-div'ing
nose'gay'
nose'piece'
nos'ey
   nos'i·er, nos'i·est
nosh
no'-show'
nos·tal'gia
nos·tal'gic
nos·tal'gi·cal·ly
nos'tril
nos'trum
nos·i·ly
nos'i·ness
nos'y
   nos'i·er, nos'i·est
not (*negative*)
   (SEE knot)
no'ta be'ne
no'ta·bil'i·ty
no'ta·ble
no'ta·bly

no'ta·rize'
  no'ta·rized',
  no'ta·riz'ing
no'ta·ry
  pl. no'ta·ries
no'ta·ry pub'lic
no'tate
  no'tat·ed, no'tat·ing
no·ta'tion
notch
  pl. notch'es
notch'back'
note
  not'ed, not'ing
note'book'
not'ed
note'pap'er
note'wor'thi·ly
note'wor'thi·ness
note'wor'thy
noth'ing
noth'ing·ness
no'tice
  no'ticed, no'tic·ing
no'tice·a·ble
no'tice·a·bly
no'ti·fi·ca'tion
no'ti·fi'er
no'ti·fy'
  no'ti·fied', no'ti·fy'ing
no'tion
no'tion·al
no'to·chord'
no'to·ri'e·ty
  pl. no'to·ri'e·ties
no·to'ri·ous
no'-trump'
not'with·stand'ing
Nouak·chott'
nou'gat
Nou·mé'a
noun
nour'ish
nour'ish·ment
nou'veau riche'
  pl. nou'veaux riches'
no'va
  pl. no'vae or no'vas
No'va Sco'tia
No'va Sco'tian

nov'el
nov'el·ette'
nov'el·ist
nov'el·is'tic
nov'el·i·za'tion
nov'el·ize'
  nov'el·ized',
  nov'el·iz'ing
no·vel'la
  pl. no·vel'las or
  no·vel'le
nov'el·ty
  pl. nov'el·ties
No·vem'ber
no·ve'na
  pl. no·ve'nae
nov'ice
no·vi'ti·ate
No'vo·caine'
  (Trademark)
now
now'a·days'
no'way'
no'ways'
no'where'
no'wise'
nox'ious
noz'zle
nth
nu
nu'ance
nub
nub'bin
nub'ble
nub'bly
nub'by
Nu'bi·an
nu'bile
nu'cle·ar
nu'cle·ate (adj.)
nu'cle·ate' (v.)
  nu'cle·at'ed,
  nu'cle·at'ing
nu'cle·a'tion
nu·cle'ic
nu·cle'o·lar
nu·cle'o·lus
  pl. nu·cle'o·li'
nu·cle·on'
nu'cle·on'ics

nu'cle·o·some'
nu'cle·us
  pl. nu'cle·i' or
  nu'cle·us·es
nu'clide
nude
nudge
  nudged, nudg'ing
nud'ism
nud'ist
nu'di·ty
  pl. nu'di·ties
nu'ga·to'ry
nug'get
nui'sance
nuke
null
nul'li·fi·ca'tion
nul'li·fi'er
nul'li·fy'
  nul'li·fied',
  nul'li·fy'ing
nul'li·ty
  pl. nul'li·ties
numb
num'ber
num'ber·less
numb'ing
numb'ly
numb'ness
nu'mer·a·ble
nu'mer·al
nu'mer·ate'
  nu'mer·at'ed,
  nu'mer·at'ing
nu'mer·a'tion
nu'mer·a'tor
nu·mer'ic
nu·mer'i·cal
nu·mer'i·cal·ly
nu'mer·ol'o·gy
nu'mer·ous
nu'mis·mat'ic
nu'mis·mat'ics
nu·mis'ma·tist
num'skull or
  numb'skull
nun (religious
  woman)
  (SEE none)

nun'ci·o
  pl. nun'ci·os

nun'ner·y
  pl. nun'ner·ies

nup'tial

nurse
  nursed, nurs'ing

nurse'maid'

nurs'er·y
  pl. nurs'er·ies

nurs'er·y·man
  pl. nurs'er·y·men

nurs'ing·home'

nur'ture
  nur'tured, nur'tur·ing

nut
  nut'ted, nut'ting

nut'crack'er

nut'hatch'

nut'meat'

nut'meg'

nut'pick'

nu'tri·a

nu'tri·ent

nu'tri·ment

nu·tri'tion

nu·tri'tion·al

nu·tri'tion·ist

nu·tri'tious

nu'tri·tive

nuts

nut'shell'

nut'ty
  nut'ti·er, nut'ti·est

nuz'zle
  nuz'zled, nuz'zling

nyc·ta·lo'pi·a

ny'lon

nymph

nymph·et'

nym'pho·ma'ni·a

nym'pho·ma'ni·ac'

O

oaf

oak

oak'en

Oak'land

oa'kum

oar (*paddle*)
  (SEE or *and* o'er *and* ore)

oar'lock'

oars'man
  pl. oars'men

o·a'sis
  pl. o·a'ses

oat

oat'cake'

oat'en

oath

oat'meal'

ob'bli·ga'to
  pl. ob'bli·ga'tos or
  (*It.*) ob'bli·ga'ti

ob'du·ra·cy

ob'du·rate

o·be'di·ence

o·be'di·ent

o·bei'sance

o·bei'sant

ob'e·lisk

o·bese'

o·bes'i·ty

o·bey'

ob·fus'cate
  ob·fus'cat·ed,
  ob·fus'cat·ing

ob'fus·ca'tion

o'bi
  pl. o'bis or (*Japn.*) o'bi

ob'i·ter dic'tum
  pl. ob'i·ter dic'ta

o·bit'u·ar'y
  pl. o·bit'u·ar'ies

ob'ject (*n.*)

ob·ject' (*v.*)

ob·jec'ti·fy
  ob·jec'ti·fied',
  ob·jec'ti·fy'ing

ob·jec'tion

ob·jec'tion·a·ble

ob·jec'tion·a·bly

ob·jec'tive

ob·jec'tive·ly

ob'jec·tiv'i·ty

ob·jec'tor

ob·jet d'*art*
  pl. ob·jets d'*art*

ob'jur·gate'
  ob'jur·gat'ed,
  ob'jur·gat'ing

ob'jur·ga'tion

ob'late

ob·la'tion

ob'li·gate' (*v.*)
  ob'li·gat'ed,
  ob'li·gat'ing

ob'li·gate (*adj.*)

ob'li·ga'tion

ob·lig'a·to'ry

o·blige'
  o·bliged', o·blig'ing

o·blig'er

ob·lique'
  ob·liqued', ob·liqu'ing

ob·lique'ly

ob'liq'ui·ty
  pl. ob·liq'ui·ties

ob·lit'er·ate'
  ob·lit'er·at'ed,
  ob·lit'er·at'ing

ob·lit'er·a'tion

ob·liv'i·on

ob·liv'i·ous

ob'long'

ob'lo·quy
  pl. ob'lo·quies

ob·nox'ious

o'boe

o'bo·ist

ob·scene'

ob·scene'ly

ob·scen'i·ty
  pl. ob·scen'i·ties

ob·scu'rant·ism'

ob·scu'rant·ist

ob·scure'
  (*adj.*) ob·scur'er,
  ob·scrur'est;
  (*v.*) ob·scured',
  ob·scur'ing

ob·scure'ly
ob·scur'i·ty
  pl. ob·scur'i·ties
ob·se'qui·ous
ob'se·quy
  pl. ob'se·quies
ob·serv'a·ble
ob·serv'a·bly
ob·serv'ance
ob·serv'ant
ob'ser·va'tion
ob·serv'a·to'ry
  pl. ob·serv'a·to'ries
ob·serve'
  ob·served', ob·serv'ing
ob·serv'er
ob·sess'
ob·ses'sion
ob·ses'sive
ob·sid'i·an
ob'so·lesce'
  ob'so·lesced',
  ob'so·lesc'ing
ob'so·les'cence
ob'so·les'cent
ob'so·lete'
ob'sta·cle
ob·stet'ric
ob·stet'ri·cal
ob'ste·tri'cian
ob·stet'rics
ob'sti·na·cy
  pl. ob'sti·na·cies
ob'sti·nate
ob'sti·nate·ly
ob·strep'er·ous
ob·struct'
ob·struc'tion
ob·struc'tion·ism'
ob·struc'tion·ist
ob·struc'tive
ob·tain'
ob·tain'a·ble
ob·trude'
  ob·trud'ed, ob·trud'ing
ob·tru'sion
ob·tru'sive
ob·tuse'

ob'verse (*n.*)
ob·verse' (*adj.*)
ob·vert'
ob'vi·ate'
  ob'vi·at'ed, ob'vi·at'ing
ob'vi·a'tion
ob'vi·ous
oc'a·ri'na
oc·ca'sion
oc·ca'sion·al
oc·ca'sion·al·ly
Oc'ci·dent
Oc'ci·den'tal
oc·cip'i·tal
oc'ci·put'
oc·clude'
  oc·clud'ed, oc·clud'ing
oc·clu'sion
oc·clu'sive
oc·cult'
oc'cul·ta'tion
oc·cult'ism
oc·cult'ist
oc'cu·pan·cy
  pl. oc'cu·pan·cies
oc'cu·pant
oc'cu·pa'tion
oc'cu·pa'tion·al
oc'cu·pa'tion·al·ly
oc'cu·pi'er
oc'cu·py'
  oc'cu·pied',
  oc'cu·py'ing
oc·cur'
  oc·curred', oc·cur'ring
oc·cur'rence
oc·cur'rent
o'cean
o'cea·naut'
o'cean·front'
o'cean-go'ing
O'ce·an'i·a
o'ce·an'ic
o'cean lin'er
o'ce·a·nog'ra·pher
o'ce·a·no·graph'ic
o'ce·a·nog'ra·phy
o'ce·lot'

o'cher *or* o'chre
o'clock'
o'co·til'lo
  pl. o'co·til'los
oc'tad
oc'ta·gon'
oc·tag'o·nal
oc·tag'o·nal·ly
oc·ta·he'dral
oc·ta·he'dron
oc'tane
oc'tant
oc'tave
oc·ta'vo
  pl. oc·ta'vos
oc·tet' *or* oc·tette'
Oc·to'ber
oc'to·ge·nar'i·an
oc'to·pus
  pl. oc'to·pus·es *or*
  oc'to·pi'
oc'to·roon'
oc'u·lar
oc'u·list
o'da·lisque
odd
odd'ball
odd'i·ty
  pl. odd'i·ties
odd' lot'
odd'ly
odd'ment
odds
odds'-on'
ode
O'din
o'di·ous
o'di·um
o·dom'e·ter
o'dor
o'dor·if'er·ous
o'dor·ous
O·dys'se·us
Od'ys·sey
oed'i·pal
Oed'i·pus
oe'no·phile'
o'er (*over*)
  (SEE oar *and or and*
  ore)

oeu'vre

of

off

of'fal (*refuse*)
(SEE awful)

off'beat' (*adj.*)

off'beat' (*n.*)

off' Broad'way

off'cast'

off'-cen'ter

off'-col'or

Of'fen·bach'

of·fend'

of·fense'

of·fen'sive

of'fer

of'fer·er or of'fer·or

of'fer·ing

of'fer·to·ry
pl. of'fer·to·ries

off'hand'

of'fice

of'fice·hold'er

of'fic·er

of'fice seek'er

of·fi'cial

of·fi'cial·ly

of·fi'cial·dom

of·fi'cial·ese'

of·fi'cial·ism'

of·fi'ci·ant

of·fi'ci·ate'
of·fi'ci·at'ed,
of·fi'ci·at'ing

of·fi'ci·a'tion

of·fi'cious

off'ing

off'ish

off'-key'

off'-lim'its

off'-line'

off'load'

off'print'

off'screen'

off'-sea'son

off'set' (*n., adj.*)

off'set' (*v.*)
off'set', off'set'ting

off'shoot'

off'shore'

off'side'

off'spring'
pl. off'spring or
off'springs'

off'stage'

off'-the-re'cord

off'track'

off'-white'

oft

of'ten

of'ten·times'

oft'times'

o·gee'

o'gle
o'gled, o'gling

o'gre

o'gre·ish

o'gress

oh (*exclamation*)
pl. oh's or ohs
(SEE owe)

O·hi'o

O·hi'o·an

ohm

ohm'me'ter

o·ho'

oil

oil' cake'

oil'can'

oil'cloth'

oil'er

oil' field'

oil'i·ness

oil'man'
pl. oil'men'

oil'skin'

oil'stone'

oil' well'

oil'y
oil'i·er, oil'i·est

oink

oint'ment

O.·K.' (*adj., adv.*)
O.·K.' (*v., n.*)
(*v.*) O.·K.'d',
O.·K.''ing;
pl. O.·K.'s'

o·ka'pi
pl. o·ka'pis or o·ka'pi

o'kay' (*adj., adv.*)

o'kay' (*v., n.*)

O'kla·ho'ma

O'kla·ho'man

o'kra

old
old'er, old'est or eld'er,
eld'est

old'en

old'-fash'ioned

old' fo'gy

old'ish

old'-line'

old' maid'

old'ster

old'-time'

old'-tim'er

old'-world'

Old World

o'le·ag'i·nous

o'le·an'der

o'le·fin

o·le'ic

o'le·o

o'le·o·mar'gar·ine

o'le·o·res'in

ol·fac'tion

ol·fac'to·ry
pl. ol·fac'to·ries

ol'i·garch'

ol'i·gar'chic

ol'i·gar'chi·cal

ol'i·gar'chy
pl. ol'i·gar'chies

Ol'i·go·cene'

ol'i·gop'o·ly

o'li·o'
pl. o'li·os'

ol'ive

ol'ive oil'

ol'la po·dri'da

O·lym'pi·a

o·lym'pi·ad'

O·lym'pi·an

O·lym'pic

O·lym'pus

O'ma・ha'
O・man'
O・man'i
om'buds・man'
　pl. om'buds・men'
o・me'ga
om・e・let or
　om・e・lette
o'men
om'i・cron'
om'i・nous
o・mis'sion
o・mit'
　o・mit'ted, o・mit'ting
om'ni・bus'
　pl. om'ni・bus'es
om・nip'o・tence
om・nip'o・ten・cy
om・nip'o・tent
om'ni・pres'ence
om'ni・pres'ent
om・nis'cience
om・nis'cien・cy
om・nis'cient
om'ni・vore'
om・niv'or・ous
on
o'nan・ism'
once
once'-o'ver
once'-o'ver-light'ly
on'com'ing
one　(single)
　(SEE WON)
one'-lin'er
one'ness
on'er・ous
one・self'
one' shot'
one'-sid'ed
one'-time' or
　one'time'
one'-on-one'
one'-to-one'
one'-track'
one'-up'man・ship'
one'-way'
on'go'ing

on'ion
on'ion・skin'
on'-line'
on'look'er
on'ly
on'o・mas'tics
on'o・mat'o・poe'ia
on'o・mat'o・poe'ic
on'o・mat'o・po・et'ic
on'rush'
on'set'
on'shore'
on'slaught'
on'stage'
on'-stream'
On・tar'i・o
on'to
on'to・log'i・cal
on・tol'o・gy
o'nus
　pl. o'nus・es
on'ward
on'wards
on'yx
oo'dles
oo'long'
oomph
ooze
　oozed, ooz'ing
ooz'y
　ooz'i・er, ooz'i・est
o・pac'i・ty
　pl. o・pac'i・ties
o'pal
o'pal・es'cence
o'pal・es'cent
o・paque'
　o・paqued', o・paqu'ing
o・paque'ly
op' art'
o'pen
o'pen air'
o'pen-and-shut'
o'pen-end'
o'pen・er
o'pen-eyed'
o'pen-faced'
o'pen-hand'ed

o'pen-heart'
o'pen-heart'ed
o'pen-hearth'
o'pen house'
o'pen・ing
o'pen let'ter
o'pen-mind'ed
o'pen-mouthed'
o'pen・ness
o'pen shop'
o'pen・work'
op'er・a
op'er・a・bil'i・ty
op'er・a・ble
op'er・a・bly
op'er・a glass'es
op'er・a house'
op'er・ant
op'er・ate'
　pl. op'er・at'ed,
　op'er・at'ing
op'er・at'ic
op'er・at'i・cal・ly
op'er・a'tion
op'er・a'tion・al
op'er・a'tive
op'er・a'tor
op'er・et'ta
oph・thal'mic
oph・thal'mo・log'ic
oph・thal'mo・log'i・cal
oph'thal・mol'o・gist
oph'thal・mol'o・gy
o'pi・ate　(n., adj.)
o'pi・ate'　(v.)
　o'pi・at'ed, o'pi・at'ing
o・pine'
　o・pined', o・pin'ing
o・pin'ion
o・pin'ion・at'ed
o'pi・um
o・pos'sum
　pl. o・pos'sums or
　o・pos'sum
op・po'nent
op'por・tune'
op'por・tune'ly
op'por・tun'ism

op'por · tun'ist
op'por · tun · is'tic
op · pos'a · ble
op · pose'
  op · posed', op · pos'ing
op'po · site
op'po · si'tion
op · press'
op · pres'sion
op · pres'sive
op · pres'sive · ly
op · pres'sor
op · pro'bri · ous
op · pro'bri · um
opt
op'tic
op'ti · cal
op · ti'cian
op'tics
op'ti · mal
op'ti · mism'
op'ti · mist
op'ti · mis'tic
op'ti · mis'ti · cal · ly
op'ti · mize'
  op'ti · mized',
  op'ti · miz'ing
op'ti · mum
  pl. op'ti · ma or
  op'ti · mums
op'tion
op'tion · al
op'tion · al · ly
op · tom'e · trist
op · tom'e · try
op'u · lence
op'u · len · cy
op'u · lent
o'pus
  pl. o'pus · es or o'pe · ra
or (alternative)
  (SEE ore and o'er and
  oar)
or'a · cle (shrine)
  (SEE auricle)
o · rac'u · lar
o'ral (spoken)
  (SEE aural)
o'ral · ly
or'ange

or'ange · ade'
or'ange · ry
  pl. or'ange · ries
o · rang'u · tan' or
  o · rang'ou · tan'
o · rate'
  o · rat'ed, o · rat'ing
o · ra'tion
or'a · tor
or'a · tor'i · cal
or'a · tor'i · cal · ly
or'a · to'ri · o
  pl. or'a · to'ri · os
or'a · to'ry
orb
or · bic'u · lar
or'bit
or'bit · al
or'ca
or'chard
or'ches · tra
or · ches'tral
or'ches · trate'
  or'ches · trat'ed,
  or'ches · trat'ing
or'ches · tra'tion
or'chid
or · dain'
or · deal'
or'der
or'der · li · ness
or'der · ly
  pl. or'der · lies
or'di · nal
or'di · nance (law)
  (SEE ordnance)
or'di · nar'i · ly
or'di · nar'y
  pl. or'di · nar'ies
or'di · nate'
or'di · na'tion
ord'nance (weapons)
  (SEE ordinance)
Or'do · vi'cian
or'dure
ore (mineral)
  (SEE or and oar and
  o'er)
ŏ're
  pl. ŏ're

o · reg'a · no'
Or'e · gon
Or'e · go'ni · an
or'gan
or'gan · dy or
  or'gan · die
or'gan · elle'
or · gan'ic
or · gan'i · cal · ly
or'gan · ism'
or'gan · is'mal
or'gan · is'mic
or'gan · ist
or'gan · iz'a · ble
or'gan · i · za'tion
or'gan · i · za'tion · al
or'gan · ize'
  or'gan · ized',
  or'gan · iz'ing
or'gan · iz'er
or · gan'za
or'gasm
or · gas'mic
or · gi · as'tic
or'gy
  pl. or'gies
o'ri · el
O'ri · ent (n., adj.)
o'ri · ent' (v.)
O'ri · en'tal
o'ri · en · tate'
  o'ri · en · tat'ed,
  o'ri · en · tat'ing
o'ri · en · ta'tion
or'i · fice
o'ri · ga'mi
  pl. o'ri · ga'mis
or'i · gin
o · rig'i · nal
o · rig'i · nal'i · ty
  pl. o · rig'i · nal'i · ties
o · rig'i · nal · ly
o · rig'i · nate'
  o · rig'i · nat'ed,
  o · rig'i · nat'ing
o · rig'i · na'tion
o · rig'i · na'tor
o'ri · ole'
O · ri'on

or'i·son
Or'lon (*Trademark*)
or'mo·lu'
or'na·ment (*n.*)
or'na·ment' (*v.*)
or'na·men'tal
or'na·men'tal·ly
or'na·men·ta'tion
or·nate'
or·nate'ly
or'ner·y
or'ni·tho·log'ic
or'ni·tho·log'i·cal
or'ni·thol'o·gist
or'ni·thol'o·gy
o'ro·tund'
or'phan
or'phan·age
Or'phe·us
or'thi·con'
or'tho·clase'
or'tho·don'tia
or'tho·don'tic
or'tho·don'tics
or'tho·don'tist
or'tho·dox'
or'tho·dox'y
  pl. or'tho·dox'ies
or·tho'e·py
or·thog'o·nal
or'tho·graph'ic
or·thog'ra·phy
  pl. or·thog'ra·phies
or'tho·pe'dic
or'tho·pe'dics
or'tho·pe'dist
Or'well
Or·well'i·an
o'ryx
  pl. o'ryx·es or o'ryx
O·sa'ka
os'cil·late'
  os'cil·lat'ed,
  os'cil·lat'ing
os'cil·la'tion
os'cil·la'tor
os'cil·la·to'ry
os·cil'lo·scope'

os'cu·late'
  os'cu·lat'ed,
  os'cu·lat'ing
os'cu·la'tion
Osh'a·wa
o'sier
O·si'ris
Os'lo
os'mi·um
os·mo'sis
os·mot'ic
os'prey
  pl. os'preys
os'si·fi·ca'tion
os'si·fy'
  os'si·fied, os'si·fy'ing
os·ten'si·ble
os·ten'si·bly
os'ten·ta'tion
os'ten·ta'tious
os'te·o·my'e·li'tis
os'te·o·path'
os'te·o·path'ic
os'te·op'a·thy
ost'mark'
os'tra·cism'
os'tra·cize'
  os'tra·cized',
  os'tra·ciz'ing
os'trich
oth'er
oth'er·wise'
oth'er world'
oth'er·world'ly
o'tic
o'ti·ose'
o·ti'tis
o'to·lar'yn·gol'o·gist
o'to·lar'yn·gol'o·gy
Ot'ta·wa
ot'ter
Ot'to·man
  pl. Ot'to·mans
Oua'ga·dou'gou
ouch
ought (*should*)
  (SEE aught)
ought'n't
Oui'ja (*Trademark*)

ounce
our (*belonging
  to us*)
  (SEE hour)
ours
our·selves'
oust
oust'er
out
out'age
out'-and-out'
out'back
out'bid'
  out'bid', out'bid'den or
  out'bid', out'bid'ding
out'board'
out'bound'
out'box'
out'break'
out'build'ing
out'burst'
out'cast'
out'class'
out'come'
out'crop' (*n.*)
out'crop' (*v.*)
  out'cropped',
  out'crop'ping
out'cry' (*n.*)
  pl. out'cries'
out'cry' (*v.*)
  out'cried', out'cry'ing
out'date'
  out'dat'ed, out'dat'ing
out'dis'tance
  out'dis'tanced,
  out'dis'tanc·ing
out'do'
  out'did', out'done',
  out'do'ing
out'door'
out'doors'
out'er
out'er·most'
out'face'
  out'faced', out'fac'ing
out'field'
out'field'er
out'fit'
  out'fit'ed, out'fit'ing
out'fit'ter

out'flank'

out'flow'

out'fox'

out'gen'er・al
out'gen'er・aled,
out'gen'er・al・ing

out'go'
pl. out'goes'

out'go'
out'went', out'gone',
out'go'ing

out'go'ing

out'grow'

out'grew', out'grown',
out'grow'ing

out'growth'

out'guess'

out'house'

out'ing

out'land'er

out'land'ish

out'last'

out'law'

out'law'ry

out'lay' (*n.*)

out'lay' (*v.*)
out'laid', out'lay'ing

out'let

out'line'
out'lined', out'lin'ing

out'live'
out'lived', out'liv'ing

out'look'

out'ly'ing

out'match'

out'mod'ed
out'mod'ed, out'mod'ing

out'most

out'num'ber

out'-of-bounds'

out'-of-date'

out'-of-door'

out'-of-doors'

out'-of-the-way'

out'pa'tient

out'play'

out'point'

out'post'

out'pour' (*n.*)

out'pour' (*v.*)

out'put'

out'rage'
out'raged', out'rag'ing

out'ra'geous

out'rank'

ou・tré'

out'reach' (*v.*)

out'reach' (*n.*)

out'ride' (*v.*)
out'rode', out'rid'den,
out'rid'ing

out'ride' (*n.*)

out'rid'er

out'rig'ger

out'right' (*adj.*)

out'right' (*adv.*)

out'run'
out'ran', out'run',
out'run'ning

out'rush'

out'sell'
out'sold', out'sell'ing

out'set'

out'shine'
out'shone', out'shin'ing

out'shoot' (*v.*)
out'shot', out'shoot'ing

out'shoot' (*n.*)

out'side' (*n.*)

out'side' (*adj., adv.,
prep.*)

out'sid'er

out'size'

out'sized'

out'skirts'

out'smart'

out'spo'ken

out'spread' (*v.*)
out'spread',
out'spread'ing

out'spread' (*adj.*)

out'spread' (*n.*)

out'stand'ing

out'stare'
out'stared', out'star'ing

out'sta'tion

out'stay'

out'stretch'

out'strip'
out'stripped',
out'strip'ping

out'vote'
out'vot'ed, out'vot'ing

out'ward

out'ward・ly

out'wards

out'wear'
out'wore', out'worn',
out'wear'ing

out'weigh'

out'wit'
out'wit'ted, out'wit'ting

out'work' (*v.*)
out'worked' or
out'wrought',
out'work'ing

out'work' (*n.*)

out'worn'

ou'zel

ou'zo

o'val

o・var'i・al

o・var'i・an

o'va・ry
pl. o'va・ries

o'vate

o・va'tion

ov'en

ov'en・bird'

ov'en・ware'

o'ver

o'ver・a・bun'dance

o'ver・a・bun'dant

o'ver・a・chieve'
o'ver・a・chieved',
o'ver・a・chiev'ing

o'ver・a・chiev'er

o'ver・act'

o'ver・ac'tive

o'ver・age'

o'ver・age

o'ver・all' (*adv.*)

o'ver・all' (*adj., n.*)

o'ver・alls'

o'ver・arch'

o'ver・arm'

o'ver・awe'
o'ver・awed',
o'ver・aw'ing

o'ver·bal'ance (v.)
  o'ver·bal'anced,
  o'ver·bal'anc·ing

o'ver·bal'ance (n.)

o'ver·bear'ing

o'ver·bid' (v.)
  o'ver·bid',
  o'ver·bid'ding

o'ver·bid' (n.)

o'ver·bite'

o'ver·blown'

o'ver·board'

o'ver·bur'den (v.)

o'ver·bur'den (n.)

o'ver·buy'
  o'ver·bought',
  o'ver·buy'ing

o'ver·call' (v.)

o'ver·call' (n.)

o'ver·cast' (adj.)

o'ver·cast' (v.)
  o'ver·cast',
  o'ver·cast'ing

o'ver·cast' (n.)

o'ver·charge' (v.)
  o'ver·charged',
  o'ver·charg'ing

o'ver·charge' (n.)

o'ver·clothes'

o'ver·cloud'

o'ver·coat' (n.)

o'ver·coat' (v.)

o'ver·come'
  o'ver·came',
  o'ver·come',
  o'ver·com'ing

o'ver·con'fi·dence

o'ver·con'fi·dent

o'ver·crowd'

o'ver·do' (do in
  excess)
  o'ver·did', o'ver·done',
  o'ver·do'ing
  (SEE overdue)

o'ver·dose' (n.)

o'ver·dose' (v.)
  o'ver·dosed',
  o'ver·dos'ing

o'ver·draft'

o'ver·draw'
  o'ver·drew',
  o'ver·drawn',
  o'ver·draw'ing

o'ver·dress' (v.)

o'ver·dress' (n.)

o'ver·drive' (v.)
  o'ver·drove',
  o'ver·driv'en,
  o'ver·driv'ing

o'ver·drive' (n.)

o'ver·due' (late)
  (SEE overdo)

o'ver·eat'
  o'ver·ate', o'ver·eat'en,
  o'ver·eat'ing

o'ver·e·lab'o·rate
  (adj.)

o'ver·e·lab'o·rate'
  (v.)
  o'ver·e·lab'o·rat'ed,
  o'ver·e·lab'o·rat'ing

o'ver·em'pha·sis

o'ver·em'pha·size'
  o'ver·em'pha·sized',
  o'ver·em'pha·siz'ing

o'ver·es'ti·mate'
  (v.)
  o'ver·es'ti·mat'ed,
  o'ver·es'ti·mat'ing

o'ver·es'ti·mate (n.)

o'ver·ex·ert'

o'ver·ex·er'tion

o'ver·ex·pose'
  o'ver·ex·posed',
  o'ver·ex·pos'ing

o'ver·ex·po'sure

o'ver·ex·tend'

o'ver·flight'

o'ver·flow' (v.)
  o'ver·flowed',
  o'ver·flown',
  o'ver·flow'ing

o'ver·flow' (n.)

o'ver·glaze' (n., adj.)

o'ver·glaze' (v.)
  o'ver·glazed',
  o'ver·glaz'ing

o'ver·grow'
  o'ver·grew',
  o'ver·grown',
  o'ver·grow'ing

o'ver·growth'

o'ver·hand'

o'ver·hang' (v.)
  o'ver·hung',
  o'ver·hang'ing

o'ver·hang' (n.)

o'ver·haul' (v.)

o'ver·haul' (n.)

o'ver·head' (adv.)

o'ver·head' (n., adj.)

o'ver·hear'
  o'ver·heard',
  o'ver·hear'ing

o'ver·heat'

o'ver·heat'

o'ver·in·dulge'
  o'ver·in·dulged',
  o'ver·in·dulg'ing

o'ver·in·dul'gence

o'ver·in·dul'gent

o'ver·joy'

o'ver·kill'

o'ver·land'

o'ver·lap' (v.)
  o'ver·lapped',
  o'ver·lap'ping

o'ver·lap' (n.)

o'ver·lay' (v.)
  o'ver·laid',
  o'ver·lay'ing

o'ver·lay' (n.)

o'ver·leap'
  o'ver·leaped' or
  o'ver·leapt',
  o'ver·leap'ing

o'ver·lie'
  o'ver·lay', o'ver·lain',
  o'ver·ly'ing

o'ver·load' (v.)

o'ver·load' (n.)

o'ver·long'

o'ver·look' (v.)

o'ver·look' (n.)

o'ver·lord'

o'ver·ly

o'ver·mas'ter

o'ver·match'

o'ver·night' (adv.)

o'ver·night' (adj.,
  n.)

o'ver·pass' (n.)

o'ver·pass' (v.)
  o'ver·passed' or
  o'ver·past',
  o'ver·pass'ing

o'ver·pay'
  o'ver·paid',
  o'ver·pay'ing

o'ver·play'

o'ver·pow'er

o'ver·price'
  o'ver·priced',
  o'ver·pric'ing

o'ver·print' (v.)

o'ver·print' (n.)

o'ver·pro·duce'
  o'ver·pro·duced',
  o'ver·pro·duc'ing

o'ver·pro·duc'tion

o'ver·pro·tect'

o'ver·rate'
  o'ver·rat'ed,
  o'ver·rat'ing

o'ver·reach'

o'ver·ride' (v.)
  o'ver·rode',
  o'ver·rid'den,
  o'ver·rid'ing

o'ver·ride' (n.)

o'ver·ripe'

o'ver·rule'
  o'ver·ruled',
  o'ver·rul'ing

o'ver·run' (v.)
  o'ver·ran', o'ver·run',
  o'ver·run'ning

o'ver·run' (n.)

o'ver·seas' (adv., n.)

o'ver·seas' (adj.)

o'ver·see'
  o'ver·saw', o'ver·seen',
  o'ver·see'ing

o'ver·se'er

o'ver·sell'
  o'ver·sold',
  o'ver·sell'ing

o'ver·sen'si·tive

o'ver·sexed'

o'ver·shade'
  o'ver·shad'ed,
  o'ver·shad'ing

o'ver·shad'ow

o'ver·shoe'

o'ver·shoot'
  o'ver·shot',
  o'ver·shoot'ing

o'ver·shot'

o'ver·sight'

o'ver·sim'pli·fi·
  ca'tion

o'ver·sim'pli·fy'
  o'ver·sim'pli·fied',
  o'ver·sim'pli·fy'ing

o'ver·size' (adj.)

o'ver·size' (n.)

o'ver·sized

o'ver·sleep'
  o'ver·slept',
  o'ver·sleep'ing

o'ver·spend'
  o'ver·spent',
  o'ver·spend'ing

o'ver·spread'
  o'ver·spread',
  o'ver·spread'ing

o'ver·state'
  o'ver·stat'ed,
  o'ver·stat'ing

o'ver·state'ment

o'ver·stay'

o'ver·step'
  o'ver·stepped',
  o'ver·step'ping

o'ver·stock' (v.)

o'ver·stock' (n.)

o'ver·stuff'

o'ver·sub·scribe'
  o'ver·sub·scribed',
  o'ver·sub·scrib'ing

o'ver·sup·ply' (n.)
  pl. o'ver·sup·plies'

o'ver·sup·ply' (v.)
  o'ver·sup·plied',
  o'ver·sup·ply'ing

o·vert'

o'ver·take'
  o'ver·took',
  o'ver·tak'en,
  o'ver·tak'ing

o'ver·tax'

o'ver-the-coun'ter

o'ver·throw' (v.)

o'ver·throw' (n.)

o'ver·time' (n., adv.,
  adj.)

o'ver·tone'

o'ver·ture

o'ver·turn' (v.)

o'ver·turn' (n.)

o'ver·use' (v.)
  o'ver·used',
  o'ver·us'ing

o'ver·use' (n.)

o'ver·view'

o'ver·ween'ing

o'ver·weigh'

o'ver·weight' (n.)

o'ver·weight' (adj.)

o'ver·whelm'

o'ver·whelm'ing

o'ver·wind'
  o'ver·wound',
  o'ver·wind'ing

o'ver·work' (v.)
  o'ver·worked' or
  o'ver·wrought',
  o'ver·work'ing

o'ver·work' (n.)

o'ver·wrought'

Ov'id

o'vi·duct'

o·vip'a·rous

o'vi·pos'i·tor

o'void

o'vo·vi·vip'a·rous

o'vu·late'
  o'vu·lat'ed, o'vu·lat'ing

o'vu·la'tion

o'vule

o'vum
  pl. o'va

owe (be indebted)
  owed, ow'ing
  (SEE oh)

ow'ing

owl

owl'et

owl'ish

own

own'er

own'er·ship'

ox
  pl. ox'en or ox'es

ox·al'ic

ox'blood'

ox'blood' red'

ox'bow'

ox'cart'

ox'eye'
  pl. ox'eyes'

ox'ford

ox'i·dant

ox′i·da′tion
ox′i·da′tive
ox′ide
ox′i·di·za′tion
ox′i·dize′
  ox′i·dized′, ox′i·diz′ing
ox′i·diz′er
ox′tail′

ox′y·a·cet′y·lene′
ox′y·gen
ox′y·gen·ate′
  ox′y·gen·at′ed,
  ox′y·gen·at′ing
ox′y·gen·a′tion
ox′y·mo′ron
  pl. ox′y·mo′ra
o′yez

oys′ter
oys′ter bed′
oys′ter·man
  pl. oys′ter·men
Oz′a·lid
  (*Trademark*)
O′zark
o′zone
o·zo′no·sphere′

P

Pab′lum
  (*Trademark*)
pab′u·lum
pace
  paced, pac′ing
pace′mak′er
pac′er
pa·chi′si
pace′set′ter
pach′y·derm′
pach′y·san′dra
pa·cif′ic
Pa·cif′ic
pac′i·fi·ca′tion
pac′i·fi′er
pac′i·fism′
pac′i·fist
pac′i·fy′
  pac′i·fied′, pac′i·fy′ing
pack
pack′age
  pack′aged, pack′ag·ing
pack′er
pack′et
pack′horse′
pack′ing
pack′ing house′
pack′ rat′
pack′sack′
pack′sad′dle
pact
pad
  pad′ded, pad′ding
pad′ding
pad′dle
  pad′dled, pad′dling

pad′dle·ball′
pad′dle·fish′
  pl. pad′dle·fish·es or
  pad′dle·fish
pad′dle wheel′
pad′dock
pad′dy
  pl. pad′dies
pad′lock′
pa′dre
  pl. pa′dres or
  (*It.*) pa′dri
pae′an (*song*)
  (SEE peon)
pa·el′la
pa′gan
pa′gan·ism′
page
  paged, pag′ing
pag′eant
pag′eant·ry
  pl. pag′eant·ries
page′boy′
pag′i·nate′
  pag′i·nat′ed,
  pag′i·nat′ing
pag′i·na′tion
pa·go′da
paid
pail (*bucket*)
  (SEE pale)
pail′ful′
  pl. pail′fuls′
pain (*suffering*)
  (SEE pane)
Paine
pain′ful
pain′ful·ly
pain′kil′ler

pain′less
pains′tak′ing
paint
paint′brush′
paint′ed
paint′er
paint′ing
pair (*two*)
  (SEE pear *and* pare)
pai′sa
  pl. pai′se
pais′ley
  pl. pais′leys
Pai·ute′
  pl. Pai·utes′ or
  Pai·ute′
pa·jam′as
Pa′ki·stan′
Pa′ki·sta′ni
  pl. Pa′ki·sta′nis or
  Pa′ki·sta′ni
pal
  palled, pal′ling
pal′ace
pal′a·din
pal′an·quin′
pal′at·a·bil′i·ty
pal′at·a·ble
pal′at·a·bly
pal′a·tal
pal′a·tal·i·za′tion
pal′a·tal·ize′
  pal′a·tal·ized′,
  pal′a·tal·iz′ing
pal′ate (*roof of
  mouth*)
  (SEE pallet *and*
  palette)
pa·la′tial

pa·lat'i·nate'

pal'a·tine'

pa·lav'er

pa·laz'zo
  pl. pa·laz'zi

pale (light; lighten; bounds)
  (adj.) pal'er, pal'est;
  (v.) paled, pal'ing
  (SEE pail)

pale'face'

Pa'le·o·cene'

Pa'le·o·gene'

pa'le·og'ra·pher

pa'le·o·graph'ic

pa'le·o·graph'i·cal

pa'le·og'ra·phy

Pa'le·o·lith'ic

pa'le·on·tol'o·gist

pa'le·on·tol'o·gy

Pa'le·o·zo'ic

Pal'es·tine'

Pal'es·tin'i·an

pal'ette (paint tray)
  (SEE palate and pallet)

pal'frey
  pl. pal'freys

Pa'li

pal'imp·sest'

pal'in·drome'

pal'ing

pal'i·node'

pal'i·sade'
  pal'i·sad'ed,
  pal'i·sad'ing

pall (become dull; dark cloud)
  (SEE pawl)

Pal·la'di·an

pal·la'di·um

Pal'las

pall'bear'er

pal'let (bed; tool)
  (SEE palate and palette)

pal'li·ate'
  pal'li·at'ed, pal'li·at'ing

pal'li·a'tion

pal'li·a'tive

pal'lid

Pall' Mall'

pal'lor

palm

pal'mate

palm'er

pal·met'to

palm'ist

palm'is·try

palm'y
  palm'i·er, palm'i·est

pal'o·mi'no
  pl. pal'o·mi'nos

pa·loo'ka

palp

pal'pa·bil'i·ty

pal'pa·ble

pal'pa·bly

pal'pate (v.)
  pal'pat·ed, pal'pat'ing

pal'pate (adj.)

pal·pa'tion

pal'pi·tate'
  pal'pi·tat'ed,
  pal'pi·tat'ing

pal'pi·ta'tion

pal'pus
  pl. pal'pi

pal'sy
  pl. pal'sies;
  (v.) pal'sied, pal'sy·ing

pal'tri·ness

pal'try
  pal'tri·er, pal'tri·est

pam'pas
  (sing.) pam'pa

pam'per

pam'phlet

pam'phlet·eer'

pan
  panned, pan'ning

pan'a·ce'a

pa·nache'

Pan'-Af'ri·can·ism'

Pan'a·ma'

Pan'a·ma'ni·an

Pan'a·ma' hat'

Pan'-A·mer'i·can

Pan'-A·mer'i·can·ism'

Pan'-Ar'a·bism'

pan'-broil'

pan'cake'
  pan'caked', pan'cak'ing

pan'chro·mat'ic

pan'cre·as

pan'cre·at'ic

pan'da

pan·da'nus
  pl. pan·da'nus·es

pan·dem'ic

pan·de·mo'ni·um

pan'der

pan'der·er

Pan·do'ra

pan·dow'dy
  pl. pan·dow'dies

pane (glass)
  (SEE pain)

pan'e·gyr'ic

pan'e·gyr'i·cal

pan'e·gyr'ist

pan'el
  pan'eled, pan'el·ing

pan'el·ing

pan'el·ist

pan'fish'
  pl. pan'fish·es or pan'fish

pan'-fry'
  pan'-fried', pan'-fry'ing

pang

pan·go'lin

pan'han'dle
  pan'han'dled,
  pan'han'dling

pan'han'dler

Pan'hel·len'ic

pan'ic
  pan'icked, pan'ick·ing

pan'ick·y

pan'i·cle

pan'i·cled

pan'ic-strick'en

pan·jan'drum

pan'nier or pan'ier

pan'o·ply
  pl. pan'o·plies

pan'o·ram'a

pan'o·ram'ic

pan'pipe'

Pan'-Slav'ism
pan'sy
　pl. pan'sies
pant
pan'ta·lets'
pan'ta·loons'
pan'the·ism'
pan'the·ist
pan'the·is'tic
pan'the·is'ti·cal
pan'the·on'
pan'ther
　pl. pan'thers or
　pan'ther
pant'ies
　(sing.) pant'ie or
　pant'y
pan'to·graph'
pan'to·mime'
　pan'to·mimed,
　pan'to·mim'ing
pan'to·mim'ic
pan'try
　pl. pan'tries
pants
pant'suit' or pants
　suit
pan'ty hose'
pant'y·waist'
pan'zer
pap
pa'pa
pa'pa·cy
　pl. pa'pa·cies
pa'pal
pa'pa·raz'zo
　pl. pa'pa·raz'zi
pa'paw
pa·pa'ya
Pa'pe·e'te
pa'per
pa'per·back'
pa'per·bound'
pa'per clip'
pa'per cut'ter
pa'per·hang'er
pa'per ti'ger
pa'per·weight'
pa'per·work'

pa'per·y
pa'pier-mâ·ché'
pa·pil'la
　pl. pa·pil'lae
pap'il·lar'y
pap'il·lo'ma
pap'il·lote'
pa·poose'
pap·ri'ka
Pap' test'
Pap'u·a
pap'ule
pa·py'rus
　pl. pa·py'ri
par
　parred, par'ring
pa·ra'
　pl. pa·ras' or pa·ra'
par'a·ble
pa·rab'o·la
par'a·bol'ic
par'a·bol'i·cal
par'a·chute'
　par'a·chut'ed,
　par'a·chut'ing
par'a·chut'ist
pa·rade'
　pa·rad'ed, pa·rad'ing
pa·rad'er
par'a·digm
par'a·dise'
par'a·dox'
par'a·dox'i·cal
par'a·dox'i·cal·ly
par'af·fin
par'a·gon'
par'a·graph'
Par'a·guay'
Par'a·guay'an
par'a·keet'
par'al·lax'
par'al·lel'
　par'al·leled',
　par'al·lel'ing
par'al·lel'e·pi'ped
par'al·lel'ism
par'al·lel'o·gram'
par·ral'y·sis
　pl. pa·ral'y·ses'

par'a·lyt'ic
par'a·lyze
　par'a·lyzed',
　par'a·lyz'ing
par'a·lyz'er
Par'a·mar'i·bo
par'a·me'ci·um
　pl. par'a·me'ci·a
par'a·med'ic　(n.)
par'a·med'ic　(adj.)
par'a·med'i·cal
pa·ram'e·ter　(key
　factor)
　(SEE perimeter)
par'a·mil'i·tar'y
par'a·mount'
par'a·mour'
par'a·noi'a
par'a·noi'ac
par'a·noid'
par'a·pet'
par'a·pher·nal'ia
par'a·phrase'
　par'a·phrased',
　par'a·phras'ing
par'a·ple'gi·a
par'a·ple'gic
par'a·pro·fes'sion·al
par'a·psy·chol'o·gy
par'a·site'
par'a·sit'ic
par'a·sit'i·cal·ly
par'a·sit'ism
par'a·si·tize'
　par'a·si·tized',
　par'a·si·tiz'ing
par'a·si·tol'o·gist
par'a·sit·ol'o·gy
par'a·sol'
par'a·sym'pa·thet'ic
par'a·thy'roid
par'a·troop'er
par'a·troops'
par'a·ty'phoid
par a·vion'
par'boil'
par'buck'le
　par'buck'led,
　par'buck'ling

par'cel
  par·celed, par'cel·ing

parch

Par·chee'si
  (*Trademark*)

parch'ment

pard

par'don

par'don·a·ble

par'don·a·bly

pare (*peel*)
  pared, par'ing
  (SEE pair *and* pear)

par'e·gor'ic

par'ent·age

pa·ren'tal

pa·ren'the·sis
  pl. pa·ren'the·ses'

pa·ren'the·size'
  pa·ren'the·sized',
  pa·ren'the·siz'ing

par'en·thet'ic

par'en·thet'i·cal

par'ent·hood'

pa·re'sis

pa·ret'ic

par ex·cel·lence'

par·fait'

pa·ri'ah

pa·ri'e·tal

par'i·mu'tu·el

Par'is

par'ish (*church
  district*)
  (SEE perish)

pa·rish'ion·er

Pa·ri'sian

par'i·ty

park

par'ka

park'ing me'ter

park'land'

park'way'

par'lance

par'lay (*bet*)
  (SEE parley)

par'ley (*conference*)
  pl. par'leys; (*v.*)
  par'leyed, par'ley·ing
  (SEE parlay)

par'lia·ment

par'lia·men·tar'i·an

par'lia·men'ta·ry

par'lor

par'lor car'

par'lor·maid'

par'lous

Par'me·san'

par'mi·gia'na

Par·nas'sus

pa·ro'chi·al

pa·ro'chi·al·ism'

par'o·dy
  pl. par'o·dies; (*v.*)
  par'o·died,
  par'o·dy·ing

pa·role'
  pa·roled', pa·rol'ing

pa·rol·ee'

pa·rot'id

par·ox·ysm'

par·ox·ys'mal

par·quet'
  par·queted',
  par·quet'ing

par'quet·ry

par'ri·cide'

par'rot

par'ry
  par'ried, par'ry·ing

parse
  parsed, pars'ing

par'sec'

Par'see

par'si·mo'ni·ous

par'si·mo'ny

pars'ley

pars'nip

par'son

par'son·age

part

par·take'
  par·took', par·tak'en,
  par·tak'ing

par·tak'er

part'ed

par·terre'

par'the·no·gen'e·sis

Par'the·non'

Par'thi·an shot'

par'tial

par·tial'i·ty
  pl. par·tial'i·ties

part'i·ble

par·tic'i·pant

par·tic'i·pate'
  par·tic'i·pat'ed,
  par·tic'i·pat'ing

par·tic'i·pa'tion

par·tic'i·pa'tor

par·tic'i·pa·to'ry

par'ti·cip'i·al

par'ti·cip'i·al·ly

par'ti·ci'ple

par'ti·cle

par'ti·col'ored

par·tic'u·lar

par·tic'u·lar'i·ty
  pl. par·tic'u·lar'i·ties

par·tic'u·lar·i·
  za'tion

par·tic'u·lar·ize'
  par·tic'u·lar·ized',
  par·tic'u·lar·iz'ing

par·tic'u·lar·ly

par·tic'u·late

part'ing

par'ti·san *or*
  par'ti·zan

par'ti·san·ship'

par·ti'ta
  pl. par·ti'tas *or* (*It.*)
  par·ti'te

par·ti'tion

par'ti·tive

part'ly

part'ner

part'ner·ship'

par'tridge
  pl. par'tridges *or*
  par'tridge

part' song'

part'–time'

par·tu'ri·ent

par·tu·ri'tion

par'ty
  pl. par'ties; (*v.*)
  par'tied, par'ty·ing

par'ty line'

par've

par′ve · nu′

pas′chal

pas de deux′
  pl. pas de deux′

pa · sha′

pasque′flow′er

pas′quin · ade′
  pas′quin · ad′ed,
  pas′quin · ad′ing

pass

pass′a · ble (that can
  be passed)
  (SEE passible)

pass′a · bly

pas′sa · ca′glia

pas′sage
  pas′saged, pas′sag · ing

pas′sage · way′

pass′book′

pas · sé′

pas′sel

pas′sen · ger

passe′-par · tout′

pass′er-by′
  pl. pass′ers-by′

pas′ser · ine

pas′si · ble (capable
  of feeling)
  (SEE passable)

pas′sim

pass′ing

pas′sion

pas′sion · ate

pas′sion · ate · ly

pas′sion · flow′er

pas′sion · fruit′

pas′sion · less

pas′sive

pas′sive re · sist′ance

pas′sive · ly

pas · siv′i · ty

pass′key′
  pl. pass′keys′

Pass′o′ver

pass′port

pass′word′

past

pas′ta

paste
  past′ed, past′ing

paste′board′

pas · tel′

pas · tel′ist

pas′tern

paste′-up′

Pas · teur′

pas′teur · i · za′tion

pas′teur · ize′
  pas′teur · ized′,
  pas′teur · iz′ing

pas · tiche′

pas · tille′

pas · time′

past′ mas′ter

pas′tor

pas′to · ral

pas′tor · ate

pas · tra′mi

pas′try
  pl. pas′tries

pas′tur · age

pas′ture
  pas′tured, pas′tur · ing

past′i · ness

past′y
  (adj.) past′i · er,
  past′i · est;
  pl. past′ies

past′y-faced′

pat
  pat′ted, pat′ting

patch

patch′work′

patch′y
  patch′i · er, patch′i · est

pate

pâ · té′

pâ · té′ de foie′ gras′
  pl. pâ · tés′ de foie′
  gras′

pa · tel′la
  pl. pa · tel′lae

pa · tel′lar

pa · tel′late

pat′en

pat′ent

pat′ent · a · ble

pat′ent · ee′

pa′ter · fa · mil′i · as
  pl. pa′ter · fa · mil′
  i · as · es or
  pa′tres · fa · mil′i · as

pa · ter′nal

pa · ter′nal · ism′

pa · ter′nal · is′tic

pa · ter′nal · ly

pa · ter′ni · ty

pa′ter · nos′ter

path

pa · thet′ic

pa · thet′i · cal · ly

path′find′er

path′o · gen

path′o · gen′ic

path′o · log′i · cal

path′o · log′i · cal · ly

pa · thol′o · gist

pa · thol′o · gy

pa′thos

path′way′

pa′tience

pa′tient

pat′i · na

pa′ti · o

pa · tis′se · rie

pat′ois
  pl. pat′ois

pa′tri · arch′

pa′tri · ar′chal

pa′tri · ar′chate

pa′tri · ar′chy

pa · tri′cian

pat′ri · cid′al

pat′ri · cide′

pat′ri · lin′e · al

pat′ri · mo′ni · al

pat′ri · mo′ny
  pl. pat′ri · mo′nies

pa′tri · ot

pa′tri · ot′ic

pa′tri · ot′i · cal · ly

pa′tri · ot · ism′

pa · tris′tic

pa · trol′
  pa · trolled′, pa · trol′ling

pa · trol′ler

pa · trol′man
  pl. pa · trol′men

pa′tron

pa'tron·age

pa'tron·ess

pa'tron·ize'
  pa'tron·ized',
  pa'tron·iz'ing

pa'tron·iz'er

pa'tron saint'

pat'ro·nym'ic

pa·troon'

pat'sy
  pl. pat'sies

pat'ter

pat'tern

pat'ty
  pl. pat'ties

pat'ty shell'

pau'ci·ty

paunch

paunch'i·ness

paunch'y
  paunch'i·er,
  paunch'i·est

pau'per

pau'per·ism'

pau'per·ize'
  pau'per·ized',
  pau'per·iz'ing

pause
  paused, paus'ing

pa·vane' *or* pa·van'

pave
  paved, pav'ing

pave'ment

pa·vil'ion

pav'ing

paw

pawl (*gear catch*)
  (SEE pall)

pawn

pawn'bro'ker

Paw·nee'
  pl. Paw·nees' *or*
  Paw·nee'

pawn'shop

pay
  paid *or* (*Naut.*) payed,
  pay'ing

pay'a·ble

pay'back'

pay'check'

pay'day'

pay·ee'

pay'er

pay'load'

pay'mas'ter

pay'ment

pay'off'

pay·o'la

pay'out'

pay' phone'

pay'roll'

pea
  pl. peas

peace (*absence of
  war*)
  (SEE piece)

peace'a·ble

peace'a·bly

peace'ful

peace'ful·ly

peace'keep'ing

peace'mak'er

peace' of'fi·cer

peace'time'

peach

peach'y
  peach'i·er, peach'i·est

pea'cock'
  pl. pea'cocks' *or*
  pea'cock'

pea'fowl'
  pl. pea'fowls' *or*
  pea'fowl'

pea'hen'

pea' jack'et

peak (*point*)
  (SEE peek *and* pique)

peaked (*pointed*)

peak'ed (*pale*)

peal (*resound*)
  (SEE peel)

pea'nut'

pea'nut gal'ler·y

pear (*fruit*)
  (SEE pair *and* pare)

pearl (*gem*)
  (SEE purl)

pearl'y
  pearl'i·er, pearl'i·est

pear'-shaped'

peas'ant

peas'ant·ry

pea'shoot'er

peat

peat' moss'

peat'y

peb'ble
  peb'bled, peb'bling

peb'bly

pe·can'

pec'ca·dil'lo
  pl. pec'ca·dil'loes *or*
  pec'ca·dil'los

pec'ca·ry
  pl. pec'ca·ries *or*
  pec'ca·ry

peck

peck'er·wood'

pec'tin

pec'to·ral

pec'u·late'
  pec'u·lat'ed,
  pec'u·lat'ing

pec'u·la'tion

pec'u·la'tor

pe·cu'liar

pe·cu'li·ar'i·ty
  pl. pe·cu'li·ar'i·ties

pe·cu'liar·ly

pe·cu'ni·ar'y

ped'a·gog'ic

ped'a·gog'i·cal

ped'a·gog'i·cal·ly

ped'a·gogue'

ped'a·go'gy
  pl. ped'a·go'gies

ped'al (*foot lever*)
  ped'aled, ped'al·ing
  (SEE peddle)

ped'al push'ers

ped'ant

pe·dan'tic

pe·dan'ti·cal·ly

ped'ant·ry
  pl. ped'ant·ries

ped'dle (*sell*)
  ped'dled, ped'dling
  (SEE pedal)

ped'dler

ped'er·ast'

ped'er·as'ty

ped'es·tal
  ped'es·taled,
  ped'es·tal·ing

pe·des'tri·an

pe'di·at'ric

pe'di·a·tri'cian

pe'di·at'rics

ped'i·cure'

ped'i·gree'

ped'i·greed'

ped'i·ment

ped'lar

pe·dom'e·ter

pe·dun'cle

peek (*look*)
  (SEE peak *and* pique)

peek'a·boo'

peel (*skin*)
  (SEE peal)

peel'ing

peen

peep

peep'er

peep'hole'

Peep'ing Tom'

peep' show'

peer (*look; equal*)
  (SEE pier)

peer'age

peer'ess

peer'less

peeve
  peeved, peev'ing

peev'ish

pee'wee' (*small one*)
  (SEE pewee)

peg
  pegged, peg'ging

Peg'a·sus

peg'board'

peg' leg'

peign·oir'

pe·jo'ra·tive

Pe'kin·ese'
  pl. Pe'kin·ese'

Pe'king'

Pe'king·ese'
  pl. Pe'king·ese'

pe'koe

pel'age

pe·lag'ic

pelf

pel'i·can

pel·la'gra

pel·la'grous

pel'let

pell'–mell' *or*
  pell'mell'

pel·lu'cid

Pel'o·pon·ne'sian

Pel'o·pon·ne'sus

pe·lo'ta

pelt

pel'vic

pel'vis
  pl. pel'vis·es *or* pel'ves

pem'mi·can

pen (*write*)
  penned, pen'ning

pen (*confine*)
  penned *or* pent,
  pen'ning

pe'nal

pe'nal·ize'
  pe'nal·ized',
  pe'nal·iz'ing

pen'al·ty
  pl. pen'al·ties

pen'ance

pence

pen'chant

pen'cil
  pen'ciled, pen'cil·ing

pen'dant (*hanging
  ornament*)

pen'dent (*hanging*)

pend'ing

pen'du·lous

pen'du·lum

pe'ne·plain'

pen'e·tra·bil'i·ty

pen'e·tra·ble

pen'e·tra·bly

pen'e·trate'
  pen'e·trat'ed,
  pen'e·trat'ing

pen'e·tra'tion

pen'e·tra'tive

pen'guin

pen'hold'er

pen'i·cil'in

pen·in'su·la

pen·in'su·lar

pe'nis
  pl. pe'nes *or* pe'nis·es

pen'i·tence

pen'i·tent

pen'i·ten'tial

pen'i·ten'tial·ly

pen'i·ten'tia·ry
  pl. pen'i·ten'tia·ries

pen'knife'
  pl. pen'knives'

pen'man
  pl. pen'men

pen'man·ship'

pen' name'

pen'nant

pen'ni
  pl. pen'ni·a *or* pen'nis

pen'ni·less

pen'non

Penn'syl·va'ni·a

Penn'syl·va'ni·an

pen'ny
  pl. pen'nies *or* (*Brit.*)
  pence

pen'ny an'te

pen'ny pinch'er

pen'ny-pinch'ing

pen'ny·weight'

pen'ny-wise'

Pe·nob'scot
  pl. Pe·nob'scots *or*
  Pe·nob'scot

pe·nol'o·gist

pe·nol'o·gy

pen'point'

pen'sion

pen'sion·er

pen'sive

pen'sive·ly

pen'stock'

pent

pen'ta·cle

pen'ta·gon'

pen·tag'o·nal

pen'ta·gram'

pen · tam'e · ter

Pen'ta · teuch'

Pen'ta · teuch'al

pen · tath'lon

pen'ta · ton'ic

Pen'te · cost'

Pen'te · cos'tal

pent'house'

pen · tom'ic

Pen'to · thal'
  (Trademark)

pent · ste'mon

pent'–up'

pe'nult

pe · nul'ti · mate

pe · num'bra
  pl. pe · num'brae or
  pe · num'bras

pe · nu'ri · ous

pen'u · ry

pe'on (worker)
  (SEE paean)

pe'on · age

pe'o · ny
  pl. pe'o · nies

peo'ple
  pl. peo'ple or peo'ples;
  (v.) peo'pled, peo'pling

Pe · o'ri · a

pep
  pepped, pep'ping

pep'er · o'ni

pep'lum
  pl. pep'lums or pep'la

pep'per

pep'per–and–salt'

pep'per · corn'

pep'per mill'

pep'per · mint'

pep'per pot'

pep'per · y

pep'pill'

pep'pi · ness

pep'py
  pep'pi · er, pep'pi · est

pep'sin

pep' talk'

pep'tic

pep'tone

Pepys

per

per'ad · ven'ture

per · am'bu · late'
  per · am'bu · lat'ed,
  per · am'bu · lat'ing

per · am'bu · la'tion

per · am'bu · la'tor

per an'num

per · cale'

per cap'i · ta

per · ceiv'a · ble

per · ceiv'a · bly

per · ceive'
  per · ceived',
  per · ceiv'ing

per · cent' or per cent'

per · cent'age

per · cen'tile

per'cept

per · cep'ti · bil'i · ty

per · cep'ti · ble

per · cep'ti · bly

per · cep'tion

per · cep'tive

per · cep'tu · al

per · cep'tu · al · ly

perch (roost)

perch (fish)
  pl. perch or perch'es

per · chance'

Per'che · ron'

per · cip'i · ent

per · cip'i · ence

per'co · late' (v.)
  per'co · lat'ed,
  per'co · lat'ing

per'co · late (n.)

per'co · la'tion

per'co · la'tor

per · cus'sion

per · cus'sive

per di'em

per · di'tion

per'e · gri · nate'
  per'e · gri · nat'ed,
  per'e · gri · nat'ing

per'e · gri · na'tion

per'e · grine

Pe · pys'

per · emp'to · ri · ly

per · emp'to · ri · ness

per · emp'to · ry

per · en'ni · al

per · en'ni · al · ly

perf'board'

per'fect (adj., n.)

per · fect' (v.)

per · fect'i · bil'i · ty

per · fect'i · ble

per · fec'tion

per · fec'tion · ism'

per · fec'tion · ist

per · fid'i · ous

per'fi · dy
  pl. per'fi · dies

per'fo · rate' (v.)
  per'fo · rat'ed,
  per'fo · rat'ing

per'fo · rate (adj.)

per'fo · ra'tion

per'fo · ra'tor

per · force'

per · form'

per · form'a · ble

per · for'mance

per · form'er

per · fume' (n.)

per · fume' (v.)
  per · fumed',
  per · fum'ing

per · fum'er

per · fum'er · y
  pl. per · fum'er · ies

per · func'to · ri · ly

per · func'to · ri · ness

per · func'to · ry

per'go · la

per · haps'

pe'ri
  pl. pe'ris

per'i · anth'

per'i · car'di · um
  pl. per'i · car'di · a

Per'i · cles'

per'i · gee'

per'i · he'li · on
  pl. per'i · he'li · a

per'il

per'il·ous
per'i·lune'
pe·rim'e·ter
   (*boundary*)
   (SEE parameter)
per'i·ne'um
  pl. per'i·ne'a
pe'ri·od
pe'ri·od'ic
pe'ri·od'ical
pe'ri·od'i·cal·ly
pe'ri·o·dic'i·ty
per'i·o·don'tal
per'i·o·don'tic
per'i·o·don'tics
per'i·pa·tet'ic
pe·riph'er·al
pe·riph'er·al·ly
pe·riph'er·y
  pl. pe·riph'er·ies
pe·riph'ra·sis
  pl. pe·riph'ra·ses'
per'i·phras'tic
pe·rique'
per'i·scope'
per'i·scop'ic
per'ish (*die*)
  (SEE parish)
per'ish·a·bil'i·ty
per'ish·a·ble
per'i·stal'sis
  pl. per'i·stal'ses
per'i·stal'tic
per'i·style'
per'i·to·ne'al
per'i·to·ne'um
  pl. per'i·to·ne'ums or
  per'i·to·ne'a
per'i·to·ni'tis
per'i·wig'
per'i·win'kle
per'jure
  per'jured, per'jur·ing
per'jur·er
per'ju·ry
  pl. per'ju·ries
perk
perk'i·ly
perk'i·ness

perk'y
  perk'i·er, perk'i·est
per'ma·frost'
per'ma·nence
per'ma·nen·cy
  pl. per'ma·nen·cies
per'ma·nent
per·man'ga·nate'
per·me·a·bil'i·ty
per'me·a·ble
per'me·a·bly
per'me·ate'
  per'me·at'ed,
  per'me·at'ing
per'me·a'tion
Per'mi·an
per·mis'si·bil'i·ty
per·mis'si·ble
per·mis'si·bly
per·mis'sion
per·mis'sive
per·mis'sive·ly
per·mis'sive·ness
per·mit' (*v.*)
  per·mit'ted,
  per·mit'ting
per'mit (*n.*)
per·mit'ter
per'mu·tate'
  per'mu·tat'ed,
  per'mu·tat'ing
per'mu·ta'tion
per·mute'
  per·mut'ed,
  per·mut'ing
per·nick'et·y
per·ni'cious
Per·nod'
  (*Trademark*)
per'o·rate'
  per'o·rat'ed,
  per'o·rat'ing
per'o·ra'tion
per·ox'ide
  per·ox'id·ed,
  per·ox'id·ing
per'pen·dic'u·lar
per'pe·trate'
  per'pe·trat'ed,
  per'pe·trat'ing
per'pe·tra'tion

per'pe·tra'tor
per·pet'u·al
per·pet'u·al·ly
per·pet'u·ate'
  per·pet'u·at'ed,
  per·pet'u·at'ing
per·pet'u·a'tion
per·pet'u·a'tor
per'pe·tu'i·ty
  pl. per'pe·tu'i·ties
per·plex'
per·plexed'
per·plex'ed·ly
per·plex'i·ty
  pl. per·plex'i·ties
per'qui·site (*benefit*)
  (SEE prerequisite)
per se'
per'se·cute'
  (*oppress*)
  per'se·cut'ed,
  per'se·cut'ing
  (SEE prosecute)
per'se·cu'tion
per'se·cu'tor
per'se·ver'ance
per'se·vere'
  per'se·vered',
  per'se·ver'ing
Per'sia
Per'sian
per'si·flage'
per·sim'mon
per·sist'
per·sist'ence
per·sist'en·cy
per·sist'ent
per·snick'et·y
per'son
per·so'na
  pl. per·so'nae or
  per·so'nas
per'son·a·ble
per'son·age
per'son·al (*private*)
  (SEE personnel)
per'son·al'i·ty
  (*character*)
  pl. per'son·al'i·ties
  (SEE personalty)
per'son·al·ize'
  per'son·al·ized',
  per'son·al·iz'ing

per'son·al·ly

per'son·al·ty
  (*property*)
  pl. per'son·al·ties
  (SEE personality)

per·son'*a* non gra'ta
  pl. per·so'nae non
  gra'tae

per·son'i·fi·ca'tion

per·son'i·fi'er

per·son'i·fy'
  per·son'i·fied',
  per·son'i·fy'ing

per'son·nel'
  (*employees*)
  (SEE personal)

per·spec'tive (*view*)
  (SEE prospective)

per'spi·ca'cious

per'spi·cac'i·ty

per'spi·cu'i·ty

per·spic'u·ous

per'spi·ra'tion

per·spire'
  per·spired', per·spir'ing

per·suad'a·ble

per·suade'
  per·suad'ed,
  per·suad'ing

per·suad'er

per·sua'si·ble

per·sua'sion

per·sua'sive

pert

per·tain'

Perth

per'ti·na'cious

per'ti·nac'i·ty

per'ti·nence

per'ti·nen·cy

per'ti·nent

per·turb'

per·tur·ba'tion

Pe·ru'

Pe·ru'vi·an

pe·ruke'

pe·rus'a·ble

pe·rus'al

pe·ruse'
  pe·rused', pe·rus'ing

pe·rus'er

per·vade'
  per·vad'ed, per·vad'ing

per·va'sive

per·verse'

per·verse'ly

per·verse'ness

per·ver'sion

per·ver'si·ty
  pl. per·ver'si·ties

per·vert' (*v.*)

per'vert (*n.*)

per·vert'ed

per'vi·ous

Pe'sach

pe·se'ta
  pl. pe·se'tas

pes'ky
  pes'ki·er, pes'ki·est

pe'so
  pl. pe'sos

pes'si·mism'

pes'si·mist

pes'si·mis'tic

pes'si·mis'ti·cal·ly

pest

pes'ter

pest'hole'

pes'ti·cide'

pes·tif'er·ous

pes'ti·lence

pes'ti·lent

pes'ti·len'tial

pes'tle
  pes'tled, pes'tling

pet
  pet'ted, pet'ting

pet'al

pet'aled

pe·tard'

pet'cock'

pe'ter

Pe'ter

pet'i·ole'

pet'it (*Law, lesser*)
  (SEE petite *and* petty)

pe·tit' bour·geois'

pe·tite' (*tiny*)
  (SEE petit *and* petty)

pe·tite' bour'geoi·sie'

pet'it four'

pe·ti'tion

pe·tit' mal'

pe'tit point'

Pe'trarch

pet'rel (*bird*)
  (SEE petrol)

pe'tri dish'

pet'ri·fac'tion

pet'ri·fy'
  pet'ri·fied',
  pet'ri·fy'ing

pet'ro·chem'i·cal

pet'ro·chem'is·try

pet'ro·dol'lar

pe·trog'ra·phy

pet'rol (*gasoline*)
  (SEE petrel)

pet'ro·la'tum

pe·tro'le·um

pe·trol'o·gist

pe·trol'o·gy

pet'ti·coat'

pet'ti·fog'
  pet'ti·fogged',
  pet'ti·fog'ging

pet'ti·fog'ger

pet'ti·ness

pet'tish

pet'ty
  pet'ti·er, pet'ti·est
  (SEE petit *and* petite)

pet'ty cash'

pet'ty ju'ry

pet'u·lance

pet'u·lant

pe·tu'ni·a

pew

pe'wee (*bird*)
  (SEE peewee)

pew'ter

pe·yo'te
  pl. pe·yo'tes

pfen'nig
  pl. pfen'nigs or
  pfen'ni·ge

pha'e·ton

phag'o·cyte'

pha·lan'ger

pha'lanx
  pl. pha'lanx•es or
  pha•lang'es

phal'a•rope'

phal'lic

phal'lus
  pl. phal'li or
  phal'lus•es

phan'tasm

phan•tas'ma•go'ri•a

phan•tas'ma•gor'ic

phan'tom

Phar'aoh

Pnar'i•sa'ic

Phar'i•see'

phar'ma•ceu'tic

phar'ma•ceu'ti•cal

phar'ma•ceu'tics

phar'ma•cist

phar'ma•co•log'i•cal

phar'ma•col'o•gist

phar'ma•col'o•gy

phar'ma•co•poe'ia

phar'ma•cy
  pl. phar'ma•cies

pha•ryn'ge•al

phar'ynx
  pl. phar•yn'ges or
  phar'ynx•es

phase (aspect)
  phased, phas'ing
  (SEE faze)

phase'–in'

phase'–out'

pheas'ant

phe•nac'e•tin

phe'no•bar'bi•tal'

phe'nol

phe•no'lic

phe'nol•phthal'ein

phe•nom'e•nal

phe•nom'e•non
  pl. phe•nom'e•na or
  phe•nom'e•nons

phe'no•type'

phe'no•typ'ic

pher'o•mone'

phew

phi

Phil'a•del'phi•a

Phil'a•del'phi•an

phi•lan'der

phi•lan'der•er

phil'an•throp'ic

phi•lan'thro•pist

phi•lan'thro•py
  pl. phi•lan'thro•pies

phil'a•tel'ic

phi•lat'e•list

phi•lat'e•ly

phil'har•mon'ic

Phi•lip'pic

Phil'ip•pine'

Phil'ip•pines'

Phil'is•tine'

phil'o•den'dron

phil'o•log'i•cal

phi•lol'o•gist

phi•lol'o•gy

phi•los'o•pher

phil'o•soph'ic

phil'o•soph'i•cal

phil'o•soph'i•cal•ly

phi•los'o•phize'
  phi•los'o•phized',
  phi•los'o•phiz'ing

phi•los'o•phiz'er

phi•los'o•phy
  pl. phi•los'o•phies

phil'ter (potion)
  phil'tered, phil'ter•ing
  (SEE filter)

phle•bi'tis

phle•bot'o•my
  pl. phle•bot'o•mies

phlegm

phleg•mat'ic

phleg•mat'i•cal•ly

phlo'em

phlox

Phnom' Penh'

pho'bi•a

pho'bic

phoe'be

Phoe•ni'cia

Phoe•ni'cian

phoe'nix

Phoe'nix

phone
  phoned, phon'ing

pho'neme

pho•ne'mic

pho•ne'mi•cal•ly

pho•net'ic

pho•net'i•cal•ly

pho'ne•ti'cian

pho•net'ics

pho'ney
  (adj.) pho'ni•er,
  pho'ni•est;
  pl. pho'nies

phon'ic

phon'i•cal•ly

phon'ics

pho'ni•ness

pho'no•graph'

pho'no•graph'ic

pho'no•log'i•cal

pho'no•log'i•cal•ly

pho•nol'o•gist

pho•nol'o•gy
  pl. pho•nol'o•gies

pho'ny
  (adj.) pho'ni•er,
  pho'ni•est;
  pl. pho'nies

phoo'ey

phos'gene

phos'phate

phos•phat'ic

phos'phor

phos'pho•resce'
  phos'pho•resced',
  phos'pho•resc'ing

phos'pho•res'cence

phos'pho•res'cent

phos•phor'ic

phos'pho•rus
  pl. phos'pho•ri'

pho'to
  pl. pho'tos

pho'to•cell'

pho'to•com•pose'

pho'to•com'po•si'tion

pho'to•cop'i•er

pho'to•cop'y
  pl. pho'to•cop'ies; (v.)
  pho'to•cop'ied,
  pho'to•cop'y•ing

pho'to・e・lec'tric
pho'to・e・lec・tric'i・ty
pho'to・e・lec'tron
pho'to・en・grave'
　pho'to・en・graved',
　pho'to・en・grav'ing
pho'to・en・grav'er
pho'to・en・grav'ing
pho'to fin'ish
pho'to・flash'
pho'to・flood'
pho'to・gen'ic
pho'to・graph'
pho・tog'ra・pher
pho'to・graph'ic
pho'to・graph'i・cal・ly
pho・tog'ra・phy
pho'to・gra・vure'
pho'to・jour'nal・ism'
pho'to・lith'o・graph'
pho・to・li・thog'ra・phy
pho'to・me・chan'i・cal
pho・tom'e・ter
pho'to・met'ric
pho・tom'e・try
pho'to・mi'cro・graph'
pho'to・mon・tage'
pho'to・mur'al
pho'ton
pho'to-off'set'
　pho'to-off'set',　pho'to-
　off'set'ting
pho'to・play'
pho'to・sen'si・tive
pho'to・sen'si・tiv'i・ty
pho'to・sphere'
Pho'to・stat'
　(Trademark)
pho'to・syn'the・sis
pho'to・syn・thet'ic
pho'to・tax'is
pho'to・trop'ic
pho・tot'ro・pism'
pho'to・vol・ta'ic
phras'al
phrase
　phrased, phras'ing
phra'se・ol'o・gy

phren'ic
phre・nol'o・gist
phre・nol'o・gy
phy・lac'ter・y
　pl. phy・lac'ter・ies
phy・log'e・ny
phy'lum
　pl. phy'la
phys'ic
phys'i・cal
phys'i・cal・ly
phy・si'cian
phys'i・cist
phys'ics
phys'i・og'no・my
　pl. phys'i・og'no・mies
phys'i・og'ra・pher
phys'i・o・graph'ic
phys'i・og'ra・phy
phys'i・o・log'i・cal
phys'i・o・log'i・cal・ly
phys'i・ol'o・gist
phys'i・ol'o・gy
phys'io・ther'a・pist
phys'i・o・ther'a・py
phy・sique'
phy'to・gen'e・sis
phy'to・ge・net'ic
pi (Greek letter;
　mix type))
　pl. pis
　pied, pi'ing
　(SEE pie)
pi'a ma'ter
pi'a・nis'si・mo'
　pl. pi'a・nis'si・mos'
pi・an'ist
pi・an'o
　pl. pi・an'os
pi・an'o・for'te
pi・as'ter
pi・az'za
　pl. pi・az'zas or (It.)
　piaz'ze
pi'ca
pi'ca・dor
　pl. pi'ca・dors or (Sp.)
　pi'ca・do'res
pic'a・resque'
Pi・cas'so

pic'a・yune'
Pic'ca・dil'ly
pic'ca・lil'li
　pl. pic'ca・lil'lis
pic'co・lo'
　pl. pic'co・los'
pick
pick'ax' or pick'axe'
　pl. pick'ax'es; (v.)
　pick'axed', pick'ax'ing
pick'er・el
pick'et
pick'et line'
pick'ing
pick'le
　pick'led, pick'ling
pick'-me-up'
pick'pock'et
pick'up'
Pick・wick'i・an
pick'y
　pick'e・er, pick'i・est
pic'nic
　pic'nicked, pic'nick・ing
pic'nick・er
pi'co・sec'ond
pi'cot
pic'ric
Pict
pic'to・graph'
pic'to・graph'ic
pic・tog'ra・phy
pic・to'ri・al
pic・to'ri・al・ly
pic'ture
　pic'tured, pic'tur・ing
pic'tur・esque'
pid'dle
　pid'dled, pid'dling
pidg'in (language)
　(SEE pigeon)
pie (pastry)
　(SEE pi)
pie'bald'
piece (portion)
　pieced, piec'ing
　(SEE peace)
pièce' de ré・sis'tance
　pl. pièces' de
　ré・sis'tance
piece'meal'

piece′work′
piece′work′er
pied
pied-à-terre′
  pl. pied-à-terre′
pier (*dock*)
  (SEE peer)
pierce
  pierced, pierc′ing
Pierce
Pierre
Pie·tà′
Pi′e·tism′
pi′e·ty
  pl. pi′e·ties
pi·e′zo·e·lec′tric
pi·e′zo·e·lec·
  tric′i·ty
pif′fle
pig
pi′geon (*bird*)
  (SEE pidgin)
pi′geon·hole′
  pi′geon·holed′,
  pi′geon·hol′ing
pi′geon-toed′
pig′gish
pig′gy
  pl. pig′gies
pig′gy·back′
pig′gy bank′
pig′head′ed
pig′ i′ron
Pig′ Lat′in
pig′let
pig′ment
pig′men·ta′tion
pig′my
  pl. pig′mies
pig′pen′
pig′skin′
pig′sty′
  pl. pig′sties′
pig′tail′
pike
  pl. pike or pikes
pik′er
pike′staff′
  pl. pike′staves′
pi·laf′

pi·las′ter
Pi′late
pil′chard
pile
  piled, pil′ing
pile′ driv′er
pile′up′
pil′fer
pil′fer·age
pil′fer·er
pil′grim
pil′grim·age
pil′ing
pill
pil′lage
pil′lar
pill′box′
pil′lion
pil′lo·ry
  pl. pil′lo·ries; (*v.*)
  pil′lo·ried,
  pil′lo·ry·ing
pil′low
pil′low·case′
pi′lot
pi′lot·age
pi′lot·house′
pi′lot lamp′
pi′lot light′
Pil′sner
Pilt′down
Pi′ma
pi·men′to
  pl. pi·men′tos
pi·mien′to
  pl. pi·mien′tos
pimp
pim′per·nel′
pim′ple
pim′pled
pim′ply
  pim′pli·er, pim′pli·est
pim′pled
pin
  pinned, pin′ning
pin′a·fore′
pi·ña′ta
pin′ball′
pin′ boy′

pince′-nez′
  pl. pince′-nez′
pin′cers
pinch
pin′check′
pinch′-hit′
  pinch′-hit′, pinch′-
  hit′ting
pinch′pen′ny
  pl. pinch′pen′nies
pin′ curl′
pin′cush′ion
pine
  pined, pin′ing
pin′e·al
pine′ap′ple
pin′feath′er
pine′ tar′
ping
Ping′-Pong′
  (*Trademark*)
pin′head′
pin′hole′
pin′ion (*wing*)
  (SEE piñon)
pink
pink′eye′
pink′ie or pink′y
  pl. pink′ies
pink′o
  pl. pink′os or pink′oes
pin′·mon′ey
pin′na
  pl. pin′nae or pin′nas
pin′nace
pin′na·cle
  pin′na·cled,
  pin′na·cling
pin′nate
pi′noch·le
pi′ñon (*tree*)
  pl. pi′ñons or (*Sp.*)
  pi·ño′nes
Pi·not′
pin′point′
pin′prick′
pin′set′ter
pin′stripe′
pin′striped′
pint

pin'to
  pl. pin'tos
pint'–size'
pint'–sized'
pin'up'
pin'wale'
pin'wheel'
pin'worm'
pin'y
  pin'i·er, pin'i·est
pin'yin'
pi'o·neer'
pi'ous
pip
pipe
  piped, pip'ing
pipe' dream'
pipe'ful'
  pl. pipe'fuls'
pipe' line' or
  pipe'line'
pip'er
pi·pette' or pi·pet'
  pi·pet'ted, pi·pet'ting
pip'pin
pip'–squeak'
pi'quant
pi'quan·cy
pique *(resentment)*
  piqued, piqu'ing
  (SEE peek *and* peak)
pi·qué' or pi·que'
  (cloth)
  pl. pi·qués' or pi·ques'
  (SEE piquet)
pi·quet' *(card
  game)*
  (SEE piqué)
pi'ra·cy
  pl. pi'ra·cies
Pi'ra·ne'si
pi·ra'nha
pi'rate
pi·rat'i·cal
pi·rosh'ki
pir'ou·ette'
  pir'ou·et'ted,
  pir'ou·et'ting
Pi'sa
pis'ca·to'ri·al
Pis'ces

pis'mire'
pis·ta'chi·o
  pl. pis·ta'chi·os
pis'til *(flower part)*
  (SEE pistol)
pis'til·late
pis'tol *(gun)*
  pis'toled, pis'tol·ing
  (SEE pistil)
pis'tol–whip'
  pis'tol–whipped', pis'tol–
  whip'ping
pis'ton
pis'ton ring'
pis'ton rod'
pit
  pit'ted, pit'ting
pi'ta
pit'a·pat'
  pit'a·pat'ted,
  pit'a·pat'ting
Pit'cairn
pitch
pitch'–black'
pitch'blende'
pitch'–dark'
pitch'er
pitch'fork'
pitch'man
  pl. pitch'men
pitch'out'
pitch' pipe'
pit'e·ous
pit'fall'
pith
pit'head'
Pith'e·can'thro·pus
pith'i·ly
pith'y
  pith'i·er, pith'i·est
pit'i·a·ble
pit'i·a·bly
pit'i·ful
pit'i·ful·ly
pit'i·less
pi'ton
pit'tance
pit'ter–pat'ter
Pitts'burgh *(Pa.)*

pi·tu'i·tar'y
  pl. pi·tu'i·tar'ies
pit'y
  pl. pit'ies
  pit'ied, pit'y·ing
piv'ot
piv'ot·al
pix'i·lat'ed
pix'y or pix'ie
  pl. pix'ies
pix'y·ish
pi·zazz'
piz'za
piz'ze·ri'a
piz'zi·ca'to
  pl. piz'zi·ca'ti
plac'a·bil'i·ty
plac'a·ble
plac'ard
pla'cate
  pla'cat·ed, pla'cat·ing
pla·ca'tion
place
  placed, plac'ing
pla·ce'bo
  pl. pla·ce'bos or
  pla·ce'boes
place' card'
place' kick' *(n.)*
place'–kick' *(v.)*
place' mat'
place'ment
pla·cen'ta
pla·cen'tal
plac'er
plac'id
pla·cid'i·ty
plack'et
pla'gia·rism'
pla'gia·rist
pla'gia·rize'
  pla'gia·rized',
  pla'gia·riz'ing
pla'gia·riz'er
plague
  plagued, pla'guing
plaid
plain *(clear)*
  (SEE plane)
plain'ly

plain'ness

plains'man
  pl. plains'men

plain'song'

plain'-spo'ken

plaint

plain'tiff

plain'tive

plain'tive • ly

plait (*pleat*)
  (SEE plate *and* plat)

plan
  planned, plan'ning

plane (*airplane;
  tool*)
  planed, plan'ing
  (SEE plain)

plan'er

plan'et

plan'e • tar'i • um
  pl. plan'e • tar'i • ums or
  plan'e • tar'i • a

plan'e • tar'y

plan'e • tes'i • mal

plan'et • oid'

plan'gent

plank

plank'ing

plank'ton

plan'ner

plant

Plan • tag'e • net

plan'tain

plan'tar (*of sole of
  foot*)
  (SEE planter)

plan • ta'tion

plant'er (*one who
  plants*)
  (SEE plantar)

plaque

plash

plas'ma

plas • mat'ic

plas'mic

plas'ter

plas'ter • board'

plas'ter cast'

plas'ter • er

plas'tic

plas'ti • cal • ly

plas • tic'i • ty

plas'ti • cize'
  plas'ti • cized',
  plas'ti • ciz'ing

plat (*plot; braid*)
  plat'ted, plat'ting
  (SEE plait *and* plate)

plat' du jour'
  pl. plats' du jour'

plate (*dish; to coat*)
  plat'ed, plat'ing
  (SEE plait *and* plat)

pla • teau'
  pl. pla • teaus' or
  pla • teaux'

plat'ed

plate'ful

plate' glass'

plate'let

plat'en

plat'er

plat'form

plat'ing

plat'i • num

plat'i • tude'

plat'i • tu'di • nous

Pla'to

Pla • ton'ic

pla • ton'i • cal • ly

Pla'to • nism'

pla • toon'

plat'ter

plat'y (*adj.*)
  plat'i • er, plat'i • est

plat'y (*n.*)
  pl. plat'y or plat'ys or
  plat'ies

plat'y • pus
  pl. plat'y • pus • es or
  plat'y • pi'

plau'dit

plau'si • bil'i • ty

plau'si • ble

plau'si • bly

play

pla'ya
  pl. pla'yas

play'a • ble

play'act'

play'back'

play'bill'

play'boy'

play'-by-play'

play'er

play'fel'low

play'ful

play'ful • ly

play'ful • ness

play'go'er

play'ground'

play'house'

play'ing card'

play'land'

play'mate'

play'-off'

play'pen'

play'room'

play'suit'

play'thing'

play'time'

play'wright'

play'writ'ing

pla'za

plea

plead
  plead'ed or plead or
  pled, plead'ing

pleas'ant

pleas'ant • ry
  pl. pleas'ant • ries

please
  pleased, pleas'ing

pleas'ur • a • ble

pleas'ur • a • bly

pleas'ure
  pleas'ured, pleas'ur • ing

pleat

plebe

ple • be'ian

pleb'i • scite'

plec'trum
  pl. plec'tra or
  plec'trums

pledge
  pledged, pledg'ing

pledg'ee'

pledg'er

Ple'ia • des'

plein′-air′

Pleis′to·cene′

ple′na·ry

plen′i·po·ten′ti·ar′y
  pl. plen′i·po·ten′
  ti·ar′ies

plen′i·tude′

plen′te·ous

plen′ti·ful

plen′ti·ful·ly

plen′ty
  pl. plen′ties

ple′num
  pl. ple′nums or ple′na

ple′o·nasm′

ple′si·o·saur′

pleth′o·ra

pleu′ra
  pl. pleu′rae

pleu′ral

pleu′ri·sy

Plex′i·glas′
  (*Trademark*)

plex′us
  pl. plex′us·es or
  plex′us

pli′a·bil′i·ty

pli′a·ble

pli′a·bly

pli′an·cy

pli′ant

pli′ers

plight

plinth

Pli′o·cene′

plis·sé′ *or* plis·se′

plod
  plod′ded, plod′ding

plod′der

plop
  plopped, plop′ping

plot
  plot′ted, plot′ting

plot′ter

plov′er

plow

plow′back′

plow′boy′

plow′man
  pl. plow′men

plow′share′

ploy

pluck

pluck′i·ly

pluck′i·ness

pluck′y
  pluck′i·er, plick′i·est

plug
  plugged, plug′ging

plug′ger

plug′-in′

plug′ug′ly
  plug′ug′lies

plum (*fruit*)
  (SEE plumb)

plum′age

plumb (*weight*)
  (SEE plum)

plumb′er

plumb′ing

plume
  plumed, plum′ing

plum′met

plump

plump′ness

plun′der

plun′der·er

plunge
  plunged, plung′ing

plung′er

plunk

plu·per′fect

plu′ral

plu′ral·ism′

plu′ral·is′tic

plu·ral′i·ty
  pl. plu·ral′i·ties

plus
  pl. plus′es

plush

plush′y
  plush′i·er, plush′i·est

plus′ sign′

Plu′to

plu·toc′ra·cy
  pl. plu·toc′ra·cies

plu′to·crat′

plu′to·crat′ic

plu·to′ni·um

plu′vi·al

plu′vi·om′e·ter

ply
  plied, ply′ing

Plym′outh

ply′wood′

pneu·mat′ic

pneu′mo·coc′cus
  pl. pneu′mo·coc′ci

pneu·mo′nia

poach

poach′er

Po′ca·hon′tas

pock

pock′et

pock′et·book′

pock′et·ful′
  pl. pock′et·fuls′

pock′et·knife′

pock′et park′

pock′et·size′

pock′et ve′to

pock′mark′

pock′marked′

po′co a po′co

pod
  pod′ded, pod′ding

po·di′a·trist

po·di′a·try

po′di·um
  pl. po′di·ums or
  po′di·a

pod′sol

Po′dunk

po′em

po′e·sy
  pl. po′e·sies

po′et

po′et·as′ter

po′et·ess

po·et′ic

po·et′i·cal

po·et′i·cal·ly

po·et′ics

po′et·ry

po′gey

po′go stick′

po·grom′

poi

poign'an·cy

poign'ant

poi'lu
  pl. poi'lus

poin'ci·an'a

poin·set'ti·a

point

point'–blank'

point'ed

point'er

Poin'til·lism'

poin'til·list

point'less

point'y
  point'i·er, point'i·est

poise
  poised, pois'ing

poi'son

poi'son gas'

poi'son·ous

poke
  poked, pok'ing

pok'er

poke'weed'

pok'ey
  (*adj.*) pok'i·er,
  pok'i·est;
  pl. pok'eys

pok'y
  (*adj.*) pok'i·er,
  pok'i·est;
  pl. pok'ies

Po'land

po'lar

po'lar bear'

Po·lar'is

po·lar'i·ty

po'lar·i·za'tion

po'lar·ize'
  po'lar·ized',
  po'lar·iz'ing

Po'lar·oid'
  (*Trademark*)

pol'der

pole (*stick*)
  poled, pol'ing
  (SEE poll)

Pole

pole'ax'
  pl. pole'ax'es; (*v.*)
  pole'axed', pole'ax'ing

pole'cat'
  pl. pole'cats' or
  pole'cat'

po·lem'ic

po·lem'i·cal

po·lem'i·cal·ly

pol'e·mist

po·len'ta

pole'star'

pole'vault' (*n.*)

pole'–vault' (*v.*)

pole'–vault'er

po·lice'
  po·liced', po·lic'ing

po·lice' dog'

po·lice'man
  pl. po·lice'men

po·lice'wom'an
  pl. po·lice'wom'en

pol'i·cli'nic
  (*outpatient clinic*)
  (SEE polyclinic)

pol'i·cy
  pl. pol'i·cies

pol'i·cy·hold'er

po'li·o

po'li·o·my'e·li'tis

pol'ish

Po'lish

Po'lit·bu'ro

po·lite'

po·lite'ly

po·lite'ness

pol'i·tesse'

pol'i·tic
  (*governmental*)
  (SEE politick)

po·lit'i·cal

po·lit'i·cal·ly

pol'i·ti'cian

pol'i·tick (*engage in
  politics*)
  (SEE politic)

po·lit'i·co
  pl. po·lit'i·cos

pol'i·tics

pol'i·ty
  pl. pol'i·ties

Polk

pol'ka
  pl. pol'kas
  pol'kaed, pol'ka·ing

pol'ka·dot'

poll (*voting*)
  (SEE pole)

pol'lack
  pl. pol'lack or pol'lacks

pol'len

pol'li·nate'
  pol'li·nat'ed,
  pol'li·nat'ing

pol'li·na'tion

pol'li·na'tor

pol'li·wog'

poll'ster

pol·lu'tant

pol·lute'
  pol·lut'ed, pol·lut'ing

pol·lut'er

pol·lu'tion

Pol'ly·an'na

po'lo

po'lo·naise'

po·lo'ni·um

pol'ter·geist'

pol·troon'

pol'y·an'drous

pol'y·an'dry

pol'y·clin'ic
  (*hospital*)
  (SEE policlinic)

pol'y·es'ter

pol'y·eth'yl·ene'

po·lyg'a·mist

po·lyg'a·mous

po·lyg'a·my

pol'y·glot'

po·lyg'o·nal

pol'y·graph'

pol'y·he'dral

pol'y·he'dron

pol'y·mer

pol'y·mer'ic

po·lym'er·i·za'tion

po·lym'er·ize'
  po·lym'er·ized',
  po·lym'er·iz'ing

Pol'y · ne'sia

Pol'y · ne'sian

pol'y · no'mi · al

pol'yp

pol'y · phon'ic

po · lyph'o · ny

pol'y · se'my

pol'y · sty'rene

pol'y · syl · lab'ic

pol'y · syl'la · ble

pol'y · tech'nic

pol'y · the · ism'

pol'y · the'ist

pol'y · the · is'tic

pol'y · un · sat'u · rate

pol'y · un · sat'u · rat'ed

pol'y · u're · thane'

pol'y · vi'nyl

po · made'
po · mad'ed, po · mad'ing

po'man · der

pome'gran'ate

pom'mel
pom'meled,
pom'mel · ing

po · mol'o · gy

pomp

pom'pa · dour'

pom'pa · no'

Pom · peii' (city)

Pom'pey (Roman
general)

pom'pon

pom · pos'i · ty
pl. pom · pos'i · ties

pomp · ous

pon'cho
pl. pon'chos

pond

pon'der

pon'der · a · ble

pon'der · o'sa

pon'der · ous

pone

pon · gee'

pon'iard

pons
pl. pon'tes

pon'tiff

pon · tif'i · cal

pon · tif'i · cal · ly

pon · tif'i · cate (n.)

pon · tif'i · cate' (v.)
pon · tif'i · cat'ed,
pon · tif'i · cat'ing

pon · toon'

po'ny
pl. po'nies; (v.)
po'nied, po'ny · ing

po'ny · tail'

pooch

poo'dle

pooh'-pooh'

pool'room'

poop

poop' deck'

poop'er-scoop'er

poor'house'

poor'ly

pop
popped, pop'ping

pop'corn'

pope

pop'eyed'

pop' fly'

pop'gun'

pop'in · jay'

pop'lar (tree)
(SEE popular)

pop'lin

pop'o'ver

pop'per

pop'py
pl. pop'pies

pop'py · cock'

pop'py seed'

pop'u · lace (people)
(SEE populous)

pop'u · lar (liked)
(SEE poplar)

pop'u · lar'i · ty

pop'u · lar · i · za'tion

pop'u · lar · ize'
pop'u · lar · ized',
pop'u · lar · iz'ing

pop'u · lar · iz'er

pop'u · lar · ly

pop'u · late'
pop'u · lat'ed,
pop'u · lat'ing

pop'u · la'tion

Pop'u · lism'

Pop'u · list

pop'u · lous
(crowded)
(SEE populace)

pop'-up'

por'ce · lain

por'ce · lain · ize'
por'ce · lain · ized',
por'ce · lain · iz'ing

porch

por'cine

por'cu · pine'

pore (ponder;
opening)
pored, por'ing
(SEE pour)

pore

por'gy
pl. por'gy or por'gies

pork

pork'er

pork'pie'

por'no

por · nog'ra · pher

por'no · graph'ic

por · nog'ra · phy

po · ros'i · ty
pl. po · ros'i · ties

po'rous

por'phy · ry
pl. por'phy · ries

por'poise
pl. por'poise or
por'pois · es

por'ridge

por'rin · ger

port'a · bil'i · ty

port'a · ble

por'tage
por'taged, por'tag · ing

por'tal

por'tal-to-por'tal

Port'-au-Prince'

port · cul'lis

porte'-co · chere' or
porte'-co · chère'

por·tend′

por′tent

por·ten′tous

por′ter

por′ter·house′

port·fo′li·o′
  pl. port·fo′li·os′

port′hole′

por′ti·co′
  pl. por′ti·coes′ or
  por′ti·cos′

por·tiere′

por′tion

Port′land

port′li·ness

port′ly

port·man′teau
  pl. port·man′teaus or
  port·man′teaux

Port′-of-Spain′

Por′to No′vo

por′trait

por′trait·ist

por′trai·ture

por·tray′

por·tray′al

Port′-Sa·lut′

Ports′mouth

Por′tu·gal

Por′tu·guese′
  pl. Por′tu·guese′

por′tu·lac′a

pose
  posed, pos′ing

Po·sei′don

pos′er (*one who
  poses*)
  (SEE poseur)

po·seur′ (*affected
  person*)
  (SEE poser)

posh

pos′it

po·si′tion

pos′i·tive

pos′i·tive·ly

pos′i·tiv·ism′

pos′i·tron′

pos′se

pos·sess′

pos·sessed′

pos·ses′sion

pos·ses′sive

pos·ses′sor

pos′si·bil′i·ty
  pl. pos′si·bil′i·ties

pos′si·ble

pos′si·bly

pos′sum

post

post′age

post′al

post′al card′

post′-bel′lum

post′box′
  pl. post′box′es

post′card′ or post′
  card′

post·date′
  post·dat′ed,
  post·dat′ing

post′di·lu′vi·an

post·doc′tor·al

post′er

pos·te′ri·or

pos·ter′i·ty

post·grad′u·ate

post·haste′

post′hole′

post′hu·mous

post′hyp·not′ic

pos·til′ion or
  pos·til′lion

Post′-Im·pres′sion·
  ism′

Post′-Im·pres′sion·ist

post′lude

post′man
  pl. post′men

post′mark′

post′mas′ter

post′mas′ter gen′er·al
  pl. post′mas′ters
  gen′er·al

post′me·rid′i·an (*of
  afternoon*)
  (SEE post meridiem)

post′ me·rid′i·em
  (*after noon*)
  (SEE postmeridian)

post′mis′tress

post-mor′tem

post′na′sal

post·na′tal

post′ of′fice

post·op′er·a·tive

post·or′bit·al

post′paid′

post′ par′tum

post·pone′
  post·poned′,
  post·pon′ing

post·pone′ment

post′script′

pos′tu·lant

pos′tu·late′ (*v.*)
  pos′tu·lat′ed,
  pos′tu·lat′ing

pos′tu·late (*n.*)

pos′tu·la′tion

pos′tu·la′tor

pos′tur·al

pos′ture
  pos′tured, pos′tur·ing

post′war′

po′sy
  pl. po′sies

pot
  pot′ted, pot′ting

po′ta·ble

pot′ash′

po·tas′si·um

po·ta′tion

po·ta′to
  pl. po·ta′toes

pot-au-feu′

pot′bel′ly
  pl. pot′bel′lies

pot′bel′lied

pot′boil′er

pot′ cheese′

po′ten·cy
  pl. po′ten·cies

po′tent

po′ten·tate′

po·ten′tial

po·ten'ti·al'i·ty
  pl. po·ten'ti·al'i·ties
po·ten'tial·ly
po·ten'ti·om'e·ter
pot'ful'
  pl. pot'fuls'
poth'er
pot'head'
pot'herb'
pot'hold'er
pot'hole'
pot'hook'
po'tion
pot'latch'
pot'luck'
Po·to'mac
pot'pie'
pot'pour·ri'
  pl. pot'pour·ris'
pot' roast'
Pots'dam
pot'sherd'
pot' shot'
pot'tage
pot'ted
pot'ter
pot'ter's field'
pot'ter·y
  pl. pot'ter·ies
pouch
Pouil·ly–Fuis·sé
poult
poult'tice
  poul'ticed, poul'tic·ing
poult'try
poul'try·man
  pl. poul'try·men
pounce
  pounced, pounc'ing
pound
pound'age
pound' cake'
pound'–fool'ish
pour (flow)
  (SEE pore)
pousse'–ca·fé'
  pl. pousse'–ca·fés'
pout
pout'er

pov'er·ty
pov'er·ty–strick'en
pow'der
pow'der puff'
pow'der room'
pow'der·y
pow'er
pow'er·boat'
pow'er brake'
pow'er·ful
pow'er·ful·ly
pow'er·house'
pow'er·less
pow'wow'
pox
prac'ti·ca·bil'i·ty
prac'ti·ca·ble
prac'ti·ca·bly
prac'ti·cal
prac'ti·cal'i·ty
prac'ti·cal·ly
prac'tice
  prac'ticed, prac'tic·ing
prac'ticed
prac'tic·er
prac·ti'tion·er
prae'tor
prae·to'ri·an
prag·mat'ic
prag·mat'i·cal·ly
prag'ma·tism'
prag'ma·tist
Prague
prai'rie
prai'rie dog'
praise
  praised, prais'ing
praise'wor'thy
pra'line
pram
prance
  pranced, pranc'ing
pranc'er
prank
prank'ster
pra'se·o·dym'i·um
prate
  prat'ed, prat'ing

prat'fall'
prat'tle
  plat'tled, prat'tling
prawn
pray (entreat)
  (SEE prey)
prayer (petition)
pray'er (one who
  prays)
prayer' book'
prayer'ful
prayer'ful·ly
preach
preach'er
preach'ment
pre'ad·o·les'cence
pre'ad·o·les'cent
pre'am'ble
pre·am'pli·fi'er
pre'ar·range'
  pre'ar·ranged',
  pre'ar·rang'ing
pre'ar·range'ment
pre'as·sem'bly
pre'as·sign'
pre'as·sump'tion
Pre·cam'bri·an
pre·can'cel
  pre·can'celed,
  pre·can'cel·ing
pre'can·cel·la'tion
pre·car'i·ous
pre·cau'tion
pre·cau'tion·ar'y
pre·cede' (go
  before)
  pre·ced'ed, pre·ced'ing
  (SEE proceed)
prec'e·dence
prec'e·dent
  (example)
pre·ced'ent
  (preceding)
  (SEE president)
pre·ced'ing
pre'cept
pre·cep'tor
pre·ces'sion (earth
  motion)
  (SEE procession)

pre′cinct

pre′ci·os′i·ty

pre′cious

prec′i·pice

pre·cip′i·tan·cy
  pl. pre·cip′i·tan·cies

pre·cip′i·tant

pre·cip′i·tate′ (*v.*)
  pre·cip′i·tat′ed,
  pre·cip′i·tat′ing

pre·cip′i·tate (*adj., n.*)

pre·cip′i·tate·ly

pre·cip′i·ta′tion

pre·cip′i·tous

pré·cis′ (*summary*)
  pl. pré·cis′

pre·cise′ (*definite*)

pre·cise′ly

pre·ci′sion

pre·clude′
  pre·clud′ed,
  pre·clud′ing

pre·clu′sive

pre·co′cious

pre·coc′i·ty

pre′cog·ni′tion

pre′-Co·lum′bi·an

pre′con·ceive′
  pre′con·ceived′,
  pre′con·ceiv′ing

pre′con·cep′tion

pre′con·di′tion

pre·cook′

pre·cur′sor

pre·da′cious *or*
  pre·da′ceous

pre·date′
  pre·dat′ed, pre·dat′ing

pred′a·tor

pred′a·to′ri·ly

pred′a·to′ri·ness

pred′a·to′ry

pre′de·cease′
  pre′de·ceased′,
  pre′de·ceas′ing

pred′e·ces′sor

pre′des·ig′nate′
  pre′des·ig·nat′ed,
  pre′des·ig·nat′ing

pre′des·ig·na′tion

pre′des·ti·na′tion

pre·des′tine
  pre·des′tined,
  pre·des′tin·ing

pre′de·ter′mine
  pre′de·ter′mined,
  pre′de·ter′min·ing

pre′de·ter′mi·na′tion

pred′i·ca·ble

pred′i·ca·bly

pre·dic′a·ment

pred′i·cate′ (*v.*)
  pred′i·cat′ed,
  pred′i·cat′ing

pred′i·cate (*adj., n.*)

pred′i·ca′tion

pred′i·ca′tive

pre·dict′

pre·dict′a·bil′i·ty

pre·dict′a·ble

pre·dict′a·bly

pre·dic′tion

pre·dic′tor

pre′di·gest′

pre′di·ges′tion

pre′di·lec′tion

pre′dis·pose′
  pre′dis·posed′,
  pre′dis·pos′ing

pre·dis′po·si′tion

pre·dom′i·nance

pre·dom′i·nant

pre·dom′i·nate′
  pre·dom′i·nat′ed,
  pre·dom′i·nat′ing

pre·dom′i·na′tion

pre·em′i·nence

pre·em′i·nent

pre·empt′

pre·emp′tion

pre·emp′tive

pre·emp′tor

preen

pre′ex·ist′

pre′ex·ist′ence

pre′ex·ist′ent

pre′fab′ (*adj., n.*)

pre·fab′ (*v.*)
  pre·fabbed′,
  pre·fab′bing

pre·fab′ri·cate′
  pre·fab′ri·cat′ed,
  pre·fab′ri·cat′ing

pre′fab·ri·ca′tion

pref′ace
  pref′aced, pref′ac·ing

pref′a·to′ry

pre′fect

pre′fec·ture

pre·fer′
  pre·ferred′, pre·fer′ring

pref′er·a·bil′i·ty

pref′er·a·ble

pref′er·a·bly

pref′er·ence

pref′er·en′ti·al

pre·fer′ment

pre·fig′u·ra′tion

pre·fig′ur·a·tive

pre·fig′ure
  pre·fig′ured,
  pre·fig′ur·ing

pre′fix (*n.*)

pre·fix′ (*v.*)

pre′flight′

pre′form′ (*v.*)

pre′form′ (*v., n.*)

preg′nan·cy
  pl. preg′nan·cies

preg′nant

pre·heat′

pre·hen′sile

pre′his·tor′ic

pre·his′to·ry
  pl. pre·his′to·ries

pre·judge′
  pre·judged′,
  pre·judg′ing

prej′u·dice
  prej′u·diced,
  prej′u·dic·ing

prej′u·di′cial

prej′u·di′cial·ly

prel′a·cy
  pl. prel′a·cies

prel′ate

pre·lim′i·nar′y
  pl. pre·lim′i·nar′ies

prel′ude
  pl. prel′ud·ed,
  prel′ud·ing

pre'ma·ture'
pre'ma·ture'ly
pre·med'
pre·med'i·cal
pre·med'i·tate'
  pre·med'i·tat'ed,
  pre·med'i·tat'ing
pre·med'i·ta'tion
pre·mier' (*chief*)
  (SEE premiere)
pre·miere' (*first
  performance*)
  (SEE premier)
prem'ise
  prem'ised, prem'is·ing
pre'mi·um
pre·mix'
pre'mo·ni'tion
pre·mon'i·to'ry
pre·na'tal
pre·oc'cu·pa'tion
pre·oc'cu·pied'
pre·oc'cu·py'
  pre·oc'cu·pied',
  pre·oc'cu·py'ing
pre'or·dain'
prep
prep'a·ra'tion
pre·par'a·to'ry
pre·pare'
  pre·pared', pre·par'ing
pre·par'ed·ness
pre·pay'
  pre·paid', pre·pay'ing
pre·pay'ment
pre·pon'der·ance
pre·pon'der·ant
pre·pon'der·ate'
  pre·pon'der·at'ed,
  pre·pon'der·at'ing
prep'o·si'tion
prep'o·si'tion·al
pre'pos·sess'
pre'pos·sess'ing
pre'pos·ses'sion
pre·pos'ter·ous
prep' school'
prep'pie or prep'py
  pl. prep'pies
pre'puce

Pre–Raph'a·el·ite'
pre're·cord'
pre·req'ui·site (*prior
  requirement*)
  (SEE perquisite)
pre·rog'a·tive
pres'age
  pres'aged, pres'ag·ing
pres'by·ter
pres'by·te'ri·an
Pres'by·te'ri·an·ism'
pre'school' (*adj.*)
pre'school' (*n.*)
pre'sci·ence
pre'sci·ent
pre·scribe' (*order*)
  pre·scribed',
  pre·scrib'ing
  (SEE proscribe)
pre·scrip'tion
pre·scrip'tive
pre·sell'
  pre·sold', pre·sell'ing
pres'ence
pres'ent (*n., adj.*)
pre·sent' (*v.*)
pre·sent'a·bil'i·ty
pre·sent'a·ble
pre·sent'a·bly
pres'en·ta'tion
pres'ent–day'
pre·sen'ti·ment
  (*premonition*)
  (SEE presentment)
pres'ent·ly
pre·sent'ment
  (*presentation*)
  (SEE presentiment)
pre·serv'a·bly
pres'er·va'tion
pre·serv'a·tive
pre·serve'
  pre·served',
  pre·serv'ing
pre·serv'er
pre–shrunk'
pre·side'
  pre·sid'ed, pre·sid'ing
pres'i·den·cy
  pl. pres'i·den·cies

pres'i·dent (*chief
  official*)
  (SEE precedent)
pres'i·dent-e·lect'
pres'i·den'tial
pre·sid'i·o
  pl. pre·sid'i·os
pre·sid'i·um
pre·sort'
press
press'er
press'ing
press'man
  pl. press'men
press'room'
pres'sure
  pres'sured, pres'sur·ing
pres'sure cook'er
pres'sur·i·za'tion
pres'su·rize'
  pres'su·rized',
  pres'su·riz'ing
press'work'
pres'ti·dig'i·ta'tion
pres'ti·dig'i·ta'tor
pres·tige'
pres·tig'ious
pres·tis'si·mo'
pres'to
  pl. pres'tos
pre·stress'
pre·sum'a·ble
pre·sum'a·bly
pre·sume'
  pre·sumed',
  pre·sum'ing
pre·sump'tion
pre·sump'tive
pre·sump'tu·ous
pre'sup·pose'
  pre'sup·posed',
  pre'sup·pos'ing
pre'sup·po·si'tion
pre·tend'
pre·tend'er
pre·tense'
pre·ten'sion
pre·ten'tious
pret'er·it or
  pret'er·ite

pre'ter · nat'u · ral

pre'ter · nat'u · ral · ly

pre'test (n.)

pre · test' (v.)

pre'text

pret'ti · fi'er

pret'ti · fy'
  pret'ti · fied',
  pret'ti · fy'ing

pret'ti · ly

pret'ti · ness

pret'ty
  (adj.) pret'ti · er,
  pret'ti · est;
  pl. pret'ties; (v.)
  pret'tied, pret'ty · ing

pret'zel

pre · vail'
  pre · vail'ing

prev'a · lence

prev'a · lent

pre · var'i · cate
  pre · var'i · cat'ed,
  pre · var'i · cat'ing

pre · var'i · ca'tion

pre · var'i · ca'tor

pre · vent'

pre · vent'a · bil'i · ty

pre · vent'a · ble

pre · vent'a · tive

pre · ven'tion

pre · ven'tive

pre'view'

pre'vi · ous

pre · vi'sion

pre'vo · ca'tion · al

pre'vue'

pre'war'

prey (victim)
  (SEE pray)

price
  priced, pric'ing

price'less

pric'ey
  pric'i · er, pric'i · est

price' war'

prick

prick'le
  prick'led, prick'ling

prick'ly
  prick'li · er, prick'li · est

prick'ly heat'

pride
  prid'ed, prid'ing

pride'ful

pride'ful · ly

prie'-dieu'
  pl. prie'-dieus' or
  prie'-dieux' or (Fr.)
  prie'-dieu'

priest

priest'ess

priest'hood

priest'ly

prig
  prigged, prig'ging

prig'gish

prim
  (adj.) prim'mer,
  prim'mest; (v.)
  primmed, prim'ming

pri'ma · cy
  pl. pri'ma · cies

pri'ma don'na
  pl. pri'ma don'nas or
  (It.) pri'me don'ne

pri'ma fa'ci · e'

pri'mal

pri · ma'ri · ly

pri'ma · ry
  pl. pri'ma · ries

pri'mate

prime
  primed, prim'ing

prim'er

pri · me'val

prim'i · tive

prim'i · tiv · ism'

prim'i · tiv · ist

pri'mo · gen'i · tor

pri'mo · gen'i · ture

pri · mor'di · al

primp

prim'rose'

prince

Prince' Ed'ward
  Is'land

prince'ly

prin'cess

prin·ci·pal (chief)
  (SEE principle)

prin'ci · pal'i · ty
  pl. prin'ci · pal'i · ties

prin'ci · pal · ly

prin'ci · ple (rule)
  (SEE principal)

prin'ci · pled

print

print'a · ble

print'er

print'ing

print'ing press'

print'mak'er

print'-out'

print' shop'

pri'or

pri'or · ess

pri · or'i · tize
  pri · or'i · tized,
  pri · or'i · tiz · ing

pri · or'i · ty
  pl. pri · or'i · ties

pri'o · ry
  pl. pri'o · ries

prism

pris · mat'ic

pris'on

pris'on · er

pris'si · ness

pris'sy
  pris'si · er, pris'si · est

pris'tine

prith'ee

pri'va · cy
  pl. pri'va · cies

pri'vate

pri'vate · ly

pri'va · teer'

pri · va'tion

priv'et

priv'i · lege
  priv'i · leged,
  priv'i · leg · ing

priv'i · leged

priv'y
  (adj.) priv'i · er,
  priv'i · est;
  pl. priv'ies

prix' fixe'
  pl. prix' fixes'

prize
  prized, priz'ing

prize'fight' or prize'
  fight'

prize'fight'er or prize'
  fight'er

prize'fight'ing or
  prize' fight'ing

prize'win'ner

pro
  pl. pros

prob'a • bil'i • ty
  pl. prob'a • bil'i • ties

prob'a • ble

prob'a • bly

pro'bate
  pro'bat • ed, pro'bat • ing

pro • ba'tion

pro • ba'tion • ar'y

pro • ba'tion • er

pro'ba • tive

probe
  probed, prob'ing

pro'bi • ty

prob'lem

prob'lem • at'ic

prob'lem • at'i • cal

prob'lem • at'i • cal • ly

pro bo'no pu'bli • co'

pro • bos'cis
  pl. pro • bos'cis • es or
  pro • bos'ci • des'

pro • caine'

pro • ce'dur • al

pro • ce'dur • al • ly

pro • ce'dure

pro • ceed' (go
  forward)
  (SEE precede)

pro • ceed'ing

pro'ceeds

proc'ess

pro • ces'sion
  (parade)
  (SEE precession)

pro • ces'sion • al

proc'es • sor or
  proc'es • ser

pro • claim'

proc'la • ma'tion

pro • cliv'i • ty
  pl. pro • cliv'i • ties

pro • con'sul

pro • cras'ti • nate'
  pro • cras'ti • nat'ed,
  pro • cras'ti • nat'ing

pro • cras'ti • na'tion

pro • cras'ti • na'tor

pro'cre • ate'
  pro'cre • at'ed,
  pro'cre • at'ing

pro'cre • a'tion

pro'cre • a'tive

pro'cre • a'tor

Pro • crus'te • an

proc • tol'o • gist

proc • tol'o • gy

proc'tor

proc'to • scope'

proc • tos'co • py

pro • cur'a • ble

proc'u • ra'tor

pro • cure'
  pro • cured', pro • cur'ing

pro • cure'ment

pro • cur'er

pro • cur'ess

prod
  prod'ded, prod'ding

prod'der

prod'i • gal

prod'i • gal'i • ty
  pl. prod'i • gal'i • ties

prod'i • gal • ly

pro • di'gious

prod'i • gy
  pl. prod'i • gies

pro • duce' (v.)
  pro • duced',
  pro • duc'ing

pro'duce (n.)

pro • duc'er

prod'uct

pro • duc'tion

pro • duc'tive

pro • duc'tive • ness

pro • duc'tive • ly

pro'duc • tiv'i • ty

prof

prof'a • na'tion

pro • fane'
  pro • faned', pro • fan'ing

pro • fane'ly

pro • fan'i • ty
  pl. pro • fan'i • ties

pro • fess'

pro • fessed'

pro • fess'ed • ly

pro • fes'sion

pro • fes'sion • al

pro • fes'sion • al • ism'

pro • fes'sion • al • ly

pro • fes'sor

pro'fes • so'ri • al • ly

pro • fes'sor • ship'

prof'fer

pro • fi'cien • cy

pro • fi'cient

pro'file
  pro'filed, pro'fil • ing

prof'it (gain)
  (SEE prophet)

prof'it • a • bil'i • ty

prof'it • a • ble

prof'it • a • bly

prof'it • eer'

prof'it shar'ing

prof'li • ga • cy

prof'li • gate

pro for'ma

pro • found'

pro • fun'di • ty
  pl. pro • fun'di • ties

pro • fuse'

pro • fuse'ly

pro • fu'sion

pro • gen'i • tor

prog'e • ny
  pl. prog'e • ny or
  prog'e • nies

pro • ges'ter • one'

prog'na • thous

prog • no'sis
  pl. prog • no'ses

prog • nos'tic

prog • nos'ti • cate'
  prog • nos'ti • cat'ed,
  prog • nos'ti • cat'ing

prog • nos'ti • ca'tion

prog • nos'ti • ca'tor

pro′gram
　pro′gramed,
　pro′gram・ing

pro′gram・ma・ble or
　pro′gram・a・ble

pro′gram・mat′ic

pro′gram・mer or
　pro′gram・er

prog′ress　(n.)

prog・ress′　(v.)

pro・gres′sion

pro・gres′sive

pro・gres′sive・ly

pro・hib′it

pro′hi・bi′tion

pro′hi・bi′tion・ist

pro・hib′i・tive

proj′ect　(n.)

proj・ect′　(v.)

pro・jec′tile

pro・jec′tion

pro・jec′tion・ist

pro・jec′tive

pro・jec′tor

Pro・ko′fiev

pro・lapse′
　pro・lapsed′,
　pro・laps′ing

pro′le・gom′e・non′
　pl.　pro′le・gom′e・na

pro′le・tar′i・an

pro′le・tar′i・an・
　i・za′tion

pro′le・tar′i・an・ize′
　pro′le・tar′i・an・ized′,
　pro′le・tar′i・an・iz′ing

pro′le・tar′i・at

pro′-life′

pro・lif′er・ate′
　pro・lif′er・at′ed,
　pro・lif′er・at′ing

pro・lif′er・a′tion

pro・lif′ic

pro・lif′i・cal・ly

pro・lix′

pro・lix′i・ty

pro′logue
　pro′logued, pro′logu・ing

pro・long′

pro・lon′gate
　pro・lon′gat・ed,
　pro・lon′gat・ing

pro′lon・ga′tion

prom

prom′e・nade′
　prom′e・nad′ed,
　prom′e・nad′ing

Pro・me′the・an

Pro・me′the・us

prom′i・nence

prom′i・nent

prom′is・cu′i・ty
　pl.　prom′is・cu′i・ties

pro・mis′cu・ous

prom′ise
　prom′ised, prom′is・ing

prom′is・so′ry

prom′on・to′ry
　pl.　prom′on・to′ries

pro・mote′
　pro・mot′ed,
　pro・mot′ing

pro・mot′er

pro・mo′tion

pro・mo′tion・al

prompt

prompt′er

promp′ti・tude′

prompt′ly

prompt′ness

prom′ul・gate′
　prom′ul・gat′ed,
　prom′ul・gat′ing

prom′ul・ga′tion

prom′ul・ga′tor

prone

prone′ly

prone′ness

prong

prong′horn′
　pl.　prong′horns or
　prong′horn′

pro・nom′i・nal

pro′noun′

pro・nounce′
　pro・ounced′,
　pro・nounc′ing

pro・nounce′a・ble

pro・nounced′

pro・nounce′ment

pro・nounc′er

pron′to

pro・nun′ci・a・men′to
　pl.　pro・nun′ci・a・
　men′tos

pro・nun′ci・a′tion

proof

proof′read′
　proof′read′,
　proof′read′ing

proof′read′er

prop
　propped, prop′ping

prop′a・gan′da

prop′a・gan′dist

prop′a・gan′dize
　prop′a・gan′dized,
　prop′a・gan′diz・ing

prop′a・gate′
　prop′a・gat′ed,
　prop′a・gat′ing

prop′a・ga′tion

prop′a・ga′tor

pro′pane

pro・pel′
　pro・pelled′,　pro・pel′ling

pro・pel′lant or
　pro・pel′lent

pro・pel′ler

pro・pen′si・ty
　pl.　pro・pen′si・ties

prop′er

prop′er noun′

prop′er・tied

prop′er・ty
　pl.　prop′er・ties

proph′e・cy
　(prediction)
　pl.　proph′e・cies
　(SEE prophesy)

proph′e・si′er

proph′e・sy′　(predict)
　proph′e・sied′,
　proph′e・sy′ing
　(SEE prophecy)

proph′et　(foreteller)
　(SEE profit)

proph′et・ess

pro・phet′ic

pro・phet′i・cal・ly

pro′phy・lac′tic

pro′phy・lax′is

pro·pin'qui·ty

pro·pi'ti·a·ble

pro·pi'ti·ate'
  pro·pi'ti·at'ed,
  pro·pi'ti·at'ing

pro·pi'ti·a'tion

pro·pi'tious

pro·pi'ti·a·to'ry

prop'jet'

pro·po'nent

pro·por'tion

pro·por'tion·a·ble

pro·por'tion·a·bly

pro·por'tion·al

pro·pro'tion·al'i·ty

pro·por'tion·al·ly

pro·por'tion·ate
  (*adj.*)

pro·por'tion·ate'
  (*v.*)
  pro·por'tion·at'ed,
  pro·por'tion·nat'ing

pro·por'tion·ate·ly

pro·pos'al

pro·pose'
  pro·posed', pro·pos'ing

pro·pos'er

prop'o·si'tion

pro·pound'

pro·pri'e·tar'y
  pl. pro·pri'e·tar'ies

pro·pri'e·tor

pro·pri'e·tor·ship'

pro·pri'e·tress

pro·pri'e·ty
  pl. pro·pri'e·ties

pro·pul'sion

pro·pul'sive

pro ra'ta

pro·rate'
  pro·rat'ed, pro·rat'ing

pro·ra'tion

pro'ro·ga'tion

pro·rogue'
  pro·rogued',
  pro·rogu'ing

pro·sa'ic

pro·sa'i·cal·ly

pro·sce'ni·um
  pl. pro·sce'ni·a

pro·sciut'to

pro·scribe'
  (*prohibit*)
  pro·scribed',
  pro·scrib'ing
  (SEE prescribe)

pro·scrib'er

pro·scrip'tion

pro·scrip'tive

prose
  prosed, pros'ing

pros'e·cut'a·ble

pros'e·cute' (*try for
  crime*)
  pros'e·cut'ed,
  pros'e·cut'ing
  (SEE persecute)

pros'e·cu'tion

pros'e·cu'tor

pros'e·lyte'
  pros'e·lyt'ed,
  pros'e·lyt'ing

pros'e·lyt·ize'
  pros'e·lyt·ized',
  pros'e·lyt·iz'ing

pros'e·lyt·iz'er

pro·slav'er·y

pro·sod'ic

pros'o·dy

pros'pect

pro·spec'tive

pros'pec·tor

pro·spec'tus
  pl. pro·spec'tus·es

pros'per

pros·per'i·ty
  pl. pros·per'i·ties

pros'per·ous

pros'ta·glan'din

pros'tate (*male
  gland*)
  (SEE prostrate)

pros·the'sis
  pl. pros·the'ses

pros·thet'ic

pros·thet'ics

pros'ti·tute'
  pros'ti·tut'ed,
  pros'ti·tut'ing

pros'ti·tu'tion

pros'trate (*lay down*)
  pros'trat·ed,
  pros'trat·ing
  (SEE prostate)

pros·tra'tion

pros'y
  pros'i·er, pros'i·est

pro'tac·tin'i·um

pro·tag'o·nist

pro'te·an

pro·tect'

pro·tec'tion

pro·tec'tion·ism'

pro·tec'tion·ist

pro·tec'tive

pro·tec'tor

pro·tec'tor·ate

pro·tec'tress

pro'té·gé' (*masc.*)

pro'té·gée' (*fem.*)

pro'tein

pro tem'

pro tem'po·re'

Prot'er·o·zo'ic

pro'test (*n.*)

pro·test' (*v.*)

Prot'es·tant

Prot'es·tant·ism'

pro·tes·ta'tion

pro·tho'no·ta'ry
  pl. pro·tho'no·tar'ies

pro'ti·um

pro'to·col'

pro'ton

pro'to·plasm'

pro'to·plas'mal

pro'to·plas'mic

pro'to·type'

Pro'to·zo'a

pro'to·zo'an

pro·tract'

pro·trac'tion

pro·trac'tor

pro·trude'
  pro·trud'ed,
  pro·trud'ing

pro·tru'sion

pro·tu'ber·ance

pro·tu'ber·ant

proud

proud'ly

Proust
prove
  proved, proved or
  prov'en, prov'ing
prov'a · bil'i · ty
prov'a · ble
prov'a · ble · ness
prov'a · bly
prove
  proved, proved or
  prov'en, prov'ing
prov'e · nance
Pro'ven · çal'
prov'en · der
pro · ve'ni · ence
prov'erb
pro · ver'bi · al
pro · ver'bi · al · ly
pro · vide'
  pro · vid'ed, pro · vid'ing
pro · vid'ed
prov'i · dence
Prov'i · dence
prov'i · dent
prov'i · den'tial
prov'i · den'tial · ly
pro · vid'er
pro · vid'ing
prov'ince
pro · vin'cial
pro · vin'cial · ism'
pro · vin'ci · al'i · ty
  pl. pro · vin'ci · al'i · ties
pro · vin'cial · ly
pro · vi'sion
pro · vi'sion · al
pro · vi'sion · al · ly
pro · vi'so
  pl. pro · vi'sos or
  pro · vi'soes
pro · vi'so · ry
pro · vo'ca · teur'
prov'o · ca'tion
pro · voc'a · tive
pro · voke'
  pro · voked', pro · vok'ing
pro'vo · lo'ne
prov'ost
pro'vost mar'shal

prow
prow'ess
prowl
prowl'er
prox'i · mal
prox'i · mal · ly
prox'i · mate
prox'i · mate · ly
prox · im'i · ty
prox'i · mo'
prox'y
  pl. prox'ies
prude
pru'dence
pru'dent
pru · den'tial
pru · den'tial · ly
prud'er · y
  pl. prud'er · ies
prud'ish
prune
pru'ri · ence
pru'ri · ent
pru · ri'tus
Prus'sia
Prus'sian
pry (v.)
  pried, pry'ing;
  pl. pries
psalm
psalm'book'
psalm'ist
psal'mo · dy
  pl. psal'mo · dies
Psal'ter
psal'ter · y
  pl. psal'ter · ies
pseu'do
pseu'do · nym
pseu · don'y · mous
pseu'do · sci'en · tif'ic
pshaw
psit'ta · co'sis
pso · ri'a · sis
psych
  psyched, psych'ing
Psy'che
psych'e · del'ic
psych'e · del'i · cal · ly

psy'chi · at'ric
psy'chi · at'ri · cal · ly
psy · chi'a · trist
psy · chi'a · try
psy'chic
psy'chi · cal
psy'chi · cal · ly
psy'cho
  pl. psy'chos
psy'cho · a · nal'y · sis
psy'cho · an'a · lyt'ic
psy'cho · an'a · lyt'i · cal
psy'cho · an'a ·
  lyt'i · cal · ly
psy'cho · an'a · lyst
psy'cho · an'a · lyze'
  psy'cho · an'a · lyzed',
  psy'cho · an'a · lyz'ing
psy'cho · bi'o · log'i · cal
psy'cho · bi · ol'o · gy
psy'cho · dra'ma
psy'cho · dy · nam'ic
psy'cho · dy · nam'
  i · cal · ly
psy'cho · dy · nam'ics
psy'cho · gen'e · sis
psy'cho · gen'ic
psy'cho · log'i · cal
psy'cho · log'i · cal · ly
psy · chol'o · gist
psy · chol'o · gize'
  psy · chol'o · gized',
  psy · chol'o · giz'ing
psy · chol'o · gy
  pl. psy · chol'o · gies
psy'cho · met'ric
psy'cho · met'ri · cal · ly
psy · chom'e · try
psy'cho · mo'tor
psy'cho · neu · ro'sis
psy'cho · neu · rot'ic
psy'cho · path'
psy'cho · path'ic
psy'cho · path'o ·
  log'i · cal
psy'cho · pa · thol'o · gy
psy'cho · sex'u · al
psy · cho'sis
  pl. psy · cho'ses

psy'cho•so'cial

psy'cho•so•mat'ic

psy'cho•ther'a•pist

psy'cho•ther'a•py

psy•chot'ic

psy•chot'i•cal•ly

ptar'mi•gan
  pl. ptar'mi•gans or ptar'mi•gan

pte•rid'o•phyte'

pter'o•dac'tyl

Ptol'e•ma'ic

Ptol'e•my

pto'maine

pto•main'ic

pty'a•lin

pub

pu'ber•ty

pu'bes
  pl. pu'bes

pu•bes'cent

pu'bic

pu'bis
  pl. pu'bes

pub'lic

pub'li•ca'tion

pub'li•cist

pub•lic'i•ty

pub'li•cize'
  pub'li•cized', pub'li•ciz'ing

pub'lic•ly

pub'lic–spir'it•ed

pub'lish

pub'lish•a•ble

pub'lish•er

puce

puck

puck'er

puck'ish

pud'ding

pud'dle
  pud'dled, pud'dling

pud'dling

pudg'i•ness

pudg'y
  pudg'i•er, pudg'i•est

pueb'lo
  pl. pueb'los

pu'er•ile

pu'er•il'i•ty
  pl. pu'er•il'i•ties

pu•er'per•al

Puer'to Ri'co

Puer'to Ri'can

puff

puff'ball'

puff'er

puff'er•y
  pl. puff'er•ies

puf'fin

puff'y
  puff'i•er, puff'i•est

pug
  pugged, pug'ging

pu'gil•ism'

pu'gil•ist

pu'gil•is'tic

pug•na'cious

pug•nac'i•ty

puke
  puked, puk'ing

puk'ka

pul
  pl. puls or pu'li

pul'chri•tude'

pul'chri•tu'di•nous

pul'er

pu'li
  pl. pu'lik or pu'lis

Pu'litz•er

pull

pull'back'

pul'let

pul'ley
  pl. pul'leys

Pull'man
  (*Trademark*)
  pl. Pull'mans

pull'–out'

pull'o'ver

pul'mo•nar'y

Pul'mo'tor
  (*Trademark*)

pulp

pulp'i•ness

pul'pit

pulp'wood'

pulp'y
  pulp'i•er, pulp'i•est

pul'sar

pul'sate
  pul'sat•ed, pul'sat•ing

pul•sa'tion

pul'sa•tor

pulse
  pulsed, puls'ing

pul'ver•i•za'tion

pul'ver•ize'
  pul'ver•ized', pul'ver•iz'ing

pu'ma

pum'ice
  pum'iced, pum'ic•ing

pum'mel
  pum'meled, pum'mel•ing

pump

pum'per•nick'el

pump'kin

pump'kin•seed'

pun
  punned, pun'ning

punch

punch'board'

punch'–drunk'

pun'cheon

punch'er

punch' line'

punch'y
  punch'i•er, punch'i•est

punc•til'i•o'
  pl. punc•til'i•os'

punc•til'i•ous

punc'tu•al

punc'tu•al'i•ty

punc'tu•al•ly

punc'tu•ate'
  punc'tu•at'ed, punc'tu•at'ing

punc'tu•a'tion

punc'tu•a'tor

punc'ture
  punc'tured, punc'tur•ing

pun'dit

pun'gen•cy

pun'gent

Pu'nic

pu'ni • ness

pun'ish

pun'ish • a • ble

pun'ish • ment

pu'ni • tive

punk

pun'ster

punt

punt'er

pu'ny
  pu'ni • er, pu'ni • est

pup

pu'pa
  pl. pu'pae or pu'pas

pu'pal (*of a pupa*)
  (SEE pupil)

pu • pa'tion

pu'pil (*student*)
  (SEE pupal)

pup'pet

pup'pet • eer'

pup'pet • ry
  pl. pup'pet • ries

pup'py
  pl. pup'pies

pup' tent'

pur'blind'

pur'chas • a • ble

pur'chase
  pur'chased,
  pur'chas • ing

pur'chas • er

pur'dah

pure
  pur'er, pur'est

pure'bred' (*adj.*)

pure'bred' (*n.*)

pu • rée'
  pu • réed', pu • ré'ing

pure'ly

pur • ga'tion

pur'ga • tive

pur'ga • to'ri • al

pur'ga • to'ry
  pl. pur'ga • to'ries

purge
  purged, purg'ing

purg'er

pu'ri • fi • ca'tion

pu • rif'i • ca • to'ry

pu'ri • fi'er

pu'ri • fy'
  pu'ri • fied', pu'ri • fy'ing

Pu'rim

pu'rine

pur'ism

pur'ist

Pu'ri • tan

pu'ri • tan'i • cal

pu'ri • tan'i • cal • ly

Pu'ri • tan • ism'

pu'ri • ty

purl (*knit*)
  (SEE pearl)

pur'lieu

pur • loin'

pur'ple
  pur'pled, pur'pling

pur'plish

pur • port' (*v.*)

pur'port (*n.*)

pur'pose
  pur'posed, pur'pos • ing

pur'pose • ful

pur'pose • ful • ly

pur'pose • less

pur'pose • ly

purr

purse
  pursed, purs'ing

purs'er

purse' strings'

purs'lane

pur • su'ance

pur • su'ant

pur • sue'
  pur • sued', pur • su'ing

pur • su'er

pur • suit'

pu'ru • lence

pu'ru • lent

pur • vey'

pur • vey'ance

pur • vey'or

pur'view

pus

push

push' but'ton

push'cart'

push'er

Push'kin

push'o'ver

push'pin'

push'up'

push'y
  push'i • er, push'i • est

pu'sil • la • nim'i • ty

pu'sil • lan'i • mous

puss

puss'y (*cat*)
  pl. puss'ies

pus'sy (*containing
  pus*)
  pus'si • er, pus'si • est

puss'y • cat'

puss'y • foot'
  pl. puss'y • foots'

pus'tu • lant

pus'tu • lar

pus'tule

put (*place*)
  put, put'ting
  (SEE putt)

pu'ta • tive

put'-down'

put'-on' (*adj.*)

put'-on' (*n.*)

put'-out'

pu'tre • fac'tion

pu'tre • fac'tive

pu'tre • fy'
  pu'tre • fied',
  pu'tre • fy'ing

pu • tres'cence

pu • tres'cent

pu'trid

pu • trid'i • ty

Putsch

putt (*golf stroke*)
  (SEE put)

put'tee

put'ter

put'ty
  pl. put'ties; (*v.*)
  put'tied, put'ty • ing

put'-up'

puz'zle
  puz'zled, puz'zling

puz′zle • ment

puz′zler

pya

Pyg • ma′li • on

Pyg′my
   pl. Pyg′mies

py′lon

py • lo′rus
   pl. py • lo′ri

Pyong′yang′

py′or • rhe′a

pyr′a • mid

py • ram′i • dal

pyre

Pyr′e • nees′

py • re′thrum

Py′rex (*Trademark*)

py′rite

py • ri′tes

py • rol′y • sis

py′ro • ma′ni • a

py′ro • ma′ni • ac

py • rom′e • ter

py′ro • tech′nics

py • rox′y • lin

pyr′rhic

Py • thag′o • ras

Py • thag′o • re′an

py′thon

pyx

Q

Qa′tar

Qi • a • na
   (*Trademark*)

qin • tar′

Quaa′lude′
   (*Trademark*)

quack

quack′er • y
   pl. quack′er • ies

quack′ish

quad

quad′ran • gle

quad′ran′gu • lar

quad′rant

quad′ra • phon′ic

quad • rat′ic

quad • rat′ics

quad • ren′ni • al

quad • ren′ni • al • ly

quad • ren′ni • um
   pl. quad • ren′ni • ums or
   quad • ren′ni • a

quad′ri • ceps′
   pl. quad′ri • ceps • es or
   quad′ri • ceps′

quad′ri • lat′er • al

qua • drille′

quad • ril′lion
   pl. quad • ril′lions or
   quad • ril′lion

quad′ri • ple′gi • a

quad′ri • ple′gic

quad′ri • par′tite

quad • riv′i • um
   pl. quad • riv′i • a

quad • roon′

quad′ru • ped′

quad • ru′ple
   quad • ru′pled,
   quad • ru′pling

quad • ru′plet

quad • ru′pli • cate′
   (*v.*)
   quad • ru′pli • cat′ed,
   quad • ru′pli • cat′ing

quad • ru′pli • cate
   (*adj., n.*)

quad • ru′pli • ca′tion

quaff

quaff′er

quag′mire′

qua′hog

Quai d′Or • say′

quail
   pl. quails or quail

quaint

quaint′ly

quake
   quaked, quak′ing

Quak′er

Quak′er • ism′

quak′y
   quak′i • er, quak′i • est

qual′i • fi • ca′tion

qual′i • fied′

qual′i • fi′er

qual′i • fy′
   qual′i • fied′,
   qual′i • fy′ing

qual′i • ta′tive

qual′i • ty
   pl. qual′i • ties

qualm

quan′da • ry
   pl. quan′da • ries

quan′ti • fi′a • ble

quan′ti • fi • ca′tion

quan′ti • fi′er

quan′ti • fy′
   quan′ti • fied′,
   quan′ti • fy′ing

quan′ti • ta′tive

quan′ti • ty
   pl. quan′ti • ties

quan′tum
   pl. quan′ta

quar′an • tin′a • ble

quar′an • tine′
   quar′an • tined,
   quar′an • tin′ing

quark

quar′rel
   quar′reled, quar′rel • ing

quar′rel • some

quar′ry
   pl. quar′ries; (*v.*)
   quar′ried, quar′ry • ing

quart

quar′ter

quar′ter • back′

quar′ter–deck′

quar′ter • fi′nal

quar′ter horse′

quar′ter–hour′

quar′ter • ly
   pl. quar′ter • lies

quar′ter • mas′ter

quar′ter note′

quar′ter rest′

quar·tet' or
　quar·tette'

quar'to
　pl. quar'tos

quartz

qua'sar

quash

qua'si

qua·si–ju·di'ci·al

qua'si–pub'lic

qua'ter·nar'y
　pl. qua'ter·nar'ies

quat'rain

quat're·foil'

quat'tro·cen'to

qua'ver

quay (pier)
　(SEE cay and key)

quea'si·ly

quea'si·ness

quea'sy
　quea'si·er, quea'si·est

Que·bec'

Que·bec'er

que·bra'cho
　pl. que·bra'chos

queen

queen'ly

queen' moth'er

queen'–size'

queer

queer'ly

quell

quench

quench'a·ble

que·nelle'

quer'u·lous

que'ry
　pl. que'ries; (v.)
　que'ried, que'ry·ing

quest

ques'tion

ques'tion·a·ble

ques'tion·a·bly

ques'tion·naire'

quet·zal'

Quet·zal'co·a'tl

queue (line)
　queued, queu'ing
　(SEE cue)

Que'zon Cit'y

quib'ble
　quib'bled, quib'bling

quiche

quick

quick'en

quick'–freeze'
　quick'–froze', quick'–
　fro'zen, quick'–freez'ing

quick'ie

quick'lime'

quick'sand'

quick'sil'ver

quick'step'

quick'–tem'pered

quick'time'

quick'–wit'ted

quick'–wit'ted

quid
　pl. quid

quid' pro quo'
　pl. quid' pro quos' or
　quids' pro quo'

qui·es'cence

qui·es'cent

qui'et

qui'e·tude'

qui·e'tus
　pl. qui·e'tus·es

quill

quilt

quilt'ed

quilt'ing

quince

qui·nel'la

qui'nine

quin·quen'ni·al

quin·quen'ni·al·ly

quin'sy

quint

quin'tal

quin·tes'sence

quin'tes·sen'tial

quin·tet' or
　quin·tette'

quin·til'lion
　pl. quin·til'lions or
　quin·til'lion

quin·tu'ple

quin·tu'pled,
　quin·tu'pling

quin·tu'plet

quin·tu'pli·cate'
　(v.)
　quin·tu'pli·cat'ed,
　quin·tu'pli·cat'ing

quin·tu'pli·cate
　(adj., n.)

quip
　quipped, quip'ping

quip'ster

quire (paper)
　(SEE choir)

quirk

quirk'y
　quirk'i·er, quirk'i·est

quirt

quis'ling

quit
　quit or quit'ted,
　quit'ting

quit'claim'

quite

Qui'to

quit'tance

quit'ter

quiv'er

qui vive'

quix·ot'ic

quix·ot'i·cal·ly

quiz (v.)
　quizzed, quiz'zing;
　pl. quiz'zes

quiz'mas'ter

quiz'zer

quiz'zi·cal

quiz'zi·cal·ly

quoin (angle)
　(SEE coin)

quoit

quon'dam

Quon'set
　(Trademark)

quo'rum

quo'ta

quot'a·bil'i·ty

quot'a·ble

quot'a·bly

quo·ta'tion

quote
  quot'ed, quot'ing

quot'er

quoth

quo·tid'i·an

quo'tient

R

Ra·bat'

rab'bet (groove)
  rab'bet·ed, rab'bet·ing
  (SEE rabbit)

rab'bi
  pl. rab'bis

rab'bin·ate

rab·bin'i·cal

rab'bit (animal)
  pl. rab'bits or rab'bit
  (SEE rabbet)

rab'ble
  rab'bled, rab'bling

rab'ble–rous'er

Rab'e·lais'

Rab·e·lai'si·an

rab'id

rab·id'i·ty

ra'bies

rac·coon'
  pl. rac·coons' or
  rac·coon'

race
  raced, rac'ing

race'course'

race' horse'

ra·ceme'

rac'er

race' track'

Rach·ma'ni·noff'

ra'cial

ra'cial·ism'

ra'cial·ly

rac'ism

rac'ist

rack

rack'et

rack'et·eer'

rac'on·teur'

rac'i·ness

rac'i·ly

rac'quet

rac'y
  rac'i·er, rac'i·est

ra'dar

ra'dar·scope'

ra'di·al

ra'di·al·ly

ra'di·ance

ra'di·an·cy

ra'di·ant

ra'di·ate' (v.)
  ra'di·at'ed, ra'di·at'ing

ra'di·ate (adj.)

ra'di·a'tion

ra'di·a'tive

ra'di·a'tor

rad'i·cal

rad'i·cal·ism'

rad'i·cal·i·za'tion

rad'i·cal·ize'
  rad'i·cal·ized',
  rad'i·cal·iz'ing

rad'i·cal·ly

rad'i·cand'

ra'di·o'
  pl. ra'di·os'; (v.)
  ra'di·oed', ra'di·o'ing

ra'di·o·ac'tive

ra'di·o·ac·tiv'i·ty

ra'di·o·broad'cast
  (n.)

ra'di·o·broad'cast'
  (v.)
  ra'di·o·broad'cast' or
  ra'di·o·broad'cast'ed,
  ra'di·o·broad'cast'ing

ra'dio car'

ra'di·o·car'bon

ra'di·o·gen'ic

ra'di·o·gram'

ra'di·o·graph'

ra'di·o·graph'ic

ra'di·og'ra·phy

ra'di·o·i'so·tope'

ra'di·o·log'i·cal

ra'di·ol'o·gist

ra'di·ol'o·gy

ra'di·o·man'
  pl. ra'di·o·men'

ra'di·om'e·ter

ra'di·o·pho'to·graph'

ra'di·o·scop'ic

ra'di·os'co·py

ra'di·o·sonde'

ra'di·o·tel'e·graph'

ra'di·o·tel'e·graph'ic

ra'di·o·te·leg'ra·phy

ra'di·o·tel'e·phone'
  ra'di·o·tel'e·phoned',
  ra'di·o·tel'e·phon'ing

ra'di·o·tel'e·phon'ic

ra'di·o·ther'a·pist

ra'di·o·ther'a·py

rad'ish

ra'di·um

ra'di·us
  pl. ra'di·i' or
  ra'di·us·es

ra'dix
  rad'i·ces' or ra'dix·es

ra'don

raf'fi·a

raff'ish

raf'fle
  raf'fled, raf'fling

raft

raf'ter

rag

rag'a·muf'fin

rage
  raged, rag'ing

rag'ged

rag'lan

ra·gout'
  ra·gouted', ra·gout'ing

rag'pick'er

rag'time'

rag′weed′
raid
raid′er
rail
rail′ing
rail′ler•y
  pl. rail′ler•ies
rail′road′
rail′way′
rai′ment
rain (*shower*)
  (SEE reign *and* rein)
rain′bow′
rain′ check′
rain′coat′
rain′ dance′
rain′drop′
rain′fall′
rain′mak′er
rain′mak′ing
rain′proof′
rain′spout′
rain′storm′
rain′ wa′ter
rain′y
  rain′i•er, rain′i•est
raise (*lift*)
  raised, rais′ing
  (SEE raze)
rais′er (*lifter*)
  (SEE razor)
rai′sin
rai′son d′ê′tre
  pl. rai′sons d′ê′tre
ra′jah or ra′ja
rake
  raked, rak′ing
rake′-off′
rak′ish
Ra′leigh
ral′ly (*v.*)
  ral′lied, ral′ly•ing;
  pl. ral′lies
ram
  rammed, ram′ming
Ram′a•dan′
ram′ble
  ram′bled, ram′bling
ram′bler
ram′bling

ram•bunc′tious
ram′e•kin
ram′ie
ram′i•fi•ca′tion
ram′i•fy′
  ram′i•fied, ram′i•fy′ing
ram′jet′
ramp
ram′page (*n.*)
ram•page′ (*v.*)
  ram•paged′,
  ram•pag′ing
ram•pa′geous
ramp′ant
ram′part
ram′rod′
  ram′rod′ded,
  ram′rod′ding
ram′shack′le
ran
ranch
ranch′er
ran•che′ro
  pl. ran•che′ros
ranch′ house′
ran′cho
  pl. ran′chos
ran′cid
ran•cid′i•ty
ran′cor
ran′cor•ous
rand
ran′dom
ra′nee
rang
range
  ranged, rang′ing
rang′er
Ran′goon
rang′y
  rang′i•er, rang′i•est
rank
rank′ing
ran′kle
  ran′kled, ran′kling
ran′sack
ran′som
rant
rant′er

rap (*strike*)
  rapped, rap′ping
  (SEE wrap)
ra•pa′cious
ra•pac′i•ty
rape
  raped, rap′ing
rape′seed′
Raph′a•el
rap′id
rap′id-fire′
ra•pid′i•ty
rap′id trans′it
rap′id•ly
ra′pi•er
rap′ine
rap′ist
rap•pel′
  rap•pelled′, rap•pel′ling
rap•port′
rap•proche•ment′
rap•scal′lion
rapt (*engrossed*)
  (SEE *pt. of* rap)
rapt′ly
rap′ture
  rap′tured, rap′tur•ing
rap′tur•ous
ra′ra a′vis
  pl. ra′rae a′ves
rare
  rar′er, rar′est
rare′bit
rar′e•fac′tion
rar′e•fy′
  rar′e•fied′, rar′e•fy′ing
rare′ly
rar′i•ty
  pl. rar′i•ties
ras′cal
ras•cal′i•ty
  pl. ras•cal′i•ties
ras′cal•ly
rash
rash′er
rasp
rasp′ber′ry
  pl. rasp′ber′ries
rasp′y
  rasp′i•er, rasp′i•est

ras'ter

rat
  rat'ted, rat'ting

rat'a·ble

ratch'et

ratch'et wheel'

rate
  rat'ed, rat'ing

rath'er'

rat'hole'

raths'kel'ler

rat'i·fi·ca'tion

rat'i·fy'
  rat'i·fied', rat'i·fy'ing

rat·i·né'

ra'tio
  pl. ra'ti·os'

ra'ti·oc'i·nate'
  ra'ti·oc'i·nat'ed,
  ra'ti·oc'i·nat'ing

ra'ti·oc'i·na'tion

ra'ti·oc'i·na'tor

ra'tion

ra'tion·al
  (reasonable)
  (SEE rationale)

ra'tion·ale' (logical
  basis)
  (SEE rational)

ra'tion·al·ism'

ra'tion·al·ist

ra'tion·al·is'tic

ra'tion·al'i·ty
  pl. ra'tion·al'i·ties

ra'tion·al·i·za'tion

ra'tion·al·ize'
  ra'tion·al·ized',
  ra'tion·al·iz'ing

ra'tion·al·ly

rat'line'

rat' race'

rats'bane'

rat·tan'

rat'ter

rat'tle
  rat'tled, rat'tling

rat'tle·brained'

rat'tler

rat'tle·snake'

rat'tle·trap'

rat'trap'

rat'ty
  rat'ti·er, rat'ti·est

rau'cous

rau·wol'fi·a

rav'age
  rav'aged, rav'ag·ing

rav'ag·er

rave
  raved, rav'ing

rav'el
  ra'veled, ra'vel·ing

ra'ven

rav'en·ing

rav'en·ous

ra·vine'

rav'ing

ra'vi·o'li

rav'ish

rav'ish·ing

raw

raw'boned'

raw'hide'
  raw'hid'ed, raw'hid'ing

ray

ray'on

raze (demolish)
  razed, raz'ing
  (SEE raise)

ra'zor (shaver)
  (SEE raiser)

ra'zor·back'

razz

raz'zle-·daz'zle

razz'ma·tazz'

re

reach

re·act' (respond)
  (SEE re-act)

re-act' (act again)
  (SEE react)

re·ac'tant

re·ac'tion

re·ac'tion·ar'y
  pl. re·ac'tion·ar'ies

re·ac'ti·vate'
  re·ac'ti·vat'ed,
  re·ac'ti·vat'ing

re·ac'ti·va'tion

re·ac'tive

re·ac'tor

read (examine
  writing, etc.)
  read, read'ing
  (SEE reed)

read'a·bil'i·ty

read'a·ble

read'a·bly

read'er

read'er·ship'

read'i·ly

read'i·ness

read'ing room'

re'ad·just'

read'out'

read'y
  (adj.): read'i·er,
  read'i·est; (v.)
  read'ied, read'y·ing

read'y·made'

read'y-to-wear'

re'af·firm'

re·a'gent

re'al (actual)
  (SEE reel)

re'al·ism'

re'al·ist

re'al·is'tic

re'al·is'ti·cal·ly

re·al'i·ty (actuality)
  pl. re·al'i·ties
  (SEE realty)

re'al·iz'a·ble

re'al·i·za'tion

re'al·ize'
  re'al·ized', re'al·iz'ing

re'al·iz'er

re'-al·ly'
  re'-al·lied', re'-
  al·ly'ing

re'al·ly

realm

re·al'po·li·tik'

Re'al·tor
  (Trademark)

re'al·ty (property)
  (SEE reality)

ream

ream'er

reap

reap'er

re'ap•pear'
re'ap•por'tion
re'ap•por'tion•ment
re'ap•prais'al
re'ap•praise'
  re'ap•praised',
  re'ap•prais'ing
rear
rear' guard'
re•arm'
re•ar'ma•ment
rear'most'
re'ar•range'
  re'ar•ranged',
  re'ar•rang'ing
rear'ward or
  rear'wards
rea'son
rea'son•a•bil'i•ty
rea'son•a•ble
rea'son•a•bly
rea'son•ing
re'as•sign'
re'as•sur'ance
re'as•sure'
  re'as•sured',
  re'as•sur'ing
re'bate
  re'bat•ed, re'bat•ing
reb'el (n., adj.)
reb•el' (v.)
  reb•elled', reb•el'ling
re•bel'lion
re•bel'lious
re•bind'
  re•bound', re•bind'ing
re•birth'
re•born'
re•bound' (v.)
re'bound (n.)
re•broad'cast'
  re•broad'cast' or
  re•broad'cast'ed,
  re•broad'cast'ing
re•buff'
re•build'
  re•built', re•build'ing
re•buke'
  re•buked', re•buk'ing
re'bus
  pl. re'bus•es

re•but'
  re•but'ted, re•but'ting
re•but'tal
re•but'ter
re•cal'ci•trance
re•cal'ci•tran•cy
re•cal'ci•trant
re•cal'cu•late'
  re•cal'cu•lat'ed,
  re•cal'cu•lat'ing
re'cal•cu•la'tion
re•call'
re•call'a•ble
re•cant'
re'can•ta'tion
re'cap'
  re'capped', re'cap'ping
re'ca•pit'u•late'
  re'ca•pit'u•lat'ed,
  re'ca•pit'u•lat'ing
re'ca•pit'u•la'tion
re•cap'ture
  re•cap'tured,
  re•cap'tur•ing
re•cast' (v.)
  re•cast', re•cast'ing
re'cast' (n.)
re•cede'
  re•ced'ed, re•ced'ing
re•ceipt'
re•ceiv'a•ble
re•ceive'
  re•ceived', re•ceiv'ing
re•ceiv'er
re•ceiv'er•ship'
re•cen'sion
re'cent
re•cep'ta•cle
re•cep'tion
re•cep'tion•ist
re•cep'tive
re'cep•tiv'i•ty
re•cep'tor
re•cess'
re•ces'sion
re•ces'sion•al
re•ces'sive
re•cher'ché
re•cid'i•vism'
re•cid'i•vist

rec'i•pe'
re•cip'i•ent
re•cip'ro•cal
re•cip'ro•cal•ly
re•cip'ro•cate'
  re•cip'ro•cat'ed,
  re•cip'ro•cat'ing
re•cip'ro•ca'tive
re•cip'ro•ca'tion
rec'i•proc'i•ty
re•ci'sion
re•cit'al
rec'i•ta'tion
rec'i•ta•tive'
re•cite'
  re•cit'ed, re•cit'ing
reck'less
reck'on
reck'on•ing
re•claim' (make
  usable)
  (SEE re-claim)
re-claim' (claim
  again)
  (SEE reclaim)
re•claim'a•ble
rec'la•ma'tion
re•cline'
  re•clined', re•clin'ing
rec'luse (n.)
rec•luse' (adj.)
rec'og•ni'tion
re•cog'ni•zance
rec'og•niz'a•bil'i•ty
rec'og•niz'a•ble
rec'og•niz'a•bly
rec'og•nize'
  rec'og•nized',
  rec'og•niz'ing
re•coil'
re•coil'less
re'-col•lect' (collect
  again)
  (SEE recollect)
rec'ol•lect'
  (remember)
  (SEE re-collect)
re'-col•lec'tion
  (collection anew)
  (SEE recollection)

rec'ol·lec'tion
(*memory*)
(SEE re-collection)

re·com'bi·nant

re'com·bi·na'tion

rec'om·mend'

rec'om·mend'a·ble

rec'om·men·da'tion

re'com·mit'
re·com·mit'ted,
re'com·mit'ting

re'com·mit'tal

rec'om·pense'

re'com·pose'
re'com·posed',
re'com·pos'ing

rec'on·cil'a·ble

rec'on·cile'
rec'on·ciled',
rec'on·cil'ing

rec'on·cil'er

rec'on·cil'i·a'tion

rec'on·dite'

re'con·di'tion

re'con·firm'

re·con'nais·sance

re'con·noi'ter

re'con·sid'er

re'con·sid'er·a'tion

re·con'sti·tute'
re·con'sti·tut'ed,
re·con'sti·tut'ing

re'con·struct'

re'con·struc'tion

re'con·ver'sion

re'con·vert'

re·cord' (*v.*)

re'cord (*n., adj.*)

re·cord'er

re·cord'ing

re·count' (*v.*)
(*count again*)
(SEE recount))

re'-count' (*n.*)
(*second count*)
(SEE recount)

re·count' (*narrate*)
(SEE re-count)

re·coup'

re'course

re·cov'er (*cover
again*)
(SEE recover)

re·cov'er (*get back*)
(SEE re-cover)

re·cov'er·a·ble

re·cov'er·y
pl. re·cov'er·ies

rec're·ant

rec're-ate' (*create
again*)
re'-cre·at'ed, re'-
cre·at'ing
(SEE recreate)

rec're·ate' (*refresh*)
rec're·at'ed,
rec're·at'ing
(SEE re-create)

rec're·a'tion

rec're·a'tion·al

re·crim'i·nate'
re·crim'i·nat'ed,
re·crim'i·nat'ing

re·crim'i·na'tion

re·crim'i·na'tive

re·crim'i·na·to'ry

re'cru·desce'
re'cru·desced',
re'cru·desc'ing

re'cru·des'cence

re'cru·des'cent

re·cruit'

rec'tal

rec'tan'gle

rec·tan'gu·lar

rec'ti·fi'a·ble

rec'ti·fi·ca'tion

rec'ti·fi'er

rec'ti·fy'
rec'ti·fied', rec'ti·fy'ing

rec'ti·lin'e·ar

rec'ti·tude'

rec'to
pl. rec'tos

rec'tor

rec'to·ry
pl. rec'to·ries

rec'tum
pl. rec'tums or rec'ta

re·cum'ben·cy

re·cum'bent

re·cu'per·ate'
re·cu'per·at'ed,
re·cu'per·at'ing

re·cu'per·a'tion

re·cu'per·a'tive

re·cur'
re·curred', re·cur'ring

re·cur'rence

re·cur'rent

re·cy'cle
re·cy'cled, re·cy'cling

red
red'der, red'dest
(SEE *pt. of* read)

re·dact'

re·dac'tion

re·dac'tor

red'-blood'ed

red'breast'

red'cap'

red' car'pet

red'coat'

Red' Cross'

red'den

red'dish

re·dec'o·rate'
re·dec'o·rat'ed,
re·dec'o·rat'ing

re'dec·o·ra'tion

re·ded'i·cate'
re·ded'i·cat'ed,
re·ded'i·cat'ing

re·deem'

re·deem'a·ble

re·deem'er

re·de·liv'er

re·demp'tion

re·demp'tive

re·demp'to·ry

re·de·ploy'

re·de·sign'

re·de·vel'op

re·de·vel'op·ment

red' fox'

red'-hand'ed

red'head'

red'-head'ed

red' heat'

red' her'ring

red'-hot'

re'di·rect'
re'di·rec'tion
re'dis·trib'ute
  re'dis·trib'ut·ed,
  re'dis·trib'ut·ing
re·dis'trict
red' lead'
red'-let'ter
red' light'
red'lin'ing
red' man'
re·do'
  re·did', re·done',
  re·do'ing
red'o·lence
red'o·len·cy
red'o·lent
re·dou'ble
  re·dou'bled,
  re·dou'bling
re·doubt'
re·doubt'a·ble
re·doubt'a·bly
re·dound'
red'-pen'cil
  red'-pen'ciled, red'-
  pen'cil·ing
re'dress (n.)
re·dress' (v.)
red'skin'
red' snap'per
red'start'
red' tape'
red' tide'
red'top'
re·duce'
  re·duced', re·duc'ing
re·duc'i·ble
re·duc'ti·o' ad
  ab·sur'dum
re·duc'tion
re·dun'dan·cy
  pl. re·dun'dan·cies
re·dun'dant
re·du'pli·cate' (v.)
  re·du'pli·cat·ed,
  re·du'pli·cat·ing
re·du'pli·cate (adj.)
re·du'pli·ca'tion
red'wing'

red'wood'
re·ech'o
  re·ech'oed,
  re·ech'o·ing
reed (grass)
  (SEE read)
re·ed'u·cate'
  re·ed'u·cat·ed
re·ed'u·ca'tion
reed'i·ness
reed'y
  reed'i·er, reed'i·est
reef
reef'er
reek (smell)
  (SEE wreak)
reel (spool; dance)
  (SEE real)
re'e·lect'
re'e·merge'
  re'e·merged',
  re'e·mer'ging
re'em·ploy'
re'en·act'
re·en'ter
re·en'try
  pl. re·en'tries
re'es·tab'lish
re'ex·am'i·na'tion
re'ex·am'ine
  re'ex·am'ined,
  re'ex·am'in·ing
re·fash'ion
re·fec'tion
re·fec'to·ry
  pl. re·fec'to·ries
re·fer'
  re·ferred', re·fer'ring
ref'er·a·ble
ref'er·ee'
  ref'er·eed', ref'er·ee'ing
ref'er·ence
  ref'er·enced,
  ref'er·enc·ing
ref'er·en'dum
  pl. ref'er·en'dums or
  ref'er·en'da
ref'er·ent
re·fer'ral
re·fill' (v.)
re'fill' (n.)
re·fill'a·ble

re·fi'nance
  re·fi'nanced,
  re·fi'nanc·ing
re·fine'
  re·fined', re·fin'ing
re·fined'
re·fine'ment
re·fin'er
re·fin'er·y
  pl. re·fin'er·ies
re·fin'ish
re·fit'
  re·fit'ted, re·fit'ting
re·flect'
re·flec'tion
re·flec'tive
re·flec'tor
re'flex (adj., n.)
re·flex' (v.)
re·flex'ive
re·for'est
re'for·est·a'tion
re·form' (improve)
  (SEE re-form)
re-form' (form
  again)
  (SEE reform)
re·form'a·tive
re·form'er
ref'or·ma'tion
re·form'a·to·ry
  pl. re·form'a·to·ries
re·formed'
re·fract'
re·frac'tion
re·frac'tive
re'frac·tiv'i·ty
re·frac'tor
re·frac'to·ry
  pl. re·frac'to·ries
re·frain'
re·fran'gi·ble
re·fresh'
re·fresh'ing
re·fresh'ment
re·frig'er·ant
re·frig'er·ate'
  re·frig'er·at·ed,
  re·frig'er·at·ing
re·frig'er·a'tion

re·frig'er·a'tor

re·fu'el
  re·fu'eled, re·fu'el·ing

ref'uge
  ref'uged, ref'ug·ing

ref'u·gee'

re·ful'gence

re·ful'gen·cy

re·ful'gent

re·fund' (v.)

re'fund (n.)

re·fund'a·ble

re·fur'bish

re·fus'al

re·fuse' (deny)
  re·fused', re·fus'ing
  (SEE BELOW)

ref'use (rubbish)
  (SEE ABOVE)

re·fu'ta·ble

re·fu'ta·bly

ref'u·ta'tion

re·fute'
  re·fut'ed, re·fut'ing

re·fut'er

re·gain'

re'gal (royal)
  (SEE regale)

re·gale' (delight)
  re·galed', re·gal'ing
  (SEE regal)

re·ga'li·a
  (sing.) re·ga'le

re'gal·ly

re·gard'

re·gard'ing

re·gard'less

re·gat'ta

re'gen·cy
  pl. re'gen·cies

re·gen'er·ate' (v.)
  re·gen'er·at'ed,
  re·gen'er·at'ing

re·gen'er·ate (adj.)

re·gen'er·a'tion

re·gen'er·a'tive

re·gen'er·a'tor

re'gent

reg'i·cid'al

reg'i·cide'

re·gime'

reg'i·men'

reg'i·ment (n.)

reg'i·ment' (v.)

reg'i·men'tal

reg'i·men·ta'tion

Re·gi'na

re'gion

re'gion·al

re'gion·al·ism'

re'gion·al·ly

reg'is·ter

reg'is·tered

reg'is·trant

reg'is·trar'

reg'is·tra'tion

reg'is·try
  pl. reg'is·tries

re·gress' (v.)

re'gress (n.)

re·gres'sion

re·gres'sive

re·gret'
  re·gret'ted, re·gret'ting

re·gret'ful

re·gret'ful·ly

re·gret'ta·ble

re·gret'ta·bly

re·group'

reg'u·lar

reg'u·lar'i·ty

reg'u·lar·ize'
  reg'u·lar·ized',
  reg'u·lar·iz'ing

reg'u·lar·ly

reg'u·late'
  reg'u·lat'ed,
  reg'u·lat'ing

reg'u·la'tion

reg'u·la'tive

reg'u·la'tor

reg'u·la·to'ry

re·gur'gi·tate'
  re·gur'gi·tat'ed,
  re·gur'gi·tat'ing

re·gur'gi·ta'tion

re'ha·bil'i·tate'
  re'ha·bil'i·tat'ed,
  re'ha·bil'i·tat'ing

re'ha·bil'i·ta'tion

re'ha·bil'i·ta'tive

re·hash' (v.)

re'hash' (n.)

re·hear'ing

re·hears'al

re·hearse'
  re·hearsed',
  re·hears'ing

Reich

Reichs'tag'

reign (rule)
  (SEE rain and rein)

re'im·burse'
  re'im·bursed',
  re'im·burs'ing

re'im·burse'ment

rein (strap)
  (SEE rain and reign)

re'in·car'nate'
  re'in·car'nat·ed,
  re'in·car'nat·ing

re'in·car·na'tion

rein'deer'
  pl. rein'deer' or
  rein'deers'

re'in·fect'

re'in·force'
  re'in·forced',
  re'in·forc'ing

re'in·force'ment

re'in·sert'

re'in·state'
  re'in·stat'ed,
  re'in·stat'ing

re'in·state'ment

re'in·sur'ance

re'in·sure'
  re'in·sured',
  re'in·sur'ing

re'in·ter'pret'

re'in·vest'

re'in·vig'or·ate'
  re'in·vig'or·at'ed,
  re'in·vig'ro·at'ing

re·is'su·a·ble

re·is'sue
  re·is'sued, re·is'su·ing

re·it'er·ate'
  re·it'er·at'ed,
  re·it'er·at'ing

re·it'er·a'tion

re·it'er·a'tive

re·ject' (v.)

re'ject (n.)

re·jec'tion
re·joice'
　re·joiced', re·joic'ing
re·join'
re·join'der
re·ju've·nate'
　re·ju've·nat·ed,
　re·ju've·nat·ing
re·ju've·na'tion
re·lapse'
　re·lapsed', re·laps'ing
re·lat'a·ble
re·late'
　re·lat'ed, re·lat'ing
re·lat'ed
re·la'tion
re·la'tion·ship'
rel'a·tive
rel'a·tive·ly
rel'a·tiv·ism'
rel'a·tiv·is'tic
rel'a·tiv'i·ty
re·la'tor
re·lax'
re·lax'ant
re'lax·a'tion
re-lay'
　re-laid', re-lay'ing
re'lay
　re'layed, re'lay·ing
re·lease' (set free)
　re·leased', re·leas'ing
　(SEE re-lease)
re-lease' (lease
　again)
　re-leased', re-leas'ing
　(SEE release)
rel'e·gate'
　rel'e·gat·ed,
　rel'e·gat·ing
rel'e·ga'tion
re·lent'
re·lent'less
rel'e·vance
rel'e·van·cy
rel'e·vant
re·li'a·bil'i·ty
re·li'a·ble
re·li'a·bly
re·li'ance

re·li'ant
rel'ic
re·lief'
re·liev'a·ble
re·lieve'
　re·lieved', re·liev'ing
re·liev'er
re·li'gion
re·lig'i·os'i·ty
re·li'gious
re·line'
　re·lined', re·lin'ing
re·lin'quish
rel'i·quar'y
　pl. rel'i·quar·ies
rel'ish
re·live'
　re·lived', re·liv'ing
re·lo'cate
　re·lo'cat·ed,
　re·lo'cat·ing
re'lo·ca'tion
re·luc'tance
re·luc'tan·cy
re·luc'tant
re·ly'
　re·lied', re·ly'ing
rem (radiation)
　(SEE REM)
REM (eye
　movement)
　(SEE rem)
re·main'
re·mains'
re·main'der
re·make' (v.)
　re·made', re·mak'ing
re'make' (n.)
re·mand'
re·mark'
re·mark'a·ble
re·mark'a·bly
Rem'brandt
re·me'di·a·ble
re·me'di·al
re·me'di·al·ly
rem'e·dy
　pl. rem'e·dies
　rem'e·died,
　rem'e·dy·ing

re·mem'ber
re·mem'brance
re·mind'
re·mind'er
rem'i·nisce'
　rem'i·nisced',
　rem'i·nisc'ing
rem'i·nis'cence
rem'i·nis'cent
re·miss'
re·mis'si·ble
re·mis'sion
re·mit'
　re·mit'ted, re·mit'ting
re·mit'tal
re·mit'tance
rem'nant
re·mod'el
　re·mod'eled,
　re·mod'el·ing
re·mon'strance
re·mon'strant
re·mon'strate
　re·mon'strat·ed,
　re·mon'strat·ing
re'mon·stra'tion
re·mon'stra·tive
re·mon'stra·tor
rem'o·ra
re·morse'
re·morse'ful
re·morse'ful·ly
re·morse'less
re·mote'
　re·mot'er, re·mot'est
re·mote'ly
re·mote'ness
re'mou·lade'
re·mount' (v.)
re'mount' (n.)
re·mov'a·ble
re·mov'al
re·move'
　re·moved', re·mov'ing
re·mu'ner·a·ble
re·mu'ner·ate'
　re·mu'ner·at'ed,
　re·mu'ner·at'ing
re·mu'ner·a'tion
re·mu'ner·a'tive

re • mu'ner • a'tor
Ren'ais • sance'
re'nal
Re • nas'cence
re • nas'cent
rend
  rent, rend'ing
ren'der
ren'dez • vous'
  pl. ren'dez • vous'
ren • di'tion
ren'e • gade'
re • nege'
  re • neged', re • neg'ing
re • neg'er
re'ne • go'ti • a • ble
re'ne • go'ti • ate'
  re'ne • go'ti • at'ed,
  re'ne • go'ti • at'ing
re'ne • go'ti • a'tion
re • new'
re • new'a • ble
re • new'al
ren'net
ren'nin
Re'noir
re • nom'i • nate'
  re • nom'i • nat'ed,
  re • nom'i • nat'ing
re'nom • i • na'tion
re • nounce'
  re • nounced',
  re • nounc'ing
ren'o • vate'
  ren'o • vat'ed,
  ren'o • vat'ing
ren'o • va'tion
ren'o • va'tor
re • nown'
re • nowned'
rent
rent'al
rent' strike'
re • num'ber
re • nun'ci • a'tion
re • oc'cu • py'
  re • oc'cu • pied',
  re • oc'cu • py'ing
re • o'pen
re • or'der
re'or • gan • i • za'tion

re • or'gan • ize'
  re • or'gan • ized',
  re • or'gan • iz'ing
re • or'gan • iz'er
rep
re • pack'age
  re • pack'aged,
  re • pack'ag • ing
re • pair'
re • pair'a • ble
re • pair'man'
  pl. re • pair'men'
rep'a • ra • ble
rep'a • ra'tion
rep'ar • tee'
re • past'
re • pa'tri • ate' (*v.*)
  re • pa'tri • at'ed,
  re • pa'tri • at'ing
re • pa'tri • ate (*n.*)
re • pa'tri • a'tion
re • pay'
re • pay'a • ble
re • pay'ment
re • peal'
re • peat'
re • peat'ed
re • pel'
  re • pelled', re • pel'ling
re • pel'lent
re • pent'
re • pent'ance
re • pent'ant
re'per • cus'sion
rep'er • toire'
rep'er • to'ry
  pl. rep'er • to'ries
rep'e • ti'tion
rep'e • ti'tious
re • pet'i • tive
re • pet'i • tive • ly
re • phrase'
  re • phrased',
  re • phras'ing
re • place'
  re • placed', re • plac'ing
re • place'a • ble
re • plac'er
re • place'ment
re • plant'

re • play' (*v.*)
re'play (*n.*)
re • plen'ish
re • plete'
re • plete'ness
re • ple'tion
re • plev'in
rep'li • ca
rep'li • cate
rep'li • ca'tion
re • pli'er
re • ply'
  re • plied', re • ply'ing
re • port'
re • port'a • ble
re • port'age
re • port'ed • ly
re • port'er
rep'or • to'ri • al
re • pose'
  re • posed', re • pos'ing
re • pos'i • tor'y
re • pos'sess'
re'pos • ses'sion
rep're • hend'
rep're • hen'si • bil'i • ty
rep're • hen'si • ble
rep're • hen'si • bly
rep're • hen'sion
rep're • sent'
rep're • sen • ta'tion
rep're • sen • ta'tion • al
rep're • sent'a • tive
re • press'
re • pres'sion
re • pres'sive
re • prieve'
  re • prieved',
  re • priev'ing
rep'ri • mand'
re • print' (*v.*)
re'print (*n.*)
re • pris'al
re • prise'
  re • prised', re • pris'ing
re'pro
  pl. re'pros
re • proach'

re·proach'a·ble

re·proach'ful

re·proach'ful·ly

rep'ro·bate'

rep'ro·ba'tion

re'pro·duce'

re'pro·duc'i·ble

re'pro·duc'tion

re'pro·duc'tive

re·proof'

re·prove'
  re·proved', re·prov'ing

rep'tile

rep·til'i·an

re·pub'lic

re·pub'li·can

re'pub·li·ca'tion

re·pub'lish

re·pu'di·ate'
  re·pu'di·at'ed,
  re·pu'di·at'ing

re·pu'di·a'tion

re·pug'nance

re·pug'nant

re·pulse'
  re·pulsed', re·puls'ing

re·pul'sion

re·pul'sive

re·pul'sive·ly

re·pul'sive·ness

rep·u·ta·bil'i·ty

rep'u·ta·ble

rep'u·ta·bly

rep'u·ta'tion

re·pute'
  re·put'ed, re·put'ing

re·put'ed

re·quest'

Req'ui·em

re·quire'
  re·quired', re·quir'ing

re·quire'ment

req'ui·site

req'ui·si'tion

re·quit'al

re·quite'
  re·quit'ed, re·quit'ing

re·run' (v.)
  re·ran', re·run',
  re·run'ning

re'run' (n.)

re·sal'a·ble

re'sale'

re·scind'

re·scis'sion

res'cue
  res'cued, res'cu·ing

res'cu·er

re·search'

re·sec'tion

re·sem'blance

re·sem'ble
  re·sem'bled,
  re·sem'bling

re·send'
  re·sent', re·send'ing

re·sent'

re·sent'ful

re·sent'ful·ly

re·sent'ment

res'er·pine

res'er·va'tion

re·serve'
  re·served', re·serv'ing

re·serv'ist

res'er·voir'

re·set' (v.)
  re·set', re·set'ting

re'set' (n.)

re·shape'
  re·shaped', re·shap'ing

re·ship'
  re·shipped',
  re·ship'ping

re·shuf'fle
  re·shuf'fled,
  re·shuf'fling

re·side'
  re·sid'ed, re·sid'ing

res'i·dence

res'i·den·cy
  pl. res'i·den·cies

res'i·dent

res'i·den'tial

re·sid'u·al

re·sid'u·al·ly

re·sid'u·ar'y

res'i·due'

re·sid'u·um
  pl. re·sid'u·a

re·sign' (give up)
  (SEE re-sign)

re–sign' (sign again)
  (SEE resign)

res'ig·na'tion

re·signed'

re·sil'ience

re·sil'ien·cy

re·sil'ient

res'in

res'in·ous

re·sist'

re·sist'ance

re·sist'ant

re·sist'er (one who
  resists)
  (SEE resistor)

re·sist'i·ble

re·sis'tor (electrical
  device)
  (SEE resister)

res'o·lute'

res'o·lu'tion

re·solv'a·ble

re·solve'
  re·solved', re·solv'ing

res'o·nance

res'o·nant

res'o·nate'
  res'o·nat'ed,
  res'o·nat'ing

res'on·na'tor

re·sorb'

re·sorp'tion

res·or'ci·nol'

re–sort' (sort again)
  (SEE resort)

re·sort' (place)
  (SEE re-sort)

re·sound'

re'source

re·source'ful

re·source'ful·ly

re·spect'

re·spect'a·bil'i·ty
  pl. re·spect'a·
  bil'·i·ties

re·spect'a·ble

re·spect'a·bly

re·spect'ful

re · spect'ful · ly
re · spect'ing
re · spec'tive
re · spec'tive · ly
re · spell'

res'pi · ra'tion
res'pi · ra'tor
res'pi · ra · to'ry
re · spire'
  re · spired', re · spir'ing
res'pite
  res'pit · ed, res'pit · ing
re · splend'ence
re · splend'ent
re · spond'
re · spond'ent
re · sponse'
re · spon'si · bil'i · ty
  pl. re · spon'si · bil'i · ties
re · spon'si · ble
re · spon'si · bly
re · spon'sive
rest (*repose;
  remainder*)
  (SEE unrest)
re · start'
re · state'
  re · stat'ed, re · stat'ing
re · state'ment
res'tau · rant
res'tau · ra · teur'
rest
rest'ful
rest'ful · ness
rest'ful · ly
rest' home'
res'ti · tu'tion
res'tive
res'tive · ly
rest'less
re · stock'
res'to · ra'tion
re · stor'a · tive
re · store'
  re · stored', re · stor'ing
re · stor'er
re · strain'
re · strain'a · ble

re · straint'
re · strict'
re · strict'ed
re · stric'tion
re · stric'tive
rest' room'
re · sult'
re · sult'ant
re · sume' (*start
  again*)
  re · sumed', re · sum'ing
  (SEE résumé)
re'su · me' or
  ré'su · mé'
  (*summary*)
  (SEE resume)
re · sump'tion
re · sur'gence
re · sur'gent
res'ur · rect'
res'ur · rec'tion
re · sus'ci · tate'
  re · sus'ci · tat'ed,
  re · sus'ci · tat'ing
re · sus'ci · ta'tion
re · sus'ci · ta'tor
re'tail
re'tail · er
re · tain'
re · tain'er
re · take' (*v*)
  re · took', re · tak'en,
  re · tak'ing
re'take' (*n.*)
re · tal'i · ate'
  re · tal'i · at'ed,
  re · tal'i · at'ing
re · tal'i · a'tion
re · tal'i · a · to'ry
re · tard'
re · tard'ate
  re · tard'at · ed,
  re · tard'at · ing
re'tar · da'tion
re · tard'ed
retch (*vomit*)
  (SEE wretch)
re · tell'
  re · told', re · tell'ing
re · ten'tion
re · ten'tive

re · ten'tive · ness
re · test' (*v.*)
re'test' (*n.*)
ret'i · cent
re · tic'u · lar
re · tic'u · late (*adj.*)
re · tic'u · late' (*v.*)
  re · tic'u · lat'ed,
  re · tic'u · lat'ing
ret'i · na
  pl. ret'i · nas or
  ret'i · nae'
ret'i · nal
ret'i · nue'
re · tire'
  re · tired', re · tir'ing
re · tired'
re · tire'ment
re · tir'ing
re · tool'
re · tort'
re · touch'
re · trace'
  re · traced', re · trac'ing
re · trace'a · ble
re · tract'
re · tract'a · ble
re · trac'tile
re · trac'tion
re · trac'tor
re · tread' (*v.*) (*put
  new tread on*)
  re · tread'ed,
  re · tread'ing
  (SEE re-tread)
re'tread' (*n.*) (*new
  tread*)
  (SEE re-tread)
re–tread' (*tread
  again*)
  re–trod', re–trod'den or
  re–trod', re–tread'ing
  (SEE retread)
re · treat'
re · trench'
re · trench'ment
re · tri'al
ret'ri · bu'tion
re · trib'u · tive
re · trib'u · to'ry
re · triev'a · ble

re·triev′al

re·trieve′
  re·trieved′, re·triev′ing

re·triev′er

ret′ro·ac′tive

ret′ro·fire′
  ret′ro·fired′,
  ret′ro·fir′ing

ret′ro·fit′
  ret′rofit′ted,
  ret′ro·fit′ting

ret′ro·grade′
  ret′ro·grad′ed,
  ret′ro·grad′ing

ret′ro·gress′

ret′ro·gres′sion

ret′ro·gres′sive

ret′ro·rock′et

ret′ro·spect′

ret′ro·spec′tion

ret′ro·spec′tive

re·turn′

re·turn′a·ble

re·turn′ee

re·type′
  re·typed′, re·typ′ing

re′u·ni·fi·ca′tion

re·u′ni·fy′
  re·u′ni·fied′,
  re·u′ni·fy′ing

re·un′ion

Ré·u′nion

re′u·nite′
  re′u·nit′ed, re′u·nit′ing

re·us′a·ble

re·use′
  re·used′, re·us′ing

rev
  revved, rev′ving

re·val′u·ate′
  re·val′u·at′ed,
  re·val′u·at′ing

re′val·u·a′tion

re·vamp′

re·veal′

rev′eil·le

rev′el
  rev′eled or rev′elled,
  rev′el·ing or
  rev′el·ling

rev′e·la′tion

rev′el·er

rev′el·ry
  pl. rev′el·ries

re·venge′
  re·venged′, re·veng′ing

re·venge′ful

re·veng′er

rev′e·nue′

rev′e·nu′er

rev′e·nue′ shar′ing

re·ver′ber·ate′
  re·ver′ber·at′ed,
  re·ver′ber·at′ing

re·ver′ber·a′tion

re·vere′
  re·vered′, re·ver′ing

Re·vere′

rev′er·ence
  rev′er·enced,
  rev′er·enc·ing

rev′er·end

rev′er·ent

rev′er·en′tial

rev′er·ie

re·ver′sal

re·verse′
  re·versed′, re·vers′ing

re·vers′ibil′i·ty

re·vers′i·ble

re·vers′i·bly

re·ver′sion

re·ver′sion·ar′y

re·vert′

re·vert′i·ble

re·view′
  (*reexamination*)
  (SEE revue)

re·view′er

re·vile′
  re·viled′, re·vil′ing

re·vil′er

re·vis′a·ble

re·vise′
  re·vised′, re·vis′ing

re·vis′er *or* re·vis′or

re·vi′sion

re·vi′sion·ism′

re·vi′sion·ist′

re·vis′it

re·vi′tal·i·za′tion

re·vi′tal·ize′
  re·vi′tal·ized′,
  re·vi′tal·iz′ing

re·viv′al

re·viv′al·ist

re·vive′
  re·vived′, re·viv′ing

re·viv′er

re·viv′i·fi·ca′tion

re·viv′i·fy′
  re·viv′i·fied′,
  re·viv′i·fy′ing

rev′o·ca·ble

rev′o·ca′tion

re·voke′
  re·voked′, re·vok′ing

re·vok′er

re·volt′

re·volt′ing

rev′o·lu′tion

rev′o·lu′tion·ar′y
  pl. rev′o·lu′tion·ar′ies

rev′o·lu′tion·ist

rev′o·lu′tion·ize′
  rev′o·lu′tion·ized′,
  rev′o·lu′tion·iz′ing

re·volv′a·ble

re·volve′
  re·volved′, re·volv′ing

re·volv′er

re·vue′
  (*entertainment*)
  (SEE review)

re·vul′sion

re·wake′
  re·waked′ or
  re·woke′, re·wak′ing

re·wak′en

re·ward′

re·wind′

re·wire′
  re·wired′, re·wir′ing

re·word′

re·work′

re·write′ (*v.*)
  re·wrote′, re·writ′ten,
  re·writ′ing

re′write′ (*n.*)

Rey′kja·vik′

re·zone′
  re·zoned′, re·zon′ing

rhap·sod′ic

rhap'so・dist

rhap'so・dize',
rhap'so・dized',
rhap'so・diz'ing

rhap'so・dy
pl. rhap'so・dies

rhe'a

rhe'ni・um

rhe'o・stat'

rhe'sus

rhet'o・ric

rhe・tor'i・cal

rhe・tor'i・cal・ly

rhet'o・ri'cian

rheum (discharge)
(SEE room)

rheu・mat'ic

rheu・mat'i・cal・ly

rheu'ma・tism'

rheu'ma・toid'

rheum'y (full of
rheum)
(SEE roomy)

Rh factor

Rhine

rhine'stone'

rhi・noc'er・os
pl. rhi・noc'er・os・es or
rhi・noc'er・os

rhi'no・plas'ty

rhi'zoid

rhi'some

rho (Greek letter)
pl. rhos
(SEE row and roe)

Rhode' Is'land

Rhodes

Rho・de'sia

Rho・di'sian

rho'di・um

rho'do・den'dron

rhom'boid

rhom'bus
pl. rhom'bus・es or
rhom'bi

Rhone

rhu'barb

rhyme (write verse)
rhymed, rhym'ing
(SEE rime)

rhythm

rhyth'mic

rhyth'mi・cal

rhyth'mi・cal・ly

ri'al

Ri・al'to

ri・a'ta

rib
ribbed, rib'bing

rib'ald

rib'ald・ry

rib'bon

ri'bo・fla'vin

ri'bo・nu・cle'ic

rice
riced, ric'ing

ric'er

rich

rich'ly

Rich'e・lieu'

rich'es

Rich'mond

Rich'ter scale'

rick

rick'ets

rick・ett'si・a
pl. ric・ett'si・ae' or
rick・ett'si・as

rick'et・y

rick'ey
pl. rick'eys

rick'rack'

rick'shaw'

ric'o・chet'
rec'o・cheted' or
ric'o・chetted',
ric'o・chet'ing or
ric'o・chet'ting

ri・cot'ta

rid
rid or rid'ded, rid'ding

rid'a・ble

rid'dance

rid'den

rid'dle
rid'dled, rid'dling

ride
rode, rid'den, rid'ing

rid'er

rid'er・ship

ridge
ridged, ridg'ing

ridge'pole'

rid'i・cule'
rid'i・culed',
rid'i・cul'ing

ri・dic'u・lous

riel

Ries'ling

rife

riff

rif'fle (shuffle)
rif'fled, rif'fling
(SEE rifle)

riff'raff'

ri'fle (weapon)
ri'fled, ri'fling
(SEE riffle)

ri'fle・man
pl. ri'fle・men

ri'fling

rift

rig
rigged, rig'ging

rig'a・to'ni

rig'ger (one that
rigs)
(SEE rigor)

rig'ging

right (correct)
(SEE rite and write)

right' an'gle

Right' Bank'

right'eous

right' field'

right'ful

right'ful・ly

right' hand'

right'-hand'

right'-hand'ed

right'ist

right'ly

right'-mind'ed

right' of way'

right'-to-life'

right' wing'

right'-wing'er

rig'id

ri・gid'i・ty

rig'ma・role'

rig'or (severity)
(SEE rigger)

rig'or mor'tis

rig'or·ous

rile
  riled, ril'ing

rill

rim
  rimmed, rim'ming

rime (*frost; write verse*)
  rimed, rim'ing
  (SEE rhyme)

Rim'sky-Kor'sa·kov'

rind

rin'der·pest'

ring (*circle*)
  ringed, ring'ing
  (SEE BELOW)

ring (*sound*)
  rang, rung, ring'ing
  (SEE ABOVE)

ring'er

ring'lead'er

ring'let

ring'mas'ter

ring'side'

ring'-tailed'

ring'worm'

rink

rink'y-dink'

rinse
  rinsed, rins'ing

Ri'o de Ja·nei'ro

Ri'o Grande'

ri'ot

ri'ot·er

ri'ot·ous

rip
  ripped, rip'ping

ri·par'i·an

rip' cord'

ripe
  rip'er, rip'est

rip'en

ripe'ness

rip'off'

ri·poste'
  ri·post'ed, ri·post'ing

rip'per

rip'ple
  rip'pled, rip'pling

rip'-roar'ing

rip'saw'

rip'tide'

rise
  rose, ris'en, ris'ing

ris'er

ris'i·bil'i·ty
  pl. ris'i·bil'i·ties

ris'i·ble

risk

risk'i·ness

risk'y
  risk'i·er, risk'i·est

ri·sot'to

ris·qué'

ri'tar·dan'do

rite (*ceremony*)
  (SEE right *and* write)

rit'u·al

rit'u·al·ism'

rit'u·al·is'tic

rit'u·al·is'ti·cal·ly

rit'u·al·ly

ritz

ritz'y
  ritz'i·er, ritz'i·est

ri'val
  ri'val·ed or ri'valled,
  ri'val·ing or
  ri'val·ling

ri'val·ry
  pl. ri'val·ries

rive
  rived, rived or riv'en,
  riv'ing

riv'er

riv'er·bank'

riv'er·bed'

riv'er·boat'

riv'er·side'

riv'et
  riv'et·ed, riv'et·ing

riv'et·er

Riv'i·er'a

riv'u·let

Ri·yadh'

ri·yal'

roach

road (*way*)
  (SEE *pt. of* ride *and* row)

road'a·bil'i·ty

road'bed'

road'block'

road' gang'

road'house'

road' map'

road'run'ner

road' show'

road'side'

road'ster

road' test'

Road' Town'

road'way'

road'work'

roam

roan

roar

roar'ing

roast

roast'er

rob
  robbed, rob'bing

rob'ber

rob'ber·y
  pl. rob'ber·ies

robe
  robed, rob'ing

Robes'pierre

rob'in

Rob'in Hood'

ro'bot

ro·bust'

Roch'es·ter

rock

rock'-bot'tom

rock'-bound'

Rock'e·fel'ler

rock'er

rock'et

rock'e·teer'

rock'et·ry

rock'fish'
  pl. rock'fish' or
  rock'fish'es

rock' gar'den

rock'ing chair'

rock'-'n'-roll'

rock'-ribbed'

rock'y
  rock'i·er, rock'i·est
Rock'y Moun'tains
ro·co'co
rod
  rod'ded, rod'ding
rode
ro'dent
ro'de·o'
  pl. ro'de·os'
Ro·din'
roe (fish eggs)
roe (deer)
  pl. roes or roe
roe'buck'
  pl. roe'bucks' or
  roe'buck'
Roent'gen
ro·ga'tion
rog'er
rogue
  rogued, ro'guing
ro'guer·y
  pl. ro'guer·ies
ro'guish
roil (stir up)
  (SEE royal)
roist'er
role (part)
  (SEE roll)
role' mod'el
roll (bread; move;
  list)
  (SEE role)
roll'a·way
roll'back'
roll' bar'
roll' call'
roll'er
roll'er coast'er
roll'er skate'
roll'er-skate' (v.)
  roll'er-skat'ed, roll'er-
  skat'ing
rol'lick
rol'lick·ing
roll'ing
roll'ing pin'
roll'mop'
roll'-on'
roll'o'ver

roll' top'
ro'ly-po'ly
  pl. ro'ly-po'lies
ro·maine'
Ro'man
ro·man' à clef'
  pl. ro·mans' a clef'
ro·mance' (n., v.)
  ro·manced',
  ro·manc'ing
ro'mance (adj.)
Ro'man·esque'
Ro·ma'ni·a
Ro·ma'ni·an
ro·man'tic
ro·man'ti·cal·ly
ro·man'ti·cism'
ro·man'ti·cist
re·man·ti·ci·za'tion
ro·man'ti·cize'
  ro·man'ti·cized',
  ro·man'ti·ciz'ing
Rom'a·ny
Rome
Ro'me·o'
  pl. Ro'me·os'
romp
rom'per
ron'do
  pl. ron'dos
rood (cross)
  (SEE rude)
roof
  pl. roofs
roof'er
roof'ing
roof'top'
rook
rook'er·y
  pl. rook'er·ies
rook'ie
room (space)
  (SEE rheum)
room'er (lodger)
  (SEE rumor)
room·ette'
room'ful'
  pl. room'fuls'
room'mate'
room'i·ness

room'y (spacious)
  room'i·er, room'i·est
  (SEE rheumy)
Roo'se·velt'
roost
roost'er
root (plant part;
  cheer; dig)
  (SEE route)
root' beer'
root' ca·nal'
root'er
root'less
root'let
root'stock'
rope
  roped, rop'ing
rop'y
  rop'i·er, rop'i·est
Roque'fort
Ror'schach
ro·sa'ceous
ro'sa·ry
  pl. ro'sa·ries
rose (flower; pt. of
  rise)
  rosed, ros'ing
  (SEE rosé)
ro·sé' (wine)
  (SEE rose)
ro'se·ate
rose'bud'
rose'bush'
  pl. rose'bush'es
rose'-col'ored
rose' fe'ver
rose'mar'y
  pl. rose'mar'ies
rose' of Shar'on
ro·se'o·la
Ro·set'ta stone'
ro·sette'
rose' wa'ter
rose'wood'
Rosh' Ha·sha'nah
Ro'si·cru'cian
ros'i·ly
ros'in
Ros·set'ti
Ros·si'ni

ros'ter
ros'trum
   pl. ros'tra *or* ros'trums
ros'y
   ros'i·er, ros'i·est
rot
   rot'ted, rot'ting
Ro·tar'i·an
ro'ta·ry
   pl. ro'ta·ries
ro'tat·a·ble
ro'tate
   ro'tat·ed, ro'tat·ing
ro·ta'tion
ro'ta·tor
   pl. ro'ta·tors *or*
   ro'ta·tor'es
ro'ta·to'ry
rote (*routine
   manner*)
   (SEE *pt. of* write)
ro'te·none'
ro'ti·fer
ro·tis'ser·ie
ro'to·gra·vure'
ro'tor
rot'ten
Rot'ter·dam'
ro·tund'
ro·tun'da
ro·tun'di·ty
   pl. ro·tun'di·ties
Rou·ault'
rou·é'
rouge
   rouged, roug'ing
rough (*uneven*)
   (SEE ruff)
rough'age
rough'-and-read'y
rough'-and-tum'ble
rough'cast'
   rough'cast',
   rough'cast'ing
rough'-dry'
   rough'-dried', rough'-
   dry'ing
rough'en
rough'-hew'
   rough'-hewed', rough'-
   hewed' *or* rough'-
   hewn', rough'-hew'ing

rough'house'
   rough'housed',
   rough'hous'ing
rough'neck'
rough'rid'er
Rough' Rid'ers
rough'shod'
rou·lade'
rou·lette'
   rou·let'ted, rou·let'ting
round
round'a·bout'
round'ed
roun'de·lay'
round'er
round'house'
round'ish
round'ly
round' rob'in
round'-shoul'dered
round' ta'ble
round'-the-clock'
round' trip'
round'up'
round'worm'
rouse
   roused, rous'ing
rous'er
rous'ing
Rous·seau'
roust'a·bout'
rout (*defeat; retreat;
   search*)
   (SEE route)
route (*way*)
   rout'ed, rout'ing
   (SEE rout)
rou·tine'
rove
   roved, rov'ing
rov'er
row (*line; quarrel;
   propel*)
   (SEE roe *and* rho)
row'boat'
row'di·ly
row'di·ness
row'dy
   pl. row'dies; (*adj.*)
   row'di·er, row'di·est

row'dy·ish
row'dy·ism'
row'el
   row'eled, row'el·ing
row' house'
roy'al (*regal*)
   (SEE roil)
roy'al·ist
roy'al·ly
roy'al·ty
   pl. roy'al·ties
rub
   rubbed, rub'bing
rub'ber
rub'ber band'
rub'ber ce·ment'
rub'ber·ize'
   rub'ber·ized',
   rub'ber·iz'ing
rub'ber·neck'
rub'ber plant'
rub'ber stamp'
rub'ber·y
rub'bing
rub'bish
rub'ble
rub'down'
rube
ru·bel'la
Ru'bens
ru·be'o·la
Ru'bi·con'
ru'bi·cund'
ru·bid'i·um
ru'ble
ru'bric
ru'by
   pl. ru'bies
ruck'sack'
ruck'us
rud·beck'i·a
rud'der
rud'di·ness
rud'dy
   rud'di·er, rud'di·est
rude (*impolite*)
   rud'er, rud'est
   (SEE rood)
rude'ly
rude'ness

ru'di·ment
ru'di·men'ta·ry
rue
  rued, ru'ing
rue'ful
rue'ful·ly
ruff (*collar*)
  (SEE rough)
ruf'fi·an
ruf'fle
  ruf'fled, ruf'fling
rug
Rug'by
rug'ged
rug'ger
Ruhr
ru'in (*destroy*)
  (SEE rune)
ru'in·a'tion
ru'in·ous
rule
  ruled, rul'ing
rul'er
rul'ing
rum
Ru·ma'ni·a
Ru·ma'ni·an
rum'ba
  pl. rum'bas; (v.)
  rum'baed, rum'ba·ing
rum'ble
  rum'bled, rum'bling
ru'mi·nant
ru'mi·nate'
  ru'mi·nat'ed,
  ru'mi·nat'ing
ru'mi·na'tion
rum'mage
  rum'maged,
  rum'mag·ing
rum'my
ru'mor (*gossip*)
  (SEE roomer)

ru'mor·mon'ger
rump
rum'ple
  rum'pled, rum'pling
rum'pus
  pl. rum'pus·es
rum'pus room'
rum'run'ner
run
  ran, run, run'ning
run'a·bout'
run'a·round'
run'a·way'
run'-down'
  (*delapidated*)
  (SEE rundown)
run'down'
  (*summary*)
  (SEE run-down)
rune (*alphabetic
  character*)
  (SEE ruin)
rung (*step; pt. of
  ring*)
  (SEE wrung)
run'-in'
run'ner
run'ner-up'
  pl. run'ners-up'
run'ning
run'ning board'
run'ning light'
run'ny
  run'ni·er, run'ni·est
run'off'
run'-of-the-mill'
runt
run'-through'
run'way'
ru·pee'

ru·pi'ah
  pl. ru·pi'ah or
  ru·pi'ahs
rup'ture
  rup'tured, rup'tur·ing
ru'ral
ruse
rush
rush' hour'
rusk
Rus'kin
rus'set
Rus'sia
Rus'sian
rust
rus'tic
rus'ti·cal·ly
rus'ti·cate'
  rus'ti·cat'ed,
  rus'ti·cat'ing
rus'ti·ca'tion
rust'i·ness
rus'tle
  rus'tled, rus'tling
rus'tler
rust'proof'
rust'y
  rust'i·er, rust'i·est
rut
  rut'ted, rut'ting
ru·ta·ba'ga
ru·the'ni·um
ruth'less
rut'ty
  rut'ti·er, rut'ti·est
Rwan'da
Rwan'dan
ry'a
rye (*grain*)
  (SEE wry)
rye' bread'
rye'-grass

S

Saar
Sab'bath
Sab·bat'i·cal
sa'ber
sa'ber-toothed'

sa'ble
  pl. sa'bles or sa'ble
sab'ot
sab'o·tage'
  sab'o·taged',
  sab'o·tag'ing

sab'o·teur'
sa'bra
sac (*pouch*)
  (SEE sack)
sac'cha·rin (n.)

sac'cha・rine (*adj.*)

sac'er・do'tal

sac'er・do'tal・ly

sa'chem

sa・chet' (*perfume*)
  (SEE sashay)

sack (*bag; plunder*)
  (SEE sac)

sack'cloth'

sack'ful
  pl. sack'fuls'

sack'ing

sac'ra・ment

sac'ra・men'tal

sac'ra・men'tal・ly

Sac'ra・men'to

sa'cred

sac'ri・fice'
  sac'ri・ficed',
  sac'ri・fic'ing

sac'ri・fi'cial

sac'ri・fi'cial・ly

sac'ri・lege

sac'ri・le'gious

sac'ris・tan

sac'ris・ty
  pl. sac'ris・ties

sac'ro・il'i・ac'

sac'ro・sanct'

sac'rum
  pl. sac'ra

sad
  sad'der, sad'dest

sad'den

sad'dle
  sad'dled, sad'dling

sad'dle・bag'

sad'dle・bow'

sad'dle・cloth'

sad'dle soap'

sad'dler

sad'dler・y
  pl. sad'dler・ies

Sad'du・ce'an

Sad'du・cee'

sad'ism

sad'ist

sa・dis'tic

sa・dis'ti・cal・ly

sad'o・mas'o・chism'

sa・fa'ri
  pl. sa・fa'ris

safe
  saf'er, saf'est

safe'-con'duct

safe'-de・pos'it

safe'guard'

safe'keep'ing

safe'ty
  pl. safe'ties

safe'ty belt'

safe'ty pin'

safe'ty valve'

saf'flow'er

saf'fron

sag
  sagged, sag'ging

sa'ga

sa・ga'cious

sa・gac'i・ty

sage
  sag'er, sag'est

sage'brush'

sage'ly

Sag'it・ta'ri・us

sa'go

Sa・ha'ra

sa'hib

said

sail (*canvas sheet*)
  (SEE sale)

sail'boat'

sail'cloth'

sail'er (*ship*)
  (SEE sailor)

sail'fish'
  pl. sail'fish' or
  sail'fish'es

sail'ing

sail'or (*boatman*)
  (SEE sailer)

saint

Saint' Ber・nard'

saint'ed

saint'hood

saint'li・ness

saint'ly
  saint'li・er, saint'li・est

Saint-Saens'

saith

sake (*purpose*)

sa'ke (*beverage*)

sa・laam'

sal'a・bil'i・ty

sal'a・ble

sa・la'cious

sal'ad

sal'ad dress'ing

sal'a・man'der

sa・la'mi

sal'a・ried

sale (*act of selling*)
  (SEE sail)

sale'a・ble

Sa'lem

sales'clerk'

sales'girl'

sales'la'dy
  pl. sales'la'dies

sales'man
  pl. sales'men

sales'man・ship'

sales'peo'ple

sales'per'son

sales'room'

sales' tax'

sales'wom'an
  pl. sales'wom'en

sal'i・cyl'ic

sa'li・ence

sa'li・en・cy

sa'li・ent

sa'line

sa・lin'i・ty

sa・li'va

Salis'bur'y

sal'i・var'y

sal'i・vate'
  sal'i・vat'ed, sal'i・vat'ing

sal'i・va'tion

Salk'

sal'low

sal'ly
  pl. sal'lies;
  (*v.*) sal'lied, sal'ly・ing

salm'on

sal'mo・nel'la
  pl. sal'mo・nel'lae

Sa·lo'me

sa·lon' (*room; shop*)
(SEE saloon)

sa·loon' (*barroom*)
(SEE salon)

sal'sa

salt

salt'–box'
  pl. salt'–box'es

salt'cel'lar

sal·tine'

Salt' Lake' Cit'y

salt'pe'ter

salt'shak'er

salt' stick'

salt' wa'ter

salt'wa'ter (*adj.*)

salt'i·ness

salt'y
  salt'i·er, salt'i·est

sa·lu'bri·ous

sal'u·tar'y

sal'u·ta'tion

sa·lu'ta·to'ri·an

sa·lu'ta·to'ry
  pl. sa·lu'ta·to'ries

sa·lute'

salv'a·ble

Sal'va·dor'

Sal'va·dor'an

sal'vage
  sal'vaged, sal'vag·ing

sal'vage·a·ble

sal·va'tion

salve
  salved, salv'ing

sal'ver

sal'vi·a

sal'vo
  pl. sal'vos or sal'voes

sam'a·ra

Sa·mar'i·a

Sa·mar'i·tan

sam'ba
  pl. sam'bas;
  (*v.*) sam'baed,
  sam'ba·ing

same

same'ness

sam'i·sen'

sam'iz·dat'

Sa·mo'a

Sa·mo'an

sam'o·var'

Sam'o·yed'

sam'pan

sam'ple
  sam'pled, sam'pling

sam'pler

sam'pling

Sam'son

sam'u·rai'
  pl. sam'u·rai'

San' An·to'ni·o'

Sa·n'a'

san'a·to'ri·um
  pl. san'a·to'ri·ums or
  san'a·to'ri·a

sanc'ti·fi·ca'tion

sanc'ti·fi'er

sanc'ti·fy'
  sanc'ti·fied',
  sanc'ti·fy'ing

sanc'ti·mo'ni·ous

sanc'ti·mo'ny

sanc'tion

sanc'ti·ty
  pl. sanc'ti·ties

sanc'tu·ar'y
  pl. sanc'tu·ar'ies

sanc'tum
  pl. sanc'tums or sanc'ta

sand

san'dal

san'dal·wood'

sand'bag'
  sand'bagged',
  sand'bag'ging

sand'bank'

sand' bar'

sand'blast'

sand'box'
  pl. sand'box'es

sand'er

sand'hog'

San' Di·e'go

sand'i·ness

San'di·nis'ta

sand'lot'

sand'man'
  pl. sand'men'

sand'pa'per

sand'pi'per

sand'stone'

sand'storm'

sand' trap'

sand'wich

sand'y
  sand'i·er, sand'i·est

sane
  san'er, san'est

sane'ly

sane'ness

San'for·ized'
  (*Trademark*)

San' Fran·cis'co

sang

sang–froid'

san·gri'a

san'gui·nar'y

san'guine

San·hed'rin

san'i·tar'i·um
  pl. san'i·tar'i·ums or
  san'i·tar'i·a

san'i·tar'i·ly

san'i·tar'y
  pl. san'i·tar'ies

san'i·ta'tion

san'i·ti·za'tion

san'i·tize'
  san'i·tized',
  san'i·tiz'ing

san'i·ty

San' Jo·sé' (*Costa
  Rica*)

San' Juan'

sank

San' Ma·ri'no

sans

San Sal'va·dor'

San'sei'
  pl. San'sei'

san'se·vi·e'ri·a

San'skrit

San'ta Claus'

San'ta Fe'

San'ti·a'go

San'to Do·min'go

São' Pau'lo

sap
  sapped, sap'ping

sa'pi·ence

sa'pi·ent

sap'ling

sap'phire

sap'py
  sap'pi·er, sap'pi·est

sap'ro·phyt'ic

sap'suck'er

sap'wood'

sar'a·band'

Sar'a·cen

sa·ran'

sar'casm

sar·cas'tic

sar·cas'ti·cal·ly

sar·co'ma
  pl. sar·co'mas or
  sar·co'ma·ta

sar·coph'a·gus
  pl. sar·coph'a·gi or
  sar·coph'a·gus·es

sar·dine'
  pl. sar·dine' or
  sar·dines'

Sar·din'i·a

Sar·din'i·an

sar·don'ic

sar·gas'so
  pl. sar·gas'sos

sa'ri
  pl. sa'ris

sa·rong'

sar'sa·pa·ril'la

sar·to'ri·al

Sar'tre

sash

sa·shay' (glide)
  (SEE sachet)

sa·shi'mi

Sas·katch'e·wan'

Sas'ka·toon'

sass

sas'sa·fras'

sas'sy

sas'si·er, sas'si·est

sat

Sa'tan

sa·tang'
  pl. sa·tang'

sa·tan'ic

sa·tan'i·cal

sa·tan'i·cal·ly

satch'el

sate
  sat'ed, sat'ing

sa·teen'

sat'el·lite'

sa'tia·ble

sa'ti·ate'
  sa'ti·at'ed, sa'ti·at'ing

sa'ti·a'tion

sa·ti'e·ty

sat'in

sat'in·wood'

sat'in·y

sat'ire

sa·tir'ic

sa·tir'i·cal

sa·tir'i·cal·ly

sat'i·rist

sat'i·ri·za'tion

sat'i·rize'
  sat'i·rized', sat'i·riz'ing

sat'is·fac'tion

sat'is·fac'to·ri·ly

sat'is·fac'to·ry

sat'is·fi'a·ble

sat'is·fy'
  sat'is·fied', sat'is·fy'ing

sa'trap

sat'u·rate'
  sat'u·rat'ed,
  sat'u·rat'ing

sat'u·ra'tion

Sat'ur·day

Sat'urn

sat'ur·nine'

sa'tyr

sa'ty·ri'a·sis

sauce
  sauced, sauc'ing

sauce'pan'

sau'cer

sau'ci·ly

sau'ci·ness

sau'cy
  sau'ci·er, sau'ci·est

Sa·u'di A·ra'bi·a

Sa·u'di A·ra'bi·an

sau'er·bra'ten

sauer'kraut'

Sauk
  pl. Sauks or Sauk

Saul

sau'na

saun'ter

sau'ri·an

sau'sage

sau·té'
  sau·téed', sau·té'ing

Sau·terne' or
  Sau·ternes'

sav'a·ble

sav'age

sav'age·ly

sav'age·ry
  pl. sav'age·ries

sa·van'na

Sa·van'nah

sa·vant'

save
  saved, sav'ing

save'a·ble

sav'er (one who
  saves)
  (SEE savor)

sav'ing

sav'ior

sa·voir-faire'

sa'vor (taste)
  (SEE saver)

sa'vor·y
  sa'vor·i·er,
  sa'vor·i·est

sa'vor·y
  sa'vor·i·er,
  sa'vor·i·est

sa'vor·y
  pl. sa'vor·ies

sav'vy
  sav'vied, sav'vy·ing

saw
  sawed, sawed or sawn,
  saw'ing

saw (pt. of see)

saw'dust'

sawed'-off'
saw'horse'
saw'mill'
saw'-toothed'
saw'yer
sax'horn'
sax'i•frage
Sax'on
sax'o•phone'
sax'o•phon'ist
say
 said, say'ing
say'a•ble
say'ing
sa'yo•na'ra
say'-so'
 pl. say'-sos'
scab
 scabbed, scab'bing
scab'bard
scab'by
 scab'bi•er, scab'bi•est
sca'bies
scab'rous
scads
scaf'fold
scaf'fold•ing
scal'a•ble
scal'age
scal'a•wag'
scald
scale
 scaled, scal'ing
scal'er
scal'lion
scal'lop
sca'lop•pi'ne or
 sca'lop•pi'ni
scalp
scal'pel
scalp'er
scal'i•ness
scal'y
 scal'i•er, scal'i•est
scam
scamp
scamp'er
scam'pi

scan
 scanned, scan'ning
scan'dal
scan'dal•ize'
 scan'dal•ized',
 scan'dal•iz'ing
scan'dal•mon'ger
scan'dal•ous
Scan'di•na'vi•a
Scan'di•na'vi•an
scan'ner
scan'sion
scant
scant'i•ly
scant'i•ness
scant'ling
scant'y
 scant'i•er, scant'i•est
scape'goat'
scape'grace'
scap'u•la
 pl. scap'u•lae or
 scap'u•las
scap'u•lar
scar
 scarred, scar'ring
scar'ab
scarce
 scarc'er, scarc'est
scarce'ly
scarce'ness
scar'ci•ty
 pl. scar'ci•ties
scare
 scared, scar'ing
scare'crow'
scarf
 pl. scarfs or scarves
scar'i•fi•ca'tion
scar'i•fy'
 scar'i•fied',
 scar'i•fy'ing
Scar•lat'ti
scar'let
scar'let fe'ver
scarp
scar'y
 scar'i•er, scar'i•est
scat
 scat'ted, scat'ting
scathe
 scathed, scath'ing

scat'o•log'i•cal
sca•tol'o•gy
scat'ter
scat'ter•brain'
scat'ter•brained'
scat'ter•ing
scat'ter•site'
scav'enge
 scav'enged, scav'eng•ing
scav'en•ger
sce•nar'i•o'
 pl. sce•nar'i•os'
sce•nar'ist
scene (view)
 (SEE seen)
scen'er•y
 pl. scen'er•ies
sce'nic
sce'ni•cal•ly
scent (odor)
 (SEE cent and sent)
scep'ter
scep'tic
scep'ti•cal
scep'ti•cal•ly
scep'ti•cism
sched'ule
 sched'uled, sched'ul•ing
sche'ma
 pl. sche'ma•ta
sche•mat'ic
sche•mat'i•cal•ly
sche'ma•tize'
 sche'ma•tized',
 sche'ma•tiz'ing
scheme
 schemed, schem'ing
schem'er
Sche•nec'ta•dy
scher'zo
 pl. scher'zos or scher'zi
schil'ling (Austrian
 money)
 (SEE shilling)
schism
schis•mat'ic
schist
schis'tose
schiz'oid
schiz'o•phre'ni•a

schiz'o•phren'ic

schle•miel'

schlepp

schlock

schmaltz

schmo
  pl. schmoes

schnapps

schnau'zer

schneck'en
  sing. schneck•e

schnit'zel

schnook

schnoz'zle

schol'ar

schol'ar•ly

schol'ar•ship'

scho•las'tic

scho•las'ti•cal•ly

scho•las'ti•cism'

school

school'bag'

school'book'

school'boy'

school' bus'

school'child'

school' day'

school'girl'

school'house'

school'ing

school'marm'

school'mas'ter

school'mate'

school'mis'tress

school'room'

school'teach'er

school'work'

school'yard'

schoon'er

schot'tische

Schu'bert

Schu'mann

schuss

schuss'boom'er

schwa

Schweit'zer

sci•at'ic

sci•at'i•ca

sci'ence

sci'en•tif'ic

sci'en•tif'i•cal•ly

sci'en•tist

sci'-fi'

scim'i•tar

scin•til'la

scin'til•late'
  scin'til•lat'ed,
  scin'til•lat'ing

scin'til•la'tion

sci'on

scis'sors

scle'ra

scle•ro'sis
  pl. scle•ro'ses

scle•rot'ic

scoff

scoff'er

scoff'law'

scold

sconce

scone

scoop

scoop'ful'
  pl. scoop'fuls'

scoot

scoot'er

scope

scor•bu'tic

scorch

scorch'er

score
  pl. scores or score;
  (*v.*) scored, scor'ing

score'board'

score'card'

score'keep'er

score'less

scor'er

scorn

scorn'ful

scorn'ful•ly

Scor'pi•o

scor'pi•on

Scor'pi•us

Scot

scotch

Scotch

Scotch'gard
  (*Trademark*)

scot'-free'

Scot'land

Scots

Scot'tish

scoun'drel

scoun'drel•ly

scour

scourge
  scourged, scourg'ing

scout

scout'craft'

scout'ing

scout'mas'ter

scow

scowl

scrab'ble
  scrab'bled, scrab'bling

scrag'gly
  scrag'gli•er, scrag'gli•est

scrag'gy
  scrag'gi•er, scrag'gi•est

scram
  scrammed, scram'ming

scram'ble
  scram'bled, scram'bling

scram'bler

scrap
  scrapped, scrap'ping

scrap'book'

scrape
  scraped, scrap'ing

scrap'er

scrap'per

scrap'ple

scrap'py
  scrap'pi•er, scrap'pi•est

scratch

scratch'i•ness

scratch' test'

scratch'y
  scratch'i•er,
  scratch'i•est

scrawl

scrawn'i•ness

scrawn'y
  scrawn'i•er,
  scrawn'i•est

scream

scream'er

screech

screech' owl'

screed

screen

screen'ing

screen'play'

screen' test'

screen'wri'ter

screw

screw'ball'

screw'driv'er

screw'y
screw'i • er, screw'i • est

scrib'ble
scrib'bled, scrib'bling

scrib'bler

scribe
scribed, scrib'ing

scrim

scrim'mage

scrim'mag • er

scrimp

scrimp'y
scrimp'i • er,
scrimp'i • est

scrim'shaw'

scrip (certificate)
(SEE script)

script (writing)
(SEE scrip)

scrip'tur • al

scrip'tur • al • ly

Scrip'ture

script'writ'er

scrive'ner

scrod

scrof'u • lous

scroll

scroll'work'

scro'tum
pl. scro'ta or scro'tums

scrounge
scrounged, scroung'ing

scroung'er

scrub
scrubbed, scrub'bing

scrub'by
scrub'bi • er,
scrub'bi • est

scrub' nurse'

scrub'wom'an
pl. scrub'wom'en

scruff

scruff'y
scruff'i • er, scruff'i • est

scrump'tious

scrunch

scru'ple
scru'pled, scru'pling

scru'pu • lous

scru'ti • nize'
pl. scru'ti • nized',
scru'ti • niz'ing

scru'ti • ny
pl. scru'ti • nies

scu'ba

scud
scud'ded, scud'ding

scuff

scuf'fle
scuf'fled, scuf'fling

scull (boat)
(SEE skull)

scul'ler • y
pl. scul'ler • ies

scul'lion

scul'pin
pl. scul'pin or scul'pins

sculpt

sculp'tor

sculp'tress

sculp'tur • al

sculp'tur • al • ly

sculp'ture
sculp'tured,
sculp'tur • ing

scum
scummed, scum'ming

scum'my
scum'mi • er,
scum'mi • est

scup'per

scup'per • nong

scurf

scur • ril'i • ty
pl. scur • ril'i • ties

scur'ril • ous

scur'ry
scur'ried, scur'ry • ing

scur'vy
scur'vi • er, scur'vi • est

scutch'eon

scut'tle
scut'tled, scut'tling

scut'tle • butt'

Scyl'la

scythe
scythed, scyth'ing

Scyth'i • a

Scyth'i • an

sea (ocean)
(SEE see)

sea' bass'

sea'bed'

Sea'bee'

sea' bird'

sea'board'

sea'borne'

sea'coast'

sea' dog'

sea'far'er

sea'far'ing

sea'food'

sea'go'ing

sea' gull'

sea' horse'

seal

seal'ant

seal'er

seal'ing wax'

seal'skin'

Seal'y • ham'

seam (juncture)
(SEE seem)

sea'man (sailor)
pl. sea'men
(SEE semen)

sea'man • ship'

seam'stress

seam'y
seam'i • er, seam'i • est

sé'ance

sea'plane'

sea'port'

sea' pow'er

sear (burn)
(SEE seer and sere)

search

search′light′
sea′scape′
sea′ shell′
sea′shore′
sea′side′
sea′son
sea′son·a·ble
sea′son·a·bly
sea′son·al
sea′son·ing
seat
seat′ belt′
seat′ing
sea′train′
sea′ trout′
Se·at′tle
sea′ wall′
sea′ward
sea′wards
sea′way′
sea′weed′
sea′wor′thy
se·ba′ceous
seb′or·rhe′a
se′cant
se·cede′
  se·ced′ed, se·ced′ing
se·ces′sion
se·ces′sion·ist
se·clude′
  se·clud′ed, se·clud′ing
se·clu′sion
Sec′o·nal′
  (*Trademark*)
sec′ond
sec′on·dar′i·ly
sec′ond·ar′y
  pl. sec′ond·ar′ies
sec′ond base′
sec′ond class′
sec′ond–class′ (*adj.*)
sec′ond–de·gree′
  (*adj.*)
sec′ond-guess′
sec′ond hand′
sec′ond-hand′ (*adj.*)
sec′ond·ly

sec′ond-rate′ (*adj.*)
se′cre·cy
  pl. se′cre·cies
se′cret
sec′re·tar′i·al
sec′re·tar′i·at
sec′re·tar′y
se·crete′
  se·cret′ed, se·cret′ing
se·cre′tion
se′cre·tive
se·cre′to·ry
  pl. se·cre′to·ries
sect
sec·tar′i·an
sec·tar′i·an·ism′
sec′tion
sec′tion·al
sec′tion·al·ism′
sec′tion·al·ly
sec′tor
sec′u·lar
sec′u·lar·ism′
sec′u·lar·i·za′tion
sec′u·lar·ize′
  sec′u·lar·ized′,
  sec′u·lar·iz′ing
se·cure′
  se·cured′, se·cur′ing
se·cure′ly
se·cu′ri·ty
  pl. se·cu′ri·ties
se·dan′
se·date′
  se·dat′ed, se·dat′ing
se·date′ly
se·da′tion
sed′a·tive
sed′en·tar′y
Se′der
sedge
sed′i·ment
sed′i·men′ta·ry
sed′i·men·ta′tion
se·di′tion
se·di′tious
se·duce′
  se·duced′, se·duc′ing
se·duc′er

se·duc′tion
se·duc′tive
se·duc′tress
se·du′li·ty
sed′u·lous
see (*perceive;*
  bishopric)
  saw, seen, see·ing
  (SEE sea)
see′a·ble
seed (*plant ovule*)
  (SEE cede)
seed′er
seed′i·ly
seed′i·ness
seed′ling
seed′time′
seed′y
  seed′i·er, seed′i·est
seek
seem (*appear*)
  (SEE seam)
seem′li·ness
seem′ly
  seem′li·er, seem′li·est
seen (*pt. of see*)
  (SEE scene)
seep
seep′age
se′er (*prophet*)
  (SEE sear *and* sere)
seer′suck′er
see′saw′
seethe
  seethed, seeth′ing
seg′ment (*n.*)
seg·ment′ (*v.*)
seg′men·tar′y
seg·men′tal
seg′men·ta′tion
se′go
  pl. se′gos
seg′re·gate′ (*v.*)
  seg′re·gat′ed,
  seg′re·gat′ing
seg′re·gate (*n.*)
seg′re·ga′tion
seg′re·ga′tion·ist
seg′re·ga′tor
seign′ior

sei · gno′ri · al

seine (*net*)
seined, sein′ing
(SEE sane)

seis′mic

seis′mi · cal · ly

seis′mo · graph′

seis′mog′ra · pher

seis′mo · graph′ic

seis · mog′ra · phy

seis · mol′o · gist

seis · mol′o · gy

seize
seized, seiz′ing

seiz′er or (*Law*)
seiz′or

sei′zure

sel′dom

se · lect′

se · lect · ee′

se · lec′tion

se · lec′tive

se · lec′tive · ly

se · lec · tiv′i · ty

se · lect′man
pl. se · lect′men

se · lec′tor

se · le′ni · um

self
pl. selves

self′-act′ing

self′-ad · dressed′

self′-ad · just′ing

self′-a · nal′y · sis

self′-ap · point′ed

self′-as · ser′tion

self′-as · sur′ance

self′-as · sured′

self′-cen′tered

self′-con′fi · dence

self′-con′fi · dent

self′-con′scious

self′-con · tained′

self′-con · trol′

self′-con · trolled′

self′-de · feat′ing

self′-de · fense′

self′-de · ni′al

self′-de · struct′

self′-de · struc′tive

self′-de · ter′mi · na′
tion

self′-dis · ci · pline

self′-ed′u · cat′ed

self′-ef · fac′ing

self′-em · ployed′

self′-es · teem′

self′-ev′i · dent

self′-ex · plan′a · to′ry

self′-ex · pres′sion

self′-gov′ern · ing

self′-gov′ern · ment

self′-im′age

self′-im · por′tance

self′-im · por′tant

self′-im · posed′

self′-im · prove′ment

self′-in · crim′i · nat′
ing

self′-in · dul′gence

self′-in · dul′gent

self′-in · flict′ed

self′-in′ter · est

self′-in′ter · est · ed

self′ish

self′-know′ledge

self′less

self′-made′

self′-per · pet′u · at′ing

self′-pit′y

self′-por′trait

self′-pos · sessed′

self′-pos · ses′sion

self′-pres′er · va′tion

self′-pro · claimed′

self′-pro · pelled′

self′-pro · tec′tion

self′-re · gard′

self′-reg′u · lat′ing

self′-re · li′ance

self′-re · li′ant

self′-re · spect′

self′-re · straint′

self′-right′eous

self′-rule′

self′-sac′ri · fice′

self′same′

self′-sat′is · fac′tion

self′-sat′is · fied′

self′-seal′ing

self′-seek′ing

self′-serv′ice

self′-start′er

self′-styled′

self′-suf · fi′cien · cy

self′-suf · fi′cient

self′-sup · port′

self′-sus · tain′ing

self′-taught′

self′-wind′ing

sell (*offer for
money*)
sold, sell′ing
(SEE cell)

sell′er (*one who
sells*)
(SEE cellar)

sell′out′

Selt′zer

sel′vage or sel′vedge

se · man′tic

se · man′tics

sem′a · phore′

sem′blance

se′men (*sperm*)
(SEE seaman)

se · mes′ter

sem′i · an′nu · al

sem′i · ar′id

sem′i · au′to · mat′ic

sem′i · cir′cle

sem′i · cir′cu · lar

sem′i · civ′i · li · za′tion

sem′i · co′lon

sem′i · con · duc′tor

sem′i · con′scious

sem′i · fi′nal

sem′i · for′mal

sem′i · month′ly
pl. sem′i · month′lies

sem′i · nal

sem′i · nal · ly

sem′i · nar′

sem'i·nar'i·an

sem'i·nar'y
  pl. sem'i·nar'ies

Sem'i·nole'
  pl. Sem'i·noles' or
  Sem'i·nole'

sem'i·of·fi'cial

se'mi·ot'ic

sem'i·per'me·a·ble

sem'i·pre'cious

sem'i·pri'vate

sem'i·pro·fes'sion·al

sem'i·pub'lic

sem'i·rig'id

sem'i·se'ri·ous

sem'i·soft'

sem'i·sol'id

sem'i·sweet'

Sem'ite

Sem·it'ic

sem'i·tone'

sem'i·trail'er

sem'i·trans·par'ent

sem'i·trop'i·cal

sem'i·vow'el

sem'i·week'ly
  pl. sem'i·week'lies

sem'i·year'ly

sem'o·li'na

sem'per fi·de'lis

sem'per pa·ra'tus

sen
  pl. sen

sen'ate

sen'a·tor

sen'a·to'ri·al

send
  sent, send'ing

send'-off'

Sen'e·ca
  pl. Sen'e·cas or
  Sen'e·ca

Sen'e·gal'

Sen'e·ga·lese'
  pl. Sen'e·ga·lese'

se·nes'cent

se'nile

se·nil'i·ty

sen'ior

sen·ior'i·ty
  pl. sen·ior'i·ties

sen'na

se·ñor'
  pl. se·ñors' or
  (*Sp.*) se·ño'res

se·ño'ra
  pl. se·ño'ras

se·ño·ri'ta
  pl. se·ño·ri'tas

sen·sa'tion

sen·sa'tion·al

sen·sa'tion·al·ism'

sen·sa'tion·al·ist

sen·sa'tion·al·ly

sense
  sensed, sens'ing

sense'less

sen·si·bil'i·ty
  pl. sen'si·bil'i·ties

sen'si·ble

sen'si·bly

sen'si·tive

sen'si·tiv'i·ty
  pl. sen'si·tiv'i·ties

sen'si·ti·za'tion

sen'si·tize'
  sen'si·tized',
  sen'si·tiz'ing

sen'sor

sen'so·ry

sen'su·al

sen'su·al·ist

sen'su·al'i·ty
  pl. sen'su·al'i·ties

sen'su·al·ly

sen'su·ous

sent

sen'tence
  sen'tenced, sen'tenc·ing

sen·ten'tious

sen'tience

sen'tient

sen'ti·ment

sen'ti·men'tal

sen'ti·men'tal·ism'

sen'ti·men·tal'i·ty
  pl. sen'ti·men·tal'i·ties

sen'ti·men'tal·ize'
  sen'ti·men'tal·ized',
  sen'ti·men'tal·iz'ing

sen'ti·men'tal·ly

sen'ti·nel

sen'try
  pl. sen'tries

Se'oul

se'pal

sep'a·ra·ble

sep'a·rate' (*v.*)
  sep'a·rat·ed,
  sep'a·rat'ing

sep'a·rate (*adj., n.*)

sep'a·rate·ly

sep'a·ra'tion

sep'a·ra'tist

sep'a·ra'tive

sep'a·ra'tor

Se'phar'dim
  sing. Se·phar·di'

se'pi·a

sep'sis

Sep·tem'ber

sep·tet' or sep·tette'

sep'tic

sep'ti·ce'mi·a

sep'tu·a·ge·nar'i·an

Sep'tu·a·ges'i·ma

Sep'tu·a·gint'

sep'tum
  pl. sep'ta

sep'ul·cher

se·pul'chral

se'quel

se'quence

se·quen'tial

se·quen'tial·ly

se·ques'ter

se·ques'trate
  se·ques'trat·ed,
  se·ques'trat·ing

se'ques·tra'tion

se'quin

se·quoi'a

se·ragl'io
  pl. se·ragl'ios

se·ra'pe

ser'aph
  pl. ser'aphs or
  ser'a·phim

se·raph'ic

Ser'bi·a

Ser'bi·an
Ser·bo-Cro·a'tian
sere (*withered*)
(SEE sear *and* seer)
ser'e·nade'
ser'e·nad'ed,
ser'e·nad'ing
ser'en·dip'i·ty
se·rene'
se·rene'ly
se·ren'i·ty
pl. se·ren'i·ties
serf (*slave*)
(SEE surf)
serf'dom
serge (*cloth*)
(SEE surge)
ser'geant
se'ri·al (*story in
installments*)
(SEE cereal)
se'ri·al·i·za'tion
se'ri·al·ize'
se'ri·al·ized',
se'ri·al·iz'ing
se'ri·al·ly
se'ries
pl. se'ries
ser'if
ser'i·graph'
se'ri·o·com'ic
se'ri·ous
ser'mon
ser'mon·ize'
ser'mon·ized',
ser'mon·iz'ing
se'rous
ser'pent
ser'pen·tine'
ser'rate
ser'rat·ed, ser'rat·ing
ser'rat·ed
ser·ra'tion
se'rum
pl. se'rums or se'ra
ser'vant
serve
served, serv'ing
serv'er
serv'ice
serv'iced, serv'ic·ing

serv'ice·a·bil'i·ty
serv'ice·a·ble
serv'ice·a·bly
serv'ice·man'
pl. serv'ice·men'
ser'vile
ser·vil'i·ty
serv'ing
ser'vi·tor
ser'vi·tude'
ser'vo·mech'an·ism'
ses'a·me
ses'qui·cen·ten'ni·al
ses'sion (*meeting*)
(SEE cession)
set
set, set'ting
se'ta
pl. se'tae
set'back'
set'off'
set'screw'
set·tee'
set'ter
set'ting
set'tle
set'tled, set'tling
set'tle·ment
set'tler
set'-to'
pl. set'-tos'
set'up'
sev'en
sev'en·fold'
sev'en·teen'
sev'en·teenth'
sev'enth
sev'en·ti·eth
sev'en·ty
pl. sev'en·ties
sev'er
sev'er·al
sev'er·al·ly
sev'er·ance
se·vere'
se·ver'er, se·ver'est
se·vere'ly
se·ver'i·ty
se·ver'i·ties

Se·ville'
Sè'vres
sew (*stitch*)
sewed, sewn or sewed,
sew'ing
(SEE so *and* sow)
sew'age
sew'er
sew'er·age
sew'ing
sew'ing ma·chine'
sewn
sex
sex'a·ge·nar'i·an
Sex'a·ges'i·ma
sex'i·ness
sex'ism
sex'ist
sex'less
sex'-linked'
sex·ol'o·gist
sex·ol'o·gy
sex'tant
sex·tet'
sex·ton
sex'u·al
sex'u·al'i·ty
sex'u·al·ly
sex'y
sex'i·er, sex'i·est
Sey·chelles'
sfor·zan'do
shab'bi·ly
shab'bi·ness
shab'by
shab'bi·er, shab'bi·est
shack
shack'le
shack'led, shack'ling
shad
pl. shad or shads
shade
shad'ed, shad'ing
shad'i·ness
shad'ow
shad'ow box'
shad'ow box'es
shad'ow·box'
shad'ow·y

shad'y
  shad'i・er, shad'i・est
shaft
shaft'ing
shag
  shagged, shag'ging
shag'bark'
shag'gi・ness
shag'gy
  shag'gi・er, shag'gi・est
Shah
shak'a・ble or
  shake'a・ble
shake
  shook, shak'en, shak'ing
shake'down'
shak'en
shak'er
Shake'speare
Shake・spear'e・an
shake'-up'
shak'i・ly
shak'i・ness
shak'ing
shak'o
  pl. shak'os or shak'oes
shak'y
  shak'i・er, shak'i・est
shale
shall
shal'lot
shal'low
sha・lom'
shalt
sham
  shammed, sham'ming
sha'man
sha'man・ism'
sham'ble
sham'ble
  sham'bled, sham'bling
shame
  shamed, sham'ing
shame'faced'
shame'ful
shame'ful・ly
shame'less
sham・poo'
  sham・pooed',
  sham・poo'ing

sham'rock
shang'hai
  shan'haied,
  shang'hai・ing
Shang・hai
Shan'gri-la'
shank
shan't
shan'tung'
shan'ty (hut)
  pl. shan'ties
  shan'tied, shan'ty・ing
  (SEE chantey)
shan'ty・town'
shap'a・ble
shape
  shaped, shap'ing
shape'less
shape'li・ness
shape'ly
  shape'li・er, shape'li・est
shape'-up'
shard
share
  shared, shar'ing
share'crop'per
share'hold'er
shar'er
shark
shark'skin'
sharp
sharp'en
sharp'er
sharp'-eyed'
sharp'ie
sharp'shoot'er
sharp'-tongued'
sharp'-wit'ted
shat'ter
shat'ter・proof'
shave
  shaved, shaved or
  shav'en, shav'ing
shav'er
Sha'vi・an
Shaw
shawl
Shaw・nee'
  pl. Shaw・nees' or
  Shaw・nee'

shay
she
sheaf
  pl. sheaves
shear (clip)
  sheared, sheared or
  shorn, shear'ing
  (SEE sheer)
shears
sheath
sheathe
  sheathed, sheath'ing
She'ba
she・bang'
shed'
  shed, shed'ding
she'd
shed'der
sheen
sheep
  pl. sheep
sheep'dog'
sheep'fold'
sheep'herd'er
sheep'ish
sheep'shank'
sheep'skin'
sheer (thin; steep;
  swerve)
  (SEE shear)
sheet
sheet'ing
sheik or sheikh (Arab
  chief)
  (SEE chic)
sheik'dom
shek'el
shelf
  pl. shelves
shelf' life'
shell
she'll
shel・lac'
  shel・lacked',
  shel・lack'ing
Shel'ley
shell'fire'
shell'fish'
  pl. shell'fish' or
  shell'fish'es
shell'proof'

shell' shock'

shel'ter

shelve
shelved, shelv'ing

Shen'an·do'ah

she·nan'i·gan

shep'herd

shep'herd·ess

Sher'a·ton

sher'bet

sher'iff

Sher'pa
pl. Sher'pas or Sher'pa

sher'ry
pl. sher'ries

Shet'land

shib'bo·leth

shield

shift

shift'i·ly

shift'i·ness

shift'less

shift'y
shift'i·er, shift'i·est

Shi·ite

shill

shil·le'lagh

shil'ling (British
money)
(SEE schilling)

shil'ly-shal'ly
(v.) shil'ly-shal'lied,
shil'ly-shal'ly·ing
pl. shil'ly-shal'lies

shi'ly

shim

shim'mer

shim'mer·y

shim'my
pl. shim'mies;
(v.) shim'mied,
shim'my·ing

shin
shinned, shin'ning

shin'bone'

shin'dig

shine
shone or shined,
shin'ing

shin'er

shin'gle
shin'gled, shin'gling

shin'gles

shin'i·ness

Shin'to

Shin'to·ism

Shin'to·ist

shin'y
shin'i·er, shin'i·est

ship
shipped, ship'ping

ship'board'

ship'build'er

ship'build'ing

ship' ca·nal'

ship'load'

ship'mate'

ship'ment

ship'pa·ble

ship'per

ship'ping

ship'ping room'

ship'shape'

ship'wreck'

ship'wright'

ship'yard'

shire

shirk

shirr

shirt

shirt'ing

shirt'-sleeve'

shirt'tail'

shirt'waist'

shish' ke·bab' or
shish' ke·bob'

Shi'va

shiv'er

shiv'er·y

shoal

shoat

shock

shock' ab·sorb'er

shock'er

shock'ing

shock'proof'

shock' troops'

shock' wave'

shod'di·ly

shod'di·ness

shod'dy
pl. shod'dies;
(adj.) shod'di·er,
shod'di·est

shoe
shod or shoed, shod or
shoed or shod'den,
shoe'ing

shoe'horn'

shoe'lace'

shoe'mak'er

shoe'mak'ing

sho'er

shoe'shine'

shoe'string'

shoe'tree'

sho'far
pl. sho'fars or
(Heb.) sho·froth'

sho'gun'

sho'gun'ate

sho'ji
pl. sho'ji or sho'jis

shone

shoo'-fly'
pl. shoo'-flies'

shoo'-in'

shook

shook up

shoot (fire gun)
shot, shoot'ing
(SEE chute)

shoot'out'

shop
shopped, shop'ping

shop'craft'

shop'girl'

shop'keep'er

shop'lift'er

shop'lift'ing

shoppe

shop'per

shop'talk'

shop'worn'

shor'an

shore
shored, shor'ing

shore' bird'

shore' leave'

shore'line'

shore' pa·trol'

shor'ing

short

short'age

short'bread'

short'cake'

short'-change'
short'-changed', short'-chang'ing

short' cir'cuit

short'com'ing

short'cut'

short'en

short'en·ing

short'fall'

short'hand'

short'-hand'ed

Short'horn'

short'-lived'

short'ly

short'-or'der (adj.)

short' shrift'

short'-sight'ed

short'stop'

short'-tem'pered

short'-term' (adj.)

short'-waist'ed

short'wave'
short'waved', short'wav'ing

short'-wind'ed

Sho·sho'ne
pl. Sho·sho'nes or Sho·sho'ne

Sho'sta·ko'vich

shot

shot'gun'
shot'gunned', shot'gun'ning

shot' put'

shot' put'ter

should

shoul'der

shoul'der blade'

should'n't

shout

shove
shoved, shov'ing

shov'el
shov'eled, shov'el·ing

shov'el·er

shov'el·ful'
pl. shov'el·fuls'

show
showed, shown or showed, show'ing

show' bill'

show'boat'

show'case'
show'cased', show'cas'ing

show'down'

show'er

show'er·y

show' girl'

show'i·ly

show'i·ness

show'man
pl. show'men

show'man·ship'

shown

show'-off'

show'piece'

show'place'

show'room'

show'y
show'i·er, show'i·est

shrank

shrap'nel

shred
shred'ded or shred, shred'ding

shred'der

shrew

shrewd

shrew'ish

shriek

shrift

shrike

shrill

shrill'ness

shril'ly

shrimp
pl. shrimps or shrimp

shrine

shrink
shrank or shrunk, shrunk or shrunk'en, shrink'ing

shrink'a·ble

shrink'age

shrink'-wrap'
shrink'-wrapped', shrink'-wrap'ping

shrive
shrove or shrived, shriv'en or shrived, shriv'ing

shriv'el
shriv'eled, shriv'el·ing

shroud

Shrove'tide'

shrub

shrub'ber·y
pl. shrub'ber·ies

shrub'by
shrub'bi·er, shrub'bi·est

shtick

shrug
shrugged, shrug'ging

shrunk

shuck

shud'der

shuf'fle
shuf'fled, shuf'fling

shuf'fle·board'

shun
shunned, shun'ning

shun'ner

shun'pike'

shunt

shush

shut
shut, shut'ting

shut'down'

shut'-eye'

shut'-in'

shut'off'

shut'out'

shut'ter

shut'ter·bug'

shut'tle
shut'tled, shut'tling

shut'tle·cock'

shy
(adj.) shy'er or shi'er, shy'est or shi'est; (v.) shied, shy'ing; pl. shies

Shy'lock

shy'ly

shy'ness

shy'ster

Si • am'

Si'a • mese'
 pl. Si'a • mese'

Si • be'ri • a

Si • be'ri • an

sib'i • lance

sib'i • lan • cy

sib'i • lant

sib'ling

sib'yl

sic (urge)
 sicked, sick'ing
 (SEE sick)

sic (Latin, so)
 (SEE sick)

Si • cil'ian

Sic'i • ly

sick (ill)
 (SEE sic)

sick' bay'

sick'bed'

sick' call'

sick'en

sick'ish

sick'le

sick'le cell'

sick'ly
 sick'li • er, sick'li • est

sick'li • ness

sick'room'

side
 sid'ed, sid'ing

side'arm'

side'board'

side'burns'

side'car'

sid'ed

side' ef • fect'

side'-glance'

side'kick'

side'light'

side'line'
 side'lined', side'lin'ing

side'long'

side'man'
 pl. side'men'

side'piece'

si • de're • al

side'sad'dle

side' show'

side'slip'
 side'slipped',
 side'slip'ping

side'split'ting

side'-step'
 side'-stepped',
 side'step'ping

side'stroke'

side'swipe'
 side'swiped',
 side'swip'ing

side'track'

side'walk'

side'ways'

side'-wheel'er

side'wind'er

side'wise'

sid'ing

si'dle
 si'dled, si'dling

siege

si • en'na

si • er'ra

Si • er'ra Le • o'ne

si • es'ta

sieve

sift

sift'er

sigh

sight (vision; view)
 (SEE cite and site)

sight' draft'

sight'less

sight'ly
 sight'li • er, sight'li • est

sight'-read'
 sight'-read', sight'-
 read'ing

sight'see'ing

sight'se'er

sig'ma

sig'moid

sign (indication)
 (SEE sine)

sig'nal
 sig'naled, sig'nal • ing

sig'nal • ize'
 sig'nal • ized',
 sig'nal • iz'ing

sig'nal • ly

sig'nal • man
 pl. sig'nal • men

sig'na • to'ry
 pl. sig'na • to'ries

sig'na • ture

sign'board'

sign'er

sig'net (seal)
 (SEE cygnet)

sig • nif'i • cance

sig • nif'i • cant

sig'ni • fi • ca'tion

sig'ni • fi'er

sig'ni • fy'
 sig'ni • fied',
 sig'ni • fy'ing

si • gnor'
 pl. si • gnors' or
 (It.) si • gno'ri

si • gno'ra
 pl. si • gno'ras or
 (It.) si • gno're

si • gno're
 pl. si • gno'ri

si'gno • ri'na
 pl. si'gno • ri'nas or
 (It.) si'gno • ri'ne

sign'post'

Sikh

Sikh'ism

si'lage

si • lence
 si'lenced, si'lenc • ing

si'lenc • er

si'lent

si • le'sia

sil'hou • ette'
 sil'hou • et'ted,
 sil'hou • et'ting

sil'i • ca

sil'i • cate

si • li'ceous

sil'i • con (chemical
 element)
 (SEE silicone)

sil'i • cone' (polymer)
 (SEE silicon)

sil'i • co'sis

silk

silk'en

silk'screen'

silk'worm'

silk'i • ness

silk'y
  silk'i • er, silk'i • est

sill

sil'li • ness

sil'ly
  sil'li • er, sil'li • est
  pl. sil'lies

si'lo
  pl. si'los
  si'loed, si'lo • ing

silt

Si • lu'ri • an

sil'ver

sil'ver • fish'
  pl. sil'ver • fish' or
  sil'ver • fish'es

sil'ver fox'

sil'ver plate'

sil'ver-plate'
  sil'ver-plat'ed, sil'ver-
  plat'ing

sil'ver • smith'

sil'ver-tongued'

sil'ver • ware'

sil'ver • y

sil'vi • cul'ture

sim'i • an

sim'i • lar

sim'i • lar'i • ty
  pl. sim'i • lar'i • ties

sim'i • le

si • mil'i • tude'

sim'mer

Si'mon • iz
  (*Trademark*)

si'mon • ize'
  si'mon • ized',
  si'mon • iz'ing

si'mon-pure'

sim • pa'ti • co'

sim'per

sim'ple
  sim'pler, sim'plest

sim'ple-mind'ed

sim'ple • ton

sim • plic'i • ty
  pl. sim • plic'i • ties

sim'pli • fi • ca'tion

sim'pli • fi'er

sim'pli • fy'
  sim'pli • fied',
  sim'pli • fy'ing

sim'ply

sim'u • late' (*v.*)
  sim'u • lat'ed,
  sim'u • lat'ing

sim'u • late (*adj.*)

sim'u • la'tion

sim'u • la'tor

si'mul • cast'
  si'mul • cast',
  si'mul • cast'ing

si'mul • ta • ne'i • ty

si'mul • ta'ne • ous

sin
  sinned, sin'ning

Si'nai

since

sin • cere'
  sin • cer'er, sin • cer'est

sin • cere'ly

sin • cer'i • ty
  pl. sin • cer'i • ties

sine (*angle ratio*)
  (SEE sign)

si'ne • cure'

si'ne di'e

si'ne qua non'

sin'ew

sin'ew • y

sin'ful

sin'ful • ly

sing

sing
  sang, sung, sing'ing

Sin'ga • pore'

singe
  singed, singe'ing

sing'er

sin'gle
  sin'gled, sin'gling

sin'gle-breast'ed

sin'gle file'

sin'gle-hand'ed

sin'gle-mind'ed

sin'gle • ness

sin'gle-space'
  sin'gle-spaced', sin'gle-
  spac'ing

sin'gle • ton

sin'gle-track'

sin'gly

sing'song'

sin'gu • lar

sin'gu • lar'i • ty
  pl. sin'gu • lar'i • ties

sin'is • ter

sin'is • tral

sink
  sank, sunk, sink'ing

sink'age

sink'er

sink'hole'

sin'ner

Sinn' Fein'

Si • nol'o • gist

Si • nol'o • gy

sin'u • os'i • ty
  pl. sin'u • os'i • ties

sin'u • ous

si'nus
  pl. si'nus • es

si'nus • i'tis

Sioux
  pl. Sioux

sip
  sipped, sip'ping

si'phon

sir

sire
  sired, sir'ing

si'ren

Sir'i • us

sir'loin

si • roc'co
  pl. si • roc'cos

sis

si'sal

sis'sy
  pl. sis'sies

sis'ter

sis'ter • hood'

sis'ter-in-law'
  pl. sis'ters-in-law'

sis'ter • ly

Sis'tine

sit
  sat, sit'ting

si • tar'

sit'com'

sit'–down'

site (*location*)
  sit'ed, sit'ing
  (SEE cite *and* sight)

sit'–in'

sit'ter

sit'ting

sit'u • ate' (*v.*)
  sit'u • at'ed, sit'u • at'ing

sit'u • ate (*adj.*)

sit'u • a'tion

sit'–up'

sitz' bath'

six
  pl. six'es

six'–pack'

six'pence
  pl. six'pence *or*
  six'penc • es

six'pen'ny

six'–shoot'er

six'teen'

six'teenth'

sixth

six'ti • eth

six'ty
  pl. six'ties

siz'a • ble *or* size'a • ble

siz'a • bly *or* size'a • bly

size
  sized, siz'ing

siz'ing

siz'zle
  siz'zled, siz'zling

skate
  skat'ed, skat'ing

skate'board'

skat'er

skeet

skein

skel'e • tal

skel'e • ton

skep'tic

skep'ti • cal

skep'ti • cal • ly

skep'ti • cism'

sketch

sketch'book'

sketch'i • ly

sketch'i • ness

sketch'y
  sketch'i • er, sketch'i • est

skew

skew'er

ski
  pl. skis *or* ski;
  (*v.*) skied, ski'ing

skid
  skid'ded, skid'ding

skid'proof'

skid' row'

ski'er

skiff

ski' jump'

ski' lift'

skill

skilled

skil'let

skill'ful

skill'ful • ly

skim
  skimmed, skim'ming

skim'mer

skimp

skimp'i • ly

skimp'i • ness

skimp'y
  skimp'i • er, skimp'i • est

skin
  skinned, skin'ning

skin'–deep'

skin'–dive'
  skin'–dived' *or* skin'–
  dove', skin'–div'ing

skin'flint'

skink

skin'ner

skin'ni • ness

skin'ny
  skin'ni • er, skin'ni • est

skin'ny–dip'
  skin'ny–dipped' *or*
  skin'ny–dipt', skin'ny–
  dip'ping

skin'ny–dip'per

skin'tight'

skip
  skipped, skip'ping

ski'plane'

ski' pole'

skip'per

skir'mish

skirt

skit

ski' tow'

skit'ter

skit'tish

skit'tles

skoal

sku'a

skul • dug'ger • y

skulk

skull (*head bone*)
  (SEE scull)

skull'cap'

skull • dug'ger • y

skunk
  pl. skunks *or* skunk

sky
  pl. skies; (*v.*) skied *or*
  skyed, sky'ing

sky'borne'

sky'cap'

sky'dive'
  sky'dived' *or* sky'dove',
  sky'dived', sky'div'ing

sky'div'er

Skye

sky'–high'

sky'jack'

Sky'lab'

sky'lark'

sky'light'

sky'line'

sky'rock'et

sky'scrap'er

sky'ward

sky'wards

sky'way'

sky'write'
  sky'wrote', sky'writ'ten,
  sky'writ'ing

slab
  slabbed, slab'bing

slack

slack'en

slack'er

slag
  slagged, slag'ging

slake
　slaked, slak'ing

sla'lom

slam
　slammed, slam'ming

slam'-bang'

slan'der

slan'der•ous

slang

slang'y
　slang'i•er, slang'i•est

slant

slant'wise'

slap
　slapped, slap'ping

slap'dash'

slap'hap'py
　slap'hap'pi•er,
　slap'hap'pi•est

slap'stick'

slash

slat
　slat'ted, slat'ting

slate
　slat'ed, slat'ing

slat'tern

slaugh'ter

slaugh'ter•house'

Slav

slave
　slaved, slav'ing

slav'er

slav'er•y

slave' ship'

Slav'ic

slav'ish

slaw

slay　(*kill*)
　slew, slain, slay'ing
　(SEE sleigh)

slay'er

slea'zi•ly

slea'zi•ness

slea'zy
　slea'zi•er, slea'zi•est

sled
　sled'ded, sled'ding

sledge

sledge' ham'mer

sleek

sleep
　slept, sleep'ing

sleep'er

sleep'-in'

sleep'ing bag'

sleep'ing pill'

sleep'less

sleep'walk'er

sleep'walk'ing

sleep'i•ly

sleep'i•ness

sleep'y
　sleep'i•er, sleep'i•est

sleep'y•head'

sleet

sleet'y
　sleet'i•er, sleet'i•est

sleeve

sleeve'less

sleigh　(*sled*)
　(SEE slay)

sleight　(*dexterity*)
　(SEE slight)

slen'der

slen'der•ize'
　slen'der•ized',
　slen'der•iz'ing

slept

sleuth

slew

slice
　sliced, slic'ing

slic'er

slick

slick'er

slide
　slid, slid or slid'den,
　slid'ing

slid'er

slide' rule'

slight　(*small; snub*)
　(SEE sleight)

slim
　(*adj.*) slim'mer,
　slim'mest;　(*v.*)
　slimmed, slim'ming

slim'ness

slime
　slimed, slim'ing

slim'y
　slim'i•er, slim'i•est

sling

sling'shot'

slink
　slunk, slink'ing

slink'y
　slink'i•er, slink'i•est

slip
　slipped, slip'ping

slip'case'

slip'cov'er

slip'knot'

slip'-on'

slip'o'ver

slip'page

slip'per

slip'per•i•ness

slip'per•y
　slip'per•i•er,
　slip'per•i•est

slip'shod'

slip'stream'

slip'-up'

slit
　slit, slit'ting

slith'er

slith'er•y

sliv'er

sliv'o•vitz

slob

slob'ber

sloe　(*fruit*)
　(SEE slow)

sloe'-eyed'

slog
　slogged, slog'ging

slo'gan

slo'gan•eer'

sloop

slop
　slopped, slop'ping

slope
　sloped, slop'ing

slop'pi•ly

slop'pi•ness

slop'py
　slop'pi•er, slop'pi•est

slosh

slot
　slot'ted, slot'ting

sloth

sloth′ful

sloth′ful・ness

slot′ ma・chine′

slouch

slouch′y
  slouch′i・er, slouch′i・est

slough

Slo′vak

slov′en

Slo・vene′

slov′en・li・ness

slov′en・ly
  slov′en・li・er,
  slov′en・li・est

slow (not fast)
  (SEE sloe)

slow′down′

slow′-mo′tion

slow′poke′

slow′-wit′ted

sludge

sludg′y
  sludg′i・er, sludg′i・est

slug
  slugged, slug′ging

slug′a・bed′

slug′fest′

slug′gard

slug′ger

slug′gish

sluice
  sluiced, sluic′ing

slum
  slummed, slum′ming

slum′ber

slum′ber・ous

slum′lord′

slump

slur
  slurred, slur′ring

slush

slush′ fund′

slush′i・ness

slush′y
  slush′i・er, slush′i・est

slut

slut′tish

sly
  sly′er or sli′er, sly′est
  or sli′est

sly′ly

smack

small

small′ arm′

small′ish

small′-mind′ed

small′pox′

small′-scale′

small′ talk′

small′-time′

smart

smart′ al′eck

smart′-al′eck・y

smart′en

smash

smash′ing

smash′-up′

smat′ter

smat′ter・ing

smear

smear′y
  smear′i・er, smear′i・est

smell

smell′y
  smell′i・er, smell′i・est

smelt

smelt′er

smid′gen or smid′gin
  or smid′geon

smi′lax

smile
  smiled, smil′ing

smil′er

smirch

smirk

smite
  smote, smit′ten or smit,
  smit′ing

smith

smith′er・eens′

smith′y
  pl. smith′ies

smock

smock′ing

smog

smog′gy
  smog′gi・er, smog′gi・est

smoke
  smoked, smok′ing

smoke′-filled′

smoke′house′

smoke′less

smok′er

smoke′ pot′

smoke′ screen′

smoke′stack′

smok′i・ness

smok′y
  smok′i・er, smok′i・est

smol′der

smooch

smooth

smooth′bore′

smooth′en

smooth′-shav′en

smooth′-spo′ken

smor′gas・bord′

smoth′er

smoul′der

smudge
  smudged, smudg′ing

smudge′ pot′

smudg′y
  smudg′i・er, smudg′i・est

smug
  smug′ger, smug′gest

smug′gle
  smug′gled, smug′gling

smug′gler

smut
  smut′ted, smut′ting

smutch

smut′ti・ly

smut′ti・ness

smut′ty
  smut′ti・er, smut′ti・est

snack

snaf′fle
  snaf′fled, snaf′fling

sna・fu′

snag
  snagged, snag′ging

snail

snake
  snaked, snak′ing

snake′bite′

snake′ dance′

snake′skin′

snak′y
  snak′i・er, snak′i・est

snap
  snapped, snap'ping

snap'-back'

snap' brim'

snap'drag'on

snap'per

snap'pish

snap'py
  snap'pi·er, snap'pi·est

snap'shot'

snare
  snared, snar'ing

snare' drum'

snarl

snatch

snaz'zy
  snaz'zi·er, snaz'zi·est

sneak

sneak'er

sneak'i·ly

sneak'i·ness

sneak' thief'

sneak'y
  sneak'i·er, sneak'i·est

sneer

sneeze
  sneezed, sneez'ing

snick'er

snide
  snid'er, snid'est

sniff

sniff'er

snif'fle
  snif'fled, snif'fling

snif'ter

snig'ger

snip
  snipped, snip'ping

snipe
  pl. snipes or snipe;
  (v.) sniped, snip'ing

snip'er

snip'pet

snip'py
  snip'pi·er, snip'pi·est

snitch

snitch'er

sniv'el
  sniv'eled, sniv'eling

snob

snob'ber·y
  pl. snob'ber·ies

snob'bish

snob'bism

snob'by
  snob'bi·er, snob'bi·est

snook'er

snoop

snoop'er

snoop'er·scope'

snoop'y
  snoop'i·er, snoop'i·est

snoot

snoot'y
  snoot'i·er, snoot'i·est

snooze
  snoozed, snooz'ing

snore
  snored, snor'ing

snor'er

snor'kel

snort

snort'er

snot

snout

snow

snow'ball'

snow'blind'

snow'bound'

snow'cap'

snow'capped'

snow'drift'

snow'drop'

snow'fall'

snow' fence'

snow'flake'

snow' job'

snow'man'
  pl. snow'men'

snow'mo·bile'

snow'plow'

snow'shed'

snow'shoe'
  snow'shoed',
  snow'shoe'ing

snow'storm'

snow'suit'

snow' tire'

snow'-white'

snub
  snubbed, snub'bing

snub'-nosed'

snuff

snuff'box'
  pl. snuff'box'es

snuff'er

snuf'fle
  snuf'fled, snuf'fling

snug
  (adj.) snug'ger,
  snug'gest; (v.) snugged,
  snug'ging

snug'ger·y
  pl. snug'ger·ies

snug'gle
  snug'gled, snug'gling

so   (thus)
  (SEE sew and sow)

soak

so'-and-so'
  pl. so'-and-sos'

soap

soap'box'
  pl. soap'box'es

soap' op'er·a

soap'stone'

soap'suds'

soap'y
  soap'i·er, soap'i·est

soar   (fly)
  (SEE sore)

sob
  sobbed, sob'bing

so'ber

so·bri'e·ty

so'bri·quet'

so'-called'

soc'cer

so·cia·bil'i·ty

so'cia·ble

so'cia·bly

so'cial

so'cial·ism'

so'cial·ist

so'cial·is'tic

so'cial·ite'

so'cial·i·za'tion

so'cial·ize'
  so'cial·ized',
  so'cial·iz'ing

so'cial•ly
so•ci'e•tal
so•ci'e•ty
  pl. so•ci'e•ties
so'ci•o•ec'o•nom'ic
so'ci•o•log'ic
so'ci•o•log'i•cal
so'ci•o•log'i•cal•ly
so'ci•ol'o•gist
so'ci•ol'o•gy
so'ci•om'e•try
so'ci•o•path'
sock
  pl. socks or sox
sock'et
sock'eye'
Soc'ra•tes'
So•crat'ic
sod
  sod'ded, sod'ding
so'da
so'da crack'er
so•dal'i•ty
  pl. so•dal'i•ties
so'da pop'
so'da wa'ter
sod'den
so'di•um
So'di•um Pen'to•thal
  (Trademark)
Sod'om
sod'o•mize
  sod'o•mized,
  sod'o•miz•ing
sod'om•y
so•ev'er
so'fa
So'fi•a
soft
soft'ball'
soft'-boiled'
soft'bound'
soft' coal'
soft'-core'
soft'-cov'er
soft' drink'
sof'ten
soft'-heart'ed

soft'ly
soft'-ped'al
soft' sell'
soft'-shell' or soft'-
  shelled'
soft'-shoe'
soft'-soap'
soft'-spo'ken
soft' spot'
soft'ware'
soft'wood'
soft'y
  pl. soft'ies
sog'gi•ness
sog'gy
  sog'gi•er, sog'gi•est
soi-di•sant'
soi•gné'
soil
soi•ree' or soi•rée
so'journ
sol (Peruvian
  money)
  (SEE soul and sole)
sol'ace
so'lar
so•lar'i•um
so'lar plex'us
sol'der
sol'dier
sole (single; fish;
  shoe part)
  soled, sol'ing
  (SEE soul and sol)
sol'e•cism'
sole'ly
sol'emn
so•lem'ni•ty
  pl. so•lem'ni•ties
sol'em•ni•za'tion
sol'em•nize'
  sol'em•nized',
  sol'em•niz'ing
so'le•noid'
so'le•noi'dal
so•lic'it
so•lic'i•ta'tion
so•lic'i•tor
so•lic'i•tous

so•lic'i•tude'
sol'id
sol'i•dar'i•ty
  pl. sol'i•dar'i•ties
so•lid'i•fi•ca'tion
so•lid'i•fy'
  so•lid'i•fied',
  so•lid'i•fy'ing
so•lid'i•ty
  pl. so•lid'i•ties
sol'id-state'
sol'i•dus
  pl. sol'i•di'
so•lil'o•quize'
  so•lil'o•quized',
  so•lil'o•quiz'ing
so•lil'o•quy
  pl. so•lil'o•quies
sol'ip•sism'
sol'ip•sist
sol'ip•sis'tic
sol'i•taire'
sol'i•tar'i•ness
sol'i•tar'y
  pl. sol'i•tar'ies
sol'i•tude'
so'lo
  pl. so'los or so'li
so'lo•ist
Sol'o•mon
So'lon
so' long'
sol'stice
sol'u•bil'i•ty
sol'u•ble
sol'u•bly
so•lu'tion
solv'a•bil'i•ty
solv'a•ble
solve
  solved, solv'ing
sol'ven•cy
sol'vent
so'ma
  pl. so'ma•ta or so'mas
So•ma'li
  pl. So•mal'is or
  So•ma'li
So•ma'li•a
So•ma'li•an

so·mat'ic
so'ma·tol'o·gy
som'ber or som'bre
som·bre'ro
  pl. som·bre'ros
some
some'bod'y
  pl. some'bod·ies
some'day'
some'how'
some'one'
some'place'
som'er·sault'
some'thing'
some'time'
some'times'
some'way'
some'what'
some'where'
som'me·lier'
som·nam'bu·late'
  som·nam'bu·lat'ed,
  som·nam'bu·lat'ing
som·nam'bu·la'tion
som·nam'bu·lism'
som·nam'bu·list
som'no·lence
som'no·lent
son (male child)
  (SEE sun)
so'nar
so·na'ta
son'a·ti'na
  pl. son'a·ti'nas or (It.)
  son'a·ti'ne
sonde
song
song'bird'
song'book'
song'fest'
song'ster
song'stress
song'writ'er
son'ic
son'ic boom'
son'-in-law'
  pl. sons'-in-law'
son'net
son'ny (male child)
  (SEE sunny)

so·nor'i·ty
  pl. so·nor'i·ties
so·no'rous
soon
soon'er
soot
sooth (truth)
  (SEE soothe)
soothe (calm)
  soothed, sooth'ing
  (SEE sooth)
sooth'er
sooth'ing·ly
sooth'say'er
soot'i·ness
soot'y
  soot'i·er, soot'i·est
sop
  sopped, sop·ping
soph'ism
soph'ist
so·phis'tic
so·phis'ti·cate (n.,
  adj.)
so·phis'ti·cate' (v.)
  so·phis'ti·cat'ed,
  so·phis'ti·cat'ing
so·phis'ti·cat'ed
so·phis'ti·ca'tion
soph'ist·ry
  pl. soph'ist·ries
Soph'o·cle'an
Soph'o·cles'
soph'o·more'
soph'o·mor'ic
sop'o·rif'ic
sop'o·rif'i·cal·ly
sop'ping
sop'py
  sop'pi·er, sop'pi·est
so·pran'o
  pl. so·pran'os
sor'cer·er
sor'cer·ess
sor'cer·y
  pl. sor'cer·ies
sor'did
sore (painful)
  sor'er, sor'est
  (SEE soar)
sore'head'

sore'ly
sor'ghum
so·ror'i·cide'
so·ror'i·ty
  pl. so·ror'i·ties
sor'rel
sor'row
sor'row·ful
sor'row·ful·ly
sor'ri·ness
sor'ry
  sor'ri·er, sor'ri·est
sort
sort'a·ble
sort·er
sor'tie
  sor'tied, sor'tie·ing
so'rus
  pl. so'ri
so'-so'
sot
sot'to vo'ce
sou·brette'
souf'fle
sough
sought
soul (spirit)
  (SEE sole and sol)
soul'ful
soul'ful·ly
soul'ful·ness
soul'less
soul' mate'
soul'-search'ing
sound
sound'box'
  pl. sound'box'es
sound' ef·fect'
sound'ing
sound'ing board'
sound'proof'
sound' track'
sound' wave'
soup
soup·çon'
soup'spoon'
soup'y
  soup'i·er, soup'i·est

sour

sour'ball'

source

sour' cream'

sour'dough'

sour'ish

sour' mash'

sour'puss'

sou'sa·phone'

souse
souse, sous'ing

south

South' Af'ri·ca

South' Af'ri·can

South' A·mer'i·ca

South' A·mer'i·can

south'bound'

South' Car·o·li'na

South' Car·o·lin'i·an

South' Da·ko'ta

South' Da·ko'tan

south'east'

south'east'er

south'east'er·ly

south'east'ern

south'east'ward

south'east'wards

south'er

south'er·ly

south'ern

south'ern·er

south'ern·most'

south'land

south'paw'

South' Pole'

south'ward

south'wards

south'west'

South'-West' Af'ri·ca

south'west'er

south'west'er·ly

south'west'ern

south'west'ward

south'west'wards

sou've·nir'

sov'er·eign

sov'er·eign·ty
pl. sov'er·eign·ties

so'vi·et'

So'vi·et' Un'ion

sow (*plant seed*)
sowed, sown or sowed,
sow·ing
(SEE **so** and **sew**)

sow'er

soy

soy'bean'

soy' sauce'

spa

space
spaced, spac'ing

space'craft'

spaced'-out'

space'less

space'man'
pl. space'men'

space'port'

space'ship'

space' shut'tle

space' sta'tion

space'suit'

space'-time'

spac'ing

spa'cious

Spackle'le
(*Trademark*)

spade
spad'ed, spad'ing

spade'ful
pl. spades'ful

spade'work'

spa'dix
pl. spa·di'ces

spa·ghet'ti

Spain

span
spanned, span'ning

span'drel

span'gle
span'gled, span'gling

Span'iard

span'iel

Span'ish

Span'ish-A·mer'i·can

spank

spank'er

spank'ing

span'ner

spar
sparred, spar'ring

spare
(*v.*) spared, spar'ing;
(*adj.*) spar'er, spar'est

spare'a·ble

spare'ly

spare'rib'

spar'ing

spar'ing·ly

spark

spar'kle
spar'kled, spar'kling

spar'kler

spark' plug'

spar'row

sparse
spars'er, spars'est

sparse'ly

Spar'ta

Spar'tan

spasm

spas·mod'ic

spas·mod'i·cal·ly

spas'tic

spas'ti·cal·ly

spat
spat'ted, spat'ting

spate

spathe

spa'tial

spa'tial·ly

spat'ter

spat'u·la

spav'in

spav'ined

spawn

spay
spayed, spay'ing

speak
spoke, spo'ken,
speak'ing

speak'-eas'y
pl. speak'-eas'ies

speak'er

spear

spear'fish'
pl. spear'fish' or
spear'fish'es

spear'head'

spear'mint'
spe'cial
spe'cial · ist
spe'cial · i · za'tion
spe'cial · ize'
  spe'cial · ized',
  spe'cial · iz'ing
spe'cial · ly
spe'cial · ty
  pl. spe'cial · ties
spe'cie (money)
  (SEE species)
spe'cies (kind)
  pl. spe'cies
  (SEE specie)
spec'i · fi'a · ble
spe · cif'ic
spe · cif'i · cal · ly
spec'i · fi · ca'tion
spec'i · fi'er
spec'i · fy'
  spec'i · fied',
  spec'i · fy'ing
spec'i · men
spe'cious
speck
speck'le
  speck'led, speck'ling
spec'ta · cle
spec'ta · cled
spec · tac'u · lar
spec'ta · tor
spec'ter
spec'tral
spec · trom'e · ter
spec'tro · scope'
spec'tro · scop'ic
spec'tro · scop'i · cal
spec'tro · scop'i · cal · ly
spec · tros'co · py
spec'trum
  pl. spec'tra or
  spec'trums
spec'u · late'
  spec'u · lat'ed,
  spec'u · lat'ing
spec'u · la'tion
spec'u · la'tive
spec'u · la'tive · ly
spec'u · la'tor

spec'u · lum
  pl. spec'u · la or
  spec'u · lums
sped
speech
speech'less
speech'mak'er
speech'mak'ing
speed
  sped or speed'ed,
  speed'ing
speed'boat'
speed · om'e · ter
speed'-read'ing
speed'ster
speed' trap'
speed'-up'
speed'way'
speed'well'
speed'i · ly
speed'i · ness
speed'y
  speed'i · er, speed'i · est
spe'le · ol'o · gist
spe'le · ol'o · gy
spell
  spelled or spelt,
  spell'ing
spell'bind'
  spell'bound',
  spell'bind'ing
spell'bind'er
spell'bound'
spell'er
spe · lun'ker
spend
  spent, spend'ing
spend'a · ble
spend'thrift'
Spen'ser
sperm
sper'ma · cet'i
sper · mat'ic
sper'ma · to · zo'on
  pl. sper'ma · to · zo'a
sperm' whale'
spew
sphag'num
sphere
  sphered, spher'ing

spher'i · cal
spher'i · cal · ly
sphe'roid
sphinc'ter
sphinx
  pl. sphinx'es or
  sphin'ges
sphyg'mo · ma · nom'
  e · ter
spice
  spiced, spic'ing
spic'i · ly
spic'i · ness
spick'-and-span'
spic'y
  spic'i · er, spic'i · est
spi'der
spi'der web'
spi'der · y
spiel
spiff'y
  spiff'i · er, spiff'i · est
spig'ot
spike
  spiked, spik'ing
spike'nard
spill
  spilled or spilt, spill'ing
spill'age
spill'o'ver
spill'way'
spin
  spun, spin'ning
spin'ach
spi'nal
spi'nal · ly
spin'dle
  spin'dled, spin'dling
spin'dling
spin'dly
  spin'dli · er, spin'dli · est
spin'drift'
spine
spine'less
spin'et
spin'na · ker
spin'ner
spin'ning wheel'
spin'-off'

Spi · no'za

spin'ster

spin'y
spin'i · er, spin'i · est

spi'ral
spi'raled, spi'ral · ing

spi'ral · ly

spire
spired, spir'ing

spir'it

spir'it · ed

spir'it · less

spir'it · u · al

spir'it · u · al · ism'

spir'it · u · al · ist

spir'it · u · al'i · ty
pl. spir'it · u · al'i · ties

spir'it · u · al · ly

spir'it · u · ous

spi'ro · chete'

spit (*expectorate*)
spit or spat, spit'ting

spit (*impale*)
spit'ted, spit'ting

spit'ball'

spite
spit'ed, spit'ing

spite'ful

spite'ful · ly

spit'fire'

spit'tle

spit · toon'

spitz

splash

splash'board'

splash'down'

splash'i · ness

splash'y
splash'i · er, splash'i · est

splat

splat'ter

splay

splay'foot'
pl. splay'feet'

spleen

spleen'ful

spleen'ful · ly

splen'did

splen'dor

sple · net'ic

splen'ic

splice
spliced, splic'ing

splic'er

splint

splin'ter

splin'ter · y

split
split, split'ting

split'–lev'el

split'–up'

splotch

splotch'y
splotch'i · er,
splotch'i · est

splurge
splurged, splurg'ing

splut'ter

Spode (*Trademark*)

spoil
spoiled or spoilt,
spoil'ing

spoil'age

spoil'er

spoil'sport'

Spo · kane'

spoke

spo'ken

spoke'shave'

spokes'man
pl. spokes'men

spokes'wom'an
pl. spokes'wom'en

spo'li · a'tion

sponge
sponged, spong'ing

sponge' cake'

spong'er

spon'gi · ness

spon'gy
spon'gi · er, spon'gi · est

spon'sor

spon·ta · ne'i · ty
pl. spon'ta · ne'i · ties

spon · ta'ne · ous

spoof

spook

spook'y
spook'i · er, spook'i · est

spool

spoon

spoon'bill'

spoon'er · ism'

spoon'–feed'
spoon'–fed', spoon'–
feed'ing

spoon'ful'
pl. spoon'fuls'

spoor (*track*)
(SEE spore)

spo · rad'ic

spo · rad'i · cal · ly

spore (*seed*)
spored, spor'ing
(SEE spoor)

spor'ran

sport

sport'ing

spor'tive

sports' car'

sports'cast'

sport' shirt'

sports' jack'et

sports'man
pl. sports'men

sports'wear'

sports'wom'an
pl. sports'wom'en

sports'writ'er

sport'i · ly

sport'i · ness

sport'y
sport'i · er, sport'i · est

spot
spot'ted, spot'ting

spot' check'

spot'less

spot'light'

spot'ter

spot'ti · ly

spot'ti · ness

spot'ty
spot'ti · er, spot'ti · est

spous'al

spouse
spoused, spous'ing

spout

sprain

sprang

sprat

sprawl

spray

spray'er

spray' gun'

spread
spread, spread'ing

spread'–ea'gle
spread'–ea'gled, spread'–ea'gling

spread'er

spree

sprig
sprigged, sprig'ging

spright'li · ness

spright'ly
spright'li · er, spright'li · est

spring
sprang or sprung, sprung, spring'ing

spring'board'

spring'bok'
pl. spring'boks' or spring'bok'

spring'–clean'ing

spring' fe'ver

Spring'field'

spring'i · ness

spring'time'

spring'y
spring'i · er, spring'i · est

sprin'kle
sprin'kled, sprin'kling

sprink'ler

sprint

sprint'er

sprite

sprock'et

sprout

spruce
(v.) spruced, spruc'ing; (adj.) spruc'er, spruc'est

sprung

spry
spry'er or spri'er, spry'est or spri'est

spud
spud'ded, spud'ding

spume
spumed, spum'ing

spu · mo'ne or
spu · mo'ni

spun

spunk

spunk'i · ly

spunk'i · ness

spunk'y
spunk'i · er, spunk'i · est

spur
spurred, spur'ring

spurge

spu'ri · ous

spurn

spurt

sput'nik

sput'ter

spu'tum
pl. spu'ta

spy
pl. spies; (v.) spied, spy'ing

spy'glass'

squab
pl. squabs or squab

squab'ble
squab'bled, squab'bling

squad'ron

squal'id

squall

squal'ly
squal'li · er, squal'li · est

squal'or

squan'der

square
(v.) squared, squar'ing; (adj.) squar'er, squar'est

square' dance'

square'–dance'
square'–danced', square'–danc'ing

square' deal'

square'ly

square'–rigged'

square' shoot'er

squash

squash'y
squash'i · er, squash'i · est

squat
squat'ted or squat, squat'ting

squat'ter

squaw

squawk

squawk' box'

squeak

squeak'y
squeak'i · er, squeak'i · est

squeal

squeal'er

squeam'ish

squee'gee
squee'geed, squee'gee · ing

squeeze
squeezed, squeez'ing

squelch

squib
squibbed, squib'bing

squid
pl. squid or squids

squig'gle
squig'gled, squig'gling

squint

squint'–eyed'

squint'y

squire
squired, squir'ing

squirm

squirm'y
squirm'i · er, squirm'i · est

squir'rel
pl. squir'rels or squir'rel; (v.) squir'reled, squir'rel · ing

squirt

squish'y
squish'i · er, squish'i · est

Sri Lan'ka

stab
stabbed, stab'bing

sta'bile

sta · bil'i · ty
pl. sta · bil'i · ties

sta · bi · li · za'tion

sta'bi · lize
sta'bi · lized', sta'bi · liz'ing

sta'bi · liz'er

sta'ble
sta'bled, sta'bling

sta'ble · mate'

stac · ca'to
pl. stac · ca'tos or stac · ca'ti

stack

sta'di·um
 pl. sta'di·ums or
 sta'di·a

staff
 pl. staves or (exc.
 assistants) staffs

stag
 stagged, stag'ging

stage
 staged, stag'ing

stage'coach'

stage'craft'

stage' door'

stage' fright'

stage'hand'

stage'-man'age
 stage'-man'aged, stage'-
 man'ag·ing

stage' man'ag·er

stage'-struck'

stag·fla'tion

stag'ger

stag'hound'

stag'ing

stag'nan·cy

stag'nant

stag'nate
 stag'nat·ed,
 stag'nat·ing

stag·na'tion

stag'y
 stag'i·er, stag'i·est

staid

stain

stain'a·ble

stain'less

stair (step)
 (SEE stare)

stair'case'

stair'way'

stair'well'

stake (post; bet;
 prize)
 staked, stak'ing
 (SEE steak)

stake'hold'er

stake'out'

sta·lac'tite

sta'lag

sta·lag'mite

stale
 stal'er, stal'ing

stale'mate'

Sta'lin

Sta'lin·ism'

Sta'lin·ist

stalk

stalk'ing-horse'

stall

stal'lion

stal'wart

sta'men
 pl. sta'mens or
 stam'i·na

stam'i·na

stam'mer

stamp

stam·pede'
 stam·ped'ed,
 stam·ped'ing

stance

stanch (stop)
 (SEE staunch)

stan'chion

stand
 stood, stand'ing

stand'ard

stand'ard-bear'er

stand'ard·i·za'tion

stand'ard·ize
 stand'ard·ized',
 stand'ard·iz'ing

stand'-by'
 pl. stand'-bys'

stand·ee'

stand'-in'

stand'ing

stand'-off'

stand'-off'ish

stand'out'

stand'pipe'

stand'point'

stand'still'

stand'-up'

stan'nic

stan'nous

stan'za

sta'pes
 pl. sta'pes or sta·pe'des

staph'y·lo·coc'cus

sta'ple

sta'pled, sta'pling

sta'pler

star
 starred, star'ring

star'board

starch

starch'y
 starch'i·er, starch'i·est

star'-crossed'

star'dom

star' dust'

stare (gaze)
 stared, star'ing
 (SEE stair)

star'fish'
 pl. star'fish' or
 star'fish'es

star'gaze'
 star'gazed', star'gaz'ing

star'gaz'er

stark'ly

stark'-nak'ed

star'less

star'let

star'light'

star'like'

star'ling

star'lit

star'ry
 star'ri·er, star'ri·est

star'ry-eyed'

Star'-Span'gled
 Ban'ner

star'-stud'ded

start

start'er

star'tle
 star'tled, star'tling

start'-up'

star·va'tion

starve
 starved, starv'ing

starve'ling

stash

state
 stat'ed, stat'ing

state'craft'

state'hood'

state'house'

state′less

state′li · ness

state′ly
  state′li · er, state′li · est

state′ment

state′room′

state′side′

states′man
  pl. states′men

state′wide′

stat′ic

stat′ics

sta′tion

sta′tion · ar′y (not
  moving)
  pl. sta′tion · ar′ies
  (SEE stationery)

sta′tion · er

sta′tion · er′y (paper)
  (SEE stationary)

sta′tion house′

sta′tion · mas′ter

sta′tion–to–sta′tion

sta′tion wag′on

stat′ism

sta · tis′tic

sta · tis′ti · cal

sta · tis′ti · cal · ly

stat′is · ti′cian

sta · tis′tics

sta′tor

stat′u · ar′y
  pl. stat′u · ar′ies

stat′ue

stat′u · esque′

stat′u · ette′

stat′ure

sta′tus

sta′tus quo′

stat′ute

stat′u · to′ry

staunch (steadfast)
  (SEE stanch)

stave
  stave or stove, stav′ing

stay
  stayed or staid, stay′ing

stay′–at–home′

stay′sail′

St.′ Ber · nard′

St.′ Cath′a · rines

stead

stead′fast′

stead′i · ly

stead′i · ness

stead′y
  stead′i · er, stead′i · est

steak (meat)
  (SEE stake)

steak′house′

steak′ knife′

steal (rob)
  stole, sto′len, steal′ing
  (SEE steel)

stealth

stealth′i · ly

stealth′i · ness

stealth′y
  stealth′i · er,
  stealth′i · est

steam

steam′boat′

steam′er

steam′i · ness

steam′roll′er

steam′ship′

steam′ shov′el

steam′y
  steam′i · er, steam′i · est

steed

steel (metal)
  (SEE steal)

steel′head′
  pl. steel′heads′ or
  steel′head′

steel′ mill′

steel′ wool′

steel′work′

steel′work′er

steel′y
  steel′i · er, steel′i · est

steel′yard′

steen′bok′
  pl. steen′boks′ or
  steen′bok′

steep

steep′en

stee′ple

stee′ple · chase′

stee′ple · jack′

steer

steer′age

steers′man
  pl. steers′men

steg′o · saur′

stein

stel′lar

stem
  stemmed, stem′ming

stem′ware′

stench

sten′cil
  sten′ciled or sten′cilled,
  sten′cil · ing or
  sten′cil · ling

Sten · dhal′

sten′o

ste · nog′ra · pher

sten′o · graph′ic

sten′o · graph′i · cal

ste · nog′ra · phy

sten′o · type′

sten′o · typ′ist

sten′o · typ′y

sten · to′ri · an

step (walk)
  stepped, step′ping
  (SEE steppe)

step′broth′er

step′child′
  pl. step′child′ren

step′daugh′ter

step′–down′

step′fa′ther

step′–in′

step′lad′der

step′moth′er

step′par′ent

steppe (vast plain)
  (SEE step)

step′per

step′ping stone′

step′sis′ter

step′son′

step′–up′

stere

ster′e · o′
  pl. ster′e · os′

ster′e · o · phon′ic

ster′e · o · scope′

ster'e·o·scop'ic

ster·os'co·py

ster'e·o·type'
  ster'e·o·typed',
  ster'e·o·typ'ing

ster'e·o·typ'er

ster'e·o·typ'i·cal

ster'ile

ste·ril'i·ty

ster'i·li·za'tion

ster'i·lize'
  ster'i·lized',
  ster'i·liz'ing

ster'i·liz'er

ster'ling

stern

stern'ness

ster'num
  pl. ster'na or ster'nums

stern'wheel'er

ster'oid

ster'ol

stet
  stet'ted, stet'ting

steth'o·scope'

steth'o·scop'ic

Stet'son (Trademark)

ste've·dore'
  ste've·dored',
  ste've·dor'ing

stew

stew'ard

stew'ard·ess

St.' Geor'ge's

stick
  stuck, stick'ing

stick'ball'

stick'er

stick'-in-the-mud'

stick'ler

stick'pin'

stick' shift'

stick'-to'-it-ive·ness

stick'up'

stick'i·ness

stick'y
  stick'i·er, stick'i·est

stiff

stiff'en

stiff'-necked'

sti'fle
  sti'fled, sti'fling

stig'ma
  pl. stig'ma·ta or
  stig'mas

stig·mat'ic

stig'ma·tism'

stig'ma·ti·za'tion

stig'ma·tize'
  stig'ma·tized',
  stig'ma·tiz'ing

stil·bes'trol

stile (steps)
  (SEE style)

sti·let'to
  pl. sti·let'tos or
  sti·let'toes; (v.)
  sti·let'toed,
  sti·let'to·ing

still

still'birth'

still'born'

still' life'
  pl. still' lifes'

still'-life' (adj.)

stilt

stilt'ed

Stil'ton

stim'u·lant

stim'u·late'
  stim'u·lat'ed,
  stim'u·lat'ing

stim'u·la'tion

stim'u·la'tive

stim'u·la'tor

stim'u·lus
  pl. stim'u·li'

sting
  stung, sting'ing

sting'er

stin'gi·ly

stin'gi·ness

sting'ray'

stin'gy
  stin'gi·er, stin'gi·est

stink
  stank or stunk, stunk,
  stink'ing

stink'weed'

stint

sti'pend

stip'ple
  stip'pled, stip'pling

stip'u·late'
  stip'u·lat'ed,
  stip'u·lat'ing

stip'u·la'tion

stip'u·la'tor

stir
  stirred, stir'ring

stir'-fry'
  stir'-fried', stir'-fry'ing

stir'rer

stir'rup

stitch

stitch'er

St.' Johns'

St.' Lou'is

stoat

sto·chas'tic

stock

stock·ade'
  stock·ad'ed,
  stock·ad'ing

stock'brok'er

stock' car'

stock'hold'er

Stock'holm

stock'ing

stock'man
  pl. stock'men

stock' mar'ket

stock'pile'
  stock'piled', stock'pil'ing

stock'room'

stock'-still'

stock'y
  stock'i·er, stock'i·est

stock'yard'

stodg'i·ly

stodg'i·ness

stodg'y
  stodg'i·er, stodg'i·est

sto'gy
  pl. sto'gies

Sto'ic

sto'i·cal

sto'i·cal·ly

Sto'i·cism'

stoke
  stoked, stok'ing

stoke'hole'

stok'er

stole

sto'len

stol'id

sto·lid'i·ty

stol'len

stom'ach

stom'ach·ache'

stomp

stone
  stoned, ston'ing

Stone' Age'

stone'-broke'

stone'cut'ter

stone'-deaf'

Stone'henge'

stone'ma'son

stone'wall'

stone'ware'

stone'work'

ston'i·ly

ston'i·ness

ston'y
  ston'i·er, ston'i·est

stood

stooge
  stooged, stoog'ing

stool

stoop (bend;
  stairway)
  (SEE stoup)

stop
  stopped, stop'ping

stop'gap'

stop'light'

stop'-off'

stop'o'ver

stop'page

stop'per

stop'watch'
  pl. stop'watch'es

stor'a·ble

stor'age

store
  stored, stor'ing

store'-bought'

store'front'

store'house'

store'keep'er

store'room'

store'wide'

sto'ried

stork
  pl. storks or stork

storm'bound'

storm' cel'lar

storm' door'

storm'i·ly

storm'i·ness

storm' sig'nal

storm' win'dow

storm'y
  storm'i·er, storm'i·est

storm'y pet'rel

sto'ry
  pl. sto'ries; (v.)
  sto'ried, sto'ry·ing

sto'ry·book'

sto'ry·tell'er

stoup (basin)
  (SEE stoop)

stout

stout'-heart'ed

stove

stove'pipe'

stow

stow'age

stow'a·way'

St.' Paul'

stra·bis'mus

strad'dle
  strad'dled, strad'dling

Strad'i·var'i·us

strafe
  strafed, straf'ing

strag'gle
  strag'gled, strag'gling

strag'gler

strag'gly
  strag'gli·er, strag'gli·est

straight (direct)
  (SEE strait)

straight' an'gle

straight'a·way'

straight'edge'

straight'en (make
  straight)
  (SEE straiten)

straight'-faced'

straight'for'ward

straight' shoot'er

strain

strained

strain'er

strait (waterway;
  distress)
  (SEE straight)

strait'en (restrict)
  (SEE straighten)

strait' jack'et

strait'-laced'

strand

strange
  strang'er, strang'est

stran'ger (newcomer)

stran'gle
  stran'gled, stran'gling

stran'gle hold'

stran'gler

stran'gu·late'
  stran'gu·lat'ed,
  stran'gu·lat'ing

stran'gu·la'tion

strap
  strapped, strap'ping

strap'hang'er

strap'less

strap'ping

strat'a·gem

stra·te'gic

stra·te'gi·cal·ly

strat'e·gist

strat'e·gy
  pl. strat'e·gies

strat'i·fi·ca'tion

strat'i·fy'
  strat'i·fied',
  strat'i·fy'ing

stra·tig'ra·phy

stra'to·cu'mu·lus
  pl. stra'to·cu'mu·lus

strat'o·sphere'

strat'o·spher'ic

stra'tum
  pl. stra'ta or stra'tums

stra'tus
  pl. stra'tus

Stra·vin'sky

straw

straw'ber'ry
  pl. straw'ber'ries

straw' boss'

straw'hat'

stray

streak

streak'i • ness

streak'y
  streak'i • er, streak'i • est

stream

steam'er

stream'line'
  stream'lined',
  stream'lin'ing

stream'lined'

street

steet'car'

street'light'

street'walk'er

strength

strength'en

stren'u • ous

strep

strep'to • coc'cus
  pl. strep'to • coc'ci

strep'to • my'cin

stress

stretch

stretch'a • ble

stretch'er

stretch'er–bear'er

strew
  strew, strewn *or*
  strewed, strew'ing

stri'a
  pl. stri'ae

stri'ate
  stri'at • ed, stri'at • ing

stri • a'tion

strick'en

strict

stric'ture

stride
  strode, strid'den,
  strid'ing

stri'dence

stri'den • cy

stri'dent

strife

strike
  struck, struck *or*
  stricken, strik'ing

strike'bound'

strike'break'er

strike'–out'

strike'o'ver

strik'er

strik'ing

string
  strung, string'ing

strin'gen • cy
  pl. strin'gen • cies

strin'gent

string'er

string'y
  string'i • er, string'i • est

string'i • ness

strip
  stripped *or* stript,
  strip'ping

stripe
  striped, strip'ing

strip'ling

strip' mine'

strip'per

strip'tease'
  strip'teased',
  strip'teas'ing

strive
  strove, striv'en, striv'ing

strobe

stro'bo • scope'

stro'bo • scop'ic

stro'ga • noff'

stroke
  stroked, strok'ing

stroll

stroll'er

strong

strong'arm'

strong'box'
  pl. strong'box'es

strong'hold'

strong'room'

strong'–willed'

stron'ti • um

strop
  stropped, strop'ping

stro'phe

struck

struc'tur • al

struc'tur • al • ly

struc'ture
  struc'tured,
  struc'tur • ing

stru'del

strug'gle
  strug'gled, strug'gling

strum
  strummed, strum'ming

strum'pet

strung

strut
  strut'ted, strut'ting

strych'nine

stub
  stubbed, stub'bing

stub'ble

stub'bly

stub'born

stub'born • ness

stub'by
  stub'bi • er, stub'bi • est

stuc'co
  pl. stuc'coes *or*
  stuc'coes; (v.)
  stuc'coed, stuc'co • ing

stuck

stuck'–up'

stud
  stud'ded, stud'ding

stud'book'

stu'dent

stud'horse'

stud'ied

stu'di • o'
  pl. stu'di • os'

stu'di • o' couch'

stu'di • ous

stud'y
  pl. stud'ies; (v.)
  stud'ied, stud'y • ing

stud'y hall'

stuff

stuffed' shirt'

stuff'i • ly

stuff'i • ness

stuff'ing

stuff'y
  stuff'i • er, stuff'i • est

stul'ti • fi • ca'tion

stul'ti·fy'
  stul'ti·fied',
  stul'ti·fy'ing
stum'ble
  stum'bled, stum'bling
stump'y
  stump'i·er, stump'i·est
stun
  stunned, stun'ning
stung
stun'ning
stunt
stu'pe·fa'cient
stu'pe·fac'tion
stu'pe·fy'
  stu'pe·fied',
  stu'pe·fy'ing
stu·pen'dous
stu'pid
stu·pid'i·ty
  pl. stu·pid'i·ties
stu'por
stur'di·ly
stur'di·ness
stur'dy
  stur'di·er, stur'di·est
stur'geon
stut'ter
St.' Vi'tus's dance'
sty
  pl. sties; (v.) stied,
  sty'ing
style (fashion)
  styled, styl'ing
  (SEE stile)
style'book'
styl'ish
styl'ist
sty·lis'tic
sty·lis'ti·cal·ly
styl'ize
  styl'ized, styl'iz·ing
styl'i·za'tion
sty'lus
  pl. sty'li or sty'lus·es
sty'mie
sty'mied, sty'mie·ing
styp'tic
sty'rene
Sty'ro·foam'
  (Trademark)

su'a·ble
sua'sion
sua'sive
suave
suave'ly
suav'i·ty
  pl. suav'i·ties
sub
  subbed, sub'bing
sub·al'tern
sub'as·sem'bly
  pl. sub'as·sem'blies
sub'a·tom'ic
sub·av'er·age
sub'base'ment
sub'cel'lar
sub'class'
sub'com·mit'tee
sub'com'pact
sub·con'scious
sub·con'ti·nent
sub·con'tract (n.)
sub'con·tract' (v.)
sub·con'trac·tor
sub·cul'ture (v.)
  sub·cul'tured,
  sub·cul'tur·ing
sub'cul'ture (n.)
sub'cu·ta'ne·ous
sub'di·vide'
  sub'di·vid'ed,
  sub'di·vid'ing
sub'di·vi'sion
sub·due'
  sub·dued', sub·du'ing
sub·fam'i·ly
  pl. sub·fam'i·lies
sub'floor'
sub'freez'ing
sub·ge'nus
  pl. sub·gen'er·a or
  sub·ge'nus·es
sub'group'
sub'gum'
sub'head'
sub·hu'man
sub·ja'cent
sub'ject (n., adj.)
sub·ject' (v.)
sub·jec'tion

sub·jec'tive
sub'jec·tiv'i·ty
sub·join'
sub ju'di·ce'
sub'ju·gate'
  sub'ju·gat'ed,
  sub'ju·gat'ing
sub'ju·ga'tion
sub'ju·ga'tor
sub·junc'tive
sub'lease' (n.)
sub·lease' (v.)
  sub·leased',
  sub·leas'ing
sub'les·see'
sub·les'sor
sub·let' (v.)
  sub·let', sub·let'ting
sub'let' (n.)
sub'li·mate' (v.)
  sub'li·mat'ed,
  sub'li·mat'ing
sub'li·mate (n., adj.)
sub'li·ma'tion
sub·lime'
  sub·limed', sub·lim'ing
sub·lime'ly
sub·lim'i·nal
sub·lim'i·nal·ly
sub·lim'i·ty
  pl. sub·lim'i·ties
sub·lu'nar
sub'ma·chine' gun'
sub·mar'gin·al
sub·mar'gin·al·ly
sub'ma·rine' (n.)
sub'ma·rine' (adj.,
  v.)
  sub'ma·rined',
  sub'ma·rin'ing
sub·merge'
  sub·merged',
  sub·merg'ing
sub·mer'gence
sub·mer'gi·ble
sub·mer'gi·bil'i·ty
sub·mer'sion
sub·mers'i·ble
sub'mi·cro·scop'ic
sub·min'i·a·ture
sub·mis'sion

sub · mis'sive
sub · mit'
  sub · mit'ted,
  sub · mit'ting
sub · nor'mal
sub'nor · mal'i · ty
sub · or'bit · al
sub · or'der
sub · or'di · nate (adj., n.)
sub · or'di · nate' (v.)
  sub · or'di · nat'ed,
  sub · or'di · nat'ing
sub · or'di · na'tion
sub · orn'
sub'or · na'tion
sub'plot'
sub · poe'na
  sub · poe'naed,
  sub · poe'na · ing
sub're'gion
sub ro'sa
sub · scribe'
  sub · scribed',
  sub · scrib'ing
sub · scrib'er
sub'script
sub · scrip'tion
sub'se · quent
sub · ser'vi · ence
sub · ser'vi · ent
sub'set'
sub · side'
  sub · sid'ed, sub · sid'ing
sub · sid'ence
sub · sid'i · ar'y
  pl. sub · sid'i · ar'ies
sub'si · di · za'tion
sub'si · dize'
  sub'si · dized',
  sub'si · diz'ing
sub'si · dy
  pl. sub'si · dies
sub'sist'
sub · sist'ence
sub'soil'
sub · son'ic
sub · spe'cies
sub'stance
sub · stand'ard
sub · stan'tial

sub · stan'tial · ly
sub · stan'ti · ate'
  sub · stan'ti · at'ed,
  sub · stan'ti · at · ing
sub · stan'ti · a'tion
sub'stan · tive
sub'sta'tion
sub'sti · tut'a · ble
sub'sti · tute'
  sub'sti · tut'ed,
  sub'sti · tut'ing
sub'sti · tu'tion
sub · stra'tum
  pl. sub · stra'ta
sub · struc'ture
sub · sum'a · ble
sub · sume'
  sub · sumed',
  sub · sum'ing
sub · sur'face
sub'ter · fuge'
sub'ter · ra'ne · an
sub'ter · res'tri · al
sub'ti'tle
  sub'ti'tled, sub'ti'tling
sub'tle
sub'tle · ty
  pl. sub'tle · ties
sub'tly
sub · to'tal
  sub · to'taled,
  sub · to'tal · ing
sub · tract'
sub · trac'tion
sub'tra · hend'
sub · trop'i · cal
sub · trop'ics
sub'urb
sub · ur'ban
sub · ur'ban · ite'
sub · ur'bi · a
sub · ven'tion
sub · ver'sion
sub · ver'sive
sub · vert'
sub'way'
sub-ze'ro
suc · ceed'
suc · cess'
suc · cess'ful

suc · cess'ful · ly
suc · ces'sion
suc · ces'sive
suc · ces'sor
suc · cinct'
suc'cor (help)
  (SEE sucker)
suc'co · tash'
Suc'coth
suc'cu · lence
suc'cu · len · cy
suc'cu · lent
suc · cumb'
such
suck
suck'er (one that
  sucks)
  (SEE succor)
suck'le
  suck'led, suck'ling
suck'ling
su'cre (money)
Su'cre (city)
su'crose
suc'tion
Su · dan'
Su'da · nese'
su'da · to'ry
sud'den
su'dor · if'ic
suds
suds'y
  suds'i · er, suds'i · est
sue
  sued, su'ing
suede or suède
su'er
su'et
Su · ez'
suf'fer
suf'fer · a · ble
suf'fer · ance
suf'fer · ing
suf · fice'
  suf · ficed', suf · fic'ing
suf · fi'cien · cy
  pl. suf · fi'cien · cies
suf · fi'cient
suf'fix
  pl. suf'fix · es

suf'fo·cate'
  suf'fo·cat'ed,
  suf'fo·cat'ing

suf'fo·ca'tion

suf'fra·gan

suf'frage

suf'fra·gette'

suf'fra·gist

suf·fuse'
  suf·fused', suf·fus'ing

suf·fu'sion

sug'ar

sug'ar cane'

sug'ar–coat'

sug'ar·plum'

sug'ar·y

sug·gest'

sug·gest'i·bil'i·ty

sug·gest'i·ble

sug·ges'tion

sug·ges'tive

su'i·cid'al

su'i·cide'

su'i ge'ne·ris

su'i ju'ris

suit (*clothes; legal
  action; cards*)
  (SEE suite)

suit'a·bil'i·ty

suit'a·ble

suit'a·bly

suit'case'

suite (*set; retinue*)
  (SEE suit or sweet)

suit'ing

suit'or

su'ki·ya'ki

Suk'koth

sul'fa

sul'fa·nil'a·mide'

sul'fate
  sul'fat·ed, sul'fat·ing

sul'fide

sul'fite

sul'fur

sul·fu'ric

sul'fur·ous

sulk

sulk'i·ly

sulk'i·ness

sulk'y
  sulk'i·er, sulk'i·est

sul'len

sul'ly
  (v.) sul'lied, sul'ly·ing;
  pl. sul'lies

sul'tan

sul·tan'a

sul'tan·ate'

sul'tri·ness

sul'try
  sul'tri·er, sul'tri·est

sum
  summed, sum'ming

su'mac

Su·ma'tra

Su·me'ri·an

sum'ma cum lau'de

sum·mar'i·ly

sum'ma·ri·za'tion

sum'ma·rize'
  sum'ma·rized',
  sum'ma·riz'ing

sum'ma·ry (*resume*)
  pl. sum'ma·ries
  (SEE summery)

sum·ma'tion

sum'mer

sum'mer·house'

sum'mer school'

sum'mer·time'

sum'mer·y (*of
  summer*)
  (SEE summary)

sum'mit

sum'mon

sum'mons

su'mo

sump'tu·ous

sun (*star*)
  sunned, sun'ning
  (SEE son)

sun' bath'

sun'bathe'
  sun'bathed',
  sun'bath'ing

sun'bath'er

sun'beam'

Sun'belt'

sun'bon'net

sun'burn'
  sun'burned' or
  sun'burnt', sun'burn'ing

sun'burst'

sun'dae (*ice cream*)
  (SEE Sunday)

Sun'day (*day of
  week*)
  (SEE sundae)

Sun'day school'

sun' deck'

sun'der

sun'di'al

sun'down'

sun'dries

sun'dry

sun'fish'
  pl. sun'fish' or
  sun'fish'es

sun'flow'er

sung

sun'glass'es

sunk

sunk'en

sun' lamp'

sun'light'

sun'lit'

Sun'ni

Sun'nite

sun'ny (*bright*)
  sun'ni·er, sun'ni·est
  (SEE sonny)

sun' porch'

sun'rise'

sun'roof'

sun'set'

sun'shade'

sun'shine'

sun'spot'

sun'stroke'

sun'suit'

sun' tan' or sun'tan'

sun'tanned

sun'up'

Sun' Yat'–sen'

sup
  supped, sup'ping

su'per

su'per·a·bun'dance
su'per·a·bun'dant
su'per·an'nu·ate'
  su'per·an'nu·at'ed,
  su'per·an'nu·at'ing
su·perb'
su'per·bomb'
su'per·car'go
  pl. su'per·car'goes or
  su'per·car'gos
su'per·charg'er
su'per·cil'i·ous
su'per·con'duc·
  tiv'i·ty
su'per·con·duc'tor
su'per·e'go
  pl. su'per·e'gos
su'per·e·rog'a·to'ry
su'per·fi'cial
su'per·fi'ci·al'i·ty
  pl. su'per·fi'ci·al'i·ties
su'per·fi'cial·ly
su'per·flu'i·ty
  pl. su'per·flu'i·ties
su·per'flu·ous
su'per·heat' (n.)
su'per·heat' (v.)
su'per·high'way'
su'per·hu'man
su'per·im·pose'
  su'per·im·posed',
  su'per·im·pos'ing
su'per·in·tend'
su'per·in·tend'ence
su'per·in·tend'en·cy
  pl.
  su'per·in·tend'en·cies
su'per·in·tend'ent
su·pe'ri·or
su·pe'ri·or'i·ty
su·per·jet'
su·per'la·tive
su'per·man'
  pl. su'per·men'
su'per·mar'ket
su·per'nal
su'per·na'tion·al
su'per·nat'u·ral
su'per·nat'u·ral·ly
su'per·no'va
  pl. su'per·no'vae or
  su'per·no'vas

su'per·nu'mer·ar'y
  pl. su'per·nu'mer·ar'ies
su'per·pow'er
su'per·scribe'
  su'per·scribed',
  su'per·scrib'ing
su'per·script'
su'per·scrip'tion
su'per·sede'
  su'per·sed'ed,
  su'per·sed'ing
su'per·sen'si·tive
su'per·son'ic
su'per·son'i·cal·ly
su'per·state'
su'per·sti'tion
su'per·sti'tious
su'per·struc'ture
su'per·tank'er
su'per·vene'
  su'per·vened',
  su'per·ven'ing
su'per·ven'tion
su'per·vise'
  su'per·vised',
  su'per·vis'ing
su'per·vi'sion
su'per·vi'sor
su'per·vi'so·ry
su·pine' (adj.)
su'pine (n.)
sup'per
sup'per·time'
sup·plant'
sup'ple
  (adj.) sup'pler,
  sup'plest; (v.) sup'pled,
  sup'pling
sup'ple·ment (n.)
sup'ple·ment' (v.)
sup'ple·men'tal
sup'ple·men'ta·ry
  pl. sup'ple·men'ta·ries
sup·pli'ant
sup'pli·cant
sup'pli·cate'
  sup'pli·cat'ed,
  sup'pli·cat'ing
sup'pli·ca'tion
sup·pli'er

sup·ply'
  (v.) sup·plied',
  sup·ply'ing; *pl.*
  sup·plies
sup·port'
sup·port'a·ble
sup·port'er
sup·port'ive
sup·pose'
  sup·posed', sup·pos'ing
sup·posed'
sup·pos'ed·ly
sup'po·si'tion
sup·pos'i·to'ry
  pl. sup·pos'i·to'ries
sup·press'
sup·pres'sant
sup·press'i·ble
sup·pres'sion
sup·pres'sive
sup·pres'sor
sup'pu·rate'
  sup'pu·rat'ed,
  sup'pu·rat'ing
sup'pu·ra'tion
su'pra
su'pra·na'tion·al
su·prem'a·cist
su·prem'a·cy
su·preme'
sur·cease'
  sur·creased',
  sur·ceas'ing
sur'charge' (n.)
sur·charge' (v.)
  sur·charged',
  sur·charg'ing
sur'cin'gle
sure
  sur'er, sur'est
sure'-fire'
sure'-foot'ed
sure'ly
sure'ty
  pl. sure'ties
surf (waves)
  (SEE serf)
sur'face
  sur'faced, sur'fac·ing
surf'board'
surf'boat'

surf′ cast′ing

sur′feit

surf′er

surf′ing

surge (*wave*)
  surged, surg′ing
  (SEE serge)

sur′geon

sur′ger•y
  pl. sur′ger•ies

sur′gi•cal

sur′gi•cal•ly

Sur′i•nam′

sur′li•ness

sur′ly
  sur′li•er, sur′li•est

sur•mise′
  sur•mised′, sur•mis′ing

sur•mount′

sur′name′
  sur′named′, sur′nam′ing

sur•pass′

sur′plice (*vestment*)
  (SEE surplus)

sur′plus (*excess*)
  (SEE surplice)

sur•prise′
  sur•prised′, sur•pris′ing

Sur•re′al•ism

Sur•re′al•ist

Sur•re′al•is′tic

sur•ren′der

sur′rep•ti′tious

sur′rey
  pl. sur′reys

sur′ro•gate′
  sur′ro•gat′ed,
  sur′ro•gat′ing

sur•round′

sur•round′ings

sur′tax′

sur•veil′lance

sur•vey′ (*v.*)

sur′vey (*n.*)
  pl. sur′veys

sur•vey′ing

sur•vey′or

sur•viv′al

sur•vive′
  sur•vived′, sur•viv′ing

sur•vi′vor

sus•cep′ti•bil′i•ty
  pl. sus•cep′ti•bil′i•ties

sus•cep′ti•ble

sus•cep′ti•bly

su′shi

sus•pect′ (*v.*)

sus′pect (*n., adj.*)

sus•pend′

sus•pend′er

sus•pense′

sus•pen′sion

sus•pi′cion

sus•pi′cious

sus•tain′

sus•tain′a•ble

sus′te•nance

su′ture
  su′tured, su′tur•ing

Su′va

su′ze•rain

su′ze•rain•ty
  pl. su′ze•rain•ties

svelte
  svelt′er, svelt′est

swab
  swabbed, swab′bing

swad′dle
  swad′dled, swad′dling

swag
  swagged, swag′ging

swag′ger

Swa•hi′li
  pl. Swa•hi′lis or
  Swa•hi′li

Swa•hi′li•an

swain

swal′low

swal′low•tail′

swal′low–tailed′

swam

swa′mi
  pl. swa′mies

swamp

swamp′land′

swamp′y
  swamp′i•er,
  swamp′i•est

swan

swan′ dive′

swank

swank′y
  swantk′i•er,
  swank′i•est

swan′s′–down′ or
  swans′down′

swan′ song′

swap
  swapped, swap′ping

sward (*turf*)
  (SEE sword)

swarm

swarth′i•ness

swarth′y
  swarth′i•er,
  swarth′i•est

swash′buck′ler

swash′buck′ling

swas′ti•ka

swat
  swat′ted, swat′ting

swatch

swath (*row cut*)
  (SEE swathe)

swathe (*wrap*)
  swathed, swath′ing
  (SEE swath)

swat′ter

sway′–back′

sway′–backed′

Swa′zi•land′

swear
  swore, sworn, swear′ing

sweat
  sweat or sweat′ed,
  sweat′ing

sweat′band′

sweat′box′
  pl. sweat′box′es

sweat′er

sweat′i•ness

sweat′ shirt′

sweat′shop′

sweat′y
  sweat′i•er, sweat′i•est

Swede

Swe′den

Swed′ish

sweep
  swept, sweep′ing

sweep′back′

sweep′er

sweep'stakes' or
  sweep'stake'

sweet (*sugary*)
  (SEE suite)

sweet'bread'

sweet'bri'er

sweet'en

sweet'heart'

sweet'meat'

sweet' pea'

sweet' talk'

sweet'-talk'

swell
  swelled, swelled or
  swol'len, swell'ing

swel'ter

swept

swept'back'

swept'wing'

swerve
  swerved, swerv'ing

swift

swig
  swigged, swig'ging

swill

swim
  swam, swum,
  swim'ming

swim'mer

swim'ming pool'

swim'suit'

swim'wear'

swin'dle
  swin'dled, swin'dling

swin'dler

swine
  pl. swine

swine'herd'

swing
  swung, swing'ing

swing'er

swin'ish

swipe
  swiped, swip'ing

swirl

swish

Swiss

Swiss' cheese'

Swiss' steak'

switch

switch'blade'

switch'board'

switch'-hit'ter

switch'man
  pl. switch'men

switch'yard'

Swit'zer·land

swiv'el
  swiv'eled, swiv'el·ing

swiv'el chair'

swiz'zle stick'

swol'len

swoon

swoop

sword (*weapon*)
  (SEE sward)

sword'fish'
  pl. sword'fish'es or
  sword'fish'

sword'play'

swords'man
  pl. swords'men

sword'tail'

swore

sworn

swum

swung

syb'a·rite'

syb'·rit'ic

syc'a·more'

syc'o·phan·cy

syc'o·phant

syc'o·phan'tic

Syd'ney

syl·lab'ic

syl·lab'i·cate'
  syl·lab'i·cat'ed,
  syl·lab'i·cat'ing

syl·lab'i·ca'tion

syl·lab'i·fi·ca'tion

syl·lab'i·fy'
  syl·lab'i·fied',
  syl·lab'i·fy'ing

syl'la·ble
  syl'la·bled, syl'la·bling

syl'la·bus
  pl. syl'la·bus·es or
  syl'la·bi'

syl'lo·gism'

syl'lo·gis'tic

sylph

syl'van

sym·bi·o'sis
  pl. sym'bi·o'ses

sym·bi·ot'ic

sym'bol (*token*)
  sym'boled, sym'bol·ing
  (SEE cymbal)

sym·bol'ic

sym·bol'i·cal

sym·bol'i·cal·ly

sym'bol·ism'

sym'bol·ist

sym·bol·i·za'tion

sym'bol·ize'
  sym'bol·ized',
  sym'bol·iz'ing

sym·met'ric

sym·met'ri·cal

sym·met'ri·cal·ly

sym'me·try
  pl. sym'me·tries

sym·pa·thet'ic

sym'pa·thize'
  sym'pa·thized',
  sym'pa·thiz'ing

sym'pa·thiz'er

sym'pa·thy
  pl. sym'pa·thies

sym·phon'ic

sym'pho·ny
  pl. sym'pho·nies

sym·po'si·um
  pl. sym·po'si·ums or
  sym·po'si·a

symp'tom

symp'to·mat'ic

syn'a·gogue'

syn'apse

sync

syn'chro·mesh'

syn'chro·nism'

syn'chro·ni·za'tion

syn'chro·nize'
  syn'chro·nized',
  syn'chro·niz'ing

syn'chro·nous

syn'chro·tron'

syn·cli'nal

syn'cline

syn'co·pate'
  syn'co·pat'ed,
  syn'co·pat'ing

syn'co·pa'tion
syn'co·pe
syn'cret'ic
syn'cre·tism'
syn'cre·tize'
  syn'cre·tized',
  syn'cre·tiz'ing
syn'dic
syn'di·cal·ism'
syn'di·cate (n.)
syn'di·cate' (v.)
  syn'di·cat'ed,
  syn'di·cat'ing
syn'di·ca'tion
syn'drome
syn·ec'do·che
syn'e·col'o·gy
syn'er·get'ic
syn'er·gism'
syn'er·gis'tic
syn'er·gis'ti·cal·ly
syn'er·gy
  pl. syn'er·gies
syn'fuel

syn'od
syn'o·nym
syn·on'y·mous
syn·on'y·my
  pl. syn·on'y·mies
syn·op'sis
  pl. syn·op'ses
syn·op'size
  syn·op'sized,
  syn·op'siz·ing
syn·op'tic
syn·tac'tic
syn·tac'ti·cal
syn·tac'ti·cal·ly
syn'tax
syn'the·sis
  pl. syn'the·ses'
syn'the·size'
  syn'the·sized',
  syn'the·siz'ing
syn'the·siz'er
syn·thet'ic
syn·thet'i·cal
syn·thet'i·cal·ly
syph'i·lis

syph'i·lit'ic
sy'phon
Syr'a·cuse'
Syr·ette'
  (Trademark)
Syr'i·a
Syr'i·an
sy·ringe'
  sy·ringed', sy·ring'ing
syr'up
syr'up·y
sys'tem
sys'tem·at'ic
sys'tem·at'i·cal
sys'tem·at'i·cal·ly
sys'tem·a·ti·za'tion
sys'tem·a·tize'
  sys'tem·a·tized',
  sys'tem·a·tiz'ing
sys·tem'ic
sys'tem·i·za'tion
sys'tem·ize'
  sys'tem·ized',
  sys'tem·iz'ing
sys'to·le'
sys·tol'ic

T

tab
  tabbed, tab'bing
Ta·bas'co
  (Trademark)
tab'by
  pl. tab'bies; (v.)
  tab'bied, tab'by·ing
tab'er·nac'le
  tab'er·nac'led,
  tab'er·nac'ling
ta'ble
  ta'bled, ta'bling
tab'leau
  pl. tab'leaux or
  tab'leaus
ta'ble·cloth'
ta'ble d'hôte'
  pl. ta'bles d'hôte'
ta'ble-hop'
  ta'ble-hopped', ta'ble-
  hop'ping
ta'ble·land'
ta'ble·spoon'

ta'ble·spoon'ful'
  pl. ta'ble·spoon'fuls'
tab'let
  tab'let·ed, tab'let·ing
  or tab'let·ted,
  tab'let·ting
ta'ble·top'
ta'ble·ware'
tab'loid
ta·boo'
  pl. ta·boos'; (v.)
  ta·booed', ta·boo'ing
ta'bor or ta'bour
tab·o·ret' or
  tab·ou·ret'
ta·bu'
  pl. ta·bus'; (v.)
  ta·bued', ta·bu'ing
tab'u·lar
tab'u·late' (v.)
  tab'u·lat'ed,
  tab'u·lat'ing

tab'u·late (adj.)
tab'u·la'tion
tab'u·la'tor
ta'cet (musical
  direction)
  (SEE tacit)
ta·chom'e·ter
tach'y·car'di·a
tac'it (implicit)
  (SEE tacet)
tac'i·turn'
tac'i·tur'ni·ty
tack
tack'i·ness
tack'le
  tack'led, tack'ling
tack'y
  tack'i·er, tack'i·est
ta'co
  pl. ta'cos
tac'o·nite'

tact
tact'ful
tact'ful・ly
tac'tic
tac'ti・cal
tac・ti'cian
tac'tics
tac'tile
tact'less
tad'pole'
taf'fe・ta
taff'rail'
taf'fy
Taft
tag
  tagged, tag'ging
tag' end'
tag' sale'
Ta・hi'ti
Ta・hi'tian
tai' chi'
tai'ga
tail (*rear part*)
  (SEE tale)
tail'back'
tail'board'
tail' coat'
tail' end'
tail'gate'
  tail'gat'ed, tail'gat'ing
tail'light'
tail'like'
tai'lor
tai'lored
tai'lor–made'
tail'piece'
tail'pipe'
tail'spin'
tail'wind'
taint
Tai'pei'
Tai'wan'
Tai'wan・ese'
Taj' Ma・hal'
take
  took, tak'en, tak'ing
take'off'
tak'er

take'out'
take'o'ver
talc
  talked or talced,
  talck'ing or talc'ing
tal'cum
tale (*account*)
  (SEE tail)
tale'bear'er
tal'ent
tales'man (*juror*)
  pl. tales'men
  (SEE talisman)
tale'tell'er
tal'is・man (*charm*)
  pl. tal'is・mans
  (SEE talesman)
talk
talk'a・tive
talk'er
talk'ing–to'
  pl. talk'ing-tos'
talk' show'
tall
Tal'la・has'see
tal'lith
  pl. tal・li'thim
tal'low
tal'ly
  pl. tal'lies; (v.)
  tal'lied, tal'ly・ing
tal'ly・ho' (*n., v.*)
  pl. tal'ly・hos'; (v.)
  tal'ly・hoed' or
  tal'ly・ho'd,
  tal'ly・ho'ing
tal'ly・ho' (*interj.*)
Tal'mud
Tal・mud'ic
tal'on
tam
tam'a・ble
ta・ma'le
tam'a・rack'
tam'a・rind
tam'bour
tam'bou・rine'
tame
  adj. tam'er, tam'est;
  (v.) tamed, tam'ing
tame'a・ble
Tam'ma・ny

tam'-o'-shan'ter
tamp
Tam'pa
tam'per
tam'pon
tan
  tanned, tan'ning
tan'a・ger
Ta・na・na・rive'
tan'bark'
tan'dem
tang
Tan'gan・yi'ka
tan'ge・lo'
  pl. tan'ge・los'
tan'gent
tan・gen'tial
tan'ge・rine'
tan'gi・bil'i・ty
tan'gi・ble
tan'gi・bly
Tan・gier'
tan'gle
  tan'gled, tan'gling
tan'go
  pl. tan'gos; (v.)
  tan'goed, tan'go・ing
tang'y
  tang'i・er, tang'i・est
tank
tank'age
tank'ard
tank'er
tank'ful'
  pl. tank'fuls'
tank' suit'
tan'ner
tan'ner・y
  pl. tan'ner・ies
tan'nic
tan'nin
tan'ta・lize'
  tan'ta・lized',
  tan'ta・liz'ing
tan'ta・lum
tan'ta・mount'
tan'trum
Tan'za・ni'a
Tan'za・ni'an
Tao

Tao'ism

Tao'ist

tap
   tapped, tap'ping

tap' dance'

tap'-dance'
   tap'-danced', tap'-
   danc'ing

tape
   taped, tap'ing

tape' deck'

tape' meas'ure

ta'per (diminish;
   candle)
   (SEE tapir)

tape'-re·cord'

tape' re·cord'er

tap'es·try
   pl. tap'es·tries; (v.)
   tap'es·tried,
   tap'es·try·ing

tape'worm'

tap'i·o'ca

ta'pir (animal)
   pl. ta'pirs or ta'pir
   (SEE taper)

tap'per

tap'pet

tap'room'

tap'root'

taps

tar
   tarred, tar'ring

tar'an·tel'la

ta·ran'tu·la
   pl. ta·ran'tu·las or
   ta·ran'tu·lae'

tar'di·ly

tar'di·ness

tar'dy
   tar'di·er, tar'di·est

tare (weight; weed)
   tared, tar'ing
   (SEE tear)

tar'get

tar'iff

tar'la·tan

Tar'mac (Trademark)

tarn

tar'nish

tar'nish·a·ble

ta'ro (plant)
   pl. ta'ros
   (SEE tarot)

ta·rot' (card)
   (SEE taro)

tar·pau'lin

tar'pon
   pl. tar'pons or tar'pon

tar'ra·gon'

tar'ry
   tar'ried, tar'ry·ing

tar'sal

tar' sand'

tar'si·er

tar'sus
   pl. tar'si

tart

tart'ness

tar'tan

tar'tar (deposit)
   (SEE Tartar)

Tar'tar (Asian)
   (SEE tartar)

tar·tar'ic

tar'tar sauce'

task

task' force'

task'mas'ter

Tas·ma'ni·a

Tas·ma'ni·an

tas'sel
   tas'seled, tas'sel·ing

taste
   tast'ed, tast'ing

taste'ful

taste'ful·ly

taste'less

tast'er

tast'i·ly

tast'i·ness

tast'y
   tast'i·er, tast'i·est

tat
   tat'ted, tat'ting

tat'ter

tat'ter·de·mal'ion

tat'tered

tat'ter·sall'

tat'tle
   tat'tled, tat'tling

tat'tle·tale'

tat·too'
   pl. tat·toos'

tau

taught (instructed)
   (SEE taut)

taunt

taupe

Tau'rus

taut (tight)
   (SEE taught)

tau·to·log'i·cal

tau·to·log'i·cal·ly

tau·tol'o·gy
   pl. tau·tol'o·gies

tav'ern

taw

taw'dri·ly

taw'dri·ness

taw'dry
   taw'dri·er, taw'dri·est

taw'ny
   taw'ni·er, taw'ni·est

tax

tax'a·bil'i·ty

tax'a·ble

tax·a'tion

tax'-de·duct'i·ble

tax'-ex·empt'

tax'i
   pl. tax'is or tax'ies;
   (v.) tax'ied, tax'i·ing
   or tax'y·ing

tax'i·cab'

tax'i·der'mist

tax'i·der'my

tax'i·me'ter

tax'o·nom'ic

tax'o·nom'i·cal

tax·on'o·mist

tax·on'o·my

tax'pay'er

T'-bar'

T'-bill'

T'-bone'

Tchai·kov'sky

tea (beverage)
   (SEE tee)

tea' bag'

tea' ball'

tea'cake'

tea'cart'

teach
  taught, teach'ing

teach'a·ble

teach'er

teach'-in'
  pl. teach'-ins'

tea'cup'

tea'cup·ful'
  pl. tea'cup·fuls'

tea'house'

teak

tea'ket'tle

teak'wood'

teal
  pl. teals or teal

team (*group*)
  (SEE teem)

team'mate'

team'ster

team'work'

tea'pot'

tear (*eye water*)
  (SEE tier)

tear (*pull apart*)
  tore, torn, tear'ing
  (SEE tare)

tear'drop'

tear'ful

tear'ful·ly

tear' gas'

tear'-jerk'er

tea'room'

tear'stained'

tease
  teased, teas'ing

tea'sel
  tea'seled, tea'sel·ing

teas'er

tea'spoon'

tea'spoon·ful'
  pl. tea'spoon·fuls'

teat

tea'time'

tech·ne'ti·um

tech'nic

tech'ni·cal

tech'ni·cal'i·ty
  pl. tech'ni·cal'i·ties

tech'ni·cal·ly

tech·ni'cian

Tech'ni·col'or
  (*Trademark*)

tech·nique'

tech·noc'ra·cy
  pl. tech·noc'ra·cies

tech'no·crat'

tech'no·log'i·cal

tech'no·log'i·cal·ly

tech·nol'o·gist

tech·nol'o·gy

tec·ton'ic

tec·ton'ics

ted'dy bear'

Te De'um

te'di·ous

te'di·um

tee (*golf peg*)
  teed, tee'ing
  (SEE tea)

teem (*abound*)
  (SEE team)

teen'-age'

teen'-ag'er

teens

tee'ny
  tee'ni·er, tee'ni·est

tee'ny·bop'per

tee'pee

tee'ter

teethe
  teethed, teeth'ing

tee·to'tal·er *or*
  tee·to'tal·ler

Tef'lon (*Trademark*)

Te'he·ran' *or* Te'hran

tek'tite

Tel' A·viv'

tel'e·cast'
  tel'e·cast' *or*
  tel'e·cast'ed,
  tel'e·cast'ing

tel'e·cast'er

tel'e·com·mu'
  ni·ca'tion

tel'e·course'

tel'e·gen'ic

tel'e·gram'

tel'e·graph'

te·leg'ra·pher

tel'e·graph'ic

tel'e·graph'i·cal

te·leg'ra·phy

tel'e·ki·ne'sis

tel'e·mark'

te·lem'e·ter

te·lem'e·try

tel'e·o·log'i·cal

tel'e·ol'o·gy

tel'e·path'ic

te·lep'a·thist

te·lep'a·thy

tel'e·phone'
  tel'e·phoned',
  tel'e·phon'ing

tel'e·phon'er

tel'e·phon'ic

te·leph'o·ny

tel'e·pho'to

tel'e·pho'to·graph'

tel'e·pho·tog'ra·phy

tel'e·play'

tel'e·print'er

Tel'e·prompt'er
  (*Trademark*)

tel'e·ran'

tel'e·scope'
  tel'e·scoped',
  tel'e·scop'ing

tel'e·scop'ic

tel'e·thon'

Tel'e·type'
  (*Trademark*)

tel'e·type'writ'er

tel'e·view'er

tel'e·vise'
  tel'e·vised', tel'e·vis'ing

tel'e·vi'sion

Tel'ex (*Trademark*)

tell
  told, tell'ing

tell'er

tell'tale'

tel·lu'ri·um

tel'pher

Tel'star' (*Trademark*)

tem′blor
  pl. tem′blors or (Sp.)
  tem · blo′res

te · mer′i · ty

tem′per

tem′per · a

tem′per · a · ment

tem′per · a · men′tal

tem′per · a ·
  men′tal · ly

tem′per · ance

tem′per · ate

tem′per · a · ture

tem′pest

tem · pes′tu · ous

tem′plate

tem′ple

tem′plet

tem′po
  pl. tem′pos or tem′pi

tem′po · ral

tem′po · rar′i · ly

tem′po · rar′y

tem′po · ri · za′tion

tem′po · rize′
  tem′po · rized′,
  tem′po · riz′ing

tempt

temp · ta′tion

tempt′er

tempt′ing

tempt′ress

tem′pu · ra′

tem′pus fu′git

ten

ten′a · ble

te · na′cious

te · nac′i · ty

ten′an · cy
  pl. ten′an · cies

ten′ant

tend

ten′den · cy
  pl. ten′den · cies

ten · den′tious

ten′der

ten′der · foot′
  pl. ten′der · foots′ or
  ten′der · feet′

ten′der-heart′ed

ten′der · ize′
  ten′der · ized′,
  ten′der · iz′ing

ten′der · iz′er

ten′der · loin′

ten′der of′fer

ten′don

ten′dril

ten′e · ment

ten′et

ten′fold′ (*adj.*)

ten′fold′ (*adv.*)

Ten′nes · se′an

Ten′nes · see′

ten′nis

ten′nis ball′

Ten′ny · son

ten′on

ten′or

ten′pin′

tense
  (*adj.*) tens′er, tens′est;
  (*v.*) tensed, tens′ing

tense′ly

tense′ness

ten′sile

ten′sion

ten′sor

tent

ten′ta · cle

ten′ta · tive

ten′ta · tive · ly

ten′ta · tive · ness

ten′ter

ten′ter · hook′

tenth

ten′u · ous

ten′ure

ten′ured

te · nu′to

te′pee

tep′id

te · qui′la

ter′bi · um

ter′cel

ter · cen′te · nar′y
  pl. ter · cen′te · nar′ies

ter′cen · ten′ni · al

ter′gi · ver · sate′
  ter′gi · ver · sat′ed,
  ter′gi · ver · sat′ing

ter′i · ya′ki

term

ter′ma · gant

ter′mi · na · ble

ter′mi · nal

ter′mi · nal · ly

ter′mi · nate′
  ter′mi · nat′ed,
  ter′mi · nat′ing

ter′mi · na′tion

ter′mi · na′tor

ter′mi · nol′o · gy
  pl. ter′mi · nol′o · gies

ter′mi · nus
  pl. ter′mi · ni′ or
  ter′mi · nus · es

ter′mite

term′ pa′per

tern (*bird*)
  (SEE turn)

ter′na · ry
  pl. ter′na · ries

terp′si · cho · re′an

ter′race
  ter′raced, ter′rac · ing

ter′ra cot′ta

ter′ra fir′ma

ter · rain′

Ter′ra · my′cin
  (*Trademark*)

ter′ra · pin

ter · rar′i · um
  pl. ter · rar′i · ums or
  ter · rar′i · a

ter · raz′zo

ter · res′tri · al

ter′ri · ble

ter′ri · bly

ter′ri · er

ter · rif′ic

ter · rif′i · cal · ly

ter′ri · fy′
  ter′ri · fied′, ter′ri · fy′ing

ter′ri · to′ri · al

ter′ri · to′ri · al′i · ty

ter'ri · to'ry
  pl. ter'ri · to'ries
ter'ror
ter'ror · ism'
ter'ror · ist
ter'ror · i · za'tion
ter'ror · ize'
  ter'ror · ized',
  ter'ror · iz'ing
ter'ror–strick'en
ter'ry
  pl. ter'ries
terse
  ters'er, ters'est
terse'ly
terse'ness
ter'ti · ar'y
  pl. ter'ti · ar'ies
tes'sel · late' (*v.*)
  tes'sel · lat'ed,
  tes'sel · lat'ing
tes'sel · late (*adj.*)
tes'sel · lat'ed
tes'sel · la'tion
tes'ser · a
  pl. tes'ser · ae
test
tes'ta · ment
tes'ta · men'ta · ry
tes'tate
tes'ta · tor
tes'ta · trix
  pl. tes · ta'tri · ces'
test' case'
tes'ti · cle
tes'ti · fi'er
tes'ti · fy'
  tes'ti · fied', tes'ti · fy'ing
tes'ti · mo'ni · al
tes'ti · mo'ny
  pl. tes'ti · mo'nies
tes'tis
  pl. tes'tes
tes · tos'ter · one'
test' pi'lot
test' tube'
tes'ti · ly
tes'ti · ness
tes'ty
  tes'ti · er, tes'ti · est
tet'a · nus

tête'–à–tête'
teth'er
teth'er · ball'
Te'thys
tet'ra
tet'ra · cy'cline
tet'ra · eth'yl
Tet'ra · gram'ma · ton'
tet'ra · he'dral
tet'ra · he'dron
  pl. tet'ra · he'drons or
  tet'ra · he'dra
te · tram'e · ter
Teu'ton
Teu · ton'ic
Tex'an
Tex'as
text
text'book'
tex'tile
tex'tu · al
tex'tu · al · ly
tex'tur · al
tex'ture
  tex'tured, tex'tur · ing
Thai
Thai'land
tha · lam'ic
thal'a · mus
  pl. thal'a · mi'
tha'ler
tha · lid'o · mide'
thal'li · um
thal'lo · phyte'
Thames
than
thane
thank
thank'ful
thank'ful · ly
thank'ful · ness
thank'less
thanks'giv'ing
that
  pl. those
thatch
thaw
the

the'a · ter *or* the'a · tre
the'a · ter · go'er
the'a · ter–in–the–
  round'
the · at'ri · cal
the · at'ri · cal'i · ty
the · at'ri · cal · ly
the · at'rics
thee
theft
thegn
their (*belonging to
  them*)
  (SEE there *and*
  they're)
theirs (*belonging to
  them*)
  (SEE there's)
the'ism
the'ist
the · is'tic
them
the · mat'ic
the · mat'i · cal · ly
theme
theme' park'
them · selves'
then
thence
thence'forth'
thence'for'ward
thence'for'wards
the · oc'ra · cy
  pl. the · oc'ra · cies
the'o · crat'ic
the · od'o · lite'
the'o · lo'gian
the'o · log'ic
the'o · log'i · cal
the · ol'o · gy
  pl. the · ol'o · gies
the'o · rem
the'o · ret'ic
the'o · ret'i · cal
the'o · ret'i · cal · ly
the'o · re · ti'cian
the'o · rist

the'o·rize'
  the'o·rized',
  the'o·riz'ing
the'o·ry
  pl. the'o·ries
the'o·soph'i·cal
the·os'o·phist
the·os'o·phy
ther'a·peu'tic
ther'a·peu'ti·cal·ly
ther'a·peu'tics
ther'a·pist
ther'a·py
  pl. ther'a·pies
there (*at that place*)
  (SEE their *and* they're)
there'a·bouts'
there'af'ter
there'at'
there'by'
there'for' (*in exchange*)
  (SEE therefore)
there'fore'
  (*consequently*)
  (SEE therefor)
there'from'
there'in'
there'in·af'ter
ther'e·min
there'of'
there'on'
there's (*there is*)
  (SEE theirs)
there'to'
there'un'der
there'up·on'
there'with'
ther'mal
ther'mic
therm'i'on
therm'i·on'ics
ther'mo·dy·nam'ic
ther'mo·dy·nam'i·cal·ly
ther'mo·dy·nam'ics
ther'mo·e·lec'tric
ther'mo·e·lec·tric'i·ty

ther·mom'e·ter
ther'mo·nu'cle·ar
ther'mo·plas'tic
ther'mos
ther'mo·set'ting
ther'mo·sphere'
ther'mo·stat'
ther'mo·stat'i·cal·ly
the·sau'rus
  pl. the·sau'ri
these
the'sis
  pl. the'ses
thes'pi·an
the'ta
they
they'd
they'll
they're (*they are*)
  (SEE their *and* there)
they've
thi'a·mine'
thick
thick'en
thick'et
thick'head'ed
thick'set' (*adj.*)
thick'set' (*n.*)
thick'skinned'
thief
  pl. thieves
thieve
  thieved, thiev'ing
thiev'er·y
  pl. thiev'er·ies
thiev'ish
thigh
thigh'bone'
thim'ble
thim'ble·ful'
  pl. thim'ble·fuls'
Thim'phu
thin
  (*adj.*) thin'ner,
  thin'nest; (*v.*) thinned,
  thin'ning
thine
thing

think
  thought, think'ing
think'a·ble
think'er
think' tank'
thin'ner
thin'ness
thin'-skinned'
third
third' base'
third' class'
third' de·gree'
third'-de·gree'
  third'-de·greed',
  third'-de·gree'ing
third'-rate'
Third' World'
thirst
thirst'y
  thirst'i·er, thirst'i·est
thir'teen'
thir'teenth'
thir'ti·eth
thir'ty
  pl. thir'ties
this
  pl. these
this'tle
this'tle·down'
thith'er
tho
thole
  tholed, thol'ing
Tho'mism
Tho'mist
thong
Thor
tho·rac'ic
tho'rax
  pl. tho'rax·es or
  tho'ra·ces'
Tho'ra·zine'
  (*Trademark*)
Tho'reau
tho'ri·um
thorn
thorn'y
  thorn'i·er, thorn'i·est
thor'ough
thor'ough·bred'

thor'ough · fare'
thor'ough · go'ing
those
thou
though
thought
thought'ful
thought'ful · ly
thought'less
thou'sand
  pl. thou'sands or
  thou'sand
thou'sandth
thral'dom
thrall
thrall'dom
thrash
thrash'er
thread
thread'bare'
thread'i · ness
thread'y
  thread'i · er, thread'i · est
threat
threat'en
three
three'-cor'nered
three'-di · men'sion · al
three'fold'
three'-piece'
three'-quar'ter
three'score'
three'some
thren'o · dy
  pl. thren'o · dies
thresh
thresh'er
thresh'old
threw (*tossed*)
  (SEE through)
thrice
thrift
thrift'i · ly
thrift'i · ness
thrift'shop'
thrift'y
  thrift'i · er, thrift'i · est
thrill

thrill'er
thrive
  throve or thrived,
  thrived or thriv'en,
  thriv'ing
throat
throat'i · ly
throat'i · ness
throat'y
  throat'i · er, throat'i · est
throb
  throbbed, throb'bing
throe (*pang*)
  (SEE throw)
throm · bo'sis
throm'bus
throne
  throned, thron'ing
throng
throt'tle
  throt'tled, throt'tling
through (*done; by*
  way of)
  (SEE threw)
through · out'
through'put'
through'way'
throw (*toss*)
  (SEE throe)
throw'a · way'
throw'back'
thrown
thru
thrum
  thrummed, thrum'ming
thrush
thrust
  thrust, thrust'ing
thru'way
thud
  thud'ded, thud'ding
thug
thumb
thumb'hole'
thumb' in'dex
thumb'nail'
thumb'nut'
thumb'screw'
thumb'tack'
thump
thump'ing

thun'der
thun'der · bird'
thun'der · bolt'
thun'der · clap'
thun'der · cloud'
thun'der · head'
thun'der · ous
thun'der · show'er
thun'der · storm'
thun'der · struck'
Thurs'day
thus
thwack
thwart
thy
thyme (*herb*)
  (SEE time)
thy'mol
thy'mus
  pl. thy'mus · es or
  thy'mi
thy'roid
thy · self'
ti · ar'a
Ti · bet'
Ti · bet'an
tib'i · a
  pl. tib'i · ae' or tib'i · as
tic (*twitch*)
  (SEE tick)
tic' dou'lou · reux'
tick (*sound; insect;*
  mark)
  (SEE tic)
tick'er
tick'et
tick' fe'ver
tick'ing
tick'le
  tick'led, tick'ling
tick'ler
tick'lish
tick'-tack-toe' or tic'-
  tac-toe'
tid'al
tid'al wave'
tid'bit'
tid'dle · dy · winks'
tid'dly · winks'

tide
  tid'ed, tid'ing
tide'land'
tide'mark'
tide'wa'ter
ti'di·ly
ti'di·ness
ti'dings
ti'dy
  ti'di·er, ti'di·est
tie
  tied, ty'ing
tie'back'
tie'-dye'
  tie'-dyed', tie'-dye'ing
tie'-in'
Tien'tsin'
tie'pin'
tier (*row*)
  (SEE tear)
tie'-up'
tiff
Tif'fa·ny
ti'ger
  pl. ti'gers *or* ti'ger
ti'ger·eye'
ti'ger·ish
ti'ger lil'y
ti'ger's-eye'
tight
tight'en
tight'fist'ed
tight'knit'
tight'-lipped'
tight'rope'
  tight'roped',
  tight'rop'ing
tights
tight'wad'
ti'gress
til'de
tile
  tiled, til'ing
till
till'a·ble
till'age
till'er
tilt
tim'bal (*drum*)
  (SEE timbale)

tim'bale (*food*)
  (SEE timbal)
tim'ber (*wood*)
  (SEE timbre)
tim'ber·land'
tim'ber line'
tim'ber wolf'
tim'bre (*sound*)
  (SEE timber)
tim'brel
Tim'buk·tu'
time (*duration*)
  timed, tim'ing
  (SEE thyme)
time' bomb'
time'card'
time' clock'
time'-con·sum'ing
time' frame'
time'-hon'ored
time'keep'er
time'-lapse'
time'less
time'li·ness
time'ly
time'-out'
time'piece'
tim'er
time'-re·lease'
time'sav'er
time'sav'ing
time' shar'ing
time'ta'ble
time'worn'
tim'id
ti·mid'i·ty
tim'ing
tim'or·ous
tim'o·thy
  pl. tim'o·thies
tim'pa·ni
tim'pa·nist
tim'pa·num
tin
  tinned, tin'ning
tinc'ture
  tinc'tured, tinc'tur·ing
tin'der

tin'der·box'
tine
tin' foil'
tinge
  tinged, tinge'ing *or*
  ting'ing
tin'gle
  tin'gled, tin'gling
tin'gly
tin'horn'
ti'ni·ness
tink'er
tink'er·er
tin'kle
  tin'kled, tin'kling
tin'kly
  tin'klier, tin'kli·est
tin'ni·ly
tin'ni·ness
tin·ni'tus
tin'ny
  tin'ni·er, tin'ni·est
tin'-plate'
  tin'-plat'ed, tin'-plat'ing
tin'sel
  tin'seled, tin'sel·ing
tin'smith
tint
tin'tin·nab'u·la'tion
tin'type'
tin'ware'
tin'work'
ti'ny
  ti'ni·er, ti'ni·est
tip
  tipped, tip'ping
tip'-off'
tip'per
tip'pet
tip'ple
  tip'pled, tip'pling
tip'pler
tip'si·ness
tip'ster
tip'sy
  tip'si·er, tip'si·est
tip'toe'
  tip'toed', tip'to'ing
tip'top'
ti'rade

Ti·ra'na

tire
tired, tir'ing

tired

tire'less

tire'some

'tis

tis'sue
tis'sued, tis'su·ing

Ti'tan

ti·tan'ic

ti·ta'ni·um

tithe
tithed, tith'ing

ti'tian

tit'il·late'
tit'il·lat'ed, tit'il·lat'ing

tit'il·la'tion

ti'tle
ti'tled, ti'tling

ti'tled

ti'tle hold'er

ti'tle page'

ti'tlist

tit'mouse'
pl. tit'mice'

ti·tra'tion

tit'tle

tit'tle-tat'tle
tit'tle-tat'tled, tit'tle-
tat'tling

tit'u·lar

tiz'zy
pl. tiz'zies

to (toward)
(SEE two and too)

toad

toad'stool'

toad'y
pl. toad'ies; (v.)
toad'ied, toad'y·ing

to'-and-fro'
pl. to'-and-fros'

toast

toast'er

toast'mas'ter

to·bac'co
pl. to·bac'cos or
to·bac'coes

to·bac'co·nist

To·ba'go'

to·bog'gan

to·bog'gan·ist

toc·ca'ta
pl. toc·ca'te

to·coph'er·ol'

toc'sin (alarm)
(SEE toxin)

to·day'

tod'dle
tod'dled, tod'dling

tod'dler

tod'dy
pl. tod'dies

to-do'
pl. to-dos'

toe (foot part)
toed, toe'ing
(SEE tow)

toe'-dance'
toe'-danced', toe'-
danc'ing

toe' hold'

toe'less

toe'nail'

tof'fee or tof'fy

to'fu'

tog
togged, tog'ging

to'ga
pl. to'gas or to'gae

to·geth'er

tog'gle
tog'gled, tog'gling

To'go

toil (work)
(SEE toile)

toile (cloth)
(SEE toil)

toi'let

toi'let·ry
pl. toi'let·ries

toi·lette'

toil'some

toil'worn'

To·kay'

to'ken

to'ken·ism'

To'ky·o'

told

tole (metalware)
(SEE toll)

To·le'do

tol'er·a·ble

tol'er·a·bly

tol'er·ance

tol'er·ant

tol'er·ate'
tol'er·at'er, tol'er·at'ing

tol'er·a'tion

toll (fee; sound)
(SEE tole)

toll'booth'

toll' call'

toll'gate'

toll'house'

Tol'stoy

tol'u·ene'

tom

tom'a·hawk'

to·ma'to
pl. to·ma'toes

tomb

tom'boy'

tomb'stone'

tom'cat'
tom'cat'ted, tom'cat'ting

tome

tom'fool'er·y
pl. tom'fool'er·ies

tom'my·rot'

to·mor'row

tom'-tom'

ton (weight)
(SEE tun)

ton'al

to·nal'i·ty
pl. to·nal'i·ties

tone
toned, ton'ing

tone'-deaf'

tone'less

tong

Ton'ga

tongs

tongue
tongued, tongu'ing

tongue'-in-cheek'

tongue'-lash'ing

tongue'-tied'

ton'ic

to·night'

ton'nage

ton·neau'
  pl. ton·neaus' or
  ton·neaux'

ton'sil

ton'sil·lec'to·my
  pl. ton'sil·lec'to·mies

ton'sil·li'tis

ton·so'ri·al

ton'sure
  ton'sured, ton'sur·ing

ton'tine

too (also)
  (SEE to and two)

took

tool (implement)
  (SEE tulle)

tool'box'
  pl. tool'box'es

tool'mak'er

tool'room'

tool'shed'

toot

tooth
  pl. teeth

tooth'ache'

tooth'brush'
  pl. tooth'brush'es

tooth'paste

tooth'pick'

tooth' pow'der

tooth' shell'

tooth'some

tooth'y
  tooth'i·er, tooth'i·est

top
  topped, top'ping

to'paz

top'coat'

top' drawer'

To·pe'ka

top'er

top'flight'

top'gal'lant

top' hat'

to'pi·ar'y
  pl. to'pi·ar'ies

top'ic

top'i·cal

top'i·cal'i·ty
  pl. top'i·cal'i·ties

top'i·cal·ly

top'knot'

top'less

top'mast'

top'most'

top'notch'

to·pog'ra·pher

top'o·graph'ic

top'o·graph'i·cal

top'o·graph'i·cal·ly

to·pog'ra·phy
  pl. to·pog'ra·phies

top'o·log'i·cal

to·pol'o·gist

to·pol'o·gy

top'per

top'ping

top'ple
  top'pled, top'pling

tops

top'sail'

top'-se'cret

top'side'

top'soil'

top'sy-tur'vy
  pl. top'sy-tur'vies

toque

tor

To'rah

torch

torch'bear'er

torch'light'

tore

tor'e·a·dor'

tor·ment' (v.)

tor'ment (n.)

tor·men'tor

torn

tor·na'do
  pl. tor·na'does or
  tor·na'dos

To·ron'to

tor·pe'do
  pl. tor·pe'does; (v.)
  tor·pe'does,
  tor·pe'do·ing

tor'pid

tor·pid'i·ty

tor'por

torque

tor'rent

tor·ren'tial

tor·ren'tial·ly

tor'rid

tor'sion

tor'so
  pl. tor'sos or tor'si

tort (civil wrong)
  (SEE torte)

torte (cake)
  pl. tortes or (Ger.)
  tor'ten
  (SEE tort)

tor·til'la
  pl. tor·til'las

tor'toise

tor'toise shell'

tor·to'ni

tor'tu·ous (winding)
  (SEE torturous)

tor'ture
  tor'tured, tor'tur·ing

tor'tur·er

tor'tur·ous (painful)
  (SEE tortuous)

To'ry
  pl. To'ries

toss

toss'up'

tot

to'tal

to·tal'i·tar'i·an

to·tal'i·tar'i·an·ism'

to·tal'i·ty
  pl. to·tal'i·ties

To'tal·i·za'tor
  (Trademark)

to'tal·ly

tote
  tot'ed, tot'ing

to'tem

to·tem'ic

to'tem pole'

tot'ter

tou'can

touch

touch'a·ble

touch'-and-go' (*adj.*)

touch'back'

touch'down'

tou·ché'

touch'i·ly

touch'i·ness

touch'-me-not'

touch'stone'

touch'-type'
 touch'-typed', touch'-
 typ'ing

touch'-up'

touch'y
 touch'i·er, touch'i·est

tough (*rugged*)
 (SEE tuff)

tough'en

tough'-mind'ed

Tou·louse'-Lau·trec'

tou·pee'

tour

tour' de force'
 pl. tours' de force'

tour'ism

tour'ist

tour'ma·line

tour'na·ment

tour'ne·dos'
 pl. tour'ne·dos

tour'ney
 pl. tour'neys; (*v.*)
 tour'ney·ed,
 tour'ney·ing

tour'ni·quet

tou'sle
 tou'sled, tou'sling

tout

tout de suite'

tow (*pull; fiber*)
 (SEE toe)

to·ward'

to·wards'

tow'a·way'

tow'boat'

tow'el
 tow'eled, tow'el·ing

tow'el·ing

tow'er

tow'er·ing

tow'head'

tow'head'ed

tow'line'

town

town' hall'

town' house'

town'ship

towns'folk

towns'man
 pl. towns'men

towns'peo'ple

tow'path'

tow'rope'

tox·e'mi·a

tox'ic

tox'i·cant

tox·ic'i·ty
 pl. tox·ic'i·ties

tox'i·co·log'i·cal

tox'i·col'o·gist

tox'i·col'o·gy

tox'in (*poison*)
 (SEE tocsin)

tox'in-an'ti·tox'in

toy

trace
 traced, trac'ing

trace'a·ble

trac'er

trac'er·y
 pl. trac'er·ies

tra'che·a
 pl. tra'che·ae

tra'che·al

tra'che·ot'o·my
 pl. tra'che·ot'o·mies

tra·cho'ma

track (*path; follow*)
 (SEE tract)

track'age

track'ing sta'tion

track'less

track' meet'

track' shoe'

tract (*area; booklet*)
 (SEE track)

trac'ta·bil'i·ty

trac'ta·ble

trac'ta·bly

trac'tile

trac'tion

trac'tor

trade
 trad'ed, trad'ing

trade'-in'

trade'-last'

trade'mark'

trade' name'

trade'-off'

trad'er

trade' school'

trades'man
 pl. trades'men

trades'peo'ple

trade' un'ion

trade' winds'

trad'ing post'

tra·di'tion

tra·di'tion·al

tra·di'tion·al·ism'

tra·di'tion·al·ist

tra·di'tion·al·ly

tra·duce'
 tra·duced', tra·duc'ing

tra·duc'er

traf'fic
 traf'ficked, traf'fick·ing

traf'fic light'

traf'fick·er

tra·ge'di·an

tra·ge'di·enne'

trag'e·dy
 pl. trag'e·dies

trag'ic

trag'i·cal

trag'i·cal·ly

trag'i·com'e·dy
 pl. trag'i·com'e·dies

trag'i·com'ic

trail

trail'blaz'er

trail'er

train

train'a·ble

train·ee'

train'er

train'load

train'man
 pl. train'men

train′mas′ter

traipse
　traipsed, traips′ing

trait

trai′tor

trai′tor • ous

tra • jec′to • ry
　pl. tra • jec′to • ries

tram

tram′mel
　tram′meled,
　tram′mel • ing

tramp

tram′ple
　tram′pled, tram′pling

tram′po • line′

tram′way′

trance
　tranced, tranc′ing

tran′quil

tran′quil • ize′
　tran′quil • ized′,
　tran′quil • iz′ing

tran′quil • iz′er

tran • quil′li • ty

tran′quil • ly

trans • act′

trans • ac′tion

trans • ac′tion • al

trans • ac′tor

trans′–A • mer′i • can

trans′at • lan′tic

trans • ceiv′er

tran • scend′

tran • scend′ence

tran • scend′ent

tran′scen • den′tal

tran′scen • den′tal • ism′

tran′scen • den′tal • ist

trans′con • ti • nen′tal

tran • scribe′
　tran • scribed′,
　tran • scrib′ing

tran′script

tran • scrip′tion

trans • duc′er

tran • sec′tion

tran′sept

trans • fer′ (v.)
　trans • ferred′,
　trans • fer′ring

trans′fer (n.)

trans • fer′a • bil′i • ty

trans • fer′a • ble

trans • fer′al or
　trans • fer′ral

trans • fer′ence

trans′fig • u • ra′tion

trans • fig′ure
　trans • fig′ured,
　trans • fig′ur • ing

trans • fix′
　trans • fixed′ or
　trans • fixt′,
　trans • fix′ing

trans • form′ (v.)

trans′form (n.)

trans • form′a • ble

trans′for • ma′tion

trans′for • ma′tion • al

trans • form′er

trans • fuse′
　trans • fused′,
　trans • fus′ing

trans • fus′i • ble

trans • fu′sion

trans • gress′

trans • gres′sion

trans • gres′sor

tran′sience

tran′sien • cy

tran′sient

tran • sis′tor

tran • sis′tor • ize′
　tran • sis′tor • ized′,
　tran • sis′tor • iz′ing

trans′it
　trans′it • ed, trans′it • ing

tran • si′tion

tran • si′tion • al

tran • si′tion • al • ly

tran′si • tive

tran′si • tive • ly

tran′si • to′ry

Tran′skei

trans • lat′a • ble

trans • late′
　trans • lat′ed,
　trans • lat′ing

trans • la′tion

trans • la′tor

trans • lit′er • ate′
　trans • lit′er • at′ed,
　trans • lit′er • at′ing

trans • lit′er • a′tion

trans • lu′cence

trans • lu′cen • cy

trans • lu′cent

trans • mi′grate
　trans • mi′grat • ed,
　trans • mi′grat • ing

trans′mi • gra′tion

trans • mis′si • ble

trans • mis′sion

trans • mit′
　trans • mit′ted,
　trans • mit′ting

trans • mit′ta • ble

trans • mit′tal

trans • mit′tance

trans • mit′ter

trans • mog′ri • fi •
　ca′tion

trans • mog′ri • fy′
　trans • mog′ri • fied′,
　trans • mog′ri • fy′ing

trans • mut′a • ble

trans′mu • ta′tion

trans • mute′
　trans • mut′ed,
　trans • mut′ing

trans′o • ce • an′ic

tran′som

tran • son′ic

trans′pa • cif′ic

trans • par′ence

trans • par′en • cy
　pl. trans • par′en • cies

trans • par′ent

tran′spi • ra′tion

tran • spire′
　tran • spired′,
　tran • spir′ing

trans • plant′ (v.)

trans′plant′ (n.)

trans • plant′a • ble

trans′plan • ta′tion

trans • po′lar

tran • spon′der

trans • port′ (v.)

trans′port′ (n.)

trans'por·ta'tion

trans·port'er

trans·pos'a·ble

trans·pose'
trans·posed',
trans·pos'ing

trans'po·si'tion

trans·sex'u·al

trans·ship'
trans·shipped',
trans·ship'ping

trans·ship'ment

trans·son'ic

tran'sub·stan·
ti·a'tion

trans'val·u·a'tion

trans·val'ue

trans·ver'sal

trans·verse'

trans·verse'ly

trans·ves'tism

trans·ves'tite

trap
trapped, trap'ping

trap' door'

tra·peze'

tra·pe'zi·um
pl. tra·pe'zi·ums or
tra·pe'zi·a

trap'e·zoid'

trap'e·zoi'dal

trap'per

trap'pings

Trap'pist

trap'shoot'ing

trash

trash'y
trash'i·er, trash'i·est

trash'i·ness

trau'ma
pl. trau'ma·ta or
trau'mas

trau·mat'ic

trau·mat'i·cal·ly

trau'ma·ti·za'tion

trau'ma·tize'
trau'ma·tized',
trau'ma·tiz'ing

tra·vail' (toil;
anguish)
(SEE travel)

trav'el (journey)
trav'eled or trav'elled,
trav'el·ing or
trav'el·ling
(SEE travail)

trav'el·er

trav'e·logue' or
trav'e·log'

tra·vers'a·ble

tra·vers'al

trav'erse
trav'ersed, trav'ers·ing

trav'er·tine

trav'es·ty
pl. trav'es·ties; (v.)
trav'es·tied,
trav'es·ty·ing

trawl

trawl'er

tray (container)
(SEE trey)

treach'er·ous

treach'er·y
pl. treach'er·ies

trea'cle

tread
trod, trod'den or trod,
tread'ing

trea'dle
trea'dled, trea'dling

tread'mill'

trea'son

trea'son·a·ble

trea'son·ous

treas'ur·a·ble

treas'ure
treas'ured, treas'ur·ing

treas'ur·er

treas'ure–trove'

treas'u·ry
pl. treas'ur·ies

treat

treat'a·ble

trea'tise

treat'ment

treat'y
pl. trea'ties

tre'ble
tre'bled, tre'bling

tre'bly

tree
treed, tree'ing

tree' house'

tree'lined'

tree'nail'

tree'top'

tre'foil

trek
trekked, trek'king

trel'lis

trem'ble
trem'bled, trem'bling

trem'bly
trem'bli·er,
trem'bli·est

tre·men'dous

trem'o·lo'
pl. trem'o·los'

trem'or

trem'u·lous

trench

trench'ant

trench'er·man
pl. trench'er·men

trench' mouth'

trend

trend'y

Tren'ton

tre·pan'
tre·panned',
tre·pan'ning

trep'a·na'tion

treph'i·na'tion

tre·phine'
tre·phined',
tre·phin'ing

trep'i·da'tion

tres'pass

tres'pass·er

tress

tres'tle

tres'tle·work'

trey (three)
(SEE tray)

tri'a·ble

tri'ad

tri'age

tri'al

tri'an'gle

tri·an'gu·lar

tri·an'gu·late (adj.)

tri·an'gu·late' (v.)
tri·an'gu·lat'ed,
tri·an'gu·lat'ing

tri·an'gu·la'tion
Tri·as'sic
trib'al
trib'al·ism'
tribe
tribes'man
 pl. tribes'men
trib'u·la'tion
tri·bu'nal
trib'une
trib'u·tar'y
 pl. trib'u·tar'ies
trib'ute
trice
tri'ceps
 pl. tri'ceps·es or
 tri'ceps
tri·chi'na
 pl. tri·chi'nae
trich'i·no'sis
tri·chot'o·my
 pl. tri·chot'o·mies
tri'chro·mat'ic
trick
trick'er·y
 pl. trick'er·ies
trick'i·ly
trick'i·ness
trick'le
 trick'led, trick'ling
trick'ster
trick'y
 trick'i·er, trick'i·est
tri'col'or
tri'col'ored
tri·cor'nered
tri'cot
tri'cy·cle
tri'dent
tri'di·men'sion·al
tried
tri·en'ni·al
tri'er
tri'fle
 tri'fled, tri'fling
tri'fler
tri'fling
tri·fo'cal
trig
 trigged, trig'ging

trig'ger
trig'ger–hap'py
tri·glyc'er·ide'
trig'o·no·met'ric
trig'o·no·met'ri·cal
trig'o·nom'e·try
tri·lat'er·al
tri·lin'gual
trill
tril'lion
tril'lionth
tril'li·um
tril'o·gy
 pl. tril'o·gies
trim
 (v.) trimmed,
 trim'ming; (adj.)
 trim'mer, trim'mest
trim'mer
tri·mes'ter
trim'e·ter
tri·month'ly
trine
Trin'i·dad'
Trin'i·dad'i·an
tri·ni'tro·tol'u·ene'
Trin'i·ty
trin'i·ty
 pl. trin'i·ties
trin'ket
tri·no'mi·al
tri'o
 pl. tri'os
tri'ode
trip
 tripped, trip'ping
tri·par'tite
tripe
trip'ham'mer
triph'thong
tri'ple
 tri'pled, tri'pling
tri'ple play'
trip'let
tri'plex
trip'li·cate' (v.)
 trip'li·cat'ed,
 trip'li·cat'ing
trip'li·cate (adj., n.)

trip'li·ca'tion
tri'ply
tri'pod
Trip'o·li
trip'per
trip'tych
tri·sect'
tri'–state'
trite
 trit'er, trit'est
trite'ly
trite'ness
trit'u·rate'
 trit'u·rat'ed,
 trit'u·rat'ing
trit'u·ra'tion
tri'umph
tri·um'phal
tri·um'phant
tri·um'vir
 pl. tri·um'virs or
 tri·um'vi·ri'
tri·um'vi·rate
tri'une
tri·va'lent
triv'et
triv'i·a
triv'i·al
triv'i·al'i·ty
 pl. triv'i·al'i·ties
triv'i·al·ly
triv'i·um
 pl. triv'i·a
tri·week'ly
 pl. tri·week'lies
tro·cha'ic
tro'che (lozenge)
 (SEE trochee)
tro'chee (poetic
 meter)
 (SEE troche)
trod'den
trog'lo·dyte'
troi'ka
Tro'jan
troll
trol'ley
 pl. trol'leys; (v.)
 trol'leyed, trol'ley·ing
trol'ley car'
trol'lop

trom · bone'

trom · bon'ist

trompe' l'oeil'

troop (*soldiers*)
(SEE troup).

troop'er (*soldier*)
(SEE trouper)

troop'ship'

trope

tro'phy
pl. tro'phies

trop'ic

trop'i · cal

tro · pism

trop'o · sphere'

trot
trot'ted, trot'ting

troth

Trot'sky

trot'ter

trou'ba · dour'

trou'ble
trou'bled, trou'bling

trou'ble · mak'er

trou'ble · shoot'er

trou'ble · some

trough

trounce
trounced, trounc'ing

troupe (*acting group*)
trouped, troup'ing
(SEE troop)

troup'er (*actor*)
(SEE trooper)

trou'sers

trous'seau
pl. trous'seaux or
trous'seaus

trout
pl. trout or trouts

trove

trow'el
trow'eled, trow'el · ing

troy

tru'an · cy
pl. tru'an · cies

tru'ant

truce

truck

truck'age

truck'driv'er

truck'er

truck' farm'

truck'ing

truck'le
truck'led, truck'ling

truck'load'

truc'u · lence

truc'u · lent

Tru · deau'

trudge
trudged, trudg'ing

true
(*adj.*) tru'er, tru'est;
(*v.*) trued, tru'ing or
true'ing

true'–blue'

true'–life'

true'love'

true'ness

truf'fle

tru'ism

tru'ly

Tru'man

trump

trumped'–up'

trump'er · y
pl. trump'er · ies

trum'pet

trum'pet · er

trun'cate
trun'cat · ed,
trun'cat · ing

trun · ca'tion

trun'cheon

trun'dle
trun'dled, trun'dling

trun'dle bed'

trunk

trunk' line'

truss

trust

trus · tee' (*guardian*)
trus · teed', trus · tee'ing
(SEE trusty)

trus · tee'ship

trust'ful

trust'ful · ly

trust'ful · ness

trust'i · ness

trust'wor'thi · ly

trust'wor'thi · ness

trust'wor'thy

trust'y (*reliable*)
(*adj.*) trust'i · er,
trust'i · est;
pl. trust'ies
(SEE trustee)

truth

truth'ful

truth'ful · ly

truth'ful · ness

try
(*v.*) tried, try'ing;
pl. tries

try'out'

try'sail mast'

tryst

tset'se

T'–shirt'

T' square'

tsu · na'mi

tub
tubbed, tub'bing

tu'ba
pl. tu'bas or tu'bae

tub'by
tub'bi · er, tub'bi · est

tube
tubed, tub'ing

tube'less

tu'ber

tu'ber · cle

tu · ber'cu · lar

tu · ber'cu · late

tu · ber'cu · lin

tu · ber'cu · lo'sis

tu · ber'cu · lous

tube'rose'

tu'ber · ose'

tu'ber · ous

tub'ing

tu'bu · lar

tu'bule

tuck

tuck'er

Tuc'son

Tu'dor

Tues'day

tuff (*rock*)
  (SEE tough)

tuff'et

tuft

tuft'ed

tug
  tugged, tug'ging

tug'boat'

tug' of war'

tu·i'tion

tu·la·re'mi·a

tu'lip

tu'lip tree'

tulle (*net fabric*)
  (SEE tool)

Tul'sa

tum'ble
  tum'bled, tum'bling

tum'ble–down'

tum'bler

tum'ble·weed'

tum'brel or tum'bril

tu·mes'cence

tu·mes'cent

tu'mid

tu·mid'i·ty

tum'my
  pl. tum'mies

tu'mor

tu'mor·ous

tu'mult

tu·mul'tu·ous

tun (*cask*)
  tunned, tun'ning
  (SEE ton)

tu'na
  pl. tu'na or tu'nas

tun'a·ble

tun'dra

tune
  tuned, tun'ing

tune'a·ble

tune'ful

tune'ful·ly

tune'less

tun'er

tune'–up'

tung'sten

tu'nic

Tu'nis

Tu·ni'sia

Tu·ni'sian

tun'nel
  tun'neled, tun'nel·ing

tun'ny
  pl. tun'nies or tun'ny

tu'pe·lo'
  pl. tu'pe·los'

tuque

tur'ban (*headdress*)
  (SEE turbine)

tur'bid

tur'bine (*engine*)
  (SEE turban)

tur'bo·charg'er

tur'bo·fan'

tur'bo·jet'

tur'bo·prop'

tur'bot
  pl. tur'bot or tur'bots

tur'bu·lence

tur'bu·lent

tu·reen'

turf
  pl. turfs

tur'gid

tur·gid'i·ty

Turk

tur'key (*fowl*)
  pl. tur'keys or tur'key

Tur'key (*country*)

Turk'ish

tur'mer·ic

tur'moil

turn (*rotate*)
  (SEE tern)

turn'a·bout'

turn'a·round'

turn'buck'le

turn'coat'

turn'down'

turn'er

tur'nip

turn'key'
  pl. turn'keys'

turn'off'

turn'out'

turn'o'ver

turn'pike'

turn'stile'

turn'ta·ble

tur'pen·tine'
  tur'pen·tined',
  tur'pen·tin'ing

tur'pi·tude'

tur'quoise

tur'ret

tur'ret·ed

tur'tle
  pl. tur'tles or tur'tle;
  (*v.*) tur'tled, tur'tling

tur'tle·dove'

tur'tle·neck'

Tus'can

tusk

tusk'er

tus'sle
  tus'sled, tus'sling

tus'sock

Tut'ankh·a'men

tu'te·lage

tu'te·lar'y
  pl. tu'te·lar'ies

tu'tor

tu·to'ri·al

tut'ti·frut'ti

tu'tu
  pl. tu'tus

tux

tux·e'do
  pl. tux·e'dos

twad'dle
  twad'dled, twad'dling

twain

Twain

twang

twang'y
  twang'i·er, twang'i·est

'twas

tweak

tweed

tweed'i·ness

tweed'y
  tweed'i·er, tweed'i·est

tweet

tweet'er

tweeze

tweez'ers

twelfth

twelve

twen'ti · eth

twen'ty
  pl. twen'ties

twerp

twice

twice'-told'

twid'dle
  twid'dled, twid'dling

twig

twig'gy
  twig'gi · er, twig'gi · est

twi'light'

twill

twin
  twinned, twin'ning

twine
  twined, twin'ing

twinge
  twinged, twing'ing

twi'night'

twin'kle
  twin'kled, twin'kling

twin'-screw'

twirl

twirl'er

twist

twist'a · ble

twist'er

twit
  twitted, twit'ting

twitch

twit'ter

'twixt

two (*number*)
  (SEE to *and* too)

two'-bit'

two'-by-four'

two'-di · men'sion · al

two'-edged'

two'-faced'

two'fer

two'fist'ed

two'fold'

two'-hand'ed

two'-piece'

two'-ply'

two'-sid'ed

two'some

two'-step'
  two'-stepped', two'-step'ping

two'-time'
  two'-timed', two'-tim'ing

two'-way'

ty · coon'

tyke

Ty'ler

tym · pan'i

tym · pan'ic

tym'pa · nist

tym'pa · num
  pl. tym'pa · nums or tym'pa · na

type
  typed, typ'ing

type'-cast' (*cast type*)
  type'-cast', type'-cast'ing
  (SEE BELOW)

type'cast' (*cast performer*)
  (SEE ABOVE)

type'face'

type'script'

type'set'
  type'set', type'set'ting

type'set'ter

type'set'ting

type'write'
  type'wrote', type'writ'ten, type'writ'ing

type'writ'er

type'writ'ing

ty'phoid'

ty · phoon'

ty'phus

typ'i · cal

typ'i · cal · ly

typ'i · fy'
  typ'i · fied', typ'i · fy'ing

typ'ist

ty'po
  pl. ty'pos

ty · pog'ra · pher

ty'po · graph'ic

ty'po · graph'i · cal

ty'po · graph'i · cal · ly

ty · pog'ra · phy

ty'po · log'i · cal

ty · ran'nic

ty · ran'ni · cal

ty · ran'ni · cal · ly

tyr'an · nize'
  tyr'an · nized', tyr'an · niz'ing

ty · ran'no · saur'

ty · ran'no · saur'us

tyr'an · nous

tyr'an · ny
  pl. tyr'an · nies

ty'rant

ty'ro
  pl. ty'ros

ty'ro · thri'cin

tzar

tza · ri'na

U

u · biq'ui · tous

u · biq'ui · ty

U'-boat'

ud'der

U · gan'da

U · gan'dan

ugh

ug'li (*fruit*)
  (SEE ugly)

ug'li · ness

ug'ly (*homely*)
  ug'li · er, ug'li · est
  (SEE ugli)

uh

u'kase

U · kraine'

U · krain'i · an

u'ku · le'le

U'lan Ba'tor

ul'cer

ul'cer·ate'
  ul'cer·at'ed,
  ul'cer·at'ing
ul'cer·a'tion
ul'cer·a'tive
ul'cer·ous
ul'na
  pl. ul'nae or ul'nas
Ul'ster
ul·te'ri·or
ul'ti·mate
ul'ti·mate·ly
ul'ti·ma'tum
  pl. ul'ti·ma'tums or
  ul'ti·ma'ta
ul'ti·mo
ul'tra
ul'tra·con·ser'va·tive
ul'tra·fash'ion·a·ble
ul'tra·fiche'
ul'tra·high'
  fre'quen·cy
ul'tra·ism'
ul'tra·ma·rine'
ul'tra·mi'cro·scope'
ul'tra·mod'ern
ul'tra·mon·tane'
ul'tra·na'tion·al·ism'
ul'tra·short'
ul'tra·son'ic
ul'tra·son'ics
Ul'tra·suede'
  (Trademark)
ul'tra·vi'o·let
ul'tra vi'res
ul'u·late'
  ul'u·lat'ed, ul'u·lat'ing
ul'u·la'tion
U·lys'ses
um'bel
um'bel·late
um'ber
um·bil'i·cal
um·bil'i·cus
  pl. um·bil'i·ci'
um'bra
um'brage
um·bra'geous
um·brel'la

u'mi·ak'
um'laut
um'pire
  um'pired, um'pir·ing
ump'teen'
un'a·bashed'
un'a·bat'ed
un·a'ble
un'a·bridged'
un'ac·com'pa·nied
un'ac·count'a·ble
un'ac·count'ed–for'
un'ac·cus'tomed
un'a·dorned'
un'a·dul'ter·at'ed
un'ad·vised'
un'af·fect'ed
un'a·ligned'
un·al·lied'
un·al·loyed'
un·al'ter·a·ble
un'–A·mer'i·can
u·nan'i·mous
un·an'swer·a·ble
un·armed'
un·asked'
un'as·sail'a·ble
un'as·signed'
un'as·sum'ing
un'at·tached'
un'at·tend'ed
un·au'thor·ized'
un'a·vail'ing
un'a·void'a·ble
un'a·void'a·bly
un'a·ware'
un'a·wares'
un·awed'
un·bal'anced
un·bar'
  un·barred', un·bar'ring
un·bear'a·ble
un·bear'a·bly
un·beat'a·ble
un·beat'en
un'be·com'ing
un'be·known'

un'be·knownst'
un'be·lief'
un'be·liev'a·ble
un'be·liev'a·bly
un'be·liev'er
un'be·liev'ing
un·bend'
  un·bent', un·bend'ing
un·bi'ased
un·bid'den
un·bind'
  un·bound',
  un·bind'ing
un·blessed'
un·blush'ing
un·bolt'
un·born'
un·bos'om
un·bound'
un·bound'ed
un·bowed'
un·bri'dle
  un·bri'dled,
  un·bri'dling
un·bro'ken
un·bur'den
un·but'ton
un·called'–for'
un·can'ni·ly
un·can'ny
un·cap'
  un·capped',
  un·cap'ping
un·cared'–for'
un·ceas'ing
un·cer·e·mo'ni·ous
un·cer'tain
un·cer'tain·ty
  pl. un·cer'tain·ties
un·chain'
un·change'a·ble
un·change'a·bly
un·char'i·ta·ble
un·chart'ed
un·chaste'
un·cho'sen
un·chris'tian
un'ci·al
un·civ'il

un·civ'i·lized'
un·clad'
un·clasp'
un·clas'si·fied'
un'cle
un·clean'
un·clean'li·ness
un·clear'
un·clench'
Un'cle Sam'
un·clog'
  un·clogged',
  un·clog'ging
un·clothe'
  un·clothed' or
  un·clad', un·cloth'ing
un·coil'
un·com'fort·a·ble
un·com'fort·a·bly
un'com·mit'ted
un·com'mon
un'com·mu'ni·ca'tive
un·com'pro·mis'ing
un'con·cern'
un'con·cerned'
un'con·di'tion·al
un'con·di'tion·al·ly
un'con·form'i·ty
  pl. un'con·form'i·ties
un·con'quer·a·ble
un·con'scion·a·ble
un·con'scion·a·bly
un·con'scious
un'con·sti·tu'tion·al
un'con·sti·tu'tion·al'i·ty
un'con·trol'la·ble
un'con·trol'la·bly
un'con·ven'tion·al
un'con·ven'tion·al'i·ty
un'con·ven'tion·al·ly
un·cooked'
un·cork'
un·count'ed
un·cou'ple
  un·cou'pled,
  un·cou'pling
un·couth'

un·cov'er
un·crit'i·cal
un·cross'
unc'tion
unc'tu·ous
un·curl'
un·cut'
un·daunt'ed
un·de·cid'ed
un·de·mon'stra·tive
un·de·ni'a·ble
un·de·ni'a·bly
un'der
un'der·a·chieve'
  un'der·a·chieved',
  un'der·a·chiev'ing
un'der·a·chiev'er
un'der·act'
un'der·age'
un'der·arm'
un'der·bel'ly
  pl. un'der·bel'lies
un'der·bid'
  un'der·bid',
  un'der·bid'ding
un'der·brush'
un'der·car'riage
un'der·charge' (v.)
  un'der·charged',
  un'der·charg'ing
un'der·charge' (n.)
un'der·class'man
  pl. un'der·class'men
un'der·clothes'
un'der·cloth'ing
un'der·coat'
un'der·coat'ing
un'der·cook'
un'der·cov'er
un'der·cur'rent
un'der·cut'
  un'der·cut',
  un'der·cut'ting
un'der·de·vel'oped
un'der·dog'
un'der·done'
un'der·draw'ers
un'der·es'ti·mate'
  (v.)
  un'der·es'ti·mat'ed,
  un'der·es'ti·mat'ing

un'der·es'ti·mate
  (n.)
un'der·es'ti·ma'tion
un'der·ex·pose'
  un'der·ex·posed',
  un'der·ex·pos'ing
un'der·ex·po'sure
un'der·feed'
  un'der·fed',
  un'der·feed'ing
un'der·foot'
un'der·gar'ment
un'der·gird'
  un'der·gird'ed or
  un'der·girt',
  un'der·gird'ing
un'der·glaze'
un'der·go'
  un'der·went,
  un'der·gone',
  un'der·go'ing
un'der·grad'u·ate
un'der·ground' (adv.,
  adj.)
un'der·ground' (n.)
un'der·growth'
un'der·hand'
un'der·hand'ed
un'der·hung'
un'der·lay' (v.)
  un'der·laid',
  un'der·lay'ing
un'der·lay' (n.)
un'der·lay'er
un'der·lie' (v.)
  un'der·lay',
  un'der·lain',
  un'der·ly'ing
un'der·lie (n.)
un'der·line'
  un'der·lined',
  un'der·lin'ing
un'der·ling
un'der·lip'
un'der·ly'ing
un'der·mine'
  un'der·mined',
  un'der·min'ing
un'der·most'
un'der·neath'
un'der·nour'ish
un'der·pants'
un'der·part'

un'der·pass'
un'der·pay'
  un'der·paid',
  un'der·pay'ing
un'der·pin'
  un'der·pinned',
  un'der·pin'ning
un'der·play'
un'der·price'
  un'der·priced',
  un'der·pric'ing
un'der·priv'i·leged
un'der·pro·duce'
  un'der·pro·duced',
  un'der·pro·duc'ing
un'der·rate'
  un'der·rat'ed,
  un'der·rat'ing
un'der·score' (v.)
  un'der·scored',
  un'der·scor'ing
un'der·score' (n.)
un'der·sea'
un'der·sec're·tar'y
  pl. un'der·sec're·tar'ies
un'der·sell'
  un'der·sold',
  un'der·sell'ing
un'der·shirt'
un'der·shoot'
  un'der·shot',
  un'der·shoot'ing
un'der·shot'
un'der·side'
un'der·sign'
un'der·size'
un'der·sized'
un'der·skirt'
un'der·slung'
un'der·staffed'
un'der·stand'
  un'der·stood',
  un'der·stand'ing
un'der·stand'a·ble
un'der·stand'a·bly
un'der·stand'ing
un'der·state'
  un'der·stat'ed,
  un'der·stat'ing
un'der·state'ment
un'der·stood'
un'der·stud'y
  un'der·stud'ied,
  un'der·stud'y·ing
  pl. un'der·stud'ies

un'der·sur'face
un'der·take'
  un'der·took',
  un'der·tak'en,
  un'der·tak'ing
un'der·tak'er
un'der·tak'ing
un'der-the-coun'ter
un'der·tone'
un'der·tow'
un'der·val'ue
  un'der·val'ued,
  un'der·val'u·ing
un'der·wa'ter
un'der·way'
un'der·wear'
un'der·weight' (n.)
un'der·weight' (adj.)
un'der·world'
un'der·write'
  un'der·wrote',
  un'der·writ'ten,
  un'der·writ'ing
un'der·writ'er
un'de·served'
un'de·sir'a·ble
un'dies
un'de·vel'oped
un·de'vi·at'ing
un·do' (reverse;
  open)
  un·did', un·done',
  un·do'ing
  (SEE undue)
un·do'ing
un·doubt'ed
un·dress'
  un·dressed' or
  un·drest', un·dress'ing
un·due' (excessive)
  (SEE undo)
un'du·lant
un'du·late' (v.)
  un'du·lat'ed,
  un'du·lat'ing
un'du·late (adj.)
un'du·la'tion
un·du'ly
un·dyed'
un·dy'ing
un·earned'
un·earth'

un·earth'ly
un·eas'i·ly
un·eas'i·ness
un·eas'y
  un·eas'i·er,
  un·eas'i·est
un·ed'u·cat'ed
un'em·ploy'a·ble
un'em·ployed'
un'em·ploy'ment
un·end'ing
un·en'vi·a·ble
un·e'qual
un·e'qualed
un·e'qual·ly
un'e·quiv'o·cal
un'e·quiv'o·cal·ly
un·err'ing
un'es·sen'tial
un·eth'i·cal
un·e'ven
un·e·vent'ful
un'ex·am'pled
un'ex·cep'tion·a·ble
un'ex·cep'tion·al
un'ex·pect'ed
un·fail'ing
un·fair'
un·faith'ful
un·faith'ful·ly
un'fa·mil'iar
un'fa·mil'i·ar'i·ty
un·fas'ten
un·fa'vor·a·ble
un·fa'vor·a·bly
un·fed'
un·feel'ing
un·feigned'
un·fet'tered
un·filled'
un·fin'ished
un·fit'
un·fit'ting
un·flag'ging
un·flap'pa·ble
un·fledged'
un·flinch'ing

un·fold'
un'fore·seen'
un'fore·told'
un·for·get'ta·ble
un·for·get'ta·bly
un·formed'
un·for'tu·nate
un·found'ed
un·friend'ly
  un·friend'li·er,
  un·friend'li·est
un·fre'quent·ed
un·frock'
un·fruit'ful
un·furl'
un·gain'li·ness
un·gain'ly
un·gen'er·ous
un·gird'
  un·gird'ed or un·girt',
  un·gird'ing
un·god'ly
  un·god'li·er,
  un·god'li·est
un·gov'ern·a·ble
un·grace'ful
un·gra'cious
un'gram·mat'i·cal
un·grate'ful
un·guard'ed
un'guent
un·guid'ed
un'gu·late
un·hand'
un·hap'py
  un·hap'pi·er,
  un·hap'pi·est
un·health'y
  un·health'i·er,
  un·health'i·est
un·heard'
un·heard'-of'
un·hinge'
  un·hinged',
  un·hing'ing
un·hitch'
un·ho'ly
  un·ho'li·er,
  un·ho'li·est
un·hook'
un·hoped'-for'

un·horse'
  un·horsed',
  un·hors'ing
un·hur'ried
un'hy·gi·en'ic
u'ni·cam'er·al
U'NI·CEF'
u'ni·cel'lu·lar
u'ni·corn'
u'ni·cy'cle
u'ni·di·rec'tion·al
u'ni·fi'a·ble
u'ni·fi·ca'tion
u'ni·fi'er
u'ni·form'
u'ni·form'i·ty
  pl. u'ni·form'i·ties
u'ni·fy'
  u'ni·fied', u'ni·fy'ing
u'ni·lat'er·al
u'ni·lat'er·al·ly
un'im·peach'a·ble
un'im·peach'a·bly
un'in·hib'it·ed
un·in'jured
un'in·tel'li·gent
un'in·tel'li·gi·ble
un'in·ten'tion·al
un'in·ten'tion·al·ly
un·in'ter·est·ed
un'in·ter·rupt'ed
un'in·vit'ed
un'ion
un'ion·ism'
un'ion·ist
un'ion·i·za'tion
un'ion·ize'
  un'ion·ized',
  un'ion·iz'ing
u·nique'
u'ni·sex'
u'ni·son
u'nit
U'ni·tar'i·an
u'ni·tar'y
u·nite'
  u·nit'ed, u·nit'ing
U·nit'ed Ar'ab
  E·mir'ates

U·nit'ed King'dom
U·nit'ed Na'tions
U·nit'ed States'
u'ni·tize'
  u'ni·tized', u'ni·tiz'ing
u'ni·ty
  pl. u'ni·ties
u'ni·ver'sal
u'ni·ver·sal'i·ty
  pl. u'ni·ver·sal'i·ties
u'ni·ver'sal·ly
u'ni·verse'
u'ni·ver'si·ty
  pl. u'ni·ver'si·ties
un·just'
un·kempt'
un·kind'
un·know'ing
un·known'
un·lace'
  un·laced', un·lac'ing
un·lade'
  un·lad'ed, un·lad'ing
un·latch'
un·law'ful
un·learn'
un·learn'ed
un·leash'
un·leav'ened
un·less'
un·let'tered
un·li'censed
un·like'
un·like'li·hood'
un·like'li·ness
un·like'ly
un·lim'ber
un·lim'it·ed
un·list'ed
un·load'
un·lock'
un·looked'-for'
un·loose'
  un·loosed', un·loos'ing
un·loos'en
un·love'ly
un·luck'y
  un·luck'i·er,
  un·luck'i·est

un·make'
  un·made', un·mak'ing
un·man'
  un·manned',
  un·man'ning
un·man'ly
un·manned'
un·man'ner·ly
un·marked'
un·mask'
un·men'tion·a·ble
un·mer'ci·ful
un·mind'ful
un'mis·tak'a·ble
un'mis·tak'a·bly
un·mit'i·gat·ed
un·mourned'
un·moved'
un·muz'zle
  un·muz'zled,
  un·muz'zling
un·nat'u·ral
un·nec'es·sar'i·ly
un·nec'es·sar'y
  pl. un·nec'es·sar'ies
un·need'ed
un·nerve'
  un·nerved',
  un·nerv'ing
un·no'ticed
un·num'bered
un'ob·tru'sive
un·oc'cu·pied'
un'of·fi'ci·al
un·or'gan·ized'
un·or'tho·dox
un·pack'
un·paid'
un·par'al·leled'
un·pin'
  un·pinned',
  un·pin'ning
un·pleas'ant
un·pleased'
un·plug'
  un·plugged',
  un·plug'ging
un·plumbed'
un·pop'u·lar
un'pop·u·lar'i·ty

un·prec'e·dent·ed
un'pre·dict'a·bil'i·ty
un'pre·dict'a·ble
un·prej'u·diced
un'pre·pared'
un'pre·vent'a·ble
un·prin'ci·pled
un·print'a·ble
un'pro·duc'tive
un'pro·fes'sion·al
un·prof'it·a·ble
un·prof'it·a·bly
un·qual'i·fied
un·ques'tion·a·ble
un·ques'tion·a·bly
un·ques'tioned
un·quote'
  un·quot'ed,
  un·quot'ing
un·rav'el
  un·rav'eled,
  un·rav'el·ing
un·read'
un·read'a·ble
un·read'i·ness
un·read'y
un·re'al
un're·al·is'tic
un're·al·is'ti·cal·ly
un·rea'son·a·ble
un·rea'son·a·bly
un·rea'son·ing
un're·con·struct'ed
un·reel'
un're·**gen**'er·ate
un're·lent'ing
un're·li'a·ble
un're·mit'ting
un're·pent'ant
un're·served'
un·rest'
un're·strained'
un·right'eous
un·ripe'
un·ri'valed
un·roll'
un·ruf'fled
un·ru'li·ness

un·ru'ly
  un·ru'li·er,
  un·ru'li·est
un·sad'dle
  un·sad'dled,
  un·sad'dling
un'sat·is·fac'to·ry
un·sat'u·rat'ed
un·sa'vor·y
un·say'a·ble
un·scathed'
un·schooled'
un'sci·en·tif'ic
un'sci·en·tif'i·cal·ly
un·scram'ble
  un·scram'bled,
  un·scram'bling
un·screw'
un·scru'pu·lous
un·seal'
un·sea'son·a·ble
un·sea'son·a·bly
un·sea'soned
un·seat'
un·seem'ly
un·seen'
un·seg're·gat·ed
un·self'ish
un·set'tle
  un·set'tled, un·set'tling
un·set'tled
un·shack'le
  un·shack'led,
  un·shack'ling
un·sheathe'
  un·sheathed',
  un·sheath'ing
un·shod'
un·shorn'
un·sight'ly
un·skilled'
un·skill'ful
un·snarl'
un'so·phis'ti·cat'ed
un·sought'
un·sound'
un·spar'ing
un·speak'a·ble
un·speak'a·bly
un·spec'i·fied'

un·spot'ted
un·sta'ble
un·stead'i·ly
un·stead'i·ness
un·stead'y
  un·stead'ied,
  un·stead'y·ing
un·stop'
  un·stopped',
  un·stop'ping
un·strap'
  un·strapped',
  un·strap'ping
un·stressed'
un·string'
  un·strung',
  un·string'ing
un·stud'ied
un'sub·stan'tial
un'suc·cess'ful
un'suc·cess'ful·ly
un·suit'a·ble
un·sul'lied
un·sung'
un·sure'
un'sus·pect'ed
un·tame'
un·tan'gle
  un·tan'gled,
  un·tan'gling
un·ten'a·ble
un·think'a·ble
un·think'ing
un·ti'dy
  (adj.) un·ti'di·er,
  un·ti'di·est; (v.)
  un·ti'died,
  un·ti'dy·ing
un·tie'
  un·tied', un·ty'ing
un·til'
un·time'ly
un·tir'ing
un·tit'led
un'to
un·told'
un'touch·a·bil'i·ty
un·touch'a·ble
un·to·ward'
un·tried'
un·true'

un·truth'
un·truth'ful
un·tu'tored
un·used'
un·u'su·al
un·u'su·al·ly
un·ut'ter·a·ble
un·ut'ter·a·bly
un·var'nished
un·veil'
un·voiced'
un·war'y
un·washed'
un·wed'
un·well'
un·whole'some
un·wield'ly
un·wield'y
un·will'ing
un·wind'
  un·wound',
  un·wind'ing
un·wise'
un·wished'-for'
un·wit'ting
un·wont'ed
un·world'ly
un·wor'ried
un·wor'thi·ly
un·wor'thi·ness
un·wor'thy
  pl. un·wor'thies
un·yield'ing
un·yoke'
  un·yoked', un·yok'ing
un·zip'
  un·zipped', un·zip'ping
up
  upped, up'ping
up'-and-com'ing
up'-and-down'
up'beat'
up·braid'
up'bring'ing
up'chuck'
up'com'ing
up'coun'try
up·date'
  up·dat'ed, up·dat'ing

up'draft'
up·end'
up'-front'
up'grade' (n.)
up'grade' (adj., adv.)
up'grade' (v.)
  up'grad'ed, up'grad'ing
up·heav'al
up'hill'
up·hold'
  up·held', up·hold'ing
up·hol'ster
up·hol'ster·er
up·hol'ster·y
  pl. up·hol'ster·ies
up'keep'
up'land
up·lift' (v.)
up'lift' (n.)
up·on'
up'per
up'per-case'
  up'per-cased', up'per-cas'ing
up·per-class'
up'per·class'man
  pl. up'per·class'men
up'per·cut'
  up'per·cut',
  up'per·cut'ting
up'per·most'
Up'per Vol'ta
up'pish
up'pi·ty
up'right'
up'ris'ing
up'roar'
up·roar'i·ous
up·root'
ups' and downs'
up'scale'
  up'scaled', up'scal'ing
up·set' (v., adj.)
  up·set', up·set'ting
up·set' (n.)
up'shot'
up'side down'
up'si·lon'
up'stage'
  up'staged', up'stag'ing

up'stairs'
  pl. up'stairs'
up·stand'ing
up'start' (*n., adj.*)
up·start' (*v.*)
up'state'
up'stream'
up'stroke'
up·surge' (*v.*)
  up·surged', up·surg'ing
up'surge' (*n.*)
up·sweep' (*v.*)
  up·swept',
  up·sweep'ing
up'sweep' (*n.*)
up'swing' (*n.*)
up·swing'
  up·swung',
  up·swing'ing
up'take'
up'thrust'
up·tick' (*v.*)
up'tick' (*n.*)
up'tight'
up'-to-date'
up'town' (*adv., n.*)
up'town' (*adj.*)
up'trend'
up·turn' (*v.*)
up'turn' (*n.*)
up'ward
up'wards
up'wind' (*adv., adj.*)
up'wind' (*n.*)
U'ral
u·ra'ni·um
U'ra·nus
ur'ban (*of a city*)
  (SEE urbane)
ur·bane' (*suave*)
  (SEE urban)
ur'ban·ism'
ur'ban·ite'
ur·ban'i·ty
  pl. ur·ban'i·ties
ur'ban·i·za'tion

ur'ban·ize'
  ur'ban·ized',
  ur'ban·iz'ing
ur'ban·ol'o·gy
ur'chin
u·re'a
u·re'mi·a
u·re'mic
u·re'ter
u·re'thra
  pl. u·re'thrae or
  u·re'thras
u·re'thral
u·ret'ic
urge
  urged, urg'ing
ur'gen·cy
  pl. ur'gen·cies
ur'gent
ur'ic
u'ri·nal
u'ri·nal'y·sis
  pl. u'ri·nal'y·ses'
u'ri·nar'y
u'ri·nate'
  u'ri·nat'ed, u'ri·nat'ing
u'ri·na'tion
u'rine
u'rin·ous
urn (*vase*)
  (SEE earn)
u'ro·log'ic
u'ro·log'i·cal
u·rol'o·gy
ur'sine
ur'ti·car'i·a
U'ru·guay'
U'ru·guay'an
us
us'a·bil'i·ty
us'a·ble
us'a·bly
us'age
use
  used, us'ing

used
use'ful
use'ful·ly
use'less
us'er
ush'er
u'su·al
u'su·al·ly
u'su·fruct'
u'su·rer
u·su'ri·ous
u·surp'
u'sur·pa'tion
u·surp'er
u'su·ry
  pl. u'su·ries
U'tah
u·ten'sil
u'ter·ine
u'ter·us
  pl. u'ter·i' or
  u'ter·us'es
U' Thant'
u·til'i·tar'i·an
u·til'i·tar'i·an·ism'
u·til'i·ty
  pl. u·til'i·ties
u'ti·liz'a·ble
u'ti·li·za'tion
u'ti·lize'
  u'ti·lized', u'ti·liz'ing
ut'most'
u·to'pi·a
u·to'pi·an
ut'ter
ut'ter·ance
ut'ter·most'
U'-turn'
u'vu·la
  pl. u'vu·las or
  u'vu·lae'
u'vu·lar
ux·o'ri·cide'
ux·o'ri·ous

va′can·cy
  pl. va′can·cies

va′cant

va′cate
  va′cat·ed, va′cat·ing

va·ca′tion

va·ca′tion·er

va·ca′tion·ist

vac′ci·nate′
  vac′ci·nat′ed,
  vac′ci·nat′ing

vac′ci·na′tion

vac·cine′

vac′il·late′
  vac′il·lat′ed,
  vac′il·lat′ing

vac′il·la′tion

vac′il·la′tor

va·cu′i·ty
  pl. va·cu′i·ties

vac′u·ole′

vac′u·ous

vac′u·um
  pl. vac′u·ums or
  vac′u·a

vac′u·um-packed′

va′de me′cum
  pl. va′de me′cums

Va·duz′

vag′a·bond′

vag′a·bond′age

va·gar′y
  pl. va·gar′ies

va·gi′na
  pl. va·gi′nas or
  va·gi′nae

vag′i·nal

va′gran·cy
  pl. va′gran·cies

va′grant

vague
  va′guer, va′guest

vague′ly

vain (futile;
  conceited)
  (SEE vein and vane)

vain·glo′ri·ous

vain′glo′ry

val′ance (drape)
  (SEE valence)

vale (valley)
  (SEE veil)

val′e·dic′tion

val′e·dic·to′ri·an

val′e·dic′to·ry
  pl. val′e·dic′to·ries

va′lence (chemical
  term)
  (SEE valance)

va′len·cy

val′en·tine′

val′et
  val′et·ed, val′et·ing

val′e·tu′di·nar′i·an

Val·hal′la

val′iant

val′id

val′i·date′
  val′i·dat′ed,
  val′i·dat′ing

val′i·da′tion

va·lid′i·ty

va·lise′

Va′li·um
  (Trademark)

Val·kyr′ie

val′ley
  pl. val′leys

val′or

val′or·ous

val′u·a·ble

val′u·a·bly

val′u·a′tion

val′ue
  val′ued, val′u·ing

val′ue-·add′ed tax′

val′ue·less

valve
  valved, valv′ing

val′vu·lar

va·moose′
  va·moosed′,
  va·moos′ing

vamp

vam′pire

vam′pir·ism′

van
  vanned, van′ning

va·na′di·um

Van Bu′ren

Van·cou′ver

van′dal

van′dal·ism′

van′dal·ize′
  van′dal·ized′,
  van′dal·iz′ing

Van·dyke′

vane (wind indicator)
  (SEE vain and vein)

Van Gogh′

van′guard′

va·nil′la

van′il·lin

van′ish

van′i·ty
  pl. van′i·ties

van′quish

van′tage

vap′id

va·pid′i·ty

va′por

va′por·i·za′tion

va′por·ize′
  va′por·ized′,
  va′por·iz′ing

va′por·iz′er

va′por·ous

va·que′ro
  pl. va·que′ros

var′i·a·bil′i·ty

var′i·a·ble

var′i·a·bly

var′i·ance

var′i·ant

var′i·a′tion

var′i·col′ored

var′i·cose′

var′i·cos′i·ty
  pl. var′i·cos′i·ties

var′ied

var′i·e·gate′
  var′i·e·gat′ed,
  var′i·e·gat′ing

var′i·e·ga′tion

va·ri′e·tal

va · ri'e · ty
  pl. va · ri'e · ties
va · ri'e · ty store'
var'i · o'rum
var'i · ous
var'let
var'mint
var'nish
var'si · ty
  pl. var'si · ties
var'y (change)
  var'ied, var'y · ing
  (SEE very)
vas'cu · lar
vas de'fe · rens'
  pl. va'sa de'fe · ren'ti · a
vase
vas · ec'to · my
  pl. vas · ec'to · mies
Vas'e · line'
  (Trademark)
vas'o · con · stric'tor
vas'o · di · la'tor
vas'o · mo'tor
vas'sal
vas'sal · age
vast
vat
  vat'ted, vat'ting
Vat'i · can
vaude'ville
vaude · vil'lian
vault
vault'ed
vault'ing
vaunt
V'-Day'
veal
vec'tor
vec · to'ri · al
Ve'da
Ve · da'ic
Ve · dan'ta
V'-E' Day'
Ve'dic
veep
veer
veg'e · ta · ble
veg'e · tal

vege · tar'i · an
vege · tar'i · an · ism'
veg'e · tate'
  veg'e · tat'ed,
  veg'e · tat'ing
vege · ta'tion
veg'e · ta'tive
ve'he · mence
ve'he · ment
ve'hi · cle
ve · hic'u · lar
V'-eight'
veil (fabric)
  (SEE vale)
veil'ing
vein (blood vessel)
  (SEE vain and vane)
ve'lar
veld or veldt
vel · le'i · ty
  pl. vel · le'i · ties
vel'lum
ve · loc'i · pede
ve · loc'i · ty
  pl. ve · loc'i · ties
ve · lour' or ve · lours'
  pl. ve · lours'
vel'vet
vel'vet · een'
vel'vet · y
ve'na ca'va
  pl. ve'nae ca'vae
ve'nal (mercenary)
  (SEE venial)
ve · nal'i · ty
ve'nal · ly
vend
vend'a · ble
vend · ee'
vend'er
ven · det'ta
vend'i · ble
vend'ing ma · chine'
ven'dor or ven'der
ve · neer'
ven'er · a · bil'i · ty
ven'er · a · ble
ven'er · ate'
  ven'er · at'ed,
  ven'er · at'ing

ven'er · a'tion
ve · ne're · al
Ve · ne'tian
Ven'e · zue'la
Ven'e · zue'lan
venge'ance
venge'ful
venge'ful · ly
ve'ni · al (forgivable)
  (SEE venal)
Ven'ice
ve · ni're · man
  pl. ve · ni're · men
ven'i · son
ven'om
ven'om · ous
ve'nous
vent
ven'ti · late'
  ven'ti · lat'ed,
  ven'ti · lat'ing
ven'ti · la'tion
ven'ti · la'tor
ven'tral
ven'tral · ly
ven'tri · cle
ven · tric'u · lar
ven · tril'o · quism'
ven · tril'o · quist
ven'ture
  ven'tured, ven'tur · ing
ven'tur · er
ven'ture · some
ven · tu'ri
ven'tur · ous
ven'ue
Ve'nus
Ve · nu'si · an
ve · ra'cious (truthful)
  (SEE voracious)
ve · rac'i · ty
  pl. ve · rac'i · ties
ve · ran'da or
  ve · ran'dah
verb
ver'bal
ver'bal · ize'
  ver'bal · ized',
  ver'bal · iz'ing

ver·bal·i·za'tion
ver'bal·ly
ver·ba'tim
ver·be'na
ver'bi·age
ver·bose'
ver·bos'i·ty
ver·bo'ten
ver'dant
Ver'di
ver'dict
ver'di·gris'
ver'dure
verge
verged, verg'ing
Ver'gil
ver'i·fi'a·ble
ver'i·fi·ca'tion
ver'i·fi'er
ver'i·fy'
ver'i·fied', ver'i·fy'ing
ver'i·ly
ver'i·si·mil'i·tude'
ver'i·ta·ble
ver'i·ta·bly
ver'i·ty
pl. ver'i·ties
ver'meil
ver'mi·cel'li
ver'mi·cide'
ver'mi·form'
ver'mi·fuge'
ver·mil'ion or
ver·mil'lion
ver'min
pl. ver'min
ver'min·ous
Ver·mont'
Ver·mont'er
ver·mouth'
ver·nac'u·lar
ver'nal
ver'ni·er
Ve·ron'i·ca
Ver·sailles'
ver'sa·tile
ver'sa·til'i·ty
verse

versed
ver'si·cle
ver'si·fi·ca'tion
ver'si·fi'er
ver'si·fy'
ver'si·fied',
ver'si·fy'ing
ver'sion
ver'so
pl. ver'sos
ver'sus
ver'te·bra
pl. ver'te·brae' or
ver'te·bras
ver'te·bral
ver'te·brate'
ver'tex
pl. ver'tex·es or
ver'ti·ces'
ver'ti·cal
ver'ti·cal'i·ty
ver'ti·cal·ly
ver·tig'i·nous
ver·ti·go'
pl. ver'ti·goes' or
ver·tig'i·nes'
verve
ver'y (extremely)
ver'i·er, ver'i·est
(SEE vary)
ves'i·cant
ves'i·cle
ve·sic'u·lar
ves'per
ves'pers
ves'sel
vest
ves'tal
vest'ed
vest'ee
ves'ti·bule'
ves'ti·buled',
ves'ti·bul'ing
ves'tige
ves·tig'i·al
ves·tig'i·al·ly
vest'ment
vest'-pock'et
ves'try
pl. ves'tries

ves'try·man
pl. ves'try·men
Ve·su'vi·us
vet
vet'ted, vet'ting
vetch
vet'er·an
vet'er·i·nar'i·an
vet'er·i·nar'y
ve'to
pl. ve'toes; (v.) ve'toed,
ve'to·ing
ve'to·er
vex
vex·a'tion
vex·a'tious
vi'a
vi'a·bil'i·ty
vi'a·ble
vi'a·bly
Vi'a Dol'o·ro'sa
vi'a·duct'
vi'al (bottle)
(SEE vile and viol)
vi'and
vi·at'i·cum
pl. vi·at'i·ca or
vi·at'i·cums
vibes
vi'bra·harp'
vi'bran·cy
vi'brant
vi'bra·phone'
vi'brate
vi'brat·ed, vi'brat·ing
vi·bra'tion
vi·bra'to
pl. vi·bra'tos
vi'bra·tor
vi'bra·to'ry
vi·bur'num
vic'ar
vic'ar·age
vi·car'i·al
vi·car'i·ous
vice (immorality)
(SEE BELOW)
vi'ce (in place of)
(SEE ABOVE and vise)
vice' chair'man

vice′ chan′cel·lor
vice′ con′sul
vice′ pres′i·den·cy
vice′ pres′i·dent
vice′-pres′i·den′tial
vice·re′gal
vice′roy
vice′ squad′
vi′ce ver′sa
Vi′chy
vi′chy·ssoise′
vi·cin′i·ty
   pl. vi·cin′i·ties
vi′cious
vi·cis′si·tude′
vic′tim
vic′tim·i·za′tion
vic′tim·ize′
   vic′tim·ized′,
   vic′tim·iz′ing
vic′tim·iz′er
vic′tim·less
vic′tor
Vic·to′ri·a
vic·to′ri·an
Vic·to′ri·an·ism′
vic·to′ri·ous
vic′to·ry
   pl. vic′to·ries
Vic·tro′la
   (*Trademark*)
vict′ual
vi·cu′ña or vi·cu′na
vi′de
vid′e·o′
vid′e·o′cas·sette′
vid′e·o·tape′
   vid′e·o·taped′,
   vid′e·o·tap′ing
vid′e·o·disc′
vie
   vied, vy′ing
Vi·en′na
Vi′en·nese′
   pl. Vi′en·nese′
Vien·tiane′
Vi′et·cong′ or Vi′et
   Cong′
Vi′et·minh′ or Vi′et
   Minh′

Vi′et·nam′
Vi·et′nam·ese′
view
view′er
view′er·ship′
view′find′er
view′point′
vig′il
vig′i·lance
vig′i·lant
vig′i·lan′te
vig′i·lan·tism′
vi·gnette′
   vi·gnet′ted, vi·gnet′ting
vig′or
vig′or·ish
vi′go·ro′so
vig′or·ous
Vi′king
vile (*evil*)
   vil′er, vil′est
   (SEE vial *and* viol)
vile′ly
vil′i·fi·ca′tion
vil′i·fi′er
vil′i·fy′
   vil′i·fied′, vil′i·fy′ing
vil′la
vil′lage
vil′lag·er
vil′lain (*evil person*)
   (SEE villein)
vil′lain·ous
vil′lain·y
   pl. vil′lain·ies
vil′lein (*serf*)
   (SEE villain)
vim
vin′ai·grette′
Vin′ci
vin′ci·ble
vin′di·ca·ble
vin′di·cate′
   vin′di·cat′ed,
   vin′di·cat′ing
vin′di·ca′tion
vin′di·ca′tor
vin·dic′tive
vin·dic′tive·ly

vine
vin′e·gar
vin′e·gar·y
vine′yard
vin′i·cul′ture
vin or·di·naire′
   pl. vins or·di·naires′
vin′tage
   vin′taged, vin′tag·ing
vint′ner
vi′nyl
vi′ol (*musical
   instrument*)
   (SEE vial *and* vile)
vi·o′la
vi′o·la·ble
vi′o·late′
   vi′o·lat′ed, vi′o·lat′ing
vi′o·la′tion
vi′o·la′tor
vi′o·lence
vi′o·lent
vi′o·let
vi′o·lin′
vi′o·lin′ist
vi·o′list
vi′o·lon·cel′list
vi′o·lon·cel′lo
   pl. vi′o·lon·cel′los
V′IP′
vi′per
vi′per·ish
vi′per·ous
vi·ra′go
   pl. vi·ra′goes or
   vi·ra′gos
vi′ral
vir′e·o′
   pl. vir′e·os′
vir′gin
Vir′gin Is′lands
vir′gin·al
Vir·gin′ia
Vir·gin′ian
vir·gin′i·ty
Vir′go
vir′gule
vir′ile
vi·ril′i·ty

vi·rol'o·gist

vi·rol'o·gy

vir·tu' (*artistic merit*)
(SEE virtue)

vir'tu·al

vir'tu·al·ly

vir'tue (*goodness*)
(SEE virtu)

vir'tu·os'i·ty

vir'tu·o'so
pl. virto·o'sos or vir'tu·o'si

vir'tu·ous

vir'u·lence

vir'u·lent

vi'rus
pl. vi'rus·es

vi'sa
pl. vi'sas
vi'saed, vi'sa·ing

vis'age

vis'-à-vis'
pl. vis'-à-vis'

vis'cer·a
sing. vis'cus

vis'cer·al

vis'cer·al·ly

vis'cid

vis·cid'i·ty

vis'cose (*solution*)
(SEE viscous)

vis·cos'i·ty
pl. vis·cos'i·ties

vis'count'

vis'count'ess

vis'cous (*thick*)
(SEE viscose)

vise (*clamp*)
vised, vis'ing
(SEE vice)

Vish'nu

vis'i·bil'i·ty

vis'i·ble

vis'i·bly

Vis'i·goth'

vi'sion

vi'sion·ar'y
pl. vi'sion·ar'ies

vis'it

vis'i·tant

vis'it·a'tion

vis'i·tor

vi'sor

vis'ta

vis'u·al

vis'u·al·i·za'tion

vis'u·al·ize'
vis'u·al·ized',
vis'u·al·iz'ing

vis'u·al·ly

vi'ta
pl. vi'tae

vi'tal

vi·tal'i·ty
pl. vi·tal'i·ties

vi'tal·i·za'tion

vi'tal·ize'
vi'tal·ized', vi'tal·iz'ing

vi'tal·ly

vi'tals

vi'ta·min

vi'ti·ate'
vi'ti·at'ed, vi'ti·at'ing

vi'ti·a'tion

vit'i·cul'ture

vit're·ous

vit'ri·fi·ca'tion

vit'ri·fy'
vit'ri·fied', vit'ri·fy'ing

vit'ri·ol
vit'ri·oled, vit'ri·ol·ing

vit'ri·ol'ic

vit'tles

vi·tu'per·ate'
vi·tu'per·at'ed,
vi·tu'per·at'ing

vi·tu'per·a'tion

vi·tu'per·a'tive

vi'va

vi·va'ce

vi·va'cious

vi·vac'i·ty
pl. vi·vac'i·ties

Vi·val'di

vi·var'i·um
pl. vi·var'i·ums or
vi·var'i·a

vi'va vo'ce

viv'id

viv'i·fi·ca'tion

viv'i·fy'
viv'i·fied', viv'i·fy'ing

vi·vip'ar·ous

viv'i·sect'

viv'i·sec'tion

vix'en

viz'ard

vi·zier'

V'-J' Day'

V' neck'

vo'ca·ble

vo·cab'u·lar·y
pl. vo·cab'u·lar'ies

vo'cal

vo·cal'ic

vo'cal·ist

vo·cal·i·za'tion

vo'cal·ize'
vo'cal·ized',
vo'cal·iz'ing

vo'cal·ly

vo·ca'tion

vo·ca'tion·al

voc'a·tive

vo·cif'er·ate'
vo·cif'er·at'ed,
vo·cif'er·at'ing

vo·cif'er·a'tion

vo·cif'er·ous

vod'ka

vogue

voice
voiced, voic'ing

voice'less

voice'-o'ver

voice'print'

void

void'a·ble

voi·ld'

voile

vol'a·tile

vol'a·til'i·ty

vol·can'ic

vol·can·ism'

vol·ca'no
pl. vol·ca'noes or
vol·ca'nos

vole

vo·li'tion

vol'ley
  pl. vol'leys; (v.)
  vol'leyed, vol'ley·ing

vol'ley·ball'

volt

volt'age

vol·ta'ic

Vol·taire'

vol·tam'e·ter

volt'-am'pere

volt'me'ter

vol'u·bil'i·ty

vol'u·ble

vol'u·bly

vol'ume

vol'u·met'ric

vo·lu'mi·nous

vol'un·tar'i·ly

vol'un·tar'y
  pl. vol'un·tar'ies

vol'un·teer'

vo·lup'tu·ar'y
  pl. vo·lup'tu·ar'ies

vo·lup'tu·ous

vo·lute'

vom'it

voo'doo
  pl. voo'doos; (v.)
  voo'dooed, voo'doo·ing

voo'-doo·ism'

vo·ra'cious
  (insatiable)
  (SEE veracious)

vo·rac'i·ty

vor'tex
  pl. vor'tex·es or
  vor'ti·ces'

vo'ta·ry
  pl. vo'ta·ries

vote
  vot'ed, vot'ing

vote'a·ble

vote'less

vot'er

vot'ing ma·chine'

vo'tive

vouch

vouch'er

vouch·safe'
  vouch·safed',
  vouch·saf'ing

vow

vow'el

vox' po'pu·li'

voy'age
  voy'aged, voy'ag·ing

voy'ag·er

vo'ya·geur'

vo·yeur'

vo·yeur'ism

vul'can·ite'

vul'can·i·za'tion

vul'can·ize'
  vul'can·ized',
  vul'can·iz'ing

vul'can·iz'er

vul'gar

vul·gar'i·an

vul'gar·ism'

vul·gar'i·ty
  pl. vul·gar'i·ties

vul'gar·i·za'tion

vul'gar·ize'
  vul'gar·ized',
  vul'gar·iz'ing

vul'gar·iz'er

Vul'gate

vul'ner·a·bil'i·ty

vul'ner·a·ble

vul'ner·a·bly

vul'pine

vul'ture

vul'tur·ous

vul'va
  pl. vul'vae or vul'vas

vy'ing

W

wack'y
  wack'i·er, wack'i·est

wad
  wad'ded, wad'ding

wad'a·ble

wad'ding

wad'dle
  wad'dled, wad'dling

wade
  wad'ed, wad'ing

wad'er

wa'di
  pl. wa'dis

wa'fer

waf'fle

waft

wag
  wagged, wag'ging

wage
  waged, wag'ing

wa'ger

wa'ger·er

wage' scale'

wag'ger·y
  pl. wag'ger·ies

wag'gish

wag'gle
  wag'gled, wag'gling

Wag'ner

Wag·ne'ri·an

wag'on

wag'on·er

wa·gon-lit'
  pl. wa·gon-lits'

wa·hi'ne

waif

wail (cry)
  (SEE wale and whale)

wain'scot
  pl. wain'scot·ed,
  wain'scot·ing

wain'wright'

waist (middle of
  body)
  (SEE waste)

waist'band'

waist'coat'

waist'-deep'

waist'-high'

waist'line'

wait (stay)
  (SEE weight)

wait'er

wait'ing room'

wait'ress

waive (*give up*)
  waived, waiv'ing
  (SEE wave)

waiv'er
  (*relinquishment*)
  (SEE waver)

wake
  waked or woke, waked
  or wok'en, wak'ing

wake'ful

wak'en

Wald'heim'

wale (*ridge*)
  waled, wal'ing
  (SEE wail *and* whale)

Wales

walk

walk'a·thon'

walk'a·way'

walk'-down'

walk'er

walk'ie–talk'ie

walk'-in'

walk'-on'

walk'out'

walk'o'ver

walk'-up'

walk'way'

wall

wal'la·by
  pl. wal'la·bies or
  wal'la·by

wall'board'

wall'cov'er·ing

wal'let

wall'eye
  pl. wall'eyes or
  wall'eye'

wall'eyed'

wall'flow'er

wal'lop

wal'lop·ing

wal'low

wall'pa'per

wall'-to-wall'

wal'nut

wal'rus
  pl. wal'rus·es or
  wal'rus

waltz

wam'pum

wan
  (*adj.*) wan'ner,
  wan'nest; (*v.*)
  wanned, wan'ning

wand

wan'der

wan'der·lust'

wane
  waned, wan'ing

wan'gle
  wan'gled, wan'gling

Wan'kel

want (*desire; need*)
  (SEE wont)

want' ad'

wan'ton

wan'ton·ness

wap'i·ti
  pl. wap'i·tis or
  wap'i·ti

war
  warred, war'ring

war'ble
  war'bled, war'bling

war'bler

war' bon'net

war' cry'

ward

war' dance'

war'den

ward'er

ward' heel'er

ward'robe

ward'room'

ward'ship

ware (*goods*)
  (SEE wear *and* where)

ware'house'
  ware'housed',
  ware'hous'ing

war'fare'

war' game'

war'head'

war'-horse'

war'i·ly

war'i·ness

war'like'

war'lock'

war' lord'

warm

warm'-blood'ed

warmed'-o'ver

warm'-heart'ed

war'mon'ger

warmth

warm'-up'

warn

warn'ing

warp

war'path'

war'plane'

war'rant

war'rant·a·ble

war'ran·tee'

war'ran·tor

war'ran·ty
  pl. war'ran·ties

war'ren

war'ri·or

War'saw

war'ship'

wart

war'time'

war'y
  war'i·er, war'i·est

war' zone'

was

wash

wash'a·ble

wash'-and-wear'

wash'ba'sin

wash'board'

wash'bowl'

wash'cloth'

wash'day'

washed'-out'

washed'-up'

wash'er

wash'er·wom'an
  pl. wash'er·wom'en

Wash'ing·ton

Wash'ing·to'ni·an

wash'out'

wash'rag'

wash'room'

wash'stand'

wash'tub'

wash'y
  wash'i•er, wash'i•est

wasp

wasp'ish

wasp'y
  wasp'i•er, wasp'i•est

was'sail

wast'age

waste (*squander*)
  wast'ed, wast'ing
  (SEE waist)

waste'bas'ket

waste'ful

waste'ful•ly

waste'land'

waste'pa'per

wast'rel

watch

watch'band'

watch'case'

watch'dog'

watch'ful

watch'ful•ly

watch'mak'er

watch'mak'ing

watch'man
  pl. watch'men

watch'tow'er

watch'word'

wa'ter

wa'ter•bed'

wa'ter•borne'

wa'ter•buf'fa•lo

wa'ter•col'or

wa'ter–cool'

wa'ter cool'er

wa'ter•course'

wa'ter•craft'

wa'ter•cress'

wa'ter•fall'

wa'ter–fast'

wa'ter•fowl'
  pl. wa'ter•fowls' or
  wa'ter•fowl'

wa'ter•fowl'
  pl. wa'ter•fowls' or
  wa'ter•fowl'

wa'ter•front'

Wa'ter•gate'

wa'ter glass'

wa'ter hole'

wa'ter•i•ness'

wa'ter•less

wa'ter line'

wa'ter•logged'

Wa'ter•loo'

wa'ter•mark'

wa'ter•mel'on

wa'ter mill'

wa'ter•pow'er

wa'ter•proof'

wa'ter-re•pel'lent

wa'ter-re•sist'ant

wa'ter•scape'

wa'ter•shed'

wa'ter•side'

wa'ter ski'

wa'ter-ski'
  wa'ter-skied', wa'ter–
  ski'ing

wa'ter-ski'er

wa'ter snake'

wa'ter-sol'u•ble

wa'ter•spout'

wa'ter ta'ble

wa'ter•tight'

wa'ter•way'

wa'ter wheel'

wa'ter•works'

wa'ter•worn'

wa'ter•y

watt

watt'age

watt'–hour'

wat'tle
  wat'tled, wat'tling

watt'me'ter

Wa•tu'si
  pl. Wa•tu'sis or
  Wa•tu'si

wave (*water; flutter*)
  waved, wav'ing
  (SEE waive)

wave'band'

wave'length'

wa'ver (*sway;*
  hesitate)
  (SEE waiver)

wav'i•ly

wav'i•ness

wav'y
  wav'i•er, wav'i•est

wax

wax' bean'

wax'en

wax' pa'per

wax'wing'

wax'work'

wax'y
  wax'i•er, wax'i•est

way (*manner; plan;*
  route)
  (SEE weigh *and* whey)

way'bill'

way'far'er

way'far'ing

way'lay'
  way'laid', way'lay'ing

way'–out'

way'side'

way' sta'tion

way'ward

we (*you and I*)
  (SEE wee)

weak (*not strong*)
  (SEE week)

weak'en

weak'fish'
  pl. weak'fish' or
  weak'fish'es

weak'heart'ed

weak'–kneed'

weak'ling

weak'ly (*sickly*)
  (SEE weekly)

weak'mind'ed

weak'ness

weal (*well-being*)
  (SEE we'll *and* wheel
  and wheal)

wealth

wealth'i•ness

wealth'y
  wealth'i•er,
  wealth'i•est

wean (*stop suckling*)
  (SEE ween)

weap'on

weap'on•ry

wear (*have on;*
impair)
wore, worn, wear'ing
(SEE ware *and* where)

wear'a · ble

wear' and tear'

wear'er

wea'ri · ly

wea'ri · ness

wea'ri · some

wea'ry
(*adj.*) wea'ri · er,
wea'ri · est;
(*v.*) wea'ried, wea'ry · ing

wea'sel
pl. wea'sels or wea'sel

weath'er (*climate*)
(SEE whether)

weath'er-beat'en

weath'er · board'

weath'er-bound'

weath'er · cock'

weath'er eye'

weath'er · glass'

weath'er · man'
pl. weath'er · men'

weath'er map'

weath'er · proof'

weath'er · strip'
weath'er · stripped',
weath'er · strip'ping

weath'er · vane'

weath'er · worn'

weave (*interlace*)
wove, wo'ven or wove,
weav'ing
(SEE we've)

weav'er

weav'er · bird'

web
webbed, web'bing

web'bing

We'ber

web'-foot'ed

web' press'

wed
wed'ded or wed,
wed'ding

we'd

wed'ding

wed'ding cake'

wedge
wedged, wedg'ing

Wedg'ie (*Trademark*)

wed'lock

Wednes'day

wee (*tiny*)
we'er, we'est
(SEE we)

weed (*plant*)
(SEE we'd)

weed'er

weed'kill'er

weed'y
weed'i · er, weed'i · est

week (*seven days*)
(SEE weak)

week'day'

week'end'

week'end'er

week'ly (*once a*
week)
(SEE weakly)

ween (*think*)
(SEE wean)

wee'nie

weep
wept, weep'ing

weep'y
weep'i · er, weep'i · est

wee'vil

weft

wei · ge'la

weigh (*measure*
heavyness)
(SEE way *and* whey)

weight (*heaviness*)
(SEE wait)

weight'i · ly

weight'i · ness

weight'less

weight' lift'ing

weight'y
weight'i · er,
weight'i · est

Wei'mar · an'er

weir (*dam*)
(SEE we're)

weird

weird'o
pl. weird'os

wel'come
wel'comed,
wel'com · ing

weld

weld'er

wel'fare'

wel'far'ism

wel'kin

well
bet'ter, best

we'll

well'ad · just'ed

well'ad · vised'

well'-ap · point'ed

well'-at · tend'ed

well'-a · ware'

well'-bal'anced

well'-be · haved'

well'-be'ing

well'-be · lov'ed

well'born'

well'-bred'

well'-con · di'tioned

well-de · fined'

well'-dis · posed'

well'-done'

well'-dressed'

well'-earned'

well'-es · tab'lished

well'-fa'vored

well'-fed'

well'-fixed'

well'-found'ed

well'-groomed'

well'-ground'ed

well'head'

well'-heeled'

well'-in · formed'

Wel'ling · ton

well'-knit'

well'-known'

well'-liked'

well'-man'nered

well'-mean'ing

well'-nigh'

well'-off'

well'-or'dered

well'-paid'

well'-read'

well'-spent'

well'-spo'ken
well'-spring'
well'-thought'-of'
well'-timed'
well'-to-do'
well'-turned'
well'-wish'er
well'-worn'
welsh
Welsh
Welsh' cor'gi
Welsh'man
  pl. Welsh'men
Welsh' rab'bit
Welsh' rare'bit
welt
wel'ter
wel'ter • weight'
Welt'schmerz'
wen
wench
wend
went
wept
were
we're
were'n't
were'wolf'
  pl. were'wolves'
wes'kit
Wes'ley • an
west
west'bound'
west'er • ly
west'ern
west'ern • er
west'ern • i • za'tion
west'ern • ism'
west'ern • ize'
  west'ern • ized',
  west'ern • iz'ing
west'ern • most'
West' In'dian
West' In'dies
West'min'ster
West' Vir • gin'ia
West' Vir • gin'ian
west'ward

wet (*damp*)
  (*adj.*) wet'ter, wet'test;
  (*v.*)
  pl. wet or wet'ted,
  wet'ting
    (SEE whet)
wet'back'
wet' bar'
wet' cell'
wet'land'
wet' nurse'
wet'-nurse'
  wet'-nursed', wet'-
  nurs'ing
wet' pack'
wet'ta • ble
wet'ting a'gent
wet' wash'
we've (*we have*)
  (SEE weave)
whack
whale (*animal*)
  pl. whales or whale
  whaled, whal'ing
    (SEE wail *and* wale)
whale'boat'
whale'bone'
whal'er
wham
  whammed, wham'ming
wham'my
  pl. wham'mies
wharf
  pl. wharves or wharfs
wharf'age
what
  pl. what
what • ev'er
what'not'
what'so • ev'er
wheal (*swelling*)
  (SEE we'll *and* wheel
  and weal)
wheat
wheat' cake'
wheat'en
wheat' germ'
whee'dle
  whee'dled, whee'dling
wheel (*disk*)
  (SEE we'll *and* wheal
  and weal)

wheel'bar'row
wheel'base'
wheel'chair'
wheeled
wheel'er
wheel'er-deal'er
wheel' horse'
wheel'house'
wheel'wright'
wheeze
  wheezed, wheez'ing
wheez'i • ly
wheez'i • ness
wheez'y
  wheez'i • er, wheez'i • est
whelk
whelp
when
whence
whence'so • ev'er
when • ev'er
when'so • ev'er
where (*at or to what
  place*)
  (SEE ware *and* wear)
where'a • bouts'
where • as'
  pl. where • as'es
where • at'
where • by'
where'fore
where • from'
where'in'
where • of'
where • on'
where'so • ev'er
where • to'
where'up • on'
wher • ev'er
where • with'
where'with • al'
wher'ry
  pl. wher'ries; (*v.*)
  wher'ried, wher'ry • ing
whet (*sharpen*)
  whet'ted, whet'ting
    (SEE wet)
wheth'er (*if*)
  (SEE weather)

whet'stone'

whew

whey (*part of milk*)
(SEE way *and* weigh)

whey'ey

which (*what one*)
(SEE witch)

which·ev'er

which'so·ev'er

whiff

whif'fle·tree'

Whig

while (*time*)
whiled, whil'ing
(SEE wile)

whilst

whim

whim'per

whim'sey
pl. whim'seys

whim'si·cal

whim'si·cal'i·ty
pl. whim'si·cal'i·ties

whim'si·cal·ly

whim'sy
pl. whim'sies

whine (*complain*)
whined, whin'ing
(SEE wine)

whin'er

whin'ny
whin'nied, whin'ny·ing

whin'y
whin'i·er, whin'i·est

whip
whipped, whip'ping

whip'cord'

whip'lash'

whip'per·snap'per

whip'pet

whip'ping boy'

whip'poor·will'

whip'saw'
whip'sawed',
whip'sawed or
whip'sawn',
whip'saw'ing

whip'stitch'

whip'stock'

whir
whirred', whir'ring

whirl

whirl'a·bout'

whir'i·gig

whirl'pool'

whirl'wind'

whirl'y·bird'

whish

whisk

whisk'broom'

whisk'er

whis'key
pl. whis'keys
(SEE BELOW)

whis'ky (*esp. Scot.
and Canadian*)
pl. whis'kies
(SEE ABOVE)

whis'per

whis'per·er

whist

whis'tle
whis'tled, whis'tling

whis'tler

whis'tle stop'

whit (*particle*)
(SEE wit)

white
(*adj.*) whit'er, whit'est;
(*v.*) whit'ed, whit'ing

white'cap'

white'-col'lar

white'face'

white'-faced'

white'fish'
pl. white'fish or
white'fish'es

White'hall'

white' heat'

white' hope'

White'horse

white'-hot'

White' House'

whit'en

whit'en·er

white'ness

whit'en·ing

white' tie'

white'wall'

white'wash'

white' wa'ter

whith'er (*where*)
(SEE wither)

whith'er·so·ev'er

whit'ing
pl. whit'ing or
whit'ings

whit'ish

whit'low

Whit'man

Whit'sun'day

Whit'sun·tide'

whit'tle
whit'tled, whit'tling

whiz or whizz

whiz'-bang'

who

who·dun'it

who·ev'er

whole (*entire*)
(SEE hole)

whole'heart'ed

whole'ness

whole' note'

whole' rest'

whole'sale'
pl. whole'saled',
whole'sal'ing

whole'sal'er

whole'some

whole'-wheat'

who'll

whol'ly (*entirely*)
(SEE holy)

whom

whom·ev'er

whom'so·ev'er

whoop (*shout*)
(SEE hoop)

whoop'-de-do' or
whoop'-de-doo'

whoop'ee (*n.*)

whoop'ee' (*interj.*)

whoop'ing cough'

whoop'ing crane'

whoops

whoosh

whop'per

whop'ping

whore (*prostitute*)
  whored, whor'ing
  (SEE hoar)

whore'house'

whorl

whose

who'so·ev'er

why
  pl. whys

wick

wick'ed

wick'er

wick'er·work'

wick'et

wick'i·up'

wide
  wid'er, wid'est

wide'-an'gle

wide'-a·wake'

wide'-eyed'

wide'ly

wide'mouthed'

wid'en

wide'-o'pen

wide'spread'

widg'eon

wid'get

wid'ow

wid'ow·er

wid'ow's mite'

wid'ow's peak'

width

wield

wield'y
  wield'i·er, wield'i·est

wie'ner

Wie'ner schnit'zel

wife
  pl. wives; (*v.*)
  wifed, wif'ing

wife'ly
  wife'li·er, wife'li·est

wig
  wigged, wig'ging

wig'gle
  wig'gled, wig'gling

wig'gly
  wig'gli·er, wig'gli·est

wig'let

wig'mak'er

wig'wag'
  wig'wagged',
  wig'wag'ging

wig'wam'

wil'co

wild

wild'cat'
  pl. wild'cats' or
  wild'cat'
  (*v.*) wild'cat'ted,
  wild'cat'ting

wild'cat'ter

wil'de·beest'
  pl. wil'de·beests' or
  wil'de·beest'

wil'der·ness

wild'-eyed'

wild'fire'

wild' flow'er

wild'fowl'

wild'-goose' chase'

wild'life'

Wild' West'

wild'wood'

wile (*cunning*)
  wiled, wil'ing
  (SEE while)

wil'ful

wil'i·ness

will
  would

will
  willed, will'ing

willed

Wil'lem·stad'

will'ful

will'ful·ly

will'ful·ness

Wil'liams·burg'

wil'lies

will'ing

wil'li·waw'

will'-less

will'-o'-the-wisp'

wil'low

wil'low·ware'

wil'low·y

will' pow'er

wil'ly-nil'ly

Wil'son

wilt

Wil'ton

wil'y
  wil'i·er, wil'i·est

Wim'ble·don

wim'ple
  wim'pled, wim'pling

win
  won, win'ning

wince
  winced, winc'ing

winch

wind
  wound, wind'ing

wind'age

wind'bag'

wind'blown'

wind'-borne'

wind'break'

wind'break'er

wind'burn'

wind' chill'

wind'ed

wind'er

wind'fall'

wind'flow'er

wind'i·ness

wind'ing

wind'ing sheet'

wind'jam'mer

wind'lass (*lifting
  device*)
  (SEE windless)

wind'less (*without
  wind*)
  (SEE windlass)

wind'mill'

win'dow

win'dow dress'ing

win'dow·pane'

win'dow seat'

win'dow shade'

win'dow-shop'
  win'dow-shopped',
  win'dow-shop'ping

win'dow-shop'per

win'dow sill'

wind'pipe'

wind'proof'

wind'row'

wind'shield'

wind'sock'

Wind'sor

Wind'sor chair'

wind'storm'

wind'-swept'

wind'up'

wind'ward

wind'y
  wind'i•er, wind'i•est

wine (*beverage*)
  wined, win'ing
  (SEE whine)

wine' cel'lar

wine'glass'

wine'grow'er

wine' press'

win'er•y
  pl. win'er•ies

Wine'sap'

wine'shop'

wine'skin'

wing

wing'back'

wing' bolt'

wing' chair'

wing'-ding'

winged

wing'foot'ed

wing' nut'

wing'span'

wing'spread'

wing' tip'

wink

win'na•ble

win'ner

win'ning

Win'ni•peg'

win'now

win'some

win'ter

win'ter•green'

win'ter•i•za'tion

win'ter•ize'
  win'ter•ized',
  win'ter•iz'ing

win'ter•kill'

win'ter•tide'

win'ter•time'

win'ter•y
  win'ter•i•er,
  win'ter•i•est

win'try
  win'tri•er, win'tri•est

wipe
  wiped, wip'ing

wip'er

wire
  wired, wir'ing

wire' cut'ter

wire'hair'

wire'-haired'

wire'less

Wire'pho'to
  (*Trademark*)
  pl. Wire'pho'tos

wire'pull'er

wire'tap'
  wire'tapped',
  wire'tap'ping

wir'i•ness

wir'ing

wir'y
  wir'i•er, wir'i•est

Wis•con'sin

Wis•con'sin•ite'

wis'dom

wise
  (*adj.*) wis'er, wis'est;
  (*v.*) wised, wis'ing

wise'a'cre

wise'crack'

wise'ly

wish

wish'bone'

wish'ful

wish'ful•ly

wish'y–wash'y

wisp

wisp'y
  wisp'i•er, wisp'i•est

wis•te'ri•a or
  wis•tar'i•a

wist'ful

wist'ful•ly

wit (*cleverness*)
  (SEE whit)

witch (*hag*)
  (SEE which)

witch'craft'

witch' doc'tor

witch'er•y
  pl. witch'er•ies

witch' ha'zel

witch' hunt'

witch'ing

with

with•al'

with•draw'
  with•drew',
  with•drawn',
  with•draw'ing

with•draw'al

with•drawn'

with'er (*shrivel*)
  (SEE whither)

with'ers

with•hold'
  with•held',
  with•hold'ing

with•in'

with•out'

with•stand'
  with•stood',
  with•stand'ing

wit'less

wit'ness

wit'ness stand'

wit'ti•cism'

wit'ti•ly

wit'ti•ness

wit'ting

wit'ty
  wit'ti•er, wit'ti•est

wiz'ard

wiz'ard•ry

wiz'ened

wob'ble
  wob'bled, wob'bling

wob'bly
  wob'bli•er, wob'bli•est

woe

woe'be•gone'

woe'ful

woe'ful•ly

wok

wold

wolf
　pl. wolves

Wolfe

wolf'hound'

wolf'ish

wolf' pack'

wol'ver·ine'

wom'an
　pl. wom'en

wom'an·hood'

wom'an·ish

wom'an·kind'

wom'an·li·ness

wom'an·ly

womb

wom'bat

wom'en·folk'

wom'en·folks'

won

won'der

won'der·ful

won'der·ful·ly

won'der·land'

won'der·ment

won'der-work'er

won'drous

wont (habit)
　wont, wont or wont'ed,
　wont'ing
　(SEE want)

won't

won' ton'

woo

wood (timber)
　(SEE would)

wood'bin'

wood'bine'

wood' block'

wood'-carv'er

wood' carv'ing

wood'chuck'

wood'cock'
　pl. wood'cocks' or
　wood'cock'

wood'craft'

wood'cut'

wood'cut'ter

wood'ed

wood'en

wood'en·ware'

wood'land'

wood'peck'er

wood'pile'

wood'shed'
　wood'shed·ed,
　wood'shed·ding

woods'man
　pl. woods'men

woods'y
　woods'i·er, woods'i·est

wood'wind'

wood'work'

wood'y
　wood'i·er, wood'i·est

woo'er

woof

woof'er

wool

wool'en or wool'len

Woolf

wool'gath'er·ing

wool'li·ness

wool'ly
　(adj.) wool'li·er,
　wool'li·est;
　pl. wool'lies

wool'y
　(adj.) wool'i·er,
　wool'i·est;
　pl. wool'ies

wooz'i·ly

wooz'i·ness

wooz'y
　wooz'i·er, wooz'i·est

Worces'ter·shire'

word

word'age

word'book'

word'-for-word'

word' game'

word'i·ly

word'i·ness

word'ing

word'less

word'-of-mouth'

word'play'

word' pro'cess·or

word' pro'cess·ing

Words'worth'

word'y
　word'i·er, word'i·est

wore

work
　worked or wrought,
　work'ing

work'a·bil'i·ty

work'a·ble

work'a·day'

work'a·hol'ic

work'bench'

work'book'

work' camp'

work'day'

work'er

work'fare'

work'horse'

work'house'

work'ing·man'
　pl. work'ing·men'

work'ing·wom'an
　pl. work'ing·wom'en

work' load'

work'man
　pl. work'men

work'man·like'

work'man·ship'

work'out'

work'room'

work' sheet'

work'shop'

work'ta·ble

work'week'

world

world'-beat'er

World' Court'

world'li·ness

world'ly
　world'li·er, world'li·est

world'ly-wise'

World' Se'ries

world's' fair'

world'-shak'ing

world'-wea'ri·ness

world'-wea'ry

world'-wide'

worm

worm'-eat'en

worm' gear'

worm'hole'

worm'wood'

worm'y
worm'i · er, worm'i · est

worn

worn'-out'

wor'ri · er

wor'ri · ment

wor'ri · some

wor'ry
v. wor'ried, wor'ry · ing;
pl. wor'ries

wor'ry · wart'

worse

wors'en

wor'ship
wor'shiped,
wor'ship · ing

wor'ship · er

wor'ship · ful

wor'ship · ful · ly

worst (most evil,
etc.)
(SEE wurst)

wor'sted

worth

wor'thi · ly

wor'thi · ness

worth'less

worth'while'

wor'thy
(adj.) wor'thi · er,
wor'thi · est;
pl. wor'thies

would

would'-be'

would'n't

wound

wove

wo'ven

wow

wrack (ruin)
(SEE rack)

wraith

wran'gle
wran'gled, wran'gling

wran'gler

wrap (enclose)
wrapped, wrap'ping
(SEE rap)

wrap'a · round'

wrap'per

wrap'ping

wrap'ping pa'per

wrap'-up'

wrath

wrath'ful

wrath'ful · ly

wreak (inflict)
(SEE reek)

wreath (floral circle)
(SEE wreathe)

wreathe (encircle)
wreathed, wreathed,
wreath'ing
(SEE wreath)

wreck (destroy)
(SEE reck)

wreck'age

wreck'er

wren

wrench

wrest (seize)
(SEE rest)

wres'tle
wres'tled, wres'tling

wres'tler

wres'tling

wretch (pitiable
person)
(SEE retch)

wretch'ed

wrig'gle
wrig'gled, wrig'gling

wrig'gler

wring (twist)
wrung, wring'ing
(SEE ring)

wring'er

wrin'kle
wrin'kled, wrin'kling

wrin'kly
wrin'kli · er,
wrin'kli · est

wrist

wrist'band'

wrist' watch'

writ

write (compose)
wrote, writ'ten, writ'ing
(SEE right and rite)

write'-down'

write'-in'

write'-off'

writ'er

write'-up'

writhe
writhed, writh'ing

writ'ing

writ'ing pa'per

writ'ten

wrong

wrong'do'er

wrong'do'ing

wrong'ful

wrong'ful · ly

wrong'-head'ed

wrong'ly

wrote

wrought

wrung

wry (twisted)
wri'er, wri'est
(SEE rye)

Wu'han'

Wun'der · kind'
pl. Wun'der · kinds' or
(Ger.) Wun'der · kin'der

wurst (sausage)
(SEE worst)

Wyc'liffe

Wy · o'ming

Wy · o'ming · ite'

X

xan'thic
x'-ax'is
  pl. x'-ax'es
X' chro•mo•some'
xe'bec
xe'non
xen'o•phobe'
xen'o•pho'bi•a

xen'o•pho'bic
xe'ro•graph'ic
xe•rog'ra•phy
xe•roph'i•lous
xe'roph•thal'mi•a
xe'ro•phyte'
Xer'ox (*Trademark*)
Xi

Xmas
X'-rat'ed
x'-ray'
xy'lem
xy'li•tol'
xy'lo•phone'
xy'lo•phon'ist
xys'ter

Y

yacht
yacht'ing
yachts'man
  pl. yachts'men
yachts'wom'an
  pl. yachts'wom'en
Ya'gi
ya'hoo
Yahr'zeit
Yah'weh
yak
  yakked, yak'king
ya'ki•to'ri
yam
yam'mer
yang
yank (*pull*)
  (SEE BELOW)
Yank (*Yankee*)
  (SEE ABOVE)
Yan'kee
Ya•oun•dé'
yap
  yapped, yap'ping
yard
yard'age
yard'arm'
yard'bird'
yard'man
  pl. yard'men
yard'mas'ter
yard'stick'
yar'mul•ke
yarn
yarn'-dyed'

yar'row
yash•mak'
yaw
yawl
yawn
yawp
yaws
y'-ax'is
  pl. y'-ax'es
Y' chro•mo•some'
ye
yea
yeah
year
year'book'
year'-end'
year'ling
year'long'
year'ly
  pl. year'lies
yearn
year'-round'
yeast
yeast'y
  yeast'i•er, yeast'i•est
yegg
yell
yel'low
yel'low fe'ver
yel'low•ish
yel'low•jack'et
Yel'low•stone'
yelp
Yem'en

Yem'en•ite'
yen (*Japanese money*)
  pl. yen
  (SEE BELOW)
yen (*desire*)
  yenned, yen'ning
  (SEE ABOVE)
yeo'man
  pl. yeo'men
yeo'man's serv'ice
yes
  pl. yes'es
ye•shi'va
  pl. ye•shi'vas or
  ye•shi'voth
yes' man'
  pl. yes' men'
yes'ter•day
yes'ter•year'
yet
yet'i
yew (*tree*)
  (SEE you *and* ewe)
Yid'dish
yield
yield'ing
yip
  yipped, yip'ping
yip'pee
Yiz'kor
yo'del
  yo'deled, yo'del•ing
yo'del•er
Yo'ga
yo'gi
  pl. yo'gis
yo'gurt or yo'ghurt

yoke (*join*)
    pl. yokes or yoke; (v.)
    yoked, yok'ing
    (SEE yolk)

yo'kel

Yo·ko·ha'ma

yolk (*part of egg*)
    (SEE yoke)

Yom Kip'pur

yon

yon'der

yoo'-hoo'

yore

Yo·sem'i·te

you (*pron.*)
    (SEE yew *and* ewe)

you-all'

you'd

you'll (*you will*)

young

young' blood'

young'ster

Young' Turk'

your (*belonging to you*)
    (SEE you're)

you're (*you are*)
    (SEE your)

yours

your·self'
    pl. your·selves'

youth
    pl. youths or youth

youth'ful

youth'ful·ly

youth'ful·ness

you've

yowl

yo'-yo
    pl. yo'-yos

yt·ter'bi·um

yt'tri·um

yu·an'
    pl. yu·an'

yuc'ca

Yu'go·slav'

Yu'go·sla'vi·a

Yu'go·sla'vi·an

Yu'kon

yule (*Christmas*)
    (SEE you'll)

yule' log'

yule'tide'

yum'my
    yum'mi·er,
    yum'mi·est

yurt

Z

za'ba·glio'ne

zai'ba·tsu'

Za·ire' (*country*)

za·ire' (*money*)

Za·ir'i·an or
    Za·ir'e·an

Zam'bi·a

Zam'bi·an

za'ni·ly

za'ni·ness

za'ny
    (*adj.*) za'ni·er,
    za'ni·est;
    pl. za'nies

Zan'zi·bar

zap
    zapped, zap'ping

zar·zue'la

z'-ax'is
    pl. z'-ax'es

za'-zen'

zeal

zeal'ot

zeal'ous

ze'bra
    pl. ze'bras or ze'bra

ze'bu

Zeit'geist'

Zen

ze'nith

ze'o·lite'

zeph'yr

Zep'pe·lin

ze'ro
    pl. ze'ros or ze'roes;
    (v.)
    ze'roed, ze'ro·ing

ze'ro-base budg'et·ing

ze'ro hour'

zest

zest'ful

zest'ful·ly

ze'ta

Zeus

zig'zag'
    zig'zagged', zig'zag'ging

zilch

zil'lion
    pl. zil'lions or zil'lion

Zim·bab'we

Zim·bab'wan

zinc
    zincked or zinced,
    zinck'ing or zinc'ing

zin'fan·del'

zing

zin'ni·a

Zi'on

Zi'on·ism'

Zi'on·ist

Zi'on·is'tic

zip
    zipped, zip'ping

zip' code'

zip' gun'

zip'per

zip'py
    zip'pi·er, zip'pi·est

zir'con

zir·co'ni·um

zit

zith'er

zlo'ty
    pl. zlo'tys or zlo'ty

zo'di·ac'

zo·di'a·cal

Zo'la

zom'bie or zom'bi

zon'al

zon'al·ly

zone
    zoned, zon'ing

zonked

zoo
 pl. zoos

zo'o·ge'o·graph'ic

zo'o·ge·og'ra·phy

zo'o·graph'ic

zo·og'ra·phy

zo'oid

zo'o·log'ic

zo'o·log'i·cal

zo'o·log'i·cal·ly

zo·ol'o·gist

zo·ol'o·gy
 pl. zo·ol'o·gies

zoom

zo'o·phyte'

zoot' suit'

Zo'ro·as'ter

Zo'ro·as'tri·an

Zo'ro·as'tri·an·ism'

zos'ter

Zou·ave'

zoy'si·a

zuc·chet'to
 pl. zuc·chet'tos or (It.)
 zuc·chet'ti

zuc·chi'ni
 pl. zuc·chi'ni or
 zuc·chi'nis

Zu'lu
 pl. Zu'lus or Zu'lu

zwie'back'

zy'gote

zy'mase

zy·mol'o·gy

zy·mot'ic

zy'mur·gy

Abbreviations

A 1 ampere; amperes 2 answer

A. 1 acre; acres 2 America 3 American 4 answer

a. 1 about 2 acre; acres 3 adjective 4 alto 5 anonymous

A.A. Associate in Arts

ab. about

A.B. Bachelor of Arts

abbr. 1 abbreviated 2 abbreviation *Also,* **abbrev.**

abr. 1 abridged 2 abridgment

abt. about

AC alternating current *Also,* **A.C., a.c.**

A/C 1 account 2 account current

A.C. before Christ

acad. 1 academic 2 academy

acct. account

ack. 1 acknowledge 2 acknowledgment

actg. acting

A.D. in the year of our Lord (*used with dates*)

add. 1 addenda 2 addition 3 address

ad int. ad interim

adj. 1 adjacent 2 adjective 3 adjutant

Adm. Admiral

adm. 1 administration 2 administrative *Also,* **admin.**

adv. 1 adverb 2 advertisement

ad val. ad valorem

advt. advertisement

aet. at the age of *Also,* **aetat.**

AF 1 Air Force 2 audio frequency

a.f. audio frequency

Afr. 1 Africa 2 African

aft. afternoon

A.G. 1 Adjutant General 2 Attorney General

agcy. agency

agr. 1 agricultural 2 agriculture

agric. 1 agricultural 2 agriculture

agt. agent

AK Alaska

a.k.a. also known as

AL Alabama

Ala. Alabama

ald. alderman

alt. 1 alteration 2 alternate 3 altitude 4 alto

Alta. Alberta

AM amplitude modulation

Am. 1 America 2 American

A.M. 1 *See* **a.m.** 2 Master of Arts

a.m. the period from 12 midnight to 12 noon

amb. ambassador

Amer. 1 America 2 American

amp. 1 amperage 2 ampere; amperes

amt. amount

anc. ancient

ann. 1 annals 2 annual

anon. anonymous

ans. answer

ant. antonym

Ant. Antarctica

A/O account of *Also,* **a/o**

Ap. April

A/P 1 account paid 2 accounts payable

a.p. additional premium

APO Army Post Office

app. 1 apparatus 2 appendix

approx. 1 approximate 2 approximately

appt. 1 appoint 2 appointment

Apr. April

apt. apartment

AR Arkansas

A/R account receivable

ar. 1 arrival 2 arrive; arrives

Ariz. Arizona

Ark. Arkansas

arr. 1 arranged 2 arrival 3 arrive 4 arrived

art. 1 article 2 artillery

A.R.V. American Revised Version

assn. association

assoc. 1 associate 2 association

asst. assistant

A.S.V. American Standard Version

at. Atomic

Atl. Atlantic

att. 1 attached **2** attention **3** attorney

Att. Gen. Attorney General

attn. attention

atty. attorney

aud. 1 audit **2** auditor

Aug. August

AUS Army of the United States

Aust. Austria

auth. 1 authentic **2** author

aux. auxiliary *Also,* **auxil.**

av. 1 avenue **2** average **3** avoirdupois

A/V 1 ad valorem **2** *Also,* **A-V** audiovisual

A.V. 1 audiovisual **2** Authorized Version

avdp. avoirdupois

ave. avenue

avg. average

A/W actual weight

AZ Arizona

B. 1 bachelor **2** bacillus **3** *Baseball,* base **4** bass **5** book **6** born **7** British

b. 1 bachelor **2** *Baseball,* base **3** bass **4** book **5** born

B.A. Bachelor of Arts

bal. balance

bar. 1 barometer **2** barometric **3** barrel

B.B.A. Bachelor of Business Administration

bbl. barrel

bc blind [*carbon*] copy

B.C. 1 before Christ **2** British Columbia

B.C.S. Bachelor of Commercial Science

bd. 1 board **2** bond **3** bound

B/D 1 bank draft **2** bills discounted **3** *Accounting,* brought down

bdl. bundle *Also,* **bdle**

B/E bill of exchange

bef. before

Belg. 1 Belgian **2** Belgium

bet. between

b.f. *Print.* boldface *Also,* **bf**

B/F *Accounting.* brought forward

B.F.A. Bachelor of Fine Arts

bg. bag

Bib. 1 Bible **2** Biblical

bibl. 1 biblical **2** bibliographical

Bibl. Biblical

bibliog. bibliography

biog. 1 biographer **2** biographical **3** biography

biol. 1 biological **2** biologist **3** biology

bk. 1 bank **2** book

bkg. banking

bkpg. bookkeeping

B/L bill of lading

bl. 1 bale **2** barrel **3** black **4** blue

bldg. building

blk. 1 black **2** block **3** bulk

B.L.S. Bachelor of Library Science

blvd. boulevard

B.O. 1 body odor **2** box office

b.o. 1 branch office **2** buyer's option

Bol. Bolivia

bor. borough

bot. 1 botanical **2** botanist **3** botany

bp. bishop

B.P. 1 bills payable **2** blood pressure

b.p. 1 bills payable **2** boiling point

bpl. birthplace

Br. 1 Britain **2** British

br. 1 branch **2** brass **3** brother **4** brown

b.r. bills receivable *Also,* **B.R.**

Brit. 1 Britain **2** British

bro. brother

bros. brothers

B.S. 1 Bachelor of Science **2** bill of sale

b.s. 1 balance sheet **2** bill of sale

B.Sc. Bachelor of Science

bsh. bushel; bushels

bskt. basket

Btu British thermal unit *Also,* **BTU**

bu. bushel; bushels

Bulg. 1 Bulgaria **2** Bulgarian

Bur. Burma

bur. bureau

bus. business

B.W.I. British West Indies
bx. box

C 1 Celsius **2** centigrade
c circa
C. 1 Cape **2** Catholic **3** Celsius
   4 Centigrade
c. 1 cape **2** carat **3** cent; cents
   4 centigrade **5** centimeter
   6 century **7** chapter **8** circa
   9 college **10** copy **11** *Also,* ©
   copyright
CA California
ca. circa
C.A. 1 chartered accountant
   2 chief accountant
CAF cost and freight
Cal. California
cal. 1 calendar **2** caliber **3** calorie
Calif. California
Can. 1 Canada **2** Canadian
Canad. Canadian
canc. 1 canceled **2** cancellation
cap. 1 capacity **2** capital
   3 capitalize **4** capitalized
caps. *Print.* capitals
Capt. Captain
car. carat
cat. catalog; catalogue
Cath. Catholic
C.B.D. cash before delivery
cc 1 carbon copy **2** cubic
   centimeter *Also,* **c.c.**
CD certificate of deposit *Also,*
   C.D.
c.d. cash discount
Cdr. Commander *Also,* **CDR**
C.E. 1 Chemical Engineer **2** Civil
   Engineer
cen. 1 central **2** century
cent. 1 centigrade **2** central
   3 century
CEO chief executive officer
certif. certificate
c/f *Bookkeeping.* carried forward
cf. 1 *Baseball.* center fielder
   2 compare
C.F. cost and freight *Also,* **c.f.**
C.F.I. cost, freight, and insurance
cg. centigram; centigrams
C.G. Coast Guard
cgm. centigram; centigrams

Ch. 1 *TV.* Channel **2** Chapter
   3 China **4** Chinese **5** Church
ch. 1 chapter **2** chief **3** church
c.h. 1 clearinghouse **2** courthouse
   3 customhouse
chap. 1 chaplain **2** chapter
chg. 1 change **2** charge
Chin. 1 China **2** Chinese
chm. chairman
chron. 1 chronicle
   2 chronological **3** chronology
chronol. 1 chronological
   2 chronology
Cia. Company
Cie. Company
C.I.F. cost, insurance, and freight
cir. 1 circa **2** circular
circ. 1 circa **2** circular **3** circuit
   4 circulation **5** circumference
circum. circumference
cit. 1 citation **2** cited **3** citizen
civ. 1 civil **2** civilian
ck. 1 cask **2** check
cl centiliter; centiliters
cl. 1 centiliter; centiliters **2** class
   3 classification **4** clause
   5 clearance **6** clerk
c.l. carload
class. 1 classic **2** classical
clk. 1 clerk **2** clock
clr. clear
cm centimeter; centimeters *Also,*
   cm.
cml. commercial
C/N 1 circular note **2** credit
   note
CO 1 Colorado **2** Commanding
   Officer **3** conscientious objector
C/O cash order
c/o 1 care of **2** carried over
   3 cash order
Co. 1 Company **2** County *Also,*
   co.
C.O. 1 cash order **2** Commanding
   Officer **3** conscientious objector
c.o. 1 care of **2** carried over
C.O.D. 1 cash on delivery
   2 collect on delivery *Also,*
   COD, c.o.d.
COL cost of living
Col. 1 Colonel **2** Colorado

col. 1 collect 2 college
3 collegiate 4 column
coll. 1 collect 2 college
3 collegiate
collat. collateral
Colo. Colorado
com. 1 commander 2 commerce
3 commercial 4 commission
5 commissioner 6 committee
7 common
comdg. commanding
coml. commercial
comm. 1 commission
2 committee 3 commonwealth
comp. 1 compiled 2 compiler
3 complete 4 composition
5 compound
Con. Consul
conf. conference
Cong. 1 Congress 2 Congressional
conj. conjunction
Conn. Connecticut
Cons. Consul
consol. consolidated
Const. Constitution
const. 1 constant 2 constitution
3 constitutional
const. construction
cont. 1 containing 2 contents
3 continent 4 continental
5 continued 6 contract
7 contraction
contd. continued
contr. contract
contrib. contributor
coop. cooperative
cor. corner
corp. 1 corporal 2 corporation
corr. 1 corrected 2 correction
3 correspondence
C.O.S. 1 cash on shipment
2 Chief of Staff
cp. compare
c.p. 1 candlepower 2 chemically
pure
C.P.A. certified public accountant
cpd. compound
CPI consumer price index
cpl. corporal
CPO chief petty officer
cr. 1 credit 2 creditor
cs. case; cases

C.S. Chief of Staff
c.s. 1 capital stock 2 civil service
C.S.A. Confederate States of
America
CST Central Standard Time *Also,*
C.S.T., c.s.t.
Ct. 1 Connecticut 2 Count
ct. 1 carat 2 cent 3 county
4 court
CT Connecticut
C.T. Central Time
ctn. carton
ctr. center
cts. cents
cu. cubic
cum. cumulative
cur. current
CWO *Mil.* chief warrant officer
c.w.o. cash with order
cwt hundredweight
cyl. cylinder
CZ Canal Zone *Also,* **C.Z.**

D. 1 December 2 Democrat
3 Democratic 4 Doctor
d. 1 date 2 daughter 3 day
4 degree 5 *Brit.* penny
6 diameter 7 died
D/A 1 days after acceptance
2 deposit account
D.A. District Attorney
dag dekagram; dekagrams
dal dekaliter; dekaliters
dam dekameter; dekameters
dB decibel; decibels *Also,* **db**
D.B. Bachelor of Divinity
dbl. double
DC 1 direct current 2 District of
Columbia *Also,* **D.C.**
dc direct current *Also,* **d.c.**
D/D days after date
D.D. 1 demand draft 2 Doctor of
Divinity
D.D.S. 1 Doctor of Dental
Science 2 Doctor of Dental
Surgery
DE Delaware
def. definite
deg. degree; degrees
Del. Delaware
del. 1 delegate 2 delegation
Dem. 1 Democrat 2 Democratic

Den. Denmark
dent. 1 dental **2** dentist
3 dentistry
dep. 1 depart **2** department
3 departure **4** deposit **5** deputy
dept. 1 department **2** deputy
D.G. by the grace of God
dg decigram; decigrams
dia. diameter
diag. 1 diagonal **2** diagram
diam. diameter
dict. 1 dictation **2** dictator
3 dictionary
diff. 1 difference **2** different
Also, **dif.**
dim. dimension
dir. director
disc. discount
dist. 1 distance **2** district
distr. 1 distribution **2** distributor
dl deciliter; deciliters
D.Litt. Doctor of Letters
D.L.O. Dead Letter Office
dlr. dealer
dlvy. delivery
DM Deutsche mark
dm decimeter; decimeters
D.M.D. Doctor of Dental
Medicine
do. ditto
D.O. 1 Doctor of Optometry
2 Doctor of Osteopathy
D.O.A. dead on arrival
doc. document
dol. dollar
Dom. Dominican
dom. domestic
doz. dozen; dozens
dpt. department
Dr. 1 Doctor **2** Drive
dr. 1 debit **2** debtor **3** drachma;
drachmas **4** dram; drams
ds decistere; decisters
d.s. *Com.* **1** days after sight
2 document signed
DST daylight-saving time *Also,*
D.S.T.
dup. duplicate
D.V. God willing
D.V.M. Doctor of Veterinary
Medicine

dwt pennyweight
dz. dozen; dozens

E 1 east **2** eastern **3** excellent
e. *Baseball.* error
ea. each
eccl. 1 ecclesiastic **2** ecclesiastical
ecol. 1 ecological **2** ecology
econ. 1 economic **2** economics
3 economy
Ecua. Ecuador
ed. 1 edited **2** edition **3** editor
4 education
edit. 1 edited **2** edition **3** editor
EDP electronic data processing
EDT Eastern daylight time *Also,*
E.D.T.
educ. 1 education **2** educational
E.E. Electrical Engineer
Eg. 1 Egypt **2** Egyptian
e.g. for example
elect. 1 electric **2** electrical
3 electricity *Also,* **elec.**
elem. 1 element **2** elementary
elev. elevation
Emp. 1 Emperor **2** Empire
3 Empress
enc. 1 enclosed **2** enclosure
encl. 1 enclosed **2** enclosure
ENE east-northeast
Eng. 1 England **2** English
eng. 1 engineer **2** engineering
engr. 1 engineer **2** engraved
Ens. Ensign
env. envelope
e.o.m. *Chiefly Com..* end of the
month
eq. 1 equal **2** equation
3 equivalent
equip. equipment
equiv. equivalent
erron. 1 erroneous **2** erroneously
ESE east-southeast
esp. especially *Also,* **espec.**
Esq. Esquire *Also,* **Esqr.**
EST Eastern Standard Time
est. 1 established **2** estate
3 estimate **4** estimated
estab. established
E.T. Eastern Time
et al. and others; etc.
Eur. 1 Europe **2** European

evg. evening

ex. 1 examination **2** example

exam. examination

exc. 1 excellent **2** except **3** exception

exch. exhange

excl. excluding

exec. 1 executive **2** executor

exp. 1 expenses **2** expired **3** export **4** express

ext. 1 extension **2** exterior **3** external **4** extra

F 1 Fahrenheit **2** farad

F. 1 Fahrenheit **2** false **3** February **4** Friday

f. 1 farad **2** female **3** feminine **4** folio **5** following **6** foot **7** franc; francs

fac. facsimile

Fahr. Fahrenheit *Also,* **Fah.**

f.b. freight bill

Feb. February

fed. 1 federal **2** federated **3** federation

Fed. Federal

fem. 1 female **2** feminine

ff. 1 folios **2** following

FIFO first-in, first-out

fig. 1 figurative **2** figuratively **3** figure; figures

Fin. 1 Finland **2** Finnish

fin. 1 finance **2** financial **3** finish

Finn. Finnish

FL Florida

Fl. 1 Flanders **2** Flemish

fl. 1 flourished **2** fluid

Fla. Florida

Flem Flemish *Also,* **Flem.**

FM frequency modulation

fm. 1 fathom **2** from

fn footnote

fol. 1 folio **2** following

foll. following

for. foreign

fp. freezing point

fpm feet per minute *Also,* **ft/min**

FPO fleet post office

fps feet per second

Fr. 1 Father **2** *pl.* **Fr., Frs.** franc **3** France **4** French **5** Friar **6** Friday

fr. 1 *pl.* **fr. frs.** franc **2** from

freq. 1 frequency **2** frequently

Fri. Friday

frt. freight

ft. foot; feet

ft. 1 foot; feet **2** fort

ft-lb foot-pound; foot-pounds

fut. future

fwd. forward

FYI for your information

g 1 good **2** gram; grams **3** *Physics.* gravity

Ga. Georgia

GA Georgia

gal gallon; gallons

G.B. Great Britain

gds. goods

Gen. 1 *Mil.* General **2** Genesis

gen. general

geog. 1 geographic; geographical **2** geography

geol. 1 geologic; geological **2** geology

geom. 1 geometric; geometrical **2** geometry

Ger. 1 German **2** Germany

GHO *Mil.* general headquarters

G.I. 1 gastrointestinal **2** general issue **3** government issue *Also,* **GI**

Gk. Greek

GNP gross national product

govt. government

G.P. general practitioner

GPO general post office

GR. 1 Greece **2** Greek

gr. 1 grade **2** grain; grains **3** gram; grams **4** gross **5** group

Gt. Br. Great Britain *Also,* **Gt. Brit.**

gtd. guaranteed

GU Guam

g.u. genitourinary *Also,* **GU**

guar. guaranteed

h. 1 hard **2** hardness **3** height **4** high **5** hour; hours *Also,* **H.**

ha hectare; hectares
H.C. Holy Communion
h.c.l. high cost of living
hd. 1 hand 2 head
hdbk. handbook
hdqrs. headquarters
HF high frequency
hgt. height
hgwy. highway
H.H. 1 His (or Her) Highness
  2 His Holiness
hhd hogshead; hogsheads
HI Hawaii
H.I. Hawaiian Islands
his. 1 historian 2 historical
  3 history
Hon. 1 Honorable 2 Honorary
hon. 1 honor 2 honorable
hor. horizontal
hort. 1 horticultural
  2 horticulture
hosp. hospital
hp horsepower *Also,* **HP**
H.P. 1 high pressure
  2 horsepower *Also,* **h.p.**
H.O. headquarters *Also,* **h.g., HQ**
hr. hour; hours *Also,* **hr**
H.R. House of Representatives
H.S. High School
ht. height
Hun. 1 Hungarian 2 Hungary
Hung. 1 Hungarian 2 Hungary
H.V. high voltage *Also,* **h.v.**
hvy. heavy
hwy. highway
hvp. 1 hypotenuse 2 hypothesis
  3 hypothetical
HZ. hertz

I. 1 Island; Islands 2 Isle; Isles
i. 1 island 2 isle; isles
IA Iowa *Also,* **Ia.**
ib. ibidem
ibid. ibidem
Ice. 1 Iceland 2 Icelandic
Icel. 1 Iceland 2 Icelandic
ID 1 *Also,* **Id., Ida.** Idaho
  2 identification
id. idem
I.D. identification
i.e. that is
IF intermediate frequency

IL Illinois
Ill. Illinois
ill. 1 illustrated 2 illustration
illus. 1 illustrated 2 illustration
illust. 1 illustrated 2 illustration
imp. 1 imperfect 2 import
  3 important 4 imported
IN Indiana
in. inch; inches *Also,* **in**
Inc. Incorporated
inc. 1 incorporated 2 increase
incl. 1 inclosure 2 including
  3 inclusive
incr. increase
Ind. 1 India 2 Indian 3 Indiana
ind. 1 independent 2 index
  3 industrial 4 industry
inf. 1 infantry 2 inferior
ins. inches
insp. 1 inspected 2 inspector
inst. 1 institute 2 institution
instr. 1 instructor 2 instrument
int. 1 interest 2 interior
  3 internal 4 international
inter. intermediate
internat. international
intl. international
intro. introduction
inv. invoice
IQ intelligence quotient *Also,*
  I.Q.
Ir. 1 Ireland 2 Irish
I.R. information retrieval
IRA individual retirement
  account
Ire. Ireland
irreg. irregular
Is. 1 Island 2 Isle
is. 1 island 2 isle
isl. 1 island 2 isle *Also,* **Isl.**
Isr. 1 Israel 2 Israeli
Ital. 1 Italian 2 Italy *Also,* **It.**
ital. 1 italic; italics 2 italicized
IUD intrauterine device

J joule *Also,* **j**
J the 10th in order or in a series
J. 1 Journal 2 Judge 3 Justice
Ja. January
J.A. Judge Advocate
Jam. Jamaica
Jan. January

Japn. 1 Japan 2 Japanese
Jav. Javanese
jct. junction
J.D. 1 Doctor of Jurisprudence 2 Doctor of Laws
Je. June
jg. junior grade *Also,* **j.g.**
jour. journal
J.P. Justice of the Peace
Jpn. 1 Japan 2 Japanese
Jr. 1 Journal 2 Junior
Ju. June
Jul. July
Jun. 1 June 2 Junior
Junc. Junction

K 1 Kelvin 2 kindergarten
k. 1 karat 2 kilogram; kilograms
Kans. Kansas
kc kilocycle; kilocycles
kc/s kilocycles per second
KD 1 kin-dried 2 *Com.* knock-down
kg. kilogram; kilograms
kHz kilohertz
km. kilometer; kilometers *Also,* **km**
kn knots; knots
K.P.H. kilometers per hour *Also,* **KPH, k.p.h., kph**
KS Kansas
Kt *Chess.* knight
kt. karat
kW kilowatt; kilowatts *Also,* **kw**
kWh kilowatt-hour *Also,* **kwhr, K.W.H.**
KY Kentucky *Also,* **Ky.**

L 1 large 2 *Brit.* pound; pounds
L. 1 Lake 2 latitude
l. 1 left 2 length 3 *pl.* **ll.** line 4 liter; liters
LA Louisiana *Also,* **La.**
Lab. Labrador
lab. laboratory
lat. latitude
lb. *pl.* **lbs., lb.** pound *Also,* **lb**
L/C letter of credit *Also,* **l/c**
l.c. 1 loc. cit. 2 *Print.* lower case
L.C.D. lowest common denominator
LCDR Lieutenant Commander

L.C.M. least common multiple
legis. 1 legislation 2 legislative 3 legislature
LF low frequency
l.f. *Print.* lightface *Also,* **lf**
lg. 1 large 2 long
lge. large
l.h. 1 left hand 2 lower half
L.H.D. Doctor of Humane Letters
Lieut. lieutenant
LIFO last-in, first-out
lin. 1 lineal 2 linear
liq. 1 liquid 2 liquor
lit. 1 liter; liters 2 literal 3 literally 4 literary 5 literature
lith. 1 lithograph 2 lithographic 3 lithography *Also,* **litho, lithog.**
Litt.D. Doctor of Letters; Doctor of Literature
ll. lines
LL.B Bachelor of Laws
LL.D. Doctor of Laws
LNG liquified natural gas
loc. cit. in the place cited
long. longitude *Also,* **lon.**
L.P. low pressure
LPG liquified petroleum gas
LPN Licensed Practical Nurse
L.S. 1 left side 2 the place of the seal
Lt. Lieutenant
lt. light
Lux. Luxembourg
lv. leave; leaves

M 1 *Mach.* 2 *Physics.* mass
M the Roman numeral for 1000
m *Metric System.* meter; meters
M. 1 Monday 2 *pl.* **MM.** Monsieur
m. 1 male 2 married 3 masculine 4 medium 5 noon 6 meter 7 mile 8 minim 9 minute 10 month
MA Massachusetts
M.A. Master of Arts
mach. 1 machine 2 machinery
Maj. Major
Mal. 1 Malay 2 Malayan
Man. Manitoba

man. manual
Mar. March
mar. 1 maritime 2 married
masc. masculine *Also*, **mas.**
Mass. Massachusetts
math. 1 mathematical 2 mathematics
max. maximum
M.B.A. Master of Business Administration
mc megacycle; megacycles
M.C. 1 master of ceremonies 2 Member of Congress
MD Maryland
Md. Maryland
M.D. Doctor of Medicine
mdse. merchandise
ME Maine
Me. Maine
M.E. 1 Mechanical Engineer 2 Mining Engineer
meas. 1 measurable 2 measure
mech. 1 mechanical 2 mechanics 3 mechanism
med. 1 medical 2 medicine 3 medieval 4 medium
M.Ed. Master of Education
meg. megohm; megohms.
mem. member
mer. meridian
Messrs. *pl. of* **Mr.**
metall. 1 metallurgical 2 metallurgy
meteorol. 1 meteorological 2 meteorology
Mex. 1 Mexican 2 Mexico
MF *Radio.* medium frequency
M.F.A. Master of Fine Arts
mfd. manufactured
mfg. manufacturing
mfr. manufacturer
mg. milligram; milligrams
Mgr. 1 Manager 2 Monseigneur 3 Monsignor
mgt. management
MHz megahertz; megahertz
MI Michigan
mi. 1 mile; miles 2 mill; mills
MIA *Mil.* missing in action
Mich. Michigan
mid. middle
mil. military

min. 1 minimum 2 minor 3 minute; minutes
Minn. Minnesota
misc. miscellaneous
mk. mark
MKS meter-kilogram-second
mkt. market
ml milliliter; milliliters
Mlle. *pl.* **Mlles.** Mademoiselle
mm millimeter; millimeters
MM. Messieurs
Mme. *pl.* **Mmes.** Madame
MN Minnesota
MO Missouri
Mo. 1 Missouri 2 Monday
mo. *pl.* **mos., mo.** month
M.O. 1 mail order 2 money order
mod. modern
Mon. 1 Monday 2 Monsignor
Mont. Montana
MP Military Police
mp. melting point
M.P. 1 Member of Parliament 2 Military Police
mpg miles per gallon *Also*, **m.p.g., MPG**
mph miles per hour *Also*, **mph., MPH**
Mr. mister
Mrs. mistress
MS 1 Mississippi 2 motor ship 3 multiple sclerosis
Ms. Miss or Mrs.
MS. *pl.* **Mss.** manuscript
ms. *pl.* **mss.** manuscript
M.S. 1 Master of Science 2 motor ship 3 multiple sclerosis
msec millisecond; milliseconds
Msgr. 1 Monseigneur 2 Monsignor
MSgt Master Sergeant *Also*, **M/Sgt**
MST Mountain Standard Time
MT Montana
Mt. 1 mount 2 mountain *Also*, **mt.**
M.T. 1 metric ton 2 Mountain Time
mtg. 1 meeting 2 mortgage
mtge. mortgage

mtn. mountain *Also,* **Mtn.**
Mts. mountains *Also,* **mts.**
mun. municipal *Also,* **munic.**
mus. 1 museum 2 music
MV motor vessel
mV millivolt; millivolts

N 1 north 2 northern
N. 1 north 2 northern
3 November
n. 1 net 2 neuter 3 north
4 northern 5 noun 6 number
N.A. 1 North America 2 not
available
nat. 1 national 2 native
3 natural
naut. nautical
nav. naval
NB note well
N.B. 1 New Brunswick 2 Note
well
NC 1 North Carolina 2 no
charge
N.C. North Carolina
NCO Noncommissioned Officer
ND North Dakota
n.d. no date
N.Dak. North Dakota *Also,*
N.D.
NE 1 Nebraska 2 northeast
3 northeastern
N.E. 1 New England 2 northeast
3 northeastern
Nebr. Nebraska
neg. negative
Neth. Netherlands
neut. neuter
Nev. Nevada
Newf. Newfoundland
Nfld. Newfoundland *Also,* **Nfd**
N.G. no good
NH New Hampshire *Also,* **N.H.**
NJ New Jersey *Also,* **N.J.**
NM New Mexico
N.M. New Mexico *Also,* **N.
Mex.**
NNE north-northeast
NNW north-northwest
no. 1 North 2 northern
3 number *Also,* **No.**
Nor. 1 Norway 2 Norwegian
Norw. 1 Norway 2 Norwegian

nos. numbers *Also,* **Nos.**
n.p. notary public *Also,* **N.P.**
N.S. Nova Scotia
NT New Testament
num. numeral; numerals
NV Nevada
NW 1 northwest 2 northwestern
NY New York *Also,* **N.Y.**
NYC New York City *Also,*
N.Y.C.
N.Z. New Zealand

O ohm
O. 1 Ocean 2 October 3 Ohio
4 Oregon
obj. 1 object 2 objective
Oct. October
oct. octavo
O.D. 1 Doctor of Optometry
2 officer of the day 3 overdraft
4 overdrawn
off. 1 office 2 officer 3 official
OH Ohio
OK Oklahoma
Okla. Oklahoma
Ont. Ontario
op. cit. in the work cited
opp. opposite
opt. 1 optical 2 optician 3 optics
4 optional
OR 1 operating room 2 Oregon
orch. orchestra
ord. 1 order 2 ordnance
Oreg. Oregon *Also,* **Ore.**
org. 1 organic 2 organization
3 organized
orig. 1 origin 2 original
3 originally
o/s out of stock
OT Old Testament
oz. ounce; ounces *Also,* **oz**

p. 1 page 2 participle 3 past
4 penny; pence 5 per 6 pint
7 *Baseball.* pitcher 8 president
9 pressure
PA 1 Pennsylvania 2 public
address (system).
Pa. Pennsylvania
P.A. 1 power of attorney 2 press
agent 3 purchasing agent

p.a. per annum
Pac. Pacific
Pan. Panama
P. and L. profit and loss *Also*,
  P. & L.
par. 1 paragraph 2 parallel
  3 parish
paren. parenthesis
parl. 1 parliament
  2 parliamentary
part. 1 participial 2 participle
  3 particular
pass. passenger
pat. 1 patent 2 patented
pat. pend. patent pending
payt. payment
p.c. 1 percent 2 petty cash
  3 postal card
pct. percent
pd. paid
P.D. Police Department
p.d. per diem
PDT Pacific daylight time
P.D. Protestant Episcopal
P.E.I. Prince Edward Island
Pen. peninsula *Also*, **pen.**
Penn. Pennsylvania *Also*,
  Penna.
per. 1 period 2 person
perf. 1 perfect 2 perforated
perh. perhaps
pf. preferred *Also*, **pfd.**
PFC *Mil.* Private First Class *Also*,
  pfc
P.G. postgraduate
pharm. 1 pharmaceutical
  2 pharmacist 3 pharmacy
Ph.D Doctor of Philosophy
phys. 1 physical 2 physician
physiol. 1 physiological
  2 physiology
pk. 1 pack 2 park 3 peak 4 peck
pkg. package
pkt. 1 packet 2 pocket
pkwy. parkway
pl. 1 place 2 plate 3 plural
P.O. 1 petty officer 2 postal order
  3 post office
POB post office box
POE 1 port of embarkation
  2 port of entry
Pol. 1 Poland 2 Polish

pol. 1 political 2 politics
polit. 1 political 2 politics
Port. 1 Portugal 2 Portuguese
pos. 1 position 2 positive
poss. 1 possession 2 possessive
  3 possible 4 possibly
POW prisoner of war *Also*,
  P.O.W.
pp. 1 pages 2 past participle
P.P. 1 parcel post 2 postpaid
  3 prepaid
ppd. 1 postpaid 2 prepaid
ppr. present participle *Also*, **p.pr.**
P.P.S. an additional postscript
  Also, **p.p.s**
P.Q. Province of Quebec
PR 1 public relations 2 Puerto
  Rico
pr. 1 pair; pairs 2 present 3 price
  4 pronoun
P.R. 1 proportional representation
  2 public relations 3 Puerto Rico
prec. 1 preceded 2 preceding
pref. 1 preface 2 preference
  3 preferred 4 prefix
prelim. preliminary
prep. 1 preparatory 2 preposition
Pres. President
pres. 1 present 2 president
prev. 1 previous 2 previously
prim. primary
prin. 1 principal 2 principle
prob. 1 probable 2 probably
  3 problem
proc. 1 procedure 2 proceedings
  3 process
prod. 1 produce 2 produced
  3 producer 4 produce
  5 production
pron. 1 pronoun 2 pronounced
Prot. Protestant
prov. 1 province 2 provincial
  3 provisional 4 provost
prox. proximo
prs. pairs
Ps. Psalm; Psalms *Also*, **Psa.**
P.S. 1 postscript 2 Public School
p.s. postscript
pseud. pseudonym
psf pounds per square foot *Also*,
  p.s.f.

psi pounds per square inch *Also,* **p.s.i.**

PST Pacific Standard Time

psych. psychology

psychoanal. psychoanalysis

psychol. 1 psychologist 2 psychology

pt. 1 part 2 past tense 3 pint; pints 4 point

P.T. 1 Pacific Time 2 physical therapy 3 physical training

p.t. 1 past tense 2 pro tempore

ptg. printing

pub. 1 public 2 publication 3 published 4 publisher 5 publishing

publ. 1 public 2 publication 3 published 4 publisher

Pft. Private

PW prisoner of war

pwt. pennyweight

PX post exchange

Q *Chess.* queen

Q. question

q. 1 quart; quarts 2 query 3 question

Q.E.D. which was to be demonstrated

qt. 1 quantity 2 quart

qty. quantity

qu. question

quad. 1 quadrangle 2 quadrant

Que. Quebec

ques. question

quot. quotation

q.v. which see

qy. query

R. 1 radius 2 railroad 3 Republican 4 right 5 river 6 road

r. 1 rare 2 rod

rad. 1 *Math.* radical 2 radio 3 radius

R&D research and development

R.C. Roman Catholic

R.C.Ch. Roman Catholic Church

Rd. Road

rd. 1 road 2 rod; rods 3 round

R.D. rural delivery

rec. 1 receipt 2 record

recd. received *Also,* **rec'd**

rect. 1 receipt 2 rectangle 3 rectangular 4 rectified

ref. 1 referee 2 reference 3 referred 4 refining 5 reformation 6 reformed 7 refund 8 refunding

refl. 1 reflection 2 reflective 3 reflex 4 reflexive

reg. 1 regiment 2 region 3 register 4 registered 5 registry 6 regular 7 regulation

rel. 1 relating 2 relative 3 released 4 religion

relig. religion

Rep. 1 Representative 2 Republic 3 Republican

rep. 1 repair 2 repeat 3 report 4 reporter

Repub. 1 Republic 2 Republican

req. 1 request 2 require 3 required

res. 1 research 2 reserve 3 residence 4 resigned 5 resolution

resp. 1 respective 2 respectively

ret. 1 retired 2 return

retd. 1 retired 2 returned

Rev. Reverend

rev. 1 revenue 2 reverse 3 review 4 revise 5 revised 6 revision 7 revolution

RF radio frequency

RFD rural free delivery

r.h. right hand

RI Rhode Island *Also,* **R.I.**

R.I.P. may he (or she) rest in peace

riv. river

rm. 1 ream 2 room

Rom. 1 Roman 2 Romania 3 Romanian

rpm revolutions per minute

rps revolutions per second

rpt. 1 repeat 2 report

R.R. 1 railroad 2 rural route

r.s. right side

R.S.V.P. please reply *Also,* **rsvp, r.s.v.p.**

rt. right

rte. route

Rum. 1 Rumania 2 Rumanian
RV recreational vehicle
RX *Med.* prescription
Ry. Railway *Also,* **Rwy**

S 1 small 2 soft 3 South
  4 Southern
s 1 small 2 soft 3 south
  4 southern
S. 1 Saint 2 Saturday 3 School
  4 Sea 5 Senate 6 September
  7 South 8 Southern 9 Sunday
s. 1 saint 2 second 3 small
  4 south 5 southern
S.A. South Africa
Sask. Saskatchewan
Sat. Saturday
S.B. Bachelor of Science
SC South Carolina *Also,* **S.C.**
S.C. South Carolina
s.c. *Print.* small capitals
Scand. 1 Scandinavia
  2 Scandinavian
sch. school
sci. 1 science 2 scientific
Scot. 1 Scotland 2 Scottish
SD South Dakota
S.D. 1 South Dakota 2 special
  delivery
S. Dak. South Dakota
SE 1 southeast 2 southeastern
sec. 1 second 2 secretary
  3 section
sect. section
secy. secretary *Also,* **sec'y**
sel. 1 selected 2 selection
sen. 1 senate 2 senator 3 senior
Sep. September
sep. 1 separate 2 separated
Sept. September
seq. the following (*one*)
ser. 1 serial 2 series
Serg. Sergeant *Also,* **Sergt.**
serv. service
SF science fiction *Also,* **sf**
Sfc Sergeant First Class
sgd. signed
Sgt. Sergeant
shpt. shipment
sig. 1 signal 2 signature
sing. singular

Slav. Slavic
sm. small
S.M. Master of Science
So. 1 South 2 Southern
s.o. 1 seller's option 2 strikeout
soc. 1 social 2 socialist 3 society
sociol. 1 sociological 2 sociology
sol. 1 soluble 2 solution
SP. 1 Shore Patrol 2 Specialist
Sp. 1 Spain 2 Spanish
sp. 1 special 2 species 3 specimen
  4 spelling
Span. Spanish
spec. 1 special 2 specifically
  3 specification
specif. 1 specific 2 specifically
sq. 1 squadron 2 square
Sr. 1 Senior 2 *Eccles.* Sister
S.R.O. standing room only
SS. Saints
S.S. 1 steamship 2 Sunday School
SSE south-southeast
SSgt Staff Sergeant
SSW south-southwest
St. 1 Saint 2 state 3 statute
  4 stone (*weight*)
s.t. short ton
sta. 1 station 2 stationary
std. standard
S.T.D. Doctor of Sacred Theology
sub. 1 subscription 2 substitute
  3 suburb 4 suburban 5 subway
subj. subject
subst. substitute
suff. 1 sufficient 2 suffix
Sun. Sunday *Also,* **Sund.**
sup. 1 superior 2 supplement
  3 supplementary 4 supply
  5 supra
supp 1 supplement
  2 supplementary *Also,* **suppl.**
supt. superintendent
svgs. savings
SW 1 short-wave 2 southwest
  3 southwestern
Sw. 1 Sweden 2 Swedish
Switz. Switzerland
syll. 1 syllable 2 syllabus *Also,*
  syl.
sym. 1 symbol 2 symmetrical
  3 symphony

syn. 1 synonym **2** synonymous **3** synonymy

syst. system

T. 1 tablespoon; tablespoonful **2** Territory **3** Testament **4** true **5** Tuesday

t. 1 teaspoon; teaspoonful **2** temperature **3** *Gram.* tense **4** time **5** ton **6** transit **7** transitive **8** troy

T&E travel and entertainment

TB tuberculosis *Also,* **T.B., Tb**

t.b. trial balance

tbs. tablespoon; tablespoonful *Also,* **tbsp**

tech. 1 technical **2** technician **3** technological

tel. 1 telegram **2** telegraph **3** telephone

temp. 1 temperature **2** temporary

Tenn. Tennessee

terr. 1 territorial **2** territory

Test. Testament

test. 1 testator **2** testimony

Tex. Texas

Th. Thursday

theol. 1 theological **2** theology

Thur. Thursday *Also,* **Thurs.**

TKO *Boxing.* technical knockout

tkt. ticket

TM trademark

TN Tennessee

tn. 1 ton **2** town **3** train

tnpk. turnpike

t.o. turn over

tp. township

tpk turnpike

tr. 1 transitive **2** translated **3** translation **4** translator **5** transpose **6** transposition **7** treasurer

trans. 1 transaction **2** transitive **3** translated **4** translation **5** translator **6** transportation

transl. 1 translated **2** translation

treas. 1 treasurer **2** treasury

T.Sgt. Technical Sergeant

tsp. 1 teaspoon **2** teaspoonful

Tues. Tuesday *Also,* **Tue.**

Turk. 1 Turkey **2** Turkish

TX Texas

U. 1 union **2** university **3** upper

u.c. *Print.* upper case

u.h. upper half

UHF ultrahigh frequency

U.K. United Kingdom

UL Underwriters' Laboratories

ult. 1 ultimate **2** ultimately **3** *Also,* **ulto. ultimo**

Univ. University

univ. 1 universal **2** university

U.S. United States *Also,* **US**

U.S.A. 1 United States Army **2** United States of America *Also,* **USA**

USAF United States Air Force *Also,* **U.S.A.F.**

USCG United States Coast Guard

USMC United States Marine Corps.

USN United States Navy

U.S.S. United States Ship

usu 1 usual **2** usually

UT Utah *Also,* **Ut.**

V 1 *Math.* vector **2** velocity **3** volt; volts

V 1 the Roman numeral for 5 **2** vanadium

v 1 velocity **2** volt; volts

V. 1 Vice **2** Village

v. 1 verb **2** verse **3** version **4** versus **5** vide **6** voice **7** volume

VA Virginia

VA. Virginia

val. 1 valuation **2** value **3** valued

var. 1 variable **2** variant **3** variation **4** variety **5** various

VAT value-added tax

ver. version

vert. vertical

VFD volunteer fire department

VFW Veterans of Foreign Wars

V.G. very good

VHF very high frequency

VI Virgin Islands *Also,* **V.I.**

vic. vicinity

VLF very low frequency

V.M.D. Doctor of Veterinary Medicine
vocab. vocabulary
vol. 1 volume **2** volunteer
V.P. Vice President
vs. 1 verse **2** versus
VT Vermont *Also,* **Vt.**

W 1 watt; watts **2** west **3** western *Also,* **w**
W. 1 watt; watts **2** Wednesday **3** weight **4** Welsh **5** west **6** western **7** width
w. 1 water **2** watt; watts **3** week, weeks **4** wide **5** wife **6** with
w/ with
WA Washington
W.A. Western Australia
Wash. Washington
W/B waybill *Also,* **W.B.**
Wed. Wednesday
Whse. warehouse *Also,* **whs.**
whsle. wholesale
WI Wisconsin
W.I. West Indies
Wis. Wisconsin *Also,* **Wisc.**
wk. 1 week **2** work
wkly. weekly

WNW west-northwest
w/o without
WO Warrant Officer
WSW west-southwest
wt. weight
WV West Virginia *Also,* **W. Va.**
WY Wyoming *Also,* **Wyo.**

xd *Stock Exchange.* without dividend *Also,* **x.div.**
x in *Stock Exchange.* without interest *Also,* **x.i., x.int.**
XL extra large
Xmas Christmas
Xn Christian

y. 1 yard; yards **2** year; years
yd. yard; yards *Also,* **yd**
yr. 1 year; years **2** your
yrs. 1 years **2** yours
Y.T. Yukon Territory
YTD year to date

z. 1 zero **2** zone
ZBB zero-base budgeting
zool. 1 zoological **2** zoology
ZPG zero population growth

How to Improve Your Spelling

The alphabet is a system for representing the sounds of a language. Ideally, each letter of the alphabet would represent only one sound, and each sound would be indicated by only one letter. Some languages—Spanish, Italian, and German, among others—come very close to such an ideal. English, unfortunately, is far from that ideal.

In English, for example, the letter *a* may appear with different sounds in such words as *cat, fate, far, any, tall,* and *alone.* Similarly, the sound *k* may appear in such different spellings as *car, character, lack, lacquer, kick, liquor,* and *Iraq.* Part of the problem in English is that we have only 26 letters in our alphabet with which to represent more than 40 distinctive sounds.

There are two other major parts of the problem. One is that the English language often retains the spelling used in the foreign language from which some words are borrowed. Second, while the pronunciation of English has been steadily changing over recent centuries, the spelling has tended to be unchanging because of the influence of the printing press.

Those who regard themselves as poor spellers, therefore, may derive some comfort in the fact that they are trying to cope with a language whose spellings are often illogical and inconsistent. They are not alone; even the best spellers make mistakes and suffer doubt and frustration. Nevertheless, many of the difficulties in spelling can be overcome by those who are willing to devote some time and energy to the task. By consulting this ready-reference book whenever they are uncertain about a spelling, they can build and steadily reinforce their knowledge of the correct spelling. In addition, they can gain from the useful suggestions and basic rules that follow.

1. The most effective way to improve your spelling is to set aside regular study sessions at which you write down and memorize a certain number of words—ten, fifteen, twenty, or more, depending upon the degree of difficulty. Memorization and drill are essential.

2. Keep a record of all your misspelled words. Practice writing them correctly again and again until you are confident that you have mastered them.

3. In memorizing a word, try to retain a visual image of the word in your mind. Because English spelling is not always phonetic, the sound of a word is not always a reliable guide to its spelling. Note

any silent letters so you will remember to include them even though they are not pronounced.

4. Use this book to find the correct spelling and syllabication of new words or problem words. Observe which syllables are stressed. Dividing words into syllables greatly simplifies the spelling of many long words which, at first glance, appear threatening. When broken up into syllables, most seemingly difficult words reveal themselves to be no more than a series of easily spelled syllables.

5. Make frequent use of your dictionary. If you do not have a reliable, up-to-date dictionary issued by a recognized publishing house, you should get one. When you encounter an unfamiliar word, look it up in the dictionary so that you will know its meaning, for, unless you understand the word, simply learning to spell the word becomes a meaningless exercise.

6. In practicing your spelling, group together those words that have similar spelling patterns: the *ie* and *ei* combinations, words ending in *ey*, words ending in *ance* and *ence*, etc.

7. Study carefully the "spelling demons" listed on pages 374 through 376. These are the commonly misspelled words that have plagued generations of users. Not all of them are necessarily your troublesome words, but it pays to review them.

8. Review the selected list of words that are often confused, appearing on pages 377 through 380, and make sure you know their meanings so that you can distinguish between them.

9. Study the basic rules of spelling that follow these suggestions. Identify those that seem to be the main sources of your problems and keep reviewing them frequently enough to change your habits. None of these rules is completely free of exceptions but they will work most of the time.

10. If possible, have someone dictate to you the words most commonly misspelled (pages 374–376), the ones in your own list of troublesome words, and random ones chosen from the general list in this book.

11. Create your own sentence, making use of the new words you have studied and concentrating especially on the troublesome words. The actual use of correctly spelled words in the context of sentences is the ultimate test of your proficiency.

Basic Rules of Spelling

Although English spelling cannot be completely covered by a set of logical rules, there are a number of guidelines that will be helpful.

I. When to use *ei* or *ie*

With only a few exceptions, the familiar rhymed spelling rule generally applies: "Write *i* before *e*, except after *c*, or when sounded like *a* as in *neighbor* and *weigh*."

Examples of ie *(Most, but not all, have the long* e *sound.):*

believe	chief	field	grief	piece
achieve	belief	brief	cashier	fierce
niece	pier	pierce	priest	relieve
shield	shriek	siege	thief	tier
wield	yield	fiend	bier	frontier
wiener	chandelier	frieze	retrieve	hygiene
friend	mischief	mischievous	sieve	

But:

either	neither	leisure	height	seize
sleight	seizure	codeine	caffeine	counterfeit
sheik	weird	forfeit	foreign	sovereign

Examples of ei *after* c:

receive	perceive	receipt	conceive
ceiling	conceit	deceit	deceive

But:

financier	ancient	species

Examples of ei *when sounded as a long* a:

neighbor	reign	beige	skein	inveigle
weigh	eight	veil	deign	heinous
heir	freight	sleigh	rein	feint
surveillance				

Note that the above rules pertain to *ie* and *ei* when the two letters represent a single sound. They do not apply when the *i* and *e* are pronounced as separate syllables. In that case, placement of the two letters depends upon the sound and meaning of the individual word. *Examples:* diet, science, reimburse, reenforce, deify, deice.

II. When to keep or drop the final *e* before a suffix

1. In words ending in a silent *e* (as in *state* and *arrive*), keep the final *e* before a suffix that begins with a consonant but drop the final *e* before a suffix that begins with a vowel. See the following applications of this rule, noting the exceptions:

Keep final silent *e* when suffix begins with a consonant:

- *love*   loved, lovely
- *hate*   hated, hateful
- *care*   cared, careful
- *use*   used, useless
- *force*   forced, forceful
- *state*   stated, stately
- *move*   moved
- *create*   created
- *advise*   advised

Drop final silent *e* when suffix begins with a vowel:

- loving, lovable
- hating
- caring
- using, usage
- forcing, forcible
- stating
- moving, movable
- creating, creator, creative
- advisable, advisory

Exceptions: awe/awful; *judge*/judgment*; *argue*/argument; *acknowledge*/acknowledgment*; *abridge*/abridgment*; *true*/truly; *due*/duly; *nine*/ninth; *possible*/possibly; *wide*/width; *whole*/wholly

Exceptions: acre/acreage; *mile*/mileage; *dye*/dyeing; *singe*/singeing

*Note: In American usage it is customary to drop the final *e* before adding the suffix -*ment*, as in *judge*/*judgment*; *abridge*/*abridgment*; *acknowledge*/*acknowledgment*. In British usage the final *e* is retained, as in *judge*/*judgement*; *abridge*/*abridgement*; *acknowledge*/*acknowledgement*.

2. Keep the final *e* of words ending in *ce* (as in *notice*) or *ge* (as in *courage*) before a suffix beginning with *a* or *o*. Retaining the *e* indicates the preservation of the soft sound of the *c* or *g*.

notice	noticeable	*but* noticing
replace	replaceable	*but* replacing
service	serviceable	*but* servicing
enforce	enforceable	*but* enforcing
courage	courageous	
outrage	outrageous	
change	changeable	*but* changing
manage	manageable	*but* managing
advantage	advantageous	

3. If a verb ending in *ie* (as *die* or *tie*) is followed by the suffix -*ing*, change the *i* to *y* and drop the *e*:

die	died	*but* dying
lie	lied	*but* lying
tie	tied	*but* tying
vie	vied	*but* vying

If the verb ends in *oe*, keep the final *e* when adding the suffix *-ing*:

canoe	canoed	canoeing
hoe	hoed	hoeing
toe	toed	toeing

III. When to drop or keep the final *y*

1. If the word ends in *y* after a consonant, change the *y* to *i* before most suffixes (except those beginning with *i*, such as *-ing*, *-ish*, and *-ist*). Note that this rule applies to all ordinal numbers from *twentieth* to *ninetieth*.

cavity	cavities	
plenty	plentiful	
try	tries, tried	*but* trying
opportunity	opportunities	
rely	relied, reliable	*but* relying
pretty	prettier, prettiest	
happy	happiness, happier	
pity	pitied, pitiful	*but* pitying
baby	babies, babied	*but* babying
copy	copies, copied	*but* copying, copyist
carry	carries, carried	*but* carrying

2. If a noun ends in *y* after a vowel, keep the *y* in forming the plurals.

attorney, attorneys	*monkey*, monkeys	*boy*, boys
chimney, chimneys	*journey*, journeys	*essay*, essays
key, keys	*turkey*, turkeys	*survey*, surveys
valley, valleys	*relay*, relays	*toy*, toys

Similarly, if a verb ends in *y* after a vowel, do not change the *y* before adding a suffix.

employ, employed, employing	*destroy*, destroyed, destroying
delay, delayed, delaying	*enjoy*, enjoyed, enjoying
convey, conveyed, conveying	*stay*, stayed, staying
play, played, playing	*survey*, surveyed, surveying
journey, journeyed, journeying	

Exceptions include:

lay	laid	*but* laying
say	said	*but* saying
pay	paid	*but* paying
slay	slain	*but* slaying
soliloquy	soliloquies	

IV. When to add *s* or *es*

1. If no additional syllable is pronounced in forming the plural of a noun or the third person singular present of a verb, add *s*.

boy, boys   *book*, books   *swim*, swims   *look*, looks

2. If an additional syllable is pronounced in forming the plural of a noun, add *es*.

church, churches   *dish*, dishes   *class*, classes

Similarly, in forming the third person singular of a verb in the present tense, add *es*.

rush, rushes   *pass*, passes   *wish*, wishes

3. If a noun ends in *o* preceded by a vowel, the plural is usually formed by adding *s*.

radio, radios	*cameo*, cameos	*rodeo*, rodeos
ratio, ratios	*tattoo*, tattoos	*folio*, folios
studio, studios	*taboo*, taboos	*embryo*, embryos
zoo, zoos	*patio*, patios	

4. If a noun ends in *o* preceded by a consonant, the plural is usually formed by adding *es*.

hero, heroes	*embargo*, embargoes
tomato, tomatoes	*motto*, mottoes (or mottos)
veto, vetoes	*cargo*, cargoes (or cargos)
echo, echoes	*zero*, zeroes (or zeros)
potato, potatoes	*volcano*, volcanoes (or volcanos)

Some nouns ending in *o* preceded by a consonant, especially some musical terms, form the plural by adding only *s*.

alto, altos	*cello*, cellos	*salvo*, salvos (or salvoes)
canto, cantos	*halo*, halos (or haloes)	*torso*, torsos
concerto, concertos	*auto*, autos	*proviso*, provisos
solo, solos	*dynamo*, dynamos	*burro*, burros
banjo, banjos (or banjoes)		
	Eskimo, Eskimos	*lasso*, lassos (or lassoes)
piano, pianos	*casino*, casinos	*silo*, silos

V. When to double the final consonant

1. Double a single final consonant in a one-syllable word if the final consonant is preceded by a *single* vowel and the suffix begins with a vowel (as -*ed*, -*er*, and -*ing*).

step, stepped, stepping   *big*, bigger, biggest
yell, yelled, yelling   *quit*, quitter, quitting*
grin, grinned, grinning

> *Since *qu* is sounded as *kw*, the *u* is treated as a consonant.

2. Double a single final consonant in a word of two or more syllables if the root word is stressed on the last syllable.

begin'	beginner	beginning
submit'	submitted	submitting
emit'	emitted	emitting
refer'	referred	referring

3. Do *not* double the final consonant in a word that has two vowels before the final consonant.

spoil	spoiler	spoiling
read	reader	reading
pair	paired	pairing
keep	keeper	keeping
applaud	applauded	applauding

4. Do *not* double the final consonant of a word that already ends with two consonants.

help, helped, helping   *camp*, camped, camping
lick, licked, licking   *park*, parked, parking
rest, rested, resting   *relent*, relented, relenting

5. Do *not* double the final consonant of a word with an unstressed last syllable.

prof'it   profited, profiting, profitable, profiteer
ben'efit   benefit, benefited, benefiting

6. Do *not* double the final consonant of a word in which the stress shifts from the final syllable to an earlier syllable when the suffix is added.

refer'	ref'erence	*but* refer'ring
infer'	in'ference	*but* infer'ring
confer'	con'ference	*but* confer'ring
defer'	def'erence	*but* defer'ring
prefer'	pref'erence	*but* prefer'ring

7. Do *not* double the final consonant of a word that ends in *x* (since *x* is sounded as a double consonant *ks*).

perplex	perplexed	perplexing
mix	mixed	mixing
box	boxed	boxing

VI. What to do with words ending in *c*

If a word ends in *c*, add a *k* before any suffix beginning with *e*, *i*, or *y* if the *k*-sound is to be preserved.

picnic	picnicked, picnicking, picnicker
frolic	frolicked, frolicking, frolicker (*but* frolicsome)
panic	panicked, panicking, panicky
traffic	trafficked, trafficking, trafficker
mimic	mimicked, mimicking, mimicker (*but* mimicry)
shellac	shellacked, shellacking

VII. When verbs end in *ceed, cede,* or *sede*

1. Only one verb in English ends in *sede*: supersede.
2. Only three verbs in English end in *ceed*: succeed, proceed, exceed.
3. All other verbs with this sound end in *cede*:

accede	antecede	cede	recede
concede	intercede	precede	secede

VIII. How to form plurals of nouns ending in f, fe, and ff

The plural of most nouns ending in *f* or *ff* is formed by the simple addition of *s*.

belief, beliefs   *chief*, chiefs
sheriff, sheriffs   *tariff*, tariffs

In the following principal exceptions, the plurals of words ending in *f* or *fe* are formed by changing the *f* or *fe* to *v* and adding *es*.

calf, calves   *thief*, thieves   *wife*, wives
half, halves   *knife*, knives   *wolf*, wolves
leaf, leaves   *loaf*, loaves   *scarf*, scarfs (*or* scarves)
life, lives   *self*, selves   *dwarf*, dwarfs (*or* dwarves)
shelf, shelves   *wharf*, wharves (*or* wharfs)

IX. Prefixes

The prefixes *dis-*, *mis-*, *il-*, *un-*, *re-*, *over-*, and *under-* do not affect the spelling of the root word that follows. When the final letter of the prefix is the same as the first letter of the root word, both letters should be retained.

disservice   illegal   underrate
dissatisfaction   illegible   underripened
misspell   reexamine   unnatural
missent   reentry   unnerved
overreact   overrun

Table of Common English Spellings

If you do not know how to spell a word, this table will help you locate it. Start by finding in the first column the specific sound you are having trouble spelling. Then go directly to the right in the second column for the most common spellings of that sound; the spellings in italicized boldface are the most frequent ones and should be tried first. The third column gives examples of words spelled in various ways for each sound.

SOUNDS:	POSSIBLE SPELLINGS:	EXAMPLES:
a as in *flat*	***a***, a'a, ach, ag, ai, au, ui	h*a*t, m*a'a*m, dr*ach*m, di*a*phr*ag*m, pl*ai*d, dr*au*ght, g*ui*mpe
a as in *cape*	***a***, ae, ag, ai, aig, ao, au, ay, é, è, ê, ea, ee, ée, eg, eh, ei, eig, eige, eigh, eilles, es, et, ey, ez	*a*te, G*ae*l, champ*ag*ne, r*ai*n, arr*aig*n, g*ao*l, g*au*ge, r*ay*, expos*é*, su*è*de, t*ê*te-à-t*ê*te, st*ea*k, matin*ee*, n*ée*, th*eg*n, *eh*, v*ei*l, f*eig*n, gr*eige*, sl*eigh*, Mars*eilles*, dem*es*ne, ber*et*, ob*ey*, laiss*ez* faire
a as in *father*	***a***, à, aa, ah, al, as, at, e, ea, oi, ua	f*a*ther, *à* la mode, baz*aa*r, hurr*ah*, c*al*m, faux p*as*, écl*at*, s*e*rgeant, h*ea*rth, reserv*oi*r, g*ua*rd
a as in *dare*	air, aire, ***are***, ayer, ear, eer, e'er, eir, er, ere, ère, ert, ey're, uerre	ch*air*, doctrin*aire*, d*are*, pr*ayer*, w*ear*, Mynh*eer*, n*e'er*, th*eir*, mal de m*er*, th*ere*, étag*ère*, Camemb*ert*, th*ey're*, nom de g*uerre*
b as in *back*	***b***, bb, bh	*b*ed, ho*bb*y, *bh*eesty
ch as in *chain*	c, ***ch***, che, tch, te, ti, tu	*c*ello, *ch*ief, ni*che*, ca*tch*, righ*te*ous, ques*ti*on, na*tu*ral

370

SOUNDS:	POSSIBLE SPELLINGS:	EXAMPLES:
d as in *deep*	*d*, 'd, dd, de, ed, ld	*d*o, we'*d*, lad*d*er, fa*d*e, pull*ed*, shou*ld*
e as in *set*	a, ae, ai, ay, *e*, è, ê, ea, eg, ei, eo, ie, oe, u, ue	*a*ny, *ae*sthetic, s*ai*d, s*ay*s, *e*bb, man*è*ge, b*ê*te-noir, l*ea*ther, phl*e*gm, h*ei*fer, l*eo*pard, fri*e*nd, f*oe*tid, b*u*ry, g*ue*st
e as in *be*	ae, ay, *e*, ea, *ee*, e'e, ei, eip, eo, es, ey, i, ie, is, oe, uay, y	C*ae*sar, c*ay*, *e*qual, t*ea*m, s*ee*, *e*'*e*n, dec*ei*ve, rec*ei*pt, p*eo*ple, dem*e*sne, k*ey*, mach*i*ne, f*ie*ld, deb*ri*s, am*oe*ba, q*uay*, pit*y*
f as in *fit*	*f*, ff, gh, lf, ph	*f*eed, mu*ff*in, tou*gh*, ca*lf*, *ph*ysics
g as in *give*	*g*, gg, gh gu, gue	*g*ive, e*gg*, *gh*ost, *gu*ard, pla*gue*
h as in *hit*	*h*, wh	*h*it, *wh*o
hw as in *what*	wh	*wh*ere
i as in *big*	a, e, ee, ei, *i*, ia, ie, o, u, ui, y	dam*a*ge, *E*ngland, b*ee*n, counterf*ei*t, *i*f, carr*ia*ge, s*ie*ve, w*o*men, b*u*sy, b*ui*ld, s*y*lph
i as in *ice*	ai, ais, aye, ei, eigh, eye, *i*, ie, igh, is, uy, y, ye	f*ai*lle, *ais*le, *aye*, st*ei*n, h*eigh*t, *eye*, *i*ce, t*ie*, h*igh*, *is*land, b*uy*, sk*y*, l*ye*
j as in *jar*	ch, d, dg, dge, di, ge, gg, gi, *j*, jj	Greenwi*ch*, gra*d*uate, ju*dg*ment, bri*dge*, sol-*di*er, sa*ge*, exa*gg*erate, ma*gi*c, *j*ust, Ha*jj*i
k as in *keep*	*c*, cc, cch, ch, ck, cq, cqu, cque, cu, gh, *k*, ke, kh, lk, q, qu	*c*ar, a*cc*ount, ba*cch*anal, *ch*aracter, ba*ck*, a*cq*uaint, la*cqu*er, sa*cque*, bis*cu*it, lou*gh*, *k*ill, ra*ke*, si*kh*, wa*lk*, Ira*q*, li*qu*or
l as in *law*	*l*, le, ll, 'll, lle, sl	*l*ive, mi*le*, ca*ll*, she'*ll*, fai*lle*, li*sl*e

371

SOUNDS:	POSSIBLE SPELLINGS:	EXAMPLES:
m as in me	chm, gm, lm, **m**, 'm, mb, me, mh, mm, mn	dra*chm*, paradi*gm*, ca*lm*, *m*ore, I'*m*, li*mb*, ho*m*e, *mh*o, ha*mm*er, hy*mn*
n as in no	gn, kn, mn, **n**, ne, nn, pn	*gn*at, *kn*ife, *mn*emonic, *n*ot, do*n*e, ru*nn*er, *pn*eumatic
ng as in sing	n, **ng**, ngg, ngue	pi*n*k, ri*ng*, mahjo*ngg*, to*ngue*
o as in ox	a, ach, au, **o**, ou	w*a*nder, y*ach*t, astron*au*t, b*o*x, c*ou*gh
o as in so	au, aut, aux, eau, eaux, eo, ew, ho, **o**, oa, oe, oh, ol, oo, os, ot, ou, ow, owe	m*au*ve, h*aut*boy, f*aux* pas, b*eau*, Bord*eaux*, y*eo*man, s*ew*, m*ho*, n*o*te, r*oa*d, t*oe*, *oh*, y*ol*k, br*oo*ch, d*os*-a-d*os*, dep*ot*, s*ou*l, fl*ow*, *owe*
o as in bought	**a**, ah, al, as, au, augh, aw, **o**, oa, ou, ough	t*a*ll, Ut*ah*, t*al*k, Ark*a*ns*as*, f*au*lt, c*augh*t, r*aw*, alc*o*hol, br*oa*d, s*ou*ght, f*ough*t
oi as in boil	aw, eu **oi**, ois, oy, uoy	law*y*er, Fr*eu*d, *oi*l, Iroqu*ois*, t*oy*, b*uoy*
oo as in book	o, **oo**, ou, oul, u	w*o*lf, l*oo*k, w*ou*ld, c*oul*d, p*u*ll
oo as in fool	eu, ew, ieu, o, oe, oeu, **oo**, ou, u, ue, ug, ui	man*eu*ver, gr*ew*, l*ieu*, m*o*ve, can*oe*, man*oeu*vre, *oo*ze, tr*ou*pe, r*u*le, fl*ue*, imp*ug*n, fr*ui*t
ou as in house	au, **ou**, ough, **ow**	land*au*, *ou*t, b*ough*, br*ow*
p as in pick	**p**, pp	*p*en, sto*pp*er
r as in rag	**r**, re, 're, rh, rr, rrh, wr	*r*ed, pu*re*, we'*re*, *rh*ythm, car*r*ot, catar*rh*, *wr*ong
s as in sell	c, ce, ps, **s**, 's, sc, sch, se, ss	*c*ity, mi*ce*, *ps*ychology, *s*ee, it'*s*, *sc*ene, *sch*ism, mou*se*, lo*ss*

372

SOUNDS:	POSSIBLE SPELLINGS:	EXAMPLES:
sh as in *shoe*	ce, ch, chsi, ci, psh, s, sch, sci, se, **sh,** si, ss, ssi, ti	o*ce*an, ma*ch*ine, fuch*si*a, spe*ci*al, *psh*aw, *s*ugar, *sch*ist, con*sci*ence, nau*se*ous, *sh*ip, man*si*on, ti*ss*ue, mi*ssi*on, men*ti*on
t as in *top*	bt, cht, ct, ed, ght, phth, *t,* 't, te, th, tt	dou*bt*, ya*cht*, *ct*enophore, talk*ed*, bou*ght*, *phth*isic, *t*oe, '*t*was, bi*te*, *th*yme, bo*tt*om
th as in *thick*	chth, **th**	*chth*onian, *th*in
th as in *that*	**th,** the	*th*en, ba*the*
u as in *up*	o, oe, oo, ou, *u*	s*o*n, d*oe*s, fl*oo*d, c*ou*ple, c*u*p
u as in *urge*	ear, *er,* err, eur, ir, or, our, *ur,* urr, yr, yrrh	l*ear*n, t*er*m, *err*, pos*eur*, th*ir*st, w*or*m, sc*our*ge, h*ur*t, p*urr*, m*yr*tle, m*yrrh*
v as in *vote*	f, ph, *v,* ve, 've, vv	o*f*, Ste*ph*en, *v*isit, ha*ve*, we*'ve*, fli*vv*er
w as in *west*	o, ou, u, *w*	ch*o*ir, *ou*ija, q*u*iet, *w*ell
y as in *yes*	i, j, *y*	un*i*on, hallelu*j*ah, *y*et
yu as in *few*	eau, eu, ew, ieu, iew, *u,* ue, ueue, yew, you, yu	b*eau*ty, f*eu*d, f*ew*, purl*ieu*, v*iew*, *u*se, c*ue*, q*ueue*, *yew*, *you*, *yu*le
z as in *zoo*	s, 's, sc, se, ss, x, *z,* ze, zz	ha*s*, who*'s*, di*sc*ern, rai*s*e, sci*ss*ors, an*x*iety, *z*one, ra*ze*, da*zz*le
zh as in *vision*	ge, s, *si,* z, zi	gara*ge*, mea*s*ure, divi*si*on, a*z*ure, bra*zi*er
neutral unstressed vowel	*a,* à, ai, *e,* ei, eo, *i,* ia, io, *o,* oi, ou, *u,* y	*a*lone, tête-*à*-tête, mount*ai*n, syst*e*m, mull*ei*n, dung*eo*n, eas*i*ly, parl*ia*ment, leg*io*n, gall*o*p, por*oi*se, curi*ou*s, circ*u*s, Abyssin*i*a
neutral unstressed vowel + *r*	ar, *er,* ir, or, our, ur, ure, yr	li*ar*, fath*er*, elix*ir*, lab*or*, lab*our*, aug*ur*, fut*ure*, mart*yr*

Commonly Misspelled Words

This list is based on statistical studies of frequently misspelled words, plus the observations of experienced teachers and editors. Mastery of this list of troublesome words, therefore, can take a poor speller a long way toward being a good speller.

absence	arguing	ceiling	decide
absorption	argument	cemetery	decision
abundance	arouse	certain	decisive
abundant	arrangement	changeable	defendant
accessible	article	changing	definite
accidentally	asked	chief	descendant
accommodate	asthma	choir	description
accumulate	athlete	clothes	desirable
achievement	attorney	collectible	despair
acquaintance	author	column	desperate
acquire	auxiliary	coming	destroy
acquittal	balance	commission	develop
across	bankruptcy	committed	development
address	beginning	committee	different
adequate	belief	comparative	dining
admittance	believable	competitive	diphtheria
against	believe	complexion	disappear
aging	beneficial	conceive	disappearance
allegiance	beneficiary	conceivable	disappoint
all right	benefit	conferred	disastrous
almost	benefited	conscience	discipline
although	boundaries	conscientious	disease
amateur	breathe	conscious	dissatisfied
among	bronchial	consistent	divide
analysis	bouyant	control	divine
analytical	bureaucracy	controlled	doesn't
analyze	burglary	convenience	easier
annual	business	counterfeit	easily
anonymous	calendar	criticism	efficient
answer	candidate	criticize	eightieth
apparent	career	curiosity	electrician
appearance	careful	cylinder	eligible
appropriate	category	debt	eligibility
Arctic	carrying	debtor	eliminate

embarrass	hypocrite	mileage	politician
environment	hypocrisy	miniature	possess
equipped	identification	miscellaneous	possession
especially	imaginary	mischievous	possessive
exaggerate	immediately	misspell	possibility
excellent	incidentally	morale	possible
exercise	incredible	muscle	practical
exhilarate	independent	naturally	practically
existence	indestructible	necessarily	practice
expense	indictment	necessary	precede
experience	inevitable	necessity	precedence
experiment	influential	neighbor	preference
explanation	innocuous	neither	preferred
extemporaneous	inoculation	nickel	prejudice
extremely	instantaneous	niece	preparatory
familiar	intellectual	ninetieth	prevalent
fascinate	intelligence	ninety	primitive
feasible	interest	ninth	privilege
February	interfere	noticeable	probably
fiend	inveigle	occasion	procedure
fierce	irrelevant	occasionally	proceed
fiftieth	irresistible	occurred	professor
finally	island	occurrence	pronunciation
foreign	jealous	omission	psychology
forfeit	judgment	omit	psychiatry
fortieth	judicial	omitted	pursuance
forty	kindergarten	opinion	pursuant
friend	knowledge	opportunity	pursue
fundamental	laboratory	optimism	pursuit
further	laid	origin	quantity
gauge	leisure	original	questionnaire
generally	length	paid	receipt
government	liaison	parallel	receivable
governor	library	paralysis	receive
grammar	license	paralyze	reciprocal
grateful	likelihood	particularly	recognize
grievance	literature	peculiar	recommend
guarantee	livelihood	perceive	reference
guard	loneliness	perform	referred
guidance	losing	performance	relieve
harass	magazine	permanent	religious
height	maintenance	permissible	repetition
heroes	maneuver	persuade	resistance
hierarchy	marriage	persuasion	responsibility
hindrance	marriageable	persuasive	restaurant
hoping	marital	planned	restaurateur
humorous	mathematics	planning	rhyme
hundredth	meant	pleasant	rhythm
hygienist	medicine	pneumonia	rhythmic

safety	similar	symmetrical	twentieth
scene	sincerely	temperament	unanimous
scenery	sixtieth	temperature	until
scenic	socially	temporarily	upholsterer
schedule	society	tendency	using
secrecy	sophomore	therefore	usually
secretary	specifically	thirtieth	vacancy
seize	specimen	thorough	vacuum
seizure	speech	thought	veil
separate	stopped	thousandth	vengeance
separately	stopping	through	villain
sergeant	strength	together	Wednesday
seventieth	studying	tragedy	weird
several	subtle	tragically	wield
shepherd	succeed	trail	writing
shining	successive	transferred	written
shoulder	supersede	transient	yacht
siege	suppress	trial	yield
significant	surprise	tries	
significance	susceptible	truly	

Commonly Confused Words

Misspellings are often the result of confusing two words that are identical or very close in their pronunciations. The words listed below are among those most commonly confused.

aboard, abroad
accept, except
advice, advise
affect, effect
air, heir
aisle, isle, I'll
all ready, already
all together, altogether
allowed, aloud
allusion, illusion
allusive, elusive
altar, alter
angel, angle
attendance, attendants
aught, ought
aural, oral
bail, bale
band, banned
bare, bear
beat, beet
berry, bury
berth, birth
beer, bier
billed, build
blew, blue
boar, bore
board, bored
boarder, border
bolder, boulder
born, borne
bough, bow
boy, buoy
brake, break
bread, bred
breath, breadth, breathe

bridal, bridle
bullion, bouillon
buy, by
calendar, colander
callous, callus
cannon, canon
canvas, canvass
capital, capitol
carat, caret, carrot
cede, seed
ceiling, sealing
cellar, seller
censer, censor, censure
cent, scent
cereal, serial
discrete, discreet
done, dun
dual, duel
dyeing, dying
elicit, illicit
elusive, allusive
emigrant, immigrant
emigrate, immigrate
eminent, imminent
except, accept
extant, extent
faint, feint
fare, fair
farther, father
feat, feet
find, fined
fir, fur
flair, flare
flea, flee
flew, flu, flue

flour, flower
for, fore, four
forbear, forebear
forego, forgo
formally, formerly
fort, forte
cession, session
choir, quire
chord, cord
chute, shoot
cite, sight, site
coarse, course
complement, compliment
confidant, confident
consul, council, counsel
core, corps, corpse
councillor, counselor
creak, creek
crews, cruise
currant, current
custom, costume
cymbal, symbol
dairy, diary
dear, deer
decent, descent, dissent
dependence, dependents
descent, dissent
desert, dessert
device, devise
dew, do, due
die, dye
dining, dinning
forth, fourth
foul, fowl
freeze, frieze
fur, fir
gait, gate
gamble, gambol
gibe, jibe
gild, guild
gilt, guilt
grate, great
grisly, grizzly
hair, hare
hale, hail
hall, haul
hangar, hanger
heal, heel
hear, here

heard, herd
heir, air
heroin, heroine
hoard, horde
hoarse, horse
hole, whole
holy, wholly
idle, idol, idyll
illicit, elicit
illusion, allusion
imminent, eminent
incidence, incidents
incite, insight
indict, indite
ingenious, ingenuous
invade, inveighed
its, it's
jibe, gibe
key, quay
knave, nave
knew, new
know, no
lead, led
lean, lien
leased, least
lessen, lesson
lesser, lessor
levee, levy
liable, libel
lie, lye
lightening, lightning
loan, lone
loath, loathe
loose, lose, loss
made, maid
mail, male
main, mane
manner, manor
mantel, mantle
marshal, martial
mean, mien
meat, meet, mete
medal, meddle
metal, mettle
miner, minor
missed, mist
mite, might
moat, mote
moral, morale

morn, mourn
morning, mourning
naval, navel
nave, knave
none, nun
oar, ore
one, won
oral, aural
ordinance, ordnance
ought, aught
overdo, overdue
pale, pail
pain, pane
pair, pare, pear
palate, palette, pallet
parameter, perimeter
passed, past
patience, patients
peace, piece
peak, peek, pique
pedal, peddle
peal, peel
peer, pier
perquisite, prerequisite
persecute, prosecute
personal, personnel
piece, peace
pistil, pistol
plain, plane
pole, poll
pore, pour
pray, prey
presence, presents
principal, principle
profit, prophet
prophecy, prophesy
quarts, quartz
quay, key
queue, cue
quiet, quite
quire, choir
rain, reign, rein
raise, rays, raze
rap, wrap
read, reed
reek, wreak
real, reel
residence, residents
retch, wretch

reverend, reverent
right, rite, write, wright
ring, wring
role, roll
root, route
rote, wrote
rye, wry
sale, sail
scene, seen
scent, sent, cent
sea, see
sealing, ceiling
seam, seem
serf, surf
seed, cede
serge, surge
serial, cereal
session, cession
shear, sheer
shoot, chute
shone, shown
shudder, shutter
sight, site, cite
sleight, slight
so, sew, sow
soar, sore
soared, sword
sole, soul
some, sum
son, sun
stair, stare
stake, steak
stationary, stationery
statue, statute
steal, steel
stile, style
straight, strait
suite, sweet
sum, some
sun, son
surge, serge
symbol, cymbal
tale, tail
tear, tier
taught, taut
team, teem
than, then
their, there, they're
therefor, therefore

threw, through
timber, timbre
to, too, two
troop, troupe
trooper, trouper
undo, undue
urban, urbane
vain, vane, vein
venal, venial
vial, vile, viol
vice, vise
waist, waste
wait, weight
waive, wave
waiver, waver
ware, wear, where
way, weigh

weak, week
weather, whether
which, witch
while, wile
whole, hole
wholly, holy
whose, who's
woman, women
won, one
wrap, rap
wretch, retch
wring, ring
write, rite, wright
wry, rye
yolk, yoke
yore, your, you're
you'll, yule

Basic Rules of Word Division

It is often necessary to divide a word at the end of a line to prevent excessive variation in the length of lines on a page. Since there are no easy rules for word division, it is best to check the recommendations in this book and to follow them consistently.

Word division in American usage is determined basically by pronunciation, in contrast with British usage, which is determined generally by derivation. All parts of the divided word, therefore, should usually be pronounceable.

1. Divide only between syllables; never divide within a syllable. Do not carry over endings such as *-ed* when they are part of a syllable.

matched	strength	width	rhythm
passed	thought	twelfth	tooth

2. Do not divide a word so that only one letter occurs alone at the end or beginning of a line. If at all possible, avoid having even two letters separated from the rest of the word.

Wrong:	criteri-a	en-lighten	ve-to
	a-vailable	month-ly	ze-ro

3. Do not divide between two letters that represent a single sound.

Wrong:	brot-hers	grap-hically	fas-hion
	tro-opers	loc-kers	churc-hman
Right:	broth-ers	graph-ically	fash-ion
	troop-ers	lock-ers	church-man

4. Do not split abbreviations, contractions, numbers, etc.

Wrong:	Ph.-D.	UNES-CO	is-n't
	17-76	YM-CA	o'-clock
Right:	Ph.D.	UNESCO	isn't
	1776	YMCA	o'clock

5. Never divide between the initials of a name.

Wrong:	G./B. Shaw	R. C./D. Lieber
Right:	G. B./Shaw	R. C. D./Lieber

6. Avoid, if at all possible, dividing an already hyphenated word except at its own hyphen.

Wrong:	self-evi-/dent	anti-Ameri-/can	twen-/ty-one
Right:	self-/evident	anti-/American	twenty-/one

7. In dividing a word that begins with a prefix, try to divide immediately after the prefix. Never divide the prefix itself.

Wrong:	prereg-ister	antimis-sile	coun-terattack
Right:	pre-register	anti-missile	counter-attack

8. In dividing a word that ends with a suffix, try to divide immediately before the suffix.

Wrong:	sis-terhood	irre-sistible	health-iness
Right:	sister-hood	iresist-ible	healthi-ness

9. Do not divide the following suffixes:

-cial	-cion	-gion	-tious
-sial	-sion	-cious	-geous
tial	-tion	-ceous	-gious

10. Do not divide the last word on a page so that part of the word must go onto the next page.

11. In dividing an unhyphenated compound word, try to split the word between the parts of the compound.

Wrong:	newspa-per	godfath-er	bandmas-ter
Right:	news-paper	god-father	band-master

12. If the final consonant of a verb is doubled before a suffix, divide between the consonants. If the root word already has a double consonant, keep the two consonants together before the division.

Wrong:	gett-ing	controll-able	sel-ling
Right:	get-ting	control-lable	sell-ing

13. If the word contains a one-letter syllable in the middle of the word, it is generally better to divide after the one-letter syllable.

Wrong:	priv-ilege	sep-aration	hand-icapped
Right:	privi-lege	sepa-ration	handi-capped

14. Since word division in American usage is usually governed by pronunciation, keep a consonant with the preceding syllable if the vowel in that syllable is short. If, on the other hand, the vowel is long or unstressed, move the consonant to the next syllable.

Wrong:	deve-lop	decis-ive	optim-ism
Right:	devel-op	deci-sive	opti-mism

15. If the word has two adjacent vowels that are individually pronounced, divide between them.

Wrong:	gradua-ted	varie-ty	curio-sity
Right:	gradu-ated	vari-ety	curi-osity

Basic Manual of Style

The style practices described in this concise guide are those generally prevalent in current English. This manual presents the more commonly accepted alternatives. noting the situations in which a particular usage is preferred. Having made a choice. the writer should maintain the same usage throughout any single document. As in all writing. consistency of style is essential.

Punctuation

PERIOD (.)
Use a period:

1. To end a declarative or imperative sentence (but not an exclamatory sentence).
    The meeting was amicable and constructive.
    Please pass the salt.
    Read the next two chapters before Friday.

2. To end an indirect question.
    He asked when the plane was leaving.

3. To end a polite request even when stated as a question.
    Will you please reply promptly.

4. To end a sentence fragment.
    Not in the least.
    A novel of suspense.

5. To follow most abbreviations.
    Mr., Mrs., Ms., Jr., Dr., N.J., etc., e.g., B.C., A.D.
    (See ABBREVIATIONS below.)

6. To separate dollars from cents in writing figures.
    $25.00 $2.98

7. To use as a decimal point in writing figures.
    98.6 degrees $3.7 million

ELLIPSIS (...or....)
Use an ellipsis mark (three or four consecutive periods) to indicate that part of a quoted sentence has been omitted.

1. If the omission occurs at the beginning or in the middle of the sentence. use three periods in the ellipsis.
    "...the book is lively...and well written."

2. If the last part of the sentence is omitted or if entire sentences are omitted. add a fourth period to the ellipsis to mark the end of the sentence.
    "He left his home....Years later he returned to find everything had changed...."

QUESTION MARK (?)
Use a question mark:

1. To end a sentence. clause. or phrase (or after a single word) that asks a question.
    Who invited him to the party?
    "Is something wrong?" she asked.
    Whom shall we elect? Smith? Jones?

2. To indicate doubt or uncertainty.
    The manuscript dates back to 560 (?) B.C.

EXCLAMATION POINT (!)

Use an exclamation point to end a sentence, clause, phrase, or even a single word that indicates strong emotion or feeling, especially surprise, command, admiration, etc.

> Go away!   Wow!
>
> What a day this has been!
>
> "Hey, there!" he shouted.

COMMA (,)

Use a comma only when you have a definite reason for doing so in accordance with the guidelines below. A safe rule to follow is, "When in doubt, leave it out."

Use a comma:

1. To separate words, phrases, and clauses that are part of a series of three or more items.

> The Dutch are an industrious, friendly, generous, and hospitable people.
>
> The chief agricultural products of Denmark are butter, eggs, potatoes, beets, wheat, barley, and oats.

It is permissible to omit the final comma before the *and* in a series of words as long as the absence of a comma does not interfere with clarity of meaning. The final commas in the examples above, while desirable, are not essential.

In many cases, however, the inclusion or omission of a comma before the conjunction can materially affect the meaning. In the following sentence, omission of the final comma might indicate incorrectly that the tanks as well as the vehicles, were amphibious.

> Their equipment included airplanes, helicopters, artillery, amphibious vehicles, and tanks.

Do not use commas to separate two items treated as a single unit within a series.

> For breakfast he ordered orange juice, bread and butter, coffee, and bacon and eggs.

But

> At the supermarket he bought orange juice, bread, butter, bacon, and eggs.

Do not use commas to separate adjectives which are so closely related that they appear to form a single element with the noun they modify. Adjectives which refer to the number, age (old, young, new), size, color, or location of the

noun often fall within this category. A simple test can usually determine the appropriateness of a comma in such instances: If *and* cannot replace the comma without creating a clumsy, almost meaningless effect, it is safe to conclude that a comma is also out of place.

> twenty happy little youngsters
>
> a dozen large blue dresses
>
> several dingy old Western mining towns
>
> beautiful tall white birches

But commas must be used in the following cases where clarity demands separation of the items in a series:

> a dozen large blue, red, yellow, and green crayons
>
> twenty old, young, and middle-aged spectators

In a series of phrases or dependent clauses, place a comma before the conjunction.

> He sold his business, rented his house, gave up his car, paid his creditors, and set off for Tahiti.
>
> They strolled along the city streets, browsed in the bookshops, and dined at their favorite cafe.

2. To separate independent clauses joined by the coordinating conjunctions *and, but, yet, for, or, nor, so.*

> Almost anyone knows how to earn money, but not one in a million knows how to spend it.

The comma may be omitted in sentences consisting of two short independent clauses.

> We missed the train but we caught the bus in time.

3. To separate a long introductory phrase or subordinate clause from the rest of the sentence.

> Having rid themselves of their former rulers, the people now disagreed on the new leadership.
>
> Although the equipment has not yet been fully developed, scientists are confident of landing astronauts on other planets.

4. To set off words of direct address, interjections, or transitional words used to introduce a sentence (*oh, yes, no, however, nevertheless, still, anyway, well, why, frankly, really, moreover, incidentally,* etc.).

Jim, where have you been?

Oh, here's our new neighbor.

Why, you can't mean that!

Still, you must agree that she knows her business.

Fine, we'll get together.

Well, can you imagine that!

5. To set off an introductory modifier (adjective, adverb, participle, participial phrase) even if it consists of only one word or a short phrase.

Politically, our candidate has proved to be very astute.

Angrily, the delegates stalked out of the conference.

Pleased with the result, he beamed at his painting.

6. To set off a nonrestrictive clause or phrase (an element which is not essential to the basic meaning of the sentence). Place commas both before and after the nonrestrictive portion.

Our professor did not agree that corporations should be protected as "persons" under the Fourteenth Amendment, although the Supreme Court had held that they were.

The old hotel, which had housed visiting celebrities for almost a century, remained outwardly unchanged.

7. To set off appositives or appositive phrases. Place commas both before and after the appositive.

March, the month of crocuses, can still bring snow and ice.

One of our major problems, narcotics, remains unsolved.

Ms. Case, chairperson of the committee, refused to comment.

8. To set off parenthetical words and phrases as well as words of direct address.

You may, if you insist, demand a retraction.

St. Peter's Place, they agreed, is one of the best schools in San Francisco.

The use of pesticides, however, has its disadvantages.

They knew, nevertheless, that all was lost.

Mr. Brown, far younger in spirit than his seventy years, delighted in his grandchildren.

You realize, Nettie, that we may never return to Paris.

9. To set off quoted matter from the rest of the sentence.

(See QUOTATION MARKS below.)

10. To set off items in dates.

Both John Adams and Thomas Jefferson died on July 4, 1826.

A comma is optional when only the month and year are given in a date.

Washington was born in February, 1732, in Virginia.

or

Washington was born in February 1732, in Virginia.

11. To set off elements in addresses and geographical locations when the items are written on the same line. Do not, however, use a comma before the zip code.

35 Fifth Avenue, New York, N.Y. 10002

1515 South Halsted Street, Chicago, Illinois 60607

He lived in Lima, Peru, for fifteen years.

12. To set off titles of individuals.

Dr. Martin Price, Dean of Admissions

Mrs. Rose Winthrop, President

13. To set off the salutation in a personal letter.

Dear Steve,

14. To set off the closing in a letter.

Sincerely yours,

Very truly yours,

15. To denote an omitted word or words in one or more parallel constructions within a sentence.

Ethel is studying Greek; George, Latin.

16. To mark off thousands in numbers of one thousand or more. (The comma is optional in numbers under 10,000.)

7,500 or 7500

11,900   250,631   3,963,426

SEMICOLON (;)

Use a semicolon:

1. To separate independent clauses not joined by a conjunction.

The house burned down; it was the last shattering blow.

The war against poverty must continue; it must be our highest priority.

2. To separate independent clauses that are joined by such conjunctive adverbs as *hence, however, therefore,* etc.

The funds are inadequate; therefore, the project will close down.

Orders exceed all expectations; however, there is a shortage of supplies.

3. To separate long or possibly ambiguous items in a series, especially when the items already include commas.

The elected officers are Jonathan Crane, president; Sarah Huntley, vice president; Edward Stone, secretary; and Susan Morrell, treasurer.

4. To separate elements that are closely related but cannot be joined without creating confusion.

Poverty is unbearable; luxury, insufferable.

5. To precede an abbreviation, word, or phrase (*e.g., i.e., namely, for example*) that introduces an explanatory or summarizing statement.

On the advice of his broker, he chose to invest in major industries; i.e., steel, automobiles, and oil.

COLON (:)

Use a colon:

1. To introduce a series or list of items, examples, or the like.

The three committees are as follows: membership, finance, and legislation.

He named his favorite poets: Langston Hughes, W. H. Auden, and Emily Dickinson.

2. To introduce a long formal statement, quotation, or question.

This I believe: All people are created equal and must enjoy equally the rights that are inalienably theirs.

Busch replied: "You are right. There can be no unilateral peace. No one will contest that view."

This is the issue: Can an employer dismiss a man simply because he is a member of a union?

3. To follow a formal salutation, as in a business letter or speech.

Dear Mr. Chadwin: Dear Madam:
Dear Ms. Sanchez: Gentlemen:
To Whom It May Concern:
My Fellow Americans:

4. To follow introductory words in a memorandum.

To: Mary Falcon
From: Andrew Casillo
Subject: Book Sales in Quebec

5. To follow the word *Attention* below both the inside and outside address when the writer wishes to bring a letter to the attention of a particular individual within an organization.

Attention: Ms. Jennie Huntley

6. To follow the name of the speaker in a play.

Ghost: Pity me not, but lend thy serious hearing to what I shall unfold.
Hamlet: Speak; I am bound to hear.

7. To separate parts of a citation.

a. Place a colon between chapter and verse numbers in biblical references.
Genesis 3:2.

b. Place a colon between volume and page numbers of periodicals.
Journal of Astronomy 15:237-261.

8. To separate hours from minutes in indicating time.

1:30 p.m. (or P.M.)
2:00 A.M. (or a.m.)

9. To indicate that an initial clause in a sentence will be further explained or illustrated by the material which follows the colon. In effect, the colon is a substitute for such phrases as "for example" or "namely."

It was a city notorious for its inadequacies: its schools were antiquated, its administration was corrupt, and everyone felt the burden of its taxes.

APOSTROPHE (')

Use an apostrophe:

1. To denote the omission of letters, figures, or numerals.

a. The contraction of a word or phrase:

nat'l   o'er   ne'er
ma'am   couldn't   he'll
I'm   you're   it's
she's   we're   they're

Do not confuse *it's* (contraction of *it is*) with the possessive *its*, which does not contain an apostrophe.

b. The contraction of a number, usually a date:

the Spirit of '76   the Class of '48

c. The omission of letters in quoting dialect:

"I ain't goin' back 'cause I'm doin' mighty fine now."

2. To denote the possessive case of nouns.

a. To form the possessive of most singular and plural nouns or of indefinite pronouns not ending in *s*, add an apostrophe and an *s*.

> the city's industries   anyone's guess
> the women's clubs
> a bachelor's degree

b. To form the possessive of singular nouns of one syllable ending in *s* or the sound of *s*, add an apostrophe and an *s* in most instances.

> the horse's mane   Bess's house
> the class's average   Lance's car

But if the addition of an *s* would produce an awkward sound or visual effect, add only an apostrophe. This rule applies more frequently, but not exclusively, to words of more than one syllable.

> Socrates' concepts   Jesus' teachings
> Moses' influence
> for old times' sake

In some cases either form is acceptable.

> Mr. Jones's (or Jones') employees
> Keats's (or Keats') poetry

c. To form the possessive of plural nouns (both common and proper) ending in *s*, add only an apostrophe.

> farmers' problems
> the Smiths' travels
> students' views
> the Joneses' relatives
> critics' reviews
> three months' delay

Note, however, that plurals not ending in *s* form their possessive by adding the apostrophe and *s*.

> men's clothing   women's hats

d. To denote possession in most compound constructions, add the apostrophe and *s* to the last word of the compound.

> anyone else's property
> one another's books
> brother-in-law's job
> the attorney general's office

e. To denote possession by two or more proper names, add the apostrophe and *s* to the last name only.

> Brown, Ross and King's law firm
> Japan and West Germany's
>   agreement
> Lewis and Clark's expedition

f. To denote individual ownership by two or more proper names, add the apostrophe and an *s* to both names.

> Bruce's and Gina's records.

3. To form the plurals of letters or figures add an apostrophe and an *s*.

> Dot the i's and cross the t's.
> 33 r.p.m.'s   +'s and −'s   C.O.D.'s
> figure 8's   the 1890's (or 1890s)   V.I.P.'s
> m's   PX's   GI's

QUOTATION MARKS
(" " – Double)   (' ' – Single)

NOTE: Unless otherwise noted, double quotation marks are used. For use of single quotation marks, see I b.

Use quotation marks:

1. To enclose a direct quotation.

a. To mark words, phrases, sentences, paragraphs, or poetic stanzas which are quoted verbatim from the original.

> Portia's speech on "The quality of mercy" is one of the most quoted passages from Shakespeare.
> It was Shaw who wrote: "All great truths begin as blasphemies."

b. To enclose a quotation within a quotation, in which case *single* quotation marks are used.

> Reading Jill's letter, Pat said, "Listen to this! 'I've just received notice that I made Dean's list.' Isn't she great?"

2. To enclose certain titles:

a. To enclose titles of newspaper and magazine articles, essays, stories, poems, and chapters of books. The quotation marks serve to distinguish such literary pieces from the books or periodicals (these are italicized) in which they appear.

> Our anthology contains such widely assorted pieces as Bacon's essay "Of Studies," Poe's "The Gold Bug," Keats's "Ode to a Nightingale," and an article on travel from *Mclean's*.

b. To enclose titles of short musical compositions and songs as distinct from symphonies and operas, which are italicized.

> The national anthem is "The Star-Spangled Banner."
> Even the youngsters laughed at the "Figaro" aria from *The Barber of Seville*.

c. To enclose titles of works of art such as paintings, drawings, photographs, and sculpture. These may also be italicized.

> Most people recognize Da Vinci's "Mona Lisa" and Rodin's "The Thinker."

d. To enclose titles of radio and television programs or of episodes within a series (in which case, the name of the series is italicized).

> a recent *Nova* special, "Children of the Forest"

e. To enclose titles of plays only if they are referred to as part of a larger collection. Referred to as single volumes, they are italicized.

> "The Wild Duck" is the Ibsen play included in this edition of *Modern European Plays*.

3. To emphasize a word or phrase which is itself the subject of discussion. Italics may be used for the same purpose.

> The words "imply" and "infer" are not synonymous.

> Such Freudian terms as the "ego," the "superego," the "id," and the "libido" are now considered part of the English language.

4. To draw attention to an uncommon word or phrase, a technical term, or a usage very different in style (e.g., dialect or unusual slang) from the context. Italics are often used for the same purpose.

> Teachers are no longer dismayed when students smirk at "square" traditions.

> In glass blowing, the molten glass is called "metal."

5. To suggest ironic use of a word or phrase.

> The radio blasting forth John's favorite "music" is to his grandfather an instrument of torture.

> Bernstein's skiing "vacation" consisted of three weeks with his leg in a cast.

NOTE: If a quotation consists of two or more consecutive paragraphs, use quotation marks at the beginning of each paragraph, but place them at the end of the last paragraph only.

Quotation marks in combination with other punctuation

1. Period. Always place a period *before* the end quotation mark.

> One angry commuter complained of "the incredible delays and breakdowns."

2. Comma.

a. Always place a final comma *before* the end quotation mark.

> "The delays and breakdowns are incredible," complained one commuter.

b. Use a comma between the quoted matter and such phrases as "according to the report," "she wrote," "he replied," "they asked," etc.

> According to the Declaration of Independence, "all men are created equal."

> "There never was a good war or a bad peace," wrote Benjamin Franklin.

(CAUTION: Do not use the comma following interrogative or exclamatory quotations. See 3 below.)

3. Question mark or exclamation point.

When a question mark or exclamation point is part of the quoted passage, place these marks *before* the end quotation mark.

> "Hurry, please, before it's too late!" she cried.

> "Is there any hope of recovering the property?" he asked.

In all other cases, place the exclamation point or question mark *after* the end quotation mark.

> Did Pangloss really mean it when he said, "This is the best of all possible worlds"?

> How absurd of him to say that "This is the best of all possible worlds"!

4. Colon or semicolon.

Always place a colon or semicolon *after* the end quotation mark.

> The boys had always called Tom "the champ"; he began to wonder if the reputation would endure.

> There were several reasons why Tom was acknowledged as "the champ": physical strength, intellectual superiority, and qualities of leadership.

5. Dash.

Use a dash to set off the name of the author following a quotation on the same line.

> "Pleasure's a sin, and sometimes sin's a pleasure." —Byron.

PARENTHESES ( )

Use parentheses:

1. To enclose material that is not part of the main sentence but is too relevant to omit.

    Faulkner's novels (published by Random House) were selected as prizes.

    The data (see Table 13) was very impressive.

2. To enclose part of a sentence that, if enclosed by commas, would be confusing.

    The authors he published (none other than Schulte, MacGregor and Johnson) were among his best friends.

3. To enclose an explanatory item that is not part of the statement or sentence.

    She wrote to *The Paris* (Illinois) *News.*

4. To enclose numbers or letters that designate each item in a series.

    The project is (1) too time-consuming, (2) too expensive, and (3) poorly staffed.

    He was required to take courses in (a) mathematics, (b) English, (c) history, and (d) geology.

5. To enclose a numerical figure used to confirm a spelled-out number which precedes it.

    Enclosed is a check for ten dollars ($10.00) to cover the cost of the order.

BRACKETS [ ]

Brackets are used in pairs to enclose figures, phrases, or sentences that are meant to be set apart from the context—usually a direct quotation.

Use brackets:

1. To set off a notation, explanation or editorial comment that is inserted in quoted material and is not part of the original text.

    According to the Globe critic, "This [*Man and Superman*] is one of Shaw's greatest plays."

    Or substitute the bracketed proper name for the pronoun: "[*Man and Superman*] is one of Shaw's...."

    "Now that the astronauts have set new records for survival in Space [84 days in *Skylab 4* and 96 days in *Soyuz 26*], space travel for the general public may be realized in our lifetime."

    "Young as they are," he writes, "these students are afflicted with cynicism, world-weariness, and *a total dis-*

regard for tradition and authority." [Emphasis is mine.]

2. To correct an error in a quotation.

    "It was on April 25, 1944 [1945—Ed.] that delegates representing forty-six countries met in San Francisco."

3. To indicate that an error in fact, spelling, punctuation, or language usage is quoted deliberately in an effort to reproduce the original statement with complete accuracy. The questionable fact or expression is followed by the Latin word *sic,* meaning "thus," which is enclosed in brackets.

    "George Washington lived during the seventeenth [*sic*] century."

    "The Missisipi [*sic*] is the longest river in the U.S.," he wrote.

4. To enclose stage directions in plays. Parentheses may also be used for this purpose.

    JULIET: [*Snatching Romeo's dagger*]...O happy dagger! This is thy sheath; [*Stabs herself*] there rest and let me die.

5. To enclose comments made on a verbatim transcription of a speech, debate, or testimony.

    MR. KRINSLEY: The steady rise in taxes must be halted. [*Applause*]

6. To substitute for parentheses within material already enclosed by parentheses. Although it is not seen frequently, this device is sometimes used in footnotes.

    [1]See "René Descartes" (M. C. Beardsley, *The European Philosophers from Descartes to Nietzsche* [New York: Random House, 1960]).

7. To enclose the publication date, inserted by the editor, of an item appearing in an earlier issue of a periodical. This device is used in letters to the editor or in articles written on subjects previously reported. Parentheses may also be used for this purpose.

    Dear Sir: Your excellent article on China [April 15] brings to mind my recent experience...

    When removing old wallpaper [*Handyman's Monthly,* June 1977] make sure that you...

DASH (—)

Use a dash:

1. To mark an abrupt change in thought or

grammatical construction in the middle of a sentence.

> We won the game—but I'm getting ahead of the story.

2. To suggest halting or hesitant speech.

> "Well—er—ah—it's hard to explain," he faltered.

3. To indicate a sudden break or interruption before a sentence is completed.

> "Eric, don't climb up that—" It was too late.

4. To add emphasis to parenthetical material or to mark an emphatic separation between parenthetical material and the rest of a sentence.

> Her influence—she was a powerful figure in the community—was a deterrent to effective opposition.

> The excursions for school groups—to museums, zoos, and theaters—are less expensive.

> The car he was driving—a gleaming black limousine—was the most impressive thing about him.

5. To set off an appositive or an appositive phrase when a comma would provide less than the desired emphasis on the appositive or when the use of commas might result in confusion with commas within the appositive phrase.

> The premier's promise of changes—land reform, higher wages, reorganization of industry—was not easily fulfilled.

6. To replace an offensive word or part of one.

> Where's that son of a b—?

SLASH (/)

Use a slash:

1. To indicate the end of a line in quoting verse.

> ...the play's the thing/Wherein I'll catch the conscience of the King.

2. To indicate alternative expressions such as *he/she, and/or,* etc. Use this device sparingly.

> The driver must show his/her license to the police.

> The tour includes Sweden and/or Norway.

> The owner/renter is required to clear the sidewalk.

HYPHEN (-)

The hyphenation of compound nouns and modifiers is often arbitrary, inconsistent, and subject to change. Practices vary. When in doubt, it is best to consult the dictionary.

Use a hyphen:

1. To spell out a word or name.
> r-e-a-s-o-n   C-a-r-l-u-c-c-i

2. To divide a word into syllables.
> hal-lu-ci-na-tion

3. To mark the division of a word of more than one syllable at the end of a line; indicating that the word is to be completed on the following line.

> It is difficult to estimate the damaging psychological effects of racism and sexism.

4. To separate the parts (when spelling out numerals) of a compound number from twenty-one to ninety-nine.
> thirty-six inches to the yard
> Fifty-second Street
> nineteen hundred and forty-three

5. To express decades in words.
> the nineteen-twenties
> the eighteen-sixties

6. To indicate a range of numbers, as in dates or pages.
> the Civil War, 1861-1865
> pages 98-130

7. To separate (when spelling out numerals) the numerator from the denominator of a fraction, especially a fraction which is used as an adjective.
> one-half cup of milk
> a two-thirds majority

When fractions are used as nouns, the hyphen is optional.
> three fourths (or three-fourths) of his constituents
> one fifth (or one-fifth) of the class

Do not use a hyphen to indicate a fraction if either the numerator or denominator is already hyphenated.
> one thirty-second
> forty-five hundredths
> twenty-one thirty-sixths

8. To form certain compound nouns.

   a. Nouns consisting of two or more words which show the combination of two or more constituents, qualities, or functions in one person or thing.
   > secretary-treasurer   city-state

teacher-counselor   AFL-CIO

b. Nouns made up of two or more words, including other parts of speech.

cease-fire	fourth-grader
coat-of-arms	hand-me-down
court-martial	has-been
cure-all	post-mortem

Do not hyphenate compound nouns denoting chemical terms, military rank, or certain governmental positions.

hydrogen sulfide
sodium chloride
carbon tetrachloride
vice admiral
lieutenant governor
justice of the peace
sergeant at arms
brigadier general
lieutenant junior grade
attorney general
private first class

9. To connect the elements of a compound modifier when used *before* the noun it modifies. In most cases, the same modifier is not hyphenated if it *follows* the noun it modifies.

They engaged in hand-to-hand combat.
They fought hand to hand.
They endured a hand-to-mouth existence.
They lived hand to mouth.
a well-known expert
an expert who is well known
an 8,000-foot peak
The peak was 8000 feet high.

Do not hyphenate a compound modifier which includes an adverb ending in *ly* even when it is used before the noun.

his loosely fitted jacket
a carefully guarded secret

But a hyphen is used when the compound modifier contains an adverb that does not end in *ly.*

a well-guarded secret
a fast-growing business

10. To distinguish a less common pronunciation or meaning of a word from its more customary usage.

CUSTOMARY USAGE:
a recreation hall
to recover from an illness
to reform a sinner

HYPHENATED FORM:
re-creation of a scene
re-cover the couch
re-form their lines

11. To prevent possible confusion in pronunciation if a prefix results in the doubling of a letter, especially a vowel.

anti-inflationary	co-op
co-ordinate	pre-empt
pre-eminent	re-enact
re-election	re-entry

The dieresis is sometimes, but less frequently, used over *e* and *o* to accomplish the same result:

coöp   reëntry

12. To join the following prefixes with *proper* nouns or adjectives.

anti	anti-American, anti-British
mid	mid-Victorian, mid-Atlantic, mid-August
neo	neo-Nazi, neo-Darwinism
non	non-European, non-Asian, non-Christian
pan	Pan-American, Pan-Slavic, Pan-African
pro	pro-French, pro-American
un	un-American, un-British

With few exceptions, these prefixes are joined to common nouns without hyphenation:

anticlimax	midsummer
nonintervention	proslavery

13. To join the following prefixes and suffixes with the main word of a compound.

all-	all-powerful, all-embracing, all-star
co-	co-chairman, co-worker, co-author
ex-	ex-sergeant, ex-mayor, ex-wife, ex-premier
self-	self-preservation, self-defeating, self-explanatory, self-educated
-elect	president-elect, governor-elect

14. To form most, but not all, compound nouns and adjectives which begin with the word elements listed below. For words not listed, it is best to consult the dictionary.

cross-

cross-examine	cross-fertilize
cross-purposes	cross-stitch

double-
- double-breasted   double-edged
- double-jointed   double-park

great-
(always used in family relationships)
- great-grandfather great-grandson
- great-hearted   great-aunt

heavy-
- heavy-handed   heavy-hearted
- heavy-duty (but heavyweight)

ill-
- ill-disposed   ill-organized
- ill-timed   ill-advised

light-
- light-fingered   light-footed
- light-hearted   light-year

single-
- single-breasted   single-handed
- single-minded

well- -
- well-behaved   well-balanced
- well-preserved   well-wisher

Division of Words

The division of a word at the end of a line should be avoided when possible. If it is necessary to divide a word, follow the syllabification shown in the dictionary.

Do not syllabify a word so that only one letter stands alone at the end or beginning of a line. Do not divide a one-syllable word, including words ending in *-ed* (such as *walked, saved, hurled*). Avoid the division of a word that carries only two letters over to the next line. The following terminal parts of words should never be divided: *-able, -ible; -cial, -sial, -tial; -cion, -sion, -tion; -gion, -ceous, -cious, -tious; -geous.*

If a word that already has a hyphen must be broken, divide the word where only the hyphen already stands.

mother- *or* mother-in- *but not* moth-
in-law   law   er-in-law

Abbreviation

In standard academic, scientific, business or other organizational reports and correspondence, abbreviations are generally avoided unless they are the commonly required ones and are specifically known and accepted terms within a particular discipline or trade.

Some abbreviations that are acceptable in journalistic or business writing may not be appropriate in extremely formal announcements or invitations in which even dates are spelled out.

Abbreviations are often used in ordering and billing, catalogs, tabulations, telephone books, classified advertising, and similar cases where brevity is essential.

In some cases, the decision to use an abbreviation is a matter of individual preference. When in doubt, it is usually prudent to use the spelled-out form. Do not, however, spell out a word in one sentence or paragraph only to use the abbreviated form elsewhere.

Use abbreviations in writing:

1. The following titles and forms of address whenever they precede a proper name: *Mr., Mrs., Ms., Dr., Mme., Mlle., M.* Do not spell out these titles even in the most formal situations.

   Mlle. Modiste   Dr. Gerner
   Mr. Carl Sandburg   Mme. Curie

2. Titles of the clergy, government officials, officers of organizations, military and naval personnel (except in an extremely formal context) provided that the title is followed by a first name or initial as well as a surname. If the title is followed only by a surname, it must be spelled out.

   Gen. Arthur Evans   General Evans
   Sgt. Ed Block   Sergeant Block
   Prof. Samuel Page   Professor Page
   Gov. Ella Grasso   Governor Grasso
   Rev. George Ryan
      The Reverend George Ryan *or*
      The Reverend Dr. (*or* Mr.) Ryan
   Hon. Frank Church

The Honorable Frank Church
or The Honorable Mr. Church

Note above that in very formal writing, the titles *Honorable* and *Reverend* are spelled out and are preceded by *The.* When the first name or initial is omitted, the title Mr. or Dr. is substituted.

3. *Jr.* or *Sr.* following a name. These abbreviations should.be added only when the names preceding them include a first name or initial.

Paul Thompson, Jr.

4. *Esq.* following a name. This abbreviation should not be used with any other title.

Gerald Hollingsworth, Esq.

5. Academic degrees: *B.A.* (Bachelor of Arts); *M.A.* (Master of Arts); *M.S.* (Master of Science); *Ph.D.* (Doctor of Philosophy); *M.D.* (Doctor of Medicine), etc. When a name is followed by a scholastic degree or by the abbreviations of religious or fraternal orders (BPOE), it should not be preceded by *Mr., Miss., Dr.,* or any other title.

Robert J. Kassan, M.D.

6. The terms used to describe business firms (*Co., Corp., Inc., Bro.* or *Bros., Ltd., R.R.* or *Ry.*) only when these abbreviations are part of the legally authorized name. In all other cases (except for brevity in tables, etc.), *Company, Corporation, Incorporated, Brothers,* and *Limited* should be spelled out.

John Wiley & Sons, Inc.

7. Except in formal writing, the names of states, territories, or possessions that immediately follow the name of a city, mountain, airport, or other identifiable geographic location. Check the dictionary for all such abbreviations.

Detroit, Mich.   San Juan, P.R.

8. Certain expressions:

i.e. (*id est*), that is
e.g. (*exempli gratia*), for example
et al. (*et alii*), and others
etc. (*et cetera*), and so forth

Do not abbreviate:

1. Names of countries, except:
   a. The U.S.S.R. (Union of Soviet Socialist Republics) because of its exceptional length.
   b. U.S. (United States) when preceding the name of an American ship. The abbreviation U.S. may also be used in tables, footnotes, etc., when modifying a government agency: *U.S. Congress, U.S. Post Office,* etc.

2. The words *street, avenue, boulevard, drive, square, road,* and *court,* except in lists requiring brevity, or when space is limited.

3. The days of the week and the months of the year except in the most informal situations or in tables.

4. Weights and measures except in lists of items, technical writing, etc.

I had hoped to lose ten pounds.
We used ten yards of cloth.

Do not use a period after the following abbreviations or shortened forms:

1. After a contraction, which is not to be confused with an abbreviation. Contractions contain apostrophes which indicate omitted letters; they never end with a period.

sec't'y or sec'y   nat'l

2. After chemical symbols.

H_2O $NaCl$

3. After *percent.*

4. After initials of military services and specific military terms.

USA	United States Army
USN	United States Navy
RCAF	Royal Canadian Air Force
RCMP	Royal Canadian Mounted Police
MP	military police
SP	shore patrol
POW	prisoner of war
PX	post exchange
GI	government issue
APO	Army post office

5. After the initials of certain governmental agencies or call letters of television and radio stations.

NATO, UNICEF, CIA, CARE, NBC, KQED, WMAQ, CBC, CBET, CFCF

6. After letters that are used as symbols rather than initials.

Let us assume that A and B are playing opposite C and D.

7. After listed items (as in catalogs, outlines, or syllabuses), if none of the items is a complete sentence. If the list includes

only one complete sentence, use a period after this and all other items on the list, including those which are not complete sentences. Consistency is essential: a pe-

riod after each item or no end punctuation whatever.

8. Points of the compass.
   NE   ESE   SW   E by NE

Capitalization

Many writers have a tendency to use capitals unnecessarily. When in doubt, one can usually learn whether a particular word is generally capitalized by consulting the dictionary. A safe guideline is to capitalize only when there is specific reason to do so.

1. Capitalize the first word of a sentence. Capitalize, also, any word (or the first word of a phrase) that stands independently as though it were a sentence.

   He is the new president of the club.
   Where is the chess set?
   Hurrah! No school!

2. Capitalize the first word of each line of verse (unless the poet specifically avoided capitals in such instances).

   Ring forth, ye bells.
   With clarion sound—
   Forget your knells.
   For joys abound.

3. Capitalize the first word of a direct quotation within a sentence (unless the quotation is a fragment).

   He replied, "Vivian prefers to enter in the fall."
   "George," she asked, "don't you want to join us for dinner?"
   He denied that he was "a neurotic editor."

4. Always capitalize the interjection *O* or the pronoun *I*. None of the other pronouns are capitalized unless they occur at the beginning of a sentence or refer to the Deity.

   Here I am.   Exult, O Shores!

5. Capitalize all proper nouns and adjectives.

   Italians   Scottish   Edwardian
   Emily Dickinson   the Cabot family
   Australia   European   Germanic
   Chicago   Chaucerian

6. The German *von* and the Dutch *van* in proper names are commonly not

printed with a capital when part of a name, but usage varies.

   Paul von Hindenburg
   Vincent van Gogh

The French particles *de* and *du* and the Italian *di* and *da* are commonly written in lower case when they are preceded by a first name or title. Without title or first name, the particle is sometimes dropped, sometimes capitalized.

   Marquis de Lafayette
   (De) Lafayette
   Count de Mirabeau
   (De) Mirabeau

In English or American names these particles are commonly capitalized in all positions:

   William De Morgan   De Morgan
   Lee De Forest   De Forest

7. Do not capitalize words derived from proper nouns but now having a special meaning distinct from the proper name:

   antimacassar   china
   pasteurize   macadam

8. Capitalize recognized geographical names:

   Ohio River   Sun Valley
   Rocky Mountains   Gulf of Mexico

9. Capitalize the following when they follow a single proper name and are written in the singular:

   Butte   County   Delta
   Canyon   Creek   Gap
   Glacier   Ocean   Range
   Harbor   Peninsula   River
   Head   Plateau   Valley

For example, the *Sacramento River*, but the *Tennessee and Cumberland rivers*.

10. Capitalize the following in the singular and plural when they follow a proper name:

   Hill   Mountain   Island   Narrows

11. Capitalize the following in the singular

whether placed before or after the name:

Bay	Sea	Gulf	Mount
Point	Cape	Isle	Peak
Strait	Desert	Lake	Plain

Capitalize in the plural when they come before the name (and sometimes following a single name). For example, *Lakes George and Champlain,* but *Malheur and Goose lakes.*

12. Capitalize geographic directions only when they designate specific regions. Capitalize also special names for regions or districts:

    Northwest Passage
    Middle Atlantic States
    the New World
    the South
    the Middle East
    Western Hemisphere

EXCEPTION: Do not capitalize merely directional parts of states.

    eastern Ohio   southern Indiana

13. Do not capitalize compass points when indicating direction.

    They went south last year but plan to go west this year.

14. Capitalize the names of streets, parks, buildings, etc.:

    Michigan Boulevard
    Royal Ontario Museum
    Metropolitan Opera House
    Golden Gate Bridge
    Empire State Building
    Yellowstone National Park
    Grand Central Parkway

EXCEPTIONS: Do not capitalize such categories of buildings as *library*, *post office,* or *museum,* written without a proper name, unless local custom makes the classification equivalent to a proper name.

15. Capitalize the various names of God or the Christian Trinity, both nouns and adjectives, and all pronouns clearly referring to the Deity. Capitalize also words that refer to the Bible or other sacred writings.

the Word	Holy Bible
the Savior	the Koran
the Messiah	Ten Commandments
Allah	to do His will
the Almighty	the Virgin Mary

16. Capitalize all personifications.

    Come, gentle Death!

17. Capitalize the names of organizations, institutions, political parties, alliances, movements, classes, religious groups, nationalities, races, etc.:

Democratic party (or Party)	Royalist Spain
Labor party	Axis powers
Republicans	Soviet Russia
Dutch Treat Club	Protestants
United Nations	Lutherans
American Legion	University of
Africans	Waterloo
	Caucasians

18. Capitalize divisions, departments, and offices of government, when the official name is used. Do not capitalize incomplete or roundabout designations:

    Department of Commerce
    Circuit Court of Marion County
    Bureau of Labor Statistics
    Congress
    Senate
    House of Commons
    United States Army
    Board of Aldermen
    the council
    the lower house (of Congress)
    the bureau
    the legislature

19. Capitalize the names of wars, battles, treaties, documents, prizes, and important periods or events:

    Battle of the Bulge
    Declaration of Independence
    Nobel Prize
    Revolutionary War
    Congress of Vienna
    Black Death
    War of 1812
    Golden Age of Pericles
    Middle Ages
    Treaty of Versailles

Do not capitalize *war* or *treaty* when used without the distinguishing name.

20. Capitalize the numerals used with kings, dynasties, or organizations. Numerals preceding the name are ordinarily spelled out; those following the name are commonly put in Roman numerals:

Second World War	World War II
Nineteenth Amendment	Henry IV
Third Army	Forty-eighth Congress

21. Capitalize titles, military or civil ranks of honor, academic degrees, decorations, etc., when written with the name,

and all titles of honor or rank when used for specific persons in place of the name:

> General Bradstreet
> the Senator from Ohio
> the Earl of Rochester
> Queen Elizabeth
> the Archbishop of Canterbury
> Your Highness

22. Capitalize the main words (nouns, verbs, adjectives, adverbs) of the titles of books, articles, poems, plays, musical compositions, etc., as well as the first word:

> The House of the Seven Gables
> All's Well That Ends Well
> The Kreutzer Sonata

23. Titles of chapters in a book are usually capitalized. Capitalize also any sections of a specific book, such as *Bibliography*, *Index*, *Table of Contents*, etc.

24. In expressions of time, *A.M.*, *P.M.*, *A.D.*, and *B.C.* are usually written or typed in capitals without space between them. It is equally acceptable to show *a.m.* and *p.m.* in lower-case letters.

> 9:40 A.M.   6:10 P.M.
> 42 B.C.   A.D. 491 (or 491 A.D.)

When A.M., P.M., A.D., and B.C. are to be typeset, one may mark them with double-underlining to indicate that small capitals are to be used.

Italics

Indicate italics by underlining in manuscript or typescript.

Use italics:

1. To emphasize a particular word, phrase or statement.

> We *must* appeal for contributions.

2. To refer to the titles of books, magazines, newspapers, motion pictures, plays, longer musical compositions, book-length poems, ships, aircraft, or any other vehicle designated by a proper name. Titles of works of art may be shown in italics or enclosed with quotation marks.

> The Catcher in the Rye   Mona Lisa
> Harper's Magazine Rodin's The Thinker
> the Philadelphia Inquirer   the Titanic
> High Noon   the Spirit of St. Louis
> Hamlet   Beethoven's Ninth Symphony
> The Raven   The Faerie Queen

3. To indicate words or phrases that, although used by English speakers or writers, are still regarded as foreign.

> In his younger days, he was a *bon vivant*.
> Formal dress was *de rigueur* at their annual dance.

4. To refer to a letter, number, word, or expression as such. Quotation marks may be used for the same purpose.

> Her favorite adjective is *fantastic*.
> The present participle ends in *ing*.

5. To indicate stage directions in a play.

> GEORGIA [*turning to* VAN]: Did you hear the bell?
> VAN: Yes, I'll answer it. [*He dashes to the door.*]

Numerals

In general, numbers that can be stated in only one or two words are spelled out.

> There were twelve girls and twenty-six boys from Montreal.
> The sweater cost twenty-five dollars.
> He gave one-tenth of his income to charity.

Other numbers are usually shown in figures.

> There are 392 members in the association.
> The radio cost him $136.50.
> The population of Chicago in 1950 was 3,620,962.

The numeral at the beginning of a sentence is usually spelled out. If this is awkward or difficult to read, rewrite the sentence to avoid beginning with a numeral.

> Three hundred and sixty students attended the dance.
>
> Twenty-six million votes were cast for him.
>
> Six thousand dollars was stolen from the safe.

It is important to be consistent in the treatment of numbers when they appear in the same series or in the same sentence or paragraph. Do not spell some out and use figures for others.

> The three chairs are 36, 72, and 122 years old.
>
> He spent $100 on rent, $30 on food, and $265 on clothes.

Use figures (generally) for dates, pages, dimensions, decimals, percentages, measures, statistical data, exact amounts of money, designations of time when followed by A.M. or P.M., and addresses.

June 29, 1945	0.9631	96.8°
124 B.C.	23 percent	86%
p. 263	75 pounds	8:30 A.M.
p. xxvi	93 miles	3:20 P.M.
2′ x 4′	$369.27	4262 Brush
10 ft. 3 in.	£ 5.9s.6d	Street

Spell out ordinal numbers whenever possible.

> sixteenth century
> Fifth Avenue
> Eighty-second Congress
> Third Republic
> Twenty-third Psalm
> Third Assembly District

Proofreaders' Marks

The conventional marks shown below are used in preparing a manuscript to be typeset or in proofreading typeset material. The mark should be written in the margin directly in line with the specific part of the text to which it refers; the text should also be marked to indicate the place of the change. If the same line has several changes, vertical or diagonal lines are placed between each of the marginal marks.

EDITORIAL MARKS

Mark in margin:	Instruction:	Mark in text:
[Show change or addition]	Insert at caret	Peter left town in hurry.
ϑ or ⸏	Delete; take out	Stephanie sent me me the book.
⸏	Delete and close up	I haven't seen theḿm for years.
stet	Make no change; keep original	They phoned both Jody and Erik.
tr	Transpose	Put the book the on table.
sp	Spell out	Lunch cost me 6 dollars.
¶	Start new paragraph	up the river. Two years later
No ¶	Do not paragraph; run in	many unnecessary additives. The most dangerous one had been in use for about ten
#	Insert space	It was a small village.
eq #	Equalize spacing	Ronnie got rid of the dog.

PUNCTUATION MARKS

Mark in margin:	Instruction:	Mark in text:
⊙	Period (.)	Claire teaches fifth grade
⸏	Comma (,)	We expect Linda, Nino, and Daniel.
⸎	Semicolon (;)	I came; I saw, I conquered.
⊙	Colon (:)	Alice worked until 6,30 P.M.
=	Hyphen (-)	Wu Pan got a two thirds majority.
⸏	Apostrophe (')	Don't mark the authors copy.
!	Exclamation mark (!)	Watch out
?	Question mark (?)	Did Mollie write to you
⸏/⸏	Quotation marks (double) (" ")	I like Rodin's The Thinker.
⸏/⸏	Quotation marks (single) (' ')	He said, "Read The Raven tonight."

398

PUNCTUATION MARKS

Mark in margin:	Instruction:	Mark in text:
(/)	Parentheses (( ))	Lillian paid 100 pesos₍13¢₎for it.
[/]	Brackets ([ ])	"The play₍Hamlet₎was performed..."
─/M	One-em dash (—)	TJ finally left₍very reluctantly.
─/N	One-en dash (–)	See pages 96₍124.

TYPOGRAPHIC MARKS

Mark in margin:	Instruction:	Mark in text:
ital	Set in *italic* type	I've read Paradise Lost twice.
bf	Set in **boldface** type	See the definition of peace.
lf	Set in lightface type	She repaired the motor easily.
rom	Set in roman type	Daphne drove to Winnipeg.
caps	Set in CAPITALS	Prabhuling deserves the nobel prize.
sc	Set in SMALL CAPITALS	He lived about 350 B.C.
c+sc	Set in CAPITALS and SMALL CAPITALS	drive slowly
lc	Set in lower case	Jeanne enjoys Reading.
u+lc	Set in UPPER and lower case	STOP!
ᵌ	Set as subscript	NaNO₃
ᵌ	Set as superscript	A² + B²
‖	Align vertically	‖from one hand to the other without spilling it.
═	Align horizontally	three days later
↓	Push down	She assigned him to Minneapolis.
×	Broken letter	They drove to Miami.
wf	Wrong font	TURN RIGHT
☊	Turn inverted letter	⅁ert proofread the book.
□	Indent one em	□Rose asked the price.
□□	Indent two ems	□□ The Use of the Comma
⊏	Move to left	⊏What's Maya's last name?
⊐	Move to right	She was born in Jersey City.
⌐	Move up	Please go now.
⌐	Move down	Well, that's that!

399

Forms of Address

The forms of address shown below cover most of the commonly encountered problems in correspondence. Although there are many alternative forms, the ones given here are generally preferred in conventional usage.

As a complimentary close, use "Sincerely yours," but, when particular formality is preferred, use "Very truly yours."

GOVERNMENT (UNITED STATES)

Addressee	Address on Letter and Envelope	Salutation
The President	The President The White House Washington, D.C. 20500	Dear Mr. *or* Madam President:
The Vice President	The Vice President United States Senate Washington, D.C. 20510	Dear Mr. *or* Madam Vice President:
Members of the Cabinet	The Honorable (*full name*) Secretary of (*name of Department*) Washington, D.C. (*zip code*)	Dear Mr. *or* Madam Secretary:
Attorney General	The Honorable (*full name*) Attorney General Washington, D.C. 20530	Dear Mr. *or* Madam Attorney General:
Senator	The Honorable (*full name*) United States Senate Washington, D.C. 20510	Dear Senator (*surname*):
Speaker of the House of Representatives	The Honorable (*full name*) Speaker of the House of Representatives Washington, D.C. 20515	Dear Mr. *or* Madam Speaker:
Representative	The Honorable (*full name*) House of Representatives Washington, D.C. 20515	Dear Mr. *or* Madam (*surname*):
Chief Justice	The Chief Justice of the United States The Supreme Court of the United States Washington, D.C. 20543	Dear Mr. *or* Madam Chief Justice:
Associate Justice	Mr. *or* Madam Justice (*surname*) The Supreme Court of the United States Washington, D.C. 20543	Dear Mr. *or* Madam Justice:

Addressee	Address on Letter and Envelope	Salutation
Judge of a Federal Court	The Honorable (*full name*) Judge of the (*name of court; if a district court, give district*) (*Local address*)	Dear Judge (*surname*):
American Ambassador	The Honorable (*full name*) American Ambassador (*City*) (*Country*)	*Formal:* Sir: *or* Madam: *Informal:* Dear Mr. *or* Madam Ambassador:
American Minister	The Honorable (*full name*) American Minister (*City*), (*Country*)	*Formal:* Sir: *or* Madam: *Informal:* Dear Mr. *or* Madam Minister:
Governor	The Honorable (*full name*) Governor of (*name*) (*City*), (*State*)	Dear Governor (*surname*):
Lieutenant Governor	The Honorable (*full name*) Lieutenant Governor of (*name*) (*City*), (*State*)	Dear (Mr., Ms., Miss *or* Mrs.) (*surname*):
State Senator	The Honorable (*full name*) (*Name of State*) Senate (*City*), (*State*)	Dear (Mr., Ms., Miss *or* Mrs.) (*surname*):
State Representative; Assemblyman; Delegate	The Honorable (*full name*) (*Name of State*) House of Representatives (*or* Assembly *or* House of Delegates) (*City*), (*State*)	Dear (Mr., Ms., Miss *or* Mrs.) (*surname*):
Mayor	The Honorable (*full name*) Mayor of (*name of city*) (*City*), (*State*)	Dear Mayor (*surname*):

GOVERNMENT (CANADA)

Addressee	Address on Letter and Envelope	Salutation
The Governor General	(His *or* Her) Excellency (*full name*) Government House Ottawa, Ontario K1A 0A1	*Formal:* Sir: *or* Madam: *Informal:* Dear Governor General:
The Prime Minister	The Right Honourable (*full name*), P.C., M.P. Prime Minister of Canada Prime Minister's Office Ottawa, Ontario K1A 0A2	*Formal:* Dear Sir: *or* Madam: *Informal:* Dear (Mr. *or* Madam) Prime Minister:
Members of the Cabinet	The Honourable (*full name*) Minister of (*function*) House of Commons Parliament Buildings Ottawa, Ontario K1A 0A2	*Formal:* Dear Sir: *or* Madam: *Informal:* Dear (Mr., Ms., Miss *or* Mrs.) (*surname*):
Senator	The Honourable (*full name*) The Senate Parliament Buildings Ottawa, Ontario K1A 0A4	*Formal:* Dear Sir: *or* Madam: *Informal:* Dear Senator:

Addressee	Address on Letter and Envelope	Salutation
Member of House of Commons	(Mr., Ms., Miss or Mrs.) (*full name*), M.P. House of Commons Parliament Buildings Ottawa, Ontario K1A 0A6	*Formal:* Dear Sir: or Madam: *Informal:* Dear (Mr., Ms., Miss or Mrs.) (*surname*):
Chief Justice of Canada	The Right Honourable (*full name*) Chief Justice of Canada Supreme Court Building Ottawa, Ontario K1A 0J1	*Formal:* Sir: or Madam: *Informal:* Dear Sir: or Madam:
Canadian Ambassador	(Mr., Ms., Miss or Mrs.) (*full name*) Canadian Ambassador to (*Country*) (*City*), (*Country*)	*Formal:* Dear Sir: or Madam: *Informal:* Dear (Mr., Ms., Miss or Mrs.) (*surname*):
Canadian Minister	(Mrs., Ms., Miss or Mrs.) (*full name*) Canadian Minister to (*Country*) (*City*), (*Country*)	*Formal:* Sir: or Madam: *Informal:* Dear (Mr., Ms., Miss or Mrs.) (*surname*):
The Premier of a Province	The Honourable (*full name*), M.L.A.* Premier of the Province of (*name*)** (*City*), (*Province*)	*Formal:* Dear Sir: or Madam: *Informal:* Dear (Mr., Ms., Miss or Mrs.) (*surname*):
Members of provincial governments	(Mr., Ms., Miss or Mrs.) (*full name*), M.L.A.* Member of the Legislative Assembly (*Name*) Building (*City*), (*Province*)	*Formal:* Dear Sir: or Madam: *Informal:* Dear (Mr., Ms., Miss or Mrs.) (*surname*):
Mayor	His or Her Worship Mayor (*full name*) City Hall (*City*), (*Province*)	Dear Sir: or Madam:

RELIGIOUS LEADERS

Addressee	Address on Letter and Envelope	Salutation
Minister, Pastor, or Rector	The Reverend (*full name*) (*Title*), (*name of church*) (*Local address*)	Dear (Mr., Ms., Miss or Mrs.) (*surname*):
Rabbi	Rabbi (*full name*) (*Local address*)	Dear Rabbi (*surname*):
Catholic Cardinal	His Eminence (*Christian name*) Cardinal (*surname*) Archbishop of (*province*) (*Local address*)	*Formal:* Your Eminence: *Informal:* Dear Cardinal (*surname*):
Catholic Archbishop	The Most Reverend (*full name*) Archbishop of (*province*) (*Local address*)	*Formal:* Your Excellency: *Informal:* Dear Archbishop (*surname*):

*For Ontario, use M.P.P.; for Quebec, use M.N.A.
**For Quebec, use "Prime Minister."

Addressee	Address on Letter and Envelope	Salutation
Catholic Bishop	The Most Reverend (*full name*) Bishop of (*province*) (*Local address*)	*Formal:* Your Excellency: *Informal:* Dear Bishop (*surname*):
Catholic Monsignor	The Right Reverend Monsignor (*full name*) (*Local address*)	*Formal:* Right Reverend Monsignor: *Informal:* Dear Monsignor (*surname*):
Catholic Priest	The Reverend (*full name*), (*initials of order, if any*) (*Local address*)	*Formal:* Reverend Sir: *Informal:* Dear Father (*surname*):
Catholic Sister	Sister (*full name*) (*Name of organization*) (*Local address*)	Dear Sister (*full name*):
Catholic Brother	Brother (*full name*) (*Name of organization*) (*Local address*)	Dear Brother (*given name*):
Protestant Episcopal Bishop	The Right Reverend (*full name*) Bishop of (*name*) (*Local address*)	*Formal:* Right Reverend Sir *or* Madam: *Informal:* Dear Bishop (*surname*):
Protestant Episcopal Dean	The Very Reverend (*full name*) Dean of (*church*) (*Local address*)	*Formal:* Very Reverend Sir *or* Madam: *Informal:* Dear Dean (*surname*):
Anglican Archbishop	The Most Reverend (*full name*) Archbishop of (*province*) (*Local address*)	*Formal:* Most Reverend Sir: *Informal:* Dear Archbishop:
Anglican Bishop	The Right Reverend (*full name*) Bishop of (*name*) (*Local address*)	*Formal:* Right Reverend Sir: *Informal:* Dear Bishop:
Anglican Archdeacon	The Venerable Archdeacon (*full name*) (*Local address*)	*Formal:* Venerable Sir: *Informal:* Dear Mr. Archdeacon:
Anglican Dean	The Very Reverend (*full name*) Dean of (*name*) (*Local address*)	*Formal:* Very Reverend Sir: *Informal:* Dear Mr. Dean:
Anglican Canon	The Reverend Canon (*full name*) (*Local address*)	*Formal:* Reverend Sir: *Informal:* Dear Canon:
Methodist Bishop	The Reverend (*full name*) Methodist Bishop (*Local address*)	*Formal:* Reverend Sir: *Informal:* Dear Bishop (*surname*):

Addressee	Address on Letter and Envelope	Salutation
Mormon Bishop	Bishop (*full name*) Church of Jesus Christ of Latter-day Saints (*Local address*)	*Formal:* Sir: *Informal:* Dear Bishop (*surname*):

MISCELLANEOUS

Addressee	Address on Letter and Envelope	Salutation
President of a university or college	Mr. (*full name*) President. (*name of institution*) (*Local address*)	Dear Mr. (*surname*):
Dean of a college or school	Dean (*full name*) School of (*name*) (*name of institution*) (*Local address*)	Dear Dean (*surname*):
Professor	Professor (*full name*) Department of (*name*) (*Name of institution*) (*Local address*)	Dear Professor (*surname*):

Weights and Measures

Customary System

LINEAR MEASURE

12 inches	= 1 foot
3 feet	= 1 yard
5½ yards	= 1 rod
40 rods	= 1 furlong
8 furlongs (5280 feet)	= 1 statute mile

MARINERS' MEASURE

6 feet	= 1 fathom
1000 fathoms (approx.)	= 1 nautical mile
3 nautical miles	= 1 league

SQUARE MEASURE

144 square inches	= 1 square foot
9 square feet	= 1 square yard
30¼ square yards	= 1 square rod
160 square rods	= 1 acre
640 acres	= 1 square mile

CUBIC MEASURE

1728 cubic inches	= 1 cubic foot
27 cubic feet	= 1 cubic yard

SURVEYORS' MEASURE

7.92 inches	= 1 link
100 links	= 1 chain

LIQUID MEASURE

4 gills	= 1 pint
2 pints	= 1 quart
4 quarts	= 1 gallon
31½ gallons	= 1 barrel
2 barrels	= 1 hogshead

APOTHECARIES' FLUID MEASURE

60 minims	= 1 fluid dram
8 fluid drams	= 1 fluid ounce
16 fluid ounces	= 1 pint
2 pints	= 1 quart
4 quarts	= 1 gallon

DRY MEASURE

2 pints	= 1 quart
8 quarts	= 1 peck
4 pecks	= 1 bushel

WOOD MEASURE

16 cubic feet	= 1 cord foot
8 cord feet	= 1 cord

TIME MEASURE

60 seconds	= 1 minute
60 minutes	= 1 hour
24 hours	= 1 day
7 days	= 1 week
4 weeks (28 to 31 days)	= 1 month
12 months (365-366 days)	= 1 year
100 years	= 1 century

ANGULAR AND CIRCULAR MEASURE

60 seconds	= 1 minute
60 minutes	= 1 degree
90 degrees	= 1 right angle
180 degrees	= 1 straight angle
360 degrees	= 1 circle

TROY MEASURE

24 grains	= 1 pennyweight
20 pennyweights	= 1 ounce
12 ounces	= 1 pound

APOTHECARIES' WEIGHT

20 grains	= 1 scruple
3 scruples	= 1 dram
8 drams	= 1 ounce
12 ounces	= 1 pound

AVOIRDUPOIS WEIGHT

$27\frac{11}{32}$ grains	= 1 dram
16 drams	= 1 ounce
16 ounces	= 1 pound
100 pounds	= 1 short hundred-weight
20 short hundred-weight	= 1 short ton

Metric System

LINEAR MEASURE

10 millimeters	= 1 centimeter
10 centimeters	= 1 decimeter
10 decimeters	= 1 meter
10 meters	= 1 decameter
10 decameters	= 1 hectometer
10 hectometers	= 1 kilometer

LIQUID MEASURE

10 milliliters	= 1 centiliter
10 centiliters	= 1 deciliter
10 deciliters	= 1 liter
10 liters	= 1 decaliter
10 decaliters	= 1 hectoliter
10 hectoliters	= 1 kiloliter

SQUARE MEASURE

100 sq. millimeters	= 1 sq. centimeter
100 sq. centimeters	= 1 sq. decimeter
100 sq. decimeters	= 1 sq. meter
100 sq. meters	= 1 sq. decameter
100 sq. decameters	= 1 sq. hectometer
100 sq. hectomers	= 1 sq. kilometer

WEIGHTS

10 milligrams	= 1 centigram
10 centigrams	= 1 decigram
10 decigrams	= 1 gram
10 grams	= 1 decagram
10 decagrams	= 1 hectogram
10 hectograms	= 1 kilogram
100 kilograms	= 1 quintal
10 quintals	= 1 ton

CUBIC MEASURE

1000 cu. millimeters	= 1 cu. centimeter
1000 cu. centimeters	= 1 cu. decimeter
1000 cu. decimeters	= 1 cu. meter

Metric and Customary Equivalents

LINEAR MEASURE

Customary Unit	Metric Unit	Customary Unit	Metric Unit
1 inch =	25.4 millimeters / 2.54 centimeters	1 yard =	0.9144 meter
1 foot =	30.48 centimeters / 3.048 decimeters / 0.3048 meter	1 mile =	1609.3 meters / 1.6093 kilometers
		0.03937 inch =	1 millimeter
		0.3937 inch =	1 centimeter
		3.937 inches =	1 decimeter

Customary Unit	Metric Unit
39.37 inches 3.2808 feet 1.0936 yards }	= 1 meter
3280.8 feet 1093.6 yards 0.62137 mile }	= 1 kilometer

SQUARE MEASURE

Customary Unit	Metric Unit
1 square inch =	{ 645.16 square millimeters 6.4516 square centimeters
1 square foot =	{ 929.03 square centimeters 9.2903 square decimeters 0.092903 square meter
1 square yard =	0.83613 square meter
1 square mile =	2.5900 square kilometers
0.0015500 square inch =	1 square millimeter
0.15500 square inch =	1 square centimeter
15.500 square inches 0.10764 square foot }	= 1 square decimeter
1.1960 square yards =	1 square meter
0.38608 square mile =	1 square kilometer

CUBIC MEASURE

Customary Unit	Metric Unit
1 cubic inch =	{ 16.387 cubic centimeters 0.016387 liter
1 cubic foot =	0.028317 cubic meter
1 cubic yard =	0.76455 cubic meter
1 cubic mile =	4.16818 cubic kilometers
0.061023 cubic inch =	1 cubic centimeter
61.023 cubic inches =	1 cubic decimeter
35.315 cubic feet 1.3079 cubic yards }	= 1 cubic meter
0.23990 cubic mile =	1 cubic kilometer

WEIGHTS

Customary Unit	Metric Unit
1 grain	= 0.064799 gram
1 avoirdupois ounce	= 28.350 grams
1 troy ounce	= 31.103 grams
1 avoirdupois pound	= 0.45359 kilogram
1 troy pound	= 0.37324 kilogram
1 short ton (0.8929 long ton)	= { 907.18 kilograms 0.90718 metric ton
1 long ton (1.1200 short tons)	= { 1016.0 kilograms 1.0160 metric tons
15.432 grains 0.035274 avoirdupois ounce 0.032151 troy ounce }	= 1 gram
2.2046 avoirdupois pounds =	1 kilogram
0.98421 long ton 1.1023 short tons }	= 1 metric ton

DRY MEASURE

Customary Unit	Metric Unit
1 quart	= 1.1012 liters
1 peck	= 8.8098 liters
1 bushel	= 35.239 liters
0.90808 quart 0.11351 peck 0.028378 bushel }	= 1 liter

LIQUID MEASURE

Customary Unit	Metric Unit
1 fluid ounce =	29.573 milliliters
1 quart =	{ 9.4635 deciliters 0.94635 liter
1 gallon =	3.7854 liters
0.033814 fluid ounce =	1 milliliter
3.3814 fluid ounces =	1 deciliter
33.814 fluid ounces 1.0567 quarts 0.26417 gallon }	= 1 liter

Metric Conversion Factors

APPROXIMATE CONVERSIONS TO METRIC MEASURES

When You Know	Multiply by	To Find
Length		
inches	2.5	centimeters
feet	30	centimeters
yards	0.9	meters
miles	1.6	kilometers
Area		
square inches	6.5	square centimeters
square feet	0.09	square meters
square yards	0.8	square meters
square miles	2.6	square kilometers
acres	0.4	hectares
Mass (weight)		
ounces	28	grams
pounds	0.45	kilograms
short tons	0.9	metric ton
Volume		
teaspoons	5	milliliters
tablespoons	15	milliliters
cubic inches	16	milliliters
fluid ounces	30	milliliters
cups	0.24	liters
pints	0.47	liters
quarts	0.95	liters
gallons	3.8	liters
cubic feet	0.03	cubic meters
cubic yards	0.76	cubic meters
Temperature (exact)		
degrees Fahrenheit	5/9 (after subtracting 32)	degrees Celsius

APPROXIMATE CONVERSIONS FROM METRIC MEASURES

When You Know	Multiply by	To Find
Length		
millimeters	0.04	inches
centimeters	0.4	inches
meters	3.3	feet
meters	1.1	yards
kilometers	0.6	miles
Area		
square centimeters	0.16	square inches
square meters	1.2	square yards
square kilometers	0.4	square miles
hectares	2.5	acres
Mass (weight)		
grams	0.035	ounces
kilograms	2.2	pounds
metric ton	1.1	short tons
Volume		
milliliters	0.03	fluid ounces
milliliters	0.06	cubic inches
liters	2.1	pints
liters	1.06	quarts
liters	0.26	gallons
cubic meters	35	cubic feet
cubic meters	1.3	cubic yards
Temperature (exact)		
degrees Celsius	9/5 (then add 32)	degrees Fahrenheit